MUIRHEAD LIBRARY OF PHILOSOPHY

An admirable statement of the aims of the Library of Philosophy was provided by the first editor, the late Professor H. J. Muirhead, in his description of the original programme printed in Erdmann's *History of Philosophy* under the date 1890. This was slightly modified in subsequent volumes to take the form of the following statement:

"The Muirhead Library of Philosophy was designed as a contribution to the History of Modern Philosophy under the heads: first of different Schools of Thought—Sensationalist, Realist, Idealist, Intuitivist; secondly of different Subjects—Psychology, Ethics, Aesthetics, Political Philosophy, Theology. While much had been done in England in tracing the course of evolution in nature, history, economics, morals and religion, little had been done in tracing the development of thought on these subjects. Yet "the evolution of opinion is part of the whole evolution".

'By the co-operation of different writers in carrying out this plan it was hoped that a thoroughness and completeness of treatment, otherwise unattainable, might be secured. It was believed also that from writers mainly British and American fuller consideration of English Philosophy than it had hitherto received might be looked for. In the earlier series of books containing, among others, Bosanquet's *History of Aesthetics*, Pfleiderer's *Rational Theology since Kant*, Albee's *History of English Utilitarianism*, Bonar's *Philosophy and Political Economy*, Brett's *History of Psychology*, Ritchie's *Natural Rights*, these objects were to a large extent effected.

'In the meantime original work of a high order was being produced both in England and America by such writers as Bradley, Stout, Bertrand Russell, Baldwin, Urban, Montague and others, and a new interest in foreign works, German, French and Italian, which had either become classical or were attracting public attention, had developed. The scope of the Library thus became extended into something more international, and it is entering on the fifth decade of its existence in the hope that it may contribute to that mutual understanding between countries which is so pressing a need of the present time.'

The need which Professor Muirhead stressed is no less pressing today, and few will deny that philosophy has much to do with enabling us to meet it, although no one, least of all Muirhead himself, would regard that as the sole, or even the main, object of philosophy. As Professor Muirhead continues to lend the distinction of his name to the Library of Philosophy, it seemed not inappropriate to allow him to recall us to these aims in his own words. The emphasis on the history of thought seemed to me also very timely; and the number of important works promised for the Library in the near future augur well for the continued fulfilment, in this and in other ways, of the expectations of the original editor.

H. D. LEWIS

MUIRHEAD LIBRARY OF PHILOSOPHY

General Editor: H. D. Lewis
Professor of History and Philosophy of Religion in the University of London

Action by SIR MALCOLM KNOX
The Analysis of Mind by BERTRAND RUSSELL
Belief by H. H. PRICE
Brett's History of Psychology edited by R. S. PETERS
Clarity is Not Enough by H. D. LEWIS
Coleridge as a Philosopher by J. H. MUIRHEAD
The Commonplace Book of G. E. Moore edited by C. LEWY
Contemporary American Philosophy edited by C. P. ADAMS and W. P. MONTAGUE
Contemporary American Philosophy, second series, edited by JOHN E. SMITH
Contemporary British Philosophy first and second series edited by J. H. MUIRHEAD
Contemporary British Philosophy third series edited by H. D. LEWIS
Contemporary Indian Philosophy edited by RADHAKRISHNAN and J. H. MUIRHEAD
    2nd edition
Contemporary Philosophy in Australia edited by ROBERT BROWN and C. D. ROLLINS
The Discipline of the Cave by J. N. FINDLAY
Doctrine and Argument in Indian Philosophy by NINIAN SMART
Essays in Analysis by ALICE AMBROSE
Ethics by NICOLAI HARTMANN translated by STANTON COIT 3 vols
The Foundations of Metaphysics in Science by ERROL E. HARRIS
Freedom and History by H. D. LEWIS
The Good Will: A Study in the Coherence Theory of Goodness by H. J. PATON
Hegel: A Re-examination by J. N. FINDLAY
Hegel's Science of Logic translated by W. H. JOHNSTON and L. G. STRUTHERS 2 vols.
History of Aesthetic by B. BOSANQUET 2nd edition
History of English Utilitarianism by E. ALBEE
Human Knowledge by BERTRAND RUSSELL
A Hundred Years of British Philosophy by RUDOLF METZ translated by J. N. HARVEY,
    T. E. JESSOP, HENRY STURT
Ideas: A General Introduction to Pure Phenomenology by EDMUND HUSSERL translated
    by W. R. BOYCE GIBSON
Identity and Reality by EMILE MEYERSON
Imagination by F. J. FURLONG

The Muirhead Library of Philosophy

EDITED BY H. D. LEWIS

COLERIDGE AS PHILOSOPHER

BY J. H. MUIRHEAD
The Use of Philosophy
The Platonic Tradition in Anglo-Saxon
Philosophy

WITH SIR H. J. W. HETHERINGTON
Social Purposes

EDITOR
Contemporary British Philosophy
Identity and Reality

COLERIDGE
AS
PHILOSOPHER

BY

JOHN H. MUIRHEAD

LONDON: GEORGE ALLEN & UNWIN LTD
NEW YORK: HUMANITIES PRESS INC

First Published in 1930

Second Impression 1954

Third Impression 1970

ISBN 0 04 192025 2

*Printed in Great Britain
by John Dickens & Co. Ltd.,
Northampton.*

TO
P. M.

"Yea, oft alone,
Piercing the long neglected holy cave,
The haunt obscure of old Philosophy,
He bade with lifted torch its starry walls
Sparkle, as erst they sparkled to the flame
Of odorous lamps tended by Saint and Sage."

COLERIDGE *A Tombless Epitaph*

"Thou that within me art, my Self! An Ey
  Or Temple of a wide Infinity!
  O What a World art Thou! a World within!
          In thee appear
          All Things, and are
  Alive in Thee! Super-Substantial, rare,
      Abov themselves, and near a-kin
          To those pure Things we find
          In His Great Mind,
  Who made the World! Tho now eclipsed by Sin,
      Yet this within my Intellect
      Is found, when on it I reflect."

THOMAS TRAHERNE *My Spirit*

PREFACE

THE following study was undertaken in the conviction, gathered from a superficial acquaintance with Coleridge's published works, that as a stage in the development of a national form of idealistic philosophy his ideas are far more important than has hitherto been realized either by the educated public or by professed students of the subject. Closer study of them further convinced me that they formed in his mind a far more coherent body of philosophical thought than he has been anywhere credited with, and that to do fuller justice to this side of his multifarious and miraculous activity a more serious attempt than any with which I was acquainted required to be made to set them in relation to the state of philosophy at the time, and to the great revival of metaphysical study in England which the latter half of the nineteenth century was to witness. There was obvious difficulty, and not less obvious risk in any such attempt.

The difficulty consisted not merely in the wide diffusion of the sources from which, in his published works, his philosophical opinions had to be gathered, but in the popular character of the writings in which the more explicit statements of them were contained. We know in our own time how much injury in respect to depth and coherence may be done by the "occasionalism" of so much of the philosophical writing of England and America. Bradley used to deplore the loss to philosophy caused by William James's continual occupation with popular exposition in lecture form. In Coleridge's case his own ardent missionary spirit combined with his straitened circumstances was a constant temptation to dissipate his powers in practical applications instead of in the systematic development of his ideas. If Lamb's gibe as to his "preaching" was an exaggeration, something like it may be said of his crusading activities against what he considered the secular and materialistic spirit of his time and country.

The risk of such an attempt as is here made is that the brilliant flashes of his innumerable *aperçus* should be robbed of their delightful element of surprise by being made to appear merely sidelights of a duller if steadier illumination, and that what was the outcome of the poetry within him finding new means of utterance, after it had died out in its proper medium of verse, should be reduced to the prose of doctrinaire philosophy.

"Coleridge suffers", writes Leslie Stephen,[1] "when any attempt is made to extract a philosophical system from his works. His admirers must limit themselves to claims for what he undoubtedly deserves, the honour of having done much to stimulate thought, and abandon any claim to the construction of a definite system."

Fortunately the light thrown upon the whole subject by the recent direction of attention to important manuscript remains has relieved the

[1] Art. "Samuel Taylor Coleridge" in the *Dictionary of National Biography*. Cp. *Hours in a Library*, essay on Coleridge, vol. iv. "Coleridge never constructed a system."

student to a large extent both of the difficulty and the risk of such an attempt. It has always been known to scholars that Coleridgean manuscripts on technical subjects existed, but the prejudice against transcendental philosophy in general, and against what was supposed to be largely a plagiarized form of it in particular has until recently caused an unmerited neglect of the matter they contain. Miss Alice D. Snyder, of Vassar College, State of New York, who has been a pioneer in the sympathetic re-examination of these manuscripts, has given an account of the chief of them in her recently published book upon *Logic and Literature in Coleridge*, and some additional details are given in the appendix to the present study. While they are far from satisfying the expectations, which the poet's own allusions to them in his letters and conversations as practically finished compositions raise, they are sufficient to show that he made a far more serious attempt to work out his ideas into clear and consistent form than is commonly supposed, and enable us to supplement and bind together into something like a real volume the "Sibylline Leaves" he so lavishly scattered in his published utterances.

Even so there will be those to whom all metaphysical philosophy appears to be "transcendental moonshine", its speculative arguments mere "logical swimming-bladders". This book is not for them. Others who are still suspicious of "metaphysic" may be reminded that it is one of the ways provided by a kindly Heaven of reaching after the Unseen, and, as Coleridge himself put it, of penetrating to the Ancient of Days under the common forms of temporal life.

It is for the above reason, and because the contents of Coleridge's published works may be assumed to be fairly familiar to the general reader, that in the more important parts of this study, the stone which the builders rejected has been made the head of the corner, and the old material used chiefly as supplementary to the new. It is unfortunate that it is not yet possible to refer the reader to chapter and verse in all cases. But Miss Snyder has made many of the passages here quoted accessible in the extracts she has printed in her book. Where this has been done I have availed myself of her annotation. For the rest, when the fuller publication, which has been undertaken by the Columbia University Press in America and the Oxford Press in England, under the editorship of Mr. Warren E. Gibbs, has been completed, I trust that the mode of reference here adopted may enable the student without much difficulty to verify the quotations. In giving them direct from the manuscripts, except in condensation for purposes of the context, and the removal here and there of the superabundant capital letters which were the fashion of the time, I have taken no other liberties with the text.

Besides my obligation to the above-mentioned American scholars, I have to express my great indebtedness first to the kindness of the Rev. Gerard H. B. Coleridge, of Leatherhead, in offering me every facility to consult the manuscripts in his possession, as well as for permission to have photographed and

reproduced as frontispiece to this volume the fine
portrait of the Poet which is in his possession; and
secondly to the Trustees of the Henry E. Huntington
Library in San Marino, California, who have permitted me to quote from the invaluable manuscript
chapters of Coleridge's *Opus Maximum* it contains.
I can only trust that my use of these sources, if
it does not repay, may at least not betray their
confidence.

What follows was itself intended to form part of
a series of studies in the History of British and
American Idealism at present in preparation, and
to be a link between the earlier seventeenth century
and the later nineteenth developments of the great
Platonic tradition in England. But for the reason
above mentioned it outgrew the limits of a section
in the larger book, as a part of which nevertheless
I should desire it to be considered. Only so can
its manifest shortcomings be in some degree covered
and a place assigned to it as an attempt to supply
a lost chapter in the historical succession of native
forms of idealistic theory. It has had the advantage
of being read in proof by Dr. James Bonar
amicorum censor amicissimus.

DYKE END
  ROTHERFIELD, SUSSEX
    May 1930

CONTENTS

REFERENCES IN FOOTNOTES TO MANUSCRIPTS
AS DESCRIBED IN APPENDIX A3

MS. Logic I and II	=	3(*a*)
MS. B, I, II and III	=	3(*b*)
MS. H	=	3(*c*)
MS. C	=	3(*d*)

INTRODUCTION

"I have not a deeper conviction on earth, than that the principles of taste, morals, and religion, which are taught in the commonest books of recent composition, are false, injurious, and debasing."

—*The Friend*

THE world into which Coleridge was born may be said to have been intellectually "out of joint". It was a period to which Hegel's phrase the "unhappy consciousness" was particularly applicable. All that was best in social and political life, in the poetry and literature of past centuries, in the Christian religion, in science itself, as the pursuit of truth guided by a sense of the essential interrelatedness of the material and the spiritual worlds, seemed to be undergoing eclipse by the application of a method which reduced everything to "disconnection dull and spiritless". Society was interpreted as the result of organized selfishness, mitigated by natural sympathy, and the transforming associations of habit; political law as the expression of some individual will, and in the end as resting in force; art and literature as the play of a fancy released from the control of fact, bound only by the formal law of "unities" carved out of the chaotic multiplicity of nature; religion as either a system of superstition maintained in the interest of the existing form of society and the morality on which it rested, or as a scheme of salvation miraculously superimposed on human life; the higher science as pledged to the view that the processes of nature and the actions of man are controlled to their inmost depths by undeviating natural law. In all this the human

mind seemed to have become estranged from the
world which it inhabited. What was highest in it,
the impulse to pass beyond itself and enter, through
knowledge, feeling and action, into union with what
is greater and more enduring than itself, was everywhere checked by the view which the prevalent
principles seemed to be forcing upon it. Instead of
spiritualizing nature, philosophy had naturalized
spirit.

Yet spirit, too, has a nature of its own, and
everywhere, even as philosophers were legislating
for it, was passing beyond the limits they would fain
have imposed upon it. Everywhere new influences
were acting upon it, and everywhere it was responding in new uncovenanted ways. Travellers were
opening up new areas of the earth's surface. His-
torians were familiarizing men's minds with the
wealth of material to be found in the Middle Ages.
From two opposite sides the idea of civic society,
as the offspring of no mere agreement for the
protection of individual liberty and property, but
of a corporate will, unconsciously feeling after the
conditions of its own moral growth: "a partnership
in all art, in every virtue, and in all perfection"
was being preached, and already being embodied in
new ways of practice in education and government,
by the disciples of Rousseau and Edmund Burke.
A great Anglo-Saxon republic had risen in the West,
which sought to found itself on the idea of the Will
of God, with whatever narrowness of vision some
of its leaders interpreted the meaning of that Will.
In religion there had been a new outburst of the

sense that man lives not by bread alone, that there is that in him which seeks for a perfection far beyond anything he can attain by his own individual efforts. Through its great preachers Robert Hall, Thomas Chalmers, and others, it was summoning congregations "to apprehend things in their relations". From the absentee God of eighteenth-century Deism men were being led to the idea of a Divine Spirit that reveals itself continuously in history and common life. In the physical sciences themselves the rise into importance of anatomy and physiology was forcing into notice the dependence of life in all its forms on a principle which works from within outwards, as a constructive organizing force, and which required an entirely different method for its interpretation from that which was in vogue. Most striking of all were the new uses, to which in the poetry and art of the end of the eighteenth century and the beginning of the nineteenth imagination was being put, and the new principles of criticism that were required for the interpretation of its work.

There have been many attempts to fix upon the characters which go to make up the spirit of romance. Mrs. Olwen Ward Campbell[1] has remarked upon the difficulty of finding a definition that will include all of them. If Scott loved "strange adventure", Lamb did not. Neither was the priest of "wild nature". And as to "wonder", Scott's happy complacency, and the shallow creed of Byron, seem curiously out of place in an age of wonder.

[1] *Shelley and the Unromantics* (1924), pp. 249 and 250.

The writer goes on to find the essence of romance in a certain kind of faith in man depending upon some sense of the inherent greatness of his soul—a hope perhaps that he is more than mortal. "If the bend of a sunlit road, a bar of music, or the glimpse of a face suddenly thrills with romance, it is because these things have brought some unexpected revelation of the value of human life;

'I did but see her passing by,
And yet I love her till I die'."

I think that this is profoundly true, but it requires to be added that what to the romantic spirit is of chief value in human life is the sense of the Infinite which is implicit in it, and is the source of all man's deepest experiences. Sometimes this presence within him is brought home by what is strange, at other times by what is familiar; sometimes it speaks in the "still sad music of humanity", and moves to tears; at other times in the oddities of the forms under which this Presence manifests itself in finite life, and moves to kindly laughter. If wit, as has been said, is the sense of the littleness of things that seem great, humour may perhaps be defined as the sense of the greatness of things that seem little. If the one is the mark of the unromantic, the other is the most certain mark of the romantic. Be this as it may, it is from this sense of man's essential relation to the infinite whole, and from this alone, that the things usually referred to as most characteristic in the art and poetry of the period can be deduced, and it was this relation that the philosophy

of the time seemed wholly incapable of justifying
to the intelligence. Was it therefore thus un-
justifiable?

There were doubtless among the representatives
of these various fields of thought and practice those
who, if they had been asked what help in the
defence of the truths, on which they had unconsciously laid hold, against the prevailing secularist
spirit of the time they might expect from philosophy,
would have rejected its offices as a "Greek gift",
more likely to betray than to bestead them, and
who would have been prepared to echo Wordsworth's appeal to "a few strong instincts and a few
plain rules" against "all the pride of intellect and
thought". But they would nevertheless have been
wrong. True, if philosophy really was what it then
appeared to be, namely, the attempt to reduce
everything by "triumphant analysis" to its component elements, and, taking these as the ultimate
realities, to treat it as a mere aggregate or
mechanical resultant, while poetry, religion, even
(as Wordsworth seemed to think) morals and
politics were matters of unanalysable feeling, there
would have been something to be said for this
attitude. But to acknowledge it as the final and only
maintainable attitude was to leave man's mind the
victim of a conflict between different "instincts",
in the end equally strong, and different "rules",
equally binding upon it, and exposed to never-
ending internal division and unrest.

Fortunately there were some to whom this result
seemed fatal and who disbelieved in its necessity.

It all depended on the true interpretation of the meaning and method of philosophy. Did it mean the abstraction of the intellectual side of experience from all the others, and the development of the view of the world that concentration on the logic of cause and effect seemed to imply? Or was it not rather the endeavour, starting from the unity of experience as a whole, to bring the different interests of the human spirit together so that it might feel itself at home in all of them? Was it not in reality what Novalis had called it, "the homesickness of the soul"? in more technical language, the effort towards the "self-recognition of that spiritual life of the world which fulfils itself in many ways, but most completely in religion"? [1]

In England of the time of which we are speaking Coleridge has the merit of being the first to perceive the significance of this problem, and to rouse himself to find an answer to it. He saw that civilization was everywhere entering on a new phase; that forms of experience were everywhere emerging, of which the popular philosophy, as represented by Locke and Hume and Hartley, was wholly unable to give any intelligible account. This came home to him primarily, and more particularly in the fields of literature and religion, with which education and temperament most closely allied him. But the wide range of his vision enabled him to realize, as none other of his contemporaries in England did, the extent of the problem as embracing besides

[1] T. H. Green in "Popular Philosophy in its Relation to Life" (*Works*, vol. iii. p. 121).

these the whole spiritual life of man, morals and
education, law and politics, science and logic themselves. He was profoundly convinced that, brilliant
as were the achievements of the philosophy of the
last century, yet owing to the narrowness of its
foundations and the defects of its method it failed
to represent what was best in philosophical tradition. He found food for this conviction in the older
writers of his own country, but he had the openness of mind to feel their limitations, and to be
ready to put himself to school in the thought of
earlier ages and other countries. More particularly
he had the insight and freedom from prejudice to
perceive that it was from Germany that the chief
light on the problem as set by his own time was
coming. Closer acquaintance convinced him that,
profound and in some respects decisive as were the
contributions of German philosophy, particularly
of Kant, to its solution, there was as little finality
in them as in those of his own country. Rich as
might be the materials he inherited from both, the
building itself must be one more precisely fitted to
the needs of the time and leaving more room for
expansion, as new needs developed or old ones
revived with new force. With a courage and per-
sistency for which he has received too little credit,
and which was even denied to him by the greatest
of his contemporaries,[1] almost alone and in spite
of the obstructions of his temperamental failings,

---

[1] "Once more", wrote Carlyle, "the tragic story of a high
endowment with an insufficient will. The courage, necessary to him
above all things, had been denied this man."—*Life of John Sterling*.

he pursued the ideal of such a comprehensive and
organized system of thought as might at last in his
own country merit the name of philosophy.

What is attempted in the following chapters is
the story of the influences under which his philosophical convictions were matured, the principles
of method he was led to adopt, the view to which
these led as to the ultimate reality of which the
world of nature and human life is the temporal
expression, and the applications he made of it in
the various departments of theory and practice.
No claim will be made for any sort of finality in
his results. On the contrary, fundamental points
will be indicated in which he manifestly failed.
But whatever be the ultimate judgment upon them,
they formed a body of doctrine, which, so far as it
was then known, exercised a profound influence on
the succeeding generation, and as we now know
it, *stat sua mole.* John Stuart Mill had little enough
sympathy with its speculative basis, but it was of
Coleridge's work as a thinker that he wrote in
1840:[1] "The name of Coleridge is one of the few
English names of our time which are likely to be
oftener pronounced and to become symbolic of
more important things in proportion as the inward
workings of the age manifest themselves more and
more in outward fact. Bentham excepted, no
Englishman of recent date has left his impress so
deeply on the opinions and mental tendencies of
those among us who attempt to enlighten their

[1] "Coleridge and Bentham," reprinted in *Dissertations and Discussions*
(1859).

practice by philosophical meditation. If it be true, as Lord Bacon affirms, that a knowledge of the speculative opinions of the men between twenty and thirty years of age is the great source of political prophecy, the existence of Coleridge will show itself by no slight or ambiguous traces in the coming history of our country."

CHAPTER I

PHILOSOPHICAL DEVELOPMENT

"A mind growing to the last."—DERWENT COLERIDGE

1. THE NATIVE HUE OF COLERIDGE'S MIND

THE philosophical development of a mind like Coleridge's, omnivorous, sensitive, growing to the last, is necessarily a tangled tale; in his case rendered more tangled still by apparently contradictory accounts of it in his own writings and conversations. There was no recorded line of thought with which he was unacquainted and with which his soul had not some bond of sympathy. I believe that the chief mistake to be avoided is that of attributing too much to any one of the multitudinous influences that went to the formation of his opinions. Yet one or two things stand clearly out, first in the native hue of his own mind modified and exaggerated in later life by certain morbid traits in his moral experience, secondly in the intellectual currents which stimulated and gave direction to his thought and in the order in which he came under their influence.

His nature was profoundly religious not only in the Platonic sense of belief in the supremacy of Good as an abstract quality, nor in the Spinozistic sense of absorption in the vision of the wholeness of things, but in the sense of a longing for a personal relation with a Mind and Will as at once the source of all reality and a living presence in the soul.

However necessary, as concerned with the grounds and conditions of religion, philosophy might be, it could never take its place. Even though philosophy shall have become the habit of referring to the Invisible as the supreme Will revealing itself in reason and pouring forth in life, this is not enough. "This is a constituent of Religion," he wrote, "but something is still wanting. To be Religion it must be the reference of an intelligent responsible Will Finite to an Absolute Will, and the reference must refer as a Will and a Life, i.e. a Person to a living I am. We may feel *from* and about a thing, an event, a quality, we can feel *toward* a Person only. The personal in me is the ground and condition of Religion, and the Personal alone is the Object."[1] It was this and not any mere attachment to a tradition that was the source of his belief in Christianity as "alone reflecting the character of religion", and in this sense "the only true religion". It was "Judaism + Greece". While in Greece the Personality of God is the esoteric doctrine, the infinite whole the exoteric, in Christianity it is the reverse. Personality is the exoteric, the whole of Good the esoteric. That this side of his philosophy obtained exaggerated emphasis in the later years of his life owing to his personal craving for a God who "answers prayer" and *forgives* is, I think, undoubtedly true and traceable to the morbid bent in his own character. But quite apart from that, it is doubtful whether he could ever have reconciled himself to any form of philosophy which seemed to

[1] MS. C, p. 115.

him to fail to do justice to what he regarded as pivotal in human life—the binding (*religio-religatio*) of man's will to a Will that is greater than itself.[1]

Leaving this for the present as belonging more particularly to his philosophy of religion, we have certain outstanding influences coming from without that mark milestones in his spiritual pilgrimage.

2. EARLY STUDIES

We need not perhaps take too seriously Lamb's picture [1] of the infant metaphysician "unfolding the mysteries of Iamblichus and Plotinus" to admiring school-fellows at Christ's Hospital. Yet we have his own word for it that while yet at school he began to experience "a rage for Metaphysics occasioned by the essays on 'Liberty' and 'Necessity' in Cato's Letters and more by theology", and that by the time he left he had already, with the aid of Voltaire's *Philosophical Dictionary*, and in spite of the flogging he received for his errancy from the

---

[1] There is a certain truth in A. W. Benn's ironical remark, "One can understand that the sense of sin conceived as an overwhelming fatality should have been particularly active with Coleridge. It is less intelligible that he should have generalized this deep and well-founded consciousness of his own delinquencies into a comprehensive indictment of human nature as such; and that he should have regarded the spirit of the Gospel as a cure for the world at large when it was proving so totally inoperative in his own particular instance" (*English Rationalism in the Nineteenth Century*, vol. i. p. 239). But the point is not his desire to convict the human race of its sin but to find a ground of pardon for his own.

[1] *Essays of Elia*, "Christ's Hospital five-and-thirty years ago".

path of scholastic routine, boxed the compass of Christian heresies.[1]

Of more importance were the influences with which he came in contact when in 1791 he proceeded to Jesus College, Cambridge. It was David Hartley's college, but there were other currents of thought in the University, and, though Cambridge Platonism is usually associated with the earlier seventeenth-century movement, it is important to remember the revival of Platonic studies in that University in these very years through the translations of Thomas Taylor,[2] of which Coleridge could hardly have failed to take notice. We shall probably be right also in referring to this period [3] his acquaintance with the Cambridge Platonists, whose writings would

[1] "At a very premature age, even before my fifteenth year, I had bewildered myself in metaphysics and theological controversies." *Works* (Shedd's edition), iii. pp. 152–3, and the biographical fragment in MS. C printed in J. Gillman's *Life of Samuel Taylor Coleridge* (1838), p. 23.

[2] These deserve more notice in any history of British idealism than they have hitherto received. They include, from Plotinus, *Ennead* i. book 6, Concerning the Beautiful (1787); An Essay on the Beautiful from the Greek of Plotinus (1792); Five Books of Plotinus (1794); from Plato, the *Phaedrus, Cratylus, Phaedo, Parmenides*, and *Timaeus* (1792–3). If, as Taylor's biographer said, his critics knew more Greek, he knew more Plato.

[3] See Professor C. Howard's *Coleridge's Idealism* (1925), useful as a corrective of the view which exaggerates German influences in Coleridge's development, but otherwise itself inclined to exaggerate the influence over him of writers whom Coleridge himself brands as a group for "ignorance of natural science; physiography scant in fact and stuffed out with fables; physiology imbrangled with an inapplicable logic and a misgrowth of *entia rationalia*, i.e. substantial abstractions". (*Notes on English Divines*, "Henry More's Theological Works", ii. p. 129.)

harmonize with what he might have learned from Plato and Plotinus, and go to deepen the mystic strain in his thought. But, aided by his intimacy with Frend,[1] the attraction of the leading representative of the Lockean tradition was too strong for him, and for the next five years he passed under the influence of David Hartley, described in his poem, *Religious Musings*, of 1794 as:

> "He of mortal kind
> The wisest; he first who marked the ideal tribes
> Up the fine fibres through the sentient brain."

In the same year he wrote to Southey: "I am a complete necessitarian, and I understand the subject almost as well as Hartley himself, and believe the corporeality of thought, namely that it is motion."[2] That this was the dominant influence in his thought up to 1796 seems proved by his allusion in September of that year to his infant son. "His name", he writes, "is David Hartley Coleridge. I hope that ere he be a man, if God destines him for continuance in this life, his head will be convinced of and his heart saturated with the truths so ably supported by that great master of Christian Philosophy." It might seem puzzling that in the poem on the *Destiny of Nations*, written apparently

[1] Gillman's *Life*, etc., p. 317.
[2] *Letters*, vol. i. p. 113 (1895 ed.). I see no reason to doubt, as Howard does, the sincerity of these words. We have the application of the doctrine of "philosophical necessity" to the ethics of revolution in the Bristol Address, also dated 1794. (See *Conciones ad Populum*, p. 21. "Vice originates not in the man but in the surrounding circumstances, not in the heart but in the understanding.")

about the same time,[1] he should have denounced those who cheat themselves

> "With noisy emptiness of learned phrase,
> Their subtle fluids, impacts, essences,
> Untenanting creation of its God",

in words that seem so precisely applicable to Hartley's materialistic psychology, were it not that in that philosopher's writings we have a conspicuous illustration of the conflict referred to in the above Introduction.

3. "THE GREAT AND EXCELLENT DR. HARTLEY"

Hartley's philosophy was, as he tells us himself at the beginning of his chief book,[2] a development on the one hand of "what Mr. Locke and other ingenious persons [3] since his time have delivered concerning the influence of associations over our opinions and affections, and its use in explaining those things in an accurate and precise way which are commonly referred to the power of habit and custom in a general and indeterminate one"; and on the other of "hints concerning the performance of sensation and motion which Sir Isaac Newton has given at the end of the *Principia* and in the questions annexed to his *Optics*". The "accuracy and precision" which Hartley claimed to have

[1] See Oxford Edition of the Poems (1912), i. p. 131.
[2] *Observations on Man: His Frame, His Duty, and His Expectations* (1749).
[3] The allusion so precisely fits Hume as to render unlikely W. R. Sorley's surmise (*History of English Philosophy*, p. 195) that Hartley had not heard of him at this time. *The Treatise of Human Nature* had appeared in 1739.

added to the older doctrine of association consisted in a fuller statement than had hitherto been attempted of its "laws", and in the application of them to explain: (1) the formation from a simpler of a more complex idea which "may not appear to bear any relation to its compounding parts"; (2) the generation of voluntary action through the connection of a sensation or an idea with a movement; (3) judgments of assent and dissent (i.e. beliefs) as only "very complex internal feelings which adhere by association to such clusters of words as are called propositions"; and (4) the constitution of intellectual pleasures and pains, such as those of imagination, ambition, self-interest, sympathy, "theopathy", and the moral sense, out of simpler constituents. The development of Sir Isaac Newton's "hints" was the doctrine of vibrations or "vibratiuncles" residing in the pores of the nerves and causing sensations, which may be said to be the first sketch of a complete physiological psychology. Into the details of this it is not necessary to enter. What concerns us is the theory of mind which in the first place reduces its action to the subconscious one of mechanical association, to the total exclusion of selective attention or imaginative construction,[1] and in the second place explains consciousness as a surface play of material movements, "the quick silverplating behind the looking-glass", as Coleridge learned to call it, enabling us

[1] Imagination has only five lines devoted to it in the whole treatise and that in a section upon Dreams, where it is distinguished from "reverie" as involving less attention to thoughts and greater disturbance by "foreign objects". *Op. cit*, part i. prop. xci.

to see what is going on, but contributing nothing to it.

If we ask how such a philosophy could come to be put forward by its author, or find any acceptance with intelligent readers as a satisfactory account of "Man, his Frame, his Duty, and his Expectations", it is only fair to both the author and his public to remember that there was no pretence of this kind. The Second Part of Hartley's treatise is devoted to an exposition of natural and revealed religion from an entirely different point of view from that of the first part, and enables the writer to pose as the defender of faiths, of which his scientific theory had destroyed the intellectual foundations.

Bearing all this in mind, we wonder less to find the same conflict of principles in Hartley's ardent disciple. I believe that a close examination of the poems of the period would show that it reflected itself there in the form of a domination of his mind by conceptions derived from a necessitarian philosophy which was in essence antagonistic to the romantic spirit of freedom that was the deepest strain of Coleridge's own intellectual being. An American critic has said of *Religious Musings* that "the principles of unity and necessity fairly jostle each other in rivalry for the reader's attention".[1]

"There is one Mind, one omnipresent Mind
    Omnific"

[1] G. F. Gingerich, in article, "From Necessity to Transcendentalism in Coleridge", in *Publications of the Modern Language Association of America*, vol. xxxv.

is the text of the poem and of this whole period of the poet's life. We have the same note in the invocation in *The Destiny of Nations* (1796) to the

> "All-conscious Presence of the Universe,
> Nature's vast ever-acting Energy!
> In will, in deed, Impulse of All to All!"

In the poems of the following years these abstractions are softened and humanized, and in the *Ancient Mariner* and *Christabel* they are wholly subordinated to the interest of the characters and incidents. It would be pedantry to look for philosophical doctrines in their magical lines. Yet the power of the first consists just in the sense it imparts of the sinister and fateful power that works in the events. If we cannot say with Gingerich that the Mariner is "a most engaging Unitarian", we can agree with him that in this poem "Coleridge has given, in a rarefied etherealized form, the exhalations and aroma of his personal experience of Necessity and Unity, the blossom and fragrancy of all his earlier religious meditations".[1] The fact that in *Christabel* the religious motive has disappeared the same writer takes as a sign that "in this direction the evolution of Coleridge's mind has gone as far as possible", and draws the conclusion that "those

[1] For the above reason I think this a truer statement of the case than Leslie Stephen's more comprehensive remark: "The germ of all Coleridge's utterances may be found—by a little ingenuity—in *The Ancient Mariner*, though we may well agree that "part of the secret (of the strange charm of the poem) is the ease with which Coleridge moves in a world of which the machinery—as the old critics called it—is supplied by the mystic philosopher."—*Hours in a Library*, vol. iv. "Coleridge".

who suppose that, if his poetic powers had remained unimpaired, Coleridge would have continued writing Ancient Mariners and Christabels imagine a vain thing". What was required was a complete reorientation of the shaping spirit of imagination within him to the new view of the world which his studies in philosophy had by this time begun to open before him. It was to this that he proved unequal. No one knew it better than himself or knew better the reason of it in the failure of the fountain within him of the "joy" that alone could bear him through the task.[1] The destroyer of this creative joy was not (as literary critics have so often said [2]) his metaphysical studies (these were his solace for the loss of it), but the fatal drug to which at this time he became addicted.[3] What in the ruin of his own poetic hopes he had the genius and the magnanimity to see was that the strength

[1] The lines in the *Ode to Dejection* (1802) are well known:

"Joy, Lady! is the spirit and the power,
Which wedding Nature to us, gives in dower
A new Earth and new Heaven."

[2] For the most part repeating Wordsworth's view that "Coleridge had been spoilt for a poet by going to Germany". His mind, Wordsworth held, had thereby been fixed in its natural direction towards metaphysical theology. "If it had not been so he would have been the greatest, the most abiding poet of his age." *Prose Works*, iii. 469.

[3] "Poetry", wrote De Quincey, who knew here what he was talking about, "can flourish only in the atmosphere of happiness. But subtle and perplexed investigations of difficult problems are amongst the commonest resources for beguiling the sense of misery." De Quincey also recognized that while dejection might stimulate to speculation, it is insufficient to sustain exertion. "Opium-eaters are tainted with the infirmity of leaving works unfinished." *Narrative Papers*, vol. ii. "Coleridge and Opium-Eating".

that was denied to him had been so richly bestowed on his friend:

> "Currents self-determined, as might seem,
> Or by some inner Power."

As Gingerich has rightly seen, the importance of the poem from which these words are quoted[1] in Coleridge's spiritual history cannot easily be over-estimated. It is with this history and the results for philosophy that we are here concerned.

4. BERKELEY AND SPINOZA

At what exact time Coleridge became aware of this conflict of principles it is difficult to determine. Different accounts are given by his biographers. Referring to the name of Berkeley which he gave to his second son, born in May 1798, J. D. Campbell[2] comments that it was "in honour of the Philosopher, the keystone of whose system was still in his disciples' eyes indestructible". He does not tell us what this keystone was, but the context seems to indicate that he had in mind the sensational basis of Berkeley's earlier thought of which Hartley's doctrine of association was a development. Turnbull, on the other hand, tells us that he named his second son "after the idealist philosopher who had now displaced Hartley, who had been in the ascendant when the first child was born".[3] This seems to find

---

[1] To William Wordsworth (1807).
[2] *Samuel Taylor Coleridge*, p. 89.
[3] *Biographia Epistolaris*, A. Turnbull (1911), vol. i. p. 162.

support in what Southey wrote in 1808, "Hartley
was ousted by Berkeley, Berkeley by Spinoza,
Spinoza by Plato",[1] and by Coleridge's own statement that when his earlier philosophy failed him [2]
and "his metaphysical theories lay before him in
the hour of anguish as toys by the bedside of a
child deadly sick", he turned again to "Plato
and the mystics, Locke, Berkeley, Descartes, and
Spinoza". The difficulty vanishes if we remember
the difference between the earlier empirical Berkeley
to whom *esse* is *percipi* and the later Platonic to
whom *esse* is *concipi*, and that the discovery of this
difference was itself one of the important steps in
Coleridge's philosophical development. Cottle
quotes him in 1796 as having said: "Bishop Taylor,
old Baxter, David Hartley, and the Bishop of
Cloyne are my men". By 1798 he may well have
discovered the difference between the last two.

At what exact time Berkeley's star began to wane
is uncertain. By the time Derwent was born (September 14, 1800) there were obvious reasons against
naming him after the philosophical idol of the
moment. We have his own word for it that in these
years he found in Spinoza's idea of God what he

[1] See Campbell, *op. cit.*, p. 165, n. 1, who quotes it without noting
the inconsistency with his own previous statement.
[2] It would be a mistake to attribute to this early period the
devastating criticism of Hartley which we have in chapters v–vii of
Biog. Lit. But the less reason we have to commit the mistake, the
more remarkable is the complete mastery he by that time had
obtained of the philosophical situation. The critical merits of these
and the following two chapters have not been sufficiently recognized
by literary critics who have been too ready to allow them to be
obscured by the evidences of "plagiarism" in the notorious
chapter xii.

describes as an "Ararat", and as late as December 1799 he could still speak of "my Spinozism".[1] But this could not remain a permanent resting-place for his ark. The Infinite of Spinoza he saw to be the negation of all "the determinations that go to make the individual". No man, Hegel said, can ever be a philosopher who has not at one time been a Spinozist; but it is also perhaps true that no philosopher who is a man has ever remained one. While the head demands the universal, the heart yearns for the particular. Coleridge saw no way to "reconcile personality" with such infinity. While "his head was with Spinoza his whole heart remained with Paul and John". The old Pantheism of Spinoza he held to be far better than the new Deism, which is "but the hypocrisy of materialism". "Did philosophy start with an *it is* instead of an *I am*, Spinoza would be altogether true."[2] But its starting-point was wrong.

Into the midst of these speculative doubts we may imagine coming his closer intercourse with Wordsworth and the co-operation which issued in the famous experiment of the *Lyrical Ballads* in 1798. His generous enthusiasm for his friend's work is a matter of literary history. He had the insight to see in it an excellence of the creative imagination, a vision of the faculty divine, which was an entirely

[1] *Letters* (1895 ed.), i. p. 319. On his admiration for Spinoza's great moral qualities as distinguished from "the whole nest of popular infidels" (including Hobbes and Voltaire), see Gillman, *op. cit.*, p. 319 foll.

[2] See H. Crabb Robinson's *Diary, Reminiscences and Correspondence*, 2nd ed., 1872, ii. 5, and *Letters*, i. 209.

new thing in poetry. But it was not merely to him a new fact. It was a summons to new thought. "This excellence", he tells us, "I no sooner felt than I sought to understand."[1] But where to find the clue to the understanding of it? There was clearly no help to be looked for in the Associationist psychology. This might account for the vagaries of fancy, though even here the images had to be formed so as to cohere in a new whole. Before the brooding spirit of imagination and the revelation of new significance in the common things of life it was helpless. Between this and merely fanciful creations there was a distinction, not of degree, but of kind. Equally helpless was the soulless pantheism which he had found in Spinoza. The clue, if clue there were, must be sought elsewhere.

5. GERMAN PHILOSOPHY

It was at this point that a new chapter of his intellectual history opened. His own account in "Satyrane's Letters" [2] of the visit which, accompanied by the Wordsworths, he paid to Germany in 1798 is familiar to students of literature. Together they visited Klopstock, the author of the once celebrated *Messiah*.[3] For the rest the difference between the two men in the use which they made of their opportunity was characteristic. To Words-

[1] How he came afterwards to understand it we know from the fine passage quoted, *Biographia Literaria*, chap. iv, from No. 5 of *The Friend*.
[2] Printed in *Biographia Literaria*.
[3] De Quincey, *op. cit.*, has given a lively account of this visit.

worth, with his essential insularity, it was simply a "change of sky". He was content to remain for the most part at Goslar wandering "among unknown men" and writing "home thoughts from abroad".[1] To Coleridge the journey was a pilgrimage of the spirit—an opportunity "to finish his education". He fared first to Ratzeburg, then to Göttingen, where he settled for the best part of a year, with the aim of "a more thorough revolution in his philosophical principles and a deeper insight into his own heart". His philosophical orientation had for the time to be postponed to a mastery of the language, to attendance on Blumenbach's lectures on physiology, and to literary studies, more particularly of Lessing,[2] that bore only indirectly upon it. But before returning to England in the following July he provided himself with the means for such a study by the purchase of thirty pounds' worth of books, chiefly metaphysics.

We get an interesting glimpse of the state of Kantian study in England at this time from the Essay of De Quincey,[3] in which he pours contempt on editors and reviewers for their failure to throw

[1] C. H. Herford's *Age of Wordsworth.*
[2] A life of whom, interwoven with a sketch of German literature, "in its rise and present state", he designed at this time. See letters of January 4 (*Letters*, i. 270) and May 21, 1799 (*Tom Wedgwood*, 1903, p. 70), in the latter of which he tells Wedgwood that one of his objects was that "of conveying under a better name than my own ever will be opinions which I deem of the highest importance". It was unfortunate that later in life, in writing *Confessions of an Inquiring Spirit*, he gave the appearance of having done the opposite with regard to the inspiration of Scripture.
[3] *Philosophical Writers* (1856).

any light on the dark places of Kant's philosophy, promises something better, but for the present contents himself with stigmatizing it as sceptical in religion and reactionary in politics. Elsewhere [1] he finds no words strong enough to denounce the "Apollyon mind" and "the ghoulish creed" of the "world-shattering Kant". On the other hand, his long Essay on the "Last Days of Immanuel Kant" [2] and his translation of the *Sketch of Universal History on a Cosmopolitan Plan* did much to stimulate the sympathetic study of Kant in the generation immediately following.

At what precise date Coleridge began the minuter examination of contemporary German philosophy it is difficult to say. At the end of 1796 he refers to Mendelssohn as Germany's profoundest metaphysician, with the exception of "the most unintelligible Immanuel Kant".[3] In his letters of 1800 there are allusions to the light he has gained on "several parts of the human mind which have hitherto remained either wholly unexplained or most falsely explained", to prolonged meditations on "the relations of thought to things", and to his "serious occupation" in metaphysical investigation of the laws by which our feelings form affinities with each other and with words.[4] Yet in connection with an unpublished memorandum of February 1801, Leslie Stephen tells us that "Coleridge writes as though he had as yet read no German philo-

[1] *Literary Remains*, pp. 171–2.
[2] *Narrative and Miscellaneous Papers* (1853).
[3] *Letters*, i. p. 203, n. 2.   [4] Campbell, *op. cit.*, p. 119.

sophy . . There is none of the transcendentalism of the Schelling kind . . He still sticks to Hartley and to the Association doctrine . . He is dissatisfied with Locke but has not broken with the philosophy generally supposed to be in the Locke line. In short, he seems to be at the point where a study of Kant would be ready to launch him in his later direction, but is not at all conscious of the change." [1]

It is probably to March of this year (1801) that we must refer the crisis. In a letter of the 16th he tells Thomas Poole that after a period of "most intense study", if he does not delude himself, he has "not only completely extricated the notions of time and space but overthrown the doctrine of association as taught by Hartley, and with it all the irreligious metaphysics of modern infidels—especially the doctrine of necessity". A week later he thinks he has unmasked the fallacy that underlies the whole Newtonian [2] philosophy, namely, that the mind is merely "a lazy Looker-on on an external world" : if this be not so, "if the mind be not passive, if it be indeed made in God's image, the Image of the Creator, there is ground for the suspicion that any system built on the passiveness of mind must be false as a system".

How far are we justified in concluding that this revolution was the result of his German studies?

[1] *Letters*, i. p. 351 n.
[2] Cp. *Table Talk*. Works (Shedd), vol. vi. p. 351, where he accuses Newton of not being able to conceive the idea of a law: "He thought it a physical thing after all".

4. Debt to Kant and Schelling

In support of the view of the dominance of their influence we have the classical passage in the *Biographia Literaria* in which he describes the general effect upon his mind of his first introduction to Kant, Fichte, and Schelling. "The writings of the illustrious sage of Koenigsberg, the founder of the Critical Philosophy, more than any other work, at once invigorated and disciplined my understanding. The originality, the depth, and the compression of the thoughts; the novelty and subtlety, yet solidity and importance of the distinctions; the adamantine chain of the logic, and, I will venture to add (paradox as it will appear to those who have taken their notion of Immanuel Kant from Reviewers and Frenchmen), the clearness and evidence of the Critique of Pure Reason, the Critique of Judgment, of the Metaphysical Elements of Natural Philosophy, and his Religion within the bounds of Pure Reason, took possession of me with a giant's hand." While it might have its attraction for a descendant of Scottish Covenanters who had inherited something of their spirit, like Carlyle, Fichte's was not a philosophy likely to find a congenial soil in the mind of a poet like Coleridge. He gives credit to Fichte for dealing the first mortal blow to Spinozism "by commencing with an act instead of a thing or substance", but he deplores his "boastful and hyperstoic hostility to Nature as lifeless, godless, and altogether unholy: while his religion consisted in the assumption of a mere *Ordo*

Ordinans which we were permitted *exoterice* to call God; and his ethics in an ascetic and almost monkish mortification of the natural passions and desires".[1] Schelling was altogether different. "It was in Schelling's *Natur-Philosophie* and *System des transcendental (en) Idealismus* that I first found a genial coincidence with much that I had toiled out for myself and a powerful assistance to what I had yet to do . . With exception of one or two fundamental ideas which can not be withheld from Fichte, to Schelling we owe the completion and the most important victories of this revolution in Philosophy." "To me", he adds, "it will be happiness and honour enough should I succeed in rendering the system itself intelligible to my countrymen and in the application of it to the most awful of subjects for the most important of purposes." From the same work we know that there was a period of his life at which he felt himself so much at one with Schelling's philosophy that he was prepared to risk his reputation for literary honesty by adopting whole portions of its text as the basis of his own theory of poetry.[2]

All this, combined with the unanimous testimony of his friends as to the impression which his conversations left upon them, would lend countenance

[1] As he puts it elsewhere, "Fichte in his moral system is but a caricature of Kant; or rather he is a Zeno with the cowl, rope, and sackcloth of a Carthusian monk. His metaphysics have gone by; but he has the merit of having prepared the ground for the dynamic philosophy by the substitution of act for thing". *Letters*, ii. p. 682.
[2] See below.

to the view that his own philosophy was little more than a transcript from the German of Kant and Schelling, from whom he selected what happened to suit him. But this would be a superficial view of the real state of the case, and one of the first results of a closer study of his philosophical opinions as a whole is the conviction of its entire baselessness.

Leaving this for the present and confining ourselves to the more external evidence, we have in the first place his own reiterated statement that the essential elements of his philosophy were already planted in his mind before he became acquainted with the later German thought.[1] While perhaps, considering the audience to which it was addressed, it would be hardly justifiable to appeal to the absence of direct allusion to German influences in the first authoritative sketch of his philosophy in the 1818 edition of *The Friend*, it is undoubtedly true, as he himself says, that this contains nothing, not even the distinction between Reason and Understanding and the "law of polarity or essential dualism",[2] which is not traceable either to Greek

[1] The most decisive passage is that in the letter to his nephew of April 8, 1825 (*Letters*, vol. ii. 735): "I can not only honestly assert but I can satisfactorily prove by reference to writings (Letters, Marginal Notes, and those in books that have never been in my possession since I first left England for Hamburgh, etc.) that all the elements, the differentials, as the algebraists say, of my present opinions existed for me before I had ever seen a book of German Metaphysics later than Wolf and Leibnitz or could have read it, if I had." Cp. this with *Anima Poetae* 106 of unrecorded date.

[2] *The Friend* (1844 ed.), i. p. 206 (Shedd, ii. p. 142) foll. and i. p. 121 (Shedd, ii. p. 91), where the latter is defined as the principle that "every power in nature and in spirit must evolve an opposite as the sole means and condition of its manifestation; and all opposition is a tendency to reunion" and expressly referred to Heraclitus.

philosophy or to "the great men of Europe from the middle of the fifteenth till towards the close of the seventeenth century", whose "principles both of taste and philosophy" he upheld.[1] But by far the most effective answer from this side to the accusation of the plagiarism of anything that was essential to his own system from Schelling is the running commentary on some of the German's works that was published by Henry Nelson Coleridge in the 1847 edition of the *Biographia Literaria*, the general line of which is to convict him of "gross materialism".[2]

The precise moment of disillusionment with Schelling is difficult to fix. If we assume that it had not taken place in 1817 (the date of the publication of the *Biographia Literaria*), a note of August 27, 1818, on Jacob Boehme's *Aurora* tells of his own early intoxication with "the vernal fragrance and effluvia from the flowers and firstfruits of Pantheism, while still unaware of its bitter root", and "pacifying his religious feelings in the meantime with the fine distinction that, though God was = the World, the World was not = God—as if God were a whole composed of parts of which the World was one". In the same note, after defining two types of error which he had found in Boehme as "the occasional substitution of the accidents of his own peculiar acts of association for processes *in universo*",

[1] *The Friend*, Appendix A.
[2] See Shedd, iii. p. 691 foll., and cp. MS. C, where Schelling is accused of having "failed to make intelligence comprehensible (as the source of definite limitation) instead of assuming it as the ground, as I myself do".

and "the confusion of the creaturely spirit in the great moments of its renascence for (with?) the deific energies in Deity itself", he goes on to attribute the first to Spinoza and both to Schelling and his followers.[1]

In view of all this, there seems to be no reason to question either the sincerity or the truth of the autobiographical statement above quoted. The acceptance of it is quite compatible with the belief, first, that the discovery of the coincidence of the teaching of Kant's *Critique* with what he had "toiled out for himself" exercised an immense confirmatory influence on his thought, and gave him a new confidence in the exposition of it; and secondly, that while still in doubt as to the full effect of the new influences, and suffering perhaps from a certain loss of nerve, he came under the spell of Schelling. But that this was only a passing phase of a mind which was "growing and accumulating to the last", is put beyond all doubt not only by the above quotations, but by his own express criticism of the views put forward in the *Biographia*, which within a month of his death has something of the solemnity of a testamentary deposition: "The metaphysical disquisition at the end of the first volume of the

---

[1] See Alice D. Snyder's article on "Coleridge on Giordano Bruno" in *Modern Language Notes*, xlii. 7, and cp. *Letters*, ii. p. 683. He thinks the coincidence between Schelling and Boehme "too glaring to be solved by mere independent coincidence in thought and intention", and in reading the former "remains in the same state, with the same dimly and partially light-shotten mists before his eyes, as when he read the same things for the first time in Jacob Boehme" (Shedd, iii. p. 695).

Biographia Literaria is unformed and immature; it contains the fragments of the truth, but it is not fully thought out. It is wonderful to myself to think how infinitely more profound my views now are, and yet how much clearer they are withal. The circle is completing; the idea is coming round to and to be the common sense."[1]

If it were worth while at this time of day to defend Coleridge's work as a whole against the charge of "plagiarism", one could not do it better than in the words which his disciple J. H. Green uses in reference to the *Confessions of an Inquiring Spirit*: "in the case of a work which is an aggregate and not a growth . . . it would be as just to reclaim, as it would be easy to detach the borrowed fragments; but where the work is the result of a formative principle which gives it unity and totality, where the thoughts and reasonings are the development of a living principle to an organic whole, it may be safely assumed that the author, who interweaves with his own the kindred products of other men's minds, is impelled only by the sense and pleasurable sympathy of a common intellectual activity, and that he would or might have arrived at the same or similar results where these are potentially contained in the principle that gave birth to his reasonings."[2]

In what sense Coleridge's philosophy is such an organic whole it is our aim in this study more

[1] See *Works*, vol. vi. p. 520.
[2] Introduction to *op. cit.*, with which might be compared what Turnbull says, *Biographia Epistolaris*, vol. ii. p. 146.

precisely to determine. Meantime the conclusion
that emerges from the above review is that in the
course of the second decade of the new century
Coleridge had passed from the pantheism not only
of Spinoza but of Schelling, and was working in
the direction of a view which should be a synthesis
of the realism which it represented with the idealism
of Kant.[1] It was on this line that he believed that
English philosophy had to be reconstructed if
justice was to be done at once to man's deepest
interests and to the outer facts of nature and
history.

The work in which already in 1814 he had
conceived the idea of developing the view he had
reached into a complete system, and which when
completed was to revolutionize "all that had been
called Philosophy or Metaphysics in England and
France since the era of the commencing predominance of the mechanical system at the restoration of the second Charles",[2] has been treated by
his biographers[3] far too much as a mere vision.
Even although it were more visionary than we now
know it to have been, his continual mention of it
from 1821 onwards is at least proof that he had
reached a stable resting-place after his long wanderings, and that whatever he thenceforth wrought

[1] See Benn, *op. cit.*, p. 244, who compares this synthesis with "the
unity of Substance and Subject" that Hegel was working out in
these same years.
[2] Letter of January 1821 (Allsop, *Letters*, etc., of *S. T. Coleridge*,
3rd ed., p. 33).
[3] See e.g. Campbell, *op. cit.*, p. 251. For allusions to it as his
Magnum Opus, see *ibid.* Index *sub verb.*

out would be as the deepening and expansion of a single principle which he had made his own. If this principle and the synthesis it represented tended in the end to ally him with Fichte rather than with Hegel, it is not the less interesting in view of the recent pronounced reaction of idealist philosophy both in England and America in the direction of Voluntarism.

In what follows no special attempt will be made to trace Coleridge's mental development further. Our object will rather be to state the broader features of the form of nineteenth-century idealism of which more than any other he was the founder, as these appear in his maturer writings, and to follow the applications he made of his principles in the different fields of philosophy.

CHAPTER II

LOGIC

"The first source of falsehood in Logic is the abuse and misapplication of Logic itself."—MS. *Logic*.

1. IDEA OF LOGIC

WHATEVER changes Coleridge's philosophical opinions underwent, one thing remained fixed and constant, the guiding star of all his wanderings, namely, the necessity of reaching a view of the world from which it could be grasped as the manifestation of a single principle, and therefore as a unity. The attempt to reach such a view was what he meant by Metaphysics, or philosophy in general. There was nothing that he deplored more than the neglect into which this study had sunk: "the long eclipse of philosophy, the transfer of that name to physical and psychological empiricism, and the non-existence of a learned philosophical class."[1] If there was one thing more than another which he regarded as his own special mission, taking precedence of any system of opinions, however dear, it was the revival of the philosophical spirit in his fellow-countrymen.

But philosophy in the sense of metaphysics was a large word and fell into various departments. Granted that it meant, as Plato defined it, the contemplation of all time and all existence, it was itself an exercise of thought, and, before the

[1] *Logic* MS. (See Snyder, *op. cit.*, p. 121.)

contemplation of time and existence must come the contemplation of thought (itself, after all, the most certain of existences), and the principles of its operation. In other words, it had to be prefaced by a study of Logic. True to this conviction, Coleridge had early become inspired with the idea of a work on Logic which should be a "propaedeutic" to the larger study.

The science of Logic in Coleridge's time was undergoing a process of change and expansion. The older Aristotelian logic still remained, and was being expounded in England and on the Continent by leading writers.[1] But new matter had been introduced into it by Kant's treatment of the categories—new wine, as it was to prove, into old bottles. Whewell's and Mill's work on Inductive Logic was still in the future, but the advances in science were making a reconstruction of the whole Science yearly more pressing. What Kant had begun in expanding the field, Hegel was already engaged in completing, and after the appearance of his *Logic* (1812–16) it was no longer possible to accept the old formal logic as anything but a more or less artificial simplification of the deeper movements of thought.

Here, as in so much else, Coleridge represented a transition stage in the coming transformation. So early as 1803 we have from him, in a letter to William Godwin,[2] the intimation that he was

[1] Coleridge mentions Leibniz, Wolff, Mendelssohn, Condillac; and in England, Hartley, Isaac Watts, William Guthrie.
[2] See A. Turnbull's *Biographia Epistolaris*, vol. i. p. 270. (Snyder, *op. cit.*, p. 50.) The omission among the names here mentioned of that of Kant is significant.

engaged on a work which was to be "introductory to a *system*" and was to include, besides the common system of Logic and an outline of the history of the science, his own "Organon veré Organon". It was to conclude with considerations as to its practical value in science, medicine, politics, law, and religion. Only fragments of this work remain,[1] but they are sufficient to indicate his view of the scope of the science, and the answer he was prepared to give some of its main problems at a time when he had not as yet realized what had been done by such writers as Mendelssohn and Kant to advance the science.

He still regards it as chiefly concerned with the syllogism, which is treated from the point of view of classification. "I think it important", he writes, "to impress the truth as strongly as possible that all logical reasoning is simply Classification, or adding to the common name, which designates the individuality and consequently the differences of things, the Generic name which expresses their resemblances." He even fails to note the distinction which the ordinary Logic makes between the Singular proposition in which an individual, and the Particular, in which "some" of a class, is the subject.[2] It is not surprising perhaps that on this basis the ordinary third figure (All M is P; all M is S ∴ Some S is P) is rejected as "a mere barren and identical proposition".[3] From this point of

[1] For these, see Snyder, *op. cit.*, p. 53 foll.
[2] "Titius is a red-haired man is a Particular Proposition. Some men are red-haired is another particular." (Snyder, p. 148.)
[3] *Ibid.*, p. 146.

view also the major premise becomes merely a summary of all the individuals that have been found to possess a certain character, among them the individual or group of individuals which is the subject of the conclusion. "In some part or other of every Syllogism we declare or imply the Character of the class, we assume that the Individual belongs to this class, and we conclude therefore that the Individual must have this Character." He seems to feel that this is to evacuate inference of something which it is usually thought to contain, namely a real advance to some fresh insight, for he goes on to ask, "But is not this merely repeating the same thing in other words? Some have thought so, and in consequence have asserted that all reasoning is made up of Identical Propositions." He admits that there is repetition, but denies that this is all. "In every Syllogism I do in reality repeat the same thing in other words, yet at the same time I do something more; I recall to my memory a multitude of other facts, and with them the important remembrance that they have all one or more property in common." It is this "recapitulation and, as it were, refreshment of its knowledge and of the operations by which it both acquires and retains it", that saves the soul of the syllogism.

The student of Mill's Logic will recognize an old friend in this proof that the syllogism is in reality a *petitio principii*: all that the major premise does being to record, as it were in shorthand, the particulars from which it is generalized, and that all inference that is not founded on complete enumeration is by mere analogy. The best that can be said for Coleridge's attempt at this stage is that he perceived the fundamental importance of the study and was already struggling with what in the succeeding generation were to become real problems. That his answer to one so central as the ground of syllogistic inference should have been that which was afterwards given by a type of philosophy, which he himself was to exert the whole power of his genius to undermine, only shows how much had yet to be done by him in the development and unification of his own thought.

The part that the study of Kant had in that development has been already referred to. By the time the manuscript which bears the name of *Logic* came to be written, Coleridge had mastered the general teaching of the *Critique of Pure Reason*, and through it arrived at an extended view of what was involved in the scientific treatment of the functions of thought, and at the same time of the limits of the science of Logic, when taken as concerned with the rules under which the understanding operates, whether considered abstractly or in connection with the concrete matter of experience. Besides the generalizing function of the mind in its commerce with experience, there is intuitive apprehension below it and a unifying organizing function above and beyond it.[1] By the time of which we are

---

[1] So little truth is there in Hort's remark (*Cambridge Essays*, London, 1856, p. 324): "Coleridge seems never to have distinctly asked what is the nature and province of logic", that his whole system may be

speaking, the distinction between these different forms of the exercise of thought, particularly that between Understanding and Reason, had become to him a fixed "frame of reference", which he applied to every subject that came within the range of philosophy, and no question goes deeper than that of its origin in his mind, the meaning he attached to it, and the relation of this meaning to that of the similar distinction in Kant. A complete answer to this question can only be given on a review of his philosophy as a whole. Here we are concerned with it as the basis of the scope he assigned to Logic.

2. REASON AND UNDERSTANDING

With regard to its origin, it has been commonly assumed that he took it over from Kant. As a matter of fact it had been before the world since the time of Plato, by whom different functions were assigned to νοῦς and διάνοια. In English writers, Shakespeare, Milton, Bacon, and the Cambridge Men,[1] we have the contrast between *discourse* of reason and the intuitive exercise of the faculty, and there is no need to question Coleridge's own statement that he found it there. All that Kant did in this case, as in others, was to confirm and give more definite form to what he had toiled out for himself. More important is the question of what he meant by it.

said to have rested on the clear convictions he had arrived at with regard to both.

[1] *Aids to Reflection*, Aphorism CVc, 9, cviii 3, and *passim*.

If we had merely the popular statements of the published works, we might suppose that it was merely an elaboration of the Platonic distinction between discursive and intuitive thought. There the understanding is defined as the "faculty of judging according to sense", that is of making generalizations from particulars given in perceptual experience, and of drawing inferences from them according to the formal laws of identity and non-contradiction.[1] As contrasted with this, reason is defined as the power of apprehending "truths above sense and having their evidence in themselves", among these the law of non-contradiction itself. Whether there ever was a time when this was all that the distinction meant to Coleridge or when he took it to be all that Kant meant, there is no need to inquire. The manuscript on *Logic* makes it quite clear that by the time it was written he had arrived, by the aid of Kant, at a far deeper apprehension of the relation of sense to understanding, and of understanding to reason in its wider and truer meaning.

Here sense is no longer spoken of as presenting us with the experience of objects from whose qualities abstraction is made, but rather as the undifferentiated background of experience, "the common or neutral boundary", as he calls it in the *Logic*, of objective and subjective.[2] Similarly

[1] In this capacity it is made the whipping-boy of prudence in morality, reliance on mere external evidence in theology, and pure expediency in politics.
[2] Long before (see *Anima Poetae* under date 1800), while his later doctrine was still forming itself in his mind, we have the aphorism,

with the Understanding. This is no longer conceived of as engaged in the discursive treatment
of objects given by sense, but as a principle entering
into the very constitution of the object, without
which there could be no experience even of the
most elementary kind. It is defined in so many
words as "the substantiating power—that by which
we attribute substance and reality to phenomena,
and raise them from mere affections into objects
communicable and capable of being anticipated
and reasoned of". Thought in this sense is constitutive "even of the simplest objects. Points, lines,
surfaces are not bodies but acts of the mind, the
offspring of intellectual motions, having their canons
in the imagination of the geometrician". Although
we cannot say that all *entia logica* are objects, yet we
can say that all objects are *entia logica*.[1] By this time,
too, he is familiar with the Kantian doctrine of space
and time as *a priori* forms of sense and of the Categories as the *a priori* principles of unity in the
matter of experience, and finally with Kant's distinction between these forms and "ideas of the reason",
the one concerned with phenomena, the other
pointing to forms of unity that carry us beyond
anything that can be verified in experience.

It is on this basis that Coleridge at the beginning of his treatise draws the distinction between

"The dim intelligence sees an absolute oneness, the perfectly clear
intellect knowingly perceives it, distinction and plurality lie
between". It might have been well if, in his later teaching, he had
kept this admirable statement of the continuity of thought in the
various levels of experience more clearly before him.

[1] *Logic*, ii. p. 396. (See Snyder, *op. cit.*, p. 100.)

Logic, as the science of the understanding oɪ
logos, in which everything is relative to the distinction between subject and object, and of objects
from one another, *Noetic*, or the science of
Nous, as referring to that which is absolute and
irrelative "because the ground of all relations",
finally *Mathematics*, as standing between them, on
the one hand starting from sensory intuition, on
the other having a necessity and absoluteness
founded on self-made postulates. Coleridge was
convinced that in the end Logic, critical though
it was itself, must submit to the higher criticism
of Noetic, but he thought it possible to allow it
provisionally to make its own assumptions as other
sciences did—chiefly that of the independence of
thought and its object—without raising the question
of their ultimate validity.[1]

3. DIVISION OF LOGIC: THE CANON

Taking Logic in this sense and distinguishing it
from mathematics as based on concepts rather than
sensory intuition, he further distinguishes between
a narrower and a wider sense of the term according
as it abstracts from the concrete matter of experience,
and aims at stating the formal canons of reasoning,
or includes a reference to the objects to which

[1] *Logic* MS., chap. i. We have a similar example of the attempt to
work out the principles of Logic independently of a philosophical
theory of the nature of truth in F. H. Bradley's book with that
title. The difference is that, while Bradley only discovers in the
course of his work that he is making this abstraction, Coleridge
starts with the clear consciousness of it.

LOGIC 69

thought has to conform. But the important distinction is between both of these and the critical, or as he prefers to call it *judicial*, treatment of the understanding to which Kant led the way.

It would be manifestly unfair to take an unrevised copy of the manuscript of a portion of Coleridge's work on Logic as a final statement of his views. But there is sufficient, when taken with the confirmation which is elsewhere supplied, to provide material for an estimate of the extent to which the contents mark an advance in logical doctrine. If we look for any real advance on his own earlier treatment of pure or syllogistic logic, we shall, I think, be disappointed. Propositions are still treated from the side of classification. His division of what he calls "logical acts" into "clusion" or "seclusion" (all men are mortal), "inclusion" (Socrates is a man), and "conclusion" (Socrates is mortal) proceeds on the assumption that the syllogism is concerned with wider and narrower classes. Nor is there anything to indicate that he does not still regard the major premise as a mere appeal to the memory of acts of inclusion.[1] The best that can be said for this part of his exposition is that he recognizes that, if the analysis of the syllogism is all that logic means, it is but "a hollow science", and "a thousand syllogisms amount merely to nine hundred and ninety-nine superfluous illustrations of what a syllogism means".[2]

[1] The long illustration (Snyder, *op. cit.*, p. 109) from the observation of the calcareousness of the whole of a common to that of a part previously included in it, proceeds on the old assumption as to the meaning of syllogistic inference.   [2] Snyder, *op. cit.*, p. 81.

It is only when we come to the section on the "Premises in all Logical Reasoning" in the later part of this section that he begins to throw off the trammels of the traditional scheme and to use his own insight. There is still little word of a logic of induction in the modern sense. The few masterly hints which Aristotle gives in the *Posterior Analytics* seem to have passed unnoticed by him, and it is another side of Bacon that interests him.[1] But at the point at which logic joins psychology in the act of perception, his unfailing sureness of touch in the latter science comes to his aid, and in the discussion of the question whether nature presents us with objects "perfect and as it were ready made", apart from any act of our own minds, he gives an answer which contains the root of the matter.[2]

After referring to the common experience that there is an education of the senses in perceiving aright, he goes on: "As there is a seeing and a hearing that belongs to all mankind, even so in the different kinds and species of knowledge there is a separate apprenticeship necessary for each. . . . In order to discuss aright the premises of any reasoning in distinction from the reasoning itself,

[1] In his notes on Mendelssohn's *Morgenstunden,* at the point where the author raises the question of imperfect and perfect Induction, Coleridge has nothing better to suggest than the need of a German word to indicate "my positiveness" as distinguished from objective "certainty".

[2] Cp. Snyder, pp. 116–18, where the passage is given at length with the comment upon it (p. 89): "Coleridge holds that perception is an art, dependent on the discipline of the senses and the development of organized bodies of knowledge". In the above quotation I have ventured to underline the important sentences.

a knowledge of the matter is the first and indispensable requisite. This may appear a truism, but,
though equally certain, it is not equally obvious
that the same necessity applies to the very means
and acts, with and by which we acquire the
materials of knowledge—*not only must we have some
scheme or general outline of the object*, to which we
could determine to direct our attention, were it
only to have the power of recognizing it, or, as
the phrase is, bring it under our cognizance when
perceived; but *the very senses by which we are to
perceive will each again require the aid of a previous* scientific insight. . . . So erroneous would the assertion
be that an object of the sense is the same as the
impression made on the senses, or that it would
be possible to conceive an act of seeing wholly
separate from the modification of the judgment
and the analogies of previous experience." From
this point of view he goes on to say it may be
seen that "the main object of logical investigation
is *most often the establishment of the object itself, which,
once established, contains, or rather is coincident with its
inferences*", and "we may therefore readily understand the observations of Lord Bacon respecting
the insignificance of common Logic, and its utter
inadequacy in the investigations of nature, and
he might safely have added in those of the pure
reason".

Readers familiar with the doctrine of appercipient
groups in modern psychology, and with the place
assigned by modern logic to the system of judgments,
into which "facts" are taken up and remoulded

in inductive inference, will be prepared to see in such a statement an anticipation of principles that may be said in recent times to have revolutionized both sciences. What was needed was that Coleridge should have brought together what he here says about the scheme or system (the pervading identity, as we might say, or "concrete universal") underlying all real inference, with what he would fain have said about the major premise, as more than a jog to memory, and the syllogism as more than a *petitio principii*. That he failed clearly to see its implications as to the true nature of inference, or only accidentally touched upon them in the phrase about the "coincidence of the establishment of the object with its inferences", is only one of many instances of the unresolved conflict in his mind between what pressed upon him with the weight of tradition and what his own insight was constantly opening up to him.

4. CRITICAL LOGIC: THE PLACE OF JUDGMENT IN GENERAL

The second part of the Logic nominally upon the "Criterion" opens with a discussion of rational and irrational questions,[1] leading to the demonstration that the question of a criterion of truth, as ordinarily put, belongs to the latter class. Truth in the sense of coincidence of thought with thing

[1] Largely taken from Mendelssohn, but leading to a different application. (See Alice D. Snyder, *Journal of English and Germanic Philology*, October 1921.)

must always be something particular corresponding to the particularity of the thing, whereas the criterion required must be a universal one. It is senseless to ask for the universal criterion of truth "when all truth is out of the question".[1] True, there is another sense in which the question might be asked, as referring to the *ground* of the coincidence as ordinarily assumed—the guarantee of "the identity of thing and thought". But in the first place "this was not the purpose of the question", and in the second place, we here introduce a reference to realities which are objects of First Philosophy (his own Noetic) not of Logic, and which "therefore cannot be submitted to a discussion or reasoning purely logical".[2] If not irrational in an absolute sense, the question is irrational from the point of view of the logic of the understanding.

If this interpretation be correct, what "Coleridge suddenly seems to realize" in this section is not, as Miss Snyder suggests,[3] that "he is giving a second criterion instead of the expected Organon", but that the whole question of a criterion is here out of place, and that what requires to be substituted for it is the proof that this is so, as that is contained in Kant's Transcendental Analysis, the effect of which has been to undermine the whole distinction between subject and object, as assumed by the ordinary logic. I agree that the retention of the title of the section is in that case highly misleading, but in the state in which the

[1] See Snyder, p. 86.   [2] *Ibid.*, p. 87.   [3] *Op. cit.*, p. 90.

work has come to us we have no reason to believe
that these headings met with the author's final
approval. Be this as it may, the interest of the rest
of the *Logic* centres round the sketch that we here
have (the first in English philosophy) of the logical
bearing of the teaching of the *Critique*, and the
special applications that are made of it to theories
still current in contemporary thought, leading to
the question of the extent to which the writer
seems prepared to accept it as final.

The central points in Kant's analysis are the
place of judgment in the structure of experience,
the distinction he draws between analytic and
synthetic judgments, and in the latter between
synthetic *a posteriori* and *a priori*. Whatever doubt
may be raised as to the first of these in Coleridge's
popular works, there is no ambiguity here. Locke's
definition of judgment as a comparison of an object
with its marks is rejected as assuming the unity
in the object, which is itself the result of judgment.
"All judgments are functions of unity in our representations—official acts by which unity is effected
among them." More particularly judgment is "the
power of determining this or that under the condition of some rule", and as such the general
condition of all rational consciousness. If it be said
that this leaves it still doubtful whether Coleridge
does not hold that "representations" give us objects,
and that all that judgment does is to abstract from
them as thus given, this might be true if the above
were all he says about it.

We reach a further point when he goes on to

explain that underlying all rational consciousness there is a distinction between subject and object, the self and its world; and that "the resolution of any given representation (his word for the modern presentation or content) into the object and the subject and the coexistence of both in one we call a judgment. At least it is the first and most generalized definition of the term judgment which is most happily expressed in the Teutonic language by *Urtheil*". It is in this Urtheil that he finds "the Archimedes standing room, from which we may apply the lever of all our other intelligent functions whereby: (1) the mind affirms its own reality; (2) this reality is a unity; (3) the mind has the power of communicating this unity; and lastly all reality for the mind is derived from its own reality".

Carrying the same thought further in a later passage, he finds in the *copula* the assertion of a whole of reality beyond the division we make in judgment between the self and the world. "It contains a truth which, being antecedent to the act of reflection and, of course therefore to all other acts and functions of the understanding, asserts a being transcendent to the individual subject in all cases, and therefore to all subjects thinking under the same laws." He admits that, so interpreted, self-conscious experience seems to imply a contradiction between subject and object. On the one hand we have the judging mind, on the other we have an object which is "assumed to contain the principle of reality in itself exclusive

of, nay, in contradiction of, whatever is mind".[1]
He himself holds that the contradiction is not an
insoluble one. But he holds also that to find the
clue to its solution we have to pass beyond the
limits of the logic which proceeds on the assumption
of the dualism of thought and its object.

Leaving this therefore for the present, and returning to the place of judgment in ordinary experience
as above defined, Coleridge illustrates it by an
acute criticism of Berkeley's form of idealism (or,
as he calls it, his "psilo-phenomenism"). On
Berkeley's view that the sole *esse* of things is the
percipi, and that the *percipi* consists in the mere
impression of the sense, we have no distinction
between subject and object. Objects "would exist
in the mind, for which they existed, no otherwise
differenced from the same than as the waves from
the collective sea". In fact "Berkeley ought to say,
not I see a chair, but I see myself in the form of
a chair".[2] His mistake consisted, as he elsewhere [3]
explains, in failing to distinguish between sensation
and developed perception: "As rationally might I
assert a tree to be a bird as Berkeley's perception
to be sensation, which is but a minimum—the
lowest grade or first manifestation of perception.
But the occasion of the error deserves notice, for

[1] The MS. here gives "not mind", which makes nonsense of the
passage.
[2] *Logic* MS., vol. ii, in chapter on "synthetic judgments *a priori*",
but the illustration from Berkeley is rather of the place of judgment
in general in self-conscious experience.
[3] MS. C, p. 10. As the passage is not given in Miss Snyder's book,
I have ventured to quote it at length as illustrative not only of his
logical views, but of Coleridge at his best in philosophical criticism.

it applies to many other schemes besides the
Berkeleian. Instead of resting at the real minimum,
it was carried downward by the imagination, or
rather by an act of the will, to the extinction of
all *degrees*, and yet thought of as still *existing*. The
true logic would in this case have been: perception
diminishing from its minimum (in which it is called
sensation) into an absolute O, sensation becomes
= O; but no! this hypothetical subliminal perception, = O, is still somewhat . . . and this, the
proper offspring of the unitive and substantiating
function of the Understanding, is, by the imagination, projected into an *ens reale*, or, still more truly,
a strange *ens hybridum* betwixt real and logical, and
partaking of both: namely, it *is*, yet it is not as
this or that, but as sensation per se; i.e. the *perceptum*, surviving its annihilation, borrows the name
by which, in its least degree, it has been distinguished and commences a new genus without
species or individual. . . . The error here noted
is only one of a host that necessarily arise
out of having only *one* starting-point, viz. the
lowest."

The criticism throughout, and particularly in the
last sentence, is one that goes to the root, not only
of Berkeley's sensationalism, but of all forms of
theory which seek to explain the higher and more
developed phases, whether of knowledge or existence, in terms of the lower and less developed,
and so ranks as a particularly lucid statement of
what might be regarded as the fundamental
principle of all later idealistic philosophy.

5. SYNTHETIC JUDGMENTS

Equally with what he says on judgment in general, his account of the important distinction between analytic and synthetic judgments, and of the existence of the latter in a form underivable from experience, and rightly therefore called *a priori*, leaves little to be desired. Whether he would himself have admitted the existence of purely analytic judgments is not clear. In his treatment of formal logic he seems to take them for granted. On the other hand, his assertion that "predicates are intermediate marks", and that "every judgment by intermediate marks is a conclusion", combined with his rejection of "immediate" inference,[1] seems to point to a different view. But the important point is his recognition that both in mathematics and in physics, not to speak of metaphysics, the existence of these sciences depends on the existence of uniting elements (in the former case equations, in the latter causal connections), which cannot be derived from experience in the sense of being generalizations from it.

The clearest case is in mathematics. The synthesis of mathematics differs from that of physics and metaphysics in being conditioned from first to last by the pre-existing forms of sense, space and time as given to intuition. Coleridge follows Kant closely in his account of these forms, but lays more stress, first, upon the fact that they are given to intuition as *infinites*, into which, for the interpre-

[1] See Snyder, p. 84.

tation of experience, determinations are introduced by limitation; and, secondly, upon their *objectivity*, in the sense that they do not depend on the individual peculiarities of our minds. Whether they exist apart from the minds of finite individuals is a question which, as falling to Noetic, he does not here discuss. For the rest, what he regards as important is "to put the student in the way of proving for himself that all Mathematical reasoning is truly Synthetic or composed of synthetic judgments *a priori*", and thus to lead him to see that other synthetic judgments have similarly "their condition and ground in the *a priori* forms of the Understanding".[1] As the doctrine of the place of judgment in general is happily illustrated from the error of Berkeley, so that of synthetic *a priori* judgments is illustrated not less happily from that of Hume.

Hume's work in general Coleridge regards as a conspicuous illustration of "the many and important advantages which truth and science derive from strict consequence even in dangerous error".[2] It was the direct outcome of Berkeley: "Berkeley's remark that we ought to speak of signals not of causes is the essence of Hume's doctrine, which was a spark that cannot be said to have fallen on incombustible materials. It produced great heat and volumes of smoke, but kindled as little light as the former." To Hume's argument it was no use appealing to common sense. Hume was neither more deficient in common sense nor more likely

---

[1] Snyder, p. 94.   [2] *Logic*, ii. p. 300. (Snyder, pp. 93–4.)

to make himself ridiculous by outraging its dictates
than Messrs. Reid, Oswald, Beattie or any other
of his opponents on either side of the Tweed.[1]
His opponents, in fact, had no idea of the depth
of the problem. They "came forward not as
investigators but as adversaries, who saw nothing
in the subject that needed investigation". Instead of
answering Hume, "they set up a Guy Faux (sic)".
What therefore happened was that "the seed which
Hume scattered was wafted and tossed about on
thè winds of literary rumour, or fell unprofitably,
till it found at length a well-fitted and prepared
soil in Kant".

Hume saw that "in judgments of causality the
assertion of a necessary connection between A and
B was not an analytic but a synthetic judgment,
seeing that A is different from B; and asked by
what right it is affirmed, and further by what right
it was transferred from physics to metaphysics. His
solution consisted in assigning the origin and ground
of the notion and the necessity conceived therein
to custom, habit, association." But this was in the
first place to confound the conception of necessity
as a positive and essential constituent of the conception of cause with a mere negative inability to
do otherwise; in the second place it was to assign,
as the cause of causality, phenomena which pre-
suppose the principle; in the third place it was to
fail to notice that experience, so far from engender-
ing the conception of causality, rather acts as a check
to the application of it, seeing that, with the unwary,

[1] *Logic*, ii. 305–6. (Snyder, p. 124.)

it is apt to flow in wherever it is not forbidden. Like breathing, in fact, it requires an express volition to suspend it. "This predisposition may be called into consciousness by occasion, but can no more be given by occasion than the form of oak can be given to the acorn by the air and light and moisture."

What blinded Hume to all this was not that he had wrongly assumed causal judgments to be synthetic, but that he had wrongly assumed that herein they differed from mathematical judgments, which he took to be purely analytic. Had he seen that these also were synthetic, and not, as he supposed, merely identical propositions, he could hardly have ventured to explain away their necessity as the result of subjective association. It was here that Kant may be said to have "begun anew and completed the work of Hume" by proving that mathematical, as well as physical and metaphysical, judgments involved a synthesis, and that, unless the very existence of the science which "hath made Earth's reasoning animal her lord" is to be denied, there must be an element in experience that was not derived from experience, as Hume interpreted it.[1]

---

[1] *Logic*, vol. ii. p. 281 foll. (Snyder, pp. 91–3.) I venture, however, to doubt the applicability, at this point, of her remark, "Here Coleridge parts company with Kant". His answer to Hume on the question of the necessity involved in causality is on all fours with Kant's. Where he might have here parted company with him, but did not, was by noting that Kant directed his criticism to the view Hume puts forward in the *Essays*, without being aware of the difference between it and that of the *Treatise*. (See E. Caird's *Critical Philosophy of Kant*, vol. i. p. 256.)

6. Parting with Kant: The Principle of Trichotomy

Freshly put as all this is, neither here nor in his account of the different forms of synthesis in judgment, which Kant had tabulated as the Categories, is there any real advance on the teaching of the *Critique*. It is only when he comes to the negative side of it, the denial of the power of the speculative reason to transcend the limits of the logical understanding, that Coleridge refuses to follow. He had himself become convinced that logic, as commonly interpreted, was an abstract science in the sense that it was based on an assumption of the relation of subject to object, thought to thing, which it had not the means of examining. The first lesson therefore which it had to learn was to keep within its own limits: "the first source of falsehood in Logic was the abuse and misapplication of Logic itself".[1] It was sure to go wrong if, for instance, it presumed to attack this problem in its own strength, and tried to resolve everything into the object (as in the "Epicurean" philosophy), or again into the subject (as in the Berkeleian), or, still again, if it were dogmatically to deny that any theory was possible, and leave us with an insoluble dualism. It was here that, by the time from which the *Logic* dates, Coleridge had discovered that the limitations of Kant's analysis were to be looked for. While therefore, as he puts it, "considered as Logic it (the transcendental analysis) is irrefragable, as philo-

[1] Snyder, p. 87.

sophy it will be exempt from opposition, and cease
to be questionable only when the soul of Aristotle
shall have become one with the soul of Plato, when
the men of *Talent* shall have all passed into the men
of *Genius*, or the men of Genius have all sunk into
men of Talent. That is *Graecis Calendis*, or when two
Fridays meet." [1]

This is picturesquely expressed, but the meaning
is clear, namely, that there is a level of thought
beyond the transcendental analysis, to which the
genius of Plato had penetrated, but which all the
talent of Kant had failed to reach. For more
detailed criticism of Kant's doctrine of experience
we have to go elsewhere,[2] but he does not leave
us in the *Logic* without a clear indication of what
he regards as the source of his failure.

If Coleridge had been asked what he considered
the most fatal of the errors of the older logic and
the point at which he would begin its reformation,
he would have said that it was the dogmatic assumption of the principle of *dichotomy*. Everywhere
in it we have terms standing in stark opposition
to each other without any attempt at mediation:
affirmative-negative, universal-particular, unity-
multiplicity, real-unreal; with the consequence
that where one of them is conceived of as denoting
something real and objective, the other is set down
as denoting something ideal and subjective. But

[1] *Op. cit.*, xi. pp. 329–30. (Snyder, p. 125.)
[2] The most penetrating occurs in a marginal note in his own copy
of the *Critique of Pure Reason*, under the modest heading, "Doubts
during a first perusal, i.e. struggles felt, not arguments objected".
See p. 91, below.

this, he held, is to contradict the very essence of reasoning itself, seeing that "the prime object of all reasoning is the reduction of the many to one and the restoration of particulars to that unity, by which alone they can participate in true being on the principle *omne ens unum*". To rely on the principle of dichotomy as final is therefore to leave us "with what is more truly eristic than logic. . . . If adopted as the only form of Logic, it excites and seems to sanction the delusive conceit of self-sufficiency in minds disposed to follow the clue of the argument at all hazards and whithersoever it threatens to lead them, if only they remain assured that the thread continues entire." But by its fruit you may know it. One of these is that "the inevitable result of all *consequent* reasoning, in which the speculative intellect refuses to acknowledge a higher or deeper ground than it can itself supply, is—and from Zeno the Eleatic to Spinoza ever has been—Pantheism, under one or other of its modes".[1] Needless to say that for Coleridge, to whom Pantheism was merely "a live Atheism",[2] this meant utter damnation.

When therefore in the *Logic* the question of dichotomy occurs, he is prepared to note Kant's attitude to it. He gives him, indeed, credit for the recognition of the higher principle of trichotomy in the triadic form in which the categories are arranged; and even speaks of this as "the prominent

[1] MS. B III (Snyder, pp. 128–9) and marginal note on Kant's *Allgemeine Naturgeschichte*. Cp. *Anima Poetae*, pp. 168–9 for other more immediate consequences in the shattering of "long deeply rooted associations or cherished opinions". [2] MS. C, p 86.

excellence of his *Critique*". But he denies that it was Kant's discovery, or that Kant had any true appreciation of its significance. He attributes the discovery of it to Richard Baxter, who in his *Methodus Theologiae* not only employed it a century before the publication of Kant's work, but "saw more deeply into the grounds, nature, and necessity of this division as a *norma philosophiae*". "For Baxter", as he elsewhere explains, "*grounds* the necessity of trichotomy as the principle of real Logic on an absolute Idea presupposed in all intelligential acts, whereas Kant adopts it merely as a fact of reflection, though doubtless as a singular and curious fact in which he suspects some yet deeper Truth latent and hereafter to be discovered". Unfortunately "the sacred fire remained hid under the bushel of our good countryman's ample folios" —to be rescued, as Coleridge hoped, from its obscurity and blown into a warming and enlightening flame by himself.[1]

[1] MS. C. (See Snyder, p. 128 n.) The doctrine of trichotomy is only the logical statement of the metaphysical doctrine of "the law of polarity or essential dualism" which Coleridge conceived of as running through all nature, and in *The Friend* (vol. i. p. 121 n.) speaks of as "first promulgated by Heraclitus, 2,000 years afterwards republished and made the foundation both of Logic, of Physics, and of Metaphysics by Giordano Bruno". In a note elsewhere on Baxter he speaks of this law as necessarily involved in the polar logic. (*Literary Remains*, iv. 141.) That he is quite right in his view of the place of trichotomy in Kant is borne out by the fact, of which Professor H. J. Paton reminds me, that "it is only in the second edition of the *Kritique* that Kant makes his point about the Categories which reminds one of the Hegelian Dialectic. His other threefold divisions (e.g. sense, imagination, understanding) seem to arise from his tendency to make very sharp distinctions and then invent a third thing to bridge the gulf"—a very different thing from what either Hegel or Coleridge meant.

For the use which he was prepared to make of the principle we have to go beyond the limits not only of the ordinary but of the critical logic, seeing that the method which trichotomy prescribes is the opposite of that which underlies both. Instead of starting with opposing concepts, in one or other of which, taken separately, we are to find the truth, we have to "seek first for the Unity as the only source of Reality, and then for the two opposite yet correspondent forms by which it manifests itself. For it is an axiom of universal application that *manifestatio non datur nisi per alterum*. Instead therefore of affirmation and contradiction, the tools of dichotomic Logic, we have the three terms Identity, Thesis, and Antithesis." [1] It is on this principle that he conceived it possible to advance beyond the limitations of Logic or the science of the Understanding to a Noetic, or science of the Reason, which should also be a science of Reality.

Meantime, whatever the defects of his own contribution to logic in the narrower sense as it was left by him, he has the undoubted merit of being one of the first to recognize the importance of a method which proceeds, as he expresses it, by "enlargement" instead of by "exclusion", [2] and by

[1] Marginal note on Kant's *Allgemeine Naturgeschichte*, etc. It was part of Coleridge's exuberance to extend this triad into a tetrad (the Tetractys of Pythagoras) and even into a pentad—an extension which may here perhaps be neglected as belonging to the eccentricities rather than the essentials of his thought.

[2] See *Anima Poetae*, pp. 168 and 301, where he speaks of "the great good of such a revolution as alters not by exclusion but by enlargement", and of the pleasure he had derived from the adage, "extremes meet", through which he was able to bring "all prob-

inner development instead of by mere external synthesis.[1] It was late in life and only to a small extent that he became acquainted with Hegel's contemporaneous attempt to revolutionize logic precisely on this basis. Short as his marginalia on the *Wissenschaft der Logik* are,[2] they are of the greatest interest as the first real attempt of an English philosopher to grapple with the difficulties of the Hegelian dialectic. They anticipate the judgment that many after him were to repeat that the treatment of the transition Being—Not-Being—Becoming is "not dialectic, but sophistry". They differ from the kind of comment that was common during the next generation and beyond it, in being founded not on any supposed outrage on the law of non-contradiction (Coleridge's doctrine of polarity had carried him past all that), but on the abstractness with which he accuses Hegel of treating of the conception of not-being or nothing. "To be (sein, εἶναι) is opposed to the 'Nothing' (Nichts), whereas the true opposite of 'To be' is 'Not to be'." Nothing, in fact, is treated as objective, whereas it is "at all times subjective. Objective Nothing is not so truly non-ens and non-sens." Had Coleridge had the

lematic results to their solution and reduce apparent contraries to correspondent opposites . . . fragments of truth, false only by negation".

[1] A favourite example was of the mathematical point which unfolds itself in the line with its opposite poles. See MS. H, p. 49, where the principle is applied to the idea of Being as the pregnant unevolved point and the identity of the opposite, actual and potential; and pp. 167–8, where he claims as an advantage of his own term "prothesis" over "synthesis" that it emphasizes identity rather than mere union.

[2] They cover only the first ninety-one pages. See Snyder, p. 162 foll.

patience to read further, he might perhaps have seen, as no one for a generation was more capable of seeing, that abstraction from the distinction between the objective and the subjective, as something logically later, was of the essence of the Hegelian exposition at this stage. He might have seen also that, whatever else is to be said of the Hegelian philosophy, it was not "Spinozism in its superficial form", and had far more points of agreement than of conflict with his own.

Be this as it may, the coincidence on the subject of this section is sufficiently remarkable, and tempts one to imagine that there must have been something in the deeper spirit of the time which it was given to these two writers, so entirely different in genius and surroundings, to seize upon and express, each in his own peculiar way. How far Coleridge's use of the principle differed from Hegel's, and how far by the consistency of his results his use of it can be justified, it will be part of our occupation in this Study to determine.

CHAPTER III

METAPHYSICS

"Let me by all the labours of my life have answered but one end
and taught as many as have in themselves the conditions of learning,
the true import and legitimate use of the term Idea and the incal-
culable Value of Ideas (and therefore of Philosophy, which is but
another name for the manifestation and application of Ideas) in
all departments of Knowledge and their indispensable presence in
the Sciences which have a worth as well as a Value to the
Naturalist no less than to the Theologian, to the Statesman no less
than to the Moralist."—MS. C, p. 33, condensed.

1. COLERIDGE'S CRITICISM OF KANT

KANT, Coleridge held, had introduced new matter
into the old logic. He had enlarged its scope, but
he had thereby only in the end brought into clearer
evidence the limitations imposed upon it by the
dualistic assumption of the independence of thought
and reality, without himself being able to get
beyond them. In effect his work had resulted only
in riveting the chains more securely to this dualism.
Yet he had indicated a way of deliverance in the
hint of a new triadic logic, and Coleridge's own
metaphysics may best be considered as an attempt
to carry the dialectic of Kant's thought a step
farther and turn criticism against the Critic.
"Kant", he had said, "had begun again and completed the work of Hume." He himself aimed, if
not at beginning Kant's work again, at any rate
at beginning where Kant had ended and completing
what he had begun. In attempting to follow him
in what he regarded as the true "Prolegomena to

all future Metaphysics", it will therefore be useful to start from a more detailed account than we had occasion to give in the preceding chapter of his criticism of Kant, before going on to what he regarded as the central point in the advance he sought to make upon him, and the logic by which he endeavoured to justify it.

We have seen how far he assimilated the positive part of Kant's teaching. Freely stated, this amounted to the claim that not only the sciences, but the very existence of an objective world of fact depended on a natural metaphysic of the mind, demanding, or postulating, necessary connections between the dispersed elements of sensory experience. Thought was not an operation superinduced upon a given world, but was necessary in order that there might be an experiencible world of any kind. But Kant's teaching had a negative side. Necessary as these forms or postulates were for the constitution of experience, they were only valid within the limits of that experience. They were not applicable to the world of reality, of which our experience presented us with only the appearance or manifestation. That there was such a reality, revealed most decisively in the moral world and the freedom which was its postulate or condition, Kant never doubted. What he denied was the possibility of *knowing* it, seeing that knowledge was only possible under forms which were inapplicable to it. It was true that beyond the partial unities, which such forms of the understanding as these of causality and substance indicated, the mind was haunted by ideals of a complete unity. It sought to bring the whole that was experienced, whether as object or as subject, or as the union of both, into a form in which it could be grasped as one. But these ideals were not to be taken as corresponding to any reality. They were useful as guiding, "regulative" principles, "ideas of the Reason", as Kant called them, borrowing so much from Plato, and as such distinguished from the concepts of the Understanding which entered into experience as constitutive of the apparent or phenomenal world; but beyond this they had no validity as a revelation of the real or noumenal world.

Coleridge accepted in the main the positive side of this teaching. But he was by no means satisfied that even here Kant had said the last word, and what he says of the form in which it was left by him is worth referring to, not only as anticipating much later criticism but as containing the germ of his own rejection of the whole Kantian metaphysic. We fortunately possess in his marginal notes upon the text of the *Critique* an authentic record of his first reactions to it, which fuller knowledge was to confirm. The force with which Kant's authority weighed upon him at the time these notes were written is indicated by the modest title, "Struggles felt not arguments objected", which he gives to the chief one. Not the less does it go straight to the weak point of the whole analysis: the relation of the "manifold of sense" to the form-giving work of the understanding: "How", he asks, "can that be called a *mannigfaltiges* ὕλη which yet contains in itself the ground why I apply one category to it rather than another? The mind does not resemble an Aeolian harp, not even a barrel-organ turned by a stream of water, conceived as many times mechanized as you like, but rather, as far as objects are concerned, a violin or other instrument of few strings yet vast compass, played on by a musician of genius. The breeze that blows across the Aeolian harp, the stream that turns the handle of a barrel organ, might be called a *mannigfaltiges*, a mere *sylva incondita*, but who would call the muscles and purpose of Linley a confused manifold?"

It was for this reason that he finds "a perpetual and unmoving cloud of darkness" hanging over Kant's work, which he goes on to attribute (surely rightly) to "the absence of any clear account of *Was ist Erfahrung?* What do you mean by a fact, an empiric reality, which alone can give solidity (Inhalt) to our conceptions? It seems from many passages that this indispensable test is itself previously manufactured by this very conceptive power, and that the whole not of our own making is the mere sensation of a mere manifold—in short, mere influx of motion, to use a physical metaphor. I apply the categoric forms of a tree. Well! but first what is this tree? How do I come by this tree?"

Coleridge has been criticized alternately for misunderstanding Kant and for accepting without demur the whole formal apparatus of the Kantian categories, but in criticisms like the above he shows that he has a better understanding of him than many of his later critics, and that we have something that goes deeper than any objection he might have taken to the form of Kant's exposition. They amount to an arraignment of the whole Kantian analysis on the ground that the "indispensable test" of truth is not there found in anything objective, but in something "previously manufactured" by the conceptive faculty, and that the only thing that is "not of our making" is a "mere sensation which may be anything or nothing".

If we compare what is here said with the passage in the *Logic* already referred to, in which he indicates the chasm which the Kantian analysis of judgment left between subject and object, we can see in it the germ of his conviction that Kant had failed to solve this fundamental contradiction, and that the source of his failure lay in his denial of the power of the reason to pass beyond the distinctions of the understanding to the unity that underlies them and gives to them such reality as they possess. Kant saw rightly that the forms of the understanding with the abstractions they involved failed to give us the truth of things. But he did human reason an injustice in placing that truth in a noumenal reality which was wholly beyond its grasp, thus leaving it a prey to an unsolved contradiction. And the reason was that he had failed to follow the clue which his idea of a trichotomic logic had put into his hands. Had he followed this out, he would have reached a point of view from which he might have seen subject and object, not as contradictions, but as complementary aspects of a being which unites them, because more than either.

It was this step that Coleridge was himself prepared to take, as he goes on in the same passage to explain, basing it on that which we must take as the definition of mind as subject. "There are many kinds of subject; *mind* is that kind which is its own object." Yet, if we confine ourselves to mind as we know it in ourselves, the contradiction remains, seeing that the subject which we know as thus object to itself is no self-subsistent being, as idealists like Fichte [1] would have it. We have therefore still to ask for the ground of its being. Descartes's method had been to start from the existence of the self, and show that on it rested all other truth: "as surely as I am, so surely this is". But this was to confuse the principle of knowledge with the principle of being, and contradictorily to assign absoluteness to the finite. Just as little can the principle of objective being be found in *all* subjects. Coleridge would have had nothing to say to the modern doctrine of "trans-subjective intercourse" as the ground of the object world. Percipient subjects, one and all, he held with the naïvest of realists, imply a *perceptum*. He goes beyond ordinary realism in demanding a real ground or ground-reality in the light of which both percipient and the perceived world shall have justice done to them, and which shall explain that strangest

[1] The criticism round which his marginal notes on Fichte's *Bestimmung des Menschen* (1800) turn is the ambiguity of the Ego in his system: "the equivoque of the word 'I' ".

and most challenging of all facts, the power of the first to respond to the second and of the second to satisfy the demands made upon it by the first in the name of coherence and unity. Was it possible to find any such ground and to justify it to the reason?

It was here that he found help in the older, and as he thought deeper, Platonic tradition, which Kant had erred by forsaking. The difference between them was that, while the emphasis in Kant was upon the conceptions of the understanding, into which the ideas of the reason entered only as regulative principles bereft of any substantiating power, in Plato the ideas were the underlying basis of the whole structure of knowledge, being not merely constitutive, but "productive". Hence, while to Kant philosophy meant the undermining of their influence over the mind, as guides to a real world beyond the phenomenal, to Plato all education was the preparation of the mind for their entrance into it and its domination by them.[1] Negative as the result of many of the Dialogues was, negative on the whole as older Platonism, in Coleridge's opinion, was, as compared with the later Neo-Platonism, everything in it was a training in the art of rising from the conceptions of the abstracting intelligence to the Ideas which are the real objects of knowledge. As he puts it: [2] "Kant supposed the Ideas to be oscillations of the same imagination, which, working determinately, pro-

[1] Cp. the motto on the title-page above from the *Principles of the Science of Method*, p. 44. In the passage which there follows he repeats what he says in *The Friend* of Bacon as the "British Plato".
[2] Note in his copy of Tennemann's *History of Philosophy*, vol. vi.

duces the mathematical intuitions, line, circle, etc., a sort of total impression made by successive constructions, each denied or negatived so soon as made, and yet the constructive power still beginning anew. Whereas, according to the true Platonic view, the Reason and Will are the Parent . . . and the Idea itself, the transcendent Analogon of the Imagination or spiritual intuition."

It was in this way that the true meaning of Ideas and the application of that meaning to the solution of the problems *first* of the nature of the ultimate reality in the World, *secondly* of man's relation to it in the different departments of human life was to Coleridge the chief occupation of philosophy. "The true import and legitimate use of Ideas" he declared to be "the most important lesson that philosophy has to teach"; philosophy itself he defines as "but another name for the manifestation and application of Ideas".

2. The Meaning of Ideas

Confining ourselves meantime to the first of these two questions, there is none which Coleridge's readers ask themselves oftener than what his "ideas of the Reason" really are. He was himself keenly alive to the difficulty, which his own distinction between them and conceptions of the Understanding seemed to have made insoluble, of finding a definition. How, he asks, teach the import without a definition? and how define without conceptions, which, just because they are conceptions, must fail to convey the reality of the thing? To ask for a conception of an idea is like asking "for an image of a flavour or the odour of a strain of music". It is even worse; for between the different senses there is at least an analogy;[1] "but Ideas and Conceptions are utterly disparate, and Ideas and Images are the negatives of each other".[2] Even language, as Pythagoras and Plato had found, fails us for the expression of ideas. The early English Platonists had a standing resource in the contrast between the physical and the mathematical sciences, the former occupied with the temporary and contingent, the latter with the eternal and necessary. But Coleridge with truer insight (doubtless aided by Kant) saw that mathematical ideas, based as they were on sensory intuition, and depending on imaginative constructions, remained infected with the weakness of their origin, and offered no easy *gradus ad philosophiam*. In this difficulty the only resource was to try to define ideas: first, *negatively* by what they are not; second, *positively* by marking the function they all perform, as something at least which they have in common; and for the rest to trust to concrete examples.

[1] "A light in sound, a sound-like power in light,
　　Rhythm in all thought, and joyance everywhere."

[2] See MS. C, p. 33 foll. (partly quoted Snyder, pp. 135–7), with which cp. the less reliable *Preliminary Treatise on Method*. It was for this reason, he quaintly notes (MS. C, p. 25), that "Plato could make nothing of Aristotle, that intellectual son of Anac (sic), whose understanding was a cloud between him and the Ideas of his great Master". The well-known Table Talk entry (July 2, 1830), "Every man is born an Aristotelian or a Platonist", etc., was to Coleridge a division into philosophical sheep and goats.

Negatively they are distinguished, not only from images and isolated conceptions, but from the systematized conceptions we call *theories*, which, as dependent on sense-given material, must always be liable to change as new sensory facts are disclosed. Nevertheless, scientific theory, in proportion to its advance, as illustrated in his own time by electric science, contrasted with "the vagaries of the magnetists", or modern chemistry, as contrasted with the older atomists, might approximate to the Idea by dropping all sensory imagery and taking the form of algebraic equations. [1]

Positively, and with reference to the common function of all Ideas, we have, as a distinguishing mark, the union in them of particular and universal. In their light the particulars are seen as the different individualized forms of a pervading identity or universal, which is the soul or individualizing principle of the particulars. Coleridge had not yet heard of Hegel's "concrete universal", or, if he had, does not refer to it; but he has the same thing in view. Seeking for a word to indicate the objective counterpart of such an identity or universal, he can find nothing better than "Law", which is itself defined as no mere synopsis of phenomena, but as "constitutive" of them, and "in the order of thought necessarily antecedent" to them—revealing fragments of the ideal world, which is thus distinguished "*not from the real, but from the phenomenal*".

[1] Cp. *The Friend,* Shedd's edition of *Works,* vol. ii. p. 436. In the present passage he goes so far as to ask whether the hypothetical atoms of physics are not merely symbols of algebraic relations "representing powers essentially united with proportions or dynamic ratios—ratios not of powers but that are powers".

But it is from the illustrations he here and elsewhere gives, particularly those from human life,
that we get the clearest indication of his meaning.
Life itself was a favourite illustration. "Take as an
instance of an idea the continuity and coincident
distinctness of nature: . . vegetable life always
striving to be something that it is not, animal life
to be itself." [1] In the history of human life, seeing
that its aim is "to present that which is necessary
as a whole consistently with the moral freedom of
each particular act", he finds the "directing idea"
to be the weaving of "a chain of necessity, the
particular links of which are free acts". There is
no reason to suppose that Coleridge was familiar
with Kant's *Idea of a Universal History*, still less with
Hegel's conception of History as the "realization
of freedom", but, apart from ambiguous details,
he would have welcomed these as illustrations on
a grand scale of what he meant by a "directing
Idea". But there was no need to go to general
history to see ideas in being in human life. "You
may see an Idea working in a man by watching
his tastes and enjoyments, though he may hitherto
have no consciousness of any other reasoning than
that of conception and facts." For "All men live
in the power of Ideas which work in them, though
few live in their light".

[1] *Table Talk*, p. 57.
[2] It is for this reason, he adds, that "you may hope to produce an
effect by referring (a man) to his own experience and by inducing
him to institute an analysis of his own acts and states of being, that
will prove the not only insufficing, but the *alien* nature of all
abstractions and generalizations on the one hand, and the limits of
the outward light upon the other".

Particularly illuminating, as we might expect, are the illustrations he draws from the field in which he was an acknowledged master. How interpret a poem, he asks, but by reference to the "charioteering genius" of the author, "the *mens poetae*, or rather *mens poeta*; the *vis vitae organica*"? [1] From the point of view of language itself "A man of genius, using a rich and expressive language (Greek, German, or English), is an excellent example of the ever individualizing process and dynamic being of Ideas. What a magnificent history of acts of individual minds, sanctioned by the collective mind of the country, a language is!"

Illuminating as these instances are, the reader is still inclined to ask what, after all, is the evidence for the existence of the object of the idea. If it is to come neither from sensory experience directly nor from the generalizations we make from its data and the inferences drawn from them, whence does it come? We seem to have only one alternative left, the old device of an appeal to innateness. That this was not Coleridge's solution ought by this time to be obvious. The doctrine of innate ideas was no part of the Platonic tradition to which

[1] In the *Preliminary Treatise on Method*, p. 41, he gives Shakespeare as the supreme example in literature of the ideal method. "In every one of his characters we find ourselves communing with the same human nature. Everywhere we find individuality, nowhere mere portraiture. The excellence of his productions is the union of the universal with the particular. But the universal is the Idea. Shakespeare therefore studied mankind in the Idea of the human race, and he followed out that Idea in all its varieties by a method which never failed to guide his steps aright." On the difference between this and what he says in *The Friend* (vol. iii. essay 4), see Snyder, *op. cit.*, pp. 34–5.

he adhered. By the great Cambridge writers of the seventeenth century to whom, in spite of what he regarded as their limitations,[1] he owed so much, it had been expressly repudiated.[2] So far from being established by Descartes, he held that it had been reduced to absurdity, by being connected with the "fanciful hypothesis" of "configurations of the brain which were as so many moulds to the influxes of the external world".[3] In so far as it seemed to be supported by Kant, it was just that which allied him to the form of idealism against which Coleridge's "spiritual realism" was directed. Yet the theory was so far right that it pointed to the configuration of the mind itself as endowed with "instincts and offices of Reason", which were essential elements in all experience, forcing it "to bring a unity into all our conceptions and several knowledges. On this all system depends; and without this we could reflect connectedly neither in nature nor on our own minds."[4] None the less the unifying idea has to be found as something rising out of experience and not something superimposed upon it.

The important point is that it is not to be found in any single object given to sense and reproducible in imagination, nor again in any generalization from selected aspects of the sense-given material. On the contrary, images and abstractions of this kind, if adhered to, may be obstructions to the rise

[1] See p. 30, above.
[2] See article by the present writer, "The Cambridge Platonists", *Mind*, N.S., vol. xxxvi. p. 172 n.
[3] *Biographia Literaria*, ch. v. n.
[4] *Aids to Reflection*, Aphorism XCVIIIc, 5.

in the mind of the unifying principle. Images have to be dissolved in the alembic of thought, and the abstractions of thought have themselves to be united and thus surmounted. What is required is openness of mind to the witness of the whole experienced fact, which is at the same time the witness of the whole experiencing mind. It is thus that such ideas as those above enumerated, *life*, the *mind* of the writer, the movement towards *freedom* in history, our own *deeper purposes*, rise in the mind, as something which is neither merely given from without nor as something merely imposed from within, but as something in which outer and inner are united, deep calling to deep in the self-evolution of truth.

But all that Coleridge says of the meaning, the source and the operation of ideas in general only leads up to what he has to say of the idea of the *ens realissimum*—that in the light of which, as the ground of all other realities, all other ideas must be seen, if we are to see them in their unity and therefore in their truth. What is this Idea? and by what logic can we establish the existence of the object corresponding to it?

3. The Idea Idearum

"The grand problem", he wrote in *The Friend*, "the solution of which forms the final object and distinctive character of philosophy, is this: for all that exists conditionally (that is, the existence of which is inconceivable except under the conditions of its dependency on some other as its antecedent)

to find a ground that is unconditioned and absolute,
and thereby to reduce the aggregate of human
knowledge to a system". That we have the idea
of such a ground Coleridge held to be indisputable,
seeing that in addition to the permanent relations, which we call laws, and which it is the
aim of the sciences to discover as the ground of
phenomena, we have the idea of a permanent
relation between the world and ourselves, a "ground
common to the world and man", forming "the link
or mordant by which philosophy becomes scientific
and the sciences philosophical".[1] It is further indisputable that this idea is constantly finding support
in experience, and in the coincidence of what we seek
with what we find—in other words of reason with
experience. But the question remains of the nature
of this ground and the nature of the reasoning, by
which it can be proved to possess that nature.

Needless at this stage to say, it is not anything
that we can reach by induction. "If we use only
the discursive reason we must be driven from
ground to ground, each of which would cease to
be a ground the moment we pressed in it. We either
must be whirled down the gulf of an infinite series,
thus making our reason baffle the end and purpose
of all reason, namely unity and system, or we must
break off the series arbitrarily and affirm an
absolute something which is *causa sui*."[2] What those
who adopt this line of argument fail to see is that

---

[1] *The Friend*, Shedd, vol. ii. p. 420.
[2] *Biographia Literaria*, xii—one of the passages supposed to be
plagiarized from Schelling. In proof that here at least Coleridge
begged *in forma divitis* we have the vivacious statement of the same

causality is a subordinate form of the human understanding under the more comprehensive one of reciprocal action, and therefore inadequate as a description of the supreme reality.[1] The idea of a *causa sui* sets us indeed on the right track, for this means a break with the logic of the understanding; but, interpreted as this was by Spinoza and others, it turns out to be no cause at all, seeing that we know nothing of anything that is causative of reality except self-conscious will.[2] It is thus the presence and priority of the will both in human and in the universal consciousness that Coleridge becomes more and more concerned to demonstrate, and it is for the additional light which his manuscript remains throw upon what he says of this in his published works [3] that they possess their chief philosophical value.

argument in MS. C, p. 45: "What our Priestleian Metaphysics call necessity is but an empirical scheme of destroying one contingency with another which is to be treated in the same manner . . the unconquerable Foe, retreating step by step and still facing the Pursuer . . the contingency playing at leap-frog vaults backwards. As if History could be thus explained; as if the motives of action were not a part of the action. Here comes the head and the neck of the Horse; but what was behind? The Tail: Ergo the Tail pushed the Head and Neck forward."

[1] See MS. H, p. 170 n., where he tells us that the very epithet "first cause," as applied to the Supreme, is borrowed from the cosmotheism of the Pagans, to whom God was one with the world.

[2] Cp. the notes on Mendelssohn's *Morgenstunden*, where he rejects the latter's criticism of Spinoza that his God is merely a collective notion: "The defect in Spinoza's System is the impersonality of God—he makes the only Substance a *Thing*, not a *Will*—a *Ground solely* and at no time a *Cause*."

[3] E.g. in the *Preliminary Treatise on Method*: "The first preconception or master-thought of our *plan* rests on the moral origin and tendency of all true Science", the first clear statement perhaps in English Philosophy of what might be called Ethical Pragmatism.

"It is at once the distinctive and constitutive basis of my philosophy", he writes in a singularly direct passage,[1] that I place the ground and genesis of my system, not, as others, in a fact impressed, much less in a generalization from facts collectively, least of all in an abstraction embodied in an hypothesis, in which the pretended solution is most often but a repetition of the problem in disguise. In contradiction to this, I place my principle in an *act*—in the language of grammarians I begin with the verb—but," he adds emphatically, "the act involves its reality." How can this implication of reality be proved?

4. How the Idea can Involve Reality

Kant denied that there was any passage by way of the speculative or logical reason from one to the other; but Coleridge had already fought his way by his principle of trichotomy beyond the limitations of Kantian logic. The defect, he writes,[2] of Kant's doctrine was that it failed to apply trichotomy to the attributes of the ὑπερούσιον, and did not see that these were united and realized in the idea of an absolute will. He was thus prepared to appeal to a wider and, as he thought, a deeper logic. In a note upon the criticism which the Kantian historian Tennemann passes upon Plotinus, he comes to the defence of the Neo-Platonist, and attributes to him "the statement in his most

[1] MS. B III.   [2] MS. H, p. 162 n.

beautiful language of the only possible form of philosophic Realism", along with "the demonstration of it by one of the most masterly pieces of exhaustive logic found in ancient or modern writings".[1] The principle, he has to explain, of this "Plotinian Logic", which Tennemann, in his blind adherence to Kant, had "so cavalierly kicked out of the ring", is the simple one that whatever is necessary to the possibility of a given reality must itself be real. More formally and fully stated: "If A relatively to X is known to be $= W$; and if no cause or reason actual or conceptual can be assigned why it should not be the same (i.e. $= W$) relatively to Y and Z; and if, supposing $A = W$ in reference to Y and Z, the consequences in *reason* are found in exact correspondence to several important phenomena, which without this supposition must remain anomalies and inexplicable, can the assumption that $A = WX$ is likewise equal WYZ be justly declared altogether groundless and arbitrary?"

Coleridge has been constantly accused of appealing to "intuition" in support of his metaphysical conclusions. It is all the more significant that in this crucial passage he expressly rejects what appears in Plotinus to be an appeal to "intellectual intuition", if that is interpreted to mean "gazing

[1] Marginal note in vol. vi. p. 64 of Tennemann's *Geschichte der Philosophie*: "Let the attempt of Plotinus have ended in failure," he goes on, "yet who could see the courage and skill, with which he seizes the reins and vaults into the chariot of the sun, without sharing his enthusiasm and taking honour to the human mind even to have fallen from such magnificent daring?"

in imagination upon Being as a vast Panorama".
But this, he holds, is not the essence of his teaching.
What Plotinus really meant was that "a knowledge
of Ideas is a constant process of involution and
evolution, different from the concepts of the understanding in this respect only that no reason can
be brought for the affirmation, because it *is* reason.
The soul (for example) contemplates its principle
(which is) the universal in itself, as a particular,
i.e. knows that this truth is *involved* and *vice versa
evolves itself from its principle.*" Accepting then this
"evolutionary" logic, the whole question resolves
itself into that of filling in the terms of the formula:
finding, that is, the reality (X), what knows it (A),
and what it knows it *as* (W), finally what is involved
in the known reality X (Y + Z).

Though rejecting Kant's logic, Coleridge had long
ago accepted what was the basis of his ethics, and
his point of contact with noumenal reality, namely,
the categorical imperative, as the sense of responsibility to something beyond the self, made known
to us in conscience. What dissatisfied him in Kant
was *first* the treatment of this as merely a mode of
our *volitional* consciousness, instead of as the foundation of all consciousness, and presupposed in it;
and *secondly* the attempt to isolate it from other
elements and interests of human nature, coupled
with the refusal to admit it as the basis of a
speculative argument. His own spiritual realism,
on the other hand, depended precisely on the power
to get beyond these limitations.

It is in disproof of the former of these mistakes

that he tries to show at a critical point of the argument in MS. B II, and in closely reasoned sequence (i) that consciousness in the proper sense of the word involves self-consciousness; (ii) that this in turn involves the consciousness of an other than self—a thou, a he, or an it; (iii) that, in distinguishing between self and other, we also unite or identify them, not, indeed, in the sense of obliterating the numerical difference, but in the sense of assigning them equal rights; (iv) that "the becoming conscious of a conscience" partakes of the nature of an act—"an act, namely, in which and by which we take upon ourselves an allegiance, and consequently the obligation of Fealty"; and finally that "the equation of the 'thou' with the 'I' by means of a free act, by which we negative the sameness in order to establish the equality, is the true definition of the conscience".

It is on the ground of the existence of this "fealty", as a fundamental fact in human nature, alone that Coleridge believes it possible to bridge the gulf which separated the finite from the Infinite. "From whichever of the two points the reason may start: from the things that are seen to the One Invisible, or from the Idea of the absolute One to the things that are seen, it will find a chasm, which the *moral* being only, which the spirit and religion of man alone, can fill up or overbridge."[1] All other arguments *either*, like that from design, assume moral attributes in the Infinite,[2] *or*, like that from the existence of law in Nature, leave them out of it

[1] MS. B III.   [2] See below.

and so deprive it of any religious significance. It was for this reason, he held, that "all the sounder schoolmen and the first fathers of the Reformation with one consent place the origin of the Idea in the Reason, the ground of its reality in the conscience, and the confirmation and progressive development (of it) in the order and harmony of the visible world". He would have admitted (he elsewhere constantly does) that there still was a "leap", but he would have insisted that it was open to demonstration that the leap was not an irrational one in the sense of leaving us with open contradiction, and therefore with mystery. On the contrary he held that we find in it the solution of the mystery which the world would *otherwise* be. "The world", in fact, "in its relation to the human soul is a mystery of which God is the only solution." [1]

Returning to the Plotinian formula, we can now see the ground on which Coleridge was prepared to fill in the terms and claim it as not only the foundation stone, but the only possible one of "philosophic Realism". "Let A", he goes on in continuation of the former quotation, "represent the Reason in Man, speculative and practical, let W stand for a knowledge, both the form and contents of which the Reason derives from itself; let X signify the Categorical Imperative of Kant; Y the absolute W, and Z the universal Reason (Y + Z = God). Then A has W, for it is realized in X. But W in X would be W (i.e. the rational knowledge would be irrational) without Y and Z. The

[1] *Lay Sermon*, Appendix C.

Idea X therefore involves the Ideas Y and Z, and the knowledge of the reality of X gives an equivalent knowledge of the reality of Y and Z."

5. COLERIDGE'S THEOLOGICAL PLATONISM

Formal, even pedantic, as it may seem, there can be no doubt as to the central importance Coleridge attaches to this argument. In the passage from which the above quotations are taken he repeats it in several forms, and, as if to leave no mistake, adds a Synopsis of it, as *"an argumentum ad hominem"* in reply to Tennemann's criticism of it. With regard to its general form, we may be prepared to share some of Coleridge's enthusiasm for it, if we are prepared to find in it an anticipation of the principle, of which later idealists, notably Bradley, have made so much, that "what is necessary and at the same time possible must be real". On the other hand, subtle and I believe original as his application of the argument is, as an attempt to establish a voluntaristic form of idealism, or as he preferred to call it "spiritual realism", at a level which similar modern attempts seldom attain, as stated by him it raises obvious difficulties not only from the formal side, but from the side of the material conclusion.

(1) After all that he has said to discredit the appeal to Logic upon final issues, why, we might ask, this anxiety to make his peace with her when it comes to real business? Without attempting to defend all that he anywhere says of the relation

between truths of the reason and logical *reasoning*, I believe that the question is capable of an answer consistent with his general view of the relation between them. Though distinguishable as higher and lower, there was in Coleridge's view no break of continuity between reason and understanding. As the laws of gravitation held as much for living as for dead things, the laws of thought hold as much for "productive" reason as for the merely "constitutive" understanding. The union of apparent opposites, which it is the function of the higher power to effect, is itself inspired by the demand for a "consistent" view of the object. These have to be united so as to escape contradiction. So far from real and logical truth being different, all truth in the end must be logical truth. Coleridge would have agreed with Bosanquet's aphorism that "logical exactitude in the full sense of the word is not a deadening but a vitalizing quality". What was required in the case of the establishment of the above ultimate metaphysical truth was not to break away from fact and its logical implications and appeal to a non-logical intuition, but to give fuller recognition first to the actual fact (the reality of the moral law in man's mind), and secondly to what was logically implied in it (the existence of a moral law, and therewith of a Lawgiver, in the world at large). The reconciliation of the existence of such a Lawgiver with other facts of the world—physical necessity, the existence of evil, individual responsibility—raised further questions which it was the business of philosophy to try to answer, and which it could only answer satisfyingly by the elimination of logical contradiction between these facts and the alleged ground of them.

(2) The difficulty raised by the material conclusion of the priority of Will to Existence—more generally of Act to Being—is a more serious one. Can will be conceived of except in relation to a world already there? Must not "act" be an effluence from being and not *vice versa*? Coleridge was himself keenly alive to this difficulty, and in MS. B tries to meet it, first by defining the priority which is claimed for the Will as purely a logical one; and secondly by showing that logical priority follows from the idea of the will itself.

Temporal relations, he insists, are inapplicable to the Absolute. Even though we conceive of will as a cause, causality itself transcends time, seeing that it merges, as we have seen, in the idea of interaction, in which cause and effect must be conceived of as contemporaneous. Attributed to the Supreme Reality, causality must therefore mean co-eternity. But he adds that it is a co-eternity in which will must be conceived of as the more fundamental factor, seeing that its very essence is to be causative of reality; to reverse this and make it a product is to destroy it as will. On the other hand, there is nothing in the conception of being which is exclusive of that of product. "So far, indeed, is the idea of co-eternal consequent from involving any rational inconceivability, that all the ancient philosophers, who, like Aristotle, asserted a Deity, but denied a creation in time, on the ground that communicativeness is an essential attribute of the Deity, admitted this in a far harsher form, for they asserted the world to be a co-eternal effect."

For himself he denies the adequacy of the whole conception of causality to express the idea of the Will, and, falling back again on Plotinus, but with a difference, goes on to explain what has to be substituted for it. This he finds in the idea of "an infinite fullness poured out into an infinite capacity . . . a self wholly and adequately repeated, yet so that the very repetition contains the distinction from the primary act, a self which in both is self-subsistent and is not the same, because the only 'only' is self-originated".

Coleridge's relation to the New Platonic philosophy has often been discussed, and as often misrepresented. We have seen how early and deeply he was impressed with its affinity to the speculative ideas, and particularly to the doctrine of the Trinity, which had become part and parcel of Christian theology. In the passages just quoted from MS. B we have a clear indication of the extent both of his agreement and of his disagreement with it. But the question is put beyond all doubt by a passage in the Huntington Library manuscript, in which he institutes a direct comparison between the Neo-Platonic scheme and his own.[1]

While prepared, as we have just seen, to adopt the Plotinian conception of the Absolute as an

[1] MS. H, p. 151 foll.

infinite power pouring itself forth like the sun as from an inexhaustible fullness, he could not accept the details of the emanation theory as an adequate counterpart, far less as the source of the Christian doctrine, and submits it to a trenchant and, so far as his own views are concerned, an illuminating criticism. He is careful at the outset to separate it from anything that could be attributed to Plato, who, he had convinced himself, does not expound, and never intended to expound, his own esoteric philosophy in the *Dialogues*. It was developed by the later. Platonists in defiance of the express warning of Plato's own immediate successor Speusippus, that the true order of the process of the Absolute was not The Good, Reason, and Soul, each identical in essence with the other, but The One, Reason, and the Good, each with a nature of its own.[1]

Passing over this difference of order, he finds a deeper objection to it in the attempt to define the supreme reality by a string of negatives as that which neither "acts", nor "thinks", nor even "is". Coleridge had thought much on the logical principle of negation,[2] and saw clearly that all intelligent negation presupposes a positive idea. Yet this is what seems to be denied in the Plotinian scheme, with the result that the idea of the Good is left quite indeterminate as a "reverential epithet", instead of being seen necessarily to involve intelli-

[1] The passages on which Coleridge seems to have relied are Aristotle, *Metaph.*, bk. vii. ch. 2 (Eng. tr. 1028b), and Stobaeus, *Eclogae* i. 58. See Ritter and Preller, *Historia Graecae Philosophiae*, 7th ed., pp. 284–5).
[2] See Snyder, *op. cit.*, p. 112.

gence and action, not to speak of being. But the chief speculative defect of the scheme is the attachment of inferiority to reason and soul as more distant emanations of the Good. Whence the inferiority? If the First be an Infinite, it must have infinite effects. In a word, Emanation assumes the possibility of a fragmentary Deity, a diluted Godhead.

Serious finally as are the speculative difficulties, the moral consequences are more serious still. For in this scheme good and evil lose all qualitative distinction, and appear as mere differences in degree of being. *Either* the idea of guilt and responsibility is altogether denied, *or* crime and evil (as mere facts) increase as guilt or the sense of them (by the degradation of Reason) diminishes.

While the modern reader would have been sorry to miss this criticism and the light it throws upon Coleridge's own doctrine of the supreme Will and its "alterity" as equivalent respectively to God the Father of the Filial Word, he will be apt to find in this theological extension of Coleridge's metaphysics a revival of what is most mediaeval, and perhaps repulsive, in English Platonism. It is, indeed, impossible to disguise in Coleridge's metaphysics the use of language that seems to subordinate philosophical doctrine to theological dogma. "The doctrine of Ideas", he writes in connection with the above exposition of it, "is antecedent, but only because ancillary, to the more important truths, by which religion rises above philosophy." But we should show an imperfect appreciation of the power of speculative truth to break through the swaddling-bands of theological dogma if we were to exaggerate the extent to which apologetic interests at this point vitiate Coleridge's results.

The stream of Greek philosophy, starting from Socrates and Plato in an atmosphere of open and untrammelled thought, had flowed for five centuries, gaining in depth, if not in clarity, from the religious interest which more and more mingled with it, and finally made itself felt in its full force in Plotinus, its "second founder". It was impossible that any one, who had inherited its leading constructive ideas and even a small portion of its free spirit, should seek merely to adapt particular parts of it, least of all what to Plato at least was only a myth or at best a "probable story", to dogmatic matter imported from alien sources. These in moments of weakness or in an atmosphere of conservative tradition might claim from Coleridge undue consideration, and even tempt him to what looks like compromise. But in a mind like his, in which speculative truth was the dominant and absorbing intellectual interest, it was these dogmas, we may believe, and not the great ideas to which it had committed itself for guidance, that had to submit to purification and reconstruction; and it is not surprising that to the most penetrating of his critics in the succeeding generation, among them John Henry Newman,[1] this should have appeared

[1] Newman speaks of him as one who "indulged a liberty of speculation which no Christian can tolerate, and advocated conclusions which were often heathen rather than Christian". *Essays*, vol. i. p. 269, quoted Benn, *Rationalism in the Nineteenth Century*, i. 270.

to be the result. Even in the above passage, while severely critical of Neo-Platonism, he shows himself anxious to save the reputation of Plato himself, and he would have distrusted any gloss upon his thought that seemed to depart from the essential sanity of the Master.

However this may be, we find Coleridge under no delusion as to what he was trying to accomplish in the exposition of the metaphysical basis of his system which we have been considering. He states it in so many words to be the offering of proof, *first* that it is possible to form an idea, consistent with all other truths, respecting the Supreme reality; *secondly* that such an idea is found in that of an Absolute Will; and *thirdly* that we have here something from which we are free to advance and to show, if we can, the sufficiency of the account to satisfy the demands made on it in the name of reason and experience. The main issue raised by his metaphysics is not Plotinus *versus* Kant, still less philosophy *versus* Christian mysticism, but the sufficiency of a theory that founds itself on the idea of the Absolute as Will. If the central line of English idealistic thought in the nineteenth century, under Hegel's influence, was destined for two generations to move in an apparently different direction, the fact of the somewhat violent reaction against it and all its works, which marks the present time, bears witness to the vitality and inherent attractiveness of the voluntaristic form of idealistic philosophy, of which Coleridge was the founder, and remains to this day the most distinguished representative.

CHAPTER IV

PHILOSOPHY OF NATURE

"In order to the recognition of himself in nature man must first learn to comprehend nature in himself and its laws as the ground of his own existence."—*The Friend*.

1. COLERIDGE'S INTEREST IN SCIENCE

IN the *Biographia Literaria* Coleridge tells us of the powerful effect upon his mind of Schelling's *Natur-Philosophie*. But after his disillusionment with Schelling, Nature-Philosophy became for him the suspicious name for a mode of thought that inevitably led to a spiritless pantheism. Yet, if this was to be met, it must be by a more adequate conception of nature as no mere finished and dead product (*natura naturata*), but as a living and creative principle (*natura naturans*).

The general intellectual atmosphere seemed favourable for this advance. The materialism with which early Platonists like Cudworth had found themselves confronted in the works of Hobbes and some of the Cartesians, was still a menace, but by the end of the eighteenth century it showed signs of having run its course. Leibnizian conceptions were exercising a powerful influence in the opposite direction. In 1747 appeared Kant's *Thoughts on the True Estimation of Living Forces*,[1] which had struck the note of a "dynamic" philosophy. His theory of knowledge, in which the material world as known

[1] Alluded to by Coleridge, *Aids to Reflection*, "Conclusion", 14 n.

to science was shown to be a construction of the mind, had undermined the ordinary arguments for materialism as a philosophical system. Biology had begun to come to its own, and the doctrine of the dependence of organic structure on a prior principle of life was being taught in high places by Dr. John Hunter (1728–93). In the early years of the new century controversy raged between his followers led by Dr. John Abernethy and their critics.

It was impossible for Coleridge to be a passive spectator of this war of ideas. He had been interested in scientific, and especially in medical investigations from early childhood, first through his brother Luke,[1] afterwards through attendance at Blumenbach's lectures in Germany, and through his friendship with Humphry Davy and his many contacts with members of the medical profession.[2] Needless to say, he was an ardent supporter of the Dynamic Philosophy. In it he saw his own dream of finding the material world, not less than the spiritual, the expression of an Idea. For this reason, if it is not quite fair to say with Miss Snyder that his concern with science was merely "the effort of a philosophic partisan to justify his philosophical position", we may agree that "there can be no adequate account of the making of his metaphysical system—the

[1] Whose medical books he read and with whom he went round the wards of the London Hospital. See Campbell's *Samuel Taylor Coleridge*, p. 12.

[2] Miss Snyder has given a scholarly account of his relations with these at various periods of his life and of the controversial atmosphere in which his own *Theory of Life* was written. *Op. cit.*, pp. 16 foll.

influences exercised by the Neo-Platonists, the English divines, the German Natur-Philosophen—that does not recognize his participation in contemporary scientific discussions, and his sense of their philosophic implications".[1]

The reader of *The Friend* is familiar with the illustrations he draws from the views of some of the writers mentioned above;[2] but it is to the posthumous essay, *Hints toward the Formation of a More Comprehensive Theory of Life* [3] that we must go for the most systematic statement of his views. In *The Friend* he had already expressed dissatisfaction with Hunter's presentation of the idea of life.[4] Hunter seems as a matter of fact to have left it open to suppose that life was merely a superimposed or emergent property of matter, which had reached through purely physical influences a particular degree of refinement and organization.[5]

Accordingly, at the beginning of the essay, after a reference to "the undeniable obscurities and

[1] *Loc. cit.*, pp. 30 and 22.
[2] E.g. vol. iii, section ii, Essays vi, vii, and ix.
[3] Edited by Seth B. Watson, 1848. On the controversy as to the editor's view of it as the joint production of Coleridge and Dr. Gillman, see Snyder, *ibid.*, pp. 16 and 17.
[4] *Loc. cit.*, Essay vii. "In his printed works the one directing thought seems evermore to flit before him, twice or thrice only to have been seized; and after a momentary detention to have been again let go: as if the words of the charm had been incomplete and it had appeared at its own will only to mock his calling." Cp. what he says of him, *Principles of the Science of Method*, p. 41.
[5] Asked by a pupil whether his theory did not make for the exploded doctrine of equivocal generation, Hunter is said to have replied, "Perhaps it does. I do not deny that equivocal generation happens. There are positive proofs neither for nor against its taking place." Article John Hunter, *Encl. Brit.* (ed. ix), p. 391.

apparent contradictions" to be found in Hunter's works, Coleridge defines his aim as "to climb up on his shoulders and look at the same objects in a distincter form, because seen from the more commanding point of view furnished by himself".

2. The Idea of Nature

We are now familiar with this "more commanding point of view" in his general metaphysical theory. To what has already been said about it we may here add a reference to one or two manuscript passages (probably of earlier date than the Essay) in which he develops the concept, or, as he prefers to call it, the "Idea" of Nature, with particular lucidity in accordance with it.

"Wonderful", he writes,[1] "are the efforts of Nature to reconcile chasm with continuity, to vault and nevertheless to glide, though in truth the continuity alone belongs to Nature, the chasms are the effect of a higher principle, limiting the duration and regulating the retention of the products. From the Vermes to the Mammalia, Organic Nature is in every class and everywhere tending to Individuality; but Individuality actually commences in Man. This and many other problems must find their solution in the right 'Idea of Nature' "

Following the sense, but preceding the date of this entry, we have a still fuller statement of the general point of view from which he would have

[1] MS. C, p. 117.

Nature regarded. "The true object of Natural Philosophy is to discover a central Phaenomenon in Nature, and a central Phaen(omenon) in Nature requires and supposes a central Thought in the Mind. The *Notional* Boundaries or *Ne plus ultras* of Nature are a part that relatively to no minor particles is a Whole, i.e. an Atom: and a Whole, which in no relation is a Part, i.e. a Universe. The System of Epicurus is that a finite Universe composed of Atoms is notionally true. But it expresses the limits and necessities of the human imagination and understanding, not the truth of Nature. An atom and a finite Universe are both alike Fictions of Mind, *entia logica*. Nevertheless, not the Imagination alone, but the Reason requires a Centre. It is a necessary Postulate of Science. That therefore which can be found nowhere absolutely and exclusively must be imagined everywhere relatively and partially. Hence the law of Bicentrality, i.e. that every Whole, whether without parts or composed of parts, and, in the former, whether without parts by defect or lowness of Nature (= a material atom), or without parts by the excellence of its Nature (= a Monad or Spirit), must be conceived as a possible centre in itself, and at the same time as having a centre out of itself and common to it with all other parts of the same System. Now the first and fundamental Postulate of Universal Physiology, comprising both organic and inorganic Nature—or the fundamental position of the *Philosophy* of Physics and Physiology—is: that there is in Nature a tendency to realize this possibility, wherever the conditions exist: and the first problem of this Branch of Science is, What are the conditions under which a Unit having a centre in the distance can manifest its own centrality, i.e. be the centre of a system and (as, in dynamics, the power of the centre acts in every point of the area contained in the circumference), be the centre and the *copula* (*principium unitatis in unoquoque Toto*) of a System. Such a Unit would have three characters:

1. It would be a component part of a System, having a centre out of itself, or, to use a geometrical metaphor, it would be a point in some one of the concentrical lines composing a common circle.

2. It would be itself the centre and copula, the attractive and cohesive force, of a system of its own.

3. *For itself* (as far as it exists *for* itself), it would be the centre of the Universe in a perpetual tendency to include whatever else exists relatively to it in itself, and what it could not include, to repel. Whatever is not contained in the System, of which it is the centre and copula, either does not exist at all *for* it or exists as an Alien, which it resists, and in resisting either appropriates (digestion, assimilation), or repels, or ceases to be, i.e. dies.

These three characters concur in every living body, and hence there necessarily arise two directions of the contemplative act. The Philosopher may either regard any body or number of bodies in reference to a common centre, the action of which centre constitutes the General Laws of the

System; in *this* view all Bodies are contemplated
as inanimate—and these, in which he can discover
none of the *conditions* indispensable to the Body's
being contemplated in any other view, he considers as positively inanimate; and the aggregate
of these we call inorganic Nature. Or he may
contemplate a Body as containing its centre or
principle of Unity in itself: and, as soon as he
ascertains the existence of the conditions requisite
to the manifestation of such a principle, he supposes Life and these bodies collectively are named
Organic Nature. In Nature there is a tendency
to respect herself so as to attempt in each part what
she had produced in the Whole, but with a limited
power and under certain conditions. N.B.—In this,
the only scientific view, Nature itself is assumed as
the Universal Principle of Life, and like all other
Powers, is contemplated under the two primary
Ideas of Identity and Multeity, i.e. alternately as
one and as many. In other words, exclusively of
degree, and as subsisting in a series of different
intensities." [1]

In this passage Coleridge stops short of naming
this principle Will, but in the parallel not less
notable passage in MS. B III, he makes it clear
that this is what he intends. Corresponding to the
criticism of "Epicurus" in the above, we there have
a protest against the view that the mind has to

[1] *Ibid.*, p. 108. I have left the capitals as indicating the importance
he attaches to the thoughts. The passage has not, so far as I know,
been printed before. This and the anticipation it contains of the
modern interest of philosophers in the Concept of Nature are
perhaps sufficient apology for the lengthy quotation.

be "weaned by aid of the analytic powers" from
the natural conception of the whole as preceding
the parts, and the reduction of Nature to nothing
but "a mere declaration of an alien strength, and
that gone ere I can arrest or question it". "This
ignores the individuality of that which is acted
upon. Aconite is poison to sheep, nutritious to
goats. Even the atoms require to differ in shape."
This difference lies beyond the reach of the reasoning
faculty, for it cannot be reduced to cause or relation.
It is presupposed in the possibility of cause. We
have as our alternatives Chance (i.e. recourse to
not thinking at all) or Will "which, if the total
sum and result of individualities or simple productive acts be in the highest degree rational,
i.e. tending in due proportion to a common unity,
must be one with reason, though in the order of
necessary connection its co-eternal antecedent". If
this is so, the several individualities must be of the
nature of a will, and therefore higher than Nature.
The spontaneity we find in Nature is not indeed
interpretable as will, but it is "of the nature of
will", and may be conceived of as the offspring
of it, as the automatism of habit in a musician's
fingers: "spontaneity in a plant must be referred
to some universal will, as the other to a particular
will". From this he again passes to the view of what
he calls the "shapes" of Nature, in contrast to the
"forms" or "shaping principles", as a progressive
series or scale.

Premising that the shapes may be of three kinds—
(1) those formed by languescence in the shaping

power, e.g. an arrow or a rocket; (2) those imposed
from without, e.g. the fluid in a containing vessel;
(3) those which are owed to an inner energy,
opposed to (2) as pure energy to pure receptivity—
we have these variously blended in an infinite
number of proportions, but the higher in the scale
the greater the proportion of the last kind. Thus
in the higher animals sensibility passes into mus-
cular power and irritability, in order to return
again upon itself and become a new sensibility;
so that in all instances the influence of the external
is mediated by and dependent upon the degree and
state of development, and we have a scale in which
"the maximum of each lower kind becomes the
base and receptive substrate, as it were, of a higher
kind, commencing through the irradiation and
transfiguration by the higher power, the base of
which it has become." "In man this law of proportions becomes fully manifest, and, in the strivings of
the will (to rise), the excess of impressibility and
receptivity of impressions from without (rises) not
only above spontaneity, not only above impulse
determined by the anticipation of outward objects,
but even above that direction of the power more
properly called voluntary, which itself predeter-
mines the object of its own knowledge, and the
previous reflection of that object in relation to
itself, but still supposes a prior state of receptivity
in overbalance during the impressions made on
the senses. Man must have an object in himself,
an object which he himself has constituted, which
is at one and the same moment the subject and

the legislator, the law and the act of obedience."
In man therefore so conceived all is energy, and
the second of the above kinds of shape (in fact
shape itself) ceases, ascending into form when the
soul receives reason and "reason is her being".

3. THE IDEA OF LIFE

It is this view of Nature as a progressive system
of embodied and individualizing activities that in
the essay is applied to the idea of Life. After stating
and rejecting some current definitions of life, such
as that it is "the sum of all the functions by which
death is resisted", and that it consists in "assimilation, growth, and reproduction", Coleridge defines
it himself as simply "the principle of individuation".
Wherever you have this, you have something that
goes beyond mere mechanism. He does not deny
the existence of mechanism, but distinguishes it
from what he calls life, as organization from without; as he epigrammatically puts it, "whatever is
organized from without is a product of mechanism;
whatever is mechanized from within is a production
of organization".[1] So defined, he finds life to be
a property of matter throughout the entire gamut

[1] See p. 385 n. of *Miscellanies Aesthetic and Literary*, where the Essay
will most conveniently be found. With its general teaching should
be compared that of J. H. Green in his Hunterian Lecture of 1840
on *Vital Dynamics* (see passages quoted in *Spiritual Philosophy*, vol. i.
pp. xxv. foll.). Green's remark that life was to be contemplated "not
as a thing, nor as a spirit, neither as a subtle fluid, nor as an intelligent soul but as a law" is of particular interest in view of present-
day controversies. Coleridge was not a vitalist in the sense, e.g. of
Driesch.

of its forms, beginning with elements or metals,[1] and going on through ever higher forms of crystals, the great vegetable and animal deposits, vegetables and animals as we know them, up to man, in whom "the whole force of organic power has attained an inward and centripetal direction". Thus, "in the lowest forms of the vegetable and animal world we perceive totality dawning into individuation, while in man, as the highest of the class, the individuality is not only perfected in its corporeal sense, but begins a new series beyond the appropriate limits of physiology. The tendency to individuation, more or less obvious, constitutes the common character of all classes, as far as they maintain for themselves a distinction from the universal life of the planet; while the degrees, both of intensity and extension, to which this tendency is realized, form the species and their ranks in the great scale of ascent and expansion".[2]

We are apt to think of individuation as a process of separation and detachment, but Coleridge insists throughout on the opposite tendency to inter-connection as an inseparable element in it, just

[1] The nugget of gold is not life, seeing that its form is accidental and *ab extra*; but gold itself is life, seeing that it is an organized system of qualities ultimately activities; for "life is an act". He seemed even prepared to convert this dictum into "all act is life": "Nature", he notes in MS. C, p. 117, "(is) always vegetative" and "therefore the vegetable creation could be anterior to the sun." The resemblance and the difference between this and the theory of monads "that yet seem With various province and apt agency Each to pursue its own self-centring end", sympathetically sketched in the early poem, *The Destiny of Nations*, are worth noting.
[2] *Op. cit.*, p. 390.

as centripetal power is necessarily presupposed in centrifugal. It is this productive power that makes life incapable of mathematical treatment. But this does not exclude it from science, as Kant would have it, for whose aphorism that science ends with mathematics Coleridge would substitute as the truer one: "the full applicability of abstract science ceases the moment reality begins".

In the vital series thus depicted as a "grand scale of ascent and expansion", each higher stage is conceived of as not merely superimposed on the lower, e.g. life on mechanism, nor as merely employing it, but as assimilating it to itself by a process which "presupposes the homogeneous nature of the thing assimilated". On any other supposition we should have a miracle comparable to that of transubstantiation—"first annihilation, then creation out of nothing".

Inquiring further through what forces this individuating principle acts, Coleridge points to magnetism, electricity, chemistry or constructive affinity as the highest that science has as yet succeeded in discovering; but he holds it conceivable that these may be found to be reducible to some other which will be more akin to life.[1] Meantime, he notes, all of them illustrate what he regards as the most general law governing the action of life in every one of its forms—the law of polarity or "the essential dualism of nature", for it is always in the identity of two counter powers that "life subsists; in their strife it consists; in their recon-

[1] *Op. cit.*, p. 400.

ciliation it at once dies, and is born again into
new forms, either falling back into the life of the
whole, or starting anew in the process of individuation".[1]

The author goes on to pursue this hypothesis
into minute details, most of which would probably
have been rejected even by the science of his own
time. But his treatment of time, space, and motion,
as "the simplest and universal, but necessary
symbols of all philosophic construction, the primary
factors and elementary forms of every calculus, and
of every diagram in the algebra and geometry of
scientific philosophy", is of particular interest in
view of recent developments of philosophy in the
direction of defining the fundamental concepts of
physical science. Needless to say, the emphasis in
Coleridge is not upon these forms as containing the
substance of the real world in any sense that
can be taken as the ground of their explanation,
but upon the active principle or *nisus* towards
individuality which expresses itself through them.

4. COLERIDGE AND EVOLUTION

The idea of an actual evolution of species ("forms",
as Coleridge called them) in time by the laws of
natural selection, as conceived by Charles Darwin,
was still in the future; but theories of their natural
origin and development in the struggle for existence
had been familiar to philosophers from the time
of Lucretius. In Coleridge's own day Erasmus

[1] *Op. cit.*, p. 390.

Darwin (1731–1802), in holding that "one and the same kind of living filaments is and has been the course of all organic life", had (in the words of his more famous grandson) "anticipated . . the views of Lamarck". Coleridge's omnivorous reading had familiarized him also with Giordano Bruno's doctrine that the Earth was "a complete ether-born animate being", which, by its union with the Sun, "successively conceives and brings to the birth from all parts of its body; so that, if the whole Earth were by some planetary accident or revolution depopulated (of its inhabitants), the Soul of the Earth would replace them: *Parens perfecta Animantum Absque ministerio coitus*".

He even goes out of his way to defend "the Philosopher of Nola" against the charge of Atheism brought against him on this ground, seeing that he everywhere considers the Earth and similar planetary souls throughout the Universe, though the "immediate maternal fount" of life, "as merely ministerial powers, and Nature, their collective name, as the Delegate, Servant, and Creature of one Supreme Being, and all-originating *Opifex*".

In view of all this, and of his own theory of the difference between what is merely prior in time and what is prior in reality and worth, and therefore in power, combined with his view of Nature as continually striving towards unity and continuity in spite of apparent "chasms", we might have expected Coleridge to have a sympathetic ear for speculations of this kind. It is all the more interesting to find him, in a carefully elaborated autograph fragment,[1] energetically repudiating them in the Lucretian and Brunian, as well as in the Darwinian form, though, as we might expect, with a pronounced preference for the former more poetic version:

"And here once for all, I beg leave to remark that I attach neither belief nor respect to the Theory, which supposes the human Race to have been gradually perfecting itself from the darkest Savagery, or still more boldly tracing us back to the bestial as to our Larva, contemplates Man as the last metamorphosis, the gay *Image*, of some lucky species of Ape or Baboon. Of the two hypotheses I should, indeed, greatly prefer the Lucretian of the Parturiency of our Mother Earth, some score thousands years ago, when the venerable Elder was yet in her Teens, and her human Litter sucked the milk then oozing from countless Breasts of warm and genial Mud. For between an hypothetical ἀπαξγινόμενον or single Incident or Event in a state and during an epoch if the Planet presumed in all respects different from its present condition, and the laws of Nature appropriate to the same . . anterior of necessity to all actual experience, and an assertion of a universal process of Nature now existing (since there is the same reason for asserting the progression of every other race of animal from some lower species as of the human race) in contradiction to all experience, I can have no hesitation

[1] British Museum MS. Egerton 2801. See Miss Snyder's article, "Coleridge on Giordano Bruno", *Modern Language Notes*, vol. xlii. No. 7, where the passage is quoted in full along with other references to Bruno.

in preferring the former, that, for which Nothing can be said, to that *against* which Everything may be said. The History I find in my Bible is in perfect coincidence with the opinions which I should form on Grounds of Experience and Common Sense. But our belief that Man first appeared with all his faculties perfect and in full growth, the anticipation exercised by virtue of the supernatural act of Creation, in nowise contravenes or weakens the assertion that these faculties . . in each succeeding Individual, born according to nature, must be preceded by a process of growth, and consequently a state of involution or latency, correspondent to each successive Moment of Development. A rule abstracted from uniform Results, or the Facet of a Sum put by the Master's indulgence at the head of the sum to be worked, may not only render the Boy's Task shorter and easier, but without such assistance he might never have mastered it or attained the experience, from which the Rule might (have been derived?)."

It is easy to seize on the reference here to Biblical authority as witness to the inveterate power of tradition over Coleridge's mind. But the real emphasis in the above passage is in the absence of proof of natural evolution on "grounds of experience and common sense". In what was clearly intended as a note to it in the same manuscript he remarks: "When experience is possible, and in points that are the fit subjects of experience, the absence of experimental proof is tantamount to an experimental proof of the contrary. *Ex. gr.*

If a man should seriously assure me that he had in the course of his Travels seen a Tree, that produced live Barnacles as its fruit, I could not in strict logic declare it contrary to all experience; for he would be entitled to reply, 'No! for I believe it on my own.' But if a Theorist should assert such a fact only because in his opinion it would be a rational account of the present parentage and existence of Barnacles, in that case I should have a right to characterize his conjecture as against all experience."

What Coleridge would have said with the "experimental" evidence of the *Origin of Species* before him it is impossible to say. Hutchison Stirling, the leader of the Idealistic revival in the 'sixties, still treated Darwinism with philosophical contempt. The fact, on the other hand, that Coleridge quotes more than once, and adopts as the motto of the *Statesman's Manual*, a fine saying of Bruno's, altogether relevant to such a situation,[1] and that he found it possible to reconcile Bruno's speculations as to the birth of man, which were not less heretical than Darwin's, with the divine origin of the whole choir of Heaven and the furniture of Earth:

Auctori laudes decantans atque ministrans,[2]

and to attribute to him "a Principle, Spirit, and eloquence of Piety and Pure Morality not surpassed

---

[1] *Ad istaec quaeso vos, qualiacunque primo videantur aspectu, attendite, ut qui vobis forsan insanire videar, saltem quibus insaniam rationibus cognoscatis.*
[2] From Bruno's *De Immenso et Innumerabilibus.*

by Fénelon"—suggests that he would have had the insight to see the distinction between a biological account of the process in time, and the inner Law or Idea of the Universe as a spiritual Whole, of which the process is only the outward manifestation, and which is the proper subject of a philosophy of Nature. We can see, at any rate, from the above quotations that he was prepared to treat such a hypothesis without the unreasoning prejudice that disfigures the references to it in Carlyle and many others, who ought to have known better, in the next generation. Securely fixed in the conviction, deepened in him by his poetic experience, of the close affinity of Nature with mind, and "with that more than man, which is one and the same in all men", and of her power of seeming "to think and hold commune with us, like an individual soul",[1] he could afford to leave to biological science the question of the way in which she produced the shapes, among them the shape of man himself, which made this intercourse possible.

It is easy to criticize the theory of Nature here set forth as an undue extension of the concept of life and a hypostatizing of Nature.[2] What is philosophically valuable in it, connecting it in a suggestive way with recent physical speculations, is, in the first place, the emphasis on the presence in all phenomena of a principle that goes beyond anything that can properly be called mechanical;

[1] *Blackwood's Magazine*, October 1821, p. 258.
[2] See Dr. Watson's Preface to the Essay, *op. cit.*, pp. 356–7.

secondly, the conception of this principle as operating throughout the whole extent of Nature, manifesting itself in ever higher forms, which constitute real differences of kind, and not merely of degree: Nature, as he puts it, "ascending not as links in a suspended chain, but as the steps in a ladder", assimilating while transcending what has gone before; thirdly, the interpretation of the law of the universe, in harmony with this idea, as "a tendency to the ultimate production of the highest and most comprehensive unity"; lastly, the clearness with which he insists that the unity must consist of individuals, becoming more and more truly such in proportion as they unite themselves with the whole, and reflect the perfections to which as an embodiment of Will it summons them.

CHAPTER V

MORAL PHILOSOPHY

"The happiness of mankind is the end of virtue, and truth is the knowledge of the means; which he will never seriously attempt to discover who has not habitually interested himself in the welfare of others."—BRISTOL ADDRESS.

1. THE SCIENCE VERSUS SCHEMES OF MORALS

IT followed from Coleridge's general theory of rational knowledge as the apprehension of Ideas, in the sense of organizing, individualizing principles, that no true theory of morals could be evolved from mere generalizations from sense experience. Sense experience might show us the conditions under which the good life has to be lived, and from which rules of prudence, varying necessarily according to circumstances, might be derived. But any claim to universality and necessity, in other words any claim to possess a system of truth that could rightly be called a moral science, must be founded on deductions from the idea of the Will itself. This is the view he expounds in the careful statement of Aphorism CIXc. 26, in the *Aids to Reflection*: "By a Science I here mean any chain of Truths that are either absolutely certain, or necessarily true for the human mind from the laws and constitution of the mind itself. In neither case is our conviction derived, or capable of receiving any addition, from outward experience, or *empirical* data—i.e. matters of fact

given to us through the medium of the senses—
though these data may have been the occasion,
or may even be an indispensable condition, of
our reflecting on the former and thereby becoming
conscious of the same. On the other hand, a connected series of conclusions grounded on empirical
data, in contradistinction from science, I beg
leave (no better term occurring), in this place and
for this purpose, to denominate a Scheme."

As illustrations of such schemes he goes on in
Aphorism CXI,[1] to give all those which, as founded
on calculations of self-interest, or on the average
Consequences of Action, supposing them *general*,
form a branch of Political Economy: "to which
let all honour be given. Their utility is not here
questioned. But, however estimable within their
own sphere such schemes, or any one of them in
particular, may be, they do not belong to Moral
Science, to which both in kind and purpose they
are in all cases *foreign* and, when substituted for it,
hostile. Ethics, or the *Science* of Morality, does
indeed in nowise exclude the consideration of
Action; but it contemplates the same in its originating spiritual *Source* without reference to Space
or Time or Sensible Existence. Whatever springs
out of 'the perfect *Law* of Freedom', which exists
only by its unity with the Will of God . . . that
(according to the principles of Moral Science) is
Good."

After so careful a definition of a subject so

[1] Under the title, "Paley not a Moralist". Cp. *Table Talk*, 1884 ed.,
p. 155.

closely related to Coleridge's central interest in
the renovation of religion, we might have expected
a large portion of a work expressly written "to
establish the distinct characters of prudence,
morality and religion" to have been devoted to
the development of this "science".

Yet neither here nor in any of his other published
works do we have any attempt of the kind. With
these mainly before him in 1856, the author of
the able essay on Coleridge in *Cambridge Essays* of
that date [1] noted as "the most striking fact about
Coleridge's moral philosophy, considering the universal supremacy which moral considerations held
in his mind", that "there is so little to say about
it". This he goes on to find all the more remarkable
as there existed, in the work of his great fellow-
countryman Butler, a body of doctrine, which
only required to be reinterpreted and freed from
ambiguous elements to form the basis of just such
a science as Coleridge had in mind. The explanation doubtless is partly to be found in the singular
fact, which this writer also notices, of Coleridge's
apparent entire ignorance of Butler,[2] but also
partly in the popular character of his own chief
published works. It is therefore natural to expect
that in the more systematic unpublished works on
which he was later engaged, there should be some
attempt to supply what was wanting.

[1] F. J. A. Hort, M.A. See p. 336.
[2] This is confirmed by the occurrence of the name of Butler in
Aids to Reflection, XLIIIc, 10 and 13, but in a context which shows
that he has Samuel and not Joseph in his mind. His hatred of the
bad Butler, who wrote *Hudibras*, seems to have blinded him to the
good Butler, who wrote the *Analogy* and the *Sermons*.

Nor are we wholly disappointed. If these do not supply us with anything approaching a complete theory of Ethics, yet they give us invaluable hints as to what must always constitute the method and the elements of such a theory. In reading them we have always to bear in mind the jungle of unanalysed notions and ambiguous terms, through which at that time anyone who sought to do justice to the moral consciousness had to hack his way. Coleridge might seem to some to be oddly equipped for such a task and to suggest rather a Don Quixote than a St. George. As a matter of fact, he possessed just that fine sense of psychological and linguistic distinctions that was most required for this work, and, comparatively meagre as his results may now appear, it is not too much to say that they all point in the right direction.

2. THE METHOD OF ETHICS

Seeing that the science of morals takes the form of a deduction from the Idea of the Will, it would seem that its foundations must be laid in the demonstration of the reality that corresponds to the idea. It was precisely this reality that was denied by "the scheme of pure mechanism, which, under all disguises, tempting or repulsive, Christian or infidel, forms the groundwork of these systems of modern and political philosophy, political economy and education, which began by manufacturing mind out of sense and sense out of sensation (and) which reduce all form to shape and all shape to impression from without".[1]

Yet here, as in the case of Ideas in general, we are faced with the difficulty of any direct proof by way of conceptual logic. Coleridge admits that no such proof is possible, but holds that "indirect arguments from extreme improbability, and motives of strongest inducement to the reconsideration of the point denied may be brought forward".[2] What makes it worth while bringing them forward is that the denier, as often as not, is unaware of all that is involved in his position: he "goes but half way, pursuing the line of declination far enough to lose sight of the true road, and yet not so far as to be aware of the whirlpool in the outward eddy of which he is wheeling round and round".[3] On the other hand, the generality of mankind are so carried along, among other things by the inertia of the moral system into which they are born, "custom, habit, imitation, the necessity of preserving character, the sympathy and supports derived from superior rank and fortune, and the consequent absence of temptation", that "they may pass through life without a single principle, and never feel the want of it from the multitude and variety of its substitutes and its counterfeits".

Negatively, then, the method will consist in forcing the mechanistic view "by a stern logic,

[1] MS. B III. See Snyder, *op. cit.*, pp. 330. On the distinction between form and shape, see Chap. IV, p. 125 above.
[2] MS. B II. Snyder, p. 129. I have here combined the gist of these two passages.
[3] MS. B III, *loc. cit.*, *supra*.

into all its consequences"; *positively* it will consist in starting from the general assent to the *postulate* of Will, in order to "mature this into distinct conceptions and by means of these to bring a consistency of thought and language in(to) all other important conceptions included in the same class truly or falsely, and in the latter instance for the purpose of transferring them to their proper department or birth-place".

It would be difficult to find a better statement of the true method of ethics or one more in harmony both with the logic which teaches that the ultimate ground of the validity of any idea is, in Bosanquet's phrase, "this or nothing", and with the definition of philosophy in general as "a criticism of categories". Anyway, it is such a form of demonstration, which, as the writer tells us, is the aim of the chapters he devotes in this work to the analysis of some of the leading moral conceptions.

3. The Idea of the Self

Disregarding the particular order of his exposition, we may start from the most comprehensive of these in the idea of the Self. In the ethical philosophy of the time, the idea of Self-love was a central one. But both the parts of this hyphenated compound were ambiguous. Leaving the latter part for the present, what, Coleridge asks, do we mean by "self"?

The prevalent empiricism, as it resolved mind

into a series of sensations, resolved the active self into a series of sensory impulses, and particularly of impulses directed to pleasure as an object. To Coleridge this meant losing hold of the unity which is of the very essence of a self. If the self is to be a real unity and not "the semblance produced by an aggregate on the mind of the beholder", we must conceive of it as "anterior to all our sensations and to all the objects towards which they are directed", seeing that without it "nothing can become the object of reflection—not even the things of perception". As that which brings unity into the variety, as the universal that expresses itself in the particulars of experience, the self is manifested to consciousness as an Idea. But ideas are known through representatives (meanings, as we might say, through images), which need not be always the same. In the case of the idea of the self it is not fixed by nature, but, on the contrary, "varies with the growth, bodily, moral and intellectual, in each individual".

So far is the *body*, for instance, from being the only representative, that it is not even the first: in the early periods of infancy the mother or the nurse is the self of the child. And "who has not experienced in dreams the attachment of our personal identity to forms the most remote from our own"? [1] Nor is the body—*given* though it is to sense, and habitually thought of as the self— prescribed by necessity as the only object of love. "Even in his life of imperfection there is a state

[1] Yes! but why only in *dreams*?

possible in which a man might truly say, 'myself loves a or b', freely constituting the object in whatever it wills to love, commanding what it wills and willing what it commands." We only in fact know what we mean by a soul or self, as the subject of weal or woe, when we cease to look for it in a single soul as one of a class, and "have learned the possibility of finding a Self in another (yea, even in an enemy)".

Taking the word in this sense, everything may be said to be *self*-love. But we apply the term rightly only when we mean "a less degree of distance and a comparatively narrowness of our moral view": its grossness being diminished "no less by distance in time than by distance in space".

Short though the treatment here is, Coleridge shows in it that he has clearly grasped the Kantian notion of all human action as a form of self-realization; further, that he is feeling his way to the all-important distinction between self-affirmation and selfishness, and to a view of moral value as dependent on the extent to which a man organizes the passing moments of his temporal self into a whole, representative of what is most permanent in him. "The good man", he wrote elsewhere, "organizes the hours and gives them a soul, and to that, the very essence of which is to fleet and *to have been*, he communicates an imperishable and a spiritual nature. Of the good and faithful servant whose energies are thus methodized, it is less truly affirmed that he lives in time than that time lives in him. His days, months, and years, as the stops and punctual marks in the records of duties performed, will survive the wreck of worlds and remain extant when Time itself shall be no more." [1]

4. WILL AND MOTIVE

Leaving for the moment the question of the good self, we have here reached a point of view from which the meaning of will and motive and their relation to each other can be more clearly defined. The common idea of will is that of a power of responding, whether freely or in a way antecedently determined, to motives conceived of as acting upon it from the outside. Coleridge saw the error of this idea, whether held by libertarian or necessitarian. "For what", he asks, "is a motive? Not a thing, but the thought of a thing. But as all thoughts are not motives, in order to specify the class of thoughts, we must add the predicate 'determining', and a motive must be defined as a determining thought. But again, what is a Thought? Is this a thing or an individual? What are its circumscriptions, what the interspaces between it and another? Where does it begin? Where does it end? Far more readily could we apply these questions to an ocean billow, or the drops of water which we may imagine as the component integers of the ocean. As by a billow we mean no more than a particular movement of the sea, so neither by a thought can we mean more than the mind thinking in some one direction. Conse-

[1] *Preliminary Treatise on Method*, 3rd ed., p. 24.

quently a motive is neither more nor less than the act of an intelligent being determining itself, and the very watchword of the necessitarian is found to be at once an assertion and a definition of free agency, i.e. the power of an intelligent being to determine its own agency".[1]

After this account of the essential continuity of the practical intelligence, Coleridge goes on to explain similarly that what we mean by will is not the source of isolated actions but "an abiding faculty or habit or fixed predisposition to certain objects". So far therefore from the will originating in the motive and the motive governing the man, "it is the man that makes the motives: and these indeed are so various, unstable, and chameleon-like that it is often as difficult as fortunately it is a matter of comparative indifference, to determine what a man's motive is for this or that particular action. A wise man will rather inquire what the man's general objects are—what does he habitually wish. Iago's apparent vacillation in assigning now one, now another motive of his action, is the natural result of his own restless nature, distempered by a keen sense of his own intellectual superiority and a vicious habit of assigning the precedence to the intellectual instead of the moral. Yet how many of our modern critics have attributed to the profound author this the appropriate inconsistency of the character itself."[2]

[1] MS. B II. Snyder, p. 132.
[2] *Ibid.* See Snyder, *op. cit.*, p. 152–3, and cp. *Omniana* Ed. T. Ashe, 1834, p. 361, on "Motives and Impulses", where this

While realizing that motives are the ideas of objects that attract us by reason of their harmony with the internal predisposition or permanent will of a man, Coleridge would do justice to the force of external circumstances. He had asked in *Aids to Reflection* [1] : "Will any reflecting man admit that his own Will is the only and sufficient determinant of all he *is* and all he does? Is nothing to be attributed to the harmony of the system to which he belongs and to the pre-established Fitness of the Objects and Agents, known and unknown, that surround him, as acting *on* his will, though, doubtless, *with* it likewise?" In the passage before us he illustrates the same point from the contrast between a change of character gradually wrought from within and the sudden change wrought by some violent influence from without: "A violent motive may revolutionize a man's opinions and professions—a flash of lightning turn at once the polarity of the compass needle—though more frequently his honesty dies away imperceptibly from evening into twilight and from twilight into utter darkness."

From the point of view of modern psychology the analysis here given is again meagre enough, but Coleridge has seized the essential point of the true relation between will and motive, and on the basis of it is prepared to discuss the nature of the Good and, incidentally, to define his position

passage occurs in slightly different form—the impulses deducible from men's habitual objects of pursuit being definitely called "the true efficient causes of their conduct".

[1] Aphorism XLIIIc, 2.

in relation both to current hedonistic theories and
the deeper ethics of Kant.

5. THE MEANING OF THE GOOD

What he says on the former has particular
interest in view of the discussion of the value of
pleasure in the good life, that was to occupy so
large a place in later nineteenth-century ethics.
Coleridge was himself prepared to define the whole
scope of moral philosophy in terms of this controversy: "The sum total of moral philosophy", he
held,[1] "is found in this one question: Is *Good* a
superfluous word, or mere lazy synonym for the
pleasurable and its causes—at most a mere modification to express degree and comparative duration
of pleasure?" But he also held that a general
case against the identification of good with pleasure
could be established by an appeal to universal
usage, on the principle that a distinction, which is
common to all languages of the civilized world,
"must be the exponent, because it must be the
consequent, of a common consciousness of man as
man". The very phrase "pleasure is a good"
implies the recognition of other goods. Otherwise
it would be a mere pleonasm = "pleasure is
pleasure". If the universality of the *desire* for
pleasure is urged in favour of the theory, he is
prepared to show that this involves the confusion
between "things which are good because they are
desired, and things which are or ought to be

[1] See *Table Talk* (ed. cit.), p. 155.

desired because they are good", as in the simple
case of different kinds of food. Here also language
refutes the theory: "the mere difference between
the particles 'to' and 'for' is sufficient to destroy
the sophism".[1] The distinctions here drawn between
good and pleasure-value, and again between the
desirable and the actually desired are of fundamental importance for ethical theory, and remind
one of the confusions, that even so clear a thinker
as John Stuart Mill would have avoided, had he
been able to learn them from Coleridge.

Not less helpful to Mill and others would have
been Coleridge's carefully drawn out distinction
between the different kinds of pleasure or satisfaction, depending on the nature of the activity
of which it is the accompaniment. Starting with the
ambiguity of "Happiness", he distinguishes between
the state that depends on favourable outward
circumstances, into which chance or "hap" enters,
and the state that depends more on our own
inward and spiritual endeavours. In the latter
again he distinguishes that which is more purely
spiritual, and to which he would assign the name
"blessedness", from that which results "when the
intellectual energies are exerted in conformity
with the laws of the intellect and its inherent
forms", for which he proposes the name "eunoia".
From both of these he finally distinguishes *hedone*
or pleasure, as comprising "all the modes of being

[1] He quotes the contemporary analyst "who has confounded the
taste of mutton with the taste for mutton, and gravely sought for
the origin of the latter in the same place with that of the former
viz. the papillae of the tongue and palate".

which arise from the correspondence of the external stimuli in kind and degree to the sensible life". Taking pleasure in this sense, we may say that the only ground of preference is the *amount*. But he acutely observes that even in extending the idea of pleasure from present amount to comparative duration and causative influence (two of Bentham's "dimensions"), we already suppose the intervention and union of motives, which are not derived from the relation between the animal life and the stimulants, but from the idea of the will or self as above defined.

Coming to the relation of these different kinds of satisfaction to "good", he sets down as alone unconditionally good that which results from the whole moral nature. But he claims a place also for *eunoia*, when the intellect is employed in the service of such spiritual good, as itself good— when not employed in its disservice, as innocent; and similarly for pleasure, under the same conditions. It was in their confusion between eunoia and hedone and in their inclusion of both in the same condemnation that he found the main error of Kant and Fichte. Eunoia is not, indeed, spiritual in the highest sense, but may yet be an instrument of the spirit, being to it "as body is to soul".

But Coleridge's criticism, both of the current empiricism and of Kantian rationalism strikes deeper than the rejection of their treatment of pleasure. Beyond this there was the acceptance by the former of the "consequences" as the ultimate criterion of the goodness of an action, the total rejection of them by the latter, and going along with this a similar antagonism in the acceptance and rejection of the sympathetic affections as a factor in the good life.

6. MOTIVE AND CONSEQUENCES

(*a*) To the first of these questions Coleridge gives his answer in the carefully elaborated criticism of Paley's doctrine that "the general consequences are the chief and best criterion of the right and wrong of particular actions", to be found in Section I, Essay XV, of *The Friend*.[1] The doctrine aims in the first place at giving us a criterion, which does not, like others, depend on the notions of the individual. But this criterion, so far from giving us this, is itself dependent on what is most individual in man, the power derived from the accidental circumstances of natural talent and education instead of from "that part of our nature which in all men may and ought to be the same: in the conscience and common sense". In the second place it aims at giving us a criterion of morality. As a matter of fact, it confounds morality with law, and "draws away the attention from the will and from the inward motives and impulses, which constitute the essence of morality, to the outward act". To suggest further, as Paley does,

[1] Edition of 1818; but it was also contained in the 1812 edition, p. 374 foll. That he marks it with a note for quotation in MS. B, where he is dealing with the same subject, shows the importance he attached to it as a statement of his own view.

that Divine Justice will be regulated in its final judgment by this rule, is to remove the grounds of the appeal to "a juster and more appropriate sentence hereafter", which is "one of the most persuasive, if not one of the strongest arguments for a future state".

It is this appeal to the inward motive that the Apostle means by faith when he appeals to it as the sole principle of justification. Nothing could be more groundless than the alarm that this doctrine may be prejudicial to utility and active well-doing. "To suppose that a man should cease to be beneficent by becoming benevolent seems to me scarcely less absurd than to fear that a fire may prevent heat or that a perennial fountain may prove the occasion of drought." True, man (and God relatively to man) must judge by works, seeing that "man knows not the heart of man; scarcely does anyone know his own". But since good works may exist without saving principles, "they cannot contain in themselves the principle of salvation". On the other hand, saving principles never did and never can exist without good works: "For what is love without kind offices (including thoughts and words) whenever these are possible?" and "what noble mind would not be offended if he were supposed to value the serviceable offices equally with the love that produced them, or if he were supposed to value the love for the sake of the services, and not the services for the sake of the love?" The doctrine of faith and the doctrine of works are "one truth considered in its two principal bearings". What man sees and can alone judge by is the outward fruits, but "what God sees and what alone justifies is the inward spring."

If we pursue the doctrine of general consequences further, we can see that to anyone who believes (as Paley does) in an overruling Providence, the criterion must be a merely imaginary one, seeing that he must hold that all actions, the crimes of Nero not less than the virtues of the Antonines, work for good. Finally it can be shown to be "either nugatory or false", seeing that the appeal is to the "general consequences" that will result on condition that all men do as we do. Passing over the source of self-delusion and sophistry that is here opened up and supposing the mind in its sanest state, "how can it possibly form a notion of the nature of an action considered as indefinitely multiplied unless it has previously a distinct notion of the single action itself, which is the multiplicand? . . . But if there be any means of ascertaining the action in and for itself, what further do we want? Would we give light to the sun? or look at our own fingers through a telescope? The nature of every action is determined by all its circumstances; alter the circumstances and a similar set of motions may be repeated, but they are no longer the same or a similar act."

To all this it is vain to reply that "the doctrine of the general consequences was stated as the criterion of the action, not of the agent". For, apart from the oversight of attributing it in that sense to the Supreme Judge, the distinction itself "is merely logical, not real and vital". The character of the agent is determined by his view of the action; and "that system of morals is alone true and suited to human nature which unites the intention and the motive, the warmth and the light, in one and the same act of mind. This alone is worthy to be called a moral principle".

(*b*) It was on this ground that Coleridge was prepared to reject no less emphatically than he rejected Paley's doctrine of consequence as the sole criterion, what he calls the "Stoic hypocrisy",[1] that would separate goodness from all idea of the consequences. "I know", he wrote, "that in order to the idea of virtue we must suppose the pure good will, or reverence for the law as excellent in itself; but this very excellence supposes consequences though not selfish ones. . . . For if the Law be barren of all consequences, what is it but words? To obey the Law for its own sake is really a mere sophism in any other sense—you might as well put Abracadabra in its place." He is there speaking of consequences extending for the individual beyond this life, but that he would apply it also to consequences, individual and social, in this life, is clear both from the above-quoted passage from *The Friend*, and from a long and interesting entry in the philosophical diary *Semina Rerum* [2] on

[1] Marginal note on p. 344 of Kant's *Vermischte Schriften*.
[2] MS. C, p. 15, representing, I think, a later stage of his own reflections, and an attempt to assign its place to the "moral sense" that had played so great a part in the ethical theories of the preceding generation. See J. Bonar's *Moral Sense*, Library of Philosophy (1930).

the place of knowledge or, as he calls it, "Sense" in the good life, as necessarily implying a reference to "interests". After distinguishing knowing for the sake of knowing as Science, from knowing for the sake of being as Sense, and in the latter that which has "exclusive reference to the responsibility of *personal* being", as Moral Sense, from the Natural Sense which has regard to the peculiar interests of the individual, he goes on :

"The perfection of human nature arises when the first (i.e. science) is allowed to be an end, but yet in subordination to the second (i.e. moral sense) as the alone *ultimate* end, and when the second existing in combination with the third (i.e. natural sense) elevates and takes it up into its own class by the habit of contemplating both the common and the peculiar interests of *all* individuals, as far as they lie within his sphere of influence, as his own individual interests. Here we have the man of practical Rectitude, with right principle, prescribing the rule, Discretion determining the objects, and Judgment guiding the application. He seeks his own happiness, and he seeks the happiness of his neighbours, and he seeks both in such a way and by such means as enables him to find each in the other." [1]

There is a certain confusion here between the moral sense and the interests that are sensed. Only the latter can, strictly speaking, be an "end". But

[1] The passage reminds us of Aristotle's treatment of the Intellectual Virtues in *Ethics*, vi, with which we may also compare what he says of the different kinds of Prudence in *Aids to Reflection*, Aphorism XXIX.

the meaning is plain, namely, the impossibility of separating the two in actual fact. That in the fullest exercise of spirit both are merged in a higher comes out in his fine treatment of Love, which brings us to the second of the above-mentioned contrasts between his own view and that both of Kant and of current empiricism, and therewith to the point at which his moral philosophy merges in his philosophy of religion.

7. LOVE THE FULFILLING OF THE LAW

It seems doubtful whether Coleridge was familiar with Adam Smith's *Moral Sentiments* and the place in the moral life assigned by writers of his school to Sympathy. In one of his longer contributions to Southey's *Omniana* he contrasts the "Good Heart" with Pharisaic righteousness and would have "the wisdom of love preceding the love of wisdom", and goes on to pay a tribute to "those who act from good-hearted impulses, a kindly and cheerful mood and the play of minute sympathies, continuous in their discontinuity like the sand-thread of the hour-glass", and to the part they have in carrying on "the benignant scheme of social nature". But he was as far as Adam Smith from trusting to what he calls these "temperamental *pro*-virtues", as the sustaining principle of the good life. Something sterner was required, which he was prepared to find with Kant in the good will alone,[1]

[1] He quotes (MS. B) the famous passage from the *Metaphysic of Ethics*, Kant's Werke (Hartenstein), vol. iv. p. 241: "It is impossible

only differing from him "so far as he differs
from the Christian code". He does not here tell
us wherein the difference consists, but it is not
difficult to gather it from other passages. His dissent from Kant's attempt to dissociate the good
will from all regard to consequences has been
already mentioned. But his criticism went deeper
and challenged Kant's whole conception of the
independence of will and affection.

So long ago as in a contribution to Southey's
Omniana (1812) and without reference to Kant,
he had written:[1] "Love, however sudden, as when
we fall in love at first sight (which is perhaps always
the case of love in its highest sense), is yet an act
of the will, and that too one of its primary, and
therefore ineffaceable acts. This is most important;
for, if it be not true, either love itself is all a
romantic *hum*, a mere connection of desire with
a form appropriated to excite and qualify it, or
the mere repetition of a day-dream; or if it be
granted that love has a real, distinct, and excellent
being, I know not how we could attach blame and
immorality to inconstancy, when confined to the
affections and sense of preference. Either, therefore, we must brutalize our notions with Pope,[2]
or we must dissolve and thaw away all bonds of

to think of anything in the world, nay of anything even outside the
world, which could without limitation be held to be good except a
good Will"—probably for the first time in English ethical literature.
[1] *Ed. cit.*, p. 410.
[2] He quotes:

> "Lust, thro' some certain strainers well refined,
> Is gentle love and charms all woman-kind."

morality by the irresistible shocks of an irresistible sensibility with Sterne."

We are not therefore surprised to find this view directly applied [1] to Kant's statement that "love is a matter of feeling not of will". "If I say I doubt this independence of love on the will, and doubt love's being in its essence a mere matter of feeling, i.e. a somewhat formed in us which is not of us and from us . . . I mean only that my thoughts are not distinct, much less adequate, on the subject —and I am not able to convey any grounds of my belief of the contrary. But the contrary I do believe. What Kant affirms of man in the state of Adam, an ineffable act of Will choosing evil, and which is underneath or within consciousness, though incarnate in the conscience, inasmuch as *it must be conceived* as taking place in the *Homo Noumenon* not the *Homo Phaenomenon*—something like this I conceive of Love, in that higher sense of the word which Petrarch understood." What he held that sense to be may perhaps be gathered from what he says in the same connection about Love "as not only contradistinguished from lust, but as disparate even from the personal attachments of habit and complex associations", which pass for it "in the vast majority of instances and into which true Love enters at best only as an *element*".[2]

[1] In a marginal note on Kant's treatment of Menschenliebe, which may perhaps be judged to be later on the ground both of the greater hesitation and the greater maturity of the thought.
[2] *Table Talk*, p. 117. Cp. "Sympathy constitutes friendship; but in love there is a sort of antipathy or opposing passion. Each strives to be the other, and both together make up one whole."

Yet in the end it remains to him "one of the five or six *magna mysteria* of human nature.[1] . . . There are two mighty mysteries—action and passion (or passive action), and love is synthesis of these, in which each is the other—and it is only *a* synthesis, or one of the syntheses of action and passion; other discoveries must be made in order to know the principle of Individuation in general and then the principle of Personality."

For what he has further to say of the mystery, we have to go to his Philosophy of Religion, and to his belief that the ground of it has to be sought in the still greater mystery of the union of men with one another by reason of their union with God. This doubtless stamps his ethical theory as a form of mysticism, but not, he would have insisted, in any other sense than that *"omnia exeunt in mysteria"*.

To Coleridge, moreover (and this was the sum and substance of his whole ethical and religious philosophy alike), it did not mean the loss of the individual in the Whole. In the passage just quoted the principle of Love is assumed to be in the end the principle of individuation. It was the growing conviction of his later years that individuality, in the only sense in which it was of moral and religious significance, consisted, not in the narrowing down of life to an exclusive point, but in the expansion of it towards the inclusion of the Whole —Man in God, doubtless, but also God in Man.

[1] Others he mentions are Will, Conscience, Carnate Evil, Identity, Growth, and Progression.

Expanded in the light of these passages and comments, we can find in the continuation of the Aphorism with which we started a summary of the answer which Coleridge was prepared to give to the one-sided ethical "schemes" of his time, whether empirical or rational, individualistic or pantheistic: "The object of Ethical Science", he there writes, "is no Compost, Collectorium, or Inventory of Single Duties; nor does it seek in the 'multitudinous Sea', in the predetermined waves, tides, and currents of *Nature*, that freedom which is an exclusive attribute of Spirit. For as the Will or Spirit, the Source and Substance of Moral Good, is one and all in every part; so must it be the totality, the whole articulated series of Single Acts, taken as Unity, that can alone, in the severity of Science, be recognized as the proper Counterpart and adequate Representative of a good Will. Is it in this or that limb, or not, rather, in the whole body, the entire Organismus, that the Law of Life reflects itself? Much less then, can the Law of the Spirit work in fragments."

Coleridge's thought, both in his published and in his unpublished writings, was too much dominated by the religious interest, and in that too much occupied with the problem of original sin, to leave him free to develop anything that could be called a balanced system of ethics. But there was no one living at the time who had a clearer idea of what was necessary as the foundation of such a system, or who went further by the acuteness of his criti-

cism of prevalent abstractions in preparing materials for it. That English philosophy had to wait
nearly half a century after his time—in fact, till
the publication of Bradley's *Ethical Studies* in 1876,
for anything better or even as good, is an interesting comment of the loss it sustained in his failure
to make these materials available to the next
generation.

CHAPTER VI

POLITICAL PHILOSOPHY

"A people are free in proportion as they form their own opinions. In the strictest sense of the word, Knowledge is Power. Without previous illumination, a change in the forms of Government will be of no avail. These are but the shadows, the virtue and rationality of the People at large are the substance of Freedom."—PROSPECTUS OF *The Watchman*.

1. COLERIDGE'S INTEREST IN POLITICS[1]

COLERIDGE lived in stirring times and his was not the temperament to allow him to live in them without their living in him. His enthusiasm for the ideas of the French Revolution is reflected in the fragment that survives of the ode he wrote on the *Destruction of the Bastille*. He tells us in the *Biographia Literaria* of "the state of thorough disgust and despondency into which he sank" when his hopes were quenched by later events. What this meant to him has been recorded imperishably in his great *Ode to France* of the year 1798. But the state of things at home, the

---

[1] Since this section was written, Dr. Alfred Cobban's book on *Edmund Burke, A Study of the Political and Social Thinking of Burke, Wordsworth, Coleridge, and Southey*, with its excellent chapter on the Political views of Coleridge, has appeared. Our chief difference is that, while he rejects Coleridge's emphasis on the "Idea" of the Constitution as pseudo-philosophy (p. 179), though crediting him with adopting a scientific empiricism in place of a metaphysical theory of politics (p. 177), in what here follows Coleridge's recognition of the Idea in the sense not of a "transcendental principle overruling and independent of experience", as Leslie Stephen expresses it (*op. cit.*, p. 364), but of the intuitively apprehended *meaning* of experience is treated as a philosophical merit.

war with France, the condition of the people after the war, the low state to which politics was in danger of sinking, the movements for reform and the troubles of Ireland, were far too clamant to permit him to rest. It was not merely as a means to a livelihood, but in the hope of affording the guidance of fixed principles in politics that he engaged for some score of years almost continuously in writing for the *Watchman*, the *Morning Post*, and the *Courier*. He tells us himself that what he thus wrote, had it been published in books, "would have filled a respectable number of volumes". As it is, his daughter has rescued some thousand pages in the three volumes of *Essays on His Own Times*.[1] It was on such a background of close observation of politics, if not of actual administrative experience, that he sketched at different periods of his life that part of his philosophy which had perhaps the greatest influence on his contemporaries and was made by John Stuart Mill the subject of his famous essay in the *Westminster Review*.[2]

[1] There seems no reason to doubt that some sort of proposal was made by Stuart that Coleridge should enter into partnership with him in the management of the *Morning Post* and the *Courier* on condition that he "would give up the country and the lazy reading of old folios". It is characteristic of the type of unmetaphysical writer, referred to in the preface above, that H. D. Traill, who had the highest opinion not only of Coleridge's talent for journalism, but of the real literary value of these essays, regrets his refusal of Stuart's proposals on the ground that "it would have been better not only for Coleridge himself but for the world at large if the editor's efforts had been successful". See his *Coleridge*, p. 86.

[2] Afterwards republished in his *Dissertations and Discussions*. The chief sources for what follows are *The Friend*, Section the First, *On the Principles of Political Knowledge*, Essays, i–iv; *Lay Sermons* (1816–17); *Church and State* (1829).

Mill has depicted in a masterly way the condition of politics in England when Coleridge wrote the essay on the *Constitution of the Church and State according to the Idea of Each*, in which he developed the hints already contained in *The Friend* and *Lay Sermons*. "We had a Government which we respected too much to attempt to change it, but not enough to trust it with any power or look to it for any services that were not compelled." On the one hand there were the Tory believers in authority, whose cry was "hands off the sacred ark of the Constitution," and the power and privilege it brought to a class. On the other hand were the Radical believers in Liberty and *laissez faire*, to whom government was at best a necessary evil: "Their cry was not 'Help us'; 'Guide us'; 'Do for us the things we cannot do; and instruct us that we may do well those which we can' (and truly such requirements from such rulers would have been a bitter jest): the cry was 'Let us alone'." There was a similar conflict in men's minds about the Church. On the one side were those who supported it in a spirit of blind conservatism or with more or less hypocrisy, as necessary for social order. On the other were those who would sweep it away as a centre of superstition and reaction "got up originally and all along maintained for the sole purpose of picking people's pockets without aiming or being found conducive to any honest purpose during the whole process". Into this welter of opinion Coleridge introduced an entirely new note by calling on men to return to the Idea or ultimate aim of both State and Church and reorient themselves in the light of it on the problem of their present duties.

2. THE ORIGIN OF POLITICAL OBLIGATION

Before the date of the publication of *The Friend*, Coleridge had arrived at clear convictions, if not as to the Idea of the Civic Community, at least as to the origin and the ends of Government, the basis of civic rights, and the extent to which moral law applied to the relations of nations to one another. He puts the formation in men's minds of steadfast convictions concerning the most important questions of politics in the forefront in enumerating the objects he had in view in the publication and devotes the central part of it to a criticism of historical theories and an exposition of his own. In the distinction between sense, reason, and understanding, which by this time was the foundation of his whole philosophy, he found a convenient starting-point for classification. From what we already know of the estimation in which he held sense and understanding as organs of truth, we might have expected to find him rejecting theories based upon them in favour of one based upon deductions from the ideas of the reason. It is all the more interesting to find him, on the contrary, reserving his most trenchant and detailed criticism for the theory which in his own time had taken this for its basis. He was himself

aware of the apparent inconsistency,[1] but trusts
to make it clear that what he objects to in it is
not its appeal to reason, but the interpretation of
reason in a sense which cuts it off from the steady-
ing influences of experience and the expediencies
to which prudence points. "Distinct notions", he
explains in a note, "do not suppose different things.
When we make a threefold distinction in human
nature we are fully aware that it is a distinction,
not a division, and that in every act of mind the
man unites the properties of sense, understanding,
and reason." From this it follows that any theory
founded on exclusive regard to any one of them is
necessarily false.

Taking the theory of Hobbes, which ascribes
the origin and continuance of government to "fear
or the power of the stronger aided by the force of
custom" as an example of systems founded on the
view that "the human mind consists of nothing
but manifold modifications of passive sensation",
he rejects it on grounds that subsequent idealistic
criticism has made familiar but that are none
the less interesting as stated by him, and as an
introduction to his own theory. The theory is
"in the literal sense of the word preposterous : for
fear presupposes conquest and conquest a previous
union and agreement between the conquerors."
Leaders in the beginning must have been in some
sense chosen. "Apparent exceptions in Asia and
Africa are, if possible, still more subversive of this
system, for they will be found to have originated

[1] *Loc. cit.* Section i, Essay iii, of later edition.

in religious imposture and the first chiefs to have
secured a willing and enthusiastic obedience to
themselves as delegates of the Deity." But the
whole theory is baseless. "We are told by history,
we learn from our experience, we know from our
own hearts that fear, of itself, is utterly incapable
of producing any regular, continuous, and calcul-
able effect even on an individual; and that the
fear which does act systematically upon the mind
always presupposes a sense of duty as its cause."
Not fear, but the spirit of law, "this is the true
necessity which compels men into the social state
now and always by a still-beginning, never-ceasing
force of moral cohesion". Hobbes had declared
that "the laws without the sword are but a bit of
parchment. How far this is true every honest
man's heart will tell him, if he will content himself
with asking his own heart and not falsify the
answer by his notions concerning the hearts of
other men. But, were it true, still the fair answer
would be—Well! but without the laws the sword
is but a piece of iron."

Coleridge had used the word contract in the
course of the criticism above condensed and the
theory of the Social Contract was still sufficiently
alive to make it necessary to guard against misunderstanding. As a theory, he regarded it as not
only dangerous but absurd, "for what could give
moral force to a contract? The same sense of duty
which binds us to keep it must have pre-existed
as impelling us to make it." In the sense in which
he uses the word, it is "merely synonymous with

the sense of duty acting in a specific direction, i.e. determining our moral relations, as members of a body politic . . a means of simplifying to our apprehension the ever-continuing causes of social union, even as the conservation of the world may be represented as an act of continued creation". Even although such a contract had been entered into, it could do no more than bind the contracting parties to act for the general good in the way that existing circumstances, internal and external, required or permitted. No more than the ideal contract could it affect the question of means and end. Taken in this sense an original (rather an ever-originating) contract is a very natural and significant mode of expressing the reciprocal duties of subject and sovereign and is far from deserving the contempt which Hume, naturally enough from his point of view, lavishes upon it.

Turning to Rousseau as the representative of the error implied in the appeal to pure reason, Coleridge lays down the excellent principle, as valid to-day as in his time, that "it is bad policy to represent a political system as having no charm but for robbers and assassins, and no natural origin but in the brains of fools or madmen, when experience has proved that the great danger of the system consists in the peculiar fascination it is calculated to exert in noble and imaginative spirits". It was to this temptation that Burke had succumbed, and that explained the small number of converts he made during his lifetime. Needless to say, Coleridge had the greatest admiration for Burke and was always ready to express his own debt to him. There was little, he held, that the political philosopher could not learn from him: "In Mr. Burke's writings the germs of almost all political truths may be found." [1] But he held also that his connection with actual politics had had the unfortunate effect of driving him into inconsistencies that a more philosophical attitude would have avoided, and in the few sentences that follow he gives us what is perhaps the best criticism extant of his great predecessor. "If his opponents are theorists, then everything is to be founded on prudence, on mere calculations of expediency; and every man is represented as acting according to the state of his own immediate self-interest. Are his opponents calculators? Then calculation itself is represented as a sort of crime . . The fact was that Burke, in his public character, found himself, as it were, in a Noah's ark, with a very few men and a great many beasts"—with the result that "he acted under a perpetual system of compromise—a compromise of greatness with meanness; a compromise of comprehension with narrowness; a compromise of the philosopher with the mere men of business, or with the yet coarser intellects who handle a truth which they were required to receive, as they would handle an ox which they were desired to purchase". For himself, Coleridge was convinced that the only true course was the opposite one. "Never can I

[1] *Biogr. Lit.*, ch. x.

believe but that the straight line must needs be the nearest; and that where there is the most, and the most unalloyed truth, there will be the greatest and the most permanent power of persuasion." Falsehoods are dangerous, chiefly because they are half-truths and "an erroneous system is best computed, not by an abuse of theory in general, nor by an absurd opposition of theory to practice, but by a detection of the errors in the particular theory. For the meanest of men has his theory, and to think at all is to theorize." [1]

True to this method, Coleridge recognizes (as Kant before him had done) the undeniable truth and the equally undeniable deductions from it with which the Rousseauite system commences. "Every man is born with the faculty of reason; and whatever is without it, be the shape what it may, is not a man or person but a thing. Hence the sacred principle recognized by all laws, human and divine, the principle, indeed, which is the ground-work of all law and justice, that a person can never become a thing, nor be treated as such without wrong." In other words, he can never be used altogether and merely as a means, but "must always be included in the end and form a part of the final cause". Hence, too, as the faculty of reason implies free agency, every rational being has the right of acting according to his own conscience, and "this right is inalienable except by guilt which is an act of self-forfeiture, and the consequences therefore to be considered as the

[1] *Loc. cit.*, essay iv.

criminal's own moral election". In this finally all men may be said to be equal, seeing that reason in this sense is a matter in which there are no degrees.

But to say this is one thing, to proceed to make the possession of reason in this sense the foundation of a system of politics prescribing the form of the Constitution, the rights of individuals, and the principles of legislation is quite another. This is to disregard "our mixed and sensitive nature", and the difficulty of adapting means to ends in the complicated circumstances of ordinary life. Yet the confusion once made, Rousseau's whole system follows with a certain mathematical precision as little applicable to human beings as pure geometry is to natural bodies. With this clue as to its fundamental error, Coleridge proceeds to trace the dialectic by which it is forced either to take account of probabilities and so abandon its first principle, or, holding to the principle, to involve itself in inconsistencies which will justify anything. This has often been done since, but perhaps never with the convincingness that, with recent events before him, Coleridge was able to impart to it.

Granting a sovereign assembly such as the principle of the possession by all equally of the qualification of reason required, consisting either of the citizens in person or of real representatives of them, the process by which the general will arising from the general reason displays itself has yet to be found. Rousseau's and (oddly enough Burke's) way was to trust to the neutralization of opposite errors, as the winds rushing from all quarters at once with equal force may for the time produce a deep calm. But so far from being a deduction from the principle, this is a mere probability against which have to be weighed other and greater probabilities: "the lust of authority, the contagious nature of enthusiasm and other of the acute or chronic diseases of deliberative assemblies", and we find ourselves already beyond "the magic circle of the pure reason". Rousseau himself allows for this contingency. It is to meet it that he introduces the distinction between the *Volonté de tous* and the *Volonté générale* (i.e. between the collective will and the casual overbalance of wills). But this amounts to the admission that all he says in the *Contrat Social* of the sovereign will to which the right of universal legislation appertains applies to no one human being, to no society or assemblage of human beings, and least of all to the mixed multitude which makes up the people.

Coleridge fails to see the deeper meaning which later idealistic writers find in Rousseau's conception of the General Will as a way of indicating what he himself calls "the permanent self" of a nation, which is always seeking expression in its laws and institutions, however imperfect these may be; but he is undoubtedly right in going on to notice that, whatever Rousseau meant by it, the distinction was lost on the legislators of the Constituent Assembly. Seeking to apply the doctrine of the inalienable sovereignty of the people in its purity, they could not proceed a step in their course of constitution-making without some glaring inconsistency. If reason is not susceptible of degrees, on what principle are women and children disfranchised? And if once you begin to introduce distinctions between classes, whence the preference for democratic or even representative institutions to any other? It was only therefore going a step farther along the same path when some of the French economists, devotees though they were of Rousseau, argued that, "no other laws being allowable but those which are demonstrably just and founded on the simplest ideas of reason, and of which every man's reason is the competent judge, it is indifferent whether one man, or one or more assemblies of men, give form and publicity to them". One step farther still and Napoleon could find justification for his claim to be the impersonation of reason, raised up and armed by Providence with irresistible power to realize its laws, in a system in which the greatest possible happiness of the people counts for nothing and the object of the governor is merely to preserve the freedom of all by coercing within the requisite bounds the freedom of each.

Returning to concrete facts, it is easy, Coleridge adds, from the single example of property, with which Governments from the first have been concerned, to show that under any circumstances except that of angelic society, an abstract equality, supposing it could be established and maintained, must be the fruitful source of all justice. "Were there a race of men, a country and a climate that permitted such an order of things, the same causes would render all government superfluous."

What emerges from the criticism of these historical systems is that, while in the search for the first principles of political obligation, we have to start from the moral nature of man as constituting him an end in himself as against Hobbes, we cannot, with Rousseau, take this in the abstract as operating in a vacuum to which circumstances, both internal and external, are irrelevant. That circumstances and general consequences could not by themselves constitute the criterion of collective any more than individual action as maintained by Paley (and Bentham) Coleridge was further prepared to show in the course of making it clear that the crying want of his time was a theory of the nature of political obligation which, while including, should go beyond these popular half-truths.

Whether because his own ideas of the implications of his metaphysical principles were not as yet clear, or, as is more likely, because of the necessity he felt himself under in *The Friend* of "bribing the attention" of his readers by connecting theory with matters of popular interest at the time, he does not here further develop his views on the nature and binding force of political constitutions. He turns instead to the question of international right which was occupying the public mind, but not before offering a definition of the ends of Government equally removed from the irresponsibility of the Hobbesian State to the ideal

of freedom and from the *laissez faire* principle of
the equal if limited freedom of all which had
emerged as the logical issue of the Rousseauite.
These were to be understood neither by the denial
of all right in the subject, nor by the assertion
of absolute and indefensible rights that could be
enumerated in "Declarations", but by reference
to the fundamental instincts and capacities of
human nature. They consist of two kinds, the
negative and the positive. "The negative ends are
the protection of life, of personal freedom, of
property, of reputation, and of religion from
foreign and from domestic attacks. The positive
ends are: First to make the means of subsistence
more easy for each individual; secondly that in
addition to the necessaries of life he should derive
from the union and division of labour a share of
the comforts and conveniences which humanize and
ennoble his nature, and at the same time the power
of perfecting himself in his own branch of industry
by having those things which he needs provided
for him by others among his fellow-citizens; the
tools and raw materials necessary for his own
employment being included. Thirdly the hope of
bettering his own condition and that of his
children"; seeing that "his Maker has distinguished
him from the brute that perishes by making hope
an instinct of his nature and an indispensable
condition of his moral and intellectual progression . . Lastly, the development of those faculties
which are essential to his human nature by the
knowledge of his moral and religious duties, and

the increase of his intellectual powers in as great a degree as is compatible with the other ends of social union and do not involve a contradiction." Instruction, Coleridge held, is one of the ends of government (not because "we must educate our rulers" but), because "it is that only which makes the abandonment of the savage state an absolute duty, and that constitution is the best, under which the average sum of useful knowledge is the greatest and the causes that awaken and encourage talent and genius the most powerful and various".[1] In this definition it is not difficult to see the germ of what he was afterwards to develop in his noted theory of the identity of Church and State. Meantime the circumstances of the time were raising wider issues.

3. THE LAW OF NATIONS [2]

As by other great wars, the question of the exention of moral law to international relations had been raised in an acute form by the Napoleonic. Coleridge had himself become involved in it by his journalistic defence of the bombardment of Copenhagen and the annexation of the Danish fleet in the conflict with Napoleon, and had been attacked by those who had denounced it as a violation of international right. By others the action had been defended in Parliament on the ground that, though a violation of right, it was justified by the urgency of the motive. In this confusion of the public mind he saw an opportunity at once

[1] *Loc. cit.*, essay ix.   [2] *Loc. cit.*, ch. xiii.

of justifying his own attitude at the time and of
stating, more clearly than he thought that Grotius,
Puffendorf and the other great writers on the
subject had done, the grounds of the difference in
identity between individual and national right.

Holding, as he does, that "morality is no accident
of human nature but its essential characteristic",
it seemed to him "absurd that individuals should be
under a law of moral obligation, and yet that a
million of the same individuals acting collectively
or through representatives should be exempt from
all law". As well suppose that a grain of corn
shall cease to contain flour as soon as it is part of
a peck or a bushel. The wise men who have
written on the law of nations have therefore been
quite right in conceiving the community of nations
after the analogy of communities of men: their
co-proprietorship of allotments in the earth's surface,
and their free agency in the disposal of them consistently with a like free agency of others constituting their national rights, and their function as
"fellow-travellers in civilization" prescribing their
national duties.[1] It is in the maintenance of these

[1] Coleridge's view of international duty with regard to the control
of disease has peculiar interest at the present time: "Every Epidemic
Disease," he writes, MS. C, p. 152, "every epidemic or endemic
imported should awaken us to the deep interest which every man
and every country has in the well-being of all men and in the
consequent progressive humanization of the surface and with it of
the atmosphere of the Planet itself. As Man, so the World he inhabits.
It is his business and duty to *possess* it and rule it, to assimilate it
to his own higher Nature. If instead of this he suffers himself to be
possessed, ruled, and assimilated by it, he becomes an animal, who,
like the African Negro or the South American Savage, is a mischief
to Man even by the neglect of his function as a Man. The neglected
Earth steams up poisons that *travel*."

rights on behalf of his fellow-countrymen and the development in them so far as possible of the faculties by which they are enabled to perform their corresponding duties that the patriot finds his true object. Such patriotism is, in fact, "itself a necessary link in the golden chain of our affections and virtues". It is therefore a false philosophy or a mistaken religion that would persuade us that "cosmopolitanism is nobler than nationality and the human race a sublimer object of love than a people". Granted that Plato, Luther, Newton, and their like belong to the world and to all ages, yet it was "in a circle defined by human affections" that they were produced—"here where the powers and interests of men spread without confusion through a common sphere, like the vibrations propagated in the air by a single human voice, distinct and yet coherent, and all uniting to express one thought and the same feeling".

From this it follows that for such patriotism we need no particular code of morals. We only require to be reminded that its objects are not to be accomplished by any system of general conquest (this would only end in the victor nation itself sinking into a mere province, probably the most abject of the empire it had created); nor by the annihilation of the State that happens to be its formidable rival, seeing that such rivalry tends to foster all the virtues by which national security is maintained. "Even in cases of actual injury and just alarm, the patriot sets bounds to the reprisal of national vengeance, and contents himself with such securities as are compatible with the welfare, though not with the ambitious projects of the nation, whose aggressions have given the provocation: for as patriotism inspires no superhuman faculties, neither can it dictate any conduct that would require such. He is too conscious of his own ignorance of the future to dare extend his calculations into remote periods; nor, because he is a statesman, arrogates to himself the cares of Providence and the government of the world."

Ten years later Coleridge was prepared to express the same view of the moral basis of national independence with even deeper conviction: "Till States", he writes, "are in that self-standingness which admits of reciprocal action, the epoch of international morality is not yet come, the Records do not as yet belong to the World of Freedom, and we read of these things (wars and conquests) as of the most interesting parts of Natural History. None but the Vulgar felt (about?) Napoleon as they do (about) Alexander the Great. Napoleon was an APE. The difference in character in the conflicting nations was wanting. Not Greeks and Persians, but a wanton wicked civil war of a depraved knot of Co-Europeans against men of the same arts, sciences, and habits. France as a State obtaining no additional means of perfecting herself, it was no expansion required in order to self-development and therefore no expansion at all. War at present", he concludes, "ought to be spoken of by all men of genius as contemptible, vulgar, the dotage of second childhood, the lechery of Barrenness." [1]

In a later passage in the same autograph note-book, referring to the events in the Netherlands of 1830, he applies the same idea to the old doctrine of Intervention. This in older times "was a *rule* and a wise one arising out of the particular state of the great European Confederacy from the Treaty of Westphalia to the French Revolution. Since then Europe has become too closely co-organized to allow of its having any practical application other than the truism . . we should do nothing without an adequate motive. On the same principle we might declare against all *War* with the proviso unless our national interests require it." But he does not think that this is any reason why we should be without "some principle from which a rule might be safely and convincingly deduced for the existing state of Europe", and he finds one in the distinction between "*the State* and the individual at the head of it and who perhaps may be at the head of three or four States, each having a distinct interest and no one of them having any interest in that Individual's being likewise the Head of a fifth State. The Emperor of Austria may have, or imagine himself to have, an interest in calling North Italy his against the will and the interest of the North Italians, but what interest

[1] MS. C, p. 85, slightly condensed. Most of us will agree to-day. We shall only ask why the limitation in the last sentence to "men of genius"?—unless we take it as an indication of the progress of opinion since Coleridge's time.

have the Bohemians, Tyrolese, Austrians in this? On the other hand, the *State* of Holland, the *State* of Prussia, and, had we had a sane ministry to see it, the *State* of Great Britain called for interference to crush the brute, insensate, ingrate rebellion of the Belgians, the monstrous hybridum of the wildest Jacobinism and the densest religious bigotry." [1] We may agree or disagree with Coleridge's judgment in the Belgian revolution of that date. But few will question the soundness of the principle he enunciates, and even this application of it suggests the question whether, had we intervened in the way he desired, the fatal events of 1914 would have been possible.

Returning to the argument in *The Friend*, having proved that "the law of nations is the law of common honesty", Coleridge has next to show [2] wherein the difference of application consists. He finds it in the one point of the comparatively small influence of example and precedent in the case of States, and goes on to find the reason of this difference in the difference of the circumstances. In the first place wherever there can be any dispute between what is required of an honest man and a true patriot, "the circumstances, which at once authorize and discriminate the measure, are so marked and peculiar and notorious, that it is incapable of being drawn into a precedent by any other State under dissimilar circumstances". This holds of ordinary cases. In extraordinary cases States simply "neither will, nor in the nature

[1] MS. C, p. 154.   [2] Essay xiv.

of things can, be determined by any other consideration but that of the imperious circumstances
which render a particular measure advisable".
But the most important difference is that "individuals are and must be under positive laws, and so
great is the advantage of the regularity of legal
decisions, that even equity must sometimes be
sacrificed to it. For the very letter of a positive
law is part of its spirit. But States neither are, nor
can be, under positive laws. The only fixed part
of the law of nations is the spirit; the letter of the
law consists wholly in the circumstances to which
the spirit of law is applied."

We may think that, in common with Hegel and
others of his time, Coleridge was too despairing of
the creation of anything like a code of positive
international law, with its appropriate system of
sanctions and precedents. Perhaps the most significant change in our own time is that while these
writers held this to be impossible, however desirable
it might be, some of us have come to think it
possible, and only differ from one another as to its
desirability in view of the extension of the reign
of force involved in the creation of an international
police. However we may differ from Coleridge in
this, few, with the facts of the Great War before
them, will disagree with the words that follow:
"It is mere puerile declamation to rail against a
country, as having imitated the very measures
for which it had most blamed its ambitious enemy,
if that enemy had previously changed all the
relative circumstances which had existed for him,

and therefore rendered his conduct iniquitous; but which, having been removed, however iniquitously, cannot without absurdity be supposed any longer to control the measures of an innocent nation, necessitated to struggle for its own safety; especially when the measures in question were adopted for the very purpose of restoring these circumstances." Still fewer, among those at least who believe in the reality of an international justice, will refuse to Coleridge the credit of having been one of the first to attempt a clear statement of the identity beneath difference between it and that which we honour in the life of "the good neighbour and honest citizen".

4. The Idea of the Body Politic

As Coleridge's ideas on the nature of political justice were developed in close contact with questions that were agitating the public mind in the middle part of his life, so the development of his ideas on the nature of a political constitution had a close connection with the questions of social and political reform that were prominent in his later years. As we might expect from what has been already said of the more and more important place that the doctrine of Ideas came to occupy in his speculations, the discussion takes the form of an exposition of what constitutes the Idea of a political society.

The allusion at the outset of the discussion in

his book on the *Constitution of Church and State* [1]
to the theory of the social contract gives it the
air of a continuation of that in *The Friend*. While
rejecting this in the form of a "conception" as
"at once false and foolish", "incapable of historic
proof as a fact and senseless as a theory", Coleridge
assigns it a central place as an *idea*. As he had
spoken in *The Friend* of "an original—more accurately an ever-originating contract" as "a very
natural and significant mode of expressing the
reciprocal duties of subject and sovereign", so now
he writes of "the idea of an ever-originating social
contract" as that which "constitutes the whole
difference between subject and serf, between a
commonwealth and a slave-plantation". [2] What is
historical about it so far as England is concerned is
that it is this difference that has been working
more or less unconsciously in "the minds of our
forefathers in their characters and functions as
public men alike in what they resisted and in what
they claimed; in the institutions and forms of
polity which they established and with regard to
those against which they more or less successfully
contended". The idea has shown its reality not
only as an actual force in their minds and con-
sciences in prescribing their duty, in their claims
and resistances, but as "the final criterion by which
all particular frames of government must be tried;

---

[1] First ed. 1829. The quotations below are made from the 1852
edition with references to the corresponding place in Shedd's edition
of the *Works*.
[2] *Op. cit.*, p. 15. Shedd, vi. p. 32.

for here only can we find the great constructive principles of our representative system in the light of which it can alone be ascertained what are excrescences and marks of degeneration; and what are native growths or changes naturally attendant on the progressive development of the original germ, symptoms of immaturity perhaps but not of disease". [1]

Important though this is for the interpretation of political history as more than a mere struggle of rival interests, Coleridge is aware that it is too general as an account of the operation of this idea in the actual working of the "constitution" and of the conditions of its health. He had rejected Rousseau's account of it under the form of a general will taken in abstraction from the actual wills of each and all, but he realized that he was thereby pledged to a better.

Starting [2] from the "metaphor so commensurate, so pregnant", of the "body politic", he makes use of it to bring out two distinctions which he considers fundamental in the working of the constitution. In the first place, corresponding to the distinction in living bodies between "the imponderable agents, magnetic or galvanic" and the ponderable fluids in the glands and vessels, we have that in the body politic between "the indeterminable but yet actual influences of intellect, information, prevailing principles, and tendencies", and "the regular definite and legally recognized

[1] *Op. cit*, p. 20. Shedd, *ibid.*, 35 (condensed).
[2] *Op. cit.*, p. 100. Shedd, *ibid.*, 78 foll.

powers". [1] There is, however, this difference, that here the imponderables are capable of being converted into the ponderable by having measured and determinate political rights and privileges attached to them. In the due proportion of these two, the generally acting spiritual forces endowed with no definitely recognized means of expression, and those which act through legally constituted channels, Coleridge finds the first condition of political health. The Greek democracies were an instance of the excess of the former, "the permeative power deranging the functions and by ephorions shattering the organic structures which they should have enlivened". Venice, on the other hand, fell owing to the contrary extreme. As illustrations of lesser disproportions, he mentions the exclusion from civil rights of classes that have qualified for their exercise and the unfair representation in Parliament of particular interests. He saw nothing but a threat to the permanence and progress of the British nation in the existing state of parties and the under-representation of the industrial, mercantile, and professional classes.

The second distinction of which Coleridge finds

[1] What he means by these imponderables is well illustrated by what he says in a letter of September 24, 1821 (Alsopp, *Letters*, etc., p. 130), of what Graham Wallas calls our "Social Heritage": "It is a source of strength and comfort to know that the labours and aspirations and sympathies of the genuine and invisible Humanity exist in a social world of their own; that its attractions and assimilations are no Platonic fable, no dancing flames or luminous bubbles on the magic caldron of my wishes; but that there are, even in this unkind light, spiritual parentages and filiations of the soul."

an analogy in the physical organism is that between the "latent or dormant" and the "actual power" in the State. It is here that he approaches the central problem and touches without naming it the question of sovereignty. In the former distinction he had in view public opinion, sectional interests, currents of national feeling so far as they are unorganized and possess no recognized means of expression. These may be different and even opposed to the organized forms of national life, but they *need* not be. The distinction may be only a kind of "polarization" of elements usually acting in unison. But in the case of which he is now speaking there is and there ought to be a real distinction, and he goes on in a passage of great insight and originality to illustrate its value in the interest of political freedom from the case of England.

What, he asks, is the secret of the degree of freedom which England has enjoyed far in excess of the most democratic republics of either ancient or modern times or of that which "the wisest and most philanthropic statesmen or the great Commonwealth's men (the stars of that narrow interspace of blue sky between the black clouds of the first and the second Charles's reign) believed compatible the one with the safety of the State, the other with the interests of Morality"? [1] His answer

[1] He has an interesting note on the supposed exception of the United States of America. He is inclined, in view of the identity of stock, etc., to deny that they form an exception. But it illustrates the impression which some travellers brought back from America at that date (1829) that he quotes an epigram of one of them (a prejudiced one, he admits) to the effect that "where every man takes liberties there is little liberty for any man".

is that whereas both in democratic republics and in absolute monarchies the nation delegates the whole of its power to the extent of leaving "nothing obscure, nothing merely in idea unevolved, or acknowledged only as an indeterminate right", in the constitution of England the nation has delegated its power only with "measure and circumspection whether in respect of the donation of the trust or the particular interests entrusted" to the Government. Lawyers indeed speak of the "omnipotence of Parliament". If this refers to "the restraints and remedies within the competence of our law courts", it is only a "puffing and pompous way of stating a mere matter of fact". If taken in any other sense, it is an hyperbole which, in view of the actual composition of the Houses of Parliament and the "sharers in this earthly omnipotence", can merely rouse laughter. What the precise nature and extent of the power which the nation thus reserves to itself and which is not contained within the rule and compass of law, it is impossible to say. By its very nature it is indeterminable *a priori*, and must be conceived of as existing and working only as an idea—except, he adds, in the rare and predestined epochs of growth and reparation when the "predisposing causes and enduring effects prove the unific mind and energy of the nation to have been in travail". But it is *there* always as the last appeal—"that voice of the people which is the voice of God". He is conscious that his account of it might seem "fitter matter for verse than for sober argument", and is content to conclude his exposition by quoting the old Puritan poet George Wither, who has given lasting expression to this idea in his *Vox Pacifica*.[1]

Short and somewhat disjointed as is the analysis here given of the elements of national consciousness and the conditions of political liberty, it marks a new achievement in English philosophy, anticipating much of the best thought of our own time as we have it in Green, Bosanquet, and others. Particularly significant in view both of recently held theories of the omnipotence of the State and the still more recent reactions against it in favour of political pluralism is the sanity with which Coleridge rejects both. "Coleridge", writes Dr. Cobban,[2] "was one of the first to denounce the theory of sovereignty in so many words, and that not because of the rival claims of any other association inside or outside the State, but because of the inherent extravagance of the conception itself. To overthrow State sovereignty

[1] London, 1645. T. H. Green, in his *Lectures on Political Obligation*, quotes Wither in a similar connection. The whole passage is worth quoting as Coleridge (though inaccurately) gives it.

> "Let not your King and Parliament in one,
> Much less apart, mistake themselves for that
> Which is most worthy to be thought upon:
> Nor think they are, essentially, the State.
> Let them not fancy that th' authority
> And privileges upon them bestown,
> Conferr'd are to set up majesty,
> A power, or a glory, of their own!
> But let them know, 'twas for a deeper life
> Which they but represent—
> That there's on earth a yet auguster thing
> Veil'd tho' it be than Parliament or King."

[2] *Op. cit.*, p. 183.

and substitute for it the sovereignty of a thousand and one petty groups, as some political thinkers have attempted to do, is a mere multiplication of evil. Coleridge goes on different principles. Against the Imperial and Papal theory of sovereignty, he asserts the national and Protestant principles of the individual conscience and the national consciousness, things which cannot be defined in terms of institutional sovereignties." I should merely add that the mention of individual conscience and national consciousness as though they were entirely different raises just the question which Coleridge's philosophy, with its doctrine of a deeper community of souls in family, nation, ultimately in the All, as the ground of the rights of sovereign and subject alike, was the attempt to give the answer.

5. PRACTICAL APPLICATIONS

Not less interesting to-day are the practical applications which he makes of these ideas. His view of the ends of government, as we have seen, was that besides what he calls the negative aims, namely, the safety of the State and the protection of life and property within it for all its members, there are great positive ends which he enumerates as: (1) making the means of subsistence easier for each individual; (2) securing to each the hope of betterment; (3) the development of the facilities essential to his humanity. However distant from the ideal mark, owing to the existing circumstances of a nation, the statesman might actually find himself, every movement, Coleridge held, ought to be in the direction of realizing these objects.

In his own time the main hindrances to the first two were to be found in the views that were held and the practices that had come to be recognized as to the rights of property. Coleridge was no revolutionary, and it is easy to find matter for ridicule in the timidity with which the philosopher sometimes expresses himself. But he is clear and consistent in the summons he addresses to the State to do all that it can to control private possessions in the interest of the community, and to refuse absolutely to recognize "claims that, instead of being contained in the rights of its proprietary trustees, are encroachments on its own rights and a destructive trespass on a part of its own inalienable and untransferable property—the health, strength, honesty, and filial love of its children".[1]

He had in view chiefly the land, which was still the main form of property in England; but these principles were valid also for what was rapidly coming to be an even more decisive factor in the national life—the private ownership of capital; and all that he says of the necessity of a reversion to the functional view of property applies equally to this. He wrote and published two pamphlets in favour of Sir Robert Peel's[2] Bill to regulate the employment of children in cotton factories in 1818, of which he speaks as the first instance of the interference of the legislature "with what is ironi-

[1] *Lay Sermons*, p. 252. Shedd, vi. 217.
[2] Lancashire manufacturer and father of the future Prime Minister.

cally called Free Labour—daring to prohibit soul-murder on the part of the rich, and self-slaughter on that of the poor". He adds: "From the borough of Hell I wish to have no representatives."[1]

It is in connection with the last of the three ends of the State as stated above that Coleridge develops his famous doctrine of the Church and its relation to the State. The Church, according to the "idea" of it, is not something separate from the State, but the State just in its function of securing this object, which in the present connection is restated as that of "providing for every native that knowledge and those attainments which are necessary to qualify him for a member of the State, the free subject of a civilized realm".[2] Valuable and indispensable as religion may be for these objects, the teaching of religion is not the chief function of the Church. Coleridge would have a "parson" in every parish, but the real "clerisy" of the nation are the learned of all denominations and professions—"in short, all the so-called liberal arts and sciences, the possession and application of which constitute the civilization of a country, as well as the theological".[3]

There is no need at this date to criticize the doctrine and the proposals which accompanied it. National development has taken a different course throughout the civilized world from that which

[1] See *Letters*, ii. p. 689 n.; *Two Addresses*, Ed. Edmund Gosse (1913); and Lucy E. Watson's *Coleridge at Highgate* (1925), p. 74 ff.
[2] *Church and State*, pp. 84 and 85. Shedd, vi. p. 70.
[3] *Op. cit.*, pp. 54–5. Shedd, vi. 53.

Coleridge hoped it would, so far as *names* are concerned. But more and more States are recognizing the objects which he emphasizes and, in proportion as their function of armed defence comes to be superseded by other more effective guarantees of security, will find themselves more and more at liberty to devote themselves to their promotion. How far in the pursuit of them they will have to ally themselves with the great religious tradition, either by seeking the aid of the Church or by embodying in their own educational system the best elements in its teaching, the future alone can show. It will largely depend on how statesmen interpret what is of essential and of permanent value in theology, and how theologians interpret the spiritual function of the State.

If we try to sum up Coleridge's view of political society we shall, I believe, find the root and essence of it in the idealistic principle which may be said to be the sum of all his thinking that the whole is more than the sum of its parts. In becoming a member of a society the individual acquires new characters and becomes something different from what he was before. "Each man", he writes, "in a numerous society is not only co-existent with but virtually organized into the multitude of which he is an integral part. His *idem* is modified by the *alter*. And there arise impulses and objects from his synthesis of *alter et idem*, myself and my neighbour." It is for this reason that when he passes from society to the State, while recognizing in the idea of the physical organism no more than a useful metaphor, he finds no better way of describing the body politic than as an organic whole. "The State", he says, "is synonymous with a constituted realm, kingdom, commonwealth or nation; that is where the integral parts, classes or orders are so balanced or so interdependent as to constitute more or less a moral unit, an organic whole." It is the mention of the "balance" and the qualification of "more or less" doubtless that leads Dr. Cobban,[1] in quoting these passages, to say that Coleridge, like Burke, "adopts a position intermediate between the organic and the mechanistic theories" of the nature of the State. We have seen to what extent Coleridge agreed with Burke and nothing could be more instructive than a comparison of their views. But there is this difference between them, besides that which Coleridge himself notices, that while in the statesman's mind the balance actually attained by the British Constitution dominated all his thinking, and the "moral unit" was interpreted in terms of what he saw before him, Coleridge regarded all actual Constitutions, including that of his own country, as temporary and imperfect embodiments of an "idea" that was slowly revealing itself on earth, if not as a city of God, at any rate as a society of seekers after Him. And the source of this vital difference was the despised metaphysical root of the poet's thought.

[1] *Op. cit.*, p. 185.

CHAPTER VII

THEORY OF FINE ART

"Beauty too is spiritual, the shorthand hieroglyphic of Truth—the mediator between Truth and Feeling, the Head and the Heart. The sense of Beauty is implicit knowledge—a silent communion of the Spirit with the Spirit in Nature, not without consciousness, though with the consciousness not successively unfolded."—MS. *Semina Rerum*, p. 97.

1. CONTEMPORARY AESTHETICS

THERE was no department in which the defects of the Hartleian philosophy were more glaring than in aesthetic [1] theory. In the *Observations on Man*, imagination is dismissed in a short paragraph in a section devoted to "Dreams". The sense of Beauty is treated of under the head of "Pleasures and Pains of Imagination". Beauty in nature is explained as a transference of "miniatures" of pleasant tastes, smells, etc., "upon rural scenes"; beauty in art, including poetry, as the result of successful imitation of Nature. When, as in the professed writers on "Taste", the hard-worked principle of Association was combined with hide-bound adherence to the neo-classical modes, and the social snobbery of the time, it is easy to imagine what the result was likely to be. [2]

[1] Though disliking the word, as unfamiliar, for "works of taste and criticism", Coleridge found it "in all respects better and of more reputable origin than billetristic", at that time its rival.—*Blackwood's Magazine*, October 1821.
[2] Treating of Colour in his *Essay on Taste* (published in 1790, in its sixth edition in 1825), Archibald Alison, the best known probably of the Scottish "aesthetic empirics", writes: "The common Colours, for instance, of many indifferent things which surround us, of the

It did not require an acquaintance with the great contemporary revival of aesthetic philosophy in Germany to convince Coleridge of the fatuity of the whole system of British aesthetics; and Saintsbury is undoubtedly right in waving aside the controversy as to the relation between him and the Schlegels, and in setting down the resemblance as "mainly one of attitude—one of those results of 'skyey influences' which constantly manifest themselves" [1] in different persons of genius and talent

Earth, of Stone, of Wood, etc., have no kind of Beauty, and are never mentioned as such. The things themselves are so indifferent to us, that they excite no kind of Emotion and, of consequence, their Colours produce no greater Emotion, as the signs of such qualities, than the qualities themselves. The Colours, in the same manner, which distinguish the ordinary dress of the common people, are never considered as Beautiful. It is the Colours only of the Dress of the Great, of the Opulent, or of distinguished professions, which are never considered in this light. The Colours of common furniture, in the same way, are never beautiful: it is the colours only of fashionable, or costly or magnificent Furniture, which are considered as such. It is observable, further, that even the most beautiful Colours (or those which are expressive to us of the most pleasing Associations), cease to appear beautiful whenever they are familiar. The Blush of the Rose, the Blue of a serene Sky, the Green of the Spring are Beautiful only when they are new and unfamiliar", and so on through what George Saintsbury calls "long chains of only plausibly connected propositions" which with the school were the substitute for actual reasoning: "the turning round of the key being too often (one might say invariably) taken as equivalent to the opening of the lock" (*History of Criticism*, pp. 165–6.) It is this kind of thing that Carlyle pillories at the beginning of his *French Revolution*. "No Divinity any longer dwelt in the world; and as men cannot do without a Divinity, a sort of terrestrial upholstery one had been got together, and named Taste, with medallic virtuosi and picture *cognoscenti*, and enlightened letter and *belles-lettres* men enough for priests."

[1] *History of Criticism*, p. 396, n. 1. The whole passage is in general harmony with the view taken in this study as to the relation of Coleridge's ideas to German philosophy.

more or less simultaneously. Saintsbury is speaking
of Coleridge as a critic—"one of the very greatest
critics in the world",[1] but what he says of him in
this capacity in respect to the Schlegels is true of
him in his capacity as philosopher in respect to
the aesthetic theories of Kant and Schelling, of
which these literary critics may be said to have
been only the most popular exponents. Yet it may
well have been under German influence that in a
letter of October 1800 he writes of an "Essay on
Poetry" as more "at his heart" than anything
else.[2]

Up to 1818 he had produced only fragmentary
essays: on *Taste* (1810), on the *Principles of General
Criticism* (1814), and on *Beauty* (1818). In the
Preliminary Treatise on Method in the latter year he
assigns to Aesthetics "a middle position" in his
formal classification of the sciences, between those
which, like physics, deal with sensory facts by
hypothetical constructions, and those which, like
metaphysics, are concerned with "laws" apprehended through the Ideas of the reason. The fine
arts, he there explains, "certainly belong to the
outward world, for they operate by the images of
sight and sound and other sensible impressions,
and, without a delicate tact for these, no man ever
was or could be either a musician or a poet, nor
could he attain excellence in any one of these arts;
but as certainly he must always be a poor and

[1] *Op. cit.*, p. 206.
[2] He adds characteristically that "its title would be on the elements
of poetry, it would be in reality a disguised system of morals and
politics". Cp. Letters of February 1801 and July 1802.

unsuccessful cultivator of the arts, if he is not impelled by a mighty inward force; nor can he make great advance in his art if in the course of his progress the obscure impulse does not gradually become a bright and clear and burning Idea".[1]

With a subject, as he tells us, so much at his heart, and with so fine a text, it is surprising that, even in one so dilatory as Coleridge habitually was, nothing approaching a systematic treatment of it was ever attempted by him, and we have to gather his views on aesthetic from even more scattered sources than in the other main heads of his philosophy, with little to supplement them in the manuscript remains. The explanation may partly have been the reluctance of a man to revisit, as a land-surveyor, a country where he had once been a prince and a ruler, but far more the concentration of his interest, as years went on, on the philosophy of religion. Fortunately in the above-mentioned fragments, combined with what he says in the more familiar passages on the subject in the *Biographia Literaria*, there is sufficient to reconstruct at least in outline his general theory of art.[2]

2. PSYCHOLOGICAL AND METAPHYSICAL DATA

In view of the defects of current theories what he felt to be required was first a psychology that would

[1] *Op. cit.*, p. 69. The passage may well have suggested to Browning his account of the poet's aim: "Not what man sees, but what God sees—the Ideas of Plato, seeds of Creation, lying burningly in the Divine Hand—it is towards these he struggles."—*Essay on Shelley*.
[2] What follows is deeply indebted to Mr. Shawcross's excellent account in his edition of this book, vol. i. pp. 47 foll.

explain the working of imagination as not merely
a reproductive, but a creative process; and, secondly,
a metaphysic that would account for the appeal
which its creations make to what is deepest in the
soul of man.

Coleridge had reflected profoundly on the process
by which poetic images are generated in the mind.
No psychologist has ever had a better opportunity
of first-hand observation of it in his own mind, and
there is no reason to believe that he here owed
anything at all to German philosophy. He had
broken with the associationist philosophy, but he
had no intention of discarding association itself as
properly interpreted. What he was led to hold as
opposed to the current intellectualistic account was
"that association depends in a much greater degree
on the recurrence of resembling states of feeling
than trains of ideas". From this it at once followed
that "a metaphysical solution (like Hartley's) that
does not instantly tell you something in the heart
is grievously to be suspected". He adds with a flash
of his usual insight:

"I almost think that ideas never recall ideas, as
far as they are ideas, any more than leaves in a
forest create each other's motion. The breeze it
is runs thro' them—it is the soul of state of feeling.
If I had said no one idea ever recalls another I
am confident that I could support the assertion." [1]

One regrets that he did not do so at length, but
in these statements, under which, as he says,
"Hartley's system totters", it is not difficult to see

[1] *Letter to Southey*, August 7, 1803 (*Letters*, 1895 ed., i. p. 428).

an anticipation of recent reforms in the psychology of association.[1] What we have since learned is that the dominating factor in the process of suggestion, whereby imagination bodies forth the forms of things, both known and unknown, is not the temporal or spatial adjacency which the psychologists call "contiguity", but "continuity of interest"[2] —the emotional occupation of the mind with a significant idea, summoning from the depths of its experience the elements necessary for its expansion into a whole of meaning. British psychology in Coleridge's time was as yet too undeveloped to provide a complete scheme, not to speak of a language, into which such a doctrine could fit. It was all the more to his credit that he was able to break away from existing schemes and affirm a principle which made them thenceforth an anachronism.

But to have demonstrated the place of emotion and interest in the process of revival was only the first step in the required reconstruction of aesthetic theory. If the work of imagination is merely revival, poetic creation is still unexplained. It was in taking this second step, probably, that Coleridge chiefly found help in his study of Kant's *Critique of Pure Reason*, particularly in the recognition, in addition to the reproductive function of imagination, of another to which he attributes not only a pro-

[1] Saintsbury, *op. cit.*, p. 166, notes as one of the main fallacies of associationist aesthetics, "the constant confusion of Beauty with interest". Cp. Bosanquet's criticism of it in *Science and Philosophy*, essay xxiii, on "The Nature of Aesthetic Emotion".
[2] G, F. Stout's phrase. See *Manual of Psychology*, 3rd ed., p. 558.

ductive activity of its own, but something of the fruitful and inexhaustible character of noumenal reality itself.[1]

It was for just such an extension of its functions that Coleridge was looking; and when he came upon it in his early excursions into German philosophy he eagerly seized upon it as giving him the desired hint. But it was only a hint. For if, as Kant held, the work of the imagination was continuous with that of the understanding, merely preparing the way for its exercise in the wilderness of the sensory manifold, and if the understanding in the end gives us no more than a world of appearance, a like limitation would have to be imposed on the deeper faculty. Under such conditions it would be impossible to find in the work of the poet and artist any analogue to the Creative Intelligence of which the world is the embodiment. Unless the activity of the productive imagination were conceived of as in some way identical with that of the Divine Imagining, it would be impossible to justify the claim of poet and artist to be seers and revealers of essential reality.

It was just this identity that Schelling [2] had sought to establish in opposition to the element of subjectivism in Kant and Fichte. Nature according to Schelling was not the creation of mind, it *was* mind, albeit as yet in unconscious form. Nature in the narrower sense of which science speaks is not

[1] See Professor Norman Kemp Smith, in *Commentary on the Critique of the Pure Reason*, p. 264.
[2] Schelling's *Ideen zu einer Philosophie der Natur* was published in 1797.

the thing-in-itself. Natural science abstracts from the meanings which Nature symbolizes and takes it as something merely finite. It is the function of art, therefore, as representing a higher level of the primeval activity of which both nature and mind are manifestations, to portray directly and concretely what science and philosophy can describe only abstractly. From the point of view thus reached it is possible to represent the work of the imagination as continuous not merely with the understanding, as Kant did, but as continuous with the creative work of the divine intelligence itself.

"To one and the same intelligence", Schelling had written, "we owe both the ideal world of art and the real world of objects. Working unconsciously it gives us the world of reality, working consciously it gives us the world of art. The world of Nature is nothing more than the primeval, though still unconscious (and therefore unpurified) poetry of the Spirit. It is for this reason that it may be said that in the Philosophy of Art we have the universal organ and the keystone of the vault of philosophy." "For", as he goes on to explain, "it is in the work of art that the problem of the division which philosophy makes between thought and things first finds its solution: in this the division ceases, idea and reality merge in the individual representation. Art thus effects the impossible by resolving an infinite contradiction in a finite product"—a result it achieves through the power of the "productive intuition" we call "Imagination".[1]

[1] See *Werke*, vol. iii. p. 349.

We can understand how, when he came on all this in Schelling, Coleridge thought he had found a "congenial coincidence".[1] He was unfortunate in the term "esemplastic", which looked like a mistranslation of the German *Ineinsbildung*:[2] he was still more unfortunate in the plagiarized passages from Schelling, which he prefixed as a kind of *apparatus criticus* to his own theory of the imagination: but he made no mistake in the value he attached to these ideas for a true theory of art in general and of poetry in particular. They only needed to be adapted to the personalistic metaphysics, which he sought to substitute for the pantheistic impersonalism of Schelling. He has suffered from his failure anywhere to work out in detail the reorientation of his views that this change involved in the theory of art, to the same extent as he did in the theory of nature. But there are abundant hints of how he came to conceive not only of the sense of beauty as a form of personal communication with the Spirit revealed in Nature, but of art as the interpreter of its life, and it is only fair to give him credit for this advance upon Schelling. Even what he says in his earlier mood of the selflessness and impersonality of genius, and the experience out of which it speaks is quite compatible with what he later came to hold of the conditions of a selfhood and individuality, which

[1] "Perhaps", observes Leslie Stephen, "the happiest circumlocution ever devised for what Pistol calls 'conveying'."—*Hours in a Library*, iv. p. 351.
[2] In *Anima Poetae* we find esenoplastic substituted for esemplastic—a less ambiguous translation.

rest on quite other foundations than "the sensation
of self",[1] however much this may be necessary as
a phase of its development.

Be this as it may, when we try to take his
philosophy of beauty and the artistic imagination
as a whole, it is easy to see that the ideas that
underlie it are, not anything for which he need
have been directly indebted to Schelling, but *first*
the old distinction between *natura naturata* and
natura naturans—Nature as a dead mechanism,
and Nature as a creative force essentially related
to the soul of man, which so often forms his
text: "Believe me", he exclaims in one of the
later manuscript passages, "you must master the
essence, the *natura naturans* which presupposes a
bond between Nature in the higher sense and the
soul of man"; and *secondly* the view that, while
Nature is truly thought and intelligence, "the rays
of intellect are scattered throughout the images
of Nature" as we know her, and require to be
focussed for us by the genius of man if we are to
have them in their full splendour: "To make the
external internal, the internal external, to make
Nature thought, and thought Nature—this is the
mystery of genius in the Fine Arts". What we call
beauty is the condensed expression of this "thought".
For "this too is spiritual, this is the shorthand
hieroglyphic of truth—the mediator between truth
and feeling, the head and the heart. The sense (of)
beauty is implicit knowledge—a silent communion
of the spirit with the spirit of Nature, not without

[1] See p. 143 above.

consciousness, though with the consciousness not successively unfolded." To the sensitive mind the beauty of a landscape, which to the sensualist is only "what a fine specimen of caligraphy is to an unalphabeted rustic", is "music", and the very "rhythm of the soul's movements".[1]

It is in the light of this general theory of the nature of beauty that the familiar passages in the *Biographia Literaria* and the fragment on *Poesy or Art* upon poetic imagination, taste, and the place of imitation must be read.

3. Poetic Imagination

His theory of the first is given in the passages, familiar to students of literature, in which, discarding the heavy German panoply, he expresses his own view of the two forms of Imagination, and of "the poet described in ideal perfection". "The Imagination then I consider either as primary or secondary. The primary Imagination I hold to be the living power and prime agent of all human perception, and as a repetition in the finite mind of the eternal act of creation in the infinite I Am.

[1] *Semina Rerum*, MS. C, p. 97. In a marginal note in his copy of *Kant's Logik* (handbook, edited by G. B. Dasche), p. 9, criticizing Kant for his approval of a writer who denies the existence of *a priori* rules determining aesthetic judgment, Coleridge writes: "This is true in part only. The principles (as it were the skeleton) of Beauty rest on *a priori* Laws no less than Logic. The Kind is constituted by Laws inherent in the Reason; it is the *degree*, that which enriches the *formalis* (*e*?) into the *formosum*, that calls in the aid of the senses. And even this, the sensuous and sensual ingredient, must be an analogon to the former."

The secondary Imagination I consider as an echo of the former, co-existing with the conscious will, yet still as identical with the primary in the kind of its agency, and differing only in degree and in the mode of its operation. It dissolves, diffuses, dissipates in order to recreate: or where this process is rendered impossible, yet still at all events it struggles to idealize and to unify. It is essentially vital even as all objects (as objects) are essentially fixed and dead. Fancy, on the contrary, has no other counters to play, but fixities and definities. The Fancy is, indeed, no other than a mode of memory emancipated from the order of space and time; and blended with, and modified by that empirical phenomenon of the will, which we express by the word Choice. But equally with the ordinary memory the Fancy must receive all its materials ready made from the law of association."[1]

Coming in the next chapter to the nature of

[1] *Biographia Literaria*, ch. xiii. Cp. ch. iv, where he illustrates the distinction between imagination and fancy in more detail. In his Essay on *Poetry as Observation and Description*, Wordsworth declares that "fancy is given to quicken and beguile the temporary part of our nature, Imagination to incite and support the eternal". Nominally Wordsworth is criticizing Coleridge's definition of the Fancy as "the aggregative and associative power" on the ground that it is "too general" (see Coleridge's reply, *Biog. Lit.*, Shawcross, p. 112 *fin.*). In reality he is developing it with his own more massive power and suggesting a phraseology to describe it, as in the phrase "meditative Imagination", which reappears in Ruskin's well-known classification in the *Stones of Venice*, of the associative, the contemplative, and the penetrative uses of this faculty. What Coleridge contributes is a metaphysics which he would have claimed makes all our thoughts upon the subject in his own phrase "corrosive on the body", by connecting the distinction with his favourite one between reason and understanding, as he does here by implication, explicitly in *Lay Sermons* (Appendix B).

poetry, he admits that there may be poems which have pleasure for their immediate object. The admission has puzzled some of his critics, who have failed to notice that the pleasure he alludes to is of a peculiar kind, corresponding to the satisfaction of no casual appetites, but to what he elsewhere calls "the two master impulses and movements of man—love of variety and love of uniformity".[1] He allows further for poetry, such as we find without metre in Plato, Isaiah, Jeremy Taylor, and even in scientific treatises which have truth for their immediate object. In this wider sense poetic imagination would be synonymous with the genius which he describes in *The Friend* as the power "to find no contradiction in the union of old and new; to contemplate the *Ancient of Days* and all his works with feelings as fresh as if all had then sprung forth at the first creative fiat", the power which "characterizes the mind that feels the riddle of the world, and may help to unravel it".[2]

But he was not the man to confuse powers in reality as different as the purpose and the material are different in poetry and philosophy, and he goes on to give his idea of the work of the poet "described in ideal perfection", as one "who brings the whole

[1] *Anima Poetae*, p. 153. Cp. the continuation of the marginal note quoted above: "It is not every agreeable that can form a component part of Beauty", and what he says of the "poetical method" in *Principles of the Science of Method*, p. 41, as requiring "above all things a preponderance of pleasurable feeling, and, where the interest of the events and characters and passions is too strong to be continuous without becoming painful, . . . what Schlegel calls a musical alleviation of our sympathy".

[2] *Op. cit.*, ch. iv.

soul of man into activity, with the subordination of its faculties to each other according to their relative worth and dignity. He diffuses a tone and spirit of unity that blends and (as it were) fuses each into each by that synthetic and magical power to which I would exclusively appropriate the name Imagination. This power, first put into action by the will and understanding, and retained under their irremissive, though gentle and unnoticed control (*laxis effertur habenis*), reveals itself in the balance or reconciliation of opposite or discordant qualities: of sameness with difference; of the general with the concrete; the idea with the image; the individual with the representative; the sense of novelty and freshness with old and familiar objects; a more than usual state of emotion with more than usual order; judgment ever awake and steady self-possession with enthusiasm and feeling profound or vehement; and while it blends and harmonizes the natural and the artificial, still subordinates art to nature; the manner to the matter; and our admiration of the poet to our sympathy with the poetry."[1]

To critics who take little interest in psychological analysis or philosophical theory such a description naturally appears to be merely ringing the changes on verbal distinctions.[2] But this is to forget the

[1] Ch. xiv.
[2] See J. W. Mackail, in *Coleridge's Literary Criticism*. Cp. *per contra* Leslie Stephen's remark: "Coleridge's peculiar service to English criticism consisted in great measure in a clear appreciation of the true relation between the faculties (poetical and logical)." *Op. cit.*, p. 350.

devastation which the emaciated accounts current in Coleridge's time of the work of the imagination had spread in men's minds upon the whole subject, and the necessity of an energetic assertion of the presence of the element of passion combined with penetrative reflection, fundamental sanity of judgment, and a form of expression that would give some sense of the inner harmony of the material presented to the mind and therewith of the essential truth of the presentation.

In view of all this there is no clause in the definition which we would willingly spare, however differently modern taste might desire to have it expressed. The account errs rather by defect than by excess, seeing that it contains no detailed reference to the kind of diction which Coleridge conceived of as essential to poetry ("the best words", as he elsewhere expresses it, "in the best order"), in the sense in which he is here using the term. But he does not forget this, and in his discussion of it later in the *Biographia*, particularly in his criticism of Wordsworth's heresy, he makes ample amends. This falls outside of our subject What we have here to note is the liberation which this new insight into the nature and the work of imagination brought to his own mind and the confidence with which it inspired him in all he afterwards wrote.

4. IMITATION IN ART

While Coleridge was more interested in poetry than in the plastic arts, and first developed his theory

of the imagination with a view to a true understanding of what was greatest in the poetry of his
own country, he enables us to see how he applied
these ideas to art in general. In his essay on *Poesy
or Art*[1] he closely follows Schelling in his discussion
of the sense in which art is imitative. If the function
of the imagination is to unite sameness with difference, art can never consist in merely copying
nature. Mere sameness as in a waxwork disgusts
because it deceives. True imitation, as compared
with mere copying, starts from an acknowledged
difference. Starting from this, every touch of Nature
gives the pleasure of approximation to truth. But
the truth is not to nature in the limited meaning
of the word, as the object of mere sense experience.
The world we meet in art is the world of sense, but
it is the world of sense twice-born, and appearing
in that "unity of the shapely and the vital which
we call beauty". It is this uniqueness and intuitive-
ness of the experience which makes it something
wholly inexplicable by "association". It often
depends on the *rupture* of association. So too with
"interest". So far from being derivable from interest
in the narrower sense of the term, "beauty is all
that inspires pleasure without and aloof from and
even contrary to interest".

Here Coleridge's idea of Nature, as above explained, came to his aid. There is an inner and an
outer nature, and the imitation must be of that
which is within. "The artist must imitate that which
is within the thing, for so only can he hope to

[1] Shawcross, ii. p. 253.

produce any work truly natural in the object, and truly human in the effect." [1]

5. THE PLACE OF TASTE

It was a merit in contemporary writers on "taste" to recognize the place in art of the emotional response which they called "sensibility". Their mistake was to interpret this as a form of self-feeling. On a view like Coleridge's the whole emphasis fell upon depth of feeling, but it was feeling for a world in which the self in any personal sense no longer occupied a place, but might be said, as in love, to have "passed in music out of sight". "Sensibility, indeed", he wrote,[2] "both quick and deep, is not only a characteristic feature, but may be deemed a component part, of genius. But it is not less an essential mark of true genius, that its sensibility is excited by any other cause more powerfully than by its own personal interests; for this plain reason, that the man of genius lives most in the ideal world, in which the present is still constituted by the future or the past; and because his feelings have been habitually associated with thoughts and images, to the number, clearness, and vivacity of which the sensation is always in inverse proportion."

Taste then there must indeed be by which the

[1] See what Miss Snyder says on Coleridge's *Theory of Imitation* as an illustration of the union of opposites, *The Critical Principle of the Reconciliation of Opposites* as employed by Coleridge, p. 50 foll.
[2] *Biographia Literaria* (Shawcross), ii. p. 65.

genuine can be distinguished from the spurious, "the proper offspring of genius from the changelings which the gnomes of vanity or the fairies of fashion may have laid in its cradle or called by its name".[1] But the word is burdened with associations derived from its primary sensory meaning, especially of passivity and natural instinctiveness, and thus fails to bring out the dependence of the thing on experience, meditation, and the acquired power of recognizing, as intuitively as the trained scientist recognizes truth by its own light, words and images fit to give "the touch of nature" to the material in hand. It is this defect that Coleridge seeks to remedy in the definition he has given to taste. Taste, he tells us, is "an attainment after a poet has been disciplined by experience, and has added to genius that talent by which he knows what part of his genius he can make acceptable and intelligible to the portion of mankind for which he writes".[2]   And again it is "such a knowledge of the facts, material and spiritual, that most appertain to his art, as, if it have been governed and applied by good sense, and rendered instinctive by habit, becomes the representative and reward of our past conscious reasonings, insights and conclusions".[3] For this reason there can be no rules for the exercise of taste any more than for imagination. "The rules of Imagination are themselves the very powers of growth and production. Could a rule be given from

[1] *Op. cit.*, ii. p. 65.
[2] Shawcross, *op. cit.*, ii. p. 281.
[3] *Op. cit.*, ii. p. 64.

without, poetry would cease to be poetry and sink
into a mechanical art." [1]

6. THEORY AND PRACTICE IN LITERARY CRITICISM

It was in this way that Coleridge carried the theory
of beauty in nature and art, and especially in the
art of poetry, as far beyond anything hitherto
current in England, as he carried the art of literary
criticism beyond anything that had been achieved
by his predecessors. Yet this union in him of a
genius for criticism, second only to the very greatest,
with the metacritical craving for a theory of
aesthetic, has aroused the same suspicion among
literary men as the union of the poet and the
metaphysician already discussed. [2]

To those who hold that aesthetic theory is a
species of "Bohemian glass" and distrust its "false
subtlety", or who accept Schlegel's witty definition
of it as "the salt which dutiful disciples are going
to put upon the tail of the Ideal (enjoined upon
them as so necessary to poetry) as soon as they
get near enough", will be prepared to ask with

[1] *Op: cit.* With these views on taste and sensibility should be taken
what Wordsworth has written to like effect. See *Prose Works*, vol. ii.
pp. 82, 87, 131, where sensibility as a mark of the poet is associated
with wide knowledge of human nature, earnest observation and
contemplation of the "goings-on of the Universe"; and p. 127,
where he declares that "the profound and the exquisite in feeling
the lofty and universal in thought and imagination; or, in ordinary
language, the pathetic and the sublime: are neither of them,
accurately speaking, objects of a faculty which could ever without
a sinking in the spirit of Nations have been designated by the
metaphor—Taste".
[2] Above, p. 44.

Saintsbury [1] whether Coleridge is not "just so much the more barren in true criticism as he expatiates further in the regions of sheer philosophy", or even with J. W. Mackail [2] to reject his whole theory of poetry as "a large incoherent abstraction inapplicable and fortunately unapplied by him to the body of the criticism of which it is the introduction".

But this would be wholly to mistake the function of a philosophy of beauty, and the distinction between it and the art of criticism. The distinction is not, as Saintsbury would have it, "that Philosophy is occupied by matters of the pure intellect; and literary criticism is busied with matters which, though not in the loosest meaning, are matters of sense".[3] It is true that philosophy is concerned with theory, but, since the theory is of life in all its departments, it is concerned with will and feeling as well as with intellect. It takes all experience: moral, aesthetic, intellectual: the sense of duty, what Saintsbury calls "the amorous peace of the poetic moment", the love of truth, as its data. If any of them is not there, philosophy cannot give it. Theory or no theory, each man has to depend on

---

[1] Who quotes these criticisms. *Op. cit.*, p. 353, n. 6, and p. 396.

[2] *Coleridge's Literary Criticism.* Introduction. (London, 1908.) With the view here implied of the relation of Coleridge's theory to his practice of criticism we may contrast that of Lowell, quoted by Miss Snyder (*op. cit.*, p. 36), according to which his philosophy of polar opposites "served to sharpen his critical insight", while the union of it with concrete observations "resulted in a criticism that does more than deepen the layman's appreciation of the works criticized".

[3] *Op. cit.*, p. 142.

his own sensitiveness to the unique quality involved in particular forms of experience. What philosophy seeks to do is to understand wherein this unique quality consists; what it implies as to the world which is thus experienced; and, finally, how these experiences and the worlds that correspond to them are related to one another. It may be able to go but a small way in this, but it is bound to go as far as it can, and is at least justified in going so far as to indicate the falsity of theories which, like that of the Associationists in the present case, not only fail to understand, but would dissolve the experience altogether by resolving it into something quite different. If there are "Happy Warriors" for truth and beauty, who find the appeal to the heart that has "felt" sufficient, and who can afford to neglect such defensive theorizing, there are others less happy, whose minds are disturbed and their feelings confused by inadequate theories, and to whom more adequate ones may be a real help to full enjoyment.

Quite apart from this, moreover, there are those to whom metaphysic may itself be a form of "that immortal fire which", as Saintsbury eloquently puts it, "each generation keeps burning to soften what is harsh, feed what is starved, anoint and cheer and clean what is stiffened and saddened and soiled in the nature of man".[1] We know at any rate that these were the things that Coleridge sought and thought that he found in metaphysics. "What is it", he asks,[2] "that I employ my metaphysics on?

[1] *Op. cit.*, p. 334.   [2] *Anima Poetae*, p. 42.

To perplex our clearest notions and living moral instincts? To extinguish the light of love and of conscience, to put out the life of arbitrament, to make myself and others worthless, soulless, Godless? No, to expose the folly and the legerdemain of those who have thus abused the blessed organ of language, to support all old and venerable truths, to support, to kindle, to project, to make the reason spread light over our feelings, to make our feelings diffuse vital warmth through our reason—these are my objects and these my subjects. Is this the metaphysic that bad spirits in hell delight in?"

If there are those to whom these words make no appeal, it might be well for them to ask whether the fault is in Coleridge or not rather in themselves. For the particular metaphysic of beauty, with which we have in this chapter been concerned, we need not be deterred even by the great authority of the writers I have named from claiming its due. Fragmentary as it is, eked out, as at one time it certainly was, by studies from Kant and Schelling, it marked a new starting-point in British aesthetics. It gave us for the first time in England the elements of a theory, in the light of which the poetry that, along with political freedom, is her most characteristic contribution to civilization, can be better understood, the enjoyment of it can be made a more understanding enjoyment.

CHAPTER VIII

PHILOSOPHY OF RELIGION

"Religion unites in its purposes the desiderata of the speculative and the practical being; its acts, including its events, are truths and objects of philosophic insight, and *vice versa* the truths in which it consists are to be considered as acts and manifestations of that being who is at once the Power and the Truth, the Power and the All-powerful, the Truth and the True."—MS. B.

1. SPECIFIC PROBLEMS OF RELIGIOUS PHILOSOPHY

THERE is a sense in which Coleridge's whole philosophy was a Philosophy of Religion. He was himself willing to speak of it as a Theosophy, even as a Theognosy—a knowledge of God, to which all other knowledges led up. "I have considered theognosy (ὡς περὶ τῶν ἀχρόνων), physiology, and anthropology", he writes,[1] "not as religion, but as the antecedent grounds and conditions of religion." This followed from his view of religion itself as the highest exercise of the human spirit. "The religion", he tells us,[2] "the cause of which I have proposed to assert, I regard as the flower and crowning blossom of the plant, formed of whatever was most vital in root, stem, and leaf, by the gradual separation and deposition of whatever was earthly and crude." It is and does all this because "it unites in its purposes the desiderata of the speculative and the practical being: its acts,

[1] MS. C.
[2] MS. B II. He cancels the actual words, but retains the sense in the passage in which they occur.

including its events, are truths and objects of philosophic insight, and *vice versa* the truths in which it consists are to be considered as acts and manifestations of that being which is at once the power and the truth".

It is not therefore surprising that it is this aspect of his philosophy that has been the storm-centre of criticism, and has drawn the fire of rationalist and orthodox alike. By the one he has been accused of using sophistical distinctions to justify him in believing what is otherwise incredible; by the other of using methods of thought which were essentially pagan, and which ended in an irreligious Pantheism. For the same reason it is from this side more than from any other that his opinions have attracted ardent defenders in the school of Broad Church theologians, of which by general consent he was the founder, and that more justice has been done to them by recent writers.[1] These writers have, however, approached their subject, as was natural, from the side of Christian theology and Biblical criticism rather than from that of his general philosophical principles. For the purposes of this Study Coleridge's relation to Christianity is secondary. What we are concerned with is primarily his general interpretation of the meaning of religion, what beliefs it seemed to him to involve, as to the nature of God and the destiny of the human soul, how far it seemed to him possible to justify these beliefs to the speculative reason, finally, and only as a corollary,

[1] Specially deserving mention are, Tulloch, Pfleiderer, Vernon Storr.

the place he assigned to the Christian religion and the theology that has come to be bound up with it.

2. THE MEANING OF RELIGION

What drove Coleridge from Unitarian Deism to Spinoza's "intellectual love of God", thence to Schelling's "intellectual vision" of Him, and forward from that again, was the failure of one and all to satisfy the demand of the heart for fellowship with God. He was himself a great, and I believe a faithful friend, and he craved friendship and faithfulness in the Source of the being of all things. Even Kant was of little help to him here. The poet in him was repelled by what seemed to him the Stoical note in a philosophy of religion that left no place for the affections; still more by its conception of God as merely the guarantor of the coincidence between virtue and happiness. He would have echoed Cook Wilson's saying, "We don't want merely inferred friends: can we possibly be satisfied with an inferred God?" What his heart craved, and what to him was the essence of religion, was Communion with God of which prayer was the medium.

There had been a time when in the strength of youth he could write of God as one

> " Of whose all-seeing eye
> Aught to demand were impotence of mind",

and still another, at which, in more miraculous verse, he could define prayer in terms of human love to "all things both great and small". But his own bitter experience of life seemed to have taught him that more was required, and that the due function of prayer was to be a refuge from the weakness and limitations of the finite will. "It is a sore evil", he writes,[1] "to be and not in God— but it is a still more dreadful evil and misery to will to be other than God." Prayer he now defines as "the mediator or rather the effort to connect the misery of the self with the blessedness of God".[2] But the same experience had also taught him that prayer must be more than mere aspiration after union with God. It necessarily and inevitably took the form of petition, involving the cancellation of the incidents of time.[3] "What a deathly *praeteritum perfectum*", he exclaims,[4] "would the denial of prayer petrify the universe into." There was no subject in his later years on which he expressed himself to his friends with greater emphasis than on his conviction that the act of prayer was the very highest energy of which the human heart was capable, and that to believe vividly that God would listen and do the thing He pleaseth thereupon was

[1] *To Charles Lamb.* Quoted in this connection by De Quincey, article *Tait's Magazine*, September 1834. See *Table Talk*, etc., *ed. cit.*, p. 80, n. 2.

[2] MS. C, p. 143.

[3] In matters spiritual at least he would have no sympathy with Omar Khayyám's

> "The Moving Finger writes; and, having writ,
> Moves on: nor all your Piety nor wit
> Shall lure it back to cancel half a Line,
> Nor all your Tears wash out a Word of it."

[4] *Ibid.*, p. 110.

the last and greatest achievement of the Christian's warfare upon earth.[1]

It was in conformity with this conviction that the main problems of the philosophy of religion shaped themselves in his mind as the possibility of justifying to the reason the belief in existence of God as more than an impersonal Absolute, in His power of transcending the natural order of cause and effect, in the destiny of the individual as capable of showing His eternity, finally and as belonging more specifically to the Christian religion the belief in the reality of sin and redemption. On all of these Kant had denied the possibility of speculative proof. These beliefs might be open to faith, but not to sight. Coleridge so far agreed that an act of faith was involved in them all, but he held that, if the object of this faith could not be *proved* to reason, it could be shown not only not to be contrary to reason as involving an inherent contradiction, but to be only another word for reason, when taken in a sense that included the practical with the speculative exercise of the faculty. It was this view of faith as the synthesis of reason and the individual will that he had expounded in the *Essay on Faith*.[2] "By virtue of the latter (the

[1] *Table Talk*, etc., *loc. cit.*

[2] *Literary Remains*, vol. iv. p. 438. Cp. the passage prefixed to the *Confessions of an Inquiring Spirit*, by the editor. Even in so purely an intellectual exercise as in working out an algebraic equation, he was prepared to note an element of faith when the algebraist "places his signs, letters, and cyphers, his $+$ and $-$ and $\sqrt{}$, etc., in their due places, drawing out the thread of its calculus, now emerging into light and now hidden in the cylinders of the machine". MS. H, 143.

will) faith must be an energy, and, inasmuch as it relates to the whole moral man, must be exerted in each and all of his constituents; it must be a total not a partial, a continuous not a desultory energy. And by virtue of the former, that is reason, faith must be a light, a form of knowing, a beholding of the truth." This is well said, but the truth had to be vindicated against the difficulties to which Kant had succumbed, the conflict, namely, between the judgments of the understanding and those to which faith prompted. Could it be shown that though all appearances as judged by sense and understanding were against such a faith yet reality might be with it? Coleridge thought that it could, and his later manuscript writings, incomplete as they are, bear witness to the earnestness with which he wrestled with these problems to the end.

3. THE IDEA OF GOD

It was, as we have seen, an essential part of Coleridge's metaphysics that the idea of a supreme reality was not anything that could be arrived at through the senses or by the ordinary processes of logical reasoning. Conviction could come only through realizing it as the common ground which is assumed in all our several knowledges. However we may separate between their several objects, (body and form, matter and life, subject and object), we assume that these all co-inhere in one supreme reality. As the basis therefore of all science, it is itself the subject of none. It is the same, substituting religious for scientific experience, with the idea of God. "I look round in vain", he writes,[1] "to discover a vacant place for a science, the result of which is to be the knowledge and ascertainment of God, i.e. of the reality and existence of the Supreme Being in the absence or rejection of the idea as the Datum, and the result anticipated and precontained in the premise." It is for this reason that we can discount in advance all "proofs" of the existence of God founded on either the direct intimations of the senses, or on reasonings from them, and the theologies that make their appeal to them. But the opportunity of illustrating his own general thesis by a review of the most important of these was not one that was likely to be lost by Coleridge, and the second of the two long chapters (unfortunately incomplete) of the Huntington manuscript is devoted to characteristic criticisms of them.

Starting from theories founded on intuition,[2] he takes as his first example the view that we know God in the same way as we behold mathematical figures — the point, line, circle, etc., of pure geometry. It seems odd that he mentions this as a mere possibility, and not as a theory that had anywhere been actually adopted, seeing that it is

---

[1] MS. H, p. 227.

[2] This may account for the absence of any allusion to Descartes's, *a priori* argument from the idea of God as the all-perfect Being, and therefore as including existence. Long ago, in *Blackwood's Magazine* of October 1821, he had rejected this on the ground that "existence is no idea but a fact, no property of a thing but its reality itself".

just to such illustrations that his own Platonizing English predecessors, notably John Norris, had constantly appealed as samples of the Ideas which were not merely in God, but which were the very mind of God. Yet the fact that it was so only adds additional interest to his criticism, as indicating the point at which, under Kantian influence, he parted company with them. The view is rejected on the ground that mathematical figures and numbers are only entitled objects in the sense that they may be anticipated in all men at all times, but that otherwise they have their sole "subsistence" in the mind or sentient faculty. It thus starts from a contradiction. Asking for that which is the ground of all reality, including the reality of the mind, and of that which is out of the mind, we are referred to one branch of the common stem as though it were the explanation of the whole. Modern Realism is not likely to accept Coleridge's characterization of mathematical objects as purely mental, and has adopted his term "subsistence" for the express purpose of indicating their essential objectivity, but he is undoubtedly right in rejecting any theory that would claim absolute existence and validity for ideas based in the end on the "sentient faculty", and consisting of abstractions from the data of sense.

Of greater historical importance, as the basis of one of the great religions of the world, is the doctrine that God is everywhere revealed to sense: "*Jupiter est quodcunque vides.*" The study of Eastern religions was still in its infancy in Coleridge's time.

It is all the more interesting to find him quoting the Bhagavad Gita as a book that "walks like the ghost of a departed world", and endeavouring to enter sympathetically into the state of mind of those of his contemporaries who had come under the spell of Brahminism.[1] As for himself, he had long outgrown the homage he had paid on his first presentation to these foreign potentates. His poetic sense was repelled by images which seemed to him the result of the combination of "mean thoughts and huge things", and he refused to find anything "Miltonic" even in the best of them. Milton would have been the last to confuse bigness with greatness. From the theological side, so far from offering the basis of a monotheistic religion, Brahminism was "in fact Atheism in the form of Polytheism". From the side finally of morality, to Coleridge the surest test in the end of theoretic validity, it offered an ethics in many respects worthy only of a Mexican Priesthood. Life gets bare recognition, while of Love, without which as the source Life has no religious bearing nor any intelligible genesis, there is no word.

Coming to the illustration of the impossibility of arriving at the idea of God by way of inference from sensory data, he gives the first place to the argument from Design. While recognizing its impressiveness, the ground on which he rejects it is not that which has been common since the time of Hume, its failure to prove more at best than the existence of a Deity limited, like a carpenter, by

[1] He mentions particularly "The late truly admirable Sir W. Jones". See Appendix C, below.

his materials. This would have been valid against the idea of an omnipotent, not necessarily against that of a personal and loving Creator. His objection struck deeper, and was nearer to modern ways of thinking in attempting to show that the argument by interpreting nature's adaptations as necessarily implying intelligence in the creative force assumes what it pretends to deduce. It reads the idea into the phenomena instead of deriving it from them.

Coleridge admits that the disproof of these arguments is in itself far from establishing the impossibility of any argument whatsoever. This can only be done by showing that, as in the case of Ideas in general, the Idea of God is something that cannot, in Locke's phrase, be "conveyed into the mind" at all. It can only be awakened and brought into distinct consciousness by the appropriate experience. He even differs from Kant in holding that though he was right in denying positive demonstrative force to the a *posteriori* arguments, we must admit that there are "inducements of such strength that a man would deserve to be deemed mad who rejected them".[1] All that he is here and elsewhere interested in showing is that the chief function of philosophy is to indicate the particular kind of experience that is fitted to awaken the idea and to remove particular obstacles to its acceptance by the reason. As the exposition we have been here following ends abruptly at the

[1] Note on Nikolais' Philosophy in the Ottery St. Mary's *Marginalia*. Cp. what he says on arguments for the immorality of the soul, p. 234 below.

point where we are led to expect some positive statements on these subjects, we are left to gather what we can upon them from kindred passages elsewhere. Leaving for the moment the former as belonging rather to the psychology than to the philosophy of religion in the strict sense, we find him in some of these keenly conscious of the difficulty of justifying to the speculative reason both those attributes in Deity which are necessary that the belief in the Absolute Will should be converted into belief in a personal God with sovereignty over the temporal order of nature, and those in man which are required for the true interpretation of his moral life as rooted in the supra-natural.

4. The Personal Being of God

In his general metaphysical theory Coleridge had tried to vindicate the priority of Will to Being in the Absolute. But personality offered further difficulty, which he was not content to solve merely as a deduction from the general position, and submits to examination in the chapter entitled "Personal and Impersonal Reason" in the portion of his *Magnum Opus* quoted above as MS. B. His solution of it has particular interest, seeing that it anticipates that which is put forward by the best-informed philosophical theists in the present day.[1]

He traces the difficulty to the habit of associating personality in ourselves with limitation and ex-

[1] E.g. by Clement C. J. Webb, in *God and Personality*, and by J. E. Turner, in *Personality and Reality*.

clusiveness. This, he holds, is founded in a mistake. Limitation cannot be its essence. Were it so, we should have to hold that "the wiser a man became, the greater (that is) his power of self-determination, with so much less propriety can he be spoken of as a person; and *vice versa* the more exclusive the limits, and the smaller the sphere enclosed—in fact the less Will he possessed—the more a person; till at length his personality would be at its maximum when he bordered on the mere animal or the idiot, when, according to all use of language, he ceased to be a person at all". The truth, on the contrary, is that, with the increase of these limitations, the personality diminishes, though it is not permitted in a responsible will ever utterly to vanish. A man may become a fiend, but hardly a brute. In reality personality becomes more perfect in proportion as a man rises above the negations and privations by which the finite is differentiated from the Absolute, the human will from the divine, man from God.

Approaching the problem from this side, we can see that "to hesitate to call God a person is like hesitating to speak of the root which is antecedent to stem and branches, lest we should be supposed to be speaking of it to the exclusion of them, and to thus cast back an eclipsing shadow of the indigent particulars on the all-sufficient basis of their common being and the originating cause of their particular existence". Yet there must remain a difference between what we know as personality in man and the same attribute in God, as including while at the same time attaining a higher grade of perfection. To meet this justifiable scruple he proposes to use the term "Personeity" to indicate what is at once personality and more than personality. God, as the modern theist would say, may be super-personal, but this must include the best we understand by personal. It is on this ground that to the idea of the Absolute as Will Coleridge feels himself justified in adding as the "second idea" that of "personal being, having the *causa sui*, or ground and principle of its being, in its own inexhaustible causative might".

In the interpretation he here gives of the meaning of personality as a circumference continually expanding through sympathy and understanding, rather than as an exclusive centre of self-feeling, and consequently of the meaning of individuality and uniqueness as something to be won, and therefore, in the end, as an element subordinate to union with the Whole and undividedness from it, he anticipates the best that later idealism had to say on the subject. So far as I know, it is the first clear statement in English philosophy of this point of view, and has the advantage of carrying us beyond the ambiguities that still infect voluntaristic schemes in our own time.[1] Its application to the life of the Absolute is a more difficult matter. Granted that personality is an ideal that progressive spirits are ever realizing in fuller degree, yet it lives in the tension between the Self and an Other beyond the self. Coleridge recognized the element of Otherness, or as he called it "Altereity" in the Infinite, but

[1] Even Royce, as I try elsewhere to indicate, is not free from them.

there is this difference, that to finite personality the Other comes as something in a real sense beyond itself, while in the Infinite it is a self-made distinction. Yet if Theism as commonly held is to be justified, it must be along the lines that Coleridge was the first to lay down.[1]

5. GOD AS SPECIAL PROVIDENCE

Even greater than the difficulty of attributing personality to the absolute Being is that of harmonizing the scientific view of the order of the world, both physical and moral, as determined by undeviating law, backed as this is by the philosophical view of God as the supreme Reason underlying that law, with the belief in Him as the hearer and answerer of prayer—a belief which, as Coleridge admitted, "seemed to rest only in the individual's secret persuasion", and to require us to accept "faith as the main evidence of the truth of the faith". For his most careful statement of the difficulty and his method of meeting it, we have, I believe, to go to the long entry in his philosophical diary, MS. C, founded on his often-repeated definition of Faith as the Fidelity of the personal will in each of us to the *moral* reason—"reason in the form of conscience, conscience in the light of reason".

The question as here put is how far this faith requires the support of "belief", in the ordinary

For an interesting up-to-date discussion of the above difficulty, see Hilda D. Oakley's *Study in the Philosophy of Personality*, p. 174 foll.

sense of the word. His answer is that faith, so
defined, does not necessarily imply belief. It may
exist without it, and, when a strong sense of the
moral issue at stake, as in Kant's case, overbears
the evidence of ordinary experience, even in contradiction to it. But he is not himself content to
leave the matter there, and he goes on in terms
of his own metaphysical conclusions to conceive
of one "who has re-examined the premises of his
reason, and, by reference to his own act of self-
affirmation, discovers that the assumption that
reason and truth are the absolutely first is a purely
arbitrary one: that there must be something before
it as the self-subsistent ground of all being, and
that this can only be conceived as Will and Good;
affirming itself in an eternal act, the source of its
own and all other reality as the Other of its own
Identity, Giver therefore of Life, i.e. of Individuality, as well as Supreme Reason; uniting Law
and Dispensation, as universal gravity does not
exclude, but includes, specific gravities; a Spirit
not only for all, but for each and every". Emancipated from the power of the understanding, even
able to use it, in spite of its uncertainty, as an ally,
such a man may possess a faith which is identical
with his pure act of will, submitting itself to reason
not merely as universal, but as the representative
of a holy Will—a faith therefore *with* belief, "but
with a belief that derives its origin and stability
wholly from the antecedent faith".

We can see in this passage, better perhaps than
anywhere else, Coleridge's heroic determination

to get beyond the merely "permissive" faith in God as a watchful Presence of the Kantian philosophy; and if prayer in the sense of petition for something for which the physical and moral constitution of the world, as we ordinarily know it, makes no provision, is to be vindicated, we may agree that it must be along some such lines as he here indicates. His argument at least possesses the advantage over that of ordinary Pragmatism that it seeks to reconcile the control of events by the "will to believe" with the existence of an eternal reality, with which our wills, if they are to attain any true individuality, have in the end to identify themselves.

Yet we may ask whether, in spite of his own deeper insight, he does not still remain too much in bondage to the Kantian doctrine of sensory experience as entirely dominated by mechanical conceptions, and of the spiritual as something brought in from some supersensual and supernatural region.[1] If the Whole is spiritual, and therefore in the end providential, it is not by having things altered from without that we have to seek the goal of union with Its spirit, but by accepting them, whether in the natural or the moral world, just as they are and turning them to the ends of the spirit. Even as man's material progress is wrought not by magic but by the ministry of physical nature, so his moral and religious progress is wrought by the ministry of psychical nature. If prayer, as Coleridge held it to be, is the effort to

[1] He objects himself to identifying the supernatural with the miraculous *Aids*, etc., Aphorism CVIII, 1.

live in the spirit of the Whole, it attains its highest level not in the assertion of our will, as in petition, but in the acceptance of God's will as including ends beyond the particular and the present, in the words "not as I will, but as Thou wilt".

6. Immortality of the Soul [1]

Belief in the soul's immortal destiny was to Coleridge, as to his Platonic predecessors in England, not only an essential part of religion, but the foundation of a rational ethics. In the marginal note on Kant's view, already referred to,[2] he protests against the attempt to separate ethics from it. "I cannot conceive", he writes, "a supreme moral Intelligence unless I believe in my own immortality, for (in that case) I must believe in a whole system of apparent means to an end which has no existence. Give up this, and virtue wants all reason. I can readily conceive that I have it in my nature to die a martyr, knowing that annihilation followed death, if it were possible to believe that all other human beings were immortal and to be benefited by it—but (not for [3]) any benefit that could affect only a set of transitory animals. Boldly should I say: O Nature! I would rather not have been; let that which is to come so soon, come now, for what is all the intermediate space, but sense and utter worthlessness?"

[1] The student of Coleridge's poetry will recall the poem on *Human Life, on the Denial of Immortality.*
[2] P. 154.
[3] Writing indecipherable. I give what seems the obvious meaning.

We may wonder at the vigour of this protest in
one who knew so well on occasion how to assert
the presence of the eternal in, as well as beyond,
the temporal. Yet we should be wrong if we took
it as merely a reflection of orthodox opinion, or of
the stock arguments in support of immortality. In
a well-known passage [1] he comments at length on
Jeremy Taylor's argument founded on the necessity
to believe in "*Another* state of things where Justice
shall rule and Virtue find her own portion". This
is too like Kant's argument to find favour in
Coleridge's eyes, and here as elsewhere the appeal,
though not explicitly, is from Kant to Plato. What
is important is not the disproportion between moral
worth and worldly prosperity, but the contradiction
in human nature itself: the presence in it of mind
and will, which ally themselves not with what is
transient and essentially unsatisfying in the objects
of sense and appetite, but with whatever has the
character of permanence amid continual flux—
"unchanging like a rainbow in a fast-flying shower,
e.g. beauty, order, harmony, law"—things that are
all "*congenera* of mind, without which they would
not only exist in vain, as pictures for moles, but
actually not *exist* at all". Finally there is the universal
presentiment, even preassurance, of a life beyond,
and the unlikelihood that, while "in every other
ingrafted word of promise Nature is found true to
her word", her first lie should be to her noblest
creature.

He makes no claim that these arguments amount

[1] *Aids*, etc., Aphorism CXXIII.

to the proof of what, as an Idea, is undemonstrable. They are only a make-weight in a balance where there is nothing in the other scale; "no facts in proof of the contrary that would not prove equally the dissolution or incapacity of the musician on the fracture of his instrument or its strings".[1] In harmony with this interpretation is the form which his appeal to the authority of St. Paul takes at the end of the passage. It is not, as we might otherwise have expected, to the argumentation of I Corinthians, chap. xv, that we are referred, but to the Epistles to the Romans and the Hebrews, where the whole question is raised to a higher level by the change of emphasis from physical to spiritual death. The salvation which Christianity offers, we are reminded, is not from temporal death or the penalties and afflictions of the present life, "but from the condemnation of the Law". The soul's question to which the Gospel gives the answer is not whether there is a judgment to come, but where may grace and redemption be found. "Not therefore *that* there is a life to come and a future state, but *what* each individual soul may hope for itself therein; and on what grounds; and that this state has been rendered an object of aspiration and fervent desire, and a source of thanksgiving and

[1] In a note on Tennemann's strictures on Socrates's argument in the *Phaedo* as "beneath a man of sound understanding" (*History of Philosophy*, vol. ii. pp. 76–8), he repeats the above in another form, adding, "surely if these taken collectively be beneath a sensible man's notice, it would be hard to say what could deserve it. But Tennemann saw everything through the spectacles of Kant, or rather Kantianism".

exceeding great joy . . . *these* are the *peculiar* and distinguishing fundamentals of the Christian Faith."

Thus spiritualized, the argument in his hands turns from one for the survival of the soul in another life, into one for its salvation in this life by rising through grace to communion with God. From this point of view he might even have been prepared to agree with the modern protest that "an over-anxious desire to prove the immortality of the soul is not by any means an evidence of a religious temper. Indeed, the belief in immortality may easily become an unhealthy occupation with a future salvation which prevents us from seeking for salvation for mankind here—unless it be that natural spring of confidence in its own supreme reality, that unbelief in death, which seems to be a necessary characteristic and concomitant of true spiritual life."[1] However this may be, it is in its assertion of the reality of moral evil and the means of salvation from it that he finds at once the power of the Christian religion and the most difficult problem that the philosophy of religion has to face.

7. NATURE AND ORIGIN OF EVIL

As religion was the highest exercise of the human spirit, Christianity, Coleridge held, was the highest exercise of religion; and its excellence consisted in its power to rouse in us the sense of the debasement

[1] E. Caird, in *Evolution of Religion*, vol. iii. p. 243.

of "slavery to the outward senses", and at the same
time "to awaken the mind to the true criteria of
reality, viz. Permanence, Power, Will manifested
in Act, and truth operating as Life".[1] It was the
conviction of this that made what he calls "the
two great moments of the Christian religion",
original sin and redemption, so important to him:
"*that* the ground, this the superstructure of our
faith".

It is not perhaps surprising that, taking this form,
his Christian apologetics should more than anything
else in his writings have given rise to the idea that,
when he came to religion, Coleridge was prepared
to abandon the appeal to philosophy. Sufficient
has already been said to show how impossible it
was for a mind like his to accept any doctrine in
an uncriticized and unrationalized form. In reality
the vividness with which he seemed to realize the
facts in his own experience, and the importance
he attached to them, were additional reasons for
the attempt to translate them into philosophical
language. He had no hope that they could be made
completely intelligible to the understanding. They
were in the end what he called mysteries. Yet, if
they could be shown to be implied in a given
experiential fact, and to be themselves possible
as free from contradiction, this was all the justification that was required.

In the form of the doctrine of "original sin" he
had discussed the question of the reality of evil
in *Aids to Reflection*, but had there been content,

[1] *Aids*, etc., Conclusion, 18.

after rejecting "the monstrous fiction of hereditary sin", to deduce it from the idea of the will itself. Given a will which is an "original", as above and contrasted with the chain of events we call Nature, there is given along with it the possibility of submitting itself to that which is behind it, instead of to its own law, and of thus becoming subject to foreign domination. Such subjection is what we know as original Sin, namely, evil which has an origin, not in Adam, but in every man, for "it belongs to the very essence of the doctrine that in respect to original sin (not Adam only but) every man is the adequate representative of *all* men".[1] Whether or not he himself recognized at this time the deeper difficulty involved in his own metaphysical theory of the Absolute as primarily and essentially Will, by the time he came to dictate the chapter in his *Opus Maximum*, entitled *On the Divine Ideas*, the whole problem had deepened, and he there set himself to deal with it as the main crux of any philosophy which, like his own, was founded on the idea of an absolute and infinite reality.

The existence of evil seems to imply the possibility of a "separated finite", of that which "in some sense or other is, yet is not God, nor one with God", and thus to create a "chasm" for who

[1] *Aids*, etc., Aphorism CIXc. 24, an interpretation of the "philosophical myth" of Genesis, which J. H. Green develops in an interesting way (see appendix to *Spiritual Philosophy*, vol. ii. p. 336 foll.). Whether it would have satisfied the orthodoxy of his own or later times may be doubted. Dr. John Tulloch mentions it (*Movements of Religious Thought in Britain in the Nineteenth Century*, p. 21) without commenting on the sophism which equates "original" with "having an origin".

can to overbridge? We might attempt to get over the difficulty by defining the finite as the mere negation of the Infinite. But it is not Nature's way to produce living shapes except from forms which are positive powers. Only in lifeless things, the arrow in the air or the fragment rent from the rock, do we have shapes that may be said to be the product of negation. Even if we admitted that the finite were a mere negation, the question of its possibility would return upon us, for just in this separation we should have the evil we set out to explain. This is the knot that has been cut rather than untied by schemes that give us either a world without God or a world that is God. On the other hand, all the great and stirring epochs in the history of Western theology have coincided with the assertion of God as absolute Will, the cause of itself and of everything else. It is further altogether to Coleridge's credit that he will have nothing to do with any attempt to solve the problem on the lines of the modern theory of God as a "Creator of creators", and as thus limited by their freedom. He has no use for a limited Godhead. God must be all in all or He is nothing. Whatever may be the value of his own attempt at a solution, it has the merit of facing the question in its ultimate and most difficult form.[1]

It starts from the view which "the oldest sages of all nations have sought to express" in the doctrine of the Divine Ideas, not as knowledge or perception as distinguished from the thing known, but as a

---

[1] On this and on the principle of solution, see p. 278 below.

realizing knowledge, a knowledge causative of its own reality, a light which knows as it is known (φῶς νοερὸν καὶ νοητόν), and therefore containing the universal and the particular, the potential and the actual, in one indivisible whole so that neither can have any true being apart from the other. From this it follows that if there is anything which we must conceive of as possessing the possibility of affirming the particular as such, this is equivalent to assigning to it the possibility of so far ceasing to be real. But this is just what we must conceive the finite to possess if it is to be a will. It is true that all willing means *self*-realization and, so far as it does so, there is a universal embodied in the particular act. But in order that it may be a *willed* act there must have been the possibility of willing this universal under the control of something foreign to it as it is in its truth: as Coleridge puts it, "under the predominance of the particular", instead of willing the particular "solely as the glory and representation of the plenitude of the universal". So long as this remains a mere possibility it is compatible with the reality of God, but in the will to actualize the possibility there is a self affirmed which is not God, and it is this that makes the difficulty—a difficulty, however, of which Coleridge thought he had the solution in the logical principle which was the foundation of his whole philosophy.

Hold by the old dichotomous logic which divides the world into actual and potential, and takes this as equivalent to real and unreal, and the problem of evil is insoluble. On the other hand, take these opposites as the two poles of one reality, and we have the key in our hands. We can see that a will which wills what is merely actual cuts itself off from its root in reality, while at the same time willing to be real—wills in fact to be and not to be in the same act. This truly is a self-contradiction, but it is one which gives the solution and not a new problem, for to be in essential contradiction with itself is precisely the state which we mean by evil. To be really actual the finite must will its subsistence in God: what it does in doing evil is to "will itself to be actual under impossible conditions, a strange and appropriate contradiction".

Concluding the long argument, here condensed, Coleridge claims for it in the first place that it enables us to avoid the mystic's conception of "the Abyss", that is of a not-Good, which is yet not evil, before the evolution of Good, a conception which he finds no better than that of chaos; in the second place that it vindicates the reality of distinct beings in the plenitude of the divine mind, whose essence is will, and whose actuality consists in their being one with God; and finally that it proves the possibility of a fall from this state, "a ceasing to be eternal and a transition into the temporal" by willing their actuality in themselves and not in God.

It was this last that he had set out to prove. It is all that philosophy can be called upon to prove. That evil actually exists is a proposition that requires no proof. It is part of the world as we know it. To realize this we have only to reflect what kind of a world that would be from which all conception of guilt is eliminated, in which we have no other distinction of value than pleasure and pain, no evils but calamities, and for a God either a demoniacal Will or no Will at all, but a mere fate, a *deus multitudo* with no higher unity than a heap of corn or a pillar of sand, the architecture of a whirlwind.[1] On the other hand, accept the patent fact of evil, with the proof of its possibility which flows from the principle on which our whole system is built, and we can see that Will is higher than Power, and that while we can think of power apart from intelligence and love, it is impossible so to think of will.

With this finally we have the answer to the question of the origin of evil. We see that it cannot be anything that is begotten of God, for in that case it would be co-eternal and co-substantial with Him. It is in fact something to which the distinction between cause and effect made by the "dividing understanding" does not apply, merging as it does in the deeper one of essence and form: something therefore which may be "represented in a fearful sense, as αὐτομήτηρ αὐτούσιος".

Looking back on the argument of this remarkable chapter of Coleridgean philosophy, we should perhaps be right in saying that there are few things of equal power in the literature of Theism. It extorts from us something of the admiration which Coleridge himself felt for the equally daring logic

[1] MS. H, p. 107.

of Plotinus.[1] We should further perhaps be right in granting that, if we start from the identification of God with the Absolute, the object of religious consciousness with that of the speculative reason, it is by some such argument that the reality of moral evil must be vindicated. It is certainly no objection to it that potential and actual seem to change places, and that *that* alone is admitted to be actual, in which the potential of the will, as one with God, is realized. We are familiar in modern Realism with views that go near to equating potentiality with reality.[2] Where it gives us pause is the assumption, which underlies it, that the problem of evil is solved by the proof of the possibility of *moral* guilt. It may be true that to the eye of faith all physical evils have their place in the divine plan, and that the tower of Siloam, and all that it symbolizes, has some deep moral significance.[3] But simply to assume this, as Coleridge seems to do throughout, is to leave what to some is the main stumbling-block in theistic schemes untouched.

Going deeper and returning to the central principle of the whole, it is legitimate to ask whether the difficulty of moral evil is not one which is raised rather than solved by the identification of the supreme reality with Will. There is nothing in which Coleridge strikes more firmly the note of

[1] See above, p. 106.
[2] E.g. in Professor A. N. Whitehead's *Process and Reality*.
[3] "Moral evil", we are told, "is the *sting* of calamity, an evil from which all else that is or can be *called* evil derives its evilness." MS. *cit.*, p. 107.

all true idealism than in his insistence that the clue to what is ultimately real is to be found in the analogy of "the highest intuitions or ideas in our own minds".[1] But if this is so, it is natural to ask whether the appeal to religious consciousness at its highest does not suggest a level of experience at which will no longer survives as will, and sin is done away with in the peace of God. Perhaps, if we had as full a treatment of Redemption, as we here have of Sin, from the point of view of Coleridge's more developed thought, we might have found that he was prepared to meet this difficulty. As it is, we have to be content with what we find upon this subject, and upon his view of the Christianity which is specifically equated with it,[2] in his earlier published works.

8. DOCTRINE OF REDEMPTION

As sin is the enslavement of the will by the rejection of its own law in favour of mere natural inclination, redemption is the resumption of the law into the will and its consequent restoration to perfect free-dom.[3] "Whenever by self-subjection to this universal light (the light of conscience) the will of the individual, the *particular* will, has become a will of reason, the man is regenerate, and reason is then the spirit of the regenerated man, whereby the

[1] MS. *cit.*, p. 37.
[2] "Christianity and redemption", he writes (*Aids*, etc., Aphorism CXVIc, 3), "are equivalent terms".
[3] *Aids*, etc., Aphorism CXIVc, 3, and XCVIIc.

person is capable of a quickening intercommunion with the Divine Spirit." The mystery of redemption just consists in the fact that this has become possible for us. "And so it is written 'The first man Adam was made a living soul, the last Adam a quickening spirit'." From what he had already said of the first Adam as the representative of all men,[1] we might have expected him to go on to say the same of the last Adam as the head of a race renewed in the spirit of their minds, all the more as he takes this to be the meaning of St. Paul's use of "the Word, on which he founds his whole reasoning",[2] and credits St. John with identifying redemption "in *kind* with a fact of hourly occurrence, expressing it by a familiar fact, the same in *kind* with that intended, though of a far lower *dignity*"—and therefore no less a mystery.[3]

That he stops short of this is doubtless partly owing to his method in this book, which sometimes leaves us in doubt whether he is giving the opinions of others or stating his own, but also and much more to the ambiguity in his use of such words as "revelation" and "miracle", which though constantly recurring are never clearly defined. But that this is his real meaning we cannot doubt from what we hear elsewhere both from himself and others of his view of what is essential in the teaching of Christianity. "Miracles", he held, "are superero-

---

[1] See above, p. 238.   [2] *Op. cit.*, Aphorism CXIVc.
[3] Aphorism CXVIIIc, 4 and cp. CXII. 2, where the mystery is explained as consisting in the fact that "The will, like the life in every act and product, supposes itself a past always present, a present that evermore resolves itself into a past".

gatory. The law of God and the great principles of the Christian religion would have been the same had Christ never assumed humanity."[1] Dealing with the same subject, his devoted disciple, J. H. Green, who is not likely to have misrepresented him in anything so fundamental, draws the parallel between Adam as "the name intended to signify primaeval man collectively", and Christ as "the Almighty Power of Goodness", his spirit "the eternal Humanity working in us", the redemptive process only another name for "all the works of creation", and therefore independent of all *profession* of Christianity.[2]

In view of these utterances, we must allow Coleridge all the credit, which Broad Church writers claim for him, of an interpretation of the Christian religion equally removed from the materialism, which left no place for it at all, and the Evangelicism, to which it was something brought in from without, and superimposed by miraculous revelation upon recalcitrant human nature. To him Christianity thus interpreted was the highest achievement of religion, itself the blossom and flower of the spirit—a position from which there is no going back for anyone who claims a future for it in the atmosphere of modern thought.

It would have been well, perhaps, if he had been content with this reading of its teaching. We might

[1] Allsop's *Letters, Conversations and Recollections*, p. 47.
[2] *Spiritual Philosophy*, vol. ii. p. 386 foll. To the same effect is Green's reference to the facts of Gospel history as admissible only "so far as they are consistent with the *Idea of the revelation of a spiritual order of events belonging to the spiritual world*", *ibid.*, p. 326 (his own italics).

have found in it an anticipation of the view made familiar to us in the leaders of the idealistic movement in our time.[1] He was himself aware of the danger that threatened the simplicity of the Gospel from preoccupation with metaphysical questions. "I am persuaded", he wrote,[2] "that the vehement widespread and long-continued Arian controversy had the effect, among other injurious effects, of fixing the mind and the heart of the Church too exclusively on the metaphysical prolegomena of the Christian religion, even to the obscuration of the Son of Man in the co-eternal Son of God. . . Too constant and partial occupation of the thoughts with the Trinity and the eternal divinity of the Word eclipses . . the mild orb of our Lord's humanity which rose with healing in its rays." As a speculative doctrine, the essence of Christianity, he held, was that "it denies the true objectivity of corporal things". For the rest, "Christianity is a growth, a becoming, a progression. . . History, therefore, and history under the form of moral freedom, is that alone in which the Idea of Christianity can be realized."[3]

---

[1] E.g. in T. H. Green's *Works*, iii. p. 230 foll., and E. Caird's *Lay Sermons and Addresses*.
[2] MS. C, p. 112.
[3] *Ibid.*, earlier entry. Cp. *Confessions*, etc., Letter vi., where the proof of the divine origin of Christianity is to be found, not in the Scriptures, but in the "progressive and still continuing fulfilment of the assurance of a few fishermen that both their own religion and the religion of their conquerors should be superseded by the faith of a man recently and ignominiously executed"—a proof that would have held "even though, as Irenaeus said, they had left no Scriptures behind them".

But he was too deeply involved in the "metaphysical prolegomena" and the Laocoon-like coils of Trinitarian theology to be content with the experiential fruits of Christianity. The Neo-Platonism of his great English predecessors, and the exaggerated sense of his own mission as a renovator of the Christian religion, blown into a flame by the adulation of some of the more fanatical of his friends, combined to inspire him with the idea of adding to his general philosophy of religion a theosophy which should establish Christianity as "alone reflecting the character of religion, its doctrines truths,[1] its narratives facts, its effects worthy of its asserted Author". All that this enterprise was thought by him to involve we know from the scheme he sketches in MS. C [2] of a treatment of Humanity "in relation to the conservative and regenerative process", which should "practically be a history of civilization from the religious side".

Impossible to complete under any circumstances, and daily for himself and his contemporaries becoming more impossible with the advance of Biblical criticism even to attempt, this was destined to remain no more than a programme, and we need not further trouble ourselves with it here. But before leaving the subject, it is only doing justice to his saner thought upon it to note the precise point at

[1] For these, see *Aids*, etc., CIII (quoted from Leighton), *Confessions*, etc., Letter i, and the "Pentad of Operative Christianity" prefixed to that work.

[2] Printed at length, Snyder, *op. cit.*, p. 3 foll., as the ground plan of "an unwritten Epic". See below, Appendix A.

which the Christian conception of redemption seemed to him to require and to lend itself to further philosophical interpretation.

Religion in general, as we have seen, rested with him on the idea of a Divine Providence acting on the individual soul through natural circumstances and the events of history, but ready to aid it in response to a right attitude of aspiration and expectation. To this Christianity added the idea of Grace and Redemption, conceived of as meeting the particular need to be saved from the misery incident to "fallen" or (as he would have been ready to say) "rising" humanity. The problem with him was not to *explain* Providence and Grace, but to show how, on the analogy of ordinary experience, and on the assumption of the difference between the apparent and the real man, they were rationally possible. It was for this reason impossible for him to accept Kant's denial of the action of outward influences upon the will. While admitting that regeneration through an act and energy of diseased human nature, aided and fostered by a supernatural one, is in the end a mystery, he finds analogies to it [1] "in the undoubted influence of example, of education, in short of all the administrants and auxiliaries of the Will. The will may be acted on not only by ourselves (through the cultivation of habits), but by the will of others, nay even by nature, by the breeze, the sunshine, by the tender life and freshness of the sensation of

[1] Note on p. 297 of Kant's *Religion innerhalb der Grenzen der bloszen Vernunft.*

convalescence, by shocks of sickness." After referring
to George Herbert's poem *The Sonne*,[1] he goes
on (tentatively enough), "Why not then an influence
of influences from the Sun of God, with the Spirit
of God acting directly on the *homo noumenon*, as well
as through the *homo phaenomenon*? This would make
a just distinction between grace and redemption
and providential aids: the direct action on the
noumenon would be the grace—the call—the
influence on the *noumenon* through the *homo phaenomenon* by the prearrangement of outward or bodily
circumstances would be, as they are commonly
called in pious language, providences. Finally, on
such a view might not Christ be the World as
revealed to human knowledge—a kind of common
sensorium, the idea of the whole that modifies all
our thoughts? And might not numerical difference
be an exclusive property of phenomena so that
he who puts on the likeness of Christ becomes
Christ?"[2]

Speculation of this kind has gone out of fashion
among philosophers, and even those who have
inherited Coleridge's reverence for the Christian

[1] "How neatly do we give one onely name
To parents' issue and the sunne's bright starre.

.   .   .   .   .

For what Christ once in humblenesse began
We Him in glorie call the Sonne of Man."

[2] *Loc. cit.* He veils these speculations in Greek and Latin terms:
$XPI\Sigma TO\Sigma = K\acute{o}\sigma\mu o\varsigma$ $\dot{\epsilon}\pi\iota\sigma\tau\eta\mu\acute{a}\tau\iota\kappa o\varsigma$ $'A\nu\theta\rho\acute{\omega}\pi\omega\nu$, sensorium quasi
commune? Idea totalis cogitationum omnium modificatrix? They
remind us of Blake's identification of Christ with the Imagination,
from which perhaps it is not very remote.

tradition, might suspect the attempt to find its essence in a distinction between the real and the apparent man, which was designed to admit of miraculous incursions from another world.[1] If the Universe is spiritual, it must be spiritual through and through, and not in streaks and patches. The belief that miracle is necessary to unite material and spiritual is really a form of unbelief. But no philosopher who is prepared to admit uncovenanted factors in our lives, such as the gift of will itself, and the sense of the need of something from beyond ourselves, wherein salvation from its weakness may be found, can fail to sympathize with any genuine attempt to show how this is possible, and how the dead bones of old theological controversies may live again in real speculative problems.

9. THE ORIGIN OF THE IDEA OF GOD IN THE SOUL

Be this as it may, it is probably with a sense of relief that some students of Coleridge's philosophy of religion will turn from speculations of this kind to what he has to say on the birth of religion in the soul, where, as always when it is a matter of psychology, he is at his best. He was profoundly convinced of the entire "naturalness of religion", in the sense in which it is advocated by idealistic writers at the present day,[2] and in a chapter

[1] Coleridge held that "Whatever is spiritual is *eo nomine* supernatural". "But", he went on to ask, "must it be always of necessity miraculous?" (*Confessions*, etc., Letter vi), where we should rather ask, "can it ever be miraculous?"
[2] See the recent book with this title by A. B. Brown and J. W. Harvey.

entitled "The Origin of the Idea of God",[1] he discusses the sources in human experience from which it springs.

He is prepared to find the beginnings of it in instinct; but this does not mean equating it with anything that is merely animal. All instincts are not alike; each kind of creature has its own; the instincts of man differ from those of the lower animals in being already pervaded by the reason which is the mark of humanity. In this sense they are "rational instincts—reason mutely prophesying of its own advent". But "rational" instincts might still mean, as they did in the current psychology, instincts directed to the preservation and well-being of the merely individual self. Needless to say, this was not Coleridge's meaning. The instinct that prophesies of religion, on the contrary, is the impulse to respond to something beyond the self, and this has its beginning in the outgoing of the child's heart to parents. "Why", he asks, "have men a faith in God? There is but one answer. The man and the man alone has a Father and a Mother. The first dawnings of (the infant's) humanity will break forth in the eye that connects the mother's face with the warmth of the mother's bosom. A thousand tender kisses excite a finer life in its lips, and their first language is imitated from the mother's smiles. Ere yet a conscious self exists the love begins, and the first love is love to an other. Beyond the beasts, yea and above the nature of which they are inmates, man possesses love and faith and the

[1] MS. B.

sense of the permanent", and this because he possesses an understanding differing, not solely by its greater extent from that of the ant or the dog, but by being "irradiated by a higher power, the power namely of seeking what it can nowhere behold, and finding that which itself has first transfused—the permanent, which in the endless flux of things can alone be known".

After showing how the bodily self by being "the image which is always present to the senses" tends, in individuals, peoples, and epochs, to usurp the place of the truly permanent, and to be the source of the corruption of religion by idolatry, ceremonialism, and magic, he goes on to insist that Nature gives no countenance to this, but draws us all the other way. "As soon as ever the heart of man is made tender by the presence of a love which has no self, by a joy in the protection of the helpless, which is at once impulse, motive and reward, so surely is it elevated to the Universal Parent." In a word, the birth of thought is also the birth of religion: "The first introduction to thought takes place in the transfer of person from the senses to the invisible. The reverence for the invisible, substantiated by the feeling of love, this, which is the essence and proper definition of religion, is the commencement of the intellectual life of humanity."

As compared with the immense literature that has grown up on the Psychology of Religion, the hints we have here and elsewhere in Coleridge may seem meagre enough. But as compared with the still meagrer and misdirected accounts of the popular psychology of his time, they have the merit of seizing the essential point by connecting religion in its beginning with that which carries the soul beyond itself and connects it, through the affections, with a larger world. To find anything comparable to it we have to come to writers of our own time, who, like him, have recognized the place of mother-love in awakening the sense of an all-encompassing, though invisible goodness.[1]

Returning to Coleridge's religious philosophy as a whole we may, after what has been already said of it, sum up in a word what may be taken to be its main achievement. This was to combine the Platonic theory of the *world* as an expression of the Divine Ideas, of *reason* as their reflection in our minds, and of *religion* as the wrapt contemplation of them, so reflected, on which the early English Platonists had mainly dwelt, with a voluntaristic theory of being and of the knowledge of it, largely Kantian, finally with a psychology essentially his own. By shifting the emphasis from God as Being or substance to God as Will, he was able to vindicate the practical nature of religion, which was later to become the keynote of the treatment of it by British and American idealistic writers,[2] and to identify Faith with Fidelity to conscience and the indications of the Will of God upon earth as

[1] See, e.g., William Wallace's similar and not less eloquent account of the birth of reason and love, and therewith of soul, in the infant through "the mother's glance and smile and touch". *Lectures and Essays*, p. 114 foll.

[2] E.g. F. H. Bradley and Josiah Royce.

rationally interpreted, instead of with belief in any system of doctrine. If, under the influence of the prevailing orthodox atmosphere in which he lived, his own morbid experience, and his conviction that the only alternative was a soul-deadening pantheism, he sought to add to this a reconstruction of orthodox Christian dogma, it only showed that, like perhaps both his masters, Plato and Kant, he was unaware of the full extent of the revolution in men's minds for which his own thought, more than that of any other writer of his time and nation, was the preparation.

CONCLUSION

"The loftiest poet and the loftiest philosopher deal with the same subject-matter, the great problems of the world and human life, though one presents the symbolism and the other unravels the logical connection of the abstract conceptions."—LESLIE STEPHEN, "Coleridge", in *Hours in a Library*.

IT might seem a natural conclusion to a study like the above to trace the influence of Coleridge's thought in the technical philosophy of the following generation. I believe that, as compared with its influence in other fields, particularly that of Anglican theology, this as a matter of fact was insignificant. There was, indeed, an apparent exception in the work of Joseph Henry Green. But it was one of those exceptions which prove the rule. Green inherited Coleridge's philosophical manuscripts, if not his prophetic mantle, and thenceforth conceived it his mission to reduce to order the materials they contained for a complete philosophy. But he felt himself overburdened by the responsibility, and somewhat after the manner of his Master spent the most of the years that remained to him, until his death in 1863, in preparation for a task that he did not live to complete on the large-scale plan he had designed. What we have from his hand in the book *Spiritual Philosophy* was somewhat hastily put together when he realized how short the available time was likely to be. Even so, it did not see the light till 1865, by which time fresh impulses were coming from Germany, that seemed to put the results of the earlier movement out of date. It was for this, among other reasons, that the book fell dead, and remains to us rather an echo of a bygone day than a uniting link filling the gap between Coleridge's death in 1834 and the writers of thirty years later.[1]

But Green was only one, and one of the lesser known of a generation of men, distinguished as few have been for intellectual interest and power to give expression to it, and, if there is little to record of Coleridge's direct philosophical influence over their thought, all the more may something seem to be required to account for this failure. "There are few middle-aged men of active intelligence at the present day", wrote H. D. Traill in the 'eighties,[2] "who can avoid a confession of having 'taken' Carlylism in their youth; but no mental constitutions not predisposed to it could ever have caught Coleridgeism at all." This is true, as many of us, who more or less belonged to Traill's generation, can remember, but it only raises the same question in the form of the reason for this difference.

The chief reason is not, I believe, to be looked for in any of those which are usually alleged. It did not consist in any radical conflict between the temperament of the poet and the philosopher as such. The example of Coleridge's great contemporary Goethe is sufficient to prove that the "ancient quarrel between poetry and philosophy" was a quarrel between friends. Coleridge himself held

[1] Yet it deserves more notice than it has hitherto received and, as it is somewhat rare, I have added in an Appendix a few further notes upon it as furnishing reliable material for studies like the present.

[2] *Coleridge*, in English Men of Letters Series (1889).

that the aim and, in a sense, the method of both were essentially the same, namely, "the union of the universal and the particular". "Plato", he wrote,[1] "was a poetic philosopher, as Shakespeare was a philosophic poet." Each doubtless had its own medium and mode of expression, and this had to be remembered according to the rôle at the time. Coleridge too often forgot it—the exuberance of his language and the vividness of his imagery were too apt to run away with him, and to lead to his frequent failure to distinguish between metaphor and argument. But a philosophical style like that of Hume or Mill or, in our own time, of Bradley, is a rare accomplishment, and its absence in him was a venial fault, often atoned for in his marginal notes (where he found himself confined within strict limits as to subject and space) by vigorous, condensed expression, which leaves little to be desired.

Nor is more than a partial explanation to be found in lack of purpose or even of will to execute what he purposed. The manuscripts he left show, on the contrary, how indefatigably he laboured in the pain and sickness of his later years to make up for wasted talents. Even his failure to complete and publish the result of these labours was of comparatively little importance. His main ideas, in their essential outlines, were well known to an inner circle of admiring disciples, including, besides Green, men like John Sterling, of whom Carlyle reluctantly records that "in after times he did not complain of Coleridge's unintelligibility or attri-

[1] *Preliminary Treatise on Method.*

buted it only to the abstruse high nature of the topics handled". After Sterling's death his master's ideas could not have had a better sounding-board than the "Sterling Club", which included among its members J. S. Mill, Alfred Tennyson, and Carlyle himself. Traill touches a deeper reason when he notes the absence in Coleridge of "any moral theory of life". But this too, as we have seen, was only partially true, and Mill's estimate on the same subject was a very different one.

The real reason is I believe to be found, in the first place, in a certain unripeness of the time for the acceptance by philosophers of these ideas. It was true that the older empiricism may be said by this time to have run its course, but under the influence of the idea of evolution it seemed possible to revive it in a new form, and at the same time to satisfy the metaphysicians, as Spencer tried to do, with a theory of the Unknowable; while for those who inherited its dislike of metaphysics in any form, Comte's Positivism seemed to be providing it with deeper roots in a new philosophy of History. Even in Scotland, that genial home of metaphysical speculation, the ground was preoccupied by a form of pseudo-Kantianism [1] which, as bad currency is said to drive out good, obstructed the spread of better knowledge.

In the second place, and even more important, was the innate conservatism, which often prevented Coleridge from following out to the bitter end the principles he had the genius to seize. "He declares

[1] Hamilton's *Essay on the Unconditioned* appeared in 1829.

great truths and principles with sufficient boldness and clearness", wrote an anonymous author, "but often fails completely in his deductions from them and his applications of them."[1] Carlyle's view of the "swimming bladders" and "transcendental life-preservers", which he threw out to orthodox opinions, is well known, and is not without justification. In general philosophy, in spite of the advance he sought to make on Kant, we have seen how he allowed himself to be too much dominated by the Kantian separation between the material and the spiritual, the causal nexus by which Nature seemed bound and the freedom of the will. In religion this meant that Christianity was made to appear to stand on a different basis, not only of spiritual appeal, but of miraculous revelation, from all other religions. In politics the same conservatism, united with the same philosophical dualism, was responsible for the distinction he drew between classes in respect to their capacity to enter into the full rights of citizenship. No more here than in religion did he ever seem completely to realize that if freedom is the soul of human life, it must have its spring in human nature itself, and must permeate the whole body. True, in Nature there are all degrees of freedom and individuality, corresponding to different natural orders. But the differentia of human life is just that in it first freedom has become a common possession, and none can

[1] The *Relation of Philosophy to Theology* (London, 1851), p. 15. The same writer probably reflects the general impression of the time when he says: "Coleridge teaches no system, not even his own." *Ibid.*, p. 7.

be really free unless all are free. In science, finally it meant that while he was prepared to welcome the treatment of individual organisms from the point of view of a single principle dominating the life of the parts, he rejected the suggestion of applying the same idea to the evolution of the animal world, including man, as a whole.

In all these respects he seemed to be setting himself against the new currents of thought and feeling, into whose deeper spirit he otherwise penetrated further than any of his English contemporaries. That in the field of literary criticism these limitations had less opportunity of showing themselves, or that his own supreme genius in it enabled him to transcend them, is perhaps the reason why it is in this field that fullest recognition has been given by succeeding generations to his greatness as a thinker.

To-day we can afford to separate between his enunciation of principles and his success in carrying them out in detailed application, and the contention of this Study is that we do him wrong if we allow his failure to influence immediately the current of philosophical thought, and the limitations, which were the cause of it, to conceal from us the place he occupies in his own right in the development of idealistic philosophy in England and America. It may perhaps in the end prove to have been in favour of his ultimate influence that there has been a certain "lag" in its power of asserting itself. Certain it is that the present reaction against the logical idealism of the latter part of the nineteenth century, and the rise of a more definitely ethical form of that doctrine, offer a more favourable atmosphere than ever before for the recognition of the Voluntarism with which his philosophy is so deeply dyed.

Be that as it may, it is more in the line of the main object of the present Study, neglecting contentious matter, to try in this Conclusion to state more precisely than there has hitherto been the opportunity of doing the place which is likely to be assigned to Coleridge in the history of Anglo-Saxon philosophy, and the feature in his teaching that is the main ground of his title to it.

1. The history in England of what at the present day is known as Idealistic Philosophy still remains to be written.[1] When it comes to be written it will, I believe, be found to be not less continuous, and not less characteristic of the English genius, than that which is commonly taken to be its main contribution to philosophy. Centuries before the age of Locke the note of this truer "way of ideas" had been struck by John Scotus Erigena, the last of the Platonists before philosophy passed under the yoke of mediaeval theology.[2] At least half a century before Locke wrote, a group of men in Cambridge, representing the best English tradition in religion and politics, revived the same note, and gave expression to it with a fullness and grace unequalled anywhere else in Europe. Though taken up and

[1] The series of studies of which this was intended to be one, shortly to be published, is intended as a small contribution to such a history.
[2] See Robert Adamson's article on him in *Encyclopædia Britannica*, Ninth Edition.

applied in new ways at the beginning of the next
century by their Oxford successors, John Norris
and Arthur Collier, it was too remote from the
empirical spirit of the time to make way against
the "new" way of ideas. Berkeley's late-born
Platonism was only a transient gleam of the old
light, and the century closed with the triumphant
domination of every field by the ideas inherited
from Locke and Hume.

To Coleridge belongs the credit of having been
the first to realize, with the sharp pang of the most
sensitive mind of his time, the inadequacy of these
ideas for the interpretation of the spiritual movements which were most characteristic of the age.
Aided by the insight which his own early transference of allegiance from the Hartleian to the
Platonic tradition gave him, he was able to develop
ideas that were in his own words *Semina Rerum* [1]—
seminal principles that, first unconsciously, then
more and more consciously as the new century
went on, were to dominate men's minds and be
translated into theory and practice.

2. After all that has been already said of them,
it is unnecessary to go into detail, but the central
idea cannot be too often stated as that of the true
meaning and place of Individuality in the world
both of nature and of man.

In nature individuality is not to be looked for
in any self-sustaining atom or cell, but in the extent
to which a structure is able to reach out to and
assimilate elements lying beyond the limits of its

[1] His title for MS. C.

own space and time existence, and thus to link
itself with the whole to which it belongs, while at
the same time rounding itself off into a self-main-
taining unit within the larger sphere. Towards such
individuality, expressing itself in ever high forms,
all nature moves, rising on stepping-stones, not of
dead but of living selves, each reflecting at its own
level and according to its own capacity the glories
of the Whole.

In human life the seat of individuality, now
become self-conscious personality, is similarly to
be sought for not in any centre of isolated and
isolating feeling, but in the degree to which a man
passes beyond the limits temporal and spiritual
within which mere feeling confines him, and
identifies himself, in thought, feeling, and action,
with the larger life about him while remaining a
self-integrating member of it. The infinite whole
of which this larger life consists may be the only
complete individual, the only completely comprehensive and self-sustaining being—therefore the
only Person in the fullest sense of the word. But
finite spirits may attain to a share in that fullness,
in proportion as they approximate to its all-
inclusive life. Life at its best is the will to approximation, perhaps in the end only an aspiration and
a prayer, but "he prayeth best who loveth best",
and love means this expansion expressed in terms
of feeling.

It does not require any deep acquaintance with
the history either of thought or practice in the
course of the last hundred years to recognize in

this conception of individuality what was to become more and more the chief moulding, epoch-making influence in national life. Coleridge held that while "in the immense majority of men, even in civilized countries, speculative philosophy has ever been, and must ever remain, a *terra incognita*, yet all the epoch-making revolutions of the Christian world, the revolutions of religion, and with them the civil, social, and domestic habits of the nations concerned, have coincided with the rise and fall of metaphysical systems". So far as the above is a correct statement of the central thought in his own system, he has the merit of first formulating the idea whose rise was in his own modest language to "coincide" with the revolutions which have since taken place in all these departments and made our national life what it is to-day.

APPENDIX A

MATERIALS FOR STUDY OF COLERIDGE'S PHILOSOPHY

REFERENCE has been made in the Preface to the sources available for the study of Coleridge's philosophical opinions, but some fuller account is called for by reason of their multifariousness. They consist of: 1, His own published prose works. 2, Letters to friends, collections of Table Talk, and reminiscences of others. 3, Various manuscript remains, as yet for the most part unpublished, including marginal notes on those of the 340 books[1] containing them, which are of philosophic interest. To these deserves to be added the book *Spiritual Philosophy*, as an exposition of the leading principles of his Master's thought by his most intimate and understanding friend, Joseph Henry Green.

1. The most important of the first group are:—

The Friend, reprinted from the numbers that appeared 1809–10 in 1812; 3 vol. ed., 1818, described by Coleridge in the Preface as "a *refacciamento* rather than a new edition", "the additions forming so large a proportion of the whole work and the arrangement being altogether new"; 3rd edition, edited by Henry Nelson Coleridge, with the author's latest corrections and appendices restoring some passages omitted in the 1818 edition.

Biographia Literaria, 1st ed., 1817; 2nd ed. (H. N. Coleridge and Sarah Coleridge), 1847; frequently edited since.

A Preliminary Treatise on Method, written as the General Introduction to the *Encyclopaedia Metropolitania*, published separately as *Principles of the Science of Method*, 1818: much

[1] See J. L. Haney's *Bibliography of Samuel Taylor Coleridge*.

"bedeviled, interpolated, and topsy-turvied" to the disgust of the author (Campbell's *Life*, p. 227 foll.).

Aids to Reflection, 1st ed., London, 1825; 2nd ed., New York, 1839; 5th ed. by Henry Nelson Coleridge, London, 1843; frequently edited since.

Confessions of an Inquiring Spirit, ed. H. N. Coleridge, 1840.

Hints toward the Formation of a more Comprehensive Theory of Life, ed. Seth B. Watson, 1848.

2. Under the second head come:—

(*a*) Collections of Letters that kept appearing up to 1911. The most important are *Letters, Conversations, and Recollections* by Thomas Allsop, 2 vols., 1836.

Letters of Samuel Taylor Coleridge, by Ernest Hartley Coleridge, 2 vols., 1895.

Biographia Literaria, by A. Turnbull, 1911.

(*b*) Joseph Cottle's *Early Recollections*, 1837, and Reminiscences of Samuel Taylor Coleridge and Robert Southey, 1847.

Henry Crabb Robinson's *Diary, Reminiscences, and Correspondence*, 1872.

Two "monologues" published in *Fraser's Magazine*, November and December 1835, on "Life" and "The Science and System of Logic", by a member of Coleridge's logic class.

3. The manuscript remains consist of (*a*) unfinished works:—

(*a*) *Two Volumes on Logic* in the British Museum (Egerton 2825 and 2826). Of these an analysis with extracts will be found in Miss Alice D. Snyder's book, *Coleridge on Logic and Learning*, pp. 78–103 and 104–27. The MS. is in the hand of several amanuenses with marginal annotations by Charles A. Ward, one time owner of it, and is undoubtedly the work alluded to in the letters of November 27, 1820, September 24, 1821, December 1822

(Allsop, *op. cit.*), in *Aids to Reflection* (ed. 1825, p. 174 n.), and in J. H. Green's *Spiritual Philosophy*, vol. i. p. 51. A list of sixteen chapters (imperfectly indicated in the MS. itself) is given at the beginning, showing as it goes from "History of Logic", "Philosophy of Education", "Logic as Canon", "Logical Acts" to a treatment of "Analytic and Synthetic Judgments", and finally of "Categories", more and more the influence of Kant's *Critique* upon Coleridge's conception of the scope of the science.

If this manuscript is the copy referred to in the last two of the above letters as practically completed and only awaiting transcription, Coleridge must have been speaking with more than his usual sanguineness. It is manifestly incomplete, and bears marks of illiteracy on every page. Miss Snyder has discussed, and on the whole justified, Green's decision against publishing it. But if, as now seems likely, the not less incomplete and unrevised *Opus Maximum* with other philosophical fragments are going to be printed, I see no reason for making an exception of the *Logic*. The study of philosophy in England and America has advanced in vain during the present generation if the student may not be trusted to select the ore and leave the dross in the work of its pioneers.

(*b*) More important for the study of Coleridge's philosophy in its later and more metaphysical developments is the manuscript preserved in three vellum-bound volumes in the possession of the Rev. Gerard H. B. Coleridge, of Leatherhead, marked conjecturally in Charles Ward's hand, vol. i, ii, iii—an order which Miss Snyder, on equally conjectural grounds, proposes to reverse. This is undoubtedly a part of the *Opus Maximum* to which Coleridge, as he tells us in a letter of 1821,[1] had devoted "more than twenty years of his life", and of which "more than half" at that time "had been dictated by

[1] Allsop, *op. cit.*, p. 82. Miss Snyder, *op. cit.*, p. 8, gives a long list of other references to it.

him so as to exist, fit for the press, to his friend and devoted pupil Mr. Green". Whether this is the actual copy referred to or not, its authenticity is guaranteed by the frequent autograph corrections in important passages.

(c) Clearly a part of the same work, and with the same marks of authenticity, is the manuscript in possession of the Huntington Library in San Marino, California. It consists of a long chapter (unnumbered) "On the Divine Ideas"[1] devoted to the discussion of the problem of moral evil followed by part of a still longer one without a title, which begins with a carefully drawn out criticism of the Plotinian idea of the Trinity as contrasted with the Christian, but is chiefly occupied with the question of the sense in which it is possible to demonstrate the existence and attributes of God either on the ground of direct intuition, or as a logical inference from the data of experience. The discussion of Brahminism as an attempt of the former kind offers scope to the imaginative as well as the critical genius of the poet-philosopher of which he is not slow to avail himself. The manuscript abruptly ends in the middle of an introduction to a discussion of Berkeley's proof of the being of God in the *Minute Philosopher*.

It is possible, perhaps even probable, that other parts of the MS. of the *Opus Maximum* survive, and may still be found. Sufficient has been quoted from those which we have to show how far, on the subjects dealt with, they supersede all that is derivable from other sources. As compared with anything we have in the published works they show a mastery of the implications of his own fundamental principles, and a command of his materials that makes their fragmentary character all the more deplorable.

[1] When residing in Los Angeles for some months in 1928 I was unaware of the existence of this manuscript, and have only been able through the kindness of Professor Alice Snyder to read it in photostat copy since my return to England.

(*d*) Of unique interest, as containing autograph notes dating apparently from 1825 of his later views on many philosophical subjects, is the manuscript commonplace book with the characteristic title, "Semina Rerum, Audita, Cogitata, Cogitanda of a Man of Letters, friendless because of no Faction, repeatedly and in strong language inculpated of hiding his Light under a Bushel, yet destined to see publication after publication abused by the *Edinburgh Review*, as the representative of one Party, and not even noticed by the *Quarterly Review* as the Representative of the other—and to receive as the meed of his labours for the Cause of freedom against Despotry and Jacobinism, of the Church against Infidelity and Schism, and of Principle against Fashion and Sciolism, Slander, Loss, and Embarrassment". At the end it contains under the date May 24, 1828, a synopsis of his metaphysical system—"more nearly approaching", as Miss Snyder notes, [1] "the epic in the quality of its conception than do any of his published prose works"— placed on record "by S. T. C., R. A., R. S. L., etc.

> Author of Tomes, whereof tho' not in Dutch,
> The Public little knows, the Publisher too much."

(*e*) Coleridge's reputation as a philosophical thinker has suffered more from the evidences of plagiarism (whether conscious or unconscious) in his writings than from any other cause. What makes the multitudinous marginal notes on philosophical books used by him, that have come down to us, of such extreme value is the comment they enable us to make on this subject, through the proof they afford of the alertness of his critical faculty in regard to the authors from whom he is alleged to have plagiarized. For illustrations on fundamental doctrines the reader may be referred to the above Study. The sources themselves are not all accessible, but the most important of the notes are gradually becoming

[1] *Op. cit.*, p. 3, where the synopsis is printed at length.

available, and those which are most important for Coleridge's relation to contemporary philosophers are fortunately to be found in copies of works used by him which are preserved in the British Museum.[1] They include:—

Moses Mendelssohn's *Morgenstunden.* Erster Theil (1790), and his *Jerusalem* (1791).[2]

Baron von Wolff's *Logic* or *Rational Thoughts on the Powers of the Human Understanding* (Eng. Tr. 1770).[3]

Kant's *Vermischte Schriften; Die Religion innerhalb der Grenzen der blossen Vernunft* (1793); *Metaphysik der Sitten* (1797).

Fichte's *Bestimmung des Menschen* (1800); *Versuch einer Kritique aller Offenbarung* (1792).

Schelling's Ideen zu einer Philosophie der Natur (1803); *System des transcendentalen Idealismus* (1800).

Tennemann's *Geschichte der Philosophie,* twelve volumes (1794).

Hegel's *Wissenschaft der Logik,* 1812–16.[4]

Besides these, the present writer has been able to consult two volumes of *Marginalia,* transcribed by E. H. Coleridge under date November 6 and 7, 1889, from the originals in possession of Lord Coleridge of Ottery St. Mary's, containing notes, among other books, on Kant's *Critique of the Pure Reason;* Jacobi's *Comments on Maas's Versuch über die Lehre d. Spinoza in Briefen an den Herrn Moses Mendelssohn*; Kant's *Allgemeine Naturgeschichte und Theorie des Himmels*; Law's *English Version of the Works of Jacob Boehme,* which had been presented to Coleridge by De Quincey.[5] If these

---

[1] See Catalogue under S. T. Coleridge, *sub fin.* They are given out to be read only in North Reading Room.

[2] Professor Snyder has given an account of these notes and their relation to the text of the MS. *Logic* in the *Journal of English and Germanic Philosophy* for October 1929.

[3] Notes printed in full, Snyder, *Coleridge on Logic and Learning,* p. 158 foll. [4] Notes printed in full, Snyder, *op. cit.,* p. 162 foll.

[5] The annotations on Boehme are printed in *Modern Language Notes* for November 1927 (vol. xlii, No. 7, p. 434 foll.) by Miss Snyder.

and his other philosophical marginalia were collated and published, as De Quincey hoped they would be, they would form a unique record not only of Coleridge's enormous reading, but, in so far as they can be dated, of the growth of his opinions. Unfortunately they are seldom dated by Coleridge himself, and we are left to the more precarious light of internal evidence.

(f) If for no other reason than that of the light it throws on the single point of Coleridge's attitude to the evolution hypothesis,[1] the miscellaneous collection of fragments (British Museum, MS. Egerton 2801) deserves mention in this Appendix. The last of the sources mentioned in the above classification is peculiar enough, and has sufficient independent interest to have separate mention in a second Appendix.

[1] See above, p. 130. For other excerpts, see Snyder, *op. cit.*, pp. 75–7, and 153 n.

JOSEPH HENRY GREEN'S SPIRITUAL PHILOSOPHY

GREEN was the most philosophically cultured and the most devoted of Coleridge's disciples. Educated for the medical profession and becoming a distinguished member of it, he held successively the Professorship of Anatomy at the Royal College of Surgeons and that of Surgery, first at St. Thomas's Hospital, afterwards (on its foundation) at King's College. He was twice President of the Royal College of Surgeons, and twice delivered the Hunterian Oration (in 1840 and again in 1847). At what precise time he became acquainted with Coleridge is not known; but it seems certain that it must have been as early as 1817, the year in which the German poet and critic Ludwig Tieck paid a visit to England and met Coleridge more than once at Green's house. Green had been appointed Demonstrator in Anatomy at St. Thomas's the year before, but with his medical studies he combined a keen interest in German philosophy, and was fired by Tieck's reports of Solger's lectures in Berlin to pay a visit to Germany, before taking up his professional duties, and obtain first-hand knowledge of what was being there taught. Solger was much taken with him, and in a letter to Tieck describes the French philosopher, Cousin, who visited him subsequently, as "a sore change from our gallant Green".[1] The manner in which on his return from Germany his friendship with Coleridge ripened is familiar matter of the poet's biography.

Left as literary executor, at his friend's death, in possession of all his manuscripts, and with complete

[1] See for these and other particulars of Green's biography Dr. John Simon's Memoir prefixed to *Spiritual Philosophy*, of which he was the editor.

discretion as to publication, and at about the same time, by the death of his father, and the inheritance of his property, finding himself free from the necessity of continuing practice as a doctor, Green decided to devote himself thenceforth to his task, as philosophical trustee, conceived with truly Coleridgean amplitude. "Theology, Ethics, Politics and Political History, Ethnology, Language, Aesthetics, Psychology, Physics and the allied sciences, Biology, Logic, Mathematics, Pathology"—his biographer tells us, "were all thoughtfully studied by him, at least in their basial principles and metaphysics, and most were elaborately written of, as though for the divisions of some vast cyclopaedic work". Meanwhile, having been born, as Traill wittily puts it, "under post-diluvian conditions",[1] lest his master's main object of the vindication of religious doctrine should remain unfulfilled, he wrote, under the title of *Religio Laici*, a first sketch of what was subsequently recast under the title Spiritual Being, finally again recast to form the second volume of *Spiritual Philosophy*, in the Appendix to which Dr. Simon has printed long extracts from the earlier manuscripts.

The circumstances under which this work was finally produced have been already referred to.[2] The book has suffered undeserved neglect for the reasons there mentioned, and, where it has received particular notice, as in Traill's *Coleridge*, has been treated with still more undeserved cynicism. It is not a great work, and suffers from the same kind of conservativism that we have noted in Coleridge himself, and (with less excuse) from the same neglect to put himself in direct touch with post-Fichtean philosophy in Germany.[3] Of the

[1] *Coleridge*, in English Men of Letters Series, p. 185.
[2] P. 256 above.
[3] His knowledge of Hegel seems to have been derived at a bad second hand from Morell's *History of Philosophy* (see *Spiritual Philosophy*, vol. ii. p. 407 n.).

"School of Hegel", he has nothing better to say than that it denies the transcendence of Deity. But he was a man of real philosophical ability, and his training in physiology gave him a method of approach to philosophical problems which lent a certain freshness to much that he wrote.[1] The two Hunterian Orations on *Vital Dynamics* and *Mental Dynamics* respectively, in which he seeks to combine Coleridgean with Hunterian ideas, witness to the breadth of his culture and his power as a writer on non-theological subjects. In his chief work we do him wrong in giving the prominence, that Traill does, to the second and more theological part. Its editor is nearer the mark in saying that the space the Author devotes to it is disproportionate to its importance, as only one of a series of deductive applications of the principles, which he had made his own; and that, had Green been longer spared, he would probably have expanded the compendious statements of the first volume "with infinitely greater amplitude".

It is at any rate to the first volume, and particularly to the second part of it, that the student to-day will turn for light upon these principles, and the development of which they were capable at the hands of a particularly clear-minded writer. Yet even in the second volume readers interested in the interpretation of the Christian tradition in the light of Neo-Kantian thought will find a striking resemblance between its teaching and that of the author's greater namesake Thomas Hill Green, as we have it in his "Lectures on the New Testament", and in his Sermons on "Faith", and "The Witness of God" (*Works*, vol. iii). The book in this respect may be said to represent the last stage in the story of the Theological Idealism which was first planted in England by Scotus Erigena, took vigorous root and flourished in seventeenth- and early eighteenth-century Platonism,

[1] I have elsewhere remarked on the debt which Philosophy owes to the medical profession (*Mind*, N.S. 36, p. 439).

was revived by Coleridge, and loaded with a luxuriance of fruit that went near to bringing it to the ground, and is here reset in a form, which the writer trusted would enable it to renew its youth in the more critical atmosphere of his own time.

APPENDIX C

Passages from the MS. in the Henry E. Huntington Library, which the Librarian kindly permits to be printed here for the first time.

THE PROBLEM OF FINITUDE AND OF EVIL

[P. 10 foll.]

ARE we struck at beholding the cope of Heaven imaged in a dew-drop? The least of the animalcula to which that dew-drop is an ocean presents an infinite problem, of which the omnipresent is the only solution. If then even the philosophy of nature can remain philosophy only by rising above nature, and by abstracting from nature, much less is it possible for the philosophy of the Eternal to evolve out of itself, that is out of the pure reason, the actual existence of change, of the beginning of that which is, yet before was not, of that which has been and is not, of that which is not yet but is to come. The organs of philosophy are ideas only, and we arrive at ideas by abstracting from time: and this truth is so obvious that even in popular language we declare it impossible to form any idea of matter, of pleasure, or of pain. Yet shall we say that these are not? Is there no history because history, or the succession of acts and agents and of phenomena, considered as the effects, products, or results of acts and agents, is not the same with philosophy though it is grounded on it? Do the mechanical powers, the lever, the pulley, the screw, not exist because they are not the same with the immediate and magical and everywhere present powers, without which the former yet could not be? The passage from the absolute to the separated finite, this is the difficulty which who shall overcome? This is the chasm which ages have tried in vain to overbridge. If the finite be in no sense separate from the infinite, if it be one with the same, whence proceeded evil? For the finite can be one with the absolute, inasmuch only as it represents

the absolute verily under some particular form. Herein
no negation is implied, nor privation, no negation from
without, for it is the position of all in the each. But that
it is the form which it is (is) so far from being the result
of negation that even in the less imperfect shapes of the
senses, those which proceed from living forms as in all
objects of the organic world (take a plant as an instance),
this shape is at once the product and the sign of the
positive power of the plant; and a form, or rather a
parent-shape proceeding from negation, either simply or
in connection with an overpowering impression from
without, is found only in the inanimate: the termination
of the path of the arrow in the air, or the form of the
fragment storm-rent from the rock or of the aggregate
of sands in the pebble, which the pressure of the waters
has compressed, and the motion of the tide rounded.
But if, on the other hand, the finite here spoken of be
separate and diverse from the absolute, we might, indeed,
explain the evil therefrom, but then the question would
return how was the finite possible? I said hastily that
from such a finite we might educe the origin of evil:
but such a finite were Evil! Still the standing room, the
δὸς ποῦ στῶ, remains unanswered, unattained.

THE PRINCIPLE OF THE SOLUTION
[P. 39 foll.]

The solution is this. To God the idea is real, inasmuch
as it is one with that will, which, as we see in its
definition, is verily *Idem et Alter*; but to itself the idea
is absolutely real, in so far only as its particular will
affirms, and in affirming constitutes its particular reality
to have no true being except as a form of the universal,
and one with the universal Will. This, however, is the
affirmation of a will, and of a particular will. It must,
therefore, contain the potentiality, that is, the power of
possibly *not* affirming the identity of its reality with the
reality of God, which is actual absolutely (*Actus purissimus*

sine ullâ potentialitate) ; or of willing to be, yet not willing
to be only because God is, and in the being of God alone.
In other words, if the essence of its being be will, and
this will under a particular form, there must be a
possibility of willing the universal or absolute under
the predominance of the particular, instead of willing
the particular solely as the glory and presentation of the
plenitude of the universal. As long as this act remains
wholly potential, i.e. implied in the holy will as its
opposite, necessarily possible because, being a holy will,
it is a will, and a particular will, so long is it compatible with God, and so long therefore hath it an actual
reality as one of the eternal, immutable ideas of God.
But in the will to actualize this potentiality, or as in
common language we should say, in the will to convert
this possibility into a reality it necessarily makes—*it*self!
shall I say? or rather *a* self that is not God, and hence
by its own act becomes alien from God. But in God
all actual reality is contained : in making therefore a
Self that is not God all actuality is necessarily lost, a
potentiality alone remains . . a causativeness must remain,
for this is the essential of the will ; but it is a causativeness
that destroys, which annihilates the actual ; and, in the
potential swallowing up all actuality so that the potential
as merely potential remains the only form of its reality,
it is an act that may be said to realize the potential in
the moment of potentializing the alone truly real. What
would follow but a world of contradictions, when the
first self-constituting act is in its essence a contradiction?
The will to make a centre which is not a centre, a will
not the same with the absolute will, and yet not contained in the absolute, that is an absolute that is not
absolute.

An Old Illustration
[P. 124 foll.]

To borrow an illustration of spiritual truths, above all
of spiritual truths so unutterably transcendent, from the

most glorious objects of the senses or the most subtle and
refined forms of the material world is not without peril.
But I will venture to anticipate those higher views of
the material world, which I trust will be opened out in
the following section of this work, and after the example
of the inspired prophets, no less than of the ancient
sages, whose philosophy approached nearest to the
doctrines of inspiration :

> "We'll try to borrow from the glorious sun
> A little light to illustrate this act,
> Such as he is in his solstitial noon,
> When in the welkin there's no cloudy tract,
> For to make gross his beams and light refract.
> Then sweep by all those globes that by reflexion
> His long small shafts do rudely beaten back,
> And let his rays have undenied projection,
> And so we will pursue this mystery's retection."

Not more impossible is it to conceive the Sun, the tri-
unity of the *focus, lux et lumen,* to be in all its splendour,
and yet rayless, than to conceive the spiritual Sun without its effluence, the essentially causative will without
its co-eternal products. As long as the rays are part of
the glory, radiant distinctly, but without division, so long
are they one with the sun, and such must be from eternity
to eternity. But these spiritual rays are themselves essentially Wills, and have their causativeness, which is one
with that of the Divine will as long as they are rays of
the Sun. But if we could conceive any number as separate
from the solar orb and no longer a prolongation of its
effluence, strangled in clouds, and born(e?) anew as it were
in rainbows and the phantoms of the air, would there
be for this any loss or change in the sun or in the solar
sphere? But to what purpose do I adduce this symbol?
If the reader beholds and contemplates it in the spirit
of the corpuscular system, the utter differences will over-
lay the shadowy and less than poetic likeness, and set
into ferment the sensuous imagination which it is our

main desideratum to keep at rest, silent, and under a
veil? . . . I have no other answer to this objection,
but that I have found it a help in my own mind
to use this image, as the philosopher of Nola had
done before, as a mental diagram for the fixing of
the attention, and the ordinance of the memory,
as, in short, the best, most comprehensive, richest and
most flexible organ of a *memoria technica*: and this the
sun with its profundity of forms and forces, of lights and
shadows will not fail to present and without risk of error,
if only the main difficulty have been once thoroughly
apprehended, and in that very apprehension overcome
and disarmed, though not removed. It is enough to have
seen that it is a difficulty which arises out of our nature,
and while that nature remains, must remain with it . .
nay, will be active, as while the ear is deeply listening
to some sweet harmony from an unknown distance, the
eyes will gaze thitherward, even though it should have
been ascertained that it was the music of the air, such
as travellers are said to have heard in Ceylon and
Sumatra, produced by currents and counter-currents,
the glancing fingers of electric fire in the higher atmosphere.

Proofs of the Existence of God
[P. 145 foll.]

If we can prove that the failure in each particular scheme
is not attributable to any fault on the part of the reasoner,
which some following reasoner might correct, but to the
very nature of the proof itself, we shall have amply
demonstrated our position, that there is no speculative
proof, no properly scientific or logical demonstration
possible. In other words, that the idea of the Godhead
is the true source and indispensable precondition of all
our knowledge of God. That consequently all that is true
and valuable in any of the so-called proofs and demonstrations, consists of expositions of this idea, or the
different means, by which the understanding is enabled

to exemplify this idea in all its experiences, whether
inward or from without, whether derived from the sense
and the senses, or by reflection on itself and on its own
operations. Nor is this all—we must add (to) the theoretic
purpose answered by thus exemplifying the idea of God
the moral one of awakening the conscious attention of
the soul to the great idea with the emotions inseparable
from its due contemplation—which, so far from the idea
or knowledge being deduced or concluded from any or
all the particulars of sensation or reflexion, is that of
deriving these as components of a world (τοῦ κόσμου and
not τοῦ χάους) from this idea. The Reason [1] as the
living source of living and substantial verities, presents
the Idea to the individual mind and subjective intellect,
which receives and employs it to its own appropriate
ends, namely, to understand thereby both itself and all
its objects—receives it, I say, uncomprehended by it,
to comprehend the universe, the world without and the
yet more wonderful world within.

[1] Autograph note: I here use the word in its highest as well
as most comprehensive sense—and not for the mere Collectaneum
of *theoretic* principles, or of such speculative truths as are accompanied with the sense of unconditional necessity and absolute
universality.

BRAHMANISM

[P. 267 foll.]

There is in almost all the Sanscrit philosophical and
religious writings, as far as they have fallen under my
notice, a character, which, it seems to me, might be
plausibly accounted for on the supposition of childish
intellects living among gigantic objects, of mean thoughts
and huge things—living Lilliputs among inanimate Brob-
dignags. Thus their Pantheism or visible God, God,
proved to them, not from, but in and by the evidence
of their senses, taken in conjunction with the languor of
a relaxing climate and the lulling influence of a deep,
sombre and gigantic vegetation, seems to me a natural
result of an imbecile understanding, producing indis-
tinction, half from indolence and half intentionally by
a partial closure of the eyelids, and when all hues and
outlines melt into a garish mist deeming it unity.

The translator of the Bhagavad Gita finds in the story
of churning the ocean for the fourteen jewels, a wonderful
affinity to—Milton! I could not, I confess, help inferring
from this remark that taste does not resemble the wines
that improve by a voyage to and from India. For if there
be one character of genius predominant in Milton it is
this, that he never passes off bigness for greatness. Children never can make things big enough, and exactly so
is it with the poets of India.

It would be more than we are entitled to expect of
the human mind, if Sir W. Jones, Mr. Wilkins, etc., great
and good as we know them to have been, had not over-
rated the merit of works, the power of understanding
which is of such rare occurrence, and so difficultly
attained. In the present instance there is an additional
excuse; an excuse which more than acquits the judges,
though it cannot prevent the reversal of their decision;
for to the writings in question all the notions, images, and
feelings, which are best calculated to excite that obscure

awe, that lies midway between religion and superstition, hang and encluster. Their undoubted antiquity is so great, and the antiquity claimed for them at once so daring and so visionary that we might almost say *"liber ipse superstat"*, the book itself walks like a ghost of a departed world. There is a superstition involved in a survival so contrary to the ordinary experience of mankind. I have myself paid this debt of homage on my first presentation to these foreign potentates by aid of the great linguists above mentioned. But having so done, I sought to purge the sight with the euphrasy of common sense, and took a second and more leisurely view before I put the question to myself, "And what then have I seen?"

"What are
These Potentates of inmost Ind?"

Shall I confess the truth? Their next neighbour of the North, the temple-throned infant of Thibet, with the Himālā behind and the cradle of the Ganges at his feet, conveys to my mind an impressive likeness, seems to me a pregnant symbol of the whole Brahman Theosophy. Without growth, without production! Abstract the enormous shapes and phantasms the Himālā, the Ganges of the fancy, and what remains?—A baby! The personality and the additional mystery of secondary impersonation, metamorphoses, incarnations, these and all the attributes of persons, dance in and out like wandering flashes, or motley aliens from a distant country, the mutes of the show, often enough to remind us of their incompatibility with the doctrines of omneity and infinity, which are the constant theme and the philosophic import of the Indian theology; but without even an attempt to resolve the riddle. These impersonations or Avatars betray themselves as fables μυθοι half verbal and built on accidents of language, and half symbolical; though nothing can be more obscure and conjectural than their direct interpretation.

INDEX OF NAMES

GEORGE ALLEN & UNWIN LTD

Head office:
40 Museum Street, London, W.C.1
Telephone: 01-405 8577

Sales, Distribution and Accounts Departments
Park Lane, Hemel Hempstead, Herts.
Telephone: 0442 3244

Athens: 7 Stadiou Street, Athens 125
Auckland: P.O. Box 36013 Auckland 9
Barbados: P.O. Box 222, Bridgetown
Bombay: 103/5 Fort Street, Bombay 1
Calcutta: 285J Bepin Behari Ganguli Street, Calcutta 12
Dacca: Alico Building, 18 Motijheel, Dacca 2
Hong Kong: 105 Wing on Mansion, 26 Hankow Road, Kowloon
Ibadan: P.O. Box 62
Johannesburg: P.O. Box 23134, Joubert Park
Karachi: Karachi Chambers, McLeod Road, Karachi 2
Lahore: 22 Falettis' Hotel: Egerton Road
Madras: 2/18 Mount Road, Madras 2
Manila: P.O. Box 157, Quezon City D-502
Mexico: Serapio Rendon, 125, Mexico 4, D.F.
Nairobi: P.O. Box 30583
New Delhi: 1/18B Asaf Ali Road, New Delhi 1
Rio de Janeiro: Caixa Postal 2537-Zc-00
Singapore: 36c Prinsep Street, Singapore 7
Sydney: N.S.W. 2000: Bradbury House, 55 York Street
Tokyo: C.P.O. Box 1728, Tokyo 100-91
Toronto: 145 Adelaide Street West, Toronto 1

Our Land Too

Line 17 on page 207 should read "over 20 per cent" instead of "about 90 per cent."

TONY
DUNBAR

OUR LAND TOO

PANTHEON BOOKS

A Division of Random House New York

LIBRARY OF CONGRESS CATALOG CARD NUMBER: 72-135-040

International Standard Book Number: 0-394-46845-7

Photo Credits
Al Clayton: Figs. ii, iii, vi, vii
Fig. i and cover photograph by Al Clayton, reprinted by permission of
The World Publishing Company from *Still Hungry in America* by
Robert Coles. An NAL book. Photographs © 1969 by Al Clayton.
Jean Martin: Figs. iv, v, viii, ix

MANUFACTURED IN THE UNITED STATES OF AMERICA

BY THE HADDON CRAFTSMEN, INC., SCRANTON, PENNSYLVANIA

Designed by A. Christopher Simon

9 8 7 6 5 4 3 2

First Printing

TO RESISTERS
everywhere in this world,
and in memory of a warm person,
JAN BECKHARDT

Introduction

I have no wish in this introduction to come forth with paragraphs of uncritical praise, seasoned with a few efforts at synopsis. Mr. Dunbar is a serious young man, and he has done a first-rate job of describing what life is like in rural Mississippi and Appalachia, among other places in this rich and powerful nation. Since he is a good writer, as well as a thoughtful and careful observer, the reader needs no interpretation, no preliminary sermon that urges, prompts, reminds, explains, and insists. The pages ahead will soon enough compel their own attention, and for that I can only thank the author, as I believe others will want to do after they have finished this book. I do, however, want to say something about *Our Land Too*; I want to say something about the tradition to which the book belongs, and if the author will forgive me, I want to say something about his youth, his utter lack of credentials, his failure to "prepare" himself with "training" for the ever-so-complicated business of "research" he has so prematurely undertaken.

In the summer of 1936 a young man in his twenties left

New York City for Alabama because he wanted to learn how sharecroppers and tenant farmers lived. With him went a photographer (they were planning to do an article for a national magazine), and no doubt it is fair to say that the two men took with them the following "research materials": some pieces of paper, a pencil or two, a fountain pen, a camera. The men had not prepared a "proposal" for foundations, nor had they spent time writing up a "design" for their "investigation" or a statement of the "methodology" they intended to pursue. Upon their return they proclaimed no "results," no "findings" or "conclusions." They said they were troubled, were confused, were torn by a whole range of conflicting feelings. And indeed, as one goes through their long book one feels on every page a certain rambling quality, a strain of indecisiveness, a tone of perplexity. And one looks in vain for "strategies" or "techniques," for a theory about this or a formulation about that. Instead, James Agee and Walker Evans give us a book with the unlikely and incurably "romantic" title *Let Us Now Praise Famous Men*; give us a book that emphasizes life's ambiguities and ironies; give us a book that seems almost dedicated to emotions like wonder, awe, admiration —in contrast, that is, to brainy self-assurance, messianic zeal, political self-righteousness or academic snobbery.

Tony Dunbar is also in his twenties, his very early twenties. Unlike James Agee he doesn't even have a college degree. In fact, the work, the *living* it was, that prompted the writing of this book was done by what we call a "dropout." After a year or two of college Mr. Dunbar felt the need to leave, to travel, to go see, to go hear, to pay attention not to himself and his hangups and his "problems" and his sense of "alienation" and his present "goals" or his future "plans"—but rather to a portion of the larger world about him. So, he set out and traveled and eventually arrived in the Mississippi Delta.

There he tried to learn from men and women and chil-

dren, who became his teachers. There he struggled, as
James Agee did, as young George Orwell did, to comprehend not "problems" or "disadvantages" or "deprivations,"
but *lives*—yes, lives heavily burdened and threatened and
terribly hurt, but lives also full of stubborn, unyielding
determination and lives marked by moments of humor and
generosity and kindness. There he also struggled to get the
facts. How much money do these particular American
citizens make? What kind of work do they find, if they can
find any? Precisely how do they live—which means in what
buildings and with what furniture or food or clothes? What
do they see ahead for themselves? Do they have much hope?
Do they lack spirit and vitality? Do they feel as sorry for
themselves as some of us are wont to feel for them—during
those occasional moments that interrupt our busy, important lives?

The result of Mr. Dunbar's failures as a college student
was a thoroughly successful monograph ("The Will to
Survive") published by the Southern Regional Council, a
group of white and black southerners who are also dropouts
of sorts, dropouts from the racism and bigotry and meanness and exploitation that have characterized that lovely,
hate-filled, much scapegoated region whose writers (William
Faulkner, Eudora Welty, Flannery O'Connor, Walker
Percy) know a thing or two about how men and women
manage to survive against high odds indeed—and I refer
not only to hurdles like poverty and the legacy of slavery,
but the peculiar loneliness and inwardness, the psychological
jeopardy it is, a "soul" can sometimes experience out in
those isolated and apparently Godforsaken villages and
hamlets of the "black belt" or in thriving but uneasy cities
like Memphis or Atlanta or New Orleans. The title of Mr.
Dunbar's monograph and the title of his book tell us how
he is inclined to look at those who are hard-pressed and
unquestionably in certain respects doomed. They suffer,
but they persist. They need our "help," but they demon-

strate certain qualities that by no means are universally found among well-to-do intellectuals: a lack of nervous self-consciousness, a certain kind of tact and grace, a faith in God that will not be deterred, a wry and detached "world-view," not unlike an existential philosopher's or a Christian theologian's. Put differently, we are to learn in this book what people *have* as well as need. Particularly in the section that takes up the world of Appalachia we must contend with (almost) the author's unwillingness to make us the comfortable philanthropists, yet again asked to take up a few more liberal causes, write out an additional check or two, maybe sign another petition.

Up those hollows and creeks live people who are proud, who want no part of us, really—who want only work and money. It *is* their land; their ancestors came to this country, as did the slaves, a long, long time ago, and they every day give to the American land all the passion and concern they can muster. They work the land for food. Some of them still wrest coal from the land. They walk the land, hunt the animals who also live off the land, catch the fish that fill up the many rivers and lakes that cover the land. They know the land's needs; know its virtues and its limitations. They also know the pain that goes with seeing kin leave the land for the city, for distant and strange and crowded places that offer a degree of sanctuary to the hungry and jobless, but also "a long sleepless night," as I once heard a mountaineer from Kentucky describe his two years in Chicago. Nor are states like Mississippi or Alabama only the property of their foul-mouthed politicians or lawless sheriffs or violence-prone State Police. The poor of those states, regardless of race, also love the land; love the pinewoods; love the promising sunrises and flaming sunsets; love the wideness of the countryside, the elbowroom, the sounds of chickens or pigs, the sight of birds and bushes and wild flowers, the feel of feet touching pine needles or grass, the feel of a worm in the hand or of a turtle or a toad.

We who live in cities and call ourselves "educated" and buy books like this one tend to overlook the attachment, even reverence a sharecropper can feel for the earth he doesn't own and often fails to subdue. Over and over again we demand justice for the poor, but are not so willing to discover what form that justice would take if the poor had *their* way. And how can we know? We have our own lives, tied as they are to cities and professions and universities and particular newspapers or magazines. When we travel it is not ordinarily to eastern Kentucky's hollows or Mississippi's back roads and dirt paths and small, dusty towns that can be entered and left within seconds when driving one of today's cars. We know statistics, and our hearts are no doubt moved when a story or an article reaches us, or when a moment of historical change comes upon us; but for the most part our sympathies can only be vague and inactive and worst of all abstract—*for* "blacks" or *against* "segregationists."

Nor do some social scientists help us. They give us more abstractions. help us feel better informed, more in command of numbers, percentages, and a host of "explanations," often phrased in language guaranteed to stop the heart and dampen the spirit and clutter the mind. And the irony of it is that for all the "studies" and "projects" done in twentieth century America only certain things get investigated— which is to say we are victims of our own particular intellectual prejudices. If we set out to "expose poverty," measure the "cultural deficits" of people, show how "retarded" they are and how saturated with apathy and ignorance and despair—then we find what we are looking for, and in the bargain spend millions of dollars on the incredible refinements of surveys and "controlled experiments" and "in-depth" analyses. Meanwhile we have as fellow citizens the mountaineers and sharecroppers and former tenant farmers Tony Dunbar has visited and lived with and tried to bring before us. Have our many methodical investigators, our thousands of social scientists, managed to tell us more about Alabama's sharecroppers than James Agee did, or more about Mississippi and Appalachia than Tony Dunbar offers in this book?

Our Land Too is the work of a keen social observer, a fine essayist—and a young social observer or a young essayist will not usually find such interests and capacities sanctioned by our universities as "academic fields" in which students can "concentrate" or "major." I hope this book is read by great numbers of young Americans who are tired of the pomposities and banalities that flourish in many of those universities. I hope many, many young Americans, yet to die in spirit, will be able to see what achievements were possible for one of their age and their inexperience.

A century ago one would talk not of the *motivations* a "researcher" had, or the *data* he accumulated, but of the *sensibility* in a young man, and what came of that sensibility when he sat down to write. Because Mr. Dunbar used his eyes and ears and head and paid attention to his heart, he was able to record faithfully two human scenes, as it were. And because he has done so, we the educated have a chance to learn what others (the uneducated) have to say, and to teach.

If I had more confidence that any number of changes are soon forthcoming in our universities and our public life, I would say that this book will inspire many colleges and universities to change their notion of what a "course" is, how students learn, what young and sensitive men and women might *do* during those four years they spend as "students" in places called "institutions of higher learning." But I fear this book will budge certain people not an inch: bureaucrats of all sorts, parochial experts, those in medicine and law and the universities and government who can always find sanctuary in the infinite recesses that professional double talk always provides. If some readers find that this book's author has done enough, even more than enough in praise of famous men James Agee and Walker Evans once sang of and hailed and grieved for and rejoiced in, then I fear others will rather quickly recognize *Our Land Too* for the threat it presents not just to entrenched political and economic interests, but to many of us who are educated to the nth degree—which often enough comes to mean stiff and haughty and self-satisfied, if not fatally compromised.

ROBERT COLES

Foreword

A nation which has existed only a few hundred years may not be expected to have too much in the way of foundations. We in America, however, have built with amazing speed, and whatever stages in the process of development we have skipped in fact we have created in our imagination. A belief very dear to us is that there was once a time when a harmonious relationship was established between men and the work which they did, that honest enterprise, untainted by exploitation, was the keystone of American growth. We like to think that the great energy which set this country on its way was provided by men whose toil was spurred on by a vision of a bountiful future for all. We have attributed to our ancestors a commonness of purpose and a simplicity of life they did not have.

Our nation today has become a very sour place to live. There is very little to promise peace, security, or satisfaction to any of us. It is our basic feeling that in some way we have deviated from the promise of America more clearly seen by our forebears. To get to the source of the problem, we search about in our society to try and find the culprits who are causing all of this trouble.

It would be better if we took an honest look at some places where the reflection of the past is still clear; where we can get a more true idea of how it was that this country was built. America has not really changed much over the years in its conduct toward land and people. Where that conduct leads us can be seen in the Delta of Mississippi and in the mountains of East Kentucky.

No two regions have figured more prominently in the growth of America than the cotton lands of the South and the coal belt of the Appalachian Mountains. The one gave us a great agricultural empire, and the other gave us the power to run our machines and the raw material to build our cities. If ever this country laid foundations, they must be found in these areas. If anywhere we can hope to find a past real enough to learn from and a clear representation of attitudes that were and are central to the American system, it is in the mountains and the Deep South.

In rural America, the greatest concentration of poor blacks is in the Deep South; the greatest concentration of poor whites is in the southern Appalachians. Both areas have had their economies geared to one central output, one main source of work. Both have experienced the shift from plentiful jobs to unemployment created by automation. Both areas lack any modern industry and are extremely vulnerable to any industry which thrives on the economic castaway—the displaced tenant farmer or the out-of-work coal miner—who can be got to work dirt-cheap.

Both areas have experienced major social upheavals. The United Mine Workers' sweep of the mountains under John L. Lewis was the greatest union spectacle in our history. Mississippi felt the impact of the civil rights movement probably more than did any other Dixie state. Both areas are still very much in turmoil.

Mississippi and Appalachia are this country's best-known poverty areas. As real places—American as Texas and Florida, as the home of real people—not creatures to be experimented with but men to be dealt with, they have been largely forgotten by outside Americans because they have been mentioned so often. They have been neglected, to our continuing loss, as places where our system's attitudes toward people, the land and its resources, and the future can be evaluated. The War on Poverty struck with unmatched fanfare in these areas. Yet only feeble efforts have been made to change things, and little has been learned here.

It is unlikely that any one book can give a sense of the great stretch of history encompassed by the mountains and the Delta. This work tries only to show where that history has left the men and women who today have inherited these regions. The author lays no claim to being entirely objective. Though nearly all the statements made on tape for the section on Kentucky were included, only about a quarter of the dialogue, taken from about two-thirds of the interviews, were included in "The Will to Survive."

Throughout this book are the thoughts, expounded by several persons, that poor people must be viewed as men and women and as neighbors, not as statistics; that the solutions to their problems lie less in welfare doles than in radical alterations of the economics governing poor communities; that the people who have a problem are most likely to have the clearest insight as to how to solve it, and that the problems of the poor in Mississippi and Kentucky are shared, though not yet felt, by each of us across this land.

Contents

Author's Note

The two sections of this book, "The Will to Survive" and "Once The Promised Land," were prepared respectively in the fall of 1968 and during all of 1969. The first is an account of conditions in the Mississippi Delta as reported by some one hundred families who live there and tenant-farm on plantations. The second is an attempt to describe the people and the problems of the Kentucky mountains as viewed by this writer and by a retired coal miner, resident of one of the state's poorest counties.

Part I

THE WILL TO SURVIVE

❴ Well, you know what I figure about it, if I treat you right, you treat me right. That's the way I feel. A man is a man regardless to the size. You're a man just like I is, only thing is you're white and I'm dark, but we're still men. I ain't gonna come back here and curse you just like you're an old dog. You know I just don't feel that's right in my book. If I curse you, why you can curse me. Kick me, hit me, treat me like a dog—why that ain't right. I've heard fellers say, Now you take that one-armed son of a bitch and knock him in the head. I say, No, ain't nobody gonna knock me.

Quit talkin' about my luck. You can have it son. I cut my arm off in a truck side-swipe, and they couldn't help me, but still, anything you ask me to do, I'm willin' to do it, see.

A black tenant farmer, beaten and shot to death in the spring of 1970 after an incident outside a "white" nightspot in Louise, Mississippi. His body was later dragged from the Sunflower River.

The Louise-Midnight area, like all the Delta, is plantation country. About half of the white men in Louise own, manage, or are agents on plantations. The others are small farmers, factory workers in Belzoni (fifteen miles to the north), or work at such jobs as service station attendants and mechanics. Almost all the black families are tenant farmers on plantations, though some are sharecroppers and small farm owners. Louise and Midnight are towns that were built originally for the convenience of planters who preferred to shop, and to have their tenants shop, at stores nearby that they themselves owned. The borders of the towns are also the borders of plantations. When U.S. 49, running north through Louise to Belzoni and south to Yazoo City, was paved in the late 1940s, they were, as it is said, put on the map.

Louise is a row of about fifteen grocery, clothing, and auto parts stores along the highway, a post office, a plantation company headquarters, a doctor's office, a cafe, a dairy bar, three gas stations, a cotton gin, and a huge bean elevator. Behind the shops on one side of the highway is a paved street where the white townsfolk live. Behind the elevator on the other side is a network of dirt roads cut by the Illinois Central Railroad, where the black families live. Regardless of the official town estimate of 481 population, Louise looks to have about three hundred people within its town limits.

Midnight is barely a town at all; it is not incorporated. It has two stores, one gas station, and two company cotton gins. The homes of the tenant farmers come right up to the highway. The town is so small that generally it will not be mentioned in this report. The Louise community can be understood to include Midnight and the surrounding area, most of which is divided into several large plantations. The large plantations have from five to twenty regularly employed tenants. There are several smaller plantations with fewer than five tenant families, and there are many individually operated farms.

I lived in the homes of poor black families in the country between Louise and Midnight for seven weeks during September, October, and November of 1968. With the help of some very courageous citizens of those towns and the receptiveness of the black community as a whole, tape recordings were made of forty-five-minute-long interviews with ninety-seven poor families in Louise and on surrounding plantations and with three community leaders. During the course of the project, only two families refused to be interviewed. The ninety-seven families whose interviews were taped have a total membership of 690 people, of whom 500 are children. The average family size is 7.1 persons. Average family income is $1,538 a year; per capita income of the 690 people is $216. The chief suppliers of income are the plantation, Social Security, and welfare.

The number of families whose statements were recorded represent approximately one-fifth of those in the black community in the Louise area, and, in fact, approximately one out of every thirty-seven families, white and black, in the county. Though the study was concerned only in an incidental way with the whole of Humphreys County, the people covered by the interviews account for one out of every twenty-nine in the total population of the county. (Each interview in the text is designated by a ⦅.)

Without exception, the black people of Louise are poor, neglected, and deprived of everything that makes life pleasant, comfortable, or simple. This report is a description of the things that make the lives of the poor in the Delta not so much liveable as possible, and why existence is becoming more difficult in each succeeding year.

The title, "The Will to Survive," was chosen, rather than one relating directly to food problems, because it is hard to say which is worse—a man's hunger, or, say, the fact that he almost froze to death in the winter because his house was unsound and unheated. Poverty does not produce situations where a family has some major problems and some minor ones. All problems are major, and all needs are filled only with great difficulty. For the poor man, however, survival implies, above all else, obtaining food, and the poorer he is, the more he is involved in trying to provide food for his family. It is for him a constant struggle and a constant searching.

❲ I think it's terrible here. Mississippi is real terrible. I think the plantation is terrible, too, because all the people have to depend on is the work on the plantation, and most of the people living on the plantation don't ever get a chance to work.

I The Plantation

October is the first cold month in the Mississippi Delta. In the very early morning hours, a mist rises from each dew-and-frost-covered plant in the long straight rows of cotton. It drifts up out of the ditches, out of the creeks, out of the swamps. The first sunlight, streaking through the fringe of trees that mark the border between one man's land and another's or between what has been cultivated and what (with all the promise of a country farmed for over 150 years and still holding out more) has yet to be cleared, brings the mist alive, making the asphalt seem to shimmer and disappear in front of a driver, obscuring the dirt roads that branch out occasionally due east and due west, and turning into dark shadows the stumps and trees that grow, five feet deep in water and mud, in the stillness of the swamps.

As the sun rises, the mist thins away and the flat fertile land of the Delta reveals itself. From Memphis, Tennessee, to Yazoo City, Mississippi, a distance of some 175 miles, there is barely a rise in the plain except for the levees that wind beside the rivers flowing toward the Mississippi. Across those miles of endless field—cotton and soybean— trees serve as landmarks ("Go on down the gravel and turn

6

down the road headin' toward that tree yonder"), and towns
three miles distant can be located by their water towers or
bean elevators. By nine o'clock tractors, mechanical cotton
pickers, and bean combines are in the field. By ten o'clock
it is hot. The land dries out. Long billowing clouds of dust
follow the old automobiles and pickup trucks as they rumble
along the dirt roads.

All day long the heat builds up. The sun shines pale
yellow in the sky. Trailers full of cotton and bean trucks take
over the blacktops, on the one side, into the fields, and on
the other toward the gins and weighing stations where the
drivers will see to the unloading of their vans and drink
a bottle of Coke.

A haze of heat, dust, crop spray, and smoke comes up
in the late afternoon. It coats the faces and arms of the
men in the fields and fouls their machines. The sun begins
to set near six o'clock. Even after it is gone, wide orange
and red streaks of light hang against the horizon like clouds
of compressed heat left behind. They are still there when,
an hour later, the men head home because it has turned
too dark and cold to work. Only rarely, when there is a
great rush to get in the crop, will men be kept at work long
after dark; then, late at night, the headlamps of their combines can be seen moving slowly up and down the fields,
through the chilly fog, while only the faraway lights of
town remain lit.

Five years ago everybody who needed to and anyone who
wanted to—men, women, and children too young for school
—would have been working in these fields in October, picking cotton at $2.50 per 100 pounds. Some of the children
would have put down their sacks to catch the school bus;
most would have kept to their work. They would have
worked through the day, eating for lunch and supper sand-
wiches that they had stuffed in their pockets. Many of the
women would have their babies with them. Each time a
bag was filled, it would be dragged to the storage shed to be

weighed and that weight logged beside the picker's name. The people would stay in the fields until well after dark, when at the signal of the agent all of the hands would stand up, straighten out their backs, and stand in line until each's name was called, the pounds each had picked totaled, and the wage, minus the rental fee for the bag, figured and paid out. The trucks would come and take them home.

❮ *How many men work this plantation now?*
They got about six of 'em, steady drivers.
Just as a guess, how many families would have been working here ten years ago?
About thirty of 'em.
Men, women, and children?
Everybody, yes sir. Them that wasn't big enough was out there. They was out there makin' a day.

❮ There used to be a whole lot more people on the plantations than there are now. The machines started long back in '50. I believe it started really back in '53, '54. Then every year they begin to get more and more, more and more, and that begin to cut people down out of pickin', you know. In other words, before that they were pickin' all the crop. Then after machines got in, they started pickin' ends, see. And so now, the biggest of 'em not pickin' none.

Almost all of the land surrounding Louise is divided into plantations. The smallest ones are only a few hundred acres; the largest are many square miles. Plantation land is farmed in two ways: by tenant farmers or by sharecroppers, all of whom are black. A tenant farmer (or what could better be called a tenant family) lives on the plantation in a house provided by the planter. In exchange for this, he is on call day or night, year round, to do any work that the planter requires, and he is paid for his work. Sharecropping, which has been considered virtually extinct for fifteen years, still persists in scattered instances around Louise. A sharecropper is given a piece of land, usually less than twenty acres, to farm. At harvest, he splits his crop between himself and the planter. Though the ratio between what the planter collects and what the cropper is left with is generally 60–40, they divide the crop evenly in Louise. To make any cash income at all, a sharecropper must double as a tenant farmer.

    (This is the way it is on the plantation. You borrow money during the winter to help take care of your family. So when you start work, you're gonna work—now a tractor driver don't make but about six to eight dollars a day, and he gotta pay this man half of this money out of his wages, for what he borrowed back in the winter. And after this, well it's gonna start rainin' and things, well he got to go back and borrow some more money. Well he's just sold there. And he just pay him anything he wants to pay him—just give him anything—because he's there. He owes the man. He can't do nothin'. He got to take what he gets. Or either run off . . . . Yeah, they'll starve you off. I once heard that they say if you can't beat 'em, starve 'em to death.

A plantation, in the real sense, is an authoritarian world, ruled by a planter, where families earn with their sweat and labor the privilege of staying alive. The plantation system easily absorbed the shift from slavery to paid labor. Workers were simply paid too little money to live and went immediately in debt to the planter. The numerous ways of putting a tenant in debt were the planter's tools in exercising his authority. Tenants exhausted their cash at company stores and began to buy on credit. At times, the exchange was simplified by paying labor in scrip for use at company-owned stores. When he needed medical care, a tenant would go see his boss, who would provide a doctor and deduct the expense from the wage. When he needed a loan to provide for his family in the winter, the tenant would go to the planter. With the advent of electricity, the planter paid tenants' light bills and reduced by that much their paychecks.

The planter remained the boss in his land. He settled all disputes between his tenants in his own way. The horrible stories of the treatment of black tenant farmers by the white overseer, now called an agent, are probably almost all true. No sheriff would arrest a tenant without the permission of the planter, and it was often withheld for some planters preferred to exact their own punishments. No sheriff would refuse to arrest a man fingered by the planter. It is quite likely that some Mississippi law enforcement officers never saw more of many plantations than the dirt road leading to the door of the planter's house where they were told to turn around and get out. The sovereignty of the planter on his own land was never questioned before or after slave days.

The transition to a wage economy did change the Delta in some ways. Many landowners found that a practical way to avoid the use of cash was to begin sharecropping their land. It was also possible for a very industrious and fortunate few of the black workers to save enough money from the wages of a tenant farmer or the proceeds from cropping to buy sections of land. Since the 1940s, a number of small farms have been set up in Humphreys County by men raised as tenant farmers. Their owners have often helped to bring relatives off the plantations by giving them pieces of the newly acquired land to sharecrop. The planter, however, retained control, at least into the 1950s, over the independent sharecropper and the small farmer. Farming income is seasonal. If any money is to be made, it will come in the late fall and will be spent by spring. Small farmers require a "furnish," a loan to cover all farm and personal expenses for the six months of the year spent in planting and waiting for the crop. The Farmers Home Administration, which offers the same type of service to the farmer that the Federal Housing Authority does to the city dweller, has loans to serve this purpose, but in the 1940s and '50s black farmers had trouble being approved for them. While many turned to the banks for furnishing, most took the familiar path and received loans from the large planters. The practice continues today though a few small farmers have begun to take advantage of the recently relaxed policies of the FHA.

For the most part, the plantation system and the relation of tenant to planter remained basically the same from its beginnings until the late 1950s. Then, the forces of the first hallelujahs of the civil rights movement, of a northward migration again getting into swing, and of a new idea in agricultural efficiency—mechanization—converged on plantation country and began to alter the system in such a way that some day its back will be broken. But in the meantime, it will take a great toll in human suffering.

❲ Now, I've seen the time when we'd come home from school, and we'd go into the fields, make about six bits, a dollar, picking cotton by the hundred. But in the fields now, there ain't nothin' doin'. It looks lonesome. Ain't nobody workin' in it 'cept cotton pickers. Machines— that's all it is . . . . I seen the time when we had great big long trailers about as long as this house. I'us pickin' then two-fifty, three, when I was in the prime, sometimes four. I could live. People ain't gettin' nowhere. They're just managing alone. I don't know. See what if there come a snow on these people. I don't know what we'd do—me and all the rest. We'd have to make snow bread or something.

In 1960, before the machines had completely taken over, a plantation of any size would have had ten to forty tenant families. Their shacks would have been strung along the dirt roads as little neighborhoods a half mile long, where every family drank from a single faucet by the road and often shared common outhouses. All of the people, perhaps numbering several hundred, would work every day that it did not rain throughout the spring, chopping cotton in the summer and picking cotton in the fall. The wage was poor, averaging three to five dollars a day for men and considerably less for women and children.

Today only the skilled men have jobs; manual labor has seen its day on Delta plantations. Poison sprayed from crop-dusting planes has ended the demand for cotton choppers. Mechanical cotton pickers, looking insect-like with their large awkward bins angling out above their tiny wheel base, have replaced hand pickers, except at the ends of the rows where the picker makes its turn and cannot reap cleanly for a stretch about fifteen feet deep in the row. Here the women still can get a few sacks. With the reduction of cotton allotments to southern planters and the wider use and availability of machines, soybeans, a crop that cannot be picked by hand, have begun to challenge King Cotton in the Delta. Some planters like to keep their bean fields neater than crop dusters can make them, and here again there is occasional work for the women and children.

¶ Now the people don't live on the plantations like they used to. All the houses are tore down. Maybe on some plantations the people are living out there, and maybe on some about ten or twelve families. Then there are some plantations here that have families there that never been further than there. They've been there all their lives.

Have they been putting people off the land?

Well, I think the people moved off the land 'cause there wasn't any work to do.

When did the people first start moving out?

About in '63. Way back. Because of the machines and this new stuff they use to kill the grass.

Men too old to learn to handle machines, but who have spent their lives on the plantation, stay on by the grace of the planter and can find no work at all.

⟨ Well, I don't do anythin' now. For the past six years—well I used to farm, but after I got in bad health, I started haulin' and hoein', but I ain't did a thing like that since they got to the place where they just about stopped pickin' cotton and hoein'. So I just take it easy now, I reckon.

Do you have any income?

No sir.

At least half of the tenants on the plantations around Louise do almost no work. They are women without husbands, old people, sick people, unskilled people. There is no evidence that there is everywhere a concerted drive on to evict them, yet nothing is being done to provide them with the means to stay alive.

⟨ *What do you do, Mrs.———?*

Well, right now, we're pickin' cotton.

About how many months out of a year do you work?

Well right now, I'd say about two because they usually put the cotton pickers in to pick the cotton.

How much did the two of you make this week?

Ten dollars and sixty-two cents.

If you did well, would you make closer to twenty dollars?

Well no, 'cause I'm not a very good cotton picker. See, you'd have to average 200 pounds a day to make twenty dollars, and I'm not a very good cotton picker. Some days I pick eighty, some days ninety. And in the morning you can't go out early because of the dew. They don't want you to pick it when it's too wet.

The unskilled men too young to be tied down by families of their own leave the Delta and the state for the jobs in the North. In Louise, there are virtually no young men between the ages of eighteen and twenty-five. Only one or two members of each class that graduates from the black high school in Louise can still be found in the county a year later.

(*Do you think your children will ever come back from Chicago?*

They would come back and go to the field if they could make anything. They don't mind, my children don't mind, real work. *But,* it's just workin' and not gettin' nothin' out of it. Now when they was here, I wasn't able to give them anything. I was glad they left.

It is difficult to operate farm machines—tractors, bull-dozers, cotton pickers, and combines—and difficult to run a cotton gin. A bean combine, for example, must be watched by a mechanic at all times, or be operated by an especially determined and talented driver. Parts break down; engine belts snap; the machine jams. A ginning operation must run constantly to process the flow of raw cotton at harvest, and something in a cotton gin will break every day. To operate and understand heavy farm machinery is not an easily acquired knack, and planters do not want to employ anyone who does not have it. A heavy-duty tractor (the kind commonly used in the Delta) costs a minimum of $5,000. A combine costs well over $20,000. The obvious risk of putting a barely-skilled or untrained man on a $20,000 machine has meant the birth, though not yet the maturity, of a competitive market for labor.

This does not imply that there is any bidding on the price of skilled labor. The minimum wage is everywhere the same for the tenant farmer: $1.00 an hour in 1967, $1.15 an hour in 1968, and $1.30 an hour in 1969. But some planters do try to entice tenants away by promising more work. It is hard, however, to foster competition among planters accustomed to cooperation. No planter in Louise has made any real attempt to improve the tenant homes or to invest in better machines, e.g., tractors with heated cabs, though these are the current bargaining factors in other areas and are guaranteed to attract the finest hands in the county. Real competition is still reserved for the giant plantations.

The small planters prefer to let workers come to them and ask for jobs. For a variety of reasons, including age, family, children, and tradition, most tenant farmers do not search around for jobs on the large or newly-organized plantations. The single men do, of course, and they follow the work to Florida, then to New York in the winter and spring, and back to Mississippi for planting and harvest. For the skilled tenant farmer, the new status has meant that he is now the breadwinner of the family, that he can, to a degree, bargain with the agent, that his economic utility is visibly equal to or greater than that of any white man, and, importantly, that if he cannot get enough work to do on one plantation, or is kicked off, he can usually find a new job.

The Minimum Wage Law of 1966, which for the first time set the wage for agricultural employees, dealt the death blow to unskilled labor and expendable skilled labor on the plantations. Until that time, the wage of the tenant farmer had fluctuated around three dollars a day, and women and children could work full time picking cotton on a piece-rate basis. All of these people, except the children, came under the new law and were entitled to one dollar an hour beginning in 1967. Though some planters in Louise do not pay the wage, or pay a straight time salary that falls below the minimum wage, or unfairly calculate the number of hours that their tenants work, most follow, more or less, the dictates of the law and in doing so cut from their work lists all but the essential laborers. In the case of large families, the law has had the unfortunate effect of putting the wife and older children out of work, placing the responsibility for earning money solely on the man, and while increasing his earnings, leaving unchanged the total family income.

(At first, the machines started throwin' people off the plantation, and after the wage law came along that made plantation owners buy more machines and put more people off.

❲ *What is the most pressing problem of the people here?*

Finance. Finance is the most pressing problem. The people need work to do. That's the problem: they can't find it . . . . If they leave, the people would have to have money to leave on. Well naturally, they don't have the money. If I was on the plantation and couldn't find any work to do, well I would have to leave here and try to find myself a job. I would have to have money to take me over until I found a job, and if I couldn't find a job right away I would have to turn around and come back before the little money I had run out. That's the main reason that people don't leave the plantations whenever they are displaced from work.

The tenant farmers are poor because they cannot earn enough to live on. Those who stay on the land work by the hour and work only when called upon by the agent. Some labor for "straight time," a minimal salary paid all year round. For most, there is no work when it rains, and it rains frequently in the farming season. For most, there is no work at all in the winter, and they then borrow heavily from the planter, accumulating a debt that reduces their spring and fall wage below any humane calculation of what it costs to raise a family.[1]

❲ *Do you work on the plantation?*
Yes.
What do you do?
I drive a tractor.
Is that a full-time job?

[1] The 1960 population of Humphreys County was 19,093. In 1966, it had fallen to 18,700. The non-white population was 65.8 per cent of the total. In 1960 there were 3,911 families in the county. According to the Social Security Administration income scale, 2,324 of the 2,493 non-white families were poor, and 484 of the 1,418 white families were poor. Thirty-five per cent of the population had failed to complete four years of school and were thus functionally illiterate. The unemployment rate in the county in 1960 was 5.9 per cent.

No sir, sure ain't.
Just part of the year?
Part of the year. I'd say just six months out of a year, six or seven good months.
How much can you make during the six months?
Oh, I don't know. About a couple thousand dollars, I reckon. Might, I doubt it.
How do you make it by the other six months?
Well, I just do the best I can.
How many people do you have living here?
Let's see. I got nine. Seven kids and my wife.

Some women work as maids or cooks or sew and quilt for neighbors. A maid in Louise is paid three dollars a day. A quilt can be sold for from three to five dollars.

《 Before I worked for CDGM² I worked as a maid. I would get three dolars a day; go to work at seven, get off at any time, for my thirteen children . . . .

《 *Do you have any income, sir?*
No sir.
Are you employed, ma'am?
I draws welfare, and sewing, that's all I do.
How much do you make from your sewing?
'Cordin' to the sewing I get. Sometimes I make four to five, six dollars per week. Sometimes I don't make nothing.
How large is your welfare check?
Fifty dollars. [a month]

《 *Where do you work?*
I works here on the farm.
What do you do on the farm?
Oh, tractor driving. Just anything in farm work he got to do.

---

² Child Development Group of Mississippi, a multi-county Head Start program which employs as teachers, aides, cooks, and drivers many poor black mothers. See pp. 67–68.

About how often do you work?

Well, I works pretty often, 'cause I'm workin' for straight time, but I count it for nothin'. I make about thirty-five dollars a week, straight through the year . . . . No raise, no cut, and really I just account that for nothing. You just can't hardly get through on it. I have all my debts to pay, doctor bills, my house expenses, all that to keep up. Doctor bills, food stamps, all of that.

Did the man who owns the plantation help you with the doctor's bills?

Well, he'll stand for them, but you got to pay him. I've got to pay him out of this weekly salary that I told you about . . . . I have a certain amount that I pays if I have to have a little extra debt. I have a certain amount to pay. I live out of about twenty-five dollars a week of that money, and I take the rest of that for my little bills . . . . Naturally, you can't pay this debt right away. Pay that and live too, you see. If I had to just pay a big amount, I wouldn't live at all. Really, I get just enough to eat on.

How large is your family?

They's ten of us—five in school.

How many hours do you usually make a day?

I don't have hours. I make from sunup to sundown and sometimes an hour or two at night, this time of year haulin' cotton. Now a straight time salary it would do pretty good—if it paid enough. There's some few, some few men in this county, pays about fifty dollars a week. If I could get the work to do steady enough, on the hour basis, I'd rather by the hour, but if I go by the hour I can't feed my family 'cause I can't get the work to do. More'n generally of us will work cheap—straight time and cheap—then you gets work all the time. It's the only way you can get work to do, but you don't get nothing for your work. But if you go by the hour then they'll swear they don't have the work to do, and you'll sit down and half the time you can't keep yourself fed. You don't get nothin' in the winter at all. You don't get nothin' in the winter.

⟨ Well, my income is poorly. I didn't have no income further than the furnish. I get six months furnish to make the crop.

In an average year, how much do you make above the furnish?

Sometime I don't make anything.

How do you get through the last six months of the year?

Well I just have to do the best I can . . . . If it takes it all to pay what I owe, well it gets it all . . . . Before I got behind—I got behind by havin' years of short crops— before I got behind I was doing pretty good. I was making twelve, fifteen hundred dollars after I cleared up my indebtedness. But now, I haven't paid that in five years. I've been behind that long. We had three bad years. It rained and the crop was very short. So that just put me in bad shape . . . This year I *might* pay out and I might not.

The small farm owner has been plagued for the last several years with crops that just will not pay the bills. He, too, has been forced by the economics of modern agriculture to abandon most manual labor. He must own a tractor to put in the crop, and most likely will have to hire a cotton picker to get the crop in. Should he, in the face of the constantly worsening market for cotton and cotton seed, choose to plant soybeans, he will have to pay a man with a combine to harvest his crop for about 15 per cent of the market value. Since price supports are based on acreage, the small landowner gets virtually no federal help. As a landowner, he is usually considered to be too well off to receive any benefits from any programs of the welfare department, including food stamps and commodities. To buy seed, fertilizer, weed poisons, and everything else that is needed to farm he must obtain a furnish to cover all non-equipment farm expenses for the six months from planting to harvest. The furnish includes a small monthly amount for living expenses. Many small farmers cannot from year to year repay their furnishes, at the normal 6 to 8 per cent interest, from the proceeds of their crop.

What is your income from farming?
My income? Well for the last two or three years, it hadn't been nothin' . . . nothin' to amount to nothin'.
Do you meet the payments on your furnish?
Well I didn't pay it last year . . . Last year I didn't make but eleven bales, and I know the way it was last year we didn't make more than $75–$80 a bale. I'll tell you the truth about how we make it. Our kids what finished school up North send us money now and then. We wouldn't make it without that.

Many are able to break even; only a few clear money above their furnish and equipment costs. While it is true that they can raise much of what they eat, their cash income is so incredibly low that in all things but food, they survive on a level at or below that of the tenant farmer.

For the last four or five years, all of us farmers done about alike. Ain't none of us made no money on the farm . . . . We got a tractor there that we pay a note on that costs $5,700 net, nothing but the tractor, $5,700 for that tractor to farm that 120 acres of land, and we have seven years to pay for it, and we have to pay $1,000 a year. And we actually haven't made no money in the last four years. All us farmers are based just about alike.
Neighbor: Look like the little people, the little farmers, he'll have to come off the farm 'cause they can't operate no farm.

There are almost no non-farm jobs for men in Louise. Belzoni is becoming a manufacturing town, but few black men are hired by local industry. The young men, both white and black, in Humphreys County for the most part want nothing to do with farming. They look at the meager return that comes from independent farming, and the indignity and low wage that is the lot of the tenant, and they leave the county. The manufacturers in Belzoni prefer to hire whites. The blacks go to Jackson, Chicago, St. Louis, and Baltimore—the farther from the farm, the better.

⟨ I have two boys who've left for Chicago.
Do you think they'll ever come back?
No, I don't think so. 'Cause there's nothing here for boys to do. Long time ago the children used to stay home; they could go to the fields and things. Now they don't need you in the field no more 'cause they've got this new chemistry that kills grass and the machines picks the cotton so they don't have anything here to do. No factories. I think there are two here: a garment factory and I don't know what kind of factory this is over here.

⟨ My wife was up there trying to sign up to go to that factory, and when the turn-out came at twelve, three colored women came up and two colored men and that was all. It was just like a school turn-out, there was so many people.

⟨ *Do you think that the one that's fourteen will stay here when he gets out of high school?*
I wouldn't think so.
Do you think he'll head North?
To make anything he's have to.

⟨ *Do you think your children will stay in Mississippi when they get out of school?*
I don't believe so. Now and then you'll catch one who'll stay, but it all needs to be changed to keep 'em here.
What needs to be changed?
The wages got to go up. They won't stand what I'll take.

⟨⟨ One time my wife wasn't working, and I didn't have no job. She just got a job this year. All right. All of 'em was lookin' right at me. There wasn't no food stamps out then. And I had to first just throw myself way behind—different things—just tryin' to make it. See I didn't want to get in debt. My boss told me I could borrow some money. I didn't want to borrow none this year. I didn't borrow none. I borrowed some from him last year, and I had a hard time trying to pay it back . . . . See, here the way he do. When I borrow some money from him, he won't give me no work to do. When he gives me a job to do, he'll take out the money, and that kind of puts me in strains . . . . So I swore I wasn't going to borrow no more money if I had to eat three months of cornbread. Something like that.

II The Planter

There are three levels of social position in the white community of Louise. Lowest are the rednecks, peckerwoods, crackers, i.e., the poor whites who are either small farmers, laborers on plantations, or blue collar workers. They are often as poor as any black man, and they suffer, as he does, the difficulties of continual indebtedness to the planter and the indignity of being excluded from participation in making decisions affecting their lives. Above the poor whites are the agents on the plantations who are responsible for seeing that the work gets done and who are paid relatively good salaries and generally provided with nice homes. They constitute a small middle class in the community, but they, too, are a group with no voice in the government of their town.

The planter governs the community. That he may or may not hold an elected office is unimportant. He exercises effective control just as certainly as does a plant manager in a small company town. Almost everyone works for him. In Louise, and elsewhere in the Delta, the interests of the plantation are the interests of the community. The planters themselves, many of whom are barely middle class by the standards of America as a whole, take on, by tradition rooted nearly two centuries deep, the role and responsibilities of the aristocracy. They act in unity—a unity which sometimes requires the expulsion from grace of one of their own—to further the economic progress of their towns, but most importantly, to maintain what is proper and good in the lives and attitudes of the people in their community. A central tenet of their view of propriety is that the races must be kept separate. To observe this command has been the life's work of many white southerners, but for most it has been the belief governing their lives: it has made sensible the alliance of rich and poor, exploiter and exploited, criminal and God-fearing, that characterizes white communities in the rural South.

There is a mayor and a city council in Louise. The councilmen with one exception are all planters, and the mayor is usually some unfortunate storekeeper who acquiesced under great pressure and accepted the position. For the twelve years prior to 1968, Louise had a Jewish mayor, the proprietor of a slowly failing grocery store.

The town officials are elected, a fact unknown to every black man interviewed: every black man in Louise with whom I talked had no idea as to how the officials got into office. Black residents call the town council "The White Citizens' Council," which it could possibly be, and they do not know whether this body is elected or privately selected. There are two polling places in Louise. Voting in county, state, or national elections is done in two makeshift stalls behind a gas station. Voting for what black people have always assumed to be the "Citizens' Council" is done at the town hall. No black man interviewed had ever walked across the street to vote in town elections. To do so would be an act of extraordinary bravery for very little return, because the man would certainly be attacked and because the "Citizens' Council," in the normal course of its business, does very little that interests or affects the black community. It is the planters' private club, and generally whites of lesser station do not know what it is doing.

The "Citizens' Council" has been credited in the past with occasional acts of meanness such as blacklisting, boycotting, threatening, or terrorizing men who challenge them. In drastic cases, they mete out almost equal treatment to white and black men alike. The president of the "Citizens' Council" is a planter. The vice-president is the town doctor. One problem that the planters have been unable to rid themselves of is that the owner of a sizeable plantation outside of Louise has for nearly twenty years been married to a black woman. He has resisted every pressure put on him by switching his ginning business to other towns, and he is reported to have been seen at night in front of his door with a gun, looking as if he'd fire at anything.

Most of the important elected offices in Humphreys County are held by plantation owners, and all appointed officials bend to the will of the planters. The chain of coercive and moral authority is thus preserved in the political as well as the social and economic spheres. One example of what this can mean is the recent conflict within the public school system. There was until the 1968–69 school year a white elementary and high school in Louise with over two hundred pupils. In 1967 Humphreys County instituted the freedom-of-choice plan for school desegregation and assigned a carefully-selected Negro teacher to Louise School. Even though no black parent chose to send his child to the white school, the hiring of the teacher caused tremendous uproar in the white community. This, added to the real possibility that some students would change schools in 1968, forced the county board of education to employ the final solution: shut down the white school and bus white children twenty miles out of their own community to Holly Bluff and Yazoo City in Yazoo County. The school building in Louise now stands empty, yet it is refused as a site for a community center or a day care center. In a tiny place like Louise the closing down of a public building for any reason is a disgrace. It was an act demonstrating unbelievable determination and dedication to old values, and it would seem madness, if the people did not accept it so naturally.

(*What does your husband make?*
When he's here on the place, he doesn't make but about five, six dollars a day. So that was puttin' us in a strain so he had to go off to get a job.
About how many hours would he work for that five or six dollars?
From six till six.
But he's got another job now?
He's workin' at the gin in Rolling Fork.
What will he do in the spring?
Work here on the place. Choppin' cotton and plowin'.
For five dollars a day?
When he's on the tractor. Now when he's choppin' cotton he gets four dollars.
The planter hasn't asked you to leave yet?
He did. Last week after my husband went off to work, he said if he could work over there he could move. So when my husband came in, he went over to talk to him Sunday morning, and he said he can't fix the house. "I ain't able to fix the house—bad a shape as that house is in. I just rather put hay in it." He told us he would like us to move so he could get hay in it. Two or three weeks, we got to move.

The tenant farmer engaged in civil rights activity has always been extremely vulnerable to the loss of his livelihood and has generally been the first to feel the wrath of the white community, though it is now a little easier to take that risk because a skilled worker can usually find work. Still, a planter with only one tenant and no prospect of running up on another would force that family to move in a minute if he heard that any member of it was engaged in what he considered to be "radical activity," which could range from registering to vote to joining the NAACP. He would do it because it made him mad. A point perhaps not yet overstated is that when people spend their lives depending upon others, the "others" do not feel like oppressors; they feel paternalistic. And, in fact, what made the plantation different from labor camps was that the planter tried to respond to the needs of his tenants as he saw them. Certainly most planters viewed the loan that they extended to get a family through the winter more as a kind act, the sort that men must perform occasionally, rather than as one link in a chain of bondage. The civil rights movement, and especially the warm reception the young northerners got from black people in the South, seemed to the planter a massive rejection of the decency with which he had tried to live his life. The kindness that might once have played a part in the relationship between planter and tenant is disappearing; it is being replaced by the callousness between management and labor.

One example of the changing times is that of the tenant's vegetable or truck garden. Until a few years ago, every family on a plantation was allowed a small patch of land to grow vegetables for its own use. Many tenants also raised hogs, chickens, and possibly a cow. Today only a few of the planters will allow even their full-time laborers to plant one or two rows of vegetables. For the rest, a garden or coops or pens for poultry and livestock are impossible because rows of cotton or soybeans now push up to the tenant's doorstep. In their drive to get the greatest possible yield from their land, the planters may force the tenants to move their toilets right up to their homes, so that every possible foot of land can be seeded and so that the machines can run straight down the rows without having to detour around the tiny, rickety privies. Even where space does permit the growing of a little truck, most tenants are prohibited from doing so because planters fear that weeds from the garden will spread to the cotton and bean fields, which they like to keep meticulously clean by spraying down poisons from the air.

Another, more important, example is the treatment accorded to families living on the plantation where the man is too old to work or there is no man to work. It is in the tradition of the plantation system that a tenant who had spent his life working on the place would be guaranteed a little bit of work here and there as long as he was able and a minimal sort of old-age security—a house to remain in until he died, occasional loans to see him through the winter, and help in paying medical expenses. What the planter could not provide, the family or neighbors of the old man or husbandless mother might contribute. Now it is likely that a man has few neighbors and that most of his family has left the Delta. There is virtually nothing, not even make-work, for the old, unskilled, or female to do on the plantation. And now, try as they may, no tenants not working regularly can believe the boss who says, "You can live here as long as you need to." They have seen too many families, believing the same promise, who were told one afternoon to leave by the next morning so that the house into which they were born could be burned and planted over in cotton.

Plantation income in the best of times is relatively unpredictable. Farming is a hazardous occupation, and men can be laid up for weeks with broken arms and legs. Whenever it rains no work can be done, and when the crop is bad everyone suffers. Yet always before, a family in trouble would not go unaided by its neighbors on the plantation, and, too, the plantation owner could be counted upon to help in difficult times if only by offering his tenant a loan. The plantation was a community in which the planter held the ultimate authority and in which each member felt common problems and common burdens. The community is now being destroyed. Each man's plight is different from that of the rest. Class distinctions, between skilled and unskilled, are being created within the ranks of the tenant farmers. The power of the planter is not guarding over them; it is seemingly aimed directly at them.

The planter is out to make money, and, viewed in this way, he is coming of age.[3] The last years in the Delta have seen tenants go homeless, truck patches on plantations prohibited or restricted, people dying or being permanently disabled because the planter would not send for a doctor, plantation huts being allowed to fall into complete disrepair, women and children by the thousands left with no way to earn money, women forced to do work for which they are physically unsuited in order to save their families from being told to move out, and countless other shameful events. This has happened, I think, not because the planters have decided to starve the black man out of the Delta, as some have said, but rather because the planters no longer care, except as it affects their own operations, what happens to the tenants on their farms; or in a larger sense, they do not care whether the black man in the Delta starves or not.

There is nothing predictable now about life on the plantation. No man knows if his home is secure, or if he will be given enough work to support his family. He does not know if he will be placed in a hospital if he is hurt on the job. He has no idea what he will do when he becomes too old to

---

[3] In 1967 seventy-two planters in Humphreys County received cash payments for land in the soil bank in excess of $20,000 a year. Six planters received cash payments of more than $100,000 a year. The largest planter in Louise received $133,764. Nine planters received between $50,000 and $100,000 a year.

work. If he falls into debt to the planter, he does not know if he will be given enough work to get in the clear. He can no longer expect the planter to give him materials with which to repair his house. If he owes the planter or cannot accumulate any savings, he has no way to leave the plantation. If he can contemplate leaving, he, who has never been one hundred miles from Louise, must face a move to Chicago which he has seen on television but does not really believe in. And what will he do in Chicago? The plantation world is all uncertainty, and the tenant farmer is economically and politically unable to make it any less so.

Those who for years, for all of their lives, have carried upon their shoulders the weight of crying, underfed children, increasing debt to "the man," and diminishing return for their labor, have a near total and perhaps unique dependency on the planter who has found himself, over the last years, labeled as an oppressor and who today, it is feared, has decided to live up to the title. The old dependency is a bond that now, when things are terribly difficult for the tenant farmer in Mississippi (and it cannot often enough be emphasized that each year the situation worsens), makes the tenant helpless to stand and fight back and unequipped to handle the role of independent laborer now imposed upon him. As an independent laborer, the tenant farmer is quickly replaceable, if not altogether dispensable; he is no longer a member of the community that was the plantation. The fear of what will be has taken hold; it has sent the young people fleeing north, and the old people wondering where to turn.

❪ *Does he (the planter) ever do anything to fix the place up?*

Well, I moved here with him last year a little before

Christmas. He put some window casings in and some windows in this old house. Old house ain't had anybody livin' in it for about five years. There's every kind of insect in it now that's in that swamp down there . . . . I laid down one night, and when I went to bed there wasn't anything wrong with that hand. I woke up the next morning, it had a knot on it. And from that it inflamed some more. It just had a little knot there—just like the end of your thumb—and that place inflamed and got sore, and course it was right on the hand and drivin' the tractors that kept it worked up . . . . And that place was sore when they treated my head about a month ago. Course, I put it to a spider bite.

Do any of your children keep catching colds all winter?

Well, they catch them that way. I feel like they catches them from the houses I live in that's not capable to live in. See, I've got to keep in the heater, when it's cold, a red hot fire. Well, to get the house hot, you have to get it too hot to live in it, see. And you get it hot and in thirty minutes it's cool, and you've already picked up a moist of sweat. That's the way I figure my kids catch so many colds . . . . You can get one real hot settin' up over that heater, and I guarantee he'll catch a cold. Your house is not built right. Just in a few minutes after your fire die out, your house is cold. And supposin' the walls is open—the air blowin' right in on you.

III   Household

In order to comprehend a man's poverty, it is not always necessary to document what he eats and what he earns. All one needs to do is to see the house in which he lives. In Humphreys County, the tenants refer to their homes as "open houses," which means that the walls are full of holes covered by cardboard, that there is no sealing (no inner layer to the walls), that the window frames hold no glass and are covered with sheets of tin, that the ground can be seen through the floor boards, that both rain and snow come in the roof and that wind blows through the house all night. Most people heat their homes with wood burned in a fireplace or in an old cast iron heater. If they leave a fire when they go to bed, the house is colder than outdoors by the time they are asleep. If they like to keep a fire going all night then they must get out of bed every hour to add wood and re-light the heater and will probably have to run outside into the freezing night to fetch more wood. There is danger involved in trying to stay warm all night. In the old rickety heaters with worn tin chimneys, a fire long unwatched can blaze too hot, sending sparks popping through the flue and threatening the whole house. The tragedy of being burned out has struck many families in Louise.

Since most black people around Louise live on plantations, most of them do not own their own homes. A fact often ignored in better days, it has now become painfully significant. One way in which it affects living conditions is that now, when the planter will do nothing to repair and maintain the homes of any but his indispensable workers, most tenants, having no job security whatsoever, are left wondering whether they dare invest money in fixing up a house that they may soon lose. It is worth noting that many tenant homes date back fifty years, and that the wood with which they were constructed came from houses which had at that time collapsed. They have seen many generations of many families. When a tenant's home burns or falls down, or when he moves on to a new plantation, he must take whatever vacant house he can find. The home into which he moves may have stood empty for months, years, or even decades. Thus, when a family takes a new house, they must first battle to reclaim the fragile wooden shell from the weeds, rot, rats, mice, rubbish, snakes, and small animals that have accumulated or moved in over the years. One company in the Louise area has constructed sixteen very nice tenant homes on its land. The company, however, is not based in Mississippi and bought the plantation only three years ago. The indigenous planters have generally made little attempt to bring the shacks of the day laborer up to any standard of decency.

❨ *Do you think your children are about as healthy as they could be?*
        No I don't think they're so healthy on account of I can't give them sufficient food and put sufficient rainments on them like they're supposed to be. You have to have shoes and clothes and a warm shelter. Well, you see, they ain't got that. See we've been here ten years, and I buy paper every year to keep warm, but it don't do any good.
        Do any of your floors have holes in them?
        They ain't no good. Ain't no good.
        What happened to your porch out there?
        It's tryin' to get away.

❨ *Is there anything in your house that needs fixing up real bad?*
        Just to tell it like it is, the whole thing needs fixin' up if that's what you want to know.
        We need a house built, let alone fix it.
        I don't know whether you could fix this trap.
        The man who owns the place, does he charge any rent?
        If he did I wouldn't live here.
        What would you do?
        I'd go somewhere else.
        Neighbor: Ain't worth it.
        Ain't worth it.
        Neighbor: Ain't worth bein' here as it is.
        That's right.
        Is your porch in good shape?

Neighbor: It's worser than the house.
Sure enough.[4]

⟨ This house doesn't have any cinders under it. This back part is setting on the ground. The only thing that's holdin' it up are the blocks on the front part. In the daytime you can mostly see how it slants—this part here up and that part there down.

The floors in most homes are full of holes. Usually there are areas in the corners of the floor and around the fireplace where it is unsafe to step. Heavy items, such as deep freezers, even if they could be afforded, cannot be installed in some homes because the floors will not support them.

⟨ *Do you use this fireplace for heat?*
Yes.
You don't have a heater?
No. Now this place right here [in front of the fireplace], it ain't nothin' but the ground. See it broke in right in here, and the fireplace fell in. It decayed all in here and it ain't nothin' but the ground. It's full of dirt. We filled it in.

⟨ *Do any of your floors have holes in them?*
Husband: Look here. Don't you see how it is?
Wife: It's a wonder you ain't falled through none of them.
Husband: House ain't no good.

After the crop is brought in, rats and mice will come out of the fields and invade the tenants' homes searching for food. Snakes and spiders follow them up through the holes in the floors.

⟨ *Are you bothered by rats, snakes in the house?*
Yeah, rats runnin' all over the place.

[4] James McBride Dabbs has described southerners as "piazza people," dwelling in a sort of cool half-life between the unbearable introspective privacy of "indoors" and the irreconcilable injustice of the public life beyond the porch. Porches are, then, inordinately important to southerners.

Have they ever bitten anybody?

One bit my wife a week ago on the foot. It was a mice.

It was the night I was trying to get my reports[5] out, and I was sittin' on the edge of the bed and something bit me. I first thought it was one of the kids under there and then I screamed.

(*Do you ever have any problems with snakes or rats in your house?*

We have rats. Plenty of rats.

Is there anything you can do to keep rats from getting in?

Well sometimes we put down poison for them—some kind of poison we put down—but then we be scared to use that on parts of the children. They might get hold to it.

(*Is there anything you'd like to talk about . . . ?*

Oh yes sir, I sure would love an indoor toilet. I sure would.

I always wished for a house that I could live in and wouldn't be bothered with the rats and snakes comin' in. We had two snakes come in here year before last. The house ain't been too good till last year. We repaired it.

(Rats and roaches like to eat me up.

Of the families surveyed 76.6 per cent are troubled by rats in their homes, and 23.4 per cent of the families have killed snakes in their homes.

The sealing of a house, one man said, is like the under-shirt on a man. It is protection against wind and cold. None of the houses of the poor black farmers in Louise is well sealed. Some have no sealing at all. In houses where a wooden inner wall was once built, it has long since begun rotting and falling apart, and only cardboard and tin hold out the wind. "Beaverboard," a thick cardboard, and "brick

---

[5] The mother of the family works at a Head Start center. Her job requires her to keep accounts of attendance and expenditures.

paper," a heavy wallpaper, are used in tenant houses where wooden sealing never was installed. Neither is particularly durable, and again, torn up cartons provide most of the protection from the elements. The walls in many houses are covered with newspaper to patch the tiny cracks, but nothing really works. In houses this old, the wind will find its way past whatever men put up to stop it.

    (| *Does the rain come in the roof?*
       Well no, it doesn't leak. With the understanding— the sealing and the outside walls, in the winter, ain't no account at all. These here, all these swollen places, see that's wind cracks where the wind comes through there. If you didn't plaster the paper over that, you see, it'd come right on in. Well naturally it do come in in places. Paper pushed away and all like that, well the wind did that.

    (| *Are your walls sealed?*
       No sir. We're outdoors. We're outdoors. If it was daylight you could just see all those—around the edges there—holes.
       They ain't no account, these old houses. They ain't fixed this house in five years.

In summer the rain comes through the roof. In winter, snow will settle lightly on the living room floor and on the beds.

There are always more people than there are beds in a household. In some homes the children must sleep wrapped in blankets on the floor. Where there are beds, the children sleep two, three, and four in each. On summer nights, when the air is heavy and hot, the children often prefer the floor to their overcrowded beds.

    (| *Where do the children sleep? In beds?*
       In beds.
       Do any sleep on mats on the floor?
       Two.

How many are in the beds?
Three in one bed, two in the other. The baby sleeps
with us.

⟪ *How many rooms do you have to sleep in here?*
Two. It ain't much for 'em to sleep.
*So all eight of the children sleep in one of the two
beds?*
Well, they share.

The children sleep an average of 2.2 in each bed. There
are never enough blankets or quilts in the wintertime. The
children sleep with their clothes on and with coats and
sweaters laid over them. Thirty per cent of the families admit to not having enough blankets in the winter.

Wood, gas, and coal are burned to heat the homes. Wood,
the traditional fuel, costs four to six dollars for a load that
will last about a week in the winter. The working men chop
their own wood; the women and old men buy theirs. A
family of women and children living alone with no neighbors close by is entirely dependent on the punctuality of the
wood dealer and on whether or not he can pass on the roads.
He is sometimes late, and the family stays cold. So do the
ones who cannot pay for the wood at all. Gas heaters are
safer, more economical, and more trustworthy than wood
heaters, but the cost of buying them and installing the
tanks is too high for most people.

⟪ I got a gas stove and I burn wood in the wintertime,
and the house ain't fit to live in. Ain't got no sealing in it
nowhere. Just one wall sittin' up there. I buy wood all
winter long.
What does the wood cost you?
I pay twenty dollars a month to buy wood. It costs
five dollars a load, and I burn four loads a month.

⟪ And that house. I like to froze last year. Wonder we,
me and her, both ain't dead. I like to froze. I went on

to the grudge ditch one morning. I prayed a good prayer that morning. I just did make it back to the house. I like to *froze*.

Why is it you say you almost froze? You couldn't buy the wood?

I didn't have the money. And when I did get some wood it wouldn't last a week. Couldn't nobody hardly get in there to bring no wood. And sometimes people, so many people, out of wood that they have to just go around as far as they could.

Water pipes do not run far out in the country, and even those with access to the pipes do not have running water. On the plantations the tenant families most often get their water from a common hydrant, which may be as far as a quarter mile from their homes, and the families are charged by the year for the use of the faucet. Most independent and share farmers have wells, but they are usually so shallow that the water is not good to drink. Everyone collects rain water to wash with. For drinking and washing clothes, the people must buy water by the barrel, which creates another major expense. The barrel itself costs $2.00; it costs twenty-five cents to fill it and fifty cents to have it hauled to the house. It can cost a family $1.50 (or $5.50 if their barrels are rusted out) to buy the bare minimum of two barrels of water a week. Well water is used for bathing. To bathe from a foot tub in an unheated kitchen in the middle of winter is an act of courage.

The only black people with inside toilets in Louise are a few who have houses that were built for white families in the town or the tenant farmers lucky enough to live in what the grander plantations once used for the maid's quarters. For every family interviewed who had an inside toilet, there was one who had no toilet at all.

❮ Where is your bathroom?
I'm rentin'.

Do you have one out back?
Sure ain't. They said they was going to build me one.

Some homes in Louise have no electricity, and some are wired for lights but the family has never been able to afford to have them turned on. On many plantations, the light bills of the tenants are sent to the planter who pays them and, once a year, adds the total bill to the debt of the tenant.

⟪ *Who owns the house?*
I'm rentin'.
How much does he charge you for rent?
Eight dollars per month.
Do you have any electricity here? Lights or anything?
There's some electricity here, but it's got to be paid. I got to pay for it to be hooked up, and I ain't got the money to pay for it.

Many families do not have a table to eat on. Almost no families have enough chairs for everyone to sit and eat together. Instead they eat standing up, or sit on old molasses drums, or on the floor. Nor can everyone eat from a plate of his own. If they do not all eat from the same plate at the same time, they must wait until the one before finishes or eat out of pans and pickle jar tops.

⟪ *Does everybody eat out of the same plate?*
Well I use some tops. Boiler tops. See I use a right smart of boilers. You put them on the fire and they burn up. So I save the tops.

⟪ *Do you have enough plates or dishes so that everyone can eat at once?*
No I sure don't.
What do you use for plates?
Bottle tops.

⟪ *Do you have enough plates and dishes to eat out of?*
Sure don't. Most I have is pans for the children to eat out of. Don't have any plates, and not many spoons, forks,

and knives. I never have been able to buy such things as that.

It is the responsibility of the county to maintain county roads and build bridges across the ditches that run beside the roads. Some of the roads and drives to the houses are in such bad shape that, when it rains, school buses cannot get near the houses and mothers must hoist their children up onto their shoulders and wade with them out to the bus or simply keep them home from school. It is a struggle for a black man to get a bridge built to his home and then to get the county to keep it in good repair. Easy access to paved or well-graveled roads is the privilege of the planter.

⟨ Unemployed woman: There's something else I'd like to say about Mississippi. The roads. The roads supervisor won't fix the roads. It's a mud hole from that road out there down to my house, and my children in the wintertime when it rains can't get out. The small ones well, I put 'em on my back and tote 'em on up to the stop. They won't even fix the roads . . . . I begged that man to put some gravel on that road to fill it up, but he just won't do it.

⟨ *Is there anything in your house that needs fixing up real bad?*

Well a lot of the windowpanes is out. I don't think there nair' a one in that room there. When it get real cold, we'll scrap a piece of tin and nail up there. In the summertime it been so hot we tear it off and tack some old screen on it. These farmers don't do anything to fix up the house any more. It don't look like none of it's like it should be.

When it rains the children can't get out to school. Sometimes they be at home for two weeks. The bus don't come down here. They have to walk out to that road . . . . but where they have to turn in to come down here off the blacktop, well all that's dirt road. Sometimes when they stand in it they can't get out.

There are never enough clothes to stay warm in the winter. On very cold days, mothers keep their children home from school rather than send them out to the bus without an overcoat. Most children have but one change of clothing and often have no underwear at all. Children miss weeks of school because their mothers will not send them improperly dressed, and later they drop out of school because they cannot buy decent clothes.

⟪ Do your children have enough clothes to get through the winter?
No sir. I won't tell you no story. That's my puzzle: clothes and shoes and money. Schoolin' wear. I have three to go to school every day. Sometimes I have to stop them to help me a little on my job.

⟪ I'll be lucky to near about give 'em lunch every day. But I don't know how long it's going to last. We're all what you say, naked. We don't have the proper change in clothes. Things like that. Well, it'll get cold, and the lunches'll have to stop. I'm gonna have to scrap clothes. Some way or somehow. These secondhand houses or something. I've just got to have them. We all is.

⟪ Do you have enough clothes for your children?
I don't have enough. We make do with what we got. We do what we be able.

Children wear out shoes quickly. The poor man cannot afford to buy a pair of new shoes for his children each time the old ones fall apart. Instead he buys, on credit, secondhand shoes that wear out before they are paid for. Some mothers will keep their kids in school no matter what they have to put on their feet. Most children, however, miss school regularly, because they own no shoes fit to wear.

⟪ Do you have enough shoes for all of your children to go to school in?
Well, I haven't been able to get no shoes yet. Some-

times the girl she'll send us some money for shoes, but she hasn't done it yet.

❲ *Have you ever had to pull a child out of school because he didn't have shoes?*
I had one last year.
How long did he have to stay out?
About a month.

❲ *Is there ever a time when you have to pull kids out of school because they don't have shoes?*
Sure. I have to stop mine sometimes three and four days at a time. And when I get a pair of shoes, I get a used pair. I have got them, and sometimes it'll be a couple of weeks payin' for 'em down at the secondhand store in Louise. Sometimes you can charge them, but you can't get more than one pair charged at a time. They got to see if they'll get paid for that one 'fore they'll charge you with another pair. Then you get a pair, and the kids wear 'em to school, and the soles liable to come off that same day . . . . It's pretty tough in this state.

❲ *Do all your children have shoes?*
Oh, I need to buy a pair now.
Have you ever had to take your kids out of school because they didn't have shoes?
Yes.
How long would they have to stay out?
About three or four days.

❲ You take last year. They's out of school on parts if they didn't have sufficient things to go in.
How long were they out?
They's out I reckon about a month 'fore I could get them straightened out into first going. 'Fore I could get 'em started to going.

❲ *How is your house heated?*
It's heated pretty good in the winter until the door comes open.
Do you have enough clothes for your children?
No, I sure don't.

Do you have enough for the winter?
Sure don't.
Are there enough shoes for the children?
No. They sure ain't got no shoes. Nothin' but these tennis.
Are there ever times when they don't have shoes to go to school in?
Sure is. Sometimes I have to keep 'em at home until I can get them some.
How long would they have to stay out?
About a week or so.

The children of 64.3 per cent of the families cannot regularly attend school because they have no shoes.

There are no federal or state standards to regulate the living conditions on the plantations, e.g., there is no agency empowered to say whether or not an outhouse shared by three families is sanitary, or whether a planter who will not provide a tenant with any toilet at all is acting in the interest of the public health. In 1960, only 21.4 per cent of the dwelling units in Humphreys County were sound: 58 per cent had no inside water; 73 per cent had no flush toilets; 79 per cent had no bathtubs; 43 per cent had no access to public water or an individual well; 57 per cent had no access to a public sewer, septic tank, or cesspool. There is no program of inspecting the homes that planters provide for their tenants to ensure that they are fit for habitation.[6]

❛ Yes sir, the house is got to be cured.

[6] Fifty-one of 73 families interviewed did not have enough blankets for the winter; children in 45 of 70 families missed school because of lack of shoes; 65 of 83 families responding did not have enough clothes for the winter. Only 32 of 70 families interviewed sat in chairs at a table when they ate; 25 of 85 families did not have enough dishes for everyone. Seventy-two of 94 families interviewed had holes in the floors of their homes; 77 of 92 were bothered by rats. Sixty-one of 91 homes were heated by woodstoves, 30 by gas heaters. Of 67 houses, 2 had "inside water," 15 had wells; families in 25 of the 67 houses got water from hydrants; 25 families bought water. Of 90 families interviewed, 7 had inside toilets, 76 had outside toilets, and 7 families had no toilet at all.

⟪ *How many days a week do you have fresh meat?*
Just one. On Saturday.
How about fish?
Oh we seldom ever have fish. Fish man used to come by, but he stopped comin' cause the people stopped buyin'.
Do you ever eat eggs?
Yes sir.
How often will you have eggs?
Well about once a week.
How much milk do you buy in a week?
Well we don't buy by the week—just when we take a notion with the cash and got the cash. Every time I get the check, I get a little milk.
What did you have for your meals today?
Wife: Not hardly anythin'.
Husband: Had some pintos. I'm gonna tell it like it is. No meat in 'em.
Is that all you had to eat today?
Yes sir.

IV Food and Diet

The abysmal poverty of the people turns their lives into a never-ending search for food. Getting something to eat, getting something to feed the family, is the overriding concern of the poor farmer; all other things are neglected for the sake of buying food. Groceries, in a more real sense than money, become the medium of exchange. Produce and home-produced meat are swapped for basic services such as hair cutting and auto repair work. It has been said that the case for the existence of "hunger" in the Delta has been overstated. For a family to go hungry for a long period means that they have no access to any federal food programs and that all of their neighbors and friends who would normally share what they had are in a similar situation. For a family to go hungry means that the entire community is going hungry. It means that there does not exist the means to bake or buy a loaf of bread to stuff down the mouths of the children. Most families can beg or buy that loaf of bread. But the real question is whether what people eat is adequate to support decent human life, or whether the normal diet of the people in Mississippi, in Louise, is one which the more comfortable in this nation are willing to let other Americans exist upon. Indeed, there are people in the Delta who are never free of the pain of hunger, as represented by shriveled children with swollen bellies. And certainly the very presence of cases such as these, and they are by no means rare, is horrifying enough to justify any display of fury and indignation which they arouse.

Far from the "meat and potatoes" of the "average" American, the staples of the poor farmer in Louise are pump water and pinto beans. In good seasons, pinto beans will alternate with other vegetables, string beans, sweet potatoes, turnip greens, and occasionally with chicken backs or necks. In the winter, pinto beans will alternate with white bread and molasses. Most families serve two meals at home: one in the morning and one in the late afternoon.

(We had some beans, some pinto beans. We had pinto beans for dinner. For breakfast it was toast and an egg, I think, and some bologna.

(I think we had some peas. Sure did. That's what we had. We had some green peas what she put up in the deep freezer. That's all. You know we don't have money enough to have a little of this and a little of that and the other. We don't have money for that. Sometimes we just have one thing and some bread. That's the truth.

❠ We had mashed potatoes and bread today. This morning we had eggs and light bread.

❠ Greens, collard greens, baked potatoes, and cornbread.

❠ We had some peas.

Most people can afford to eat meat only on the weekends. They eat fish about once every six weeks. Perhaps the children will be given a little fruit every other week. Because the price of eggs has gone up so high, most families are able to serve them only about three times in two weeks.

❠ *Are you ever able to buy fresh meat for your family?*
Sure do. Sometimes I do.
How many days a week would you eat meat?
Sometimes I eat it two days a week. Sometimes not at all. I don't eat it that often.
Do you ever buy fish?
No, sure don't buy no fish at all.
How about eggs?
Sometimes . . . Just when I happen to have them.
Do you ever buy fresh fruit?
Yes, sometimes I do.
Are you able to buy enough milk for your children?
Sometimes I get a quart; and sometimes I get two quarts.
Are you usually able to buy a quart every week?
No, sir, I sure ain't.

❠ *Do you ever buy fresh meat?*
No.
How about fresh fish?
I don't know. I haven't had that in so long a time.
Do you ever buy eggs?
Well, no. [She explained they get some eggs from chickens.]
Are you able to buy enough milk for your children?
I buys a little bit, but I can't buy it all the time.
How often do you buy it?
About three or four times a month.

How much do you buy when you buy it?
About a pint.
What did you have for your meals today?
I had some string beans and white potatoes.
Do you usually have the one meal a day?
No, two. Just two.
What did you have for breakfast this morning?
I had an egg.

(| *What did you have for your meals today or yester-day?*
Well, we had butterbeans. I don't hardly eat no breakfast.

(| *Do you ever have fruit?*
Very seldom. Every Christmas mostly.

Only the children in Head Start regularly eat a meal between seven in the morning and five at night. It is a treat for a child to be given the fifteen cents he needs to buy a hot lunch at school. It is not unusual for a child to have bread and syrup in the morning, or no breakfast at all, and wait until dark to have bread and syrup for supper.[7]

[7] Of 93 families interviewed, 10 ate meat daily; 7 ate meat three or four days a week; 19, two to three days a week; 40, one to two days a week; 3 families had meat one or two days a month; 9 families ate meat "rarely"; and 5 families "almost never" ate meat. Of 91 families interviewed, 86 had fresh fruit one or two days a month, "rarely," or "almost never." Of 90 families responding, 17 had eggs one or two days a week; 13, two to three days a week; 9, three or four days; 15 had eggs daily. Three families had eggs one or two days a month; 21 had them "rarely"; 12 families "almost never" had eggs.
Of the 89 families responding, 4 bought three or more gallons of milk per week; 13 families bought two gallons a week; 25 bought between one gallon and one quart per week; 9 bought up to a quart a week. Four families bought up to a quart per month; 5 rarely bought milk; and 29 families bought no milk at all.
Out of 70 families interviewed, 20 (representing 73 children) were able to afford lunch at school daily for their children; 8 families (representing 33 children) were able to give their children lunch at school three or four days a week; the 103 children of 20 families ate lunch at school two or three days a week; 56 children of 10 families ate lunch one or two days a week; the 9 children in one family ate lunch at school one or two days a month; 54 children belonging to 11 families "rarely or never" ate lunch at school.

⟨ *Your children in school, do they get lunch every day?*
Wife: Not all days.
Husband: I have seven children goin' to school practically every day. Two of 'em goin' to that little school
around there. It's the kindergarten school—The Friends of
the Children[8]—and the others are goin' to the public
school . . . . Some mornings we don't be able to get them
anything. Sometimes my wife will fix them a lunch to
carry along with them. We won't be able to give them
anything here in the winter.

⟨ *How often can your children in school buy lunches?*
Wife: To tell you the truth, you just can't manage.
Husband: That lunch. That really is a problem.
Do they buy milk at school?
They buys milk when they haves the money. It's four
cents.
How often can you give them the money?
Not too regular, 'cause most times we don't hardly
have the money to care for them. We just give them a
nickel or things like that.

⟨ *Are any of your students who can eat no breakfast,
buy no lunch, and who work in crowded homes able to do
well in school?*
A student would have to be especially dedicated and
intelligent to get good marks under these conditions.
[assistant principal of a black high school in Belzoni]

The coming of winter carries with it the threat of starva-
tion for many families in Louise. The least affected by the
ending of the crop season are those, of course, who have
regular non-farm jobs and those who receive welfare, social
security, or veterans' checks, or are paid "straight time" on
a plantation. But for the tenant, sharecropper, and small
farmer, there is, from mid-November until April, no money
coming in. To get through the winter he must borrow from

[8] The Friends of the Children of Mississippi is a four-county Head
Start program administered, locally, by poor people. See pp. 67ff.

the planter and buy on credit from the stores. He will often have to share food with his neighbors; any hogs or cows straying loose on the roads are considered fair game by the first hungry man that comes along.

It is one of the luxuries of the small farmer that he can raise a garden. Throughout the autumn, he will pack away peas, beans, and tomatoes in his deep freeze to have something to fall back on in the winter. Most farmers raise hogs, and they will slaughter a shoat or hog late in the fall so that the family may enjoy a little meat occasionally in the long cold months. Some tenant farmers are accorded the privilege of planting a small garden and some are allowed to raise hogs. The greater number of tenants, however, are not allowed gardens, or have such restrictions placed upon the size of them that too little can be grown to make it practical to invest in a deep freeze. Many tenants are forbidden to raise livestock, though the cost of raising hogs prohibits most from wanting to in any case. Very few poor farmers can afford to own a cow because federal and state agencies require each cow to have a barrage of expensive vaccinations to ensure that it is free of disease. The black residents of Louise do not eat well, they do not eat much, and they do not eat often.

(*Does anybody in your family have high blood?*
I have a touch of it.
How about sugar diabetes?
Well, my little boy, what I was tellin' you about, he was born with this sweet blood the doctor said, and he has epileptic spells, and they sent him to Jackson and they gave him medicine for it.
Do any of your children catch colds and keep them pretty much all winter long?
Yes sir. I got some that way now. My baby . . .

Do any of your children develop sores or scabs on their arms and legs?

Lord. There's some broke out here. My baby got them worms. The doctors says it's ringworms, and she's kinda breakin' out around her neck.

Have any ever had their stomachs bloated out?

Yes sir. The doctor said it's worms. He keeps sayin' it's worms.

Have any of the other children with something wrong inside of them ever seen a doctor?

I got another girl in there. The doctor said she had thin tissue. When she was six months old (she's fourteen now), I like to lost her. Said she had it so long that the food she's given like to pass right back through her. Said her intestines like to grow together. I have a lot of trouble out of her for that.

V Health

The health of the people of Louise is incredibly poor. The community is ridden with sickness, disease, and chronic illness. While people's low income severely limits the medical care they may receive, many find themselves often living in the doctor's office. ("I'm just a doctor victim. I stays in the doctor's.") Barely a household is free of a case of high blood pressure, which shows itself in the swollen ankles of the women, results in a weakened heart, fainting spells, "nervous breakdowns," and demands an abstinence from pork. Throughout the winter the children are plagued by colds that turn occasionally into pneumonia. Cases of asthma are not rare. Running sores and scabs dot the bodies of most children in the summer. While often a symptom of a dietary deficiency, they are caused in the main by unsanitary conditions which turn tiny cuts into painful infections. Diabetes is a common disease. Cases of tuberculosis and amoebic dysentery are not hard to find. Many children have a variety of internal parasites.[9]

⟦ This baby right here; he'll cough and go out of breath, and you can't disturb him. He'll go out of breath. I don't seem to know what makes him do that. If you make him over-average mad, if he thinks you scold him some way or the other, he'll just go right out of breath. Sometimes it don't look like he'll get his breath back no way. That child there, she complains right smart about her stomach, and I taken her out to Belzoni to the doctor. Well the doctor said she might have worms and he gave me some worm medicine for her, but I don't know if she was taking it like she should have 'cause I was trying to go to school in order to pay him . . . Sometimes they [sores] just break out all over in the summertime. I've got another boy here who looked like he just never would get well of his sores.

People visit doctors most often for "high blood" pills and for cold medicine for the children. For matters more or less serious than these, the expense of treatment is beyond the reach of the poor man; he would prefer to suffer through the illness or resort to home remedies. There is not in the Delta the hearty farm family of American folklore, living simply but comfortably and enjoying robust good health; instead there are people blighted by low income, inadequate food, and disease.

There were many complaints in the interviews that people were unable to get doctors to come to their homes, even as in the cities.

⟦ We ain't been checked by a doctor in so long I can't tell you what condition the family's in.

[9] Over 57 per cent of families interviewed complained of heart disease or high blood pressure; 7 per cent had diabetes; 9.3 per cent reported that a member of the family had asthma; 2.1 per cent had tuberculosis; 51.8 per cent reported frequent or continuous colds; members of 59.7 per cent of all families complained of sores or scabs on their bodies; 21.4 per cent of the families had family members who were continually tired or listless.

About 13 per cent of the black community in Louise has never seen a doctor. Also, about 49 per cent of the people have never seen a dentist. Due to the cost, people only see dentists when their teeth need to be pulled, and when that point is reached, many people choose to pull their own teeth.[10]

⟨ *How many of your children have ever seen a doctor?*
I've got one in the family. It wasn't from sickness though. Had a little fat boy of mine. He went out to the outside bathroom one day. When he got ready to come back in, he went to zip up his pants, and he caught hisself in the zip. I taken him to the doctor. It was on a Wednesday; he takes Wednesday off, and you can't get him back to that office. So when I got to his office, he was gone. I never did try to go to his home to get him. We have a pretty favorable doctor up there in Midnight. He's real old; he'll practice till a certain hour in the evenin' and then he's through. Well, I went up there and his hours was up. Well I just kep' a goin' then. I went to Belzoni to take him to the hospital—I couldn't afford to wait because he's sufferin'—and they got it off.

There were numerous complaints about the federally-supported hospital in Belzoni. The people said patients, even emergency cases, not able to produce cash have been denied admission to the hospital and directed to hospitals in Vicksburg and Jackson where some cost reductions are granted to indigent patients. Stories were told of suffering and death resulting from the drive to these cities, each seventy miles away.

[10] Twenty-one of 36 respondents were too sick to work; 44 of 85 heads of households reported that some or all of their children had colds all winter; 49 of 82 said that their children had sores; 15 of 70 had children who were sleepy or listless all day; 45 of 81 respondents reported that a member or members of the family "often felt like fainting."
One hundred forty-eight of the 690 people in the families interviewed had never seen a doctor; 532 had never seen a dentist.

❙[I worked there at the hospital a long time. I worked over there about six or eight years. Now the hospital has changed a whole lot 'cause when I was over there we was gettin' $14 a week—go to work at seven, get off at five . . . . They take in black patients. Some, but it is so high over there that black people just can't pay it, and if you go in there and don't have the money, well, you have to go somewhere else . . . . I know a cousin of mine, on the Fourth of July, she had a miscarriage, and they carried her over there, and they wouldn't take her in. They had to rush her to Vicksburg and operate on her at once. Now, that could have been a life saved. At this hospital, you have to have money . . . . When I was there, they kept them [babies] separate . . . . The black babies stay in the nursery for a while, and then they bring them up and puts them in the diet kitchen, you know, on the colored side. Now that's what they were doing when I was there. I don't know what they're doing now.

As far as the wards are concerned, the hospital consists of, I think, thirty-four rooms that is used by patients, and eight of those rooms is used by black patients. . . . I wouldn't say they handle them any different, but it's seldom they handle any black patients. If you go to the hospital to have anything done, they will always refer you to another hospital—Jackson or Vicksburg.

The cost of medicine is one of those expenses that nags endlessly at a poor man. The shots or pills needed to check diabetes, the pills needed for high blood pressure, the non-prescription pills and syrups needed to fight the colds all winter are items which cut unbearable holes in the budget of the black man in the Delta. It is a bitter joke for a tenant farmer to pay ten dollars for an examination that shows he has "high blood" and must pay four dollars each month of his life for pills. The money is just not there. Rather than follow the doctor's instructions, he will buy, if he is able, a month's supply of pills and make them last six months.

❰ *Do you have to take medicine regularly for your sugar or high blood?*

Sure does. Course I'm not able to buy the sugar pills. I take the shots or either take the sugar pills. And I'm not able to get the sugar pills . . . .

Because they're too expensive?

Too expensive. And the doctor put me in on health department sugar shots, and the lady wrote and told me to come up there, and said the government said I'd have to pay fifty cents a week to take this treatment. And I wasn't able to pay fifty cents a week. And I didn't ever go back, and that was last year. So I have to go to the doctor in Midnight, and I haven't been there in three, four months, near about four months, to get a sugar treatment 'cause I got light bills, burial club . . . . I get a little money and it goes.

Some people treat serious diseases with home remedies. They do so out of habit, certainly, but they are no more able to afford professional treatment now than when the practices began. Those who need medicine the most can afford it the least.

❰ *When they were babies, did either of them have large stomachs?*

No sir. Well, you take that boy. When he was a baby he had a large navel, but he didn't have a large stomach.

You mean stuck way out?

Yeah, a navel you know would stick out way in front of him. Well, a lady gave my wife a remedy; told her to take a fifty-cent piece and bandage it, you know, tie it around him. That's when he was young, and it seems it went back in place.

How old was he then?

He's about eleven months old, I imagine.

Most babies in the black community of Louise are born in the home and are delivered by a midwife with the occasional assistance of a doctor. The number of miscarriages and infant deaths is startlingly large. (The infant death rate in 1964 in Humphreys County was 2,941 per 100,000 live births, compared to the national norm of 1,700.) Recent medical research indicates that it is during the second through the twelfth month of a child's infancy that his death may most characteristically be attributed to the fact that the nourishment which he received before and after his birth was insufficient to provide for his growth. When a woman is undernourished during pregnancy, her baby may be undernourished at birth. There have been 4 infant deaths for every 100 live births accounted for.[11]

⟮ *All of these children, were they born here at home or in a hospital?*

Well, I got three was born in the hospital. The rest of 'em was born here in this house.

The ones born here in the house, were they brought in by a doctor or a midwife?

Well, I used to have trouble, and I needed a doctor's help.

Have you ever had any miscarriages?

I sure is. I've had twenty-six and I've only saved ten.

This is you?

And I only saved those with the doctor's help.

Husband: We lost a lot in one year like that.

⟮ *Has your wife ever had any miscarriages?*

Three.

[11] Of the 690 people covered by the interviews, 107 are women who have borne children or at one time been pregnant. They have had a total of 607 live births. Of these, 2 were born in a clinic, 60 in a hospital, 16 at home attended by a doctor, 481 at home attended by a midwife, and 48 under unspecified conditions. Sixty-one of the women, who have had a total of 311 of the live births, have had a total of 140 miscarriages and 24 children lost in infancy. On the average, every mother has had 1.31 miscarriages and lost .22 children in infancy. The fetal death rate is 247 per 1,000 live births. The infant death rate is 39.5 per 1,000 live births. It must be noted that the 607 births span a large number of years, and presumably health conditions have improved somewhat with the passage of time.

Has she ever had any babies that didn't live?
Well, we had one that lived about three hours after she was born, then died.
So out of the five pregnancies you got the girl?
We got the girl.

((*Where were your children delivered?*
All of mine was in the home.
By a doctor or midwife?
By a midwife.
Have you ever had any miscarriages?
Husband: Many of them.
How many have you had?
About five.

Many women in Louise eat cornstarch when they are pregnant. Some keep the habit and continue to eat as much as they can get after childbirth as a means of filling themselves up. The same is true of baking soda. And the same is true of clay.[12] There was a time when most women in Louise ate clay and starch while they were pregnant. Now, one out of every four eats starch, and one out of every three eats clay. The best clay is said to come from the hill country around Canton or Yazoo City. Farmers passing through will pull off the roads and shovel the dirt into bags for their wives and friends. When a woman cannot get hill clay she may take a bagful out of the side of an irrigation ditch. She lets the clay dry out, or may bake or freeze it, and she will later break off little chunks to suck. Sometimes you can see a woman at work in the fields after mealtime pick a piece of dirt off the ground and pop it into her mouth.

At the hospital in Belzoni, there are beds for one out of every 534 people in the county. In Humphreys County, there are five doctors, one for every 3,740 people. There are two dentists, one for every 9,350 people. There are four nurses,

[12] Of the 77 women interviewed, 20 ate starch "at least during pregnancy," and of 76 interviewed, 25 ate clay.

one for every 4,675 people. Where the poverty of the people is so great, their health so poor, their ability to afford medical care so hampered, and the availability of medical services so limited, there is a crying need for public health programs. The Mississippi State Board of Health does not have the budget or the manpower to provide fully all of its designated services. For the eighteen counties in the Delta, there are only ten medical directors, i.e., doctors, for the county health departments. One doctor serves as the director for six separate health departments, and one of these serves two counties. The director of the Humphreys County Health Department also directs the Yazoo County department. The Humphreys County department is staffed by two nurses and a sanitarian. In the areas that most directly benefit the poor, maternity and infant care and immunization against communicable diseases, much has yet to be done. It is estimated that 35 per cent (more than twice the national average) of the children in Mississippi from one day to nine years of age have not received basic immunizations, i.e., polio, diphtheria, smallpox, and typhoid fever. It can be inferred that the percentage is quite high in Humphreys County. One problem is that in Mississippi, where for ten years there has been no compulsory school attendance law, many children, especially those of poor families, miss getting their shots because they either do not attend school at all, or attend it very irregularly. Shots are given to all children in the Head Start centers.

❲ *Have any of your children been to see a doctor?*
I know those she [a sister] left are going to have to go. They needs a check-up. . . . See she had tuberculosis and she left here about two weeks ago, and they was comin' around to check the kids, but they got on the wrong road.
In other words, they been lookin' for us, but they got throwed off and didn't find here. It was the Public Health Department that was lookin' for 'em, but they didn't find this place.

Maternity and child care services in Humphreys County barely exist. None of the people talked with in Louise could recall ever having heard of any lectures or courses being offered in child care. When medical problems arise during pregnancy or during a child's infancy that force a mother to go to the health department in Belzoni, she will be referred to a private physician for treatment that she often cannot afford. The department supervises 14 "granny" midwives in the county. Many mothers are assisted in their delivery by women who call themselves "midwives" but are under no supervision from the county. There are no nurse-midwives in the county.

What is desperately lacking in Humphreys County is free or inexpensive medical help and enough dentists, free or inexpensive hospital care and enough hospital beds, and free medicine. There are at this time no programs, federal or state, operating in the county aimed at fulfilling these needs.

VI The Disintegration of the Black Community

The community of the poor in Louise was built around the plantation. Plantation life was both secure and terrible. To ease the painful, and to maintain and strengthen the bonds of community, the people had their churches, their weekend gathering spots, and their schools. That these institutions were able to sustain the spirit, and, in a fashion, the economy of the poor community when conditions on the plantation were at their best, is in itself a miracle. But now the security provided by the plantation system has collapsed. Neither the old institutions themselves nor the forces created by them are capable of handling the overwhelming social, political, and economic problems faced by the poor of Louise today. The following is a description of the part that these several forces have played in holding together the poor community in the past and why there cannot now grow from the primary institutions, the church and the schools, the true leadership needed to build a new framework to replace that of the plantation.

The Church

It has been said that services at the small country backwoods churches provided for the black poor a release for the pressures that must build up in men living in continual poverty and subjected to constant racial slander. The emotional outpourings, from whatever sources they flow, of congregations at church services around Louise are certainly dramatic, exciting, and exhausting. Three Sundays out of four, at any given church, only the children will meet in the morning for their lesson, and, in a few churches, the older folks will gather in the evening to sing and pray with the deacons. The fourth Sunday, though, is "pastoral day." It is the day that the traveling preachers, hailing from Belzoni or Vicksburg but spreading the word to congregations a hundred miles apart, complete their circuits and return again to hold services.

In and around Louise there are a dozen little churches, calling themselves New Hope, Big Mount Zion, Love Feast, and other biblically inspired names, and every Sunday there will be a pastoral day at one of them. The considerable anticipation that precedes a preacher's visit turns the fourth Sunday into a true holiday, and it is perhaps so as not to mar the pleasure of the occasion that few members of a congregation will give in to temptation and attend pastoral day services at another church mid-month. Also, most congregations have considerable pride in their preachers. Where religious excitement is so real to a people, and feel-

ing the touch of the Master's hand is an accepted phenomenon, the preacher has a clear role—that of bringing God to
the people and raising the spirits of the congregation to a
pitch where they may see God—and it is according to his
ability to perform this duty that he maintains his reputation
and holds the devotion of congregations. During the long
hours of each service, the preacher will slowly spin out his
story as the faithful get the spirit in them and shout and
moan and dance, struggling with each other and with the
passion inside them. When the right pitch is reached, when
the sorrows and ecstasy of the folk have poured out, then the
preacher will end his tale. The church, alone in a cotton
field and miles from the highway, will have sheltered a
spectacular resurgence of the spirit of the people.

The church has played a singular role within the black
community. It is quite certainly the single most important
institution. It is the center for community news and information, which means that it has served as a place where
political issues can be debated and community policy decided. The church has been the medium through which civil
rights workers have stated their intentions, and it remains
the place where the most people can be reached the most
quickly. Things can be accomplished very rapidly with
the church's blessings, and only with difficulty with the
church's opposition.

It has been rare for preachers to take definite stands
against changes in the status quo, but it has been equally
rare for preachers to rise up and fight to improve the lot of
their people. For the most part, they have remained neutral
and disinterested in times of political or civil rights turmoil
unless personally attacked for their inaction. It has been
the deacons of the church, elected by the congregation, who
have formed the worldly or political arm of the black church.
They have in the past taken active stands in civil rights, offering the use of the church building for community meetings,

working to organize their communities, and, in a very real sense, often providing the elected leadership of the black community.

Because its deacons are responsive to the wishes of the congregation and because the church holds the allegiance of so many, it should now be playing a principal part in striving to create a unified black community out of the fragments left by the demise of the plantation system, and it should be speaking for and helping the poor who make up each congregation. The black churches of Louise have shown themselves to be immobilized on all social, economic, or political issues. Part of the problem is that over the last several years their congregations have been changing and getting smaller. Pastoral services would once have lasted throughout the afternoon, and there would have been a prayer meeting that night and once or twice more during the week. The Sunday school would have filled a third of the church, and the congregation would have overflowed the pews. Now pastoral service is a morning affair; the crowd is not large enough to sustain it all day long. The Sunday school class is conducted in a corner of the first few pews, and the whole congregation can barely fill the rest. The church organization does not include as many people as it once did. Nor does it now reach the same people. Once everyone attended church. Now the congregation is filled mostly with women and children, the young men having left and the working men perhaps feeling out of place among all the wives. This, too, has meant a change in the effectiveness of the church as a force in shaping community policy. For where once men could be reached directly through the church, now only women can be. And where once women bore the dual role of bringing up the family and working as long as the men in the fields, and saw themselves as figures of extraordinary strength with the responsibility of concerning themselves with the public welfare, they now, no longer being wage earners, have seemed to relinquish to their men, in a subtle way, the second responsibility of community concern. The transition is far from complete, but, as it does occur, the church, as has sometimes been suggested, becomes less relevant to the lives of the people. It still supports their spirit, but it cannot channel that spirit into matters of this world.

THE CLUBS, JUKE JOINTS, AND SATURDAY NIGHT

Many black men in Louise and Midnight are members of the Masons or Elks. As far as the whole community is concerned, the clubs do very little, but they do allow their members a chance for a little fun once a month and hold dances that draw the youngsters from all over the county. What is important, however, is that their meeting halls, virtually the only large, black-owned buildings in the small towns of the South, have been available for use as a community centers, Head Start centers, and halls for civil rights meetings. In Lousie, one of the two Head Start centers leases the Masons' Hall. In Belzoni, the NAACP holds meetings three times a week in the Taborin Hall of the Elks' club, which at one time also housed a Head Start center.

The clubs, juke joints, or roadhouses have sometimes been as cooperative with their facilities as the fraternal societies. Head Start centers, in crying need of space to handle countless children, have been forced to move into private clubs where every morning the teachers would arrange and decorate the room, and every evening patiently re-package the toys and remove the children's paintings from the walls. The roadside beer and sandwich establishment is perhaps the field most fully exploited by the black entrepreneur. Because men like a place to eat their lunches and gather after work, because there has to be some place to go on Friday night, and because these facilities are denied, or not provided in the right style, by white businesses, juke joints have cropped up in the black communities. They swarm with people on weekend nights. Many are men yet dirty from the fields, worn out after a week of heavy work and anxious to mix and relax; such a man wants to remember (as W. J. Cash says of the white southerner) that he's one hell of a fellow. The girls come to dance, the boys to show off, the married couples because it is the only place that they have had to go to for most of their lives, and the old men to watch. Groups of people wander in and out, usually without buying anything. The ladies are dressed in whatever might pass for a party dress. Occasionally, outside amidst the cars jammed together, a fight will get started among the few boys. In Belzoni, the police force claims several Negro officers (with no power to arrest a white man) whose job is to roam the night spots and to keep things quiet. In Louise there is a "colored law" (who lacks the authority to arrest anyone) whose job is to snoop around the roadhouses and dairy bars to find out, for the white folks, what his neighbors are up to.

⟨ There's not a colored law in the state of Mississippi that's my friend. If a friend of mine becomes a cop, he's not my friend. If he's a law in Mississippi, I don't know him.

Saturday is payday, and Saturday night is the real farmers' night. The most accurate method of taking a census in a community like Louise would be to make a head count in town on Saturday night. From all the surrounding country, men and women come to "make provisions." Most hardware, clothing, and groceries are bought on Saturday night. It is an occasion more widely recognized than any other. Everyone wears not his age-old Sunday dress, but just the nicest, cleanest clothing he can put together. Young people and children beg or borrow money from their parents so that they can buy something in town, and along the street they can be seen walking slowly, peeping into shop windows, flirting with one another. The old men lean back against the store fronts in their straw chairs, watching the world go by, or make conversation on the street corners, often negotiating over the price of a bottle of sealed or unsealed whiskey. The whites are out too with their slicked-down hair shining from beneath their finest cowboy hats. The planters show off their big new cars and wave and yell at friends and workers as they drive slowly down the street. Everything, and most everyone, is pleasant. Acquaintances are renewed. People that folks were "worried about" show up on Saturday night. It is the night for cashing the check, paying off debts, buying fruit for the children, and getting special things for Sunday dinner. Anything that interests anybody will be widely discussed on sidewalks, and everyone gets an excellent chance to pick up rumors. In the big towns, country boys come in on Saturday to get drunk and make noise. In the little towns, they come to shop, and talk to friends.

The stores stay open until the last man is off the street. After they lock up, Louise is dark and quiet, except for the steady rumble and pounding as cotton is baled at the gin where the tenant hands have been at work since early in the afternoon.

THE SCHOOLS

By all accounts, the quality of education has changed little over the last few years. On the side of the good, however, it is in the schools that first begins that network of friendships and acquaintances which enables everyone in the county to know everyone else. Associations develop here that make it possible for the county to be what the small town cannot—what economists call a market, where goods and services and labor can be peddled and located. Were the towns of Louise and Midnight to burn down one night, the only loss to the major part of the population would be convenience to certain stores. These towns serve as the geographical center of the community, but they are unessential to the economic and social life of the area. What is necessary to these is the knowledge of every man's skills—who is a trustworthy tractor driver, who can make a good quilt—the knowledge of every man's habits—which men get too drunk to work on Monday, where certain white men will be at a certain time of night—the knowledge of each man's situation—who needs help, who will jump at the chance to pick a little cotton—and the knowledge of who are the troublemakers, killers, and bums.

Negro teachers and school administrators have been outrageously reluctant to assume any position of leadership in their communities, or even an interest in the affairs of the families whose children they teach. Holding, like Negro policemen, jobs created by the dual system of government yet being expected to serve their white superiors and not their own community, Negro teachers and principals live in fear of the white establishment.

In Midnight, there is a black elementary school and in Louise a black high school, which had over four times as many pupils as the white school (when the latter existed) but fewer than twice the number of teachers. What teachers there are, however, have probably not registered to vote for fear of jeopardizing their jobs. They, in the natural positions of leadership that fall to the teacher and professional, have consistently resisted all pleas to involve themselves in the struggles of their community. Of course, across the South there have been many exceptions to the general apathy of the public school personnel. Many college professors and administrators, and some high school teachers, have worked hard on behalf of civil rights. Some county school systems in the South have released schools for summer Head Start centers at the insistence of black principals. Some public school teachers have worked with children in OEO[13] day care centers. In Humphreys County, a teacher sits on the county committee of the Friends of the Children of Mississippi (FCM) Head Start system. Still, the involvement of teachers in community action has been even less than that of the preachers, who can point to members or prospective members of their ranks in the Southern Christian Leadership Conference, the Student Non-Violent Coordinating Committee, and Congress of Racial Equality of the early 1960s, and in local groups like the Delta Ministry[14] (a project of the National Council of Churches), located in Washington County (Greenville) which borders on Humphreys County. The teachers, hamstrung by being employees of the county and set apart by their complicity in a disgraceful and unconstitutional educational system, have themselves withdrawn and forgotten the needs of their people.

It has thus become clear that no new arrangement of community development will spring from the old leadership of the black community, the churches and the schools. It can also be seen that the institutions and routines that were built around the plantation system will not now be useful in creating something which will sustain those people who have been displaced from the plantation as it undergoes its transition toward modern efficiency. The last years of civil rights turmoil have brought great hope to the black men in Mississippi. In Louise there has been developed a new program, Head Start, which was not born of the plantation system, and which has drawn for its local leadership upon a too-long-neglected source—the independent black small farmer.

[13] The Office of Economic Opportunity; called by some: The War on Poverty.

[14] The Delta Ministry does research, gives out clothes, sets up conferences, and supports community projects.

VII   Civil Rights and
Community Organizations

Louise and Midnight were passed over, as were many little towns, by the civil rights activity in the Delta in 1963 and 1964. Belzoni was not:

❲ When it first started, COFO [Council of Federated Organizations] came here and set up a voter registration drive. That lasted about a year. After that we organized the NAACP. We organized the NAACP in 1967, and that was when the biggest push in the civil rights movement came in Humphreys County. We've put on quite an effective boycott against the stores and brought suits against the schools, in fact against the whole county . . . . Reverend Lee was killed back in '55 and Gus Courts was shot . . . . I believe he was shot for pushin' for the right to vote . . . . They had some kind of autopsy on Reverend Lee and they found the pellets in his jaw, shotgun pellets, but they said it was dental fillings so that was as far as it went . . . . They [Sunflower and Sharkey Counties] had more activity in them than Humphreys County has . . . .
Has anything been done in Louise and Midnight?
No, not yet. Some people in Louise joined the NAACP, but no one down there is really active. So Louise sort of stands off by itself. The people are kind of scared of what might happen. [Willie Hazelwood, Director of the NAACP, Humphreys County.]

A few men and women in Louise harbored civil rights workers from Sharkey County and became active in the precinct affairs of that county's Mississippi Freedom Democratic Party (MFDP), but it was not until 1966, when one column of the Meredith March Against Fear came proudly

down U.S. 49 through Belzoni, through Midnight, through
Louise, that the people first began going in numbers to the
courthouse to register to vote. One man tells it this way:

> ⟨[The Meredith March came right down the highway
> here. There was a long line of them, singing and shouting.
> People came running out of the fields to see and wave.
> A lot of them started in marchin'. At school they tried to
> keep them in, but the kids ran out and got in the line
> with them and started marchin'. Some of them went all
> the way to Jackson. Mr. ——— boarded up his drink
> machines so they couldn't buy a pop. In Louise all of the
> stores closed. There wasn't a white man in them streets
> .... A lot of us registered behind the Meredith March. I
> did. A whole lot of people did.

The boycott effort in Belzoni has united the black community there in a way that nothing else ever has, but it
has yet done little to Louise and Midnight. The Negro
police officer in Louise was added to the force primarily because the white merchants wanted a way to learn about and
to stop any attempts at spreading the boycott to those little
towns. The state of political organization in Louise, however, is not what it is in Belzoni. There are perhaps fifteen
members of the NAACP in Louise and not all of these
attend meetings in Belzoni or in Sharkey County.

Louise has two precious Head Start centers. The confusing and sorry history of the CDGM, MAP (Mississippi
Action for Progress), FCM conflict is well illustrated by the
battle in Humphreys County. In 1965 the Child Development Group of Mississippi (CDGM) was funded by OEO
to administer Head Start centers in twenty-two counties,
including Humphreys. Two centers were set up in Belzoni.
CDGM's concept of how a preschool center should be
run was novel at that time. It felt that the people who
best knew how to care for children were mothers of children, and almost all of its centers across the state were

staffed by poor, previously unemployed women, trained by CDGM in the techniques of bringing words, music, colors, and sounds alive in the minds of three-to-five-year-olds. In this way, poor women who had never in their lives earned more than three dollars a day chopping cotton were given the opportunity to earn a decent salary. It was, and remains, an outrage in the white establishment's view of things that money it does not control is placed in the hands of black people. In October, 1966, OEO bowed to pressures, charged CDGM with mishandling of funds, and terminated the grant. But the centers in Humphreys County and in several other counties did not close down. In buildings offered free by their black owners and by churches, women worked without pay to see that the children, even if they could no longer regularly get a hot meal at the center, got loving attention each day. To raise funds for the approximately seventy-five centers operating on a volunteer basis, Friends of the Children of Mississippi was established.

To fill the void left by CDGM, an organization with more compromising policies, MAP, was formed and funded by OEO. In its beginning, MAP was more rigid in determining the qualifications of its personnel, especially for its county staff, and many women who had been resource teachers, teacher guides, and center directors with CDGM found that they could not be hired by MAP, and were determined to keep working with what, in any case, were overflowing numbers of children. In January, 1967, CDGM was refunded, but did not include Humphreys County which was to be exclusively MAP. The old CDGM centers in five counties including Humphreys (plus a sixth that had not been CDGM) refused to be administered by MAP and organized themselves under the name of Friends of the Children of Mississippi. Financed, barely, by stopgap grants from a foundation and the Board of National Missions of the United Presbyterian Church, FCM was able to provide some assistance in keeping the centers going and bringing in a bit of food and clothing for the children. FCM maintained through most of the next year two centers in Belzoni and set up one in Louise. MAP moved into Belzoni in the spring of 1967 where, in competition with FCM, it opened two centers and into Louise where it opened the second Louise center.

For seventeen long months, FCM functioned in what was officially a MAP county. The MAP centers, when they were opened, were well equipped, the children well fed, and the teachers paid. The FCM centers were furnished with handmade toys, the children had no milk, and the teachers had no money. In a final reshuffling, after pleas for a settlement "in the name of the children" from citizens and organizations all over the country, FCM was funded for four of the six counties (including Humphreys) served by both FCM and MAP.

In Louise, the results of the conflict can still be seen. What was at one time the MAP center is a large, well-constructed building, paneled on the inside and filled with new toys, plastic cushions for the children to sleep on, and piles of story books. Three doors away the old FCM center is only now recovering from its year and a half without money. The building is tiny and cramped, the walls are full of cracks, and all last winter the wind blew steadily through the one-room building. The center has three units of seventeen children each that must be accommodated in that space, or in a tiny play area separated from U.S. 49 by a wire fence. The toys are mostly handmade. The children play with tires in the yard. There are barely enough plates to feed all of the children at once. During the last week that I lived in Louise, money was finally allocated to build an extension to the building that will allow for two more units of children. Slowly, a trickle of new books, new equipment, new plates, and new toys is beginning to arrive at the center.

❨ I'm a county teacher guide for FCM. I work with the teachers and the children. Help train the teachers, and work with the children. We try to get the children interested in things. We let the children pick different alphabets and put them together. We make puzzles. We're trying to teach them themselves. We make puzzles and put them together. We have songs about my eyes, my nose, my mouth. We're trying to get the children acquainted with themselves, and after we get them acquainted with themselves then they'll know—we're trying to let them know—that they're just as important as anybody else. And to really let them know that they are important, they first have to know about themselves.

Head Start has had an especially wonderful effect upon the Louise community. When the first visions of the life-giving power of federal assistance were stolen away, the people, rather than recoiling in bitterness, determined to make good themselves the OEO promise of a place where withdrawn and underfed children could be made to laugh and to play together, and to learn to understand and enjoy the world of people and things: a place run by poor men and women elected in community meetings, a place staffed by poor men and women (carefully selected by the center council), a place where children could eat a hot lunch, and, most important, a place of their own where everything and everybody connected with it would be decent. It has been the first step in community action ever taken in the long history of the black people in that plantation town.

To keep the center going, they used their sparse resources. Near the end, when small salaries were being given out, the center was forced to move into a smaller building. Two units of children were cut; their teachers were left jobless. The remaining teachers divided their salaries so that even those hurt in the cutback received an equal share of what little there was. When OEO finally approved FCM's budget and the center was required to come up to federal standards of adequacy, the people in the community contributed money to seal the walls, to put linoleum over the holes in the floor, and to buy a shield for the gas heater.

The nomination and election of members for the center committee defined which men in Louise would be responsible for the affairs of the community. Almost all of those elected are small farm owners. They have taken their role seriously, and having once been proclaimed leaders will continue to be leaders in whatever concerns their small town.

When FCM first was established in Louise, the white community put up a stiff fight to get rid of it. Tenants were forbidden to work for the center or to drive children there. The welfare checks of the teachers and cooks were threatened and generally cut back, even though FCM could not afford to pay salaries. Women on the plantations were told not to send their children to the "civil rights school." Men were refused employment because their wives worked for Head Start. But all of this, for the most part, has ended. In place of resistance there is nastiness. For example, the town has not moved the "65 MPH" sign on the road out of Louise past the center. Tourists' cars continue to roar by as the children pile out of station wagons that bring them to school. But the larger struggle seems almost won. It has been a meaningful one, intended not so much to prove, as simply not to be deterred from, a belief that the poor best know what's best for the poor.

⟨ It seems that we did more for the county last year, working volunteer, than we did when we were workin' for CDGM, because the reason I say this is that we got a lot of children in school that didn't have birth certificates, we got a lot of children clothes and shoes that hadn't ever been in school, and we found lots of families that was fastened up in the house that people didn't even know was in the county; and we helped a lot of children with doctor care . . . . Some of them would be just lined with sores

and their little stomachs would be pushed out. So I think
FCM has done a wonderful job. We had some little children that when they walked in the door couldn't even
stand up. We worked so long without any money that
really what we were working for was not a salary. There
was one thing that we wanted to prove: that we could do
something if we was allowed a chance. That's why we
worked two years for nothing. We just wanted to prove
that we could do it and do a good job, and we did do a
good job.

There are now in Louise five units of children in Head
Start centers. In all of Humphreys County there are approximately twenty-six units, for a total of 450 children. This is
the maximum number allowed for in the budget. There are
approximately 800 children of poor families between three
and five years of age in the county for whom there is no
room in the centers.

❨ *Could you make a guess as to how much you spend
on food in a month?*
I spend so much. I don't spend no more'n I have. I
spend all of my check, and sometimes I have to go back
and take up debt before the month is out.

VIII **Problems with Assistance Programs**

WELFARE

While most agencies of the county government, such as
those concerned with roads and agriculture, are controlled
and administered by the planters for the planters, there is

only one agency, excepting the public school system, concerned mainly with the black community, and that is the
welfare department. Though in many matters the welfare
department abides by standardized regulations and becomes
an overly objective bureaucracy, heartless and pitiless, it is
frequently used as a tool to manipulate the black man and
thus in that aspect becomes too personal. It gives the
planter, then, yet another avenue of control over the black
and the poor. In Humphreys County, as in the rest of the
state, one encounters reports that welfare checks were cut
off in the early 1960s as a means of stopping black people
from registering to vote. More recently, it is said, early participants and staff members of the Head Start programs in
Humphreys County had their checks stopped or reduced to
force them out of the project. Head Start center personnel,
who received their salaries only in spurts, have seen their
welfare checks reduced each time a little money was paid out,
and the cuts not restored until long after the money stopped
coming. The boards of supervisors in Mississippi, which in
the Delta is to say the planters, have no legal authority over
the county welfare departments, but do have their considerable influence to wield against them. Those tenants on the
supervisors' plantations in Humphreys County having any
claim to eligibility receive welfare benefits that seem guaranteed for the elected term of their boss. This guarantee, which
acts as an incentive for good work, also serves the planter
as an assurance that none of his tenants will cause any
trouble.[15]

It should be noted that things are improving. It only
rarely happens now that county welfare departments will
ignore an explicit rule set down by the state. The right of an

[15] In an OEO, HEW, USDA listing of the 255 most needy counties in
the nation, Humphreys County ranks 54th. In a recent report by the
Citizens' Board of Inquiry into Hunger and Malnutrition, HUNGER,
USA, a list of statistics on "hunger counties" showed that 71.5 per cent
of the population of Humphreys County were in poverty, but only 12.1
per cent of the poor were on welfare.

applicant to appeal the decision of the county agent to a state board is more widely known and understood. The county, however, controls the speed with which it handles cases; the difference between an application's being approved one month or the next can be the difference between subsistence and acute hunger. A more vital point, and one which will be returned to later, is that while eligibility for welfare and the size of the check are established by a schedule of income set by the state, the county welfare agent has the responsibility for determining an applicant's income. It is very difficult to ascertain the annual income of a tenant farmer who works irregularly and by the hour, and who most likely keeps no records; so the welfare department can set a man's income at almost any point that it likes without being challenged. The agent often gets from the planter his figures for the income of his tenant, which again gives the power over the check back to the planter. The county welfare department also administers either the surplus commodities or food stamp program of the U. S. Department of Agriculture and handles these programs in much the same way, and to the same ends, as it does the welfare checks.

The welfare system, as has often been remarked, has certain built-in shortcomings. Though the federal government contributes the major portion of the welfare budget in Mississippi—83.3 per cent in the case of Aid to Dependent Children (ADC) payments—the state still has too little money to give substantial assistance to welfare recipients. Payments in the categories of Aid to the Permanently and Totally Disabled (APTD), Aid to the Blind (AB), and Old Age Assistance (OAA) are usually $50 a month. Though $600 a year is a very small amount, it is still almost three times as large as the per capita income of the poor people in Louise. Most recipients of APTD and OAA, however, support families with their checks. The amount paid out for Aid to Dependent Children is clearly inadequate for actual child support.

Maximum ADC payments in Mississippi are based roughly on the formula of $25 a month for the first child and $10 a month for each other child under eighteen years of age. The state sets the standard of living scale for families of all sizes, and the above-mentioned maximum payments are approximately 27 per cent of what the state estimates to be a minimal standard of living. But most families cannot claim the maximum allowance. For a mother and three children living on a plantation where their home is provided, the state establishes the living requirements at $125 a month. If the mother earns approximately $72 a month as a maid, the size of her ADC check will be figured on the basis of the $53 that she falls short of the standard. The established payment is $15 a month, about 28 per cent of the difference. Three children are supported on $18 a week from the mother's earnings and $5 a month apiece from the welfare department.

The states with the greatest percentage of poor people, and thus the smallest budgets, are the least capable of providing decent welfare assistance. And, in racially divided Mississippi where the white man runs the welfare department and the poor are predominantly black, the possibility of fair administration of the system, especially on the local level, is quite remote.

⁅ *What do you do?*
I works by the day.
On the plantation?
Yes.
Do you work all year round or are there parts of the year when you don't work?
Well, I chops a little bit, and I picks a little cotton.

Do you work about every day?

No sir, not every day. I make about two or three days a week.

Could you give me an idea of what your income is in a month or a year?

Well, near as I can get at it, about $75 or $80.

A month?

No, I don't make that much a month. I make that much in the run of about two or three months.

Are you getting food stamps?

No. They said I was makin' too much. I couldn't see how I was makin' too much for food stamps.

COMMODITIES AND FOOD STAMPS

The federal government has two main programs to assist low-income families in obtaining adequate amounts of food: direct distribution or surplus commodities, and the food stamp program. The commodity distribution program has existed since 1949. Its purpose is to prevent the waste of agricultural surpluses, created mainly through the price support operations of the USDA, by distributing free the surplus, unmarketable goods to the poor. The basic commodities, cornmeal, corn grits, rice, flour, non-fat dry milk, peanut butter, and rolled wheat, are given out each month in counties that have requested and been approved for the program. From month to month, the basic goods will be supplemented with several of the fifteen other staples purchased by the USDA. People in households receiving federal welfare assistance and all persons deemed to be needy by the local welfare agency are eligible for the program.

In 1964, the food stamp program was begun. It was intended to remedy some of the problems of the commodity program, such as the difficulties and the expense of distributing large quantities of food, the low nutritional level provided by a diet of surplus food, and the burden it placed on poor people who have no ready access to transportation and little storage space in their homes but who had to transport and store a month's supply of food at one time. Also, the program was created as an answer to the complaints of merchants who felt that the free distribution of certain foods hurt their businesses. Under the food stamp program, a person declared eligible by the welfare department will, according to his income and size of his family, pay a set amount each month for food coupons distributed by the welfare department. These coupons are worth a certain amount more than is paid for them and can be used just like cash in the purchase of food at cooperating stores. Thus, the food purchasing power of the poor man is increased, and he may select his own groceries at the store of his choice.

Counties may elect to sponsor either program; no county may have both unless the Secretary of Agriculture declares an emergency. The food stamp program is slowly phasing out the commodity program in counties where it existed, and is beginning to be administered in counties that have never had any food program.

Until August, 1968, Humphreys County used the surplus commodities program. Of the black families in Louise, 89.2 per cent were on the program. The remaining families were generally denied participation because they owned too much land or their income was considered to be too high. One family was denied because they had fixed up their house; another was reported stricken from the rolls because the father had been blacklisted by a planter. Almost 95 per cent of those who got commodities had to buy some food to supplement them. The rest of the families were not able to buy groceries and lived solely on the surplus food. Not everyone ate all the foods that were distributed. Many mothers said that the powdered milk made their children sick, and almost no one used it for anything but cooking. Only a few ate the powdered eggs. Everyone viewed the raisins, only recently distributed, with suspicion because a great many boxes in the first month's shipment were infested with bugs. If people had a choice, they would not eat the canned "luncheon" or "commodity" meat (mostly composed of pork) which was usually given out. Members of fifty-three families could not eat it because they had high blood pressure, and their doctors had warned them against eating pork. Much of the commodity food was stored away for use in the winter.

In August, 1968, Humphreys County started the food stamp program. In setting it up, the county followed guidelines that were designed to clear up some of the difficulties other areas had encountered, notably: that the poor have little transportation, that prior indebtedness to stores often makes it difficult for a poor man to free enough cash to make an initial purchase of stamps, and that a time lapse between the end of the commodity program and the beginning of the food stamp program can be disastrous to poor families. Stamps are sold twice a month in Louise, and every weekday in Belzoni. The first month's stamps were half-price. The transition from one program was made smoothly. However, in Louise, participation in the food programs dropped by 20.1 per cent.[16] The reasons for this can be seen by examining several examples of food stamp costs per month.

The average black family in Louise has about seven members and an income of about $1,538 a year, or $128 a month. The stamp price to that family every month is $54 for stamps valued at $98, for a bonus of $44.

The family must each month pay $54 cash for stamps. This is the amount that the Department of Agriculture feels

[16] Eighty-three of the 93 families interviewed had received surplus commodities when the county participated in the program; only 4 families got all the food they needed from commodities. When the county adopted the food stamp program, 9 of the 97 families interviewed were rejected; 67 families had bought the stamps, and 21 did not apply. Only 31 of 47 respondents had purchased the stamps every month, however. The stamps lasted an average of three weeks.

a family of this size and income would "normally" spend on food. Normally, however, that family had been getting surplus commodities and spending perhaps $20 each month to supplement the free food. The extra cash outlay, even though netting a $44 "bonus," is too much for many families to make, and so they do not buy the stamps.

For two ladies living together, eating nothing but commodities and whatever their neighbors contribute, and *who earn no cash income*, the price in 1967 was $1 for stamps worth $30 (a $29 bonus).

Where are they to get the $1 a month needed to buy stamps? And how are they to eat on $15 a month? Sixty-nine percent of the families in the black community of Louise now get food stamps. Many others heard about how much the stamps might cost and never bothered to apply. One out of every ten who applied was rejected as having too high an income.

The welfare department in Humphreys County has the responsibility for determining each applicant's income, and thus who is eligible for the program and how much each must pay for stamps. Farm workers earn money in spurts and only in certain seasons. There is no standard income for the tenant farmer, skilled or unskilled; there can be great differences in the calculated income of one tenant and another. What this can mean in the cost of stamps can be seen below in two cases taken from this survey.

NUMBER IN FAMILY	MONTHLY INCOME	STAMP PRICE	"BONUS"	VALUE OF STAMPS
8	$210-229	$78	$38	$116
8	130-139	58	48	106

To avoid relying on the applicant's information, the welfare department usually demands of the tenant an affidavit signed by the planter, telling what the employee's income is. No official will question the judgment of a planter concerning his tenants; it is the opinion of many poor people that their bosses state that their income is too high.

The value of stamps that a given family receives fluctuates as their income rises and falls. In the poor community of Louise, however, incomes are so low as to put families at a level of bare subsistence. Everyone needs everything equally badly. It might be wondered why, in setting a stamp value schedule in an assistance program for the destitute, the USDA should determine that families with the same number of mouths to feed should be given different limits on the value of stamps that they may buy.

Though a person may purchase stamps at the beginning and at the end of the month in Louise, and at any time in Belzoni, he must always buy either a whole month's supply or a half-month's supply, and he must buy the same supply every month. It is very difficult for a poor man to amass that amount of cash at one time. He does not earn his money all at once, but irregularly, by the day. Most poor people in Louise have been accustomed, partially because of the commodity program, to buying food only as they need it. If they have developed any normal pattern of expenditures, it certainly does not allow for spending a great amount of cash for anything on any given day. If no money is available until the third week of the month, a man will have to do without stamps altogether for that month or purchase an entire month's supply for the last week.

Some tenants borrow the money for stamps from their bosses and try to pay them back out of their month's wages. On some plantations, it is said, the planter himself will purchase the stamps for his tenants and sell them to his workers as he sees fit. The real problem in Louise arises as work begins to slack off in the winter. Most tenants have absolutely no income in the winter months. There is no provision in the Food Stamp Act for lowering the cost of stamps in areas where the income of most people is seasonal, though this is recommended by the USDA. Even if the prices that the tenant farmers in Louise are charged for stamps are decreased to the minimum, they will probably not be able to afford them. It is likely that most tenant farmers will rely on the planters to pay for the stamps. The food stamp program will then serve to reinforce the old plantation planter-dominated system that the poor must be helped to escape from.

Food stamps, in the amounts now allotted, do not last most people all month. On the average, they carry people in Louise through for about three weeks. The families for whom the stamps do last all month are those who have no choice but to make them last. Everyone must spend his stamps sparingly. Using the stamps, people may, for the first time in years, buy an occasional piece of fresh meat. But people would rather use their food stamps to purchase foods that will go a long way: rice, grits, meal, beans, flour. There is nothing to indicate that more, or even as much, meat is eaten now than when the commodities program gave it away.

(Everything I buy since we got stamps has gone up. I don't know nothin' that the price has stayed the same . . . .
Can you buy more with the stamps now than before with cash?
Well you can't. Cause the prices was down before you started gettin' stamps, and by you gettin' the food cheaper you could buy just as much and maybe more than with the stamps because the food's all gone up. Even the bread, the light bread, a loaf has gone up.

The most striking effect that the food stamp program has had in Louise has been to cause stores to raise their prices for food. The items that have gone up the most are those that were distributed free under the surplus commodities program.

❪ *Has the price of food gone up since stamps came to the county?*
It sure has.
Has any specific thing gone up?
Not just one thing. It looks to me like everything's gone up.

One example is that eggs one week reached a peak of eighty cents a dozen from a low there in the county of forty cents. The merchants themselves were benefitting from the "bonus" provided by the stamps.

❪ *Did you happen to notice if the price of food went up after stamps came to the county?*
Yes sir, I sure did. It climbed a good bit up. We talks about it every day . . . . Now this evening—I made $3.10 today picking cotton—I know something in there I'd been payin' about a dollar for, the grocer he told me a dollar nineteen. A bag of smoked sausage. But I'd been payin' a dollar for it, and before the food stamps got here we didn't even pay that. I think we'd been payin' about ninety-five cents. But I paid for it, and on the way home I told the fellow I was drivin' with that pretty soon it'd be $3.15.

In one way or another, people using stamps pay more for food items than people using cash. There were reports of instances in Louise of merchants openly reducing cash register receipts when they learned that their customers were not paying with food stamps. It is reportedly a common practice to tax each item in a string of groceries and then tax the total, when the customers are paying with food stamps. USDA regulations made all this illegal, but they lack any means for enforcement.

The smallest food stamp denomination is fifty cents. Merchants must make change for purchases made with stamps, either with a fifty-cent stamp or with an official "due bill" for the amounts under fifty cents. He cannot make change for stamps in money. Some merchants in Louise refuse to render "due bills." If they owe a customer forty-nine cents in change, they will instruct him to pick up two loaves of bread and a bar of candy. The customer often finds himself buying things he does not need, or when he does not need them. No merchant will give a "due bill" for an amount under ten cents. Pieces of candy and boxes of matches are used for change instead. In fact the price of matches has been raised to two cents for ease in making change. If a customer does receive a "due bill," he must use it later at that same store. The stores in Louise do not price their goods competitively; a merchant is not inclined to price a can of soup three cents lower than others charge, because his customers must spend their stamps in multiples of fifty cents, or are tied to him by "due bills."

Many poor people in Louise, three months after the beginning of the food stamp program, still ate for breakfast and supper the rice and meat that was left over from that distributed through the commodity program. Commodity food formed a large portion of everyone's diet, and supplemented what could be purchased with food stamps. Some people who could not afford stamps still ate nothing but surplus food. It is wrong to replace a program from which everyone benefits with a program, even a better one, from which only some benefit.

In the face of the gradually declining ability of the black community of Louise to make do, the price of food, since the initiation of the food stamp program, has risen sharply and has absorbed much of the "bonus" allotted in the purchase of food stamps. The hardest hit are those who cannot afford to buy food stamps. They are caught in the price squeeze that stamps have created; yet they are too poor to buy them and benefit from the "bonus" that they provide. Those who need food the most pay the highest price for it.

IX Conclusions

Over the next ten or fifteen years, the black community of Louise and of Humphreys County will gradually become more vocal in its opposition to the political and social order reigned over by the wealthy planters; and it can eventually be expected to have the power to control all of the local elected offices. In time, when almost all employees on plantations are skilled, they will quite likely organize themselves and be able to bargain successfully for a living wage. These will be the final results of the dissolution of the old plantation system. They will only come about after all of the hundreds of economically expendable men, women, and children in Louise have died, or moved away; only after all of the young men have gone north; only after many successive years of increasing poverty and worsening conditions. The complete transition will involve many years of the meanest possible existence for people. It will be a horrifying period of wasted humanity.

Until now, it has been possible for most of the poor black people of Louise to make some sort of living. The per capita income of the poor people there is slightly more than $200 a year. There is absolutely no flexibility to the budgets of people living at this level. If someone gets sick, it means that money that should be spent for clothes goes to pay doctor's bills. If someone gets sick and someone's shoes wear out, then money set aside for food is otherwise spent. These things of course do happen, and they require a constant reshuffling of funds that are never quite sufficient to meet the needs. Men must always struggle to find money to handle emergencies as they happen and to provide a buffer against future bills. This is necessary for survival.

It is an extraordinary demonstration of human persever-ance and creativity that families do manage to survive. The poor men of Louise have explored every possible means of earning money with little initial capital. In the late summer evenings, when work on the plantations has ended for the day, there will be men in the forests chopping and sawing down trees to sell as fuel for heaters in the winter. Some women make dresses, and some make quilts. Men hire out their trucks to haul water barrels from Louise to people's homes. A tenant not called to work for a week on a plantation might spend his time fishing and peddle his catch to his neighbors. A man who can fix a car can usually find work to do. Some farmers sell a few vegetables, and sometimes milk and eggs to neighbors. Others, if they own machines, hire themselves out to harvest the crops of other small farmers. There is always a market for homemade whiskey, and many do their best to exploit it. Even in a town the size of Louise, there are dozens of little jobs that men must do—work at service stations, paint and repair white folks' homes, clean the streets, mind the stores, and many more—which usually go to white men but still have been held, at one time or another, by almost every black in the area.

One reason that everyone knows everyone else in the county is that, over the years, everyone has worked to-gether. There is a continual flow of labor around the county, and a very reliable grapevine that spreads news, hints, and rumors of jobs from Yazoo City to Rolling Fork, from Holly Bluff to Belzoni, from Anguilla to Isola, from In-verness to Silver City, and to every working man's home in Louise. And men's reputations build, so that planters come looking for combine operators, farmers know where to find mechanics, and girls preparing for graduation know where the dressmakers are. The men in Louise call this job search "scrapping." When things are rough, they have to scrap up something to do. It would be my guess that scrapping brings under $100 additional each year to a family, but these are the dollars that make it possible for most to stay alive.

(We don't have no medical care here, or nothin', and I'll tell you, what we scrap up, we've got to try and live. It's either that or sink. The only way we could swim is what little we scrap up. Now I didn't say make a living. I said we do that to try to live—keep from starving. That's what I mean.

Each year it gets harder. The techniques for "making it," which could never do more than supplement farm income, show themselves to be more and more inadequate for supporting a family as the direct income from the plantation decreases.

There is just no real money to be made on the plantations today, and money is necessary now for survival. The vast numbers of the unskilled work a few days scattered throughout the year, and they hold down the incomes of the skilled by draining off countless little jobs and performing them for almost nothing. To make the final resolution of this situation come about sooner and less painfully it will be necessary to draw labor off the farm, make a variety of home industries more profitable, and improve the lot of the small farmer so that he can compete with the plantations.

The government's efforts to end poverty in the Mississippi Delta have been met with a good deal of passive resistance. In the latter part of the 1960s, the U.S. Department of Labor has started running a large project in the Delta, called the Concentrated Employment Program, which coordinates all of the federally-funded and state-managed programs in the area related to basic education, vocational and technical training, and employment. The project has been aimed at approximately 13,000 unemployed in the Delta, of whom it might possibly train and place in full-time jobs considerably fewer than half, and its scope is such that it cannot include the tens of thousands of men and women in the Delta who are very much underemployed.

Several men and women in Louise are taking, through the project, basic education or vocational courses, which, however, promise no jobs. One aspect of the program is a declared effort to re-locate men to industrial areas, hopefully out of the state. Public efforts to encourage migration from Mississippi have not been widely successful.

The one effective government program, Head Start, was withdrawn mainly because it worked. The resulting fight for community-run child care centers brought people together in a way rare and wonderful in isolated towns.

One product of the Friends of the Children of Mississippi struggle and other on-going civil rights efforts in Humphreys County has been the uniting of men in the county who can help to articulate community goals and who can help to devise effective routes for protest as well as economic development programs. This last is of course crucial, for the situation in plantation areas has now reached a point where the entire economic system of the plantation must be replaced for thousands of people. The alternative to replacing that system is to stand by while those thousands go unemployed, underemployed, homeless, and hungry in the Delta, or drift northward to swell the bloated ghettos of our once great cities.

X   Profiles of the People

§ The head of the family is a very old widow who at the time of the interview kept three of her grandchildren and now keeps four. They farm 4 of their 72 acres and rent out the rest. The little money from the cotton and her Social Security check bring in $892 to $2,192 each year, depending on the crop. Three of the children have never seen a dentist because the cost is too high.

§ The mother of eight is a tenant but works as a teacher at one of the Head Start centers. Her $77 welfare check was stopped when she began work for FCM even though she had received her salary only three times at the date of the interview. She can no longer afford food stamps because the cost was raised to $82 a month. On the day of the interview she ate pinto beans, cornbread and kool-aid for supper. Their home burned two weeks before the interview, and the house they are now in is bare. The children sleep on the floor. The family income is $1,129 a year.

§ The husband is a tractor driver on a plantation. The wife is a teacher for FCM. One of their seven children has asthma. The children are covered with sores and have regular colds all winter. The family income is $2,008 a year.

§ The husband has been laid off on the plantation. He is unskilled and had been tending the few cows, but they are being sold, and his job is gone. They can no longer buy food stamps. The children sleep four in one bed, three in another. The family income is $1,300 a year.

§ The mother of five—three at home—farms her own 120 acres which she bought twenty-five years ago from her wages as a tenant farmer. The farm, which is supposed to support three families, a total of fourteen people, has lost money for the last four years. The families share the work and the debts. A boarder at the house who has returned after seven years in New York works and contributes some money. Their income is $950 a year.

§ The daughter of the woman above and her five children. She attends an adult education school. Her house is a shell; her walls have no sealing. She has no toilet. Her income from school, APTD, and ADC checks is $1,292 a year.

§ The husband does most of the work on a 120-acre farm to support two of the families mentioned above and his own wife and two children. All that they owned was lost in a fire five years ago, and they have been recovering ever since. His wife is director of a Head Start center. The family income is between $2,400 and $2,900 a year, depending on the crop.

§ The husband drives a tractor on a plantation. They have eight children at home. They cannot buy food stamps because their welfare check was stopped and the cost of stamps simultaneously raised. Their home is in poor shape. Their income is about $1,000.

§ Both husband and wife are too sick to work. They keep two children and four grandchildren. The mother was hospitalized after a heart attack and they owe $180 for her bills. She has raised ten children and had sixteen miscarriages. Their whole house is collapsing; they cook over an open fire. Social Security and ADC checks provide $948 a year.

§ The woman lives with her grandchild. She did not apply for food stamps because she feared the cost. APTD and ADC checks provide $768 a year.

§ The father is a skilled and very needed worker on a plantation. He earns about $50 a week year round. His wife is director of a Head Start center. Their house, like all the others on the plantation, is old and unsound. Total income for the family of eight is $3,580 a year.

§ The husband does hand labor on a small plantation for three dollars a day. He applied for food stamps but was told his income was too high. The day of the interview they ate butterbeans for supper. Income, including Social Security, is between $846 and $976 a year.

§ The family farms their own 80 acres. For supper on the night of the interview they had peas. The father has had a heart attack; the son, for reasons unknown, is often too weak to get out of bed in the morning. He owes $5,500 on farm equipment. From his furnish, ADC, and APTD checks, he makes $1,084 a year.

§ The household is made up of a husband, his wife, their child, and a boarder. They farm their own 40 acres, thus their applications for food stamps and commodities were rejected. The farm has been in debt for five years. Their total income from the furnish is $600 a year.

§ The family farms their own 80 acres. The wife is a driver for FCM. They repaired their house in 1963 and as a result were cut from the commodities program. During the months not covered by the furnish, they get by on what their children in Chicago send them. Their income this year was between $1,300 and $1,900.

§ The father services and installs butane tanks for gas heaters. His wife is a teacher for FCM. They have a relatively nice home for which they pay $25 a month rent. But the windows have no panes; their toilet is outside; and two of the children have to sleep on the floor. The income for the ten people is $3,512 a year.

§ The father works on a plantation. The mother is a Head Start teacher. They own some land which they have rented out. They do not buy food stamps because of the cost. The income for the three people is $1,550 a year.

§ The father is a highly skilled machine operator on a large plantation. The mother has raised six children, had two miscarriages, and lost one child in infancy. She cannot afford medicine for her high blood pressure. Their porch steps have collapsed. Income for the family of eight is $2,924 a year.

§ A mother and three children are supported by a $41-a-month ADC check. She is charged $22 a month for food stamps. The family almost never eats meat, fish, or eggs. For supper they usually eat beans or canned spaghetti. They have no toilet.

§ The mother supports her ten children by working as a maid for three dollars a day. She must pay $16 a month for food stamps and $8 a month for rent. She buys medicine on credit for her blood pressure and diabetes. The income for the family is $936 a year.

§ The husband is too old to do much work on the plantation. His wife works for FCM. Their oldest son is too disabled to work. Their application for ADC was rejected because their income was too high. The mother has raised three children and had five miscarriages. Their income is $1,928 a year.

§ The father does hand labor on the plantation. His wife sews. Their granddaughter and her two children live with them. Income for the family is $700 a year.

§ A mother and her adult daughter. They do whatever work they can find. The daughter will be enrolled in a CEP[17] program this winter. Their neighbors contribute food. Their home sits on the ground and on a slant. Their income is $334 a year.

§ The family of six is supported solely by the father's earnings from the cotton gin in the fall. Their income is $334 a year.

[17] Concentrated Employment Program, a vocational training program of the Labor Department which has as one of its objectives the relocation of poor people to job centers outside of Mississippi.

§ A woman alone, unemployed. She will sometimes cook a meal for a white family and earn a little money. She missed buying food stamps because she had doctor's bills. She eats mostly what her neighbors contribute. Her income might be as high as $260 a year.

§ The father drives a tractor on a plantation. The six children rarely eat meat, fish, or fruit. On the day of the interview, they had mashed potatoes and cornbread. Two children sleep in one bed, four in the other. Their income from farm work is $1,632 a year.

§ The father is a skilled tenant farmer. He is paid a straight time salary of $35 a month and $9 per day worked. On the day of the interview, the family ate three meals: sausage for breakfast, dry beans for dinner, dry beans for supper. None of the ten in the family has ever seen a dentist. Their income is $1,635 a year.

§ The father is a tractor driver and supports his wife, twelve children, and a grandchild. The mother eats clay and starch to satisfy her appetite. One child was born with diabetes; another now has intestinal worms; another is blind and retarded; one died when he was four months old. The mother has had five miscarriages. Including an APTD check, the income for the fifteen is $2,992 a year.

§ The father is a skilled tenant farmer. His seven-year-old son cannot enter school because he has no birth certificate. The family does not get food stamps because of their expense. There are two rooms—a bedroom and kitchen—for the eight in the family. Their income is $1,920 a year.

§ The father works straight time on a plantation for $35 a week. He works about eighty hours a week, six months a year, twenty hours a week thereafter. He was hurt on the job and could not buy food stamps one month. His eight children can never buy lunches at school in the winter;

they all have colds all winter. Their house offers barely any shelter against the elements. Their income is $1,820 a year.

§ The household is made up of a twenty-three-year-old-woman and her two children. The mother is unemployed. She pays six dollars a month for stamps; after they run out, the family lives on beans. They cannot afford wood to burn in their heater. They get a $25-a-month ADC check.

§ The father is an unskilled tenant farmer. The mother is a cook at the Head Start center. They have raised seventeen children. The father has not seen a doctor since 1942. Total income for the family of eight is $900 a year.

§ The father drives a tractor. The family cannot afford food stamps. For supper on the day of the interview, the thirteen in the family ate beans. The walls of the two bedrooms are not sealed. Rain comes in the roof. The family income is $1,081 a year.

§ The father farms his own 40 acres of land with a furnish from a planter. After the six months covered by the furnish, the family borrows from the planter to stay alive. Total income for the family of four is $480 a year.

§ The father farms his own 80 acres and actually clears money on his land. Because of this, he was rejected for food stamps. He has eight children at home by his second wife, and helps to support four more by his first wife. Only one of the eight has ever seen a dentist. The family income is $2,550 a year.

§ The father drives a tractor; he does not earn enough ($910 a year) to buy food stamps so he prefers the commodities program. Three of his children have had intestinal worms; all have colds in the winter and skin infections in the summer. They eat their meals on the floor. Their toilet is inside because theirs is the old cook's house.

§ The father is a skilled tenant farmer. He did not apply

for food stamps because he feared the cost would be too high. On the day of the interview, the family ate only green peas and rice. Three children sleep in a bed; four sleep on a cot. Total income for the family of eleven is $1,960 a year.

§ The household is made up of an unemployed twenty-three-old woman and her four children. They cannot afford food stamps. They never eat meat, fish, or eggs. They drink about three or four pints of milk a month. None of the five has ever seen a dentist. They own no blankets, no stove, no furniture except a bed and a chair. Their house has no electricity. The ADC check provides $54 a month.

§ Both husband and wife are elderly and unemployed. They left the plantation last year because their home was collapsing and they could not get wood to burn. They get $74 a month from Social Security.

§ The husband is a saw operator at a lumber mill. He was not allowed to get commodities or food stamps. He has just installed a toilet inside his home and he is laying pipes for inside running water. Income for the family of eight is $3,380 a year.

§ The father drives a tractor. The mother works for FCM. Most of their five children have colds all winter and running sores on their bodies in the summer. The family income is $1,780 a year.

§ The father drives a tractor. He can buy food stamps, but they last him only two weeks. The family gets its water one-half mile away at the county barn hydrant. Total income for the family of four is $1,800 a year.

§ The father suffered a stroke and cannot work. The mother is a maid. Their house is made of cinder blocks, but still they are bothered by rats and snakes coming in.

Total income, including ADC and APTD checks, is $2,900 for the family of ten.

§ The father drives a tractor on a plantation and supports a wife and two grandchildren. Rats have eaten holes in the sealing on the walls; the roof leaks. The family income, counting Social Security, is $1,764 a year.

§ The father drives a tractor on a plantation. His eight children do not eat lunch at school in the winter; they taste fruit "every Christmas mostly." Rats have eaten away the paper sealing on his walls. The income for the ten people is $900 a year.

§ The father is old and too disabled to work; the mother is a part-time maid. Their twenty-three-year-old daughter and her three children live with them. The daughter has had two miscarriages and lost one child in infancy. The family income, including welfare, is $1,753.

§ The father drives a tractor and supports his wife and four children and four of his sister's children (their mother died; they were transferred to another sister who developed tuberculosis, were sent to live with him). None of the children ever gets milk to drink, and the five in school never eat lunch. The two-year-old has asthma. The family owns no blankets, few clothes, and almost no shoes. Four children sleep on one bed, two on another, two on the floor. The family has no toilet. Total income for the ten people is $1,514 a year.

§ The father is a skilled tenant farmer. His home is very nice. The eldest of his nine children works also, but does not contribute his earnings to the family; the family was rejected for food stamps because he lives there. The mother has had one miscarriage, and three children died in infancy. The family income, including ADC, is $2,584 a year.

§ An old couple who farm 40 rented acres. Their total income is $440 a year from the furnish and the crop.

§ The family farms their own 100 acres. The price that they pay for food stamps was raised $22 per month when the father began attending an adult education school that pays him $30 a week expenses. They buy almost all of their food on credit. They own almost no clothing and all of the children do not have shoes. They are badly in debt. Income is $1,140 a year for the six people.

§ The father drives a tractor on a plantation. The family could afford food stamps only once. Total income for the five people is $1,170 a year.

§ The household is made up of a mother and her thirteen children, her father and her three brothers. All of the adults do occasional hand labor on the plantation. The two younger brothers and the thirteen children have never seen a doctor. All eighteen sleep in three rooms. The family income is $2,400 a year.

§ The father farms 37 acres of which he rents 17. His oldest child has been crippled for four years for unknown reasons. Total income for the family of seven, counting all checks, is $1,342 a year.

§ The husband owns, and sometimes works at, an auto repair shop. He was denied commodities because he owned a car, and he did not apply for food stamps. With him live his wife and an adopted child. He is very old and sick, and buying pain killers takes most of his $360-a-year income.

§ The father drives a tractor on a plantation. The floors of his home are full of holes, and he is bothered by rats. His mother-in-law, living with the family, spends $10 to $12 a month for pills for her high blood pressure. Total income, including all checks, for the family of ten, is $1,612.

§ The husband was driving a tractor on a small plantation for four dollars a day, but he found a better-paying job at a cotton gin, and his family is now being evicted from their home. None of the six children, except for an eleven-year-old girl who has rheumatism, has even seen a doctor or a dentist. Income for the family of eight is $1,860 a year.

§ The family farms a rented 27 acres. The mother also works at an adult school. Her nine children have colds all winter and sores on their bodies all summer. The thirteen-year-old has rheumatic fever. Their floors have holes in them; the sealing on the walls is rotting. Income for the ten is $2,456 a year.

§ The mother works on her father-in-law's farm. She has nine children. With her lives a sixty-three-year-old aunt who keeps the family from getting food stamps because she cannot produce her doctor bills. The children eat on the floor out of pans. Wind blows through the walls; windowpanes are missing. Their income is $2,412 a year.

§ The mother is unemployed and was hospitalized recently with heart trouble. The family almost never has meat, fruit, fish, eggs, or milk. The six children in school never eat lunch. From inside their house you can see the ground below and the sky above. Total income, including ADC, for the seven people, is $732 a year.

§ The family, an elderly couple and usually about three grandchildren, farms their own 180 acres. The mother has raised nine children, and has had five miscarriages. Their income is $600.

§ The father drives machines on a plantation. His wife sharecrops 13 acres. Two of their five children had hernia operations in their second year. They have an inside toilet because their house was built for a white man. The family income is $1,540 a year.

§ Husband and wife are both too old to do much work. They could not get commodities because a planter "blackballed" them. There are large cracks in the walls of their home; there are no panes in the windows. They receive $720 a year from Social Security.

§ The father does hand labor on a plantation. None of his eleven children has ever seen a dentist. They eat from jar tops on the floor. The twelve people are supported by $700 a year from Social Security.

§ The father is too old to work. All eleven children are bothered by sores and continuous colds. The seventeen-year-old girl has asthma. The mother likes to eat clay. Welfare and Social Security checks total $1,540 a year.

§ The mother is unemployed. Two of her nine children work in the summer when school is out; the family will not be able to get food stamps for the next few months because they need to buy shoes. One son has epilepsy. One has asthma. Their present house is in very poor condition. Their old one, a better house, burned down in the spring. The family income, including ADC and APTD, is $2,380 a year.

§ The household is made up of a husband and wife, their three children, and the mother, two brothers and a sister of the wife, and the three children of one of them. The husband does mechanical work in the shop of a plantation. They get their water from a well a quarter mile away. Income for the twelve people is $2,320.

§ The mother is unemployed. She has been hospitalized recently for a bladder operation and she is now recovering. Her seven children get colds in the winter and sores in the summer, and some are sleepy and listless all day. They can no longer buy lunches at school. The family has no toilet; their porch is collapsing. They get $67 a month ADC.

§ The household is made up of two brothers and their wives, ten children, and the mother of one of the wives. One brother works on the plantation; the other attends an adult school. Between them, the two wives have had five miscarriages and lost one child in infancy. The children eat on the floor. Two sleep on the floor. Income for the fifteen is $3,472 a year.

§ The father drives a tractor on a plantation. His twelve children eat their meals on the floor and sleep up to four in each bed. Income for the fourteen people is $2,160 a year.

§ The mother of five attends an adult school. One of her five children has asthma. None of them has even been to see a dentist. None of the walls in the kitchen is sealed. All seven in the family are supported by $1,702 a year.

§ A seventy-three-year-old man alone. He does odd jobs on a friend's farm. The farmer built him a little house to live in. It is sound but has no electricity. He has never been to see a doctor. He receives $50 a month welfare.

§ The household is made up of a mother, her mother, and eight children. The mother does a little hand labor on the plantation. Six of the children have never seen a doctor; seven have never been to see a dentist. Three children sleep with their mother and two with their grandmother. Income is $1,108 a year.

§ The father, sixty years old, does hand labor on a plantation. He has not been able to afford food stamps since the first month. On the day of the interview, the family ate mashed potatoes for breakfast and butterbeans for supper. The oldest of the five children is blind. The father has a bad heart and diabetes but cannot afford to buy medicine. Income for the seven people is $700 a year.

§ The father is a non-tenant machine operator. He was

kicked off a plantation because his wife was a block organizer for a store boycott in another town. He was not allowed to receive commodities and he cannot afford food stamps. He refuses to pay rent for his house until his landlord repairs the porch and the windows. He supports his wife and child on $1,200 a year.

§ The father attends a vocational school; his wife works. Because of the money from school, the family made roughly $6,000 in 1968. He was rejected for commodities and he does not get food stamps because he got tired of responding to the welfare department's inquiries about his income. He is trying to send one of his sons through college.

§ The father is too old to work. He needed doctor's treatment one month and has not been able to afford food stamps since. There are three in the family supported by Social Security and welfare checks totalling $1,104.

§ The father farms 4 of his father's 30 acres; he is furnished by a planter. The family's food stamp allotment lasts them two weeks after which they begin skipping meals. The five children in school are able to buy lunch about once a week. None of the six children has ever seen a dentist. Total income, including a veteran's check, for the family of eight, is $432.

§ The father is a skilled tenant farmer. On the day of the interview, the family ate dry cereal for breakfast and pinto beans for supper. The two children in school can buy lunches most days; their mother will keep them home if she cannot give them the money. She has raised six children, had three miscarriages, and lost two children in infancy. The family income is $1,680 a year.

§ The father works very infrequently on a plantation. He has not purchased food stamps since the first month. The three-year-old child has had worms three times in the last year which parents have gotten rid of by spreading turpentine on her stomach. The family has no toilet. Their income is $900 a year.

§ The father drives a tractor on a plantation. His seven children in school almost never eat a lunch. He usually cannot buy food stamps. His two children eligible for Head Start were not enrolled because they did not have enough clothes at the time. Total income for the family of twelve is $1,260 a year.

§ The household is made up of a father, his working son, his daughter and her five children, and a younger son. The father is not skilled in the operation of any farm machines and lives on a plantation that relies solely on machine work. His son supports them. None of the six children has ever seen a dentist. "Wind comes through the whole house." Income for the nine people is $1,690 a year.

§ The mother is a maid. Her two eldest sons found two week's work this summer. One son sends a little money from Chicago. Including a Social Security check, income is $1,380 a year.

§ The father is a skilled plantation worker. His sixteen-year-old daughter has asthma. The mother has raised six children, had two miscarriages, and lost one child to disease at eight years of age. Income for the four is $832 a year.

§ The mother of three is too old to farm her 120 acres of land and has rented it out. Because the family owned the land, they could not get commodities, and though the husband died last year, they could not get stamps. They eat meat once a week; they never eat fish, fruit, or eggs. The family has no toilet. The four people live on $2,240 a year.

§ A mother and her adult daughter. The daughter is a driver for one Head Start center. They could not get commodities because their income from sharecropping was too high; they cannot get stamps because the FCM salary is too high. The two women have raised a total of six children and had a total of eleven miscarriages. Including Social Security, their income is $2,642 a year.

§ The family sharecrops 6 acres. Including all checks, they make an average of $108 a month out of which they must pay $50 for food stamps. There are five children in the household.

§ The husband and wife are too old to work. The mother has never birthed any live children, but they have raised several "sets" of other people's. They are now raising two. The husband is quite ill; the wife suspects he has cancer. From Social Security and welfare, they get $1,795 a year.

§ The father drives a tractor. The mother has a bad heart and diabetes. One of their four children has rheumatism. There are no screens for the windows. Total income for the six people is $1,930 a year.

§ The mother of three is unemployed. Food stamps do not last the family but two or three weeks and after that they do not eat much but bread and syrup. They are supported by an ADC check—$43 a month.

§ The father is a machine operator on a plantation. The house is in extremely poor condition. The cracks in the walls are very large. Including all checks, the income of the four people is $2,810 a year.

§ Husband and wife farm 17 acres of rented land. Because they had land, they were rejected for commodities and OAA. Usually neither can afford the medicine needed for heart condition. Social Security provides them with $84 a month.

§ The father works on a plantation and sharecrops 15 acres. The eleven children catch colds all winter. The walls of their house are not sealed. Total income for the family is $775 a year.

§ The household is made up of eight children, their mother, and their grandmother, neither of whom are employed. The mother has recently been in the hospital for heart and kidney ailments, and that expense means that the family will be unable to buy food stamps for some time. One child has asthma. None of the eight children has ever seen a dentist. They eat their meals on the floor. Social Security and ADC provide the ten people with $92 a month.

§ An old couple and their six grandchildren. They cannot afford food stamps. Five of the children have never seen a doctor or a dentist. The wife has high blood pressure but cannot afford medicine. Social Security provides them with $1,668 a year.

§ The sixty-four-year-old father works on a plantation. One of his sons quit school because he did not have decent clothing. Their daughter cannot hear well. The wife has high blood pressure. One of her children died after six years of heart trouble. Total income for the three at home is $1,700 a year.

§ The household is made up of a mother, eight children, and one grandchild. The mother was badly injured doing heavy work on the plantation, and rather than stand for her needed operation, the planter evicted her. Because of her medical bills, she cannot afford food stamps. Two children have quit school to earn money. All must eat from pans on the floor. Neighbors contribute money and food. Their total income, including ADC, is about $1,708 for the ten people.

XI The Will to Survive

The poor people of Louise have virtually nothing; yet their wants, as they articulate them, are quite simple and are things taken for granted by most Americans. They want to work. They want to be able to log enough hours in a week to make a good income. They want to be able to give their children enough food so that they will survive their childhood and grow up to be strong. They want for them something better than a daily fare of bread and molasses. They want a way to keep their children from having intestinal worms, sores on their bodies, colds all winter. They want homes that can be kept warm and dry in the winter and do not have rats in them. They want to be treated with the respect that they have earned by working, all of their lives, as hard and as often as they could. And most of them do not want to leave Mississippi or Louise—their state and their community.

⟨ I have a hard way to go along so far as my living affairs. If I could get me a job that was worthwhile to where I could live, where I could school my children, then I could overlook some other few things that's happened. I would love to be able to get my kids clothes, keep 'em in school to where they could get a fair learning. And I would love to live inside my house, too, well, decent. Other outside affairs, the worldly part—it don't bother me so bad. We have a heap of unfair things to go through with. Right now, I wouldn't make any complaints against them. I would like to make my complaints long toward my house and what I would call my wages affairs, what I work for, my earnings, and so I could see to my own family. That's where I stand right now . . . .

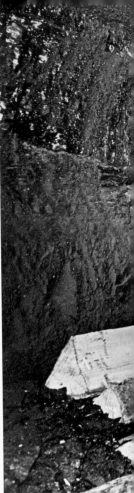

Above: Reclamation, three years later

Right: Reclamation, over ten years later

Part II

ONCE THE PROMISED LAND

❨ I wouldn't advise none of my children to go into the coal mines . . . . I took one boy in . . . . There wasn't nothin' else he could do here . . . . I said don't go. But he said I've got to work . . . . I told him not to go and I'll tell the next boy not to go. Fer there's nothin' in the coal mines. You get the rock dust. You get the black lung. You work like a slave.

It is not easy to make the shift from the Delta to the Kentucky mountains, for the regions are very different. They are not alike in geography, culture, climate, or custom. But both have been used to further the interests of a nation bent on out-producing all others. And they have been used in a manner contemptuous of the land and the people. The ultimate sign of that contempt is the condition in which the men and women who have made the cotton grow and have brought the coal from the ground must now live.

It is somehow easier to convey a picture of the flat land of the Delta than it is to describe, for the benefit of one who has never seen them, the cramped hilltops of Kentucky. It is also easier to understand the compact world of the Delta than it is to understand the far-flung mountain region, of which East Kentucky is just one part, and which has a history more murky and probably less familiar to the outsider than any other part of this country.

It is not possible to learn about the mountains today by looking at one town or one county, for there is no town or county which is typical of the mountains. While all are tied together and can tell much the same story about the past and the present, the wall of hills which separates the

Appalachians from the outside world also cuts off each mountain creek, town, and county from the others. People speak about "the mountains" and about their own community. They do not have much feeling for what is happening in a neighboring county. It becomes necessary, in writing, to switch frequently from the vantage point of one creek or community to one overlooking the entire Kentucky region. The same forces are at work everywhere, but there is no one place where they can all be seen with equal clarity.

As in the Delta, many people in the Kentucky mountains are farmers, of one sort or another, who live away from and around small towns. Few men are steadily employed. But it has been coal, the companies that took it out, its union, and its modern-day production methods, and not racism, that have dominated and shaped life in the mountains.

The mountains of southeastern Kentucky seem a place quite mysterious to the outsider. In the winter, the snowy hills and fields, marked with smoke from the chimneys of occasional homes, are scenes for Christmas cards. In the spring, bright dogwood and red buds burst from every slope. In summertime, green forests, appearing almost virginal, blanket the hills. And in the fall, the splendor of reds and yellows is matched in but a few other places in this land. Throughout the year dawns are cloaked in fog and mist that fills up the fields and valleys and rises gently to the mountain caps. In the night time, the hills are without scattered lights, and they are in silence. Always the mountains seem impenetrable, lacking a geography that is sensible or that is familiar to the outsider. East and West, North and South become muddled. There are no straight lines. Roads and creeks and hilltops follow directions set by natural, not human, plan. The eye travels only so far as the next rising slope. The horizon is above you and near to you. All that is around you speaks of isolation.

The people who inhabit the mountains are a rough

breed who have given of themselves, their customs, culture and remembrances only sparingly, and as needed, to the outside world. Clothes, speech, food, actions, and attitudes hint of times past. The mountaineers are very close to their past and to feelings sprung from a long history. They are an identifiable and in-bred people who have worked hard to maintain themselves as a separate group. To be from East Kentucky means to have shared a life style with thousands of others in a more distinct way than, for example, to be from New York City means to have things in common with eight million others. To be a hillbilly is to be raised in a certain way, to react to things in a certain way, to have certain things going for you and certain things going against you, and to be distinctly different from anyone else in the United States—anyone who is not a hillbilly.

Spanning this beautiful land is an earthen storehouse of slick, black coal. Throughout nineteen counties in southeastern Kentucky, the coal is everywhere, and so are the evidences of the attempts to extract it: operating and abandoned mines; working tipples, billowing coal dust, and old and crumbling tipples at played out shafts; coal towns where companies crammed together homes for their miners, now crowded and dirty, or abandoned and falling; Mack trucks, speeding along the highway, loaded with twenty or thirty tons of mineral; the blasts from a mountainside excavation where an auger is to be set to drill out the coal; and a barren, eroded, acid-ridden, mountain shelf where a strip mine has been run and the hilltop, now useless, has been left to wash away down the once clear streams of the mountain glory. Out of the mountaineers' homes, hidden far up the precious streams, come clouds of black and dusty smoke to foul with coal walls, yards, cars, clothes, and children. Mining, mine accidents, mine problems, mine wages, these are a part of life.

Clay County lies within the mountain coal fields of Kentucky. Here, and in a score of counties like it in the state, can be seen the interplay between the highlands—a barrier against outside influence and a fortress to shelter the unhindered development of a people, the fact of coal, and a severe and stifling poverty that has settled upon the mountaineer largely because of the hills and the coal. It is to explain and summarize one view of the problems known in East Kentucky that the second section of this book was prepared. It is not, as was "The Will To Survive," a survey of conditions in a town or country. It is rather an attempt to provide a perspective on the situation of the poor in the Kentucky mountains from the primary vantage point of a single county.

This second section is not a study. It is an expression of two individuals' thoughts about the problems of the mountains; it is a mutual work between an outsider and a local man, Robert Messer of Clay County. Both share the conviction that the nation has not yet come to terms with what has been done to this region. Mr. Messer has lived in Goose Creek of Clay County for most of his adult life. For about twenty-five years he mined coal. For the last three years he has been trying to organize the poor people of his own and two other communities. All of the dialogue in "Once the Promised Land" consists of words spoken into a tape recorder by Mr. Messer.

No other voices were taped because this was conceived of as a project between two men and because it was felt that it was not just to question, for public ear, men about the condition of their homes, or the state of their health, income, or diet. For most families, home, land, and food are things for which they have struggled, the only things that they can claim as actually gotten by work, a source of bitter pride, and possessions ferociously defended.

Not so in Mississippi where living conditions are caused by a white-dictated plantation system. There men do strive to expose what they have been subjected to for they feel an economic betrayal that needs to be made public. In the

Delta, a rotting house is the boss's house. In Kentucky, the old shack is a family homestead.

Another reason for not extensively taping conversations in Clay County is that mountaineers have no special desire to, and no personal need to, mention publicly what troubles them. In Mississippi it takes an unbelievable degree of bravery to speak out at all, and it was an assertion of courage to state exactly how bad things are in that state. Robert Messer's narrative is that of a man who has lived in poverty and has definite ideas on how the poverty of his region can be combatted. The conversations recorded in Mississippi were in themselves part of a fight of the people against the problems of that area.

"Once the Promised Land" was prepared during 1969 in Goose Creek, Kentucky, under the partial sponsorship of the Appalachian Volunteers, Inc., an organization for which the writer worked for most of that year.

Spreading northward from the Cumberland River the mountains of Kentucky are laden with riches in timber, natural gas, and coal. The first great western frontier, it was settled by free-spirited, renegade indentured servants from Georgia, Virginia, and the Carolinas, who saw the apparent boundlessness but not the value of the resources beneath and around them in the virgin mountain lands that to them offered escape from the ties and the crampedness, and perhaps the settledness, of the old nations and the already founded colonies. The wealth of minerals and forests has been, in this century, discovered and exploited, first by the hand of those who braved the highlands and later by those who came to join the work at the direction of powers largely unseen—the northern businessmen. And while the appetites of a growing industrial America have been met by the energy from these hills, and while some her greatest fortunes have been founded here, the people who live here and who have so contributed to the development of their country, have as their reward poverty in isolation, slums, welfare, social security, unemployment, sickness, rock dust, black lung, soup beans, and food stamps.

The inhabitants of the southern Appalachians, by first matching their savagery with the Indians and overcoming the terrible hardships of pioneering and, later, the horrors of an exceptionally rending Civil War experience, had set down generations-old roots in the land and a claim to a share in whatever good might come from the pains of building a nation by the time that strangers first appeared to buy up the coal. When did it become the idea of the clever men of this country that they could, in fairness, travel to such a place as East Kentucky, bringing with them money and perception enough to see the possibilities of a new national industry founded on the extraction of coal, offer to those who lived there a wage for their labor only high enough to outshadow the return from subsistence farming, and later, themselves much richer, the nation much richer, leave behind a region emptied of its wealth, with a history of unrewarding employment and mine disasters and a future of unending poverty? When did it become their idea that the acumen and profits of a few made right the destroyed lives of many? When did the notion of national interest come to include the ruin of a region?

All that the mountains had to offer America at the turn of this century was its people, a grand pioneering heritage, great high timber forests, and an abundance of coal, locked in hillsides from Alabama and Georgia to Ohio and Pennsylvania. It was the timber and coal that made the mountains important, not to those who lived here but to those who foretold a growing nation. So they came, in the years before the First World War, surveying the hills and buying for real cash dollars, from the astute but unknowing hillbilly— ever ready to take a buck that's being given away, for how else could money paid out for an "X" on an illegible document be viewed—the right to extract the minerals hidden in the earth "sometime in the future." But it was not made clear that the four-foot seams of coal running through a man's mountain would serve, in part, as foundation for some of our largest corporations. It was not understood that the tall poplar and oak hardwood forests, sold freely in the years preceding the Great Depression, were so highly prized in those parts of the country where the building, not the tearing down, was to be done. It certainly was not imagined that the deeding away of one's mineral rights would mean, half a century later, that coal companies would send earth-moving machines to cut great gashes along the mountainsides, allowing tons of earth to pile up and land precariously on the hills above mens' homes, in the enterprise called strip mining, all without necessary compensation.

Eastern Kentucky lies midway in the northeastward sweep of the Appalachian chain. Unlike the majestic Smokies and Blue Ridges of North Carolina and Virginia, the gentle, cleared slopes of Tennessee, and the neatly laid mountains and valleys of West Virginia, the Kentucky hills form a tangled, forbidding system of small mountains so enmeshed that sunlight strikes some spots for no more than a few hours each day. Tightly nestled between the peaks, in the "hollers" where the streams flow downward through the woodlands, are the homes of those who settled here, preferring the privacy of isolation to ample or even sufficient farming land. Between ridges, long strings of flat-topped mountains that, as a chain, are in no way apparent from the ground, are "bottoms," wider areas of level land opening the terrain up to the sky. Here the branches of streams converge to form creeks along which crops can actually be sown.

In East Kentucky, the land is not something to be worked and made productive under man's hand. For the most part it cannot be cultivated; tractors cannot manage the sheer inclines. It is not a land that can be made to work for men as can the fertile South and Midwest. The mountains can be cleared for pasture, and coal can be cut from within them. In the past, men cleaned huge areas of timber; now they strip mine it. But aside from these ventures, which have a dramatic and purely destructive effect upon the land, the mountains have been taken as they were found. They force upon people the impression of a changeless world, and a world full of natural imponderables like the terrible floods of '49 and '59, '63 and '66. These were so unmanageable that creek beds in many places still serve as roads, and in these parts roads, once built, cannot even hopefully be kept in good repair. A world where customs and a timeless religion form laws governing most daily action. One where strangers had seldom set foot and are now met with open suspicion. A world of people very much perplexed by modern America.

Well, I was born in Clay County in 19 an' 11, the twenty-seventh day of March. My daddy was raised in Knox County then and stayed till I was about sixteen years old. Then we moved back to Clay County. And when I didn't work my mother made me go to school, but I had to work. I had another brother and we farmed in the mountains. We tended ten, fifteen acres of corn. We had to work through the summers, an' we had to work in the field, an' we had school merely half a day. An' I had a teacher that when we went to school, we played up an' down the road. We lived by a river, a creek, an' we'd get out an' swim an' play about. The teacher was my neighbor that I'd been raised up with all my life, an' he didn't try to learn us anythin'. And that's the reason I'm in the shape I'm in today. That don't sound very good, I guess, to you, but it's the truth.

I had one good teacher one year. I guess she was a pretty good teacher. She tried to learn us. But we actually hadn't any learnin'. It was very hard to learn, at least with me. You know how boys was. And this boy an' me, we'd do all we wanted to do.

There was a lot more people lived further away than I did. My daddy lived closest to the school. The schoolhouse was on my daddy and mother's land. That was in Knox County.

My daddy he made cross ties, he peddled, he peeled tan bark, and he worked around. He had a team and a wagon, and when I was just that high, a small boy, I drive a team of mules to Fat Lick from Knox County up here by my own self many a day. An' I had to work you see. I had to peddle, an' I had to do everything to help my dad raise his family . . . Now I've got a family an' I've told 'em all about this. You know when I was at home, and I made any money, I give it to my daddy an' mother. My young'uns never did me that way. But I've never asked for that. I've been blessed; I've had a little money, but not much. That's the way I was raised buddy. When they needed a dollar, when I had the money, I come in an' give it to my mommy and daddy. Had to. You had to do that to get by.

What did we peddle? We peddled eggs. You talk about the gov'ner pickin' blackberries, we picked blackberries in the summer an' peddled them. I've helped pick many a lard can full o' blackberries. And we'd take them to Straight Creek, there was plenty of work at that time in Bell County, and we'd peddle chickens; we'd peddle geese, anything. We raised a acre of cane. I've sot many a day at the cane mill with my hands freezin' off. We'd grab the cane a week at the time. A mule an' the cane and a three-roller mill. And we'd sell the molasses, but we didn't bring too much: fifty, seventy-five cents a gallon then. A dollar is about the average price of molasses. That's when I was raised. We made it on the farm. If we had twenty-five dollars in the spring to make out on, we thought we was rich.

Well, when I was fifteen years old, like I tol' you, I worked in the cornfields for people. You know there was a few men had money, and they could hire fellers to help them hoe corn. And when I didn't have to work at home,

I'd help these people hoe corn or anything else they had to do on the farm. They'd hire me everytime they got the chance. I hadn't got no job to make money on. It was a cheap price but then stuff was cheap. I've hoed corn all day for a dollar a day, and seventy-five cents a day, and back down to fifty cents. I've worked for fifty cents a day since I've been married. I didn't have no money. But that was the year I was married, I worked for fifty cents a day, rollin' logs and sawin'.

Well as I got older, I went to work anytime I could get a job. I went to work in the timberwoods, anywheres to make a dollar. I didn't work very much at public work till I got married. I was twenty-two, tweny-three I believe, when I got married.

From fifteen up to twenty-three, oh sure, I worked all the time. On the job at home, we farmed like I told you. You see they was a bunch of us kids at home, I believe it was eight of us, and we all worked. An' if I wasn't workin' at home, I was workin' at somebody else's to get the dollar, dollar an 'a half, or what ever it'd be, an' peddlin' and everythin'. I worked all the time. In the wintertime we didn't work too much. We had the stuff we made out o' the farm. We had winters then; we didn't have them like we do now. I've seen the ice stay froze over the creek, son, for two weeks, three, at a time. An' hard enough thay you could run a wagon over it tendin' mules.

Well, my mother was born in Clay County. It was where her home's at on Mill Creek. We took a notion to leave Knox County by some means, and my daddy, he wanted to come over too. An' we moved over here in Clay County, an' we've lived here ever since. When we first moved to Clay County, we moved up the holler here to Ike's. We rented a house up there, an' we stayed there three or four years. Where my daddy lives now, we built that house. An' we, me an' my brother, he got killed in the war number two, we hauled them logs out for the house. It's a log house, an' we peeled them logs with an ax in the wintertime, an' we built out of poplar logs, except, I guess, some o' the ceilin' an' stuff. Well me an' my brother, an' my daddy too, we hewed them logs in the winter an' built that house. We hewn the bark off with an ax.

Well, me an' Daisy, when we got married, we went to Knox County an' stayed one year. It was up in summer when we got married, an' there was a feller in Knox County, an' him an' his woman that summer had separated, and they had a real garden. An' he wanted to sell it to me. Well I gave him five or ten dollars for that. And we made plenty of stuff. We just stayed there one year when we came back to Clay County. But I got good pay on that money you see. He had about three or four acres of corn plowed up, an' I got it all. An' I jest stayed there that one summer, an' come back to Clay County, an' I've been in Clay County 'bout ever since.

When I came back to Clay County. . . . My grandaddy had a place, an' he died, an' I didn't have to pay any rent at all. I stayed there about four or five years, an' I didn't have to pay no rent on account o' it was ours. Then we bought a little place over in Knox County, at the head of Jeffs Creek, an' I made enough timbers over there, minin' timbers an' pulp wood, to pay fer that place about twice. When I left there, I come here. From then on I went to work in the coal mines. I worked in the coal mines about twenty-five years off an' on. I may have missed two or three years. Harlan County, Bell County, and Clay County.

I The Curse of Coal

At the center of the mountain economy during this century has been coal mining. Untold billions of tons of coal have been removed from the mountain region since 1900. For sixty years coal hoppers have been hauling the resources of Appalachia north to Pittsburgh, south to Birmingham, and east and west to the great industrial centers of the United States. The story of what has been given the mountain people—the coal camps, mine tragedies, and low pay—in exchange for turning out to America the material on which its industry has been built has become a part of union and popular folklore. The wage for a coal loader in 1969 is about thirteen dollars per shift, or maybe eighteen dollars and up in a union mine, and higher for the perhaps five machine operators whose skill it is to excavate a mountain ridge or level a mountaintop for a strip mine.

In most coal mines there are jobs for operators of cutting machines, for men who shoot, or dynamite, the coal, for those who load the coal into the cars inside the mines, for the drivers of the jeeps that pull the coal cars out of the shaft, and for those who man the tipples through which coal is funneled into trucks or rail cars. All of the men working inside the mine spend their day cramped in areas the height of the coal seams: fifty inches would be "big coal," twenty-eight inches would be "little coal." The air is not good: it is filled with dust. For the main body of miners, coal loaders, wages are paid according to the number of tons or the number of cars loaded. Generally in mines without union contracts the rate is about $1.75 per three-ton car. The market price for that coal is around $24.00 in Kentucky, around $100.00 elsewhere. Not only are the wages for this labor extraordinarily low, but there are of course innumerable ways to get hurt in the mines. Landslides and rockfalls have killed and injured many men. Explosions in gaseous deep mines have caused the most horrible industrial disasters in our history. The driver of a "jeep," a long, flat, battery-powered vehicle weighing approximately three tons and sitting about two feet high, might rise too far from the fetal position in which he does his job, and rake his back along the mine top. The cutting machine's cable might snap, wrenching a man's body out of shape. Everyone working within the mines breathes in dust from the rock above and below the coal seam, and dust from the coal itself. Miners almost inevitably are left with some degree of "rock dust" (silicosis) or "black lung" (pneumoconiosis) both of which are deadly pulmonary diseases. It is perhaps the most hazardous occupation in this country. To gain compensation for anything other than hospital bills, e.g., compensation for an injury that is permanently disabling, the worker must, in fact, contest with his employer the degree to which he is hurt. This means that the company will send the claimant to "their" doctors, and he will go to "his" doctors if he can afford them and if he can find them. The case is settled by a board of attorneys appointed by the governor, and the claimant is almost certain to be denied workmen's compensation unless he is represented skillfully by a lawyer, to whom would go 25 or 50 per cent of the miner's settlement.

Clay County lies on the periphery of the Kentucky mountain coal fields. To the north and west begin the foothills that slip down into the bluegrass country. Southward and eastward are the more important mining counties: Bell, where some of the first strip mines were cut; Leslie, where big coal is still found; and Harlan, site of the state's hardest fought union battles and still one of the top producers of coal in Kentucky. Mining in Clay County is now a small industry; only about a dozen sizable operations still survive. The miners of Clay County work mostly in Leslie, but Clay has the rail headings to which all nearby areas must send their coal. There are four major tipples in the county where the coal is sorted from rock, separated, and graded according to size of the blocks, then sent on its way in long strings of rail cars.

All day, along U.S. 421, Clay County's main artery, there is a roar of the flying coal trucks, emblazoned with titles ("Ruth," "The Bomb") like fighter planes, and covered with STP stickers, coal chunks shooting off the overloaded thirty-ton beds as they round the sharp mountain curves, drivers straining to make an unlikely four runs in one day from Leslie County to Manchester, at seven dollars a load. Manchester is Clay's county seat. It is a small town of eighteen hundred residents greatly devoted to the coal business. Its other main interest is the farmer, and there are several feed, hardware, and heavy equipment suppliers. There are only three factories.

Well, I've worked in some good coal mines and I've worked in some bad coal mines. But I'll tell you about a man workin' in the coal mines now. A man has got to know how to take care of hisself workin' in the coal mines. The easiest money I ever made in the coal mines was in Harlan County in about '45, fer we had big coal. An' that's the first time I ever went to work in the coal mines jest about. Way big coal.

Me an' Perry Jackson's worked in places where they had jacks six foot long holdin' it up, and we'd take these two-by-sixes and two-by-tens an' make a cross out o' that to hold it up. An' I've seen jacks on things that the tops'd be so soft that sometimes it'd go up in that. And we'd have to cut that like that.[18]

You know once I walked out on a feller, it was a bad place, and . . .I was afraid of it actually. It was a great big bunch of us one mornin' went in an' looked at it. Well I was afraid of it, an' I come out. An' I had Gib . . . . I took Gib, that was my brother, I took him in, broke him in. An' that mornin' I was afraid of the place actually. I'd been in there and seen a lot of timbers that was a' poppin' an' a' crackin'.

[18] Mechanical jacks, wood planks, timber props, and even long four-foot bolts are used in mine shafts to brace the rock top that is undercut to remove the coal.

We had fellers that had gone on an' looked at it too, an' they said they wouldn't work it. An' the boss come around, I'd already come out of the place, an' he said, "You gonna work that place?" an' I said, "No, I don't think I will, I'm afraid of it." I said, "Buddy that's dangerous in there, man may get killed." An' he said, "No, it's not dangerous." An' I said, "How do you know?" I said, "Both of these other fellers has seed it an' they're afraid of it." I said, "You're a boss, an' you can see through that top jest as far as I can see. Nother thing," I said, "I don't have to work fer you without I want." An' he said, "Now I'll tell you what you do. You go back in there an' clean that place up." He said, "There's no danger in it."

I would o' quit in a minute if it hadn't been fer Gib. He needed the work. An' I said, "All the way I'll ever clean that place up is if you go right back in there an' sit with me. An' if it catches you, you'll go mashed all to heck right with me." He got mad at me 'cause o' these other men. He knowed these other men'd all be fer me. I could quit him right there. He tried to force me. You can't force me to work where I think it's dangerous. In the coal mines you gotta use your own mind.

He 'us a pretty good boss, but he got mad that mornin'. An' I was mad too, I didn't care. An' I said you go back an' sit in there with me till the cut o' coal is cleaned out. Set timbers, I'll go back. An' I said the reason I'm going back is on account o' Gib, not fer me. You had to have some experience to get jobs in the coal mines. An' I told him, "I've got the experience an' I could get a job where Gib couldn't." But I said, "If you'll go back there an' stay till I clean it up, then I'll go back." An' he said OK. An' that's the way I done it. We cleaned that cut up, but it scared me. I'll tell you. He went right back in there with me an' sot till it was cleaned up. I told him if I ever go back, you'll go in an' sit with me, brother. I said, I knowed you'd push a man anywheres.

*I've had to run some races. I've had to run a lot o' races
to keep it from fallin' on me. I've cleaned up cuts o' coal
son, an' the safety poppin' an' breakin' in front of me.
That's a big tale, but that's the way it does when you go to
robbin'. They won't let you drive in the coal mines unless
you got . . . three entries. You've gotta have a air course;
you gotta have two ways out. The danger in drivin' a narrow place is a lot of fellers gets killed with big slugs a'fallin'.
But I've seen many of a timber break, an' many of a top
fall. I've seed 'em fall in. You know I've help drive a mine
up maybe a mile, two mile long. An' then we'd pull 'em
back. You stand at the back an' pull 'em all back out. It's
nothin' dangerous. I mean it's dangerous; you gotta watch.
If you don't, you're gonna get it.*

*Oh God, I worked where it'd fall in an' all on 'em. You
get this cut o' coal here, an' you move on to another one
an' get it, an' you jest keep on movin'. You get out five or
six cuts, an' five or six o' those pillars, it'll every bit fall in
back here. I've seed a many of them fall in. I've seen one
man get his leg broke, but it wasn't a rock, it'us a jeep. They
had jeeps. The feller worked the jeep, he got off the jeep, an'
he knocked the brake here an' he hit the starter, an' it kept
rollin' an' rolled over that man an' broke his leg. That was
a good man.*

*How much head room? Well I've worked in some fifty-
inch coal; you know what that is. I've worked in thirty-two.
Why I've worked in twenty-eight-inch coal. An' you know
how that is. I've crawled fer as a hundred foot at a time.*

*In Harlan, that was a union mine. You paid your dues.
That was the best money I made. That was durin' the war,
an' it was all shift work. It's been all worked out. That was
a union mine. You could make a good livin' at that price.
I think, we'us gettin' about twelve, fourteen dollars. We'us
makin' good money. I boarded up in Harlan. I didn't live
there; I boarded up in there.*

I worked in Leslie; I worked in Clay some; I worked in

Bell, an' I worked in Harlan County. I went to Detroit a while durin' the war, but I didn't stay too long. A month or two. I didn't like Detroit. It was too cold. I worked there in the wintertime an' it froze me to death buddy, everytime I got out. An' I took one of the awfulest colds. It'us a sight. I'us workin' in a factory where they made war materials. Course I was mostly helpin' unload freight an' stuff off of the railroad cars an' things like that. It'us a big munitions factory.

They never had too much coal work in Knox County. They had some, but not like they had in Clay County. They had a lot o' coal in Clay County, but it's about gone now. They got a lot of coal, but it's small; I couldn't work in it. Anyhow, I've had my part of it. I can get by. I may have to go back to it, I don't know.

I've seed many places I wouldn't work. You know when you get afraid. I've always heard said, in the coal mines, when you get too afraid of a place, you better not work it. I've turned plenty of places down, an' I've seen plenty of men turn places down they wouldn't work in the coal mines. An' they'd jest tell the boss they wouldn't work in. Course the only thing they could do is fire you. I've left cuts o' coal I didn't get. Course that feller was anxious to get that cut. We'd worked it; we'd set out timbers. In the coal mines you've got to take care of yourself. You can't let a boss all the time tell you. A boss might put you under there to get a block o' coal. I've worked enough to know pretty well when it's dangerous.

I quit a mine once. That's been about ten or twelve years ago. We'd drive up a coal mine, an' we'd started back, an' it all fell in. We had one way in. The air course had fell in, an' we had about 102 foot to go with jest one way in. It was beginnin' to fall in all around us, an' poppin' an a' crackin' all the time. Crit, the day before that, was drivin' a jeep, an' there'us enough rock fell on his jeep if it had hit him would have mashed him up. Well we went in there that mornin', an' it looked awful bad. There'us about eight or ten of us. We said, "Boys, let's get out of here: we'll get killed." Well the boss wasn't in there. We, every man of us, loaded in the jeep, an' come back outside.

When we come back out, the boss said, "Boys, what you fellers come back out here fer?" "Well," we said, "we quit." An' he said, "What you quit fer?" We said we was afraid to go in there with one way, afraid that would fall in an' we'd be shut up in there, an' they'd be a time a' gettin' us out if they ever got us out. "Oh," he said, "there's no danger in that." There's about five or six of us. All of us had quit but about three men. Well he talked two or three of them men into goin' back. Well, I pulled my shovel out when I come out. If I tell you I'm gonna quit a thing an' come out, I'm gonna quit. So I quit, an' I don't know, five or six of us. I went an' signed up on the Rockin' Chair money, an' they held us up fer six weeks over quittin' a job, but we drawed it because there wasn't but one way in, an' you can't work a man in the coal mines if there isn't more than one way in. You've gotta have two or three ways out, an' we had one. They knowed that we had them, an' we Rocked.

You know they sent me down, unemployment sent me down below Manchester one day for a job. Well I went down there jest to look at the job, an' when I went down there it'us jest a pony mine. An' the mud, it looked to me, was about six inches deep. Well, I went to the boss, an' I said, "How much you make a day here buddy?" He said, "from two to fifteen dollars." An' I said, "From the looks of it, there's more twos than they is fifteens, ain't it?" He said, "Well, you heard me." An' I said OK. Well, I come back an' tol' the unemployment men, I said, "I don't want that job." An' they said why? An' I said, "I didn't make my money in Clay County in the pony mines, an' " I said, "I'm not takin' it." Well, they helt me up six weeks on the Rockin' Chair money fer refusin' to take that job, which I thought was unfair.

An' I felt that if a man couldn't tell me no better story than from two to fifteen dollars, than I didn't have no business goin' in that mine. In a pony mine they have track, an' they have little steel cars, an' they haul that out with the ponies. They haul that trailer out with the ponies. Yes sir. Drive 'em son. It goes a lot slower. They used to have plenty pony mines in this country. There's a company didn't have too much money. He could get some steel, an' he could get some cars an' haul it out with them ponies. That's the truth buddy.

I've worked in coal mines where we'd have two or three sections of men working. That's what you've gotta have. I've seed eight or ten men in one section, or maybe more than that. You know they have eight, ten or fifteen places. When you go to drivin' entries, you'll have fifty-foot pillars an' you'll have breaks an' all such as that. It's hard fer you to know about that till you've gone in an' seed it. But they can make the money.

You'll have six or eight men loadin' coal. They're worked to death. You need two jeeps fer six or eight men. A lot of places, they have timber men. An' they have men who cover your top. I've worked where we had to have two men to bolt the top. If you had a bad top, they bolt it, an' that holds it up with about thirty-eight, forty-inch bolts. An' they have a shootin' man. Men who cuts coal generally cuts it an' somebody else shoots it. You have to shoot it. It sits there till you shoot it. Then when you shoot it, it all busts up in blocks. Lot of times I've seen 'em go back an' have to shoot it over. You don't shoot it heavy enough, it won't break down. They have several shootin' men, an' the boss.

I've loaded as high as thirty ton o' coal a day. But you've got to do a day's work to load coal like that. It's accordin' to what the minimum wage is right now, how much you *gotta load. You know, last work I done, if you couldn't load ten, twelve dollars a day, they couldn't work you. They had to pay you anyway, an' you had to make it or they wouldn't keep you too long. They'd get shet of you.*

I've done shift work, an' I've loaded coal too, an' I could always pay my way. I never was fired. I could always quit a job, an' go back to the same place an' get a job. But I wouldn't want to ever go back to the coal mines. I've made many of a dollar. I've made twenty dollars a day loadin' coal. Shamrock Coal Company. Twenty dollars by the car. I loaded by the car mostly. I have worked for twelve, fifteen dollars a shift. I have worked for ten. I've made twelve many a time for Shamrock Coal Company. You know they paid diff'rent prices 'cordin' to what you done. They paid ten dollars for some; maybe if you're gonna help run a coal machine, they pay you twelve or fifteen dollars.

Yeah, I have a little rock dust. The Health Department asked me if I was goin' back to the coal mines, an' I said I didn't know, I might have to. You see, I take X-rays all along, an' they said I advise you not to go back. They say that rock dust won't kill you, but it'll cut your wind off awful bad. I can tell the diff'rence.

Lord have mercy, I've seed men that had it hard. Yeah, I've seen fellers had it very bad. I know a feller right now, I don't want to give his name, he sued ———— Coal Company, an' he got a big settlement. Which I was goin' to do, but it costs a lot o' money. An' I didn't do it, but should I guess. If you win the company, you're all right. If you don't, you're hurtin'. That's the reason I didn't tackle it. I know one feller I worked with had rock dust, an' he sued them an' they beat him. An' I know another feller sued 'em, an' he winned. They tell me if you get it too bad, it cuts your breath off. I can't tell much diff'rence right now, but I might in a year or two. The Health Department had a X-ray sittin' on the thing that comes in the truck. I went down an' took an X-ray, an' I got a notice in a little while to come back an' take it over. They took skin tests, they took everythin', an' they come out an' said it was rock dust. They call this here coal dust black lung. I don't know what they call this other stuff, but it's not too bad yet.

THE GOOD THINGS

For all that can be said about the injustices and dangers of mine work, few miners would willingly change their occupation. They may flee the lowly wage, but the work is not thought of badly. The coal industry is part of the mountain way of life. It was the importer of the idea of "the job" as separate from the farm, and still, in much of Kentucky, getting a job means going into the mines. For that reason, it is respected as no other occupation could be. Mining, for poor Kentuckians, is an understandable and natural way to make a living. It is what every poor man does who cannot collect welfare, who will not migrate, and who prefers the wage to the farm. And coal miners think highly of themselves. They realize full well that theirs is the hardest, dirtiest, unhealthiest, and least safe work that a man can do. There is pride in their talk as they emerge from the shafts, black with dust from boot to hard hat, and make their way home. Everyone agrees, "You've got to know how to watch out for yourself in the mines." But also, "Mines is cool in the summer and warm in the winter."

After ten or twenty years in the mines, should his lungs or back force him to quit, a man has a hard time adjusting to the prospect of changing occupations. Even if he had other jobs to choose from—which he would not have in most of mountain Kentucky—he might be inclined to sit back and rest, feeling that he had fulfilled his obligation to work. The realization of the grace he has been afforded in staying alive through his working years fills him with the peace of accomplishment and the urge to enjoy his remaining days as he pleases. But this is natural, and accepted, for in Kentucky, options being few, a poor man is expected to support his family either by farming all of his life, which is highly difficult, or by loading coal, but only so long as he is able. It is no disgrace, at thirty-five, to quit the labor of twenty years with decaying lungs and say I can no longer work, for to the poor man in the mountains, inability to mine means inability to work. And when a man can no longer work in the mines, he is expected to rest.

I liked it pretty good, buddy. It was when the coal didn't get under thirty-six . . . . You see I'm big an' tall. When the coal was around thirty-six, I liked it good, if the top was good. In the summertime it's very cool, an' in the wintertime it was good. There wasn't no snow nor rain workin', an' we worked every day too. We didn't hardly miss any. I liked the coal mines all right.

Unions

The union movement never gained a foothold in Clay County. There has never been a union mine operating in the county, though companies worked in Clay whose mines in other counties were under union contract. At the time of the big union pushes in neighboring counties during the 1920s and 30s, Clay County had not yet had its boom days in coal. In the middle 50s when organizers began talking among the county's miners, the years of "big coal" were almost over—one reason that pro-union sentiment never gained much foothold in Clay. Another is the opposition put up by the operators; but then the opposition in other counties, like Harlan and Bell, had been much stiffer than it ever was in Clay. A third reason might be that by the time the United Mine Workers was well enough established to take on the operators in the lesser coal counties, it was too content of its strength to become truly aggressive again. The contention that the UMW has for the last several years been inattentive to its rank and file was strengthened in the spring of 1969 when 42,000 miners in West Virginia, almost the entire UMW membership in that state, went on strike to force passage of a workmen's compensation bill covering such illnesses as black lung and rock dust. They did this largely without the support and encouragement of the union itself. Much was said about the corruption of the UMW hierarchy during the 1969 fight for the union presidency between William Anthony ("Tony") Boyle, the incumbent, and Joseph A. ("Jock") Yablonski, the first major challenger to the union leadership since the retirement of John L. Lewis. Before he, his wife, and daughter were murdered on January 5, 1970, Yablonski was attempting to get a federal investigation into the activities of the UMW bosses.

Wages in Clay County mines are a good deal—about 30 per cent—below those in union mines. And workers in Clay lack the dubious benefit of a UMW pension upon retirement which, as many union men have found out, is a hard thing for many to get. The word union is, of course, anathema to the coal operators of Clay County; but it also makes the working men uneasy for it means troubles—trouble that at this late date might as well be avoided.

Well that's been about ten or fifteen years ago. They tried to come in here you know. They did some people join, an' they paid them so much a week to try to organize Clay County. But they never did get nowheres. They never did get organized. The operators was agin it. They caused a lot of trouble, was one thing did it. They claimed the reason they couldn't organize . . . . You take haulin' coal from Leslie County; they said they couldn't pay the union price. They didn't have no railroad, an' they couldn't truck that coal far an' pay the union price, is what they said. That's what I was told.

Well, they was afraid, buddy. They didn't want any union. It was in Harlan an' all those places. Why they had guards, I've been told, in Clay County a' watchin' fer the union to come in. If they had come in I guess they would have had a lot of trouble maybe. But they never did come. They wanted the men to work, I guess, without it. An' like I tol' you, they was glad it didn't come like in Harlan. But I didn't work in Harlan then, but I heard lot o' talk that it'us a rough place.

I remember when they first started talkin' about it. There was a lot of people in this country that I've seed they tried . . . you know, they joined the union. An' they'd go around in other places. An' they had them paid. They was tryin' to get them to organize the people, you know. Like they'd give me, the union'd give me, so much a week or somethin' to help 'em organize. An' I know of one feller had to leave Clay County. I was told that now, that that was the reason he left Clay County. I don't know. He left all right. An' I was told that they [mine operators] told him to go, an' he better go. An' he's never been back in Clay County. He got a lot of money off the union to try to organize the people in Clay County, an' he'd a been workin' in the coal mines before he done this. An' he didn't organize nobody. They told him he'd better go, if he didn't he'd be the next feller that was buried. An' I imagine at that time, if he hadn't a left, he would have went, fer there used to be a lot of people in Clay County was afraid. They didn't want nobody to come around that they didn't know. And you know, that's very bad.

AUTOMATION

For twenty-five years, mining has been becoming a more and more mechanized operation. The pony mines where coal cars are hauled from the shafts by ponies are now hard to find. Everywhere, while coal production stays high, men are losing their jobs to machines. The greatest change in conventional mining came with the introduction, three decades ago, of the continuous coal loader, called a Joy, from the Joy Mine Machine Corporation of Pennsylvania. It was not until the 1950s that the Joys began to be used in almost all underground mines in Kentucky, displacing about six human coal loaders per machine.

Two men can run a coal machine. They've got machines now, but I've never seed 'em, they've got coal machines now will cut the coal an' drill it an' everythin'. With two or three men. But two is all ever had to run a coal machine where I worked.

A Joy is a thing that loads coal; it takes men, but it's run by machinery. See that cut out a lot of coal loaders when they got a Joy. A Joy can load all a cut o' coal in fifteen minutes; maybe fifty, sixty, seventy-five ton of coal. It's got big arms. It's run by juice, you know an' it's got a big broad thing in front, an' it jest digs that coal right out. It's got arms will fly over an' jerk that coal right up on that pan, so it's got a pan down there. They got a car that goes with the Joy. They push a car up on the Joy. It's got a big tail piece on it, like a belt on it, an' goes in the car. They drive the car back out.

They been here for years an' years you know. I've knowed of 'em ever since I worked in the coal mines. It's been in Clay County about ten or fifteen years, but they've had 'em always in the union mines. Big coal back in Harlan an' Bell County, they had 'em. First time I ever worked in coal mines they had Joys. They make a lot of noises. They scare you to death. You can't hear. Lot of men gets killed that way. I don't like to work around them. They make so much noise, if a rock falls you can't hear it ner nothin' else.

Automation of a Kentucky mine has few redeeming factors except that it makes more profitable the production of coal. It does not allow men more time for leisure. It does not create new jobs, except for those who run the machines. It does not free men for other labor. What other work can a man do anywhere when he quit the fourth grade at the age of fifteen to work at a semi-skilled job, and stayed at that job for twenty-five years? In Kentucky, he can do nothing, for there are no jobs but coal work for the generally unskilled and illiterate worker. Automation in Kentucky does nothing but create unemployment, and unemployables.

In the last few years a new type of mining has been perfected, an almost totally mechanized operation—strip mining. A strip mine runs on the principle that rather than dig entries in the mountainside and drive underground to clean out a coal seam, it is far quicker and less expensive to remove the earth above the seam, which might include the top of a mountain, and scoop out the exposed coal. Or, another method, to cut a ledge along a mountain ridge revealing the coal seam and ram huge augers—drills as much as seven feet across, that can be extended well over a hundred feet—into the mountainside. The coal pulled back by the spinning augers is fed by an automatic conveyor into waiting trucks. This operation requires three men. The enormous D-9 bulldozers that create a twenty-five-foot-wide terrace out of what once was a steep slope, or remove the mountaintop, take one man to run. The tons of earth and trees that are excavated are pushed over the side; this is the overburden. It is liable, at the first heavy rainfall, to come sliding down the hillside, snapping over the trees in its path.

BULLDOZERS LEVEL THE MOUNTAINS

Many conventional mines are opened on land for which only the mineral rights, not the property itself, is owned by the mining companies. Most men do not greatly mind a conventional mine operating on their property because it does not cause excessive damage. But strip mines are another story. They destroy the timber and beauty of a mountain. The run-off from the overburden pollutes the streams and creeks with mud and acid. As the creek banks turn red with mineral deposits, all animal and plant life in the water dies. A strip mine violates the unwritten understanding between mine owner and worker that they are mutually dependent, that everybody needs coal mines. For while a strip mine, like all others, greatly profits the owner and extracts the source of mountain wealth—a state of things accepted as necessarily unalterable in mining communities, it does also what other mines never have—ruins the mountains and the streams, and offers virtually no employment.

Opposition and Broad Form Deed: It is estimated that in Pike, Floyd, Perry, Harlan, Letcher, Knott, and Bell counties, title to the minerals has been separated from title to the general surface over at least 90 per cent of the land on the basis of so-called "broad form" deeds signed for the most part in the first ten years of this century.[19]

This means that the coal from almost every acre of the rich fields of eastern Kentucky does not belong to the actual landowner and that most land can be strip mined without the landowner's permission. It is, of course, astonishing and infuriating to the mountain landowner—who

[19] No figures have been compiled to show exactly how much land in Clay County is covered by "broad form" deeds. Since 1958 only 3 per cent of all the acres in eastern Kentucky permitted for stripping have been in Clay County. In 1962, 27 per cent (10 acres) of the land in Clay permitted for stripping was on land where the ownership of the minerals was separate from the ownership of the land. Yet in 1967, all of the land permitted for stripping was on the land for which the minerals and the surface were singly owned. This has meant that, for the most part, Clay County has been spared the conflicts, familiar to some other counties, that arise when a coal company, armed with a sixty-year-old deed giving it ownership of the coal, tries to run a strip mine over the land of an unwilling property owner.

takes so to heart the inviolate nature of property ownership and who often has only the productivity of his land to stand between himself and destitution—to consider the possibility that his mountains and timber and streams, and perhaps even his pastures and his home itself might be totally destroyed on the basis of a deed signed half a century before when surface mining of the mechanized and auger sort was not even conceived of. His opposition to this legalized plunder has been continuous and at times powerful.

In 1955 a Knott County man brought a case in the circuit court challenging the validity of the "broad form" deed covering the minerals underneath his land, which was about to be overrun by bulldozers. Circuit Court Judge Cornett upheld the deed but ruled that coal companies must pay for damages to the surface land. The case was taken to the Kentucky Court of Appeals where it was decided that the owner of the land surface had no claim to damages caused by the removal of underlying minerals.

In 1967, another Knott County man whose land was in danger of being stripped challenged the "broad form" deed, signed in 1905, which covered his ninety acres. That deed, not dissimilar to most "broad form" deeds, conveyed in part:

> . . . all the coals, minerals, and mineral products, all the oils, gases, all salt minerals and salt water, fire and potters clay, all iron and iron ore, all stone and such of the standing timber as may be . . . deemed necessary for mining purposes . . . , and the exclusive rights of way for any and all railroads and ways and pipe lines, telegraph or telephone lines that may hereafter be located on said property by the Grantee . . . together with the rights to enter upon said land, use and operate the same and surface thereof, and make use of and for this purpose divert water sources . . . in any and every manner that may be deemed necessary or convenient for mining . . . and in the use of said

land and in the surface thereof by the Grantee, its successors or assigns shall be free from and is and are hereby released from liability or claim of damage to the said grantor, their liens, responsibilities or assigns.

In return for signing this remarkable document, the then landowner, who likely could not read, was paid three dollars an acre, which at that time, in the mountains, was a large sum.

Circuit Court Judge Cornett ruled as he had done in 1956, that the deed was valid, but that the waiver of damages included in the deed covered only damages done to the surface in accord with the operator's right to use the surface responsibly to remove the coal, but that the operator did not have the right to destroy the land and that damages must be paid to the landowner. The case was taken to the Kentucky Court of Appeals where, in a 4–3 ruling in 1968, Judge Cornett's decision concerning payment of damages was reversed. Arguing that since the payment made in 1905 for mineral rights was often higher than the land value itself at that time—a highly questionable judgment—then the estate of the minerals was superior to the estate of the surface. In other words, if to get the coal the land must be irrevocably damaged, the weight of the law must side with the owners of the mineral, finally defined as coal and clay and not simply those minerals which compose the actual earth.

This was a particularly disastrous decision for the welfare of Kentucky, and it left thousands of mountain landowners with no protection under the law for the defense of their property. Appeals Court Judge Hill, in his dissent, stated, "I contend first that inasmuch as the parties to the broad form deeds never contemplated the use of the then unknown method of strip mining and never dreamed of the cataclysmic destruction of the surface, the Grantee and his successor in title have no right to remove the coal by stripping methods. Secondly, I contend that if rules of construction are so modified and distorted as to authorize the Grantee to use stripping methods, he should be answerable in damages to the surface owners for just compensation"; and he wondered, "that the court of last resort in the beautiful state of Kentucky would ignore the logic and reasoning of the great majority of other states and lend its approval and encouragement to the diabolical devastation and destruction of a large part of the surface of this fair state without compensation to the owners thereof."

With the repeated refusal of the Kentucky courts to intervene to halt strip mining in the mountains, opposition to this devastation of land has taken other forms. In June of 1967, Jink Ray, a Pike County resident, whose land was about to be stripped, stopped the bulldozers at his property line by standing in their path. He appealed to then Governor Breathitt to revoke the mining company's permit (Puritan Coal) on the grounds that the provisions of the 1966 Strip Mining Law (to be discussed below) prohibited surface mining on his land. His appeal to the courts against an injunction barring him from obstructing the bulldozers was denied. Over two hundred East Kentuckians met with the governor in early July saying they would die trying to protect their land. After the state investigators decided that almost all of Mr. Ray's land could be legally stripped, Governor Breathitt, in an unprecedented move, cancelled Puritan's permit stating as his reason the "strong likelihood of damage" that would exist if the land were stripped. Though this was in itself a victory, retaliation was swift, and three community organizers in Pike County were arrested under the state sedition law, which was subsequently found unconstitutional. Said Robert Holcomb, President of the National Independent Coal Operators Association and the Pike County Chamber of Commerce, about the arrests, "You might say we spearheaded the investigation." As tempers rose on the subject of "outsiders," a Canadian film producer, Hugh O'Conner, was shot and killed in Letcher County while making a film on American life.

In other counties, anti-strip mine groups, generally involved in the vocal and widespread Appalachian Group to Save the Land and the People, tried to mobilize the opposition to surface mining. The organization publicly disassociated itself from violence as a weapon against mine operators. Yet some men did turn the skills they had acquired "shooting coal" in the mines to the disadvantage of the operators. In June, 1967 while Jink Ray was keeping the bulldozers from his land, a $50,000 shovel was dynamited at a Knott County operation. In August of that year, $300,000 worth of equipment was blown up at a Perry County strip. At the end of August, 1968, two months after the Kentucky Court of Appeals had upheld the "broad form deed," bulldozers, shovels, and other equipment, valued at $750,000, were exploded at a Leslie County mine. And in December of 1968, almost $1,000,000 in gear was dynamited at a strip mine in Jellico, Tennessee, on the border of Whitely County, Kentucky. Yet strip mining still continues, apparently unhampered by the courts, by sabotage, by individual resistance, by pleas of landowners and conservationists, by a restrictive state law, or by federal legislation.

Reclamation: There is no doubt that strip mining lays to waste thousands of mountain acres each year. The surface mining industry shares with deep mining the responsibility for having polluted, by drainage of sulfuric acid, almost every mile of East Kentucky streams, leaving them devoid of any significant aquatic life. The tons of rubble and earth that are carved from mountainsides to permit augering are dumped over the hillside, forming the overburden. One effect of this is the pollution, and in some cases, the damming of streams with mud. Richard M. Kirby, in a study for the Conservation Foundation, concluded that, "Like acid drainage, erosion from strip mining operations has significant off-site effects. In the form of sedimentation and flooding, it constitutes, together with the acid problem, total detrimental effect of strip mining on water quality."[20] With heavy rainfall the overburden may drift down the hillside, leaving the entire mountain slope a field of mud and splintered timber. There have been repeated cases of damage done to houses and pastures from strip mine landslides and of homes endangered by floods caused by creeks blocked with brush and rocks brought down from the mountaintops.

As a result of popular indignation over the disastrous effects of strip mining, Kentucky had passed, in 1966, what was then boasted of as the most comprehensive and restrictive strip mine control law in the nation. The main provisions of the law are that in order to receive a permit to disrupt land with a strip mine, the operator has to submit a plan for reclamation and put up bond of from $100 to $500 per acre to ensure that the reclamation statutes are followed, that no stripping is to be allowed on slopes over thirty-three degrees (the average slopes in eastern Kentucky are thirty-one degrees), that vegetation must be planted on the overburden, and that the Division of Reclamation has the authority to fine, deny a permit to, or revoke the permit of any strip mine operator who violates the provisions of the law. Surface mining industry spokesmen voiced the fear before passage of the law that the costs of land restoration demanded by law would cripple strip mining in the mountains.

This did not come about, however. The law has had seemingly little effect on the industry in eastern Kentucky. In 1965, 4,288 acres in eastern Kentucky were permitted for strip mining. In 1967, after the law was in effect, 6,898 acres were laid open to strip mining. Coal companies were

[20] "The Curse of Coal: Policy Issues of Strip Mining in Eastern Kentucky," memorandum of the Conservation Foundation (Washington, D.C., August 1967), p. 12.

approved for 288 strip mine operations in 1965. They received permits for 422 in 1967. Clearly the law did not disturb the expansion of the industry.

Has the law had the effect of forcing the restoration of stripped lands? It should be remembered that the property that Jink Ray defended in 1967 was carefully examined by state investigators and found to be suitable for stripping under that 1966 law. Breathitt's action in revoking the company's permit was the first and only such use of that provision in the law. In July of 1967, a landslide from a strip operation near Harlan kept up for twenty-two hours, covered a section of U.S. 119, two homes, and narrowed the Cumberland River channel from fifty feet to ten feet. In August 1968, boulders from an approved strip mine operation smashed one vacant house in the valley below and careened through the wall of a Knott County family's home. At old mine sites across the state, feeble pine shrubs can be seen, uprooted by erosion, slipping down the overburden; and sod grass, poking through layers of mud, can be found in valleys far below where they were first planted. Little reclamation, meaning making land useful again— much less restoration, making land become as it once was—has occurred.

There are several reasons for this. One is that the state has not been strict in applying the strip mine law. One coal company, Peabody Coal, was granted three forty-five-day extensions without fines by the Reclamation Division, starting in mid-July, 1969, when it was bound by law to have concluded its reclamation efforts. This was done though state investigators had repeatedly reported that company's violations. Also, as Mr. Kirby notes, "Enforcement too is a large problem. Consider, for example, the strip miner with a creek valley under permit. Out of ten miles of proposed bench, a mile could easily lie on slopes steeper than thirty-three degrees, a mile the miner cannot strip only because of a state (or federal) inspector. The inspector earns perhaps $10,000 a year; the mile will bring in (on the average) about $270,000. One can draw one's own conclusion; but it is clear that no government can afford to get in a bidding match for the loyalties of the inspectors."[21]

But the basic problem, so far as reclamation of stripped mountain land goes, is that repair of the land is impossible. Since it is the principle of strip mining that rather than dig underground to cut out the coal, it is cheaper to remove the tons of soil and rock that lie above the seam, the end result of stripping is a gutted mountain with either the entire top pushed over the side or with a ledge, or bench, like a monstrous terrace cut along the mountain ridge. There is no way to replace the earth cut from the hillside, grade it back to a slope, restore the timber and vegetation, or bring back the pollutants that have despoiled the waterways. As was asserted in the 1967 challenge of the "broad form" deed led by a Knott County citizen, "Once the soil is turned upside down by explosives and machinery, the topsoil and timber buried, and the surface covered with a jumble of rocks and acid subsoil in the manner common to hillside strip mining, the land is, for all practical purposes, permanently destroyed."

It can also be said that no real economic use can be found for highlands gutted by strip mines. To demonstrate to the contrary, a few operators have developed "show piece" strip mine excavations where pine trees and even peach orchards have been planted on the bench left behind by the strip. It is sheer nonsense to say that these frail efforts indicate that stripped land can indeed be made productive, that strip mines are necessary as a means to create land for ventures of this sort, that anything can be done to restore the mud-covered slope itself, or that the creation of an orchard on the shelf of a strip mine compensates for

---

[21] "The Curse of Coal," p. 65.

the enormous waste and destruction of hillsides and streams and the violation of the landowner's claim to property rights.

It is maintained by many citizens of East Kentucky that the 1966 legislation in itself prohibits mountain surface mining. "They point out that the law calls for: '*all measures* . . . to eliminate property damage to members of the public, their real and personal property, public roads, streams, and all other public property from soil erosion, falling stones and overburden, water pollution and hazards dangerous to life and property,' and authorizes the Commission to 'require any measure whatsoever to accomplish the purpose of this chapter.' Certainly the plain purpose of the chapter is to prevent damage of the sort described, by any means necessary."[22]

It is clear to anyone who has witnessed the carnage left behind by a strip mine that the operation, by its nature, falls into conflict with this mandate of the legislature. And it is clear that the stripping of mountain land is one of the most inexcusable endeavors of modern industry and nothing less than a rape of the beauty, the bountifulness, and the productivity of the earth.

At the head of Goose Creek, in Clay County, is the Mountain Clay Coal Company, Strip and Auger Mine. It has been operating for about three years, following two seams of coal through two ridges over a distance of more than three miles. At one point, the top of a small outcrop ridge had to be cut clean away to get the coal. The ledge of the strip is used as a road by the trucks hauling coal the twenty miles into Manchester. It forms a better road than the state-maintained blacktop that the mine road leads off of. In accordance with the state law, Mountain Clay Coal Company hydraulically seeded all of the overburden resulting from their strip, but their efforts were not very effective.

[22] "The Curse of Coal," p. 42.

Well a strip mine . . . . They tear the whole top of the mountain off, an' they auger it, is all I can describe it. An,' I don't like it. Destroys all the timber, the water, it damages it, an' everythin' else. You've seed it, an' it's a bad thing.

Well, it's not hurt the water up here . . . but a lot of places. . . . You know coal's got sulfer in it, an' it kills the fish an' dries, 'cording to how it is, dries up your wells an' everythin' else. Now this strip mine up here, it's so high up I don't think it'll ever come down here on anythin'. You know, there could come a slip up here an' it could destroy everythin'. You see all that dirt's been pushed over the hill up there, where they tore everything up, that could come off that mountain, if a big flood came, an' damage a lot o' people up in that holler.

I never did work around strip mines. You got bulldozers an' you got these shovels. It don't take as a many men. It's all machinery work. It's not like coal mines. I imagine they pay high. I don't know what they pay. Anytime you run machinery, you get more money. If you run a coal machine they pay you more than anythin' else. Pay you fifteen, eighteen dollars a day on a coal machine, but I expect never to work around another. Jesus Christ, that there's hard work, buddy. An' the man that does that, you eat coal dust all day long. It's bad.

When first people came to Kentucky, they survived as most Americans did then by scratching enough out of their land to feed their families. But when other areas began to develop cash crops, East Kentucky was faced with the fact that there is not sufficient land to grow much of anything in the mountains. For a time, a great deal of livestock was raised, but the South and Midwest better supplied that market. When the coal industry began to spread, many young men quit the farm and began to draw the first regular paychecks of their lives. As that industry now begins to mechanize fully, many disabled and unemployed miners have nothing to do but try and cultivate their small plots of ground to feed their families. As employment in the industry withers, the young head for the cities. Poor communities in the mountains are filled largely with old men, injured men, their wives, and their children. The work in the automobile plants of Detroit and Atlanta is done by young whites from the mountains as well as young blacks from the Deep South. Here in Kentucky is another tragic example of what dependence on one industry can do. Here live people that supplied the coal the nation burned, and who now have to borrow money to buy coal to heat their homes in winter. Here miners and miners' sons stand in line to buy food stamps. What will the mountains get in exchange for their coal; the poor for their contribution to the nation; the mountaineer for his loss of dignity?

Talk about poor people, well I don't know. I don't know if I'm actually right, but what I think makes poor people poor is they was born poor, I guess, an' they stayed poor all their lives. An' the cause o' that is they was raised up in the head o' these hollers, an' they didn't have no money to get started to make money with. An' a lot of 'em's on welfare, an' the welfare jest draws . . . they jest give 'em enough money on the welfare to barely live. They can't get ahead or nothin'. They jest stay poor. That's the way I see it. A lot of people I know don't have a garden. An' until they get somethin' to make somethin' with, they don't have no land, an' they stay poor. I don't know if that's right or not, but that's the only way I see. If they set you down up in the head of one of these hollers here, you jest have enough income to live on, an' it takes money to make money with, an' if you don't have it, you can't make it.

II   Poor People and a Great Invention: The Poverty War

Clay County stands in the middle of the Daniel Boone National Forest, a monument to the long forgotten days of the frontier. Ranked by median family income, it is the fifty-ninth poorest county in the United States. Flung out from Manchester, back in the hills, are dozens of small communities, generally found along, and named for, major creeks where the land spreads out a bit. Each little settlement is different from the others. Three, out of many, are Granny's Branch, Mud Lick, and Goose Creek.

THREE COMMUNITIES: A SKETCH OF CONDITIONS

Granny's Branch shelters a collection of about forty homes crammed together along a mile and a half of creek. There is no land to cultivate, except at the mouth of the creek, and the people living there have a rather nice garden. What brought so many people together on a piece of land that would support so few is a mystery. Perhaps they were lured from further back in the hill by early-day jobs in Manchester, which is six miles away along U.S. 421. Most of the families living there now are related to each other by marriages, and the accumulated homes of each generation leave barely any open space in the community. Some young couples build small two-room shacks in parents' back yards to which they return after each unsuccessful foray for jobs in the cities. The houses are pressed so tightly together in some spots that twenty feet does not stand between them. To find space to build, men have had to dig out and level places along the hillside. This is rural poverty at its worst. People with no land to grow food on must find jobs, and there are no jobs to be had. Children born into such communities have no base to strike out from. There is no money to clothe them for school; there is no money to carry them north to look for paying work. Probably half the families on the branch draw welfare. The rest have no money coming in or live by occasional jobs in the mines or in town. Even for the thrifty parent, welfare provides barely enough to feed and clothe a family. The children—who are faced with rising up out of a poverty that offers no chances—are the ones most damaged by living in a community of landless welfare recipients. Others, the sons of poor farmers, can at least scratch together a little spending money working in their neighbors' gardens. Clay County has done little to change the state of things in Granny's Branch. In fact it seems to have balked, in every possible way, at improving the lot of the community. Not until 1969 was a road begun along the creek. Until that time, cars and children, hiking out to the highway to go to school, had to negotiate the only open passageway, the creek itself.

The community of Mud Lick or Sand Hill, sits atop a high and very beautiful pine-covered mountain in the backwoods of Clay County. Geographically, it is about the most isolated community of its size, about forty-five families, in the county, and recent improvements in the miles of long dirt roads that snake their way up the ridge hardly make it any less cut off. Three creeks flow down from the top, and along each is a road, one of which is not generally passable, and each represents a strung-out but self-contained (by virtue of family ties) community. From the top, where the ground spreads out enough to allow a tiny hillside garden, it is about seven miles to the nearest school (by a dirt road that cannot be crossed in snowy or wet weather), and an almost equal distance to a store where more than a few canned goods can be bought. People must stock up provisions for the winter months; the children cannot reach school. Only a few families have wells, for they must be sunk quite deep to reach the first water sources. The traditional occupation of men on Mud Lick has been cutting timber, when it can be found, and paper wood, poor growth or young trees used to make pulp, when the market price is up, from around their homes. There is little left now that can be cut and sold. Thousands of the surrounding acres have been put under the protection of the National Forest Service. More and more land is constantly being purchased —often from elderly people who surrender the land title at the time of their death—in what is apparently an attempt at the conservation of mountain beauty through buying out whole communities of mountain people. Little thought, it seems, is given to the conservation of the mountains as a place where people can live. Some on Mud Lick mine; some dig coal out of little "dog hole" mines to sell to their neighbors; some still cut paper wood; there are many who draw welfare.

Well, the worst thing about bein' poor, there's a lot o' things. You know poor people, buddy, they live on such a little stuff. They don't have enough money to buy nothin' with very good. They live very hard. Man, I know people that lives very bad, son. You take no money or no jobs to make money off, an' you're gonna be in very bad shape. You don't have nothin' to eat half the time like you oughta have, an' that's a very bad life. You take four or eight kids an' have to live on maybe jest so many food stamps, an' you know you're gonna eat them up pretty directly, an' there you sit. Live very hard.

If a man makes under $3,000 a year an' he's got much of a family, he's very poor, he's a poor man. You know some people don't have $2,000 a year to live on, an' a lot of 'em, you'd say, don't have $1,500. An' they have a little garden maybe. 'Cordin' to your family 'bout how you live. I know three thousand ain't no money now. Used to be, if you had $3,000, you'd be in good shape, but now it's gettin' hard. You go in these supermarkets an' take $15, an' you can pack it out under your arm.

Goose Creek is one of the major little communities in the county. Defined by the last half of a twelve-mile-long black-top road running beside the creek which ties together a network of lesser roads winding back through the mountains and into other counties, Goose Creek claims about sixty homes. Few families are without a large garden because the land there is level and good. Most of the older men on the creek have experienced long years of mining, but few are still willing or able to go back to that work. Almost all of the young men past school age work in other states or have gone to Vietnam. A good number of men here, as in all the county's communities, work for the Concentrated Employment Program's Operation Mainstream at public works jobs. Most of the people on the creek spring from seven or eight main families.

There is a community center near the head of the creek, housing a Head Start classroom for about twenty children and a workshop. It is used for fairly regular community meetings.

Almost everyone on the creek has two trades, of which one is farming. The other might be mining, carpentry, auto mechanics, logging, coal hauling, truck driving, or, a full-time job itself, drawing welfare. Tobacco is the cash crop; hogs are virtually the only stock raised to sell. The community is touched with a less rigid sort of poverty; a life where people raise much of what they eat but where cash incomes are extremely low. There is access, by a passable road, to both schools and town. Yet lack of real money shows itself in homes too frail to withstand the winter cold, too small to shelter properly the large numbers who live in them. The difficulties that the mountains themselves place in the way of economic development are felt here as much as elsewhere: treacherous roads that tear apart cars and trucks and which translate thirty miles into an hour's drive; lack of plumbing and waste disposal which, along with such unnatural things as strip mines, results in spoiled creeks and rivers; floods which destroy the little that men have built; general isolation, by distance, from towns which themselves are isolated from cities; a history of one-room schools—of which there were, until the last few years, three in the Goose Creek area—made necessary by the far-flung communities and at which little was taught.

Housing

A more specific sketch of conditions that prevail all over the county can be made by looking at Goose Creek. In the county, 64 per cent of all the housing units are unsound. In Goose Creek, nine out of ten of the homes are not as good as the log houses that some old couples still live in. They are constructed from old lumber, often with just one outside wall and no insulation at all except wallpaper or newspapers and, in rare cases, plasterboard. They are extremely difficult to keep warm in the bitter mountain winters, and, in many structures, no attempt at all is made to heat back rooms like kitchens. Most houses have two rooms and a kitchen, and most families range in size from seven to ten. It is common practice for newly wed couples to live in one- or two-room frames built beside a parent's home. In other communities, conditions are more severe:

Well, I could 'scribe what I seen on the inside. I went there long back. It was sometime last spring. An' I don't believe I ever seed no nastier house in my life, but these are old people. An' I went in, an' I went in the back door an' came through the kitchen. Come through the door to come to a fireplace. An' I'd say it was full of women. Two of 'em was very old, an' one of 'em was in bed. One of 'em had three or four pigs on a bottle. It was very cold. An' I don't know buddy, I coulda took a broom or a shovel an' swept dirt up in the kitchen. They had a wood stove, an' there was ashes all over the place. I believe it's against the health department to have a house such as that. I've never seen such a dirty house. She said her roof leaked, but it was covered with this roofin' paper an' it had lumber under that. Well the walls looked pretty good, but it was a bad house, and the floors, I've never seen such a dirty floor in my life.

Before they fixed it, Jimmy's house, it was a very bad house. It was built low, I had to stoop right over to get in. It was about the worst little house, I mean jest as far as livin' in, it was a bad house. But now he's done some work on it, an' he's fixed it up real nice. Best as I remember it had four rooms an' there must have been about ten children.

Well, I don't want to tell you the names, but I could take you to some houses that's jest box houses. And the floors are bad. You know when I say a box house I mean a house that's jest boxed up out of old lumber, you say, an' got paper on the inside. You got a wall of lumber here, an' nothin' but paper on these walls, then you got a bad house to live in this winter. Sometimes they'll take a little roofin' paper an' put it on the inside, an' that makes it a little bit warmer. But any time you got a box house, jest one box, an' little strips over them cracks, then you've got the worst house you've ever seed. You can't hardly keep them warm; the air'll get in around that. An' there's plenty o' them houses in this country. There's not as many in this creek as there is in the head of Mud Lick or Flat Creek. In Granny's Branch there's several of 'em, I looked at three or four the other day, up a holler where you've never been. I went up there to look at a house way in the head of a holler up there. It'us a bad house.

If you had a real good log house, an' had it notched and daubed . . . . See old people'd build log houses an' daub 'em with clay mud, an' that makes a good warm house. It makes a thick house; you ain't jest got a little inch plank. There's not many of 'em left in this country. I remember my grandaddy way back had a log house, but his was with big thick logs. They was a foot thick or two, an' they hewed 'em out with a broad ax, an' he had that daubed with mud. You

*know when you hew lots of logs down here, you think
you're gettin' them close together, but you're not. You
put a plank inside over that, an' then you fill that outside
in with mud, clay mud, I call it, and smooth it over, an'
you've got a good warm house.*

HEATING

People use coal to heat their homes, and in the winter it
takes about a ton a month to warm even a small house.
That much coal costs eight dollars, and the man who hauls
it charges an extra three dollars on each ton. Coal stoves
burn out at night leaving the walls, which often seem to
do no good at all, as the only protection against the cold outside. Ideally, the tin pipes which take out the smoke should
be replaced each year because the heat from the stove burns
holes in them. When they are not, they become very dangerous, and almost every year someone's house on the creek
will catch fire and burn down. It is not always possible for a
poor man to pay out, all at once, the sixty or seventy dollars
needed to buy enough coal to last the winter. He must take
the chance that when his small supply of coal runs out, the
roads will be clear enough that another one month's load
can reach him.

*Well, if you got plenty of clothes you can keep warm I
guess. They get used to it, but it's mighty hard. But you
know, people gets used to winter as it comes on, an' you
got to have maybe ten, twelve tons of coal. It's mighty hard
fer them people to find it, and a lot o' people have to take
wood in this country. They get by, but it's bad.*

WATER

For water to drink, to cook and to wash with, many people
rely on the small streams that come off the mountains.
They must, of course, walk to get their water, and in the

wintertime they may have to break the ice to fill their bucket. In summer months these streams, and most of the wells, dry up for a time, leaving people waiting days for a rainfall.

If you don't have a well, a lot o' times there'll be a spring. They get it out of a spring or a branch. You could call it a branch. I don't call it a creek. This out here is a creek; it's bigger down here. An' that's where them people gets their water here around. An' you study 'bout how you have to drink water at this time of the year, comin' out of the branch, how warm it is. An' that woman told me how she raised eight or nine kids, an' she's lived up there I guess all her life. An' she has to pack water to wash; she has to pack water to cook with, an' she has to go right up that hill an' pack it straight up and down.

No it's not good. It's not good to drink. It's too much sulferous in it to be good water. But that's all they got.

I wouldn't drink that out of this creek at all, fer it's not good. I wouldn't drink that no way fer it's got things in it above here I wouldn't want to drink. You'd have to go up the hill, or somewhere down the holler. Now you see down this road here is four or five houses, an' they got a well, an' they started haulin' water from here yesterday. Out here they got some outside toilets over it. And they got a strip mine up there that's pushed a lot o' mud down it, an' it stays too muddy an' nasty. We couldn't drink outa that. We used to wash outa that creek down there, before the strip mines ever got started up here. Out by that barn, is a big hole o' water. It stayed there pretty an' clear all summer. But ever since they started that, it stays black an' muddy.

GARBAGE

The standard solution to getting rid of garbage is to drop it in the creek. There is no place else to put it. Most mountain streams that run through inhabited areas are full of cans and bottles, stray auto parts and other refuse. Only animal carcasses are not pushed over the side, for they poison the water. A constant cause for dispute is whether a neighbor's toilet drains into the creek, which is contrary to law.

One of the outstanding sights along mountain roadways is the number of junked and stripped automobile bodies. Driving is so rough on vehicles that to keep one car running requires the parts from several others. Often these empty hulks are turned over into creek beds to shore up the embankments and to divert the rushing water of springtime floods.

Where do they dump it? They dump it anywheres to get it out of the basket. They burn the papers up, and they dump bottles over the creek or anywheres to get shet of it up here. It's not good fer the creeks, but it's the only place I seed. Or on the roads. . . . You can see old cans dumped over.

No garbage pickup around here; that's what we need. There's no dump or nothin'.

In Goose Creek, there's sixty–seventy homes, and none of 'em's hardly got a inside bathroom.

ROADS

In the mountains, roads—and Clay County's are not exceptions—are terribly bad. Blacktop roads generally stick to the wide bottoms where there is at least a possibility of easy construction and repair. When a major road is forced to wind through and over the mountains, the problems of building it so that sections do not wash away in rainy seasons or rock falls do not cover it are much increased. In the mining areas, the big trucks, loaded far over their legal limits with coal, tear up any roads that they travel. Most people, however, do not live on the blacktops; they live miles and miles up roads that often are a combination of rocky, rutted dirt trails and creek beds. It is no little accomplishment to build a road at all through mountain country, and probably the greater part of the people in Clay County do not find their road passable three months out of the year. It is the poor condition of the roadways that people most often complain about, and it is for roads that taxpayers most willingly see their money spent. Where once, it is said, people valued the inaccessibility of their homes to others, they now argue mightily for a way to get a truck to their door. Such is the change that occurs when people lose, or grow out of, as some would say, their self-sufficiency and begin to require speed of transport and the services of others.

It's hard gettin' out of here in the winter. If it comes a big snow and falls on this road here, we might have to stay up here till it thaws off. Without you put chains on. A lot o' times they grade it, but they don't grade up here like they do on the highway. It's awful bad up these dirt roads. You take this branch right here. If they get ice in that creek, they can't get up in here. Or they might have to walk fer a week or two up that branch. I'm afraid of slick roads.

Course they go to school now better than they used to. Used to, I'd say they didn't go to school three, four, five months a year. But we have better roads now than we used to have. Course when it's too bad up here fer the school buses to run, see, they don't go to school at all. An' they can't drive the bus till it fairs up. An' they make up time in the summer which causes school to run late. But I'd say they go to school now better than they used to. They ride the bus, and they don't drive the bus when it's too dangerous on the kids.

Before you got here, up Granny's Branch was a creek road. Now do you believe that? That means you had to go up the creek all the way to the head of Granny's Branch. The first time I went up Granny's Branch, I went up the

*creek, an' I didn't think I was aimin' to get out o' the creek.
I had that same truck I'm drivin' now, an' it was trees
stickin' over the holler an' I like to hit my mirror on one.
The first time I went up Granny's Branch, I'll tell you why
I went up there. You notice when you go up, the road up
there forks, an' a man lives right in the fork. I heared he
had some hogs to sell, it was in the wintertime, which he
did have the hogs. Well I went up that branch, buddy, an'
I didn't think that I'd ever get up through there. I went
right up to his house an' asked did he have some hogs. I
couldn't buy 'em; he was too high fer me. I asked the man,
"What kind of road you got up here?" and he said, "We
ain't got no road, buddy. We been promised a road fer years
and years." I said, "Buddy that's the one place I've seen
where you ain't got anything." But they built a road in
Granny's Branch when you came here. An' last winter they
filled it out o' that creek, an' it got so muddy an' froze last
winter. I could see it doin' that. But if they put a lot of
gravel on it, they might have a better road. Jesus Christ, that
was the worst road I'us ever on. An' they had to walk out,
all the kids did, to go to school. I guess that's a mile and a
half from the head o' that holler. Maybe two miles. I imagine it's close to forty families. It's more'n that. I guess
forty-five.*

CLOTHES

Mountain winters are cold, and it is a problem that all
must face to provide clothing and shoes for their children.
Often, of course, children are kept from school because
they lack warm coats. Shoes do not last long if the trail
that leads to the store or to the school bus is a muddy or
hard-frozen and rocky branch. Kids run barefoot in the
summertime to save their footwear, and in some households,
even the winter does not mean that children can wear their
shoes after school.

No, they don't have near enough clothes. Plenty of 'em don't. I could say one thing, that's the reason a lot of young-'uns drops out of school. They're very poor, an' they don't have the right kind of clothes they think they should have to wear to school. An' 'fore they go to high school they quit. They can't afford the clothes that maybe someone can afford, an' they feel very bad about goin' down to where two or three hundred, or maybe five hundred kids are, an' them not dressed as well as other people. I've heard people say that they couldn't send their kids to school because they didn't have enough clothes to wear.

It's plenty o' times in the wintertime that kids'll wear their shoes out. I have to buy mine maybe two or three pairs a year. If they get too bad, they're not gonna go to school. When they get gone they'll say I have to have a pair of shoes, an' I'll have to manage to get them 'em or they'll quit.

FOOD

Setting out a good dinner ranks high in mountain traditions. In the summer and fall, when the gardens have borne well and for some there have been hogs to slaughter, most eat better and more heartily than do city dwellers. Winter brings a sparser table, especially for families who had no garden from which to store up jars of food. Even a family in good luck can count only on store-bought beans, fresh milk, and cornbread. A family in "hard times" might sustain itself on biscuits and watery gravy. Meat, with the exception of bologna, is a rarely seen commodity for most. A large percentage of the people in the county receive food stamps each month. The help that these give is most times not great, but they make the difference between cornbread and cornbread with soup beans.

You know, I've seed a lot of people who eats very bad. A lot of people don't have the money to buy what they need. They might eat good a while, but you take people on food stamps. If they don't have a garden—as many people don't have a garden as do—they live pretty hard. They don't have half enough to eat. They can't afford it.

When I say half enough, they may have nothin' but gravy an' biscuits, an' the gravy'll be made up outa water, stirred up out of flour dough an' water. They may not have milk to put in it. You want to have good gravy, you got to have milk an' other stuff to put in it. I went to a place here long back, an' they was eatin' breakfast, an' had nary a thing but gravy an' a little biscuits. And that looked bad to me. They had a great bunch o' kids, but they was eatin' it, very happy seemed to me.

I doubt if they eat meat more'n once a month. If they got it. They'd have to go down to the supermarket to get it, an' it's high. It's the highest thing they got. An' all they got to be careful what they buy to make them food stamps go far enough. You can't buy much meat. If you do, you're gonna run out of money directly.

AGRICULTURE

For many, in the right seasons, there is abundance in the mountains. A good deal is actually raised on the roughly 12 per cent of Clay County that is level. In fact, much is grown on the hillsides that a midwesterner would not consider planting. Families with a little space plant cabbages, beans, tomatoes, corn, potatoes, and cucumbers. That part of the harvest which is not eaten at once is canned for the winter. Blackberries grow wild in the hills and are picked for canning and to sell. Poke, a strange wild plant tasting like turnip or mustard greens, can be picked in the woods. Men raise bees in homemade bee "gums" and try to sell honey. Each spring and fall, those who have hogs slaughter them for meat, and pigs are sold to neighbors for ten dollars apiece. Calves, however, are not killed for beef, but rather sold in London, Kentucky, at the stock market. There is a feeling that God put hogs on the earth to be eaten, but that cows were put here to give milk and not to be killed by those who raise them.

Years ago, before there were stock laws and before blight destroyed the chestnut trees, hogs were allowed to roam free on the hills and fatten themselves on nuts for the fall slaughter. Now, when owners must take upon themselves the responsibility of raising their own stock, most cannot afford the expense and must forego the pleasure of fresh meat. The only real cash crop that is grown is burley tobacco, but the government makes strict allotments of the amount a farmer can grow. Not every farmer who wants one can get an allotment, or "tobacco base." Most of the tobacco bases held by poor men are in the neighborhood of 7/100 of an acre to 3/10 of an acre. The crop grown on 7/100 of an acre might bring eighty to one hundred dollars. Tobacco prices are very high, but it is also very costly to raise as it must be repeatedly sprayed and fertilized, and stored in barns to dry out for weeks after cutting, and in the wintertime the land must be sown with a good cover crop like rye grass. Another source of income, for those with the time to go after it, is the collecting of medicinal roots—ginseng, apple root, May root, corn root, and others which can be sold to medicine manufacturers. Ginseng, the most valuable, brings about three dollars an ounce.

Basically, this is the extent of agriculture in Clay County. The mountains are unsuited to the plow, yet the plow has broken that rocky land for well over one hundred years.

HEALTH

All diseases and health problems that plague men in our relatively sanitary society are seen in amazing proportions in Clay County. The mines and the rigors of mountain life have made their contribution—pulmonary diseases, back and bone infirmities, and all manner of crippling injuries—

to the general unhealthiness seen in mountain communities. Problems such as tuberculosis, intestinal worms, sugar diabetes, and malnutrition often enter serious stages before they are diagnosed because people are frequently hard put to travel to doctors and to pay their bills. Most medical treatment is extremely impersonal; it is administered through state agencies for public health and mental health, tuberculosis clinics, or by overworked physicians with claim to far too few hospital beds. In Clay County there are two private hospitals—one of which is church supported—and together these are staffed by five doctors. In addition there are three doctors in Manchester. Though this is barely adequate for the twenty thousand people in Clay County, there is the additional load from Jackson County, where there is only one doctor and no hospital. In 1969 Clay County broke ground for a new hospital, but even when it is completed, most patients will still have to report to those places where treatment is inexpensive: the small Red Bird Mission Hospital in Clay County, and the Appalachian Regional hospitals in Harlan and Pineville—all over an hour's drive from most points in the county.

Though mothers are diligent in their attempts to keep their children neat, the notion of cleanliness has little bearing in the mountains where in cold winter even the air is heavy with coal smoke. Unsanitary conditions, certainly increased by outside toilets, polluted streams, and lack of garbage disposal, strengthen the foothold of disease in mountain communities. Homes that cannot be heated in winter, insufficient clothing, poor food—all play a role.

Though most women have their babies delivered by doctors in one of the hospitals, Clay County has an infant death rate of 45.7, which lists fourth from the top among the 120 counties in Kentucky.

County doctors handle emergency cases as best they can, often sending accident victims by ambulance to the hospital at the University of Kentucky in Lexington, one hundred miles away. Patients suffering from the usual range of problems see doctors on a first-come, first-served basis in the hospitals. On busy days, it requires several hours of waiting to see a physician.

A lot of people seems to be more sick than they was when I was growin' up. Seems to me like they weren't a'goin' every day to the doctors like they are now. Half the people you see it seems are sick or say they are, an' they're goin' to see the doctor.

I couldn't offhanded tell you how many's got it, but a lot of people's got the sugar diabetes. Lot of people's got TB. But I'd say more people's got the sugar diabetes than they have that. Tell me if you don't let the TB get too big a start on you, you can cure the TB pretty quick. But I don't know, I never had it I reckon, an' never had the sugar diabetes, or if I had, I didn't know it. I'll tell you about that. That sugar diabetes is a bad disease. You know it does people awful bad. A lot o' times you have to have one of your legs cut off, or one of your feet took off. It's a bad disease.

Yeah we got worms. We used to have worm medicine, they had it in bottles way back, but now you go to the drugstore, you can buy different kinds. My mother used to get it in the bottles. Christ, it'us the worst tastin' stuff I ever seed in my life. I'd rather do anythin' than take a dose o' that. Now they got different stuff; it don't taste so bad. If it gets bad enough you can go see a doctor. There's different kinds of worms: pin worms and big worms. They'll kill you too, brother, if you don't get them out. I've seed kids had 'em pretty bad. They had to go to the doctor to get 'em out. Lots of kids have worms in this country.

WELFARE SYSTEM

All welfare recipients and unemployed fathers are allowed medical cards for their families. These provide for general medical treatment and some hospital care, the money coming through the welfare department under the category of Aid to Families with Dependent Children. Unfortunately, Kentucky claims to be unable to meet the demands of the program and is curtailing it throughout the state.

In general, the welfare system in Kentucky is no worse, no more arbitrary, or more bureaucratic than anywhere else. It is a victim of the same extraordinarily confining categories of assistance that all states must work within, and the same ill-timed rulings that the federal government sets forth—such as the recent freeze on the size of the Aid to Families with Dependent Children grants that state may receive. In Mississippi, the means by which the AFDC regulations can be used against recipients—such as the notorious midnight raids on homes to see that no man lives there—have been much heralded. In Kentucky, where the number of injured and disabled men in their twenties, thirties, and forties is staggering, much the same is the case with the categories of the Aid to the Permanently and Totally Disabled and AFDC-Incapacity. In the former category, a claimant must prove that he is permanently and totally unable to perform any substantial gainful activity. Neither partial nor temporary disability can be compensated for by reason of the federally defined category. Thus an applicant, who may be bedridden, is forced to see doctors who, for the welfare department's fee of five dollars, are expected to make comprehensive judgments about their patient's ability to work. If a doctor does affirm that the patient is permanently and totally disabled, then the welfare department will send him to a State Examining Physician, usually in Lexington, who frequently will conclude from the same medical evidence that the applicant is only totally and temporarily disabled or permanently and partially disabled, thus collapsing the applicant's case. To contest this, the applicant must produce more medical reports indicating disability than the department can produce indicating fitness.

If a man has enough Social Security quarters to apply for benefits under that agency's APTD category, he must prove that he is unable to engage in substantial gainful activity anywhere within the *national economy*. Applicants are sometimes told that they could be trained for a type of work done in Texas or Oregon. These glaring absurdities, it seems, have not yet impressed themselves on the lawmakers of this country.

Perhaps the most humane program to aid those unable to work is welfare's AFDC-Incapacity. To receive benefits under this category, a father or mother must only prove inability to return to a former occupation, which for men is most often mining, or to perform any other gainful activity in the county or community. Difficulties here are that single or childless men are not eligible for benefits and that "other gainful activity" is often construed to mean night watchman or service station attendant, which are jobs that few but the bedridden could not theoretically perform.

None of these programs takes the availability of employment into consideration. That a given job exists, whether or not it is available, is a sufficient criterion for denying a man welfare. That seems to be a theory running throughout all programs of assistance to the disabled—that a man is morally responsible to perform a job until his dying breath, and that state agencies are morally responsible to keep a man from spending a single more relaxed day than can be helped. Is it unfair to assume that the working men who have done the heavy labor of this country deserve a little more leisure—if that is what you can call the state a man with a disarranged spine or rock dust finds himself in—than Sunday off once a week? How greatly does it increase the productivity of our labor force to run an injured man through a mill of doctor's exams, welfare fieldworker's inquiries and home visits, and a lengthy, humiliating appeals process for the sake of determining that he can still stand and therefore might still be able to chalk up six more months on the job?

In some ways, the Kentucky welfare system excels in comparison with those of other states. Payments to families with dependent children are based on 87 per cent of a fifteen-year-old standard of living scale, whereas in Mississippi, the ceiling is 27 per cent. Yet while many cities and states have taken upon themselves the expense of non-federally sponsored programs like general public assistance, Kentucky has no such category.

The state, like all others, offers unemployment compensation to those who swear they are able and available to work. To receive benefits (Rocking Chair pay) or to get a medical card on the grounds of unemployment, a man cannot refuse any job offered him. This provides a complication for a disabled man, denied welfare, who has registered with the employment office only to get medical assistance, for, while he is in fact disabled, he must assert that he can and will take any job offered him. The employment offices administer a Manpower Training and Development program which requires for admission a level of education which few have reached. The Bureau of Rehabilitation Services, which does the bulk of the vocational training and re-training in the state, forces men to leave their homes to attend the training sites, which for some might be several counties away. All training programs are faced with the fact that there are virtually no private, non-mining jobs in the mountains, and what jobs there are are heavily competed for by the young.

I Rocked about three times to my knowin's. Never drawed no welfare. Never got no food stamps. And way back, I got a little commodity, you know. You know when

they first bring it in here, I got some of it one or two times,
I was drawin' some Rockin' Chair money. An' they wouldn't
let me have commodity. Said I was drawin' too much.
"Well OK," I said, "Keep it."

HOW IT FEELS TO BE POOR

The poor people of Kentucky have been made subject
to an incredible number of programs designed for their
betterment. All of Franklin D. Roosevelt's great plans were
tested in the mountains. All manner of public works
projects have been here and gone. Where the WPA left
off the Happy Pappies (some twenty-five years later)began,
and when that program ended the Nelson and Mainstream
programs rushed in. Public assistance has probably achieved,
in spite of itself, record caseloads here. And surely the
rediscovery of Appalachia had great effect on the creation
of President Johnson's War on Poverty. Kentucky has seen
a missionary movement, a union movement, and representatives of the Southern Conference Educational Fund,
the Christian Appalachian Movement, the Council of
Southern Mountains, the Save the Children Federation,
the Appalachian Volunteers, the Volunteers in Service
to America, and literally scores of other organizations trying to promote their solutions to the mountains' problems
and, in rare cases, trying to effect the solutions that the
poor themselves have devised. Appalachia, and Kentucky
more than other states, and Clay County as much as any
county, have been worked over to a greater extent than
even prime areas like Mississippi and Harlem or even the
lands of the American Indians. The main thrust of these
agencies and groups has been to improve the hillbilly
through give-away programs—that people are often forced
by circumstance to participate in or are degraded by having
to fight to participate in—or by channeling the people's
energy through the often fallacious theories and plans of

an outsider who considers he knows "the way" or "a way" toward a better life. There have been some notable exceptions to this, many of which have been provided by the inspirations of indigenous people working for several of the already mentioned organizations.

There have also been, unfortunately, a lot of examples of an outsider damaging the spirit that moves people of a community to strike out for a better life. One Clay County man, not an organizer but simply a coal truck driver with some insights into the problems he and his neighbors face, complained that his community had been virtually wrecked through the efforts of a VISTA worker. The organizer, he said, succeeded in exciting the people about the things they could do if they met together and acted together. At the first gathering people began talking with each other about the ways of cleaning up the community's creeks and roads. At the next meeting, however, the organizer had something else on her mind and lectured the people on that. Community interest and the organization itself deteriorated as, at each subsequent meeting, the organizer dominated the discussion, which was always about some new topic of her choosing. People lost interest in coming to meetings and have since resisted all other attempts by outsiders to "organize them."

It is the observation of one long-time community worker in the mountains that the outside organizers have maintained a fine record of discouraging militancy among poor people. He believes that it is the natural reaction of an organizer when presented, for example, with a situation where disgruntled welfare claimants decide to march around the courthouse carrying shotguns to emphasize their grievances, to argue that that is a bad plan, which could only lead to arrest, and to point out that it is not so correct an approach as petitioning, getting legal help, etc. What occurs in a case like that is that poor people bow to the voices of "wisdom," as they have been trained to follow the dictates of whoever is educated and sophisticated and are deterred from testing out which of the approaches to a problem are in fact wise, and which will be effective. They have been denied a chance to learn how they can accomplish their goals by an outsider who has theories of his own about how things should be done. It would be better if people exercised the methods that come naturally to them—better that they march around the courthouse, get arrested, and then decide, on that basis, whether that is the best tactic—than that they do nothing but follow the advice of one educated outsider about how they can free themselves from the rule of the more polished individuals, welfare workers, politicians, and program planners who make the decisions which control the lives of the poor.

The kinds of political activity that mountain poor people have engaged in when they have followed their own inclinations have been more militant and no less successful than movements arranged by outsiders. In 1969, a group of Whitely County citizens, angered that their pleas for repair on a road used by all and by school buses were consistently ignored, elected to declare the road unsafe for travel and to close it off. They set up road blocks and refused to let traffic pass. As each group of men were arrested, others appeared to take their place. Finally a much embattled highway department agreed to resurface the road.

The struggle against strip mining was largely carried out at the direction of mountain people. The real commitment on the part of the men everywhere in the mountains to put a stop to the terrible waste caused by surface mining was a stronger showing of the real wants of the mountain people than anything that has been seen since. Though they were not successful in their main purpose of outlawing stripping on mountain slopes, they did force strip mines into the most costly battle they have ever had to wage.

It is essential that people can learn from their own efforts how change can be won. Most programs and program planners have failed to see that oppression is not primarily a matter of little money and bad homes: it is essentially a problem of a people's spirit. Giving people money and rebuilding homes is a good and generally necessary thing, but no one has yet come up with the wherewithal to give all poor mountain people good incomes and nice homes. Although most programs aspire to provide pathways that will lead people out of poverty, the planners seem to forget that they are manhandling people's lives. They try to give new tools to people, yet they are foreign tools and make people ashamed of the tools they themselves have. They try to impose, by fragments, the features of a modern America on communities with very beautiful, if old-fashioned, cultures. At every step, each little bit of modernity is met with resistance by a much larger force of old methods of doing and thinking of things. Those bent on obliterating poverty can either overpower it—and the culture and traditions that go with it—by constructing a thousand factories and a million homes in the mountains, or they can seek other ways, not the least of which might be ending the humiliating, self-righteous programs our government now operates. It might be better to let the poor go it alone and try to solve their problems in their own way than to dispatch them bits and pieces of the good life —a little adult education here, a little welfare there. Hopefully, while the government concerns itself with some of the most severe material elements of poverty—bad food, bad clothing, bad homes—the poor people of the mountains will continue to use their wits to overcome a world seemingly bent on showing its superiority to them.

OEO: Almost all programs and outsiders seem, intentionally or not, to try to impress upon the mountaineer the error of his ways, or the boat that he is missing. As an example, OEO is here singled out, in part because it is the least offender.

The Office of Economic Opportunity came to Kentucky in the form of multi-county Community Action programs, or CAP's, whose boards of directors were filled with professional and political townspeople. In the Cumberland River Valley, of which Clay County is a part, there was begun, in 1964, an eight-county "politicians' " CAP. Poor people's groups throughout the area fought against this, and by dint of their own persistence, succeeded in persuading OEO to defund the monolith in 1966. In its place were set up four single- and double-county groups, one being the Jackson-Clay Community Action Agency, whose boards were made up almost entirely of low-income people. Thus the organized poor had succeeded in bringing home to themselves what was to be the master solution to poverty. In Clay County, the CAP helped to set up local community poor people's groups to which VISTA volunteers were dispatched. The efforts of almost all organizers and organizations were aimed at implementing the CAP structure of board-controlled community groups, organization presidents, parliamentary procedure, etc.

But the idea had two main failings. One was that, while attempting to be a grass-roots organization, it was forced by the nature of OEO's own programs to be a top-down arrangement. Community organizers were mostly outsiders, or dominated by outsiders, and it was their job locally to implement OEO projects. But these were projects not designed by mountain people, and it is likely they were designed not with the mountains, but with the nation, in mind; and they were hopelessly complex. Who in a poor community can handle the intricate job of writing proposals, reading guidelines, locating personnel, and preparing budgets? Even though they sit on the boards that approve the programs, how can they gain a feeling of control of or participation in operating these programs? For most

of the poor people, the CAP has become another agency—
though by far the most benign one—that has taken a hand
in running their lives.

The other failing is the sadder one. Almost all of the
efforts of the organized poor are channeled into or directed
by the CAP. When it comes down to it, the CAP's are not
prepared to fight the many fronts of poverty. All that they
are able to do is to administer OEO programs such as
child care, but only for a few, Emergency Food vouchers,
but not for all, Self-Help programs like home improvement,
but not for all, certain home services like sewing classes,
the VISTA program, and a few others. It cannot engage
itself in many activities, notably political ones, and has
little contact with the sort of problems that poor men
come up with when they talk informally out in the fields.
If the welfare department were controlled by poor people,
it would still only be equipped to administer welfare. OEO
is another grand project aimed at eradicating, in some
measure, the visible aspects of poverty. Its often ill-tailored
programs are planned in Washington and obviously not by
poor people. It is not geared to learning the desires of the
poor, and it would probably be prohibited by law from
meeting those desires if it knew them.

Town and Country: One problem faced by those who
run agencies to benefit the poor is the ingrained prejudice
of the mountain poor against towns, town dwellers, all
the things that are done in town and at the courthouse,
and men, except preachers, who wear ties. It is a general
feeling that the people in town, who are usually the middle
class, care little about the poor, do not want to hear them,
and believe themselves better than those in the country.
Many come to take on the assumption that townspeople
are right—this is the most degrading and probably most
destructive part of poverty. Those people who have made
it, who have money in the bank, do not much care for you,

think you were born to serve, treat you as subhuman, and in time succeed in convincing you that that is what you are. But not quite, because most poor people retain a spark within them that makes them burn with bitterness and resentment toward those with economic and political power. The gratification that fills a man after he has joined a successful mine strike or the boycott of a white-owned store in the South, pays for years of indignities, of feeling shabby, uneducated, inarticulate, clumsy, of being poor. It is this sort of striking out that eases the real burdens of poverty.

Sure I can see a lot o' diff'rence in the poor man an' the well-off man in how they treat him. I think a lot o' times, the big feller, they want to keep the poor man down anyway. They want to keep him down so maybe he can depend on them. An' they want him to stay poor probably so they can tell him what to do. So he'll listen to them, and they'll get his vote. Sometimes I think the poor people's been treated pretty bad. Take the big shots, they'll shake hands with you every four years, and you're a good man. But after that four years, you probably don't see them again till the next four years. They've been treated bad. See, they don't get up in the hollers to see how people live. They stay downtown. But every four years they come up in the hollers, an' they see, an' you're fine people then. They're wantin' your votes.

The good things about livin' around here are you're out from a town, an' you don't see much goin' on. You don't hear all that noise you hear about town. It's very quiet an' a diff'rent place than town. That's the reason I say it's a very good place. I don't like to live in a town myself. It's all crowded up. I don't have nothin' against town people myself, but I don't like to live there. It's less botherin' you here. I know it suits me better, an' I know most o' the people'd rather live up here than down in Manchester.

III   Political Powerlessness, the "Courthouse Gang"

It is not strange that poor people in the mountains should feel some distrust and dislike for those who run the towns. They have been badly treated, in a very obvious way, by the political and economic powers that be. The Kentucky political system on the county level, like that of a few other states in the East, remains essentially colonial. Local government is supposed to rest in the hands of the elected county judge and four magistrates, or squires, who are elected by districts. Each magistrate, who is not required to have legal training, is empowered to judge minor suits, mainly traffic cases, that arise in his district and to levy fines. The county judge, who also may not have legal training, presides over most cases that arise in the county. Together the magistrates and the judge administer all county revenue and much of the federal and state money that comes in for such things as roads. These men join other important officials—the high sheriff, the county court clerk, the circuit court clerk, and the county and commonwealth attorneys—in deciding what goes on in their county.

In the past, mine operators played a great part in county politics because the courthouse is in charge of things like assessing coal lands for taxes, road maintenance, attracting or discouraging outside industry, and enforcing the tonnage limits on coal trucks. However, as the number of men engaged in mining, and thus the number that would be susceptible to company pressure, has declined, so has the direct influence of the individual operators diminished. In their place has come an equally powerful force, the School System. By virtue of its permanently employing far more men and women than any other agency or industry, it has become the seat of power in Clay and most other mountain counties. It is generally thought that the school superintendent, who in Clay County has been in office for years, dictates most of what is done by other county officials as well as how money is spent. In Clay County that power is further compounded by the fact that the husband of the school superintendent is the chairman of the county Republican party, which is by far the stronger party in the county. The school superintendent is not elected but is appointed by the five school board members, who could not themselves be elected without the support of the incumbent school superintendent. Political power, which is centered in the figures of the school superintendent, county judge, magistrates, and county court clerk, is built upon all the votes of the county and town employees, state highway department employees, welfare recipients, and school system employees, and is maintained throughout the county by a network of minor politicos who are entrusted with rallying support during election campaigns. The resulting situation for the poor is one in which nothing seems to come down to them from their local governments and there is no immediate way apparent to get anything out of their local governments, which, it is clear, are main elements of political oppression.

Election time, which in Clay County means the Republican primary, is heralded months in advance by the appearance everywhere of candidates' posters and stickers. The public campaign is quite exciting, and it is cause for much heated discussion out in the country—reviving old feuds, suspicions, and grievances concerning the candidates. For some offices, like jailer or coroner, there are often as many as a dozen men and women running, each backed by his or her own nucleus of family and friends. Elections, like most other important matters in the county, are very much involved with family allegiances. The mountain voter puts great weight on pleas for support by "my wife's daddy's cousin," and considerable respect is accorded to the bearer of certain distinguished names. Often a candidate enjoys a victorious campaign by letting his wife's family do the work for him, and, on occasion, a father with a good deal of pull will do the campaigning for his relatively unknown son. Before the election there are mass rallies at the county's larger schools where all candidates may speak. These are usually the scene of loud and underhanded debates between the various contenders for an office. Every so often the audiences get enough into the spirit of the occasion that fights or even shootings flare up. During the campaign, the candidates cover as much ground as possible, slapping as many backs and shaking as many hands as are presented to them across the county.

A private campaign is also waged by the hangers-on to the political bosses. There are men in each community who at every election time come out on the side of the incumbent and go around to their neighbors handing out campaign cards and, where it will do any good, passing out money for assurances of a right vote at the ballot box. It has been said that, in the past, word was spread to welfare recipients and men on county and state payrolls that they were expected to vote the party choices—mostly twenty-year men—back in, but even without being told, most of these men and women feel their own vulnerability and would vote the old ticket for fear of repercussions if they did not. In such a manner is political power won in the mountains. No one quite understands why control over the county's purse strings holds such attraction for men in politics, but it is widely believed that big payoffs go with the jobs to enable officials to leave office more wealthy than they entered and seemingly to spend more money on campaigns than they make in salary.

County officials could not, probably, do all of the things poor people think they should do even if they were not, as it is thought, "crooked." But there remain many areas where, by its inactivity, the "courthouse gang" does its part to keep poor people poor, and many instances where it acts more for the continuance of its own power than in the interests of the approximately 70 per cent of the people in Clay County who are poor. The county does not lobby the state for extensive strip mine control or wider workmen's compensation coverage. The county puts little pressure on an equally uninterested state highway department to pave roads or to build or properly maintain roads through poor communities—unless there is the desire to consolidate power in a certain area. The county judge, who must assign Operation Mainstream men to jobs, puts them to work sweeping schoolhouses and county buildings rather than planning jobs that might actually train men for something. Highway jobs, a traditional source of patronage, do not go to the very poor, but rather to men at peace, more or less, with the business or political powers. The school system, which once locked community people out of the county schoolhouses to keep them from meeting to discuss the ills of the first Cumberland Valley CAP, now, in Goose Creek of Clay County, has refused the community's request for adult education classes in a well-lighted, heated, and spacious community building and offered instead to allow classes to be held in an ancient one-room schoolhouse nearby. The school system, too, casts covetous glances at the CAP-run Head Start program. When the school board administered a Head Start program in the summer of 1969, many thought that the staff hired to run the centers could have been drawn from needier families. Clearly there are things that the government of Clay County could do for the poor yet there is nothing in its recent history of which it could be rightly said, "This was to benefit the poor people."

In the past three or four years it's been the school system, the county judge, the circuit court clerk, the county attorney

. . . the school system. How come they got the power? Well, they stayed in office so long. An' the school system is the biggest . . . it hires more people than any other thing in Clay County. They got more jobs. An' they got people teachin' school, an' they got people doin' jobs that the school superintendent tells, "You vote for this man right here." Then he's got that kind of power, an' he can go to the county judge an' say, I put that man in there an' you'll do what I say.

The school superintendent is elected by the school board, an' they got these districts set up where they know they got the most people workin'. An' it's very hard to beat 'em out. But I think the day's comin'.

We got five school board members in Clay County. You take three of them an' you can hire a school superintendent. Other two might be agin her, I don't know. But she's got the power over 'em. They stand with her. And they're gonna promise to hire her or they're not gonna get elected. An' when the board members get elected, they hire the school system. If they don't do what she says, she'll put them out in the next two or three years. An' I knowed of one board member who's been in there since I knowed him. An' he ain't got out an' run a campaign nowheres. He jest sat an' rocked on his porch. They elected him. All he got to say is, "You've got the school board, you'll be the superintendent." That's where they get their power.

Politics is enjoyed with great intensity in mountain counties. The personalities and actions of officials, who for the most part stay quite aloof from their constituents, can provoke honest hatred among mountain men. In the last ten years one or two Kentucky mountain counties have lost their courthouses to arsonists. In 1969, the sheriff of Clay County was killed by a shotgun blast on a back road after his successor had already been elected.

The politics of the county are not democratic, except in that word's crudest sense. Entreaties from the poor for better roads and bridges, for more free lunches in school, are generally ignored or put off by claims of too little money, which, in some cases, are true. In fact, the county does not need to serve the organized poor: county officials already satisfy enough people to get elected—by dispensing little loans, gifts, or services, though often only by taking advantage of a man's poverty. And they are not especially eager to encourage greater participation in government. They sometimes, however, overestimate the strength of their positions. In the 1969 primary, a candidate pledging to "serve all the people" and urging voters not to be pushed around by political "bosses," ousted the incumbent county judge, a man who had held that office for twenty years, by twelve votes. There was considerable shock over the outcome of that race, and some speculation that the new county judge would move to redraw the voting precincts used in school and county elections, which were gerrymandered in 1962 to the benefit of the loyal school board members who choose the superintendent.

No, I've never seed nobody jest throw money out an' give nobody; they slip it. They go around behind a car, an' you can see 'em goin' to that car like bees. Now that's somethin' I never did pay much attention to. I knowed they was buyin' it, but I never ask around in a man's business an' try to see him handin' out money to someone. Which I don't like. That money comes off our county. You know if you buy an office, it's yours, an' it'll take you four years to get your money back. That's why a lot o' times you don't get nothin' done in your county for four years. Takes him four years to get his money back.

You know, it has been, they'll say you vote this way or we'll take you off welfare. Well they've caught up with

*that, an' now they're about afraid to tell people somethin'
that's false. They can't take you off 'cordin' to how you
vote, but they used to say they could.*

*I think if we had a man to do the job, an' enough
knowledge, an' he come out o' the head o' these hollers
as poor as could be, I think he'd have more feelin' for the
poor people. An' if he had any money to do anythin' with,
like buildin' roads, the county, you know, builds roads, I
think he'd be a'tryin' to build some roads up in these hollers
an' not waste it. Somebody who's up an' got a lot o' money,
they're not carin' 'bout the poor man. If they are, I've not
seed too many of 'em. An' I think that the poor man would
be a'feelin' fer the other poor men.*

*The reason there's never been a poor man elected is he's
never had a chance. He didn't have no money, an' actually,
I don't agree with buyin' votes myself, there wouldn't be no
use in his a'runnin'. They'd laugh at him. "He can't run
that county judge's office noway. He can't get it, an' he
don't need it noway." He can't get it if he don't have no
money to buy nobody with. That's a pretty bad thing to
say. If you have to buy a vote to win. I won't sell my vote.
I'll vote fer the man that'll do fer the poor people.*

*I'd like to see a poor man in the county judge's office. If
he had enough ability, enough experience, to do the job.
I don't think poor people'd laugh at him noway. The county
judge we've had has not been too rich a man, but he's been
handled by these people. He'd a been a pretty good man,
but he let other people tell him what to do. You know,
money can hurt or money can help. You know the poor
people don't have money to go down there an' offer the
county judge, an' maybe somebody like the school system
has an' can say you do this or that. I'm against the big shots
takin' over. We need the poor people in office.*

*It's been some people's wore the seats out in the school
buses. They never gets a new man. They keep that same*

bunch on an' on. An' that's the reason they're goin' down the drain. Poor people's wakin' up today, an' they're gonna put them out. I'd say in a couple of years there'll be a new bunch. I don't think that no office is made for one person to stay in a lifetime. There's some new ideals needs to be scattered around.

One thing that makes an oppressive political system harder to fight in the mountains, than say, in the southwest counties of Mississippi where Mrs. Geneva Collins, Charles Evers, and some others have won hard election battles, is that the arm of mountain politics reaches well into poor communities, while in the South, the old political powers never sought any involvement in the black community. In Kentucky it is much harder to isolate the true villains in the political structure, for there is not the separation of black and white, nor really even of rich and poor. There are many fairly poor people in local office and many extremely poor men who cater to their wishes by campaigning for them. The ones who hang around the courthouse and fraternize with the county court clerk are mostly old men with government pensions—and they are actually important parts of the political machine: they control votes. In every poor community are men who would turn over the people's votes to incumbents, which is to say that most poor people in poor communities are related to someone who believes himself to carry some weight in the courthouse. Of course, there are not a whole lot of rich people in Clay County. And many poor men run for jobs like jailer because it is one of the few things that offers a good steady income. All of this means not that the county officials have the needs of the poor at heart, but rather that the poor have a more difficult time arranging themselves to challenge the system itself. Almost everyone in the mountains is poor, and common expectation is that if a less than wealthy man is clever enough to swing a majority vote, he will try, while in office, to get every dollar he can to enrich himself, and this expectation of the people is not usually dashed.

STATEMENT OF PROTEST

I think it's come a time when the poor people's got to wake up. They've got to go a'doin' somethin' about this, place o' lettin' people run everythin' over them. I've seen people run over poor people all my life, an' I'm gettin' tired of it fer my part.

You take in this county right here; they're good people long as you go down an' vote fer 'em. Then they'll come back in the next four years an' pat you on the back an' say, "We're gonna give you jobs." You never see 'em no more— till the next four years. Then you'll see 'em come up. "Well, it's the election. You gonna vote fer old man Charlie this time?" Well, a lot of them will go down there, an' they'll ease around, an' they'll do this, an' they'll say they're Christians. Then they'll reach around there, an' they'll give 'em two dollars, an' people'll stick it in their pockets. An' they'll vote four years against their own interests fer two an' a half or two dollars. That's right. They ought not to do that. They ought to be votin' fer a man who'll do somethin' fer them. If you can find him. If you got a man in four years doesn't do nothin' fer you, put him out, an' put in a man that will do it. Jest keep on till you try to find that kind o' man. That's the way I see the poor people's gonna have to do. If they don't, they're gonna be trod right down on their feet, an' these big politicians'll jest be cheatin' them alive to get 'em to vote fer 'em every four years . . . . That's right, buddy, I know it. I'm gettin' sick about it.

An' we got the poorest folk there ever was. An' they'll come around an' say, "Let's have a community meetin'." I've been goin' to community meetin's fer the last four years, an' we got plenty people goin' out to meetin's. I ain't got anythin' to offer 'em myself. I'm gonna be honest about that. I ain't got nothin'. But we got people who got money, the OEO. They'll say, "We'll do somethin' about it. You set up a meetin' an' we'll do somethin'." An' when you set that meetin' up, you'll never see 'em about it, an' they'll never do nothin' about it. We talked about buyin' a well rig. People's drinkin' out o' the creek in Clay County, out o' the branches, an' they got Self-Help money to buy a well rig, an' I don't know what's the reason they won't buy it. I believe if I had the money I'd buy it. I wouldn't stop till I found it.

I don't know what to do about it. We oughta jest walk down an' say, "Stop all of it," say, "Boys, this is the time to change over. We come atter you." You believe that'd work? I think that's the only way you're gonna solve the problems.

Now I believe in people havin' jobs. An' that's the only way you can solve the problem a lot o' times. But if you go an' give one man $12,000 or $14,000 a year to run the CAP an' the poor people are gettin' nothin', that's not right either. Why don't you pay a man a salary he can live at, an' take some o' that 12,000 you're givin' him an' let that come down to the poor people to give them somethin'. And the poor people are livin' on $1500, some of 'em a thousand. They're scratchin' any way to get by.

And them Mainstream men, they got jobs sweepin' school-houses. They need takin' out o' the schoolhouse though. They need takin' out o' this an' get up there an' build roads an' bridges where people won't have to wade the creek to their knees. Our taxpayers pay fer the schools to be cleaned. They're knockin' people out o' jobs.

And what makes me so sick, the school system won't have nothin' to do with the CAP much. If they got a community building, they want people to go down yonder to the schoolhouse fer adult education class. A woman told me yesterday she wouldn't go. Then she told me she'd go to adult education if it weren't up at the schoolhouse. I told her I wasn't gonna go up to the schoolhouse. We're gonna have it in our own buildin'. We've got a buildin' in Goose Creek. We built it. An' that's where we're gonna hold our meetin's at. What's the reason they can't have it in this center? We got lights. We got plenty o' water in here.

Q. How much do they pay the county judge and the school superintendent?

The county judge? I don't know what they pay him. I don't know what they pay the school superintendent. $7,000, $8,000 a year. I understand they're raisin' it, but I guess the judge'll make around $6,000 a year.

Q. How much do they spend on campaigns?

Oh God! About $20,000, $30,000 every four years. He stays there every year, an' it takes him four years to get that money back. If you buy an office here, you see, you've got to stay there four years to get your money back, about it. They don't get it all off o' the county. They get part of it, but they get other things. That's the reason they don't do nothin'; they got to get that money back. An' that's the way the school system is; they buy it. But they don't be out as much on their politics as the county judge would. They got their districts cut up where they can get elected where they pull. But that day's comin' where they won't have that.

See a good man ain't got a chance. A poor man ain't got a chance now. That's the way they run it, an' that's the way they've had it. It wouldn't be worth nothin' to run down here fer an office. Why they'd jest laugh at me. "Why he ain't got no money." And I've knowed a lot of poor men to run, an' they jest laughed, "Oh, that man can't make it." No wonder he couldn't make it. He didn't have the money to back him. I ain't a'figurin' on runnin' fer nothin'. It wouldn't be no use. I ain't got no money. The people's goin' to have to get behind the election office an' say, "Look here, buddy, that's agin the law." We're gonna have to get shet o' these people, though, that's been a'doin' that an' elect new people. An' then we're gonna stop all that.

I'll tell you the reason the people takes the two dollars. You know, two dollars looks pretty big to the poor man when he's got nothin' to live on. You know, they go to the election, they know they're gonna get the two dollars that day. But they don't have no promise fer a job the day atter. An' I think that if everybody was up on the standard of livin', that they would turn that two dollars down.

You take a poor man today that ain't got a sack o' meal in his house or somethin' like that, two dollars looks pretty big to him. But I wouldn't take the two dollars myself. I'd beg the two dollars 'fore I'd sell my vote fer two dollars. I'd say, buddy, I ain't got a bite, but I don't want your two dollars. But you know a lot o' poor people does that, an' that's a bad thing. I'd like to see that broke up. But one thing that'd do it is fer poor people to get on their feet. They wouldn't be beholdin' to people. Then they'd say we don't have to sell out. We got the money. We've got a job. I believe that'd be one of the answers. I see a poor man, he's got a big bunch o' kids, two or three dollars will help him a big lot sometimes. I've seed the time myself if I had three dollars it'd help me a lot. Sure have.

You know buddy, you take a lot o' these rich people, they want to stay in power. I don't think we should have selfishness, selfish people. I think we should have all alike. But we've got some people that's got respect of persons an' that's all right with your relations, but I don't think that you should go down in that county judge's office an' make diff'rences in people, I think that you should treat everybody alike. You should not send a bulldozer down to the *lower end of the county and maybe blacktop a road and never send one to the head of Goose Creek in four years. That's not treatin' your tax money right.*

These fellers have been in power so long, an' they got a certain bunch o' people. That's the way they get 'em to stick to 'em. They do that much fer so many people. An' the poor people, they don't do nothin' fer the poor people. The only thing they look at is every four years. You're good people fer three or four months; they shake hands with you to beat the world. An' atter the election, they won't shake hands with you till the next four years. I can tell jest as good, if I fergit about an election, when it's comin' up. They go shakin' hands with you, buddy, an' you know somethin' up. They're out to get elected again. An' if the poor people'd stay away from those elections . . . . They oughta wake up their eyes an' say, "Buddy, we're shet of you. We're gonna put a poor man in who'll do somethin' fer us."

But a lot o' things, the OEO money, I'm gettin' sick of it. They say they're gonna help the poor people. Then they get it all made up an' it's too much, we can't do nothin' fer you, you're not in the category. That's what they say. Let's not talk about helpin' people. If we're gonna help 'em, let's do somethin' about it. I've seed so many things that ain't right, I don't know what to do against it.

I think that the strip minin' coal industry has damaged Kentucky worse than anythin' I've ever seed. It's tore the beauty of the mountains up. And the poor man didn't get anythin' out of it. It went out to the big fellers. That's the way I see the strip mines. But coal mines has helped a lot. If it hadn't been fer some o' that in Clay County, the poor people would o' fared bad. They sure would. They had to work at somethin'. If they couldn't get the big price, they had to work at something to feed their families. But they worked many a day that they didn't get what pay they oughta have. They had to work at it. I've had to work at it; I've had to feed my young'uns. It was the only thing I could get to make any money at all. I could work out in the timber woods or somethin' like that, but I could make more money in the coal mines than I could that. But strip minin' has destroyed this country.

See, our road's tore up right here. And what did Goose Creek get out of this here strip mine? They never got one five cents off o' this. They should of had tax come off o' this went back to build some things. You know, we didn't get anythin' out of it. But that's the people lettin' 'em get away with it. If everybody'd walk up an' say, "Here!" an' our county officials went along, then we could collect it. We gotta have somebody down in them tax boards to say, "Here, buddy, you're takin' all this away from us." But these fellers an' them has always stood together.

It's like me. I ain't any richer now than when I was workin' in the coal mines. I had jest as much then. An' I haven't got any of it now, so how do you figure I could be any richer.

You know a lot of this land was leased way back on some kind of a broad form deed they talk about. And I've heard said that they didn't get nothin' fer it much. But their parents way back had done this, and there's nothin' I could do about it now 'lessen I lawed the broad form deed.

There's gonna have to be somethin' in East Kentucky besides coal mines. There's gonna have to be some jobs come in fer the young people. You take a feller fifteen years old right now. There's not gonna be any coal. There's not much coal here now in Clay County 'cept little bitty stuff. An' I ain't gonna work in it myself; I can't stand it.

I wouldn't advise none of my children to go into the coal mines, fer I don't want them to go through what I went through. I took one boy in. He got married when he wasn't too old. Well I took him in the mines, an' I had a time gettin' him out o' the mines. There wasn't nothin' else he could do here, but I didn't want him to go in. I said don't go. But he said I've got to work. And I agreed to take him *in the mines to work with me. I broke him in. I told him not to go and I'll tell the next boy not to go. Fer there's nothin' in the coal mines. You get the rock dust. You get the black lung. You work like a slave. No easy work in the coal mines.*

Young people they don't want to leave the state. They'd rather stay in Clay County or in Kentucky if there's jobs fer them to do. If they could get a job here an' make as much money . . . they'd come back to make a lot less money. But they go to Lexington. They go to Detroit. They go to Ohio. They go to Georgia. They go to Indianapolis, Indiana. Anywhere they can find work. They work at General Motors. They work at Ford's. And they work at regular jobs. A lot of these boys go off an' do construction. They work on the railroads. People out o' Goose Creek works on the railroads. Anybody who's got a high school education generally gets a job at a factory.

They don't see nothin' here right now. And they're young people. And they don't know what steps to take to get somethin' in here, to get shet o' politics an' get somethin' in here. I've talked to a lot of big people, an' they say, "You ain't got no roads in Clay County." If a business tries to start up here, I've heard said that they've said we don't need no business, but I don't know if that's true. Let me tell you somethin'. The reason they didn't want business here is they had a right smart o' coal work here at one time, an' they wanted these men to work in the coal mines fer them. And they knowed if there come a decent job here, that they're gonna quit an' go to it. An' these young men all stopped workin' in the coal mines an' left here. The coal operators in Clay County didn't want the WPA in here. They didn't want the Happy Pappies in here. They was mad. They say we can't hire a man to work in our coal mines. But they didn't care about the rock dust I was eatin' or the black lung I was gettin'. Let me go to heck; they're gonna hire another man the next day if they can get him. That's how I feel about it. They don't want these gov'ment programs. They don't want these OEO programs.

IV   The Mountain Community and the Outside World

There is only one true institution in the poor communities of Clay County, and that is the church. Though church-going may not be the focal point of mountain life, it is one of the few things that people do regularly and together; and it is one of the few subjects about which controversies arise that serve to split communities almost irrevocably. There are many Protestant denominations in Clay County—Brethren, Methodist, Pentecostal, Baptist, Missionary Baptists, and others—and one small Catholic church, and the differences or imagined differences of each group in its practice of faith causes great consternation among the rival sects. Methodists are accused of baptizing children who are too young to understand the vows that they take. Baptist churches argue among themselves about dropping the old tokens of faith, like foot washing, from their ceremonies. Pentecostals attack all others for deviating from, or modernizing, the Bible. Congregations which handle poisonous snakes look down upon those who do not. And Catholicism is greatly feared by most mountain Protestants—as it has been from the time men first left European countries to venture to America. A good deal of anti-Catholic feeling is vented in the more fundamentalist Protestant churches, as is much anti-Semitism.

We've got a few churches in this country that say they're the only ones right. Some of 'em won't go to other churches, which I disagree with that. You know they got 'nominations. A Baptist, a Missionary, a United. You know Christ is the head of the church. An' I don't care; a Missionary, a United or somethin' like that is nothin'. That's jest a man-made organization. Christ is the head of the church. It belongs to him, an' he belongs to all o' the people. There's a lot o' people in this country handle snakes. I don't believe in that. I'm afraid o' rattlesnakes. There's some people handlin' snakes in this country got bit an' died an' everythin' else.

We had one preacher preached down here said if you didn't go to his church, you weren't nothin'; you were gone. Everybody's gone if they didn't go to that church. An' I quit goin' to it on account o' that. But he don't live around here now. If you didn't go to his church you were wrong. I've been there, an' I've heard him preach funerals. An' he said, "Well, that brother or sister, he belonged to this church, an' he's sure goin' to heaven." And I said, buddy, you're jest a man yourself. You don't know where she's goin' to, I said the Good Ol' Man above knows; not you, preacher.

But the various churches manage to coexist with one another, and likely as many people attend some service as do not. There is no great compulsion to go to a church. It is frowned upon not to, more so for a woman than a man, whose disinclination to endure an inactive two hours is fairly well accepted. But most people enjoy church; it offers the only real opportunity for neighbors to gather together and for boys to meet girls. Most mountain churches serve only small congregations which are generally from the same community, and often made up of only three or four extended families; this makes it more of a congenial gathering. After services, people move on to neighbors' homes to share dinner, which during the summertime can be a fancy production. Often this will amount to a large family get-together if sons and brothers have come back from the city for the weekend.

Most country preachers are not seminary trained, but

simply men who have felt called upon to preach the gospel. Especially good preachers are widely competed for and are often called upon to preach revivals. In Clay and Knox counties, the Reverend Homer Jackson is a much acclaimed preacher, and the revivals which he leads generally pack the church. Preachers in the mountains are expected to preach, to be possessed with the Glory of God in the delivery of their sermons, and to transfer that fervor to their listeners. Methodist and Brethren ministers, who are mainly missionaries from the Midwest, sometimes have difficulty attracting followings because they are trained in a soft-spoken, reasoning style, in contrast with the loud, repetitive exhortations of the country Baptist. However, with the exception of the Pentecostals, once tagged "Holy Rollers," most mountain churches see less and less of the chanting and "shaking" by spirited listeners than they once did, and sermons are often directed at this distressing movement away from actual religious excitement.

There is much concern that people's faith, like the old rituals, is wasting away. The great sinners in the mountain religions are hypocrites, deceivers, selfish people, and Christians who debase their religion by turning from the old ways. To some, there is a much wider variety of sinners—men with long hair, women who cut their hair, people who play ball, young people who dance, and, of course, people who drink whiskey, which is to name just a few. Mountain religion dictates only one thing that must be done: accept Christ as the personal savior; outside of this, the beliefs of some sects are concerned mainly with the things not to be done, and the many sins that are so easy to commit. Above all else is the promise of heaven, where no one is troubled and no one is poor. Indeed, some hold the belief that poverty on this earth is in accord with God's plan and should not be complained of. When people do get somewhere in business, or land a good job, they, like thousands elsewhere, thank the "Ol' Man upstairs."

COMMUNITY GROUPS

In many communities throughout Clay County, the poor have gathered together to form community associations, neighborhood action councils, or improvement associations. These have been attacked by some preachers as being, among other things, communist, and they have been encouraged by as many more. County officials have done what they could to subvert these groups—from refusing community schools as meeting places to confiding their displeasure to all who would listen. In the main, the function of community organizations has been to see that available OEO and other government programs reach their communities and to mobilize people for various CAP affairs and area-wide meetings of the poor on such issues as black lung compensation legislation and the struggle for poor people's participation on the newly created Area Development District boards which, apparently, the Nixon administration hopes to use nationally to channel federal monies into areas lacking economic development. Much of the energy of these groups, as suggested previously, is invested in OEO-CAP programs. Three of the most highly organized community groups in the county were made "delegate agencies" by the CAP and given Head Start programs. Approximately one hundred children in the county attend Head Start.

Some of the community groups have succeeded in erecting buildings for centers, and some of them have begun to create small businesses using mostly the Self-Help program funds of the CAP. None has moved into areas like welfare rights, voter registration, or political activity, though OEO-sponsored groups and independent organizations in other mountain counties have, largely because these are not areas in which the CAP is involved. Community groups in Clay County did not come together to strike out at the forces which oppress them, as they did in the South. They were organized with the help of VISTA workers, Appalachian Volunteers, and the CAP staff to move against the physical manifestations of poverty—poor housing, no water systems, etc. This is clearly a far different approach than poor people in some other areas have taken, and one of the problems that it brings is that, with the gradual de-funding by OEO of the largest anti-poverty group in the mountains, the Appalachian Volunteers, and the general deflation of the CAP's power and budget over the last year or two, community groups in Clay County have been forced into a sort of lull in their activities.

Still, poor people's organizations continue to meet in the county, and people still look forward to the chance to come together and enjoy themselves talking. Some of the finest storytelling is heard among the men outside, and the choicest gossip is passed among the women; crops and weather are discussed, and occasionally, problems that confront the community are settled. And perhaps it is enough if an organization accomplishes these things.

CLASSES

There is a good deal of what might be called class aware-ness voiced in poor communities in the county. Towns-people are generally lumped together as the non-poor, controlling class, and, as noted before, no little antipathy is directed toward the doctors and lawyers, mine bosses, bankers, elected officials, and welfare and state employees —all of whom it is felt care nothing for the poor and, in fact, hope to keep the poor down. Some townsfolk do stress that they are not "country," and, as many of their young people grow up, they want nothing more than to go to an urban college or secretarial school and be considered worldly. It is quite likely that many people in town do not realize the extreme poverty in which others in their county live. Not knowing this makes more understandable the state-ments one hears about "those no-account hillbillies."

There are also two fairly distinct classes within the poor community: the working class and the welfare class. The mountaineers' view on welfare is rather mixed, and, of course, it is biased by whether he is, or is not, on public support. It is pretty much accepted that if a man needs help, he ought to have it. "Needs help" usually means "too sick to work." There is always the suspicion, however, that the man who does draw a check is not really unable to work, but, if that were actually the case, most would say of him that "he used his head," for while it is somewhat disapproved of not to work when able, it is a good sign if a man is clever. There are some men who would die before accepting welfare, either because they do not believe in "handouts" or because they do not want to undergo the considerable difficulty and humiliation involved in dealing with the welfare department. There are some people who look down on all welfare recipients, and many welfare recipients who take the reasonable view that they are just getting some of their tax dollars back and that it's nobody's business but their own. Everybody agrees that it is right to protect widows and orphans, but in the mountains many grown men draw a check, or have a medical card due to unemployment, or purchase food stamps. There is also the case of the disabled man, who for one of many possible reasons, cannot get approved for welfare, who cannot get a job, and who must keep up a home and family. The haggard, worn parents, the dirty, ill-clothed children, and the little one-room tar-paper-covered shack can make even his poor neighbors count their blessings. But often it will cause him to be spurned by his neighbors, as townspeople spurn the poor. Poor people are often insensitive to each other's problems, and in this sense, there is no compelling feeling of themselves as a class.

Well if they're sick, an' can prove that they're sick, they think it's a good thing. But I've heard a lot of people say, "I wish I could get on the welfare. I have to work." "The

welfare, it ain't no 'count," they say. Which I think that
they're wrong. I believe that the people ought to be honest.
I don't know, but I've been told . . . I'm jest gonna tell you
what I've been told . . . that you could go down there an'
get on the welfare if you stood in the right corner. You could
give the doctor somethin' an' he'd pass you, say you're
bad off. But I think that the welfare's a good thing if people
needs it an' are sick. They oughta have some income. But I
don't think people oughta tell a lie or try to get something
to get on welfare. If they can get jobs, I believe they oughta
work fer it. I feel it's a good thing. I won't say nothin' about
nobody that's on the welfare.

The workin' man, he knows he's a'gettin' his honest.
He's a'workin' fer it. An' he knows his neighbor's gettin'
it give to him. An' if he knows that his neighbor's gettin'
his honest, an' is sick, then he's not gonna say nothin'
about it. But if he feels that he's tricked 'long the line somewhere, he'll say he oughta be workin'. If I knowed that my
neighbor right out yonder was on the welfare, an' me a'
workin' eight hours a day in the coal mines, an' if he had
got that without bein' sick, then I don't think he ought to
have it. But if he is sick, I'd feel good about it. And I think
everybody else feels jest about the same way.

I know that there's a lot o' these kids that needs somethin' bad. And I feel that there's a lot of people that ought
to be on the welfare. I don't know no man's feelin's. Nor
I don't want to say nothin' agin him no way. You know I
might have to get on welfare myself some day. And they're
gonna say the same thing about me that I said. If you're
sick, you oughta have the welfare. You know, I'm no doctor,
an' if a doctor OK's a man, he ought to be an honest man.
He ought to do the straight business. But I've heard people
say that there's people on welfare who oughtn't to be. I
don't know. I know there's people, I don't know what their
trouble is, but they look like they need somethin'.

I feel that the poor man can't help himself. An' that's

what's wrong with the world today. They're lookin' down on that poor man place o' helpin' him. If the people had somethin' to help that man in Granny's Branch, or ever where he lives, I think that they'd be a'doin' a better thing than they're doin'. I think that they're a'punchin' that man down when they oughta be a'givin' him somethin'. As long as we talk about our neighbors an' say he's too poor fer us to fellowship with, if we're up above that man a little bit an' can lend a helpin' hand to that man, we oughta be a'doin' it. An' that's what's the matter with the world today.

You know I don't have any money much myself, but if I seed a man like that an' lived close to that man, an' if he needed five dollars, I'd give him five dollars in money or somethin' jest as free as I could. If he'll try to help hisself. An' he's a sick man. But if a man jest sits down, I mean if he ain't no account . . . . But I don't know, you see. I think the man's sick jest to look at him. Or somethin's wrong with him. I don't know what it is. But you know they got a lot o' people in the world today is sick people, an' the people needs to be a'helpin' them people. An' that's one thing that's the matter with the people today. They don't help one another much.

THE MOUNTAIN PERSONALITY

Mountain people are often characterized as being independent. Perhaps the nature of that independence bears examining here. It does not strictly mean that mountain people refuse to follow any but their own lead. More truly it means that they do not like to be told what to do; they do not like to bend to the will of the majority; they do not like people such as county officials, sheriffs, congressmen, presidents, game wardens, etc.; they do not like people who deny their own nature, e.g., wear a tie; they don't think the idea of "working together" is a requisite for getting things done; they believe in settling their own disputes;

they think they're tougher, but also friendlier, than most other people. Much has been made of this attribute of independence by those who extol "traditional American virtues," and it has been much lamented by outsiders intent on organizing mountain communities or serving the mountain poor. They are not very easy to serve, for they even have a hard time getting along with themselves, except within their own family structures. The well-understood need to go one's own way often comes in conflict with the rigid codes of conduct laid down by church and custom, and men and women find themselves chastised by their neighbors for this or that breach of unwritten, or maybe biblical, law. Within the confines of the little mountain settlements, grievances are not soon forgotten but tend to break into small-scale feuds that sometimes end in shootings or trips to the penitentiary.

They think too much agin their neighbors. I think that is one thing that is ruinin' the world today, that they don't share their loads with one another, their burdens with one another enough. They look on another feller, they might think he's got a little more'n he has, they'll try to knock him out o' somethin'. That's wrong. I don't care what somebody else has got; I'm not gonna try to knock him out o' nothin'. I don't know how you get that out o' people. But you know that's true. They're agin their neighbors; they talk about their neighbors an' say, "There's nothin' to that feller," an' all such as that. I call it selfish. I think that that keeps 'em down a lot o' times. I think that that's one of our problems. I've tried to tell people to fergit about such as that and do somethin' to help somebody because holdin' a grudge, old grudges . . . lot o' people got old grudges against one another, an' they'll die with that in 'em. You know I think that you've got to forgive people. If I had anythin' agin you, I'd come right out an' tell you. I don't believe in gettin' out all over the country an' talkin' about it. If I got somethin' agin you

*right now, or you done somethin' I don't like, place o' me
a'goin' up an' down this road a'sayin' you done somethin', I
oughta go to you an' tell you an' say you ought not do that
no more. An' that stops it right there. But if I go tellin' it to
my neighbors, an' they go tellin' it outside, it don't get no
smaller, it gets bigger everytime it's told.*

*You should not fight your neighbors; I never have tried
to fight nobody. An' I didn't see that I could fight people an'
live. It's people today who'll tell anythin' in the world, an'
try to down you. Sometime I get nervous, but I've had
persecutin' all my life. That doesn't hurt me. I've done a
lot o' things that I'm glad of, an' I don't care fer nobody
a'talkin' about me. But now if you've never got people to
talk about you, you've never done nothin'. When you find
a man that nobody never speaks nothin' of, you say, well
that man never did nothin' no way. You can't have people
talk good about you all the time.*

The mountain man is quick to anger, and in return for
some offenses against him, he is expected to mete out his
own punishments. A man must guard his own property,
and disputes about ownership of stock or dogs can provoke
lengthy gun battles along the moonlit, winding roadways.
Young men do not take lightly the idea of courting a girl
in another settlement or "across the hill." He knows he
might have to fight it out with her neighboring suitors.
Should he mistreat the girl, he might be ambushed on
the darkened roads by her brothers. There is no crime worse
than adultery or ill-treatment of another's wife. It is expected of the aggrieved husband that he will kill the offender, and for this reason men go out of their way to show
no signs of interest in each other's wives. That mountaineers
strive vigorously to settle their scores is shown by the fact
that in Clay County there is a shooting or other violent
crime on the average of about once a month.

Usually, people have little use for the law. They prefer to

settle their differences in their own way. When a sheriff is summoned to settle a complaint, it is most often a woman, not a man, who has called him. Few are the men who have not spent a night in jail or paid a fine, but sheriff's deputies are not overly anxious to take in men because the men often put up a good fight before they go.

On summer days, men like to go squirrel hunting which, like fishing, is mostly an art of sitting still waiting for something to move. The Clay County game warden is kept busy stalking up steep mountainsides trying to locate the roaring shotgun blasts of an out-of-season hunt. On fall nights, men loose their dogs to track down the big coon that less and less roam the forests. A good hunter is as highly regarded as a good mechanic, and a good coon dog is more highly regarded than just about anything else.

Dogs, hunting rifles, and knives are continually being traded in the informal markets of downtown street corners and country general stores. Some claim to make their living by alternately trading and selling. The true trader deals in the "antique"—the World War II high-powered automatic, old "Case" brand knives, or "Old Timers" without the USA on the blade—and men might travel miles to find the owner of such a gem. It is no small gift when a father passes on to his son a 1918 officer's pistol.

A time-honored mountain profession not as yet mentioned is moonshining. In a county that has optioned "dry," such as Clay, there is a considerable demand for good home-made whiskey. Pure corn liquor is a virtual myth to the moonshine drinker, as it is extremely expensive to make and generally substituted for by much diluted mixtures, and it is heard about only once every few years in a given county when a moonshiner, moved by sheer benevolence, runs off a small batch for his best customers and friends. The moonshiner is a well-known figure in most communities, but he, unlike the bootlegger who sells beer at fifty cents a can, is left fairly unmolested by county law officers.

There is also in the mountain character a lot of simple country goodness. The usual parting words between people are, "Stay with us; spend the night," "Gotta go, y'all come with us," and people are not usually put out if you take them up on their offer. Anyone visiting a home at mealtime is expected to stay for dinner. People do not mind stopping on the road to help each other with car troubles. Work like "robbing" bee gums (so called because farmers traditionally raised bees in hollowed sections of gum trees rather than in manufactured hives), fixing tractors, and loading trucks is shared without comment. But picking beans, canning, and hoeing fields, which were once community efforts where all who could joined in, going from house to house, are now jobs you must pay others to help you with. This lost magic of working together is often talked about and wondered at by mountain people, and no one seems to know why it is no longer there, except, "people stopped doin' it." It is speculated that the World War, or maybe welfare, had something to do with it, but to no one is the connection quite plain.

RELATIONS TO OUTSIDERS AND THE MODERN WORLD

The mountains of Kentucky, which for many decades were little visited or heard about by people elsewhere, have seen their share of outsiders in the last few years. They, in the persons of anti-poverty workers, community organizers, and government men from Frankfort or Washington, are generally met fairly, if with some curiosity and aloofness—though the outsider, with his peculiar dress, manner, speech, and ideas, sticks out like a sore thumb. People are usually willing to listen to what an outsider has to say, and often they are willing to be dominated by his decisions, for he represents all that people have been taught is better than themselves—the urban born, the educated, and the sophisticated. Of course there are some who will speak bitterly about "all those people comin' in here tryin' to civilize us," and often outsiders will arouse scornful criticism by openly violating what is considered proper conduct between the sexes, by admitting to a disbelief in God, or by talking about the draft and the war.

From time to time preachers or small businessmen will begin to worry about communists and do a good bit of talking about these "strange foreigners," but for the most part poor people put the outsider into one of two categories: the suspect, not to be fully trusted; or the benevolent protector who will fight off welfare departments and school systems. Regardless of which group he falls into, the outsider is not really approved of. This is because most outsiders come to the mountains with the desire to help, in an obvious way, and most mountain people, much as they want to see justice done them, vaguely resent the idea of being helped. For all this, there comes an occasional outside organizer who can quickly adjust to a new people and be accepted by them and quietly draw people together. Yet any outsider, by his presence, serves as proof that the people where he comes from, the people in the towns and cities, do not need help, that, somehow, they have made it.

I'll tell you, I guess that outside people is all right. I've seen a lot of outside people myself, an' it takes a outside person who comes in here a long time to get used to how the mountain people lives. I can see where they can do a lot o' good things, but they got to get used to the people before they can do anything. I think outside people's been a lot o' help to us. Course, you know, a lot o' people, when they come in here, they say, "Well, maybe they're spies, or communists, or somethin' like that," which is wrong.

We live diff'rent here than they do in the cities. You know we have outside . . . houses. We don't have like they do in the cities. An' actually we eat diff'rent, I guess. I guess you do know that. We raise what we eat here mostly. That's hard fer people to get used to . . . . You jest can't come in this place right here an' people take up with you right now in a few days. You got to stay around till people learns you before they'll pay too much attention to you.

If you go up this branch right here this evenin', you're a strange man, they want to know what you're up here fer. An' if you come in here like a VISTA. . . . They say they're comin' up here to, you could say, organize or to help the people. But I've never seen any of 'em come up here right off the reel an' know plumb blank what they was comin' up here fer. I can't go in a place, not knowin' what I'm a' goin' fer an' tell the people what I'm about. Now it looks to me if I go in a strange place in this country or anywheres they got to find out what I'm doin' in there an' pretty quick. And that's the way the VISTA's are, or anybody else. They want to know what you're here for, an' you've got to tell them what you're here for. Of course, it's nobody here that I know of that'd have anythin' agin people, but they jest don't understand what they're here for. I feel that VISTA's supposed to be here to help people. What I mean to help people, to get people to help themselves. I believe in people tryin' to do somethin' to help themselves. Until they do, I don't see much.

They's plenty of 'em comes down, they don't know what they're doin'. Yes sir, there's plenty of 'em comes here don't know. If you go up in these hollers to work with these people, you got to have somethin' to tell these people. If you jest go up there an' talk about organizin' people, well that's all right, but people gonna ask you directly what you're gonna organize them for. I'm gonna have to tell these people what kind o' resource I'm gonna give 'em. To help these people so they can help themselves.

It's not too many people in this country worry about communists. It's a lot o' things goes around if you're a outside man. You got some people in this country'll say that's communist. Well I don't believe in callin' people communist until I know who they are. I don't think there's been any communists around this area here. You know they've heard talk o' Russia, an' it's been said to me long back that, you know Russia's communist people, that they're gonna come in here an' they're gonna do this an' that. If you was an outside person, why I could ruin you here, buddy. I could say you're a communist, and, brother, you wouldn't do no more good here. I could kill you in Goose Creek in three days if I wanted to. I could go an' say you're nary a thing but a communist, and boy they'd be through with you then. They'd say, we'd better not fool with him.

I know of some outsiders who's caused some troubles back in Otter Creek, but that's over with now. There was a girl who made some mistakes. A girl can't come in this country and know right from the start . . . well, you gotta know how to act. I had a girl in Otter Creek, an' she made some bad mistakes, and it's not out o' some people yet.

Q. Are there any rules that you'd make for an outsider coming here to organize?

Well, if it was a girl come in here, I'd lay down a rule that they should not be out with men after dark. And they should wear their clothes more decently, a lot o' times. Like shorts an' things like that, in this country, don't work. It ain't right, but a lot o' old people an' a lot o' other people talks about 'em. You know, it ain't none o' my business what other people wears. But I know what the people says. But you know we watch people. We talk about their dress bein' too short. Up to here, you know, up to 'round here. Jesus Christ. That's right.

The mountain people feel a deep wonder at the outside world that makes the news and builds the machines and steals away their young. Some of the feeling is that things have gotten out of their hands, and that their lives are being directed from Washington, Detroit, and Cincinnati. It seems that all that is important is being done in the cities, and that they, far up the mountain back roads, are no longer a part of what America has come to be. The things that go on in the cities do not please the mountain people. They hear of riots and hoodlums and painted women, beer joints and slums, and neighbors you never meet. The cities seem a terrible place where anyone can get mugged on the street, or have his wallet stolen, and where you must carry a gun in your car. The fact that so many of their sons and daughters have moved there increases the worry.

Well, it's a lot diff'rent from here, the cities. They live diff'rent. An' a lot o' people have never been in the cities too much. Some of 'em has. They live diff'rent ways. They seem to be crowded up more. An' I don't like the city myself to live in. But I don't have no kin to people in the cities.

I don't like to stay right in a crowded up place. I've been all over the cities. I jest don't like to get there an' jest sit down on the porch an' sit there. An' in the cities I've been, I don't see them visitin' people too much. I don't know. I don't like to go down to Manchester an' stay there fer over an hour. Long as I can get out o' that town. I want out. Now that's the way I see it. Which I got nothin' agin nobody in the cities. I jest don't like a town, not any crowded up place. I want to get away from it.

Drinkin' an' gamblin' is very bad in the cities. I mean they say. I never seed much of it. You know you can go anywheres they got beer an' whiskey, an' they go on more, an' they have more goin's on than we do here. We don't have no whiskey in Clay County. We have plenty of it, too, but it's not legal; they bootleg it.

I wouldn't say that people thinks they're an evil place. I've heard people say that there's a lot o' meanness goes on in a city, but I don't know. See I know we got mean people anywheres we go, but I wouldn't want to say the cities, like Manchester, was an evil place. I can't judge people.

There is a strong sense in mountain communities that the world is turning into a very evil place, and that all of these modern things, which are so hard to grasp, are very wrong. Movies, dancing, television, and other entertainments are considered by many to be "the devil's work," and to see them enjoyed so widely in the cities and accepted by the young people in the mountains makes the whole modern tide seem unholy. Much of the preaching heard in mountain churches concerns the way in which the world is turning away from Christ. Even those who sit and watch the news on their televisions become greatly fearful about what is happening in "modern America," and what they have come to know will dominate their future.

They don't like that modern stuff. They say that's what's ruinin' the world today. It's modern stuff. I think, jest to tell you the truth about it, that a lot o' people don't want to go in the cities. For they can't dress . . . that big tie an' that suit. An' away from here, in the cities, you got to dress pretty well or they won't let you eat in the restaurant, unless you got a big tie. I've heared it said that you have to have on the right kind of suit or they won't look at you. An' that's one reason that a lot o' people don't like the cities. You know the way people dresses in the cities, we can't afford it here. These poor mountain people can't. They're not able to get that kind o' suit. They don't have no jobs to buy the clothes with. An' they never been away too much, an' that's what they think about it. They say that's too modern fer us. We don't want in that place.

There's some people in Goose Creek don't believe in a television. They say if you got a television it's wrong. They show some movies on the television, an' things like that, an' they say it's wrong to look at that. That you should not be a'lookin' at movies.

Well, I don't think it's wrong. I think the TV is a good thing. What I think about it, it's a lot o' trainin', a lot o'

experience. An' they can't prove to me it's wrong. If I had
a TV an' I didn't go to church or do somethin' but watch
that TV, or wouldn't turn my hand to help people that
needed it. I'd say then I'm a'doin' wrong. But I got a TV
up here, an' if anythin' comes on I don't want to watch it's
got a knob there I can turn off. An' I got a conscience that
teaches me when I do wrong or steal or anythin' else, but
not about a TV.

If you got a TV, I don't know if they think too bad about
you, but they might say, "That feller might do anythin',"
if he had a TV. Which I've got one, an' I'm gonna keep
it till I'm ready to get shet of it. I think this is a free world
an' a free America, an' I think every individual's got a right
to his own beliefs, an' that's the way I'm gonna believe
it. An' if you can cite me any diff'rences, I'm not gonna
fall out with you, but I might get shet of you.

There's some women here, if they went to the city, they'd
say that the very devil's right here. She'd see the women
with the short dresses on, shorts, an' then she might see
some o' that beer an' stuff that they got in them joints.
She's say, "Lordy Mercy, the world's gonna end right now."
She'd see long hair. She'd say, "That's nary a thing but the
devil; them's them hippies." That's right. Better not let your
hair get long around here.

You can't do no good in this country with long hair. Lot
o' people would talk about you wearin' a long hairdo. They
say that the Bible says that a woman's hair is her glory,
and a man's hair . . . I forget how the Bible says it, but
anyway, they want a man to have short hair.

The moon landing in 1969, which so inspired men elsewhere, was largely upsetting in mountain communities.
Very few people believed that men actually had done what
the government said they had done, and many of those who
did believe it doubted that it was a right thing to do. Many
declared, before the landing took place, that God would

prevent it, quoting scriptures that said God placed the moon in the heavens to give light and arguing that man should not try to change what God has arranged and that living men could not enter heaven. After the news of the successful landing was broadcast, many shook their heads and called it a fake, and from the pulpits of not a few churches it was called "the great deceit" and part of the ascendancy of hypocrites and sinners to power, part of what is going wrong in the world today. Many people, it is sure, saw in the triumphant speeches and parades after the moon shot a very important step being taken by the world towards evil and evil modern ways, and away from the truer, more trustworthy path that has led poor people in the mountains through lives of greater hardship and suffering than many of our modern people would like to think about.

Well, they said he didn't go. Several people said he didn't go. I was asked that yesterday; the preacher asked me that yesterday. He ate dinner with me, and he'd heard about it, an' he asked me did I believe the man went to the moon. An' my daddy-in-law was up there. An' I said I believed the man went to the moon. I'll tell you the reason I believe it. I told him that I don't believe the government, the federal government, would get on the microphone an' talk to the people an' try to deceive the people like that. I believe he went to the moon, and I believe he walked on it. Ed was sittin' right there. I don't believe Ed thinks they went to the moon. I said the reason I think that, preacher, is that the Lord give man the knowledge to make the thing, an' if it hadn't been His will to go there, we would not o' went there. An' I said, I'm believin' he went, an' I looked right at him. An' the preacher said, "I guess you're right." An' Ed never would say too much. Ed said that they could take a picture of anythin' an' show it to people.
Some people feels that the Lord put the moon up there, an' He put it up there to give light. Not for people to fool

*with. That's what some o' them people says. But you know
I feel, goin' to the moon, we wasn't tryin' to do nothin' to
the moon to hurt nothin'. And that's the reason that I
believe that we went to the moon. A lot of people, you know,
don't believe that the moon is as big as this whole earth. A
lot of people thinks that the moon is jest that little light
that you see. That's what Ed believes about it. "The moon's
as big as this whole earth, Ed," I said. "No," he said, "not
nearly." Well I couldn't afford to argue with him.*

*I believe that we beat Russia to the moon, an' I believe
that we're the sharpest nation in the world, an' I believe
we went to the moon, an' I don't know, we might go
further. I'm very proud o' them men a'goin' there. Well,
we need the money down here. We need the money. But
that showed Russia that they wasn't the smartest nation in
the world. It took a lot o' money to get to the moon, but
you don't know, that could help bring peace quicker'n'
anythin' in the world. I've studied about that. But you
know that the poor people needed some money down here.
Maybe we'll have money to do that job an' this one too. I
don't know whether we can do that, but we can solve this
thing jest as soon as people get together an' go to doin' things
to get money. I've had to work all my life, an' I've raised
eight kids. I've worked for fifty cents a day, an' I never did
starve. Now I don't have too much, but I think if the people
will try to do things, we can get something to do here.*

V The Past and the Future

People look back on times past in the mountains with
longing. They are remembered as days when there was
plenty of good timber on the hillsides, when there was big
coal to be mined, when meal and flour and lard could be
bought cheap, and when young men and women would
settle down close by and raise big families. It is a tragic, and

by no means necessary, thing that all of this is gone now. Wiser men might have looked ahead and seen that no good comes from methodically pillaging a region, building for its people no industries for the future, and allotting them no place in the fantastic growth of America. For now the mountains are as they were first conceived by the mining corporations—large mounds of rocky dirt surrounding tiny valleys of worn-out soil—except that now there is no longer the timber that once could be seen covering every mountaintop. A land of poorly educated, hard working, but tired-out people. Why was big business so hasty about removing the coal? Surely there was a better way to do it—a way that would not cause the miner to say, "The thing that's wrong with this coal business is a few men gets it all, an' the rest of us is jest slaves."

It's been a change in livin' the last twenty, thirty years, a lot. Way back, you see, we made what we got. When I was growing up myself, we didn't go to stores for things. We made it on the farm. An' the farms is wore out, an' the hillsides is washed away. Of course wages got higher, an' the people stepped up from what they was. They couldn't live now like they used to live. If I had to back up in these mountains, it's all right maybe, but like we used to farm, ten hours a day from six till five in the evenin', we couldn't live. The mountains won't make it. An' they got more jobs, a lot more jobs. But it's not enough jobs. They have more people now than they used to be here. It's stepped up so high, is one thing. Costs is got so high. People have to pay more, an' they have to get money fer other things. They haven't nothing to get on by.

They used to pick beans. They used to farm. They used to swap o' work. If a man's fields got weedy, they went out an' hoed it out. That's the past about it. Now they won't, but you know there's not too many people around here farms to do that. I think if I needed accommodation, I think the people around here would do that. I don't know about money. Used to they did without money. I remember way back, my daddy he took sick one summer, an' he never was in the hospital but once or twice that I knowed of in his life, an' we had a great big field of corn yonder. I wasn't grown. An' the people came in an' hoed that out. The weeds was knee high.

It's been a lot o' diff'rence. Used to we went to church, an' we rid a mule. I've seed 'em hitched up all day. I mean they rid five or six miles to church. An' now they got automobiles to ride, an' nine times outa ten, place o' goin' to church they go to a drive-in or somewheres else. And when they had to ride their mules, they went to church. They had 'em standin' underneath the shade trees. I've seen forty, fifty mules standin' out from that church on Mill Creek down by that schoolhouse. Hitched all over that hill in the bottoms. They'd ride five or ten miles. Now, they got a car, an' they go other places.

What the future holds for the mountains of Kentucky seems quite bleak. Eventually enough industry may move in to employ the bulk of those who have not by that time left. What will happen to those who cannot or will not leave for the city, who cannot wait for a job fifteen years from now, or who will be too old, unschooled, or unskilled to get a job if ever they are plentiful—this is a question that no one has answered. Presumably these people, who number in the thousands in each mountain county of the state, will be left to scratch out a living as best they can, to grovel for food stamps, and to die. If this is what does happen, much that is beautiful will die with them. A large part of America will die. That mountain culture with its proud people, its beautiful gospel hymns, its fierce religion—it will be gone. A people as distinct from others as are the southern white, southern black, American Indian, or Mexican-American will have been erased. And that part of the American litany which calls for human dignity and the general welfare of man will have held itself up to be called worthless again.

It should be noted that the triumph of one generation can burden the next. The Tennessee Valley Authority, a monument to the New Deal, through displacing hundreds of families, served to create cheap electric power for the mountains and the South where there had been no power before. It opened the way over large areas for the coming and the growth of industry.

By far, the greatest users of the TVA's incredible output today are government military installations, principally the atomic research complex at Oak Ridge, Tennessee. One source of Oak Ridge's power is a TVA steam plant which sends virtually all its current to Oak Ridge. The steam that produces the electricity is created by the speedy burning of low-grade coal from the mountains of Kentucky. The purchaser of about 90 per cent of the strip mine coal from the mountains of Kentucky is the Tennessee Valley Authority.

The great pride we feel, and the major interest we have in the development of inexpensive power, need to be re-evaluated in light of the fact that we currently sponsor the annual destruction of thousands of mountain acres, and that we are in conflict with the needs and hopes of poor people in the Kentucky mountains.

The mountains have been made so much as the target area for the War on Poverty that now its many planners and its shrinking population have become somewhat battle weary. The poverty war partly succeeded in achieving the goals of its many projects, but it failed to dent, much less eradicate, the poverty of this region. Too little money—and certainly too little thought—was given to the fight. Appalachia stands as testimony to the many blunders of our American system. These are not to be corrected by the investment of a few million dollars spread across an area of such size; too much damage has been done for that.

The mountains have been carelessly and wantonly ravaged during this century. Billions of tons of coal have been removed at an enormous expense in lives and hardship. Not one ton had taxes levied upon it to enrich the counties from which it came. Not one miner shared in the profits of the coal companies. Surface mining in eastern Kentucky has done violent harm to the beauty of the mountains, has polluted and deadened creeks, and has left scars that only serious land reclamation, not time, could ever heal. The coal industry gave jobs, but no roads were built from the profits of the coal, for coal is moved by rugged trucks along main highways and by rail cars. The coal industry spawned no economic development because, aside from machines and trucks, it requires no secondary industry to supply its needs. Business did not follow the coal companies because miners' wages were too low to encourage buying. Water systems were not built because mines need no water. Waste removal systems were not created because rock and slag could be dumped down the mountainside or piled up in valleys. No power lines were laid because mines can more cheaply use generators. The coal industry could come and go, leaving nothing behind it.

Yet the industry has not gone; only that part of it which offered plentiful jobs. In 1968, more than 100,000,000 tons of coal were taken from Kentucky, a record total. Close to half of this was taken from the flat land of western Kentucky where mechanized operation is much easier to employ. More and more small mines were shut down, leaving more otherwise unskilled coal miners unemployed. A rise was seen in the number of large underground mines, the sort in which horrible disasters have occurred—like the one in Farmington, West Virginia, where seventy-eight men were killed by a gas explosion.

The mountains still hold plenty of coal; what they do not have are enough jobs to go around. Resentment against this state of affairs flared openly during the still smoldering anti-strip mine fight. And hopefully the miners' anger will continue to make itself heard. A great debt is owed Kentucky and the people who live there. They have not only surrendered the mineral that once gave their region hope of prosperity, but they have given of themselves, as laborers in a killing occupation. That debt will not be repaid by inviting industry to the mountains—that would follow the pattern set forth by big coal: industry that will destroy land, take without giving, and pay only as high a wage as is needed to ensure an "abundant labor supply."

The debt could only be repaid by diverting what is left of Appalachian coal to the benefit of the region, toward building roads and schools; by returning, through government, some of what has been taken to promote industry owned and run by mountain people; by halting the destruction of mountain lands with surface mining; and by paying heed to the voices that can be heard in the mountains—voices of poor people who have seen for themselves the worst that America can do and who have more hope than most groups that our society can be reshaped to the benefit of all.

I imagine there's a lot o' people yet who's never got on their feet from the Depression. You take a lot o' people in Clay County; they've got no money to make money with. An' they can't get out. You take you jest barely gettin' enough money to get by with; if you ain't got a job that you can make a little money with, to lay it up to make money with, you always stay poor.

You take the people on the welfare; they jest barely got enough money to live on, an' they owe their check jest as quick as they get it to some store down here. Well, they take that check an' give it to that store; they live one month on the credit. They ain't got $50 or $100 ahead that they could go out an' buy somethin' that they knowed they could make $25 or $30 with.

I call that pretty poor myself. An' there's plenty of 'em in Clay County today. And until they got that broke, they'll stay poor. Now I've been here long enough to know that. And I've actually been that way myself. You know if you work fer the coal mines all week, an' you make $75, or $300 a month, you can owe a lot o' debt. I've been in debt 16, $1800 at one time. Well by the time I paid that an' run my family, I didn't have no money to make nothin' else with. I had to pay these debts. An' that's the reason that today you ain't makin' enough money. You're jest makin' enough to pay your debts an' sort o' breathe by, not livin' like you oughta live, an' send your young'uns to school. You had to be mighty careful to do that. Now buddy that's true.

I believe in payin' anybody for their work, but we got a lot o' things that some people can make 'em $10,000 a year. An' I pay as much tax as them $10,000 a year men on one job. I don't think that anybody ought to have big money. I don't think they ought to have 12, $15,000 a year an' a poor man down here gettin' maybe $3,000. That's what's the matter with the world. All the big men's got all the money, an' the poor man ain't got nothin'. I don't know if that sounds right or not, but that's the way I see it.

I can tell the truth. I've worked all my life. From a boy up. You know, I guess I done as much work as anybody. It's not been easy work; it's been hard work. It's been with a shovel. It's been with a cross-cut saw. It's been workin' in stave woods. It's been workin' in a saw mill. I've cut trees with a cross-cut saw. They got power saws now; we didn't have a power saw. Comin' from the coal mines, I'd have to scoot fifty feet off a hill, couldn't walk. Do you believe that? My legs hurt me so bad in the calves of my legs I jest couldn't make the next step. I got out an' scooted off they was so sore. But that was when I started work in the coal mines. I said I'll never stand this. But I did stand it. I got used to it.

VI   Remarks on the Changing Times

Well, I could see a change in the people. I could see a change in the land. You know, back twenty years ago, we had plenty timber in this country. It was plenty timber work. You could get a job. Well, that timber's all gone now. And people's got to look fer somethin' besides timber fer a job. And one way people has changed from what they was twenty years ago, they've learned a lot more things about a lot o' things than they used to know. I'd say thirty or forty years ago, if they went to Manchester they rode a mule. They didn't know what was goin' on up in Manchester then; they thought that was somethin'. Now when they go, they go in a car. They go faster. They don't ride a mule. And they've caught on to the racket some. They know what's goin' on.

I've rid a mule from right here on Mill Creek into Manchester. Since the cars have come along, they've quit the mules and they've changed. They learned a lot more about the world than they knowed twenty or thirty years ago. I can see a lot o' changes in everythin'. There's a lot o' poor people yet. Nobody wants to up an' own that they're poor. They're tryin' to hold their heads up, but they are poor. You know it used to be big chestnut oak, white oak, that they made staves out of. That's all gone now. And you have to look to somethin' else fer a job.

I would say it's changed from what it used to be. One way, if it's carried out, we got stricter laws than there used to be over the mine system. Used to, you would have an inspector . . . you've got 'em now, but they are a little bit harder than they used to be. But they're not hard enough.

In places it's worser. Used to be, you wouldn't ride down these roads an' see the whole top of a mountain slipped off. That was all there in timber. An' where's that at? I think a lot of it's they took the coal out an' 'stroyed the young timber, and hurt somebody and made their earth poorer. For the young generation. And the coal didn't do a lot o' poor people any good. Helped the big man, but not the worker. I can see on Mill Creek, there's a whole lot of level land up there, I can see, if time keeps on another twenty, thirty years an' people increases like they are, I can see that full o' houses up there.

I don't know. I can see it may be a tough place, if nothin' comes in diff'rent. I can see, I guess I shouldn't say it, people gettin' weaker. We live in a world right now that, I don't know how to say it, but I think ther'll have to be somethin' done to make our state a better place to live in. We got a lot o' young people who's comin' up, an' they're comin' up wrong. I don't know if you agree with me or not. I don't think they're teachin' 'em too good. I think that they should teach 'em to treat everybody alike when they come up, an' not have a group o' people sayin', "Oh, there's nothin' to that man. There's nothin' to that woman." That's no way to raise kids. They ought to be raised to treat everybody alike, an' I believe we'd have a better world to live in. That might sound foolish to you.

Our people today is wantin' you to give 'em somethin'. Now that's a pretty bad thing to say, but I'm tellin' the truth. They've been that way fer a long time. We have a community meetin' right here, an' they can have forty or fifty people. And you sit right here an' ask 'em what they want to do, an' they'll sit right up there an' wait fer you to come up with the answer. If I knowed somethin' I could get fer people to help 'em, then I oughta get that. But I think that there ought to be a group o' people start talkin' about what they want to do. Long as you sit right where you are and depend on someone else doin' it for you, you ain't gonna do no good.

You've heard talk of welfare. You've heard talk of com-

modity. *You've heard talk of food stamps. You heard talk of OEO programs, which I'll say ain't got down to where they oughta been. But they think there's a lot o' money they can get. Now it's gonna take people to get these people doin' jobs. They're gonna have to go around. They're gonna have to sit on their porches. They gotta tell 'em what they could do, an' try to get these people learnt to go to talkin' . . . organizing.*

That's the worst thing that I ever done was to promise a man that I was gonna do somethin' an' I can't do that. That's a'killin' me right there. They'll say that man promised me somethin' an' now he let me down.

And another thing that makes it bad. You take all these diff'rent churches, diff'rent 'nominations, and they'll say that they are the best people. The United Missionary or Holiness or what have you, we're the people that's right. They're wrong. I don't think that 'nominations mean anythin'. They're jest mountain folk. We got a lot o' preachers that need straightenin' out. They oughta preach the Bible, an' quit talkin' about 'nominations.

The CAP's have done some things to bring people together, and they've done some things to draw 'em away. They've done some things, an' they've hurt too. They have brought some people together, I'll state that, but they've brought not enough people together. Nothin' like it. They've not done what they oughta do to bring people together.

The Mountains and the South

COMPARISON TO THE SITUATION OF SOUTHERN BLACKS

Much can be said in comparing the situations of the poor blacks in the Mississippi Delta and the poor whites in the mountains of Kentucky. Here an attempt is made only to illustrate certain areas of similarities and differences.

The rich, flat, burning land of the Mississippi Delta yielded naturally to the development of huge, many-thousand-acre plantations. In such earth, agricultural industry can grow, and cotton, a nation-building crop, was well suited to the Delta. It was for the sake of cotton, and of the great farming empires, that the black man was brought to work the land. Little has happened to change the positions of rich white landowner, impoverished black worker, and struggling small farmer. When the plantation aristocracy decided to mechanize their farms, it wreaked spectacular havoc throughout the whole system. The black tenant farmers and sharecroppers had nothing of their own to fall back on, no alternate sources of employment, no land, no history of diverse occupation. The particularly terrible conditions that prevail in the Delta today are blamable on the too long unchallenged life of the plantation system. With each man's job, income, home, and all the political power held in the hand of the plantation owner, it is impossible to expect a rising out of poverty. A family cannot even repair its own home because there is no money and because the home is not its own to repair. A family cannot build another, because there is no money and because it owns no land to put a house on. A powerless people deprived of the right to produce has no choice but to make the best of poverty— a poverty unparalleled in this country today—or to strike out against the collection of forces that hold them bound— an alternative that is being taken more and more often in the cities where the southern family has found more subtle and complex barriers to a decent life.

The political and economic systems developed quite differently in the mountains of Kentucky. The men who settled the mountains came to make a living and a new life, not to make money. There was no question of industry, agricultural or otherwise. Men hunted, farmed, and built what they could to support themselves. It was not until the coal industry moved in at the turn of the century that any real change took place, and even then, except near the big mechanized mines where sprawling coal camps were erected, most men farmed or kept a little farm going while they worked in the mines. The operators of the large-scale, northern-owned coal companies controlled the politics and the police of the principal mining counties—Harlan, Perry, and others—and theirs was a regime so bitter that it provoked the bloody union battles in the state. The power of the coal barons was never complete in the outlying coal counties, like Clay, where most of the mines were small, "shovel" mines that were owned by mountain interests, if not locally. In these counties, few men came rich or got rich. The ones who ran things were more successful businessmen and farmers who were not so far in stature above the poor man himself. Miners and other laborers, for the most part, retained ownership of their land and did not forsake it for the lure of the coal camp where the good wage was coupled with exorbitant rent and company store prices. When the coal boom in Clay died out in the 1950s, closing down many of the smaller mines and diminishing the influence of the large companies, the miner still had his little patch of land where he could grow a little to tide him by. So the problem left by mechanization, was, in Kentucky, a crisis of no jobs, not as in Mississippi, a tragedy of no jobs, no homes, no lands, and no gardens.

Without a job, a man in the mountains must either get by on what little he can raise on his acre or two of level ground and what he can buy with food stamps, or he must leave the mountains for the cities. The men who are crippled by injury or too enfeebled to work must try to cope with a welfare system that is destructive in all aspects, terribly inefficient, and frustratingly hostile. If a man had never owned a house and farm out of town, but instead had been born into one of the semi-rural, semi-urban, slum hollers near town where he had no room for a garden, then he would be totally at the mercy of the welfare department—left destitute by its denial of benefits or left forever in debt because the check would not make ends meet.

In itself, there may not be too much wrong with living in an old, half-sound house up a dirt back road if the man can make sixty dollars a week at a garage, and the woman has an acre of land on which to tend vegetables—though most families in such situations might wish there were more chances to do better. But most people are not that well off. Either the acre of land is missing, or the sixty dollars a week is missing or substituted for by thirty-five dollars welfare, or both land and income are missing. There are many families, lacking everything but irregularly available food stamps, who live in conditions no better than does the displaced tenant farmer in Mississippi. In general, however, the coal mining generations survived their working years with a little more, mainly in terms of land, than did the cotton farming generations of Mississippi—though in both places there are left no jobs, few young people, and hard times. It is difficult, though, to calculate the loss to Kentucky of its mountain resources, which truly seemed to give little but misery to the people who inherited the rich mountain lands from their forefathers of one hundred and fifty years ago.

Poor people view their plight from much different perspectives in the Delta and in the mountains. The history of the black man in the Delta is one of slavery, racial oppression, economic exploitation, violent suppression, and political disfranchisement. He accurately sees the roots of his present troubles in the white planter's and businessman's unconcern for himself as a black working man and in the lack of power he himself holds in the politics and economics of his community. He sees no help coming to him from the federal government which manifests itself in the Delta in the form of welfare departments, employment programs encouraging him to leave the state or requiring him to take a job that no white man would be given, and in the Head Start programs, most of which were at one time or another defunded by OEO. He directs his struggles largely through independent groups such as the NAACP and the Freedom Democratic Party whose battlefields have mainly been street demonstrations, economic boycotts of stores, and political campaigns for local office. Poor people, to him, means "black people," though he believes that small farming whites also have been victims of the "big man's" system; and he shows great unity of hopes and of purposes with his neighbors. Everyone has been treated alike, and everyone has understood that treatment from the cradle up. Though many have been immobilized or dispirited by years of revolving indebtedness and the family ties of the plantation, just as many have shown that they will still fight as people from the plantations in Humphreys County fought to build their Head Start. A movement for human dignity still continues, though sometimes underground, and is felt in Mississippi.

In Kentucky, most men agree that things are hard because there are no jobs. The man who does have a job or works in a mine knows he cannot make anything because, "the big man at the top takes it all." Past that point, people have had trouble isolating things that should be blamed for all their grievances. County officials and the welfare department are uniformly distrusted, and it is believed that these people do not encourage, and probably hinder, factories coming into the area. It is hard for people to log blame against the rich man, for outside of the big mine operators and truck fleet owners who are considered to be exploiters, there are not many rich people in the mountains. A kind of formless hostility is felt for the "big man," the man seen as a directing force on county and state politics, who lives comfortably, who owns a lot of property scattered around a county, who can hand out jobs on the highway department or the county, who puts money into elections and tries to coerce the poor people to vote a certain way. But there are too many "little men" or poor men who try to achieve these same things, or who pass money for or fraternize with the powerful men; this sort of corrupt, oppressive maneuvering reaches so far down into poor communities and is so much a part of mountain life that little is done to fight it.

Southeastern Kentucky miners were once united in their struggle for higher wages, better conditions, and a union, but there has been since that time no other movement in poor mountain communities to compare with the movement that has been seen in Mississippi and the South.

There have been, however, many counties where people have united for the purpose of achieving specific goals. During the 1960s, statewide movements addressed to specific problems have been seen: in the West Virginia miners' strike for black lung legislation, and in the anti-strip mine campaign, active primarily in Kentucky. Most of these efforts have been extremely militant, and if they have not all been successful in the sense of winning their causes, they have succeeded in the sense that people decided for themselves what needed to be done and tried hard to do it. Most of them, for that matter, have been more effective in achieving their goals than have the programs directed by outsiders, and virtually all have been more important, in terms of people learning that they too have the right to speak out, than anything that the government has offered (except possibly the first rare moments of the War on Poverty when mountain men felt that the project might be important enough to fight for and remove from the hands of local politics).

But the mountain poor have not been confronted with such an obvious array of hostile forces as have the black poor in Mississippi, nor have they been able, across the region, to unite as poor people. Faults in the American economic system, callousness toward land, labor, people, and the future lies behind most of what has beset the mountains today. In Mississippi, the problem lies less with the inhumanity of an economic structure than with the inhumanity born of racial oppression. It is hard, in Kentucky, to strike out at the economic system because, in large measure, it does not function there. There is no big business; there are no factories to treat men unjustly, and it is hard to perceive who might be responsible or before whom grievances ought to be laid. So, lesser enemies have been selected —the highway department that builds no roads, the welfare department that operates unfairly, and county and school officials who provide nothing to ease the burden of poverty. Yet people have rarely rallied against these bodies because while they do little for the poor, they control more non-farm jobs in a given county than any single industry, and because they can wield great power against any individual family or community that struggles against them. For the most part, then, when poor people have joined together to do things over the last few years, their interest has been mainly to make use of programs, primarily OEO—to right some of the conspicuous aspects of poverty, inadequate pre-school care, bad housing, inadequate food, illiteracy, and insufficient clothing. Whether these are to be the sum of a nation's efforts to repair a region spanning the eastern seaboard and to repay the debt of extracted coal remains a question.

COMPARISON TO THE SITUATION OF SOUTHERN WHITES

The Appalachians run deep into Georgia and Alabama, cover one-third of Tennessee, much of North Carolina and Virginia, and a corner of South Carolina. In the mountain parts of these states the men like to consider themselves rednecks about as much as hillbillies, and this is also the case for a goodly number of Kentuckians. It is perhaps valuable to draw some distinctions between the attitudes of poor white Kentucky hillbillies and poor white southern rednecks. It would not be correct to identify Kentucky with the South, for while cars may sport Confederate-flag license tags, and while Atlanta has attracted many young men from the hills, eastern Kentucky as a whole thinks of itself as more allied with states like West Virginia, and has come more under the influence of Ohio, Indiana, and Michigan than of the industrial South.

White southerners, in farming areas, feel themselves to be in league with the large planters, businessmen, and politicians who run their county and state. They are used to the system where the prosperous and powerful, who must rely for their support on somebody, look out for what they believe to be the interests of the poor white, in terms of jobs, welfare, debt paying, and other matters. Their own situation, as they see it, is that if they are to make a living on a small farm, they must have the help of the successful farmers and businessmen; and if they are to make a living at a factory job, they must not be made to compete with a greater number of poor blacks who also need work. They fear the black man getting their jobs more than they dislike the rich whites for excluding them from political and economic decisions. So, in areas like the Mississippi Delta, where whites seldom openly contest each other in local politics and where there is a central authority—the planter— the poor whites abide by the decisions that reach them and do as they are bid. But in the larger areas of the South, less dominated by traditional powers and where the status quo cannot be so smoothly maintained, the poor whites can become as bitterly frustrated in their needs as can poor men in Kentucky or poor black men in the South. Often enough they will turn to the Klan for a way out, but the Klan just tells them that the poor whites are in a fight every step of the way with the black men who wants the same things, and the black men have got the government behind them. And it is quite true that agencies like OEO have succeeded, in the South, in serving mainly the black poor (or the white politicians and civic leaders who have assumed control of the programs).

In the mountains of Kentucky, relations between poor whites and poor blacks are very confused. In most counties blacks number only three or four per cent of the population, and that is almost entirely concentrated around the county seats. Some counties, like Harlan, have large black communities, for men came up out of the coal fields of Alabama and Tennessee to work the mines of Kentucky. Where whites and blacks have worked together, there is virtually no animosity between the groups, and indeed, it is likely that before the dual ascendancy of the civil rights movement and television in the late 50s and early 60s, most Kentucky whites knew little of the racial situation in other areas. Mountain people have always figured that everybody is different in one way or another, and that there is not much you can do about it. In Clay County, whites do not really think one way or another about the black community in Manchester; it has never been a cause of concern for them. All area-wide poor people's groups join together, whites and blacks, and the fiercest speakers in the Cumberland Valley are black ministers and miners. Adjoining Clay County is Jackson County, and there no black family has ever been allowed to settle down. It is the only Kentucky mountain county of which that is true, and it is a rather inexplicable phenomenon. Of course the news from the cities on TV has disturbed some whites, but a lot of poor whites have remarked, "What we need down here is one of those black power people. Then we'd get organized."

It should be stressed that the poor white in the South is caught between those two identifications: poor and white. To too many, the "southern white" represents the ruling class of the South, and therefore also the poor. And it is the particular problem of the poor white that he has too long relied on his affluent neighbor to see him through times of trouble. Now he is in the rather helpless position of seeing black men around him pulling themselves up faster than he can, and the only lasting organization open to poor whites in the South, the Klan, has been unable to come up with a solution to his problems yet.

The Deep South is very unlike the mountain areas such as eastern Kentucky in that it views itself much as a rival civilization to the rest of America. Southern values, especially those built upon race and religion, have been spurned by the North. The divide between the Protestant fundamentalism of Georgia and the libertinism of New York that is portrayed on southern TV and radio is really enormous. Mountain people in Kentucky share some of these attitudes about northern cities, but they are manifested as dismay and wonder that such things could go on, whereas many white southerners think of their region as a last entrenchment against heathen free thinking. Young people in the rural South differ little from their parents on these issues, but in the mountains young people are very casual about city influences, and some wear long hair and sport mustaches and listen to the rock music broadcast from Lexington and Cincinnati.

Southern whites are extremely concerned about halting communism, and they consider themselves, in that respect, very patriotic. The Vietnam war is much supported in the South, though little faith is put in Washington's ability to handle it. Mountain people, too, consider themselves patriotic, but rarely involve themselves with issues like "communism." They are willing to go to war if everybody else is going because they do not believe themselves any better than other people. Most mountain communities were left almost bereft of men during the Second World War. Thousands of men left for the war plants in Detroit and Oak Ridge, and thousands more dug coal at the big mines which were kept open during the war. Barely a family did not lose a relative in combat. Those years left the mountain people with little enthusiasm for wars, and the war in Vietnam has been widely hated as being for no good purpose. It is part of an ingrained distrust for elected men that mountain people do not really accept the excuses for fighting there that this country has offered. Neither are they comfortable at having sons so far from home.

Conclusion

One of the most remarkable things about the 1960s was that people who were not themselves poor or as a group actually oppressed did show their willingness to become involved in America's social movements toward economic and political justice. But the problems of this nation's poor people have shown themselves to be not so simple that those unfamiliar with each group's specific wants could lead the struggle. It is difficult enough to suggest massive solutions to the poverty of the Mississippi Delta or the Kentucky mountains without searching for solutions that will fit throughout the South, the Appalachians, or the country.

Though their thinking is often ignored by professional poverty fighters, poor people themselves have desires for and about change. These desires are often not well articulated, but sometimes they are quite clear. The black movement throughout the South, the store boycotts in Mississippi, the development of Head Start centers through organizations like the Child Development Group of Mississippi and Friends of the Children of Mississippi, the fight against strip mining on mountain land waged in Kentucky, Tennessee, and West Virginia—all have been

225

efforts poor people carried through for definite ends. These were not movements where the outsider conceived the problem and rallied the poor around him to support the cause. They were all expressions of anger and of hope that sprang directly from the needs and frustrations of people who have been kept down and left to waste away.

If it is not his wish to abort or to redirect the desperate want for change in poor communities, the concerned outsider can play a definite role by helping poor people to come together so that they may better express the changes that they seek. Too often, that role is overstepped and the outsider gives in to the temptation to lead the people who all of their lives have been led this way and that, and always been denied the chance to run things themselves.

What the outsider, be he a representative of a government agency, church group, or a private agency, may well not understand is that his solution to poverty, which usually involves the creation of "opportunities" for individual improvement, though excellent in itself, does not address itself to the main problem. The essential responsibility is not the poor man's to try to adapt himself to "opportunities" which, in fact, are not generally provided by the solutions of the outsider; rather it is the responsibility of the nation, as represented by government and business, to pay off the debt owed men and women who, after well-serving the builders of the twentieth century, have found that they have had taken from them virtually all the things which were important to them and all the things which made them important in the eyes of the world. Whatever the form of the repayment, it must be more substantial than increased "opportunities." It might be enough if the debt were admitted and the process halted—the process by which people are used and then discarded for the sake of the production and progress.

The need is for social change. It is fruitless to expect that this will be spawned from within the social, economic, or political structure, from within the system, for laws and institutions are by their nature inflexible; they do not foster change but, at best, yield to change after it has begun to occur. Social change comes from people, people for whom change is a necessity—the industrial worker during the first decades of this century, the southern black during the 1960s. We make the mistake when looking for solutions to poverty of thinking in terms of huge efforts, dramatic legislation, mammoth inventions like OEO. This creating of new institutions does little to encourage the energetic development of society. It is a dead-end process, both when the institution is manufactured by the government, as was OEO, and when it is a product of a social movement, as are the modern trade unions. For many working men, their union is a problem just like their employer. For many poor people, OEO is a problem along with the forces they feel are oppressing them.

America's problems are many, and they are not so simple that they can be solved through handouts to the poor or by giving jobs to the unemployed as a means of elevating them. This is no longer a country in which it is a pleasure to work, to physically build. It is no longer a country in which the good life can go untainted. As a nation, we have lost our spiritual footing. We have built too much too fast, created and became enmeshed in too large a structure, a bureau-structure that is programmed only for "progress," and we no longer have an understanding of what we have done, are doing, or what we want.

We have developed two terrible traits. We feel unable to stand up and air our own beliefs and grievances because— in a society that is not highly integrated but enormously complex and virtually incomprehensible—we have lost the sense of our own self-importance. And we have developed a conservatism within us that is suspicious of, and that causes us to obstruct, the outcries of those who have found it within themselves to stand up. We have come to believe that our problems can best be solved through institutional leadership. We resent those who deny this.

America needs new voices. We need to cherish each new voice and to cherish our own. We need, for the benefit of each of us, not to encourage the extension of what has become the American way of life to the millions who now exist apart from the system—the black, the poor white, etc. —for they will not, as cultural identities, fit into the system but will be crushed by it, leaving it unchanged; rather, we need to encourage their separate development, encourage their willingness to challenge the system, so that perhaps they will reinvigorate us all, make us remember that we too have a right to be dissatisfied and that we too have a right to seek satisfaction.

When we look around us at what has become an uncomfortable society and realize the horrible fact that it has coughed up some twenty to forty million souls for whom it has decided that there is no further use, let us not be hasty to play more games with those men's lives by redirecting our institutions toward their material improvement but instead encourage them to fight back so that we might know how such a fight is waged.

This book proposes no solutions to the problems of poor people or of poverty as a national fault, except that of calling upon the reader to support or at least stand out of the way of men who, from a sense of anger, of need, and of social justice, have come to represent by many methods, and to many ends, their interests as they perceive them.

It might be better if, as you read this, another document about the pain and unfairness of poverty in America, you did not first wonder what could be done to help these people but instead wonder how it happened that a society which, in founding, paid more than lip service to the idea of free men, became emptied of joy and unconscious of the worth of men, and look for a means of personal, not just national, salvation.

Postscript

During the time that has gone by since *Our Land Too* was finished, some important things have happened in Louise and in the mountains.

The schools of Yazoo City complied with federal order and peacefully desegregated during the 1969–70 year. The children of many of Louise's white families had been going to these schools since the white school of Louise was shut down to avoid desegregating. Most of these children have now begun going to a private school in Silver City, Humphreys County.

In the spring of 1970, Rainey Pool, a one-armed, black plantation worker, was beaten and shot to death in Louise after an incident outside a "white" nightspot. The murder stunned both the white and the black communities, for in the Delta, land of the gentleman planter, public killings are not supposed to take place. The black community reacted by beginning a boycott of the town's businesses. It is the first concerted act of resistance seen in Louise, and it has brought out resentments which for years have been buried within people. When the Sunflower River was dragged for Rainey Pool's body, the bodies of two other black men were discovered. The parents of both young men had thought they were in Chicago.

Kentucky and West Virginia in the summer of 1970 have seen coal strikes which have kept up to twenty thousand men away from work. The work stoppage has been caused by picket lines manned by disabled union miners. The picketers have been demanding that their union grant them hospital benefits from the time they become disabled, rather than withholding them until the miner reaches retirement age. The men who are staying off their jobs complain that the Federal Mine Safety Act is not being enforced either by the government or by the union.

It was the feeling among the strikers that the president of the United Mine Workers, Tony Boyle, has not been sensitive to his men's demands. He has declared that the UMW welfare and retirement fund, one of the richest union treasuries in the country, cannot afford to increase benefits; and, on top of the increase he gave during his re-election campaign in 1969 and the fund's notorious ill-management, he may be right. He tells the men that if they want a more prosperous union, they should return to work, for on each ton of coal they mine, the company pays forty cents into the union's welfare fund.

One result of this confrontation between men and the union which has ceased to represent them is that coal production in the United States dropped 20 per cent. The operating mines of eastern Kentucky have been working extra shifts to capitalize on the national demand. A ton of coal now costs fifteen dollars in the mountains. They say that by the winter it will be twenty.

In June 1970, the fiscal court of Knott County, in a meeting attended by several hundred angry landowners, banned strip mining within the county limits. It is questionable under Kentucky law whether or not a county has that authority. The Reclamation Department apparently decided that Knott County did not, for it issued permits to several companies to begin stripping operations.

A controversy has begun to rage concerning the damage that coal trucks do to public roads. The trucks, weighing with their coal as much as fifty tons, carry licenses good only to half that amount and drive roads that often have a weight limit as low as ten tons. Both the battle against the strippers and the battle against the trucks have seen, during the course of this summer, armed citizens demanding relief from the law.

Clay County seems to be in for a new boom in coal. A great deep mine is about to open, promising to employ 150 men and operate throughout the decade. At the same time, four new stripping operations have begun. To leave the main highway and travel to what was only a few months ago near-virgin countryside is to see the ruin that a bulldozer, in just a week or two, can make of a rugged and wild green mountain.

—TONY DUNBAR

Goose Creek, Kentucky
August 13, 1970

Harvard Semitic Monographs

Volume 5

THE DIVINE WARRIOR IN EARLY ISRAEL

Patrick D. Miller, Jr.

Harvard University Press

Cambridge, Massachusetts

1973

This book is dedicated to my father

Patrick D. Miller, Sr.

who very early taught me that the life of the mind

is part of the service of God

PREFACE

Any reader familiar with the subject matter of this volume will recognize at once my indebtedness to Frank M. Cross of Harvard University. I would like to express my gratitude to him for his wise counsel and critical encouragement through the years.

The Ugaritic texts are cited according to Cyrus Gordon's classification in *Ugaritic Textbook* (Rome, 1965) with Herdner's citation listed in parentheses immediately following. Although Herdner's system in *Corpus des tablettes en cuneiformes alphabetiques* (Paris, 1963) is slowly becoming the international standard, Gordon's *Textbook* continues to be the most nearly complete and the most accessible and widely used collection of the Ugaritic material.

I am grateful to the editors of *Vetus Testamentum* for permission to reprint a portion of my article, "The Divine Council and the Prophetic Call to War," *VT*, 18 (1968), 100-107; *Catholic Biblical Quarterly* for permission to use part of my article, "Fire in the Mythology of Canaan and Israel," *CBQ*, 27 (1965), 256-261; and *Harvard Theological Review* for allowing me to quote from my articles, "Two Critical Notes on Psalm 68 and Deuteronomy 33," *HTR*, 57 (1964), 240-243 and "El the Warrior," *HTR*, 60 (1967), 411-431.

I would like to thank Mrs. F. S. Clark for her editorial and secretarial help in the several revisions of this manuscript and my student James Benson Sauer for his careful and efficient work in compiling the indexes.

Patrick D. Miller, Jr.

Union Theological Seminary in Virginia

CONTENTS

ABBREVIATIONS

AJSL	*American Journal of Semitic Languages and Literatures*
ANET	*Ancient Near Eastern Texts Relating to the Old Testament*, ed. J. B. Pritchard, 2nd ed.
ARI	W. F. Albright, *Archaeology and the Religion of Israel*
ASD	M. J. Dahood, "Ancient Semitic Deities in Syria and Palestine," *Le antiche divinità semitiche,* ed. S. Moscati
BASOR	*Bulletin of the American Schools of Oriental Research*
BZAW	*Beihefte zur Zeitschrift für die alttestamentliche Wissenschaft*
CBQ	*Catholic Biblical Quarterly*
CML	G. R. Driver, *Canaanite Myths and Legends*
CTA	*Corpus des tablettes en cunéiformes alphabétiques,* ed. A. Herdner
EUT	Marvin Pope, *El in the Ugaritic Texts*
HKAT	*Hand-Kommentar zum Alten Testament*
HTR	*Harvard Theological Review*
HUCA	*Hebrew Union College Annual*
ICC	*International Critical Commentary*
IDB	*The Interpreter's Dictionary of the Bible*
IEJ	*Israel Exploration Journal*
JAOS	*Journal of the American Oriental Society*
JBL	*Journal of Biblical Literature*
JCS	*Journal of Cuneiform Studies*
JNES	*Journal of Near Eastern Studies*

ABBREVIATIONS

JPOS	*Journal of the Palestine Oriental Society*
JSS	*Journal of Semitic Studies*
LXX	*The Septuagint*
MT	*The Masoretic Text*
OT	*Oudtestamentische Studien*
PRU	*Le Palais royal d'Ugarit*, 5 vols.
1QH	*The Thanksgiving Psalms from Qumran Cave I*
1QM	*The War Scroll from Qumran Cave I*
SVT	*Supplements to Vetus Testamentum*
TLZ	*Theologische Literaturzeitung*
UM	C. H. Gordon, *Ugaritic Manual*
UT	C. H. Gordon, *Ugaritic Textbook*
VT	*Vetus Testamentum*
WM	*Wörterbuch der Mythologie*, ed. H. W. Haussig, vol. I
WMANT	*Wissenschaftliche Monographien zum Alten und Neuen Testament*
ZA NF	*Zeitschrift für Assyriologie, Neue Folge*
ZAW	*Zeitschrift für die alttestamentliche Wissenschaft*
ZDMG	*Zeitschrift der Deutschen Morgenländischen Gesellschaft*
ZNW	*Zeitschrift für neutestamentliche Wissenschaft*
ZTK	*Zeitschrift für Theologie und Kirche*

The Divine Warrior in Early Israel

INTRODUCTION

This monograph is a study of one of the major images of God in the Old Testament and its background in the mythology of Syria-Palestine. The conception of God as warrior played a fundamental role in the religious and military experience of Israel, one that has been recognized but not fully treated or analyzed in its various dimensions. One can go only so far in describing the history of Israel, or its religion, or the theology of the Old Testament without encountering the wars of Yahweh. In prose and poetry, early and late materials alike, the view that Yahweh fought for or against his people stands forth prominently. The centrality of that conviction and its historical, cultic, literary and theological ramifications can hardly be overestimated. Some of these matters have been dealt with in previous works; other dimensions are taken up in the present study. It is in no sense exhaustive. There are many facets of the subject which do not receive attention here, but I hope in what follows to highlight some aspects of Israel's understanding of the wars of Yahweh that have not received as much attention in other studies and to point to some wider implications of the divine warrior motif as it comes to expression in the documents of the Old Testament. That task cannot be accomplished apart from indebtedness and relationship to the work of others. It is necessary, therefore, at the beginning to say briefly how my study grows out of previous

contributions and what the particular focus and point of departure of these pages will be.

Among those works of the last three decades which have been
seminal and influential in Old Testament studies, Gerhard von
Rad's small monograph *Der Heilige Krieg im alten Israel* occupies
a place of first rank. Although earlier scholars such as
Schwally and Weber had called attention to the special character
and importance of the early wars in Israel's history, von Rad
succeeded in accurately describing the phenomenon which he and
others have called holy war, distinguishing it from other conflicts and tracing the influence of these holy wars on the later
history of Israel. Like all reconstructions of the early history
of Israel, von Rad's work is subject to criticism and, particularly in more recent times, has received an increasing amount of
critical comment. Nevertheless, his study was carefully done and
essentially sound, even though criticisms of particular issues,
such as his virtual relegation of holy war to Israel's defensive
operations in the period of the Judges, may be justified. He has
made us aware of the extent to which the history and faith of
early Israel centered in the wars of the tribal league.

In its brief length and limited scope there were certain related matters which von Rad's monograph did not take up. For one
thing, he did no extended comparison of the holy wars of Israel
with military practices in other countries of the ancient Near
East. Further, while von Rad has paid attention to some of the
theological dimensions involved, he has not dealt extensively
with the theological imagery which pictures Yahweh as divine war-

rior. This latter area, which is the principal concern of this
book, was investigated in an earlier work by H. Fredriksson entitled *Jahwe als Krieger*. Fredriksson divided the *Gottesbild* cf
Yahweh as warrior into different categories under the large headings of Yahweh as leader of an army and Yahweh as individual
fighter. Under these headings he took up one by one the different kinds of armies Yahweh leads, the various ways he functions
as single warrior and the weapons he employs, and some of the
technical terms associated with Yahweh's warring activity.

Fredriksson's work performed a valuable service in bringing
together most of the Old Testament evidence for this remarkable
imagery. Sometimes, however, his judgments and observations are
less than accurate, as, for example, when he remarks that the
ideas of Yahweh as leader of an army of heavenly beings appear
sporadically in older sources as mere remnants with little influence on the general religious development. Further, the work
suffers from being largely a list and a brief discussion of categories. It covers the whole of the Old Testament in a very ec-
lectic way without focusing in depth at any point to see the role
that imagery played. Nor does it give any serious attention to
the mythological background of the imagery in the literature of
the ancient Near East. So, while he has cited most of the relevant material in the Old Testament, Fredriksson has not exhausted
by any means the work that needs to be done on this important
subject.

One sees this most clearly in two recent articles by Frank
M. Cross which take up this theme anew: "The Divine Warrior in

Israel's Early Cult" and "The Song of the Sea and Canaanite Myth." In a fresh way, by focusing on the role of the divine warrior, Cross has broken through some old impasses, particularly on the relationship between myth and history and the nature of the early Israelite cultus, and suggested some new directions and approaches. A summary of his articles is unnecessary at this point because they are used and discussed throughout the following pages. In part, what follows is an outgrowth of Cross's work, but, even more, it represents a parallel approach to what he has been doing, with more attention to the mythological and less to the cultic aspects, though the two are not wholly separable. This work had its earliest form as part of a dissertation prepared under Cross's direction and submitted in 1963, three years prior to the publication of the first article mentioned above but while Cross was working on the subject matter. The constant dependence upon his work, not only in these two articles but also in many others, will be immediately evident to the reader.

Before describing briefly the approach I have taken, some mention should be made of a terminological issue that has arisen in the discussion of von Rad's work. In the more recent literature some scholars such as R. Smend and H.-M. Lutz have preferred to use the term "war of Yahweh" instead of "holy war" because the former expression is used in the Old Testament for the early wars and the latter is not. While Smend has rightly called attention to the Old Testament terminology, it is not necessary to make the modern designation precisely dependent upon Old Testament usage.

In the following pages "holy war" will be used generally because
it has become established as the usual designation and will probably continue as such, as Smend acknowledges. Occasionally, for
variation, the terms "sacral war" or "Yahweh war" will also be
used. In any case, we are confronted in the early period with a
sacral kind of warfare both in the involvement of the deity and
the existence of certain cultic practices. Obviously other wars
have or had a sacral character, but the designation in this case
is applied to the "wars of Yahweh" in the premonarchic period
and where elements or aspects of the early theory of warfare
appear in later materials.

The focus of this work is upon divine warfare in ancient
Israel, its mythological background, and its relationship to the
wars of Israel. That is, I have sought to look at the mythologi-
cal-theological conceptions which were associated with Israel's
early wars, her reflections on them, and the divine involvement
in them. Although later materials are drawn in, the basic source
material is found in the corpus of early poetry as that has been
worked out and defined particularly in the studies of W. F. Albright, F. M. Cross, and D. N. Freedman. By concentrating here,
one has a reasonable chance to get at the understanding of the
divine warrior in the early period. Special attention is given
in the following discussion to the role of the divine or cosmic
hosts of Yahweh in Israel's conceptions of how Yahweh was involved in her wars and fought for her. It is my contention that
this was a far more significant factor in the imagery of divine
warfare than is usually recognized, and one of the aims of this

study is to point that out.

That the God of Israel should be regarded as the commander
of divine or heavenly armies should not be surprising when one
considers conceptions of divine warfare in other parts of the
ancient Near East. Until the studies by Frank Cross, this
heavily mythological motif does not appear to have been examined
in the light of other ancient Near Eastern representations of
divine warriors. In this work I have sought to fill this gap in
a partial way be devoting a significant part of the study to the
extra-biblical materials from Syria-Palestine, specifically the
Ugaritic texts and the work of Philo Byblius. Thus the divine
warrior motif and the patterns that evolve out of the biblical
data may be seen against this background out of which they come,
although not without their own particular character.

A more extensive study would have to take into account Egyptian, Mesopotamian, and Hittite texts. Except in specific cases
these are for several reasons excluded from treatment here. Although they are important to the general picture, they do not
appear to give a decisively different approach to the matters at
hand. Further, they are less directly and extensively related to
the literature and religion of Israel (see Part I), and the inclusion of such material would greatly alter the scope of this
study without significantly altering our basic understanding.

Although this book is a study of one aspect of Yahwistic
faith, it becomes a way into larger matters. It enables us to
understand better the origins of that faith and its continuity
and discontinuity with the religious world of which it was a

part. In a concluding section I have suggested also that the
ancient epic of Israel's origins, which is in large part an account of the various conflicts through which the people moved to
the establishment of a home and place in which to live and serve
God, took its shape at least in part out of the hymnic accounts
of God's leading his armies in the primal march of holy war and
conquest. If that suggestion should be on the right track, then
continuing attention to the question of the growth of the Penta-
teuch/Hexateuch is in order. Finally, I have underscored an observation that cannot be ignored when one engages oneself with
the subject matter of these pages. That is the fact that the
view of Yahweh as warrior can hardly be a peripheral matter in
the effort to work out a biblical theology. Rather, it lies at
the theological center and much of the traditional substance of
God-talk when given content from an Old Testament perspective
confronts one directly with the wars of Israel and the God who
was active in them.

PART ONE

DIVINE WARFARE IN THE LITERATURE OF SYRIA-PALESTINE

This part deals with what is generally known as Canaanite religion, that is, the religion of Syria-Palestine.[1] The religion of Canaan and its mythological roots were a part of the general culture of the ancient Near East, which had, despite many differences, a certain basic homogeneity to it due to various factors including geographical proximity, language similarities, and cultural interpenetration and influence.[2] Nevertheless, that religion was an independent entity which grew out of its own soil while it was borrowing from and assimilating neighboring religions. Its significance in this context, however, lies in the fact that the material involved was closely tied to the world of the Old Testament, the history and religion of Israel. The influence of Egyptian and Mesopotamian history and culture on Israel was of course considerable. From Egypt Israel's life as a nation had its beginning. In Mesopotamia it reached its end for all intents and purposes. But it was on Syro-Palestinian soil that Israel's history and religion were cultivated, and that en-

vironment had an inevitable influence upon her, both by Israel's
reaction against and her accommodation to the phenomena which
she met in her surroundings.[3] The study at hand deals with only
one aspect of this overall problem.

Sources

The main sources for the following analysis are two -- the
Ugaritic texts and Philo Byblius' account of the "Phoenician History" of Sanchuniathon (Phoen. *Sakkun-yatōn*). The Old Testament
and inscriptional material are brought in where enlightening, but
these other sources are the foundation upon which any study of
Canaanite religion must be based. Use of the Ugaritic texts
needs no explanation. They speak for themselves as a primary
source.

Philo's report, however, is another matter. Though regarded
with great suspicion as to its accuracy, Philo was, until the
discoveries at Ugarit, the main source for knowledge of Canaanite
or Phoenician religion. The dubious regard in which his account
was held was not without justification. Philo belonged to the
first century A. D., a time when the flourishing religion of Canaan in the second and first millennia B. C. had long passed. His
source was Sanchuniathon, who probably wrote around the sixth
century B. C.,[4] although his date is still not entirely certain.
Hellenistic influence, including a tendency toward theological
speculation, was to be expected in Philo's account. The possibility of very late and secondary material being inserted was also a very live option. Indeed, all these possibilities are at

least in part probabilities as far as Philo Byblius is concerned.
The fact remains, however, that since the discovery and publication of the Ugaritic texts as well as some Hurrian mythological
texts, Philo's history has been vindicated and shown to be far
more reliable than ever suspected, having been based on quite ancient and authentic sources.[5] Although some of his data may be
late or secondary, still other parts of his or Sanchuniathon's
reconstruction may represent an even earlier stage in the history
of Canaanite mythology than that represented in the Ugaritic
texts.[6]

    That the Ugaritic texts and Philo Byblius should be valuable
for the religion of Syria-Palestine throughout the second and
first millennia is not surprising. Albright and Dahood have both
properly stressed the homogeneity of the culture and civilization
of that region during those two millennia.[7] The religion and
culture were relatively stable not only over the *time* span, but
also over the *geographical* span, although there were particular
nuances and developments in certain regions. The texts from
Ugarit did not have their origin and influence only in northern
Syria; some of them (for example, the Keret epic) may have come
from Phoenicia or even farther south. The deities worshiped at
Ugarit were also worshiped throughout Palestine. Conversely, in
the Old Testament, Psalm 29, probably a very early modified Canaanite hymn, may have had its origins in northern Syria.[8]

    A careful analysis of extra-biblical materials has to start
from the fact that the type of literature that is used as a
source makes some difference in the information or conclusions

derived therefrom. That is to say, different forms of literature
stress different aspects of the world of the gods, though these
emphases may represent parts of the same overall conception.
Various gods of the ancient Near East and their assemblies function at times as warrior forces. The purely mythological literature tends to stress the battles among the gods, while the
historical texts emphasize the involvement of the heavenly war-
rior(s) in earthly affairs, and the hymnic literature often represents a mixture of these two aspects. The principal Ugaritic
texts are heavily mythological though not entirely so. The
Legend of Aqhat involves the relationships of the gods and goddesses to men, and the Keret epic is even more a narrative of
human endeavors including a major military expedition, probably
having a historical core or background.[9] But even here the gods
play a definite role. The character of the existing material is,
of course, important in itself inasmuch as these texts do not
represent a merely casual find but are the literary remains of a
key Syrian crossroads uncovered in a large amount of material by
systematic excavation.

With regard to the Ugaritic texts, the emphasis in this section is placed on the Baʿal and ʿAnat cycle,[10] though reference
is also made to other relevant texts. The Baʿal epic is primary
because it furnishes the most information concerning Canaanite
conceptions of the matter at hand, that is divine warfare -- war
among the gods and their hosts and the participation of these cosmic forces in human battles, both aspects being derivative from
or a reflection of the other. The analysis revolves around the

divine assembly as such and the three major deities of the text,
El, Ba‘al and ‘Anat, with reference to the other gods or goddesses as they relate to these three. The nature and role of the
assembly are looked at in some detail both separately and in relation to the major deities. While most Ugaritic studies deal
only briefly with the divine council and its role, its function
is a major part of this study.[11]

The Nature and Role of the Divine Assembly

In Syria-Palestine, as in Mesopotamia and to some degree in
Egypt and elsewhere, the assembly of the gods included among its
constituency many of the familiar named deities, who involved
themselves in one way or another in the activities of the celestial council. First place belonged to the great gods and goddesses: El, the theoretical head of the council, Ba‘al, ‘Anat,
Aṯirat, ‘Aṯtart, Yamm, and Mot.[12] Among other deities mentioned
in the Ugaritic texts as playing more or less significant roles
were Šapš, Koṯar-wa-Ḫassis, ‘Aṯtar, and Yariḫ. Still others,
such as Ḥoron, Rešeph, and Dagan, are mentioned but according to
our present knowledge do not play what can be regarded as a significant part in the Ugaritic texts.[13] These were not all the
named deities; other gods and goddesses, some not yet precisely
identified, belonged to the pantheon,[14] but it is not intended at
this juncture to go into any lengthy discussion of them.

The assembly was, however, a much broader and more encompas-
sing entity than the total of the gods listed above.[15] It was
the totality of all the gods, the *pḫr ilm*. This phrase, which

was also the common designation for the divine assembly in Akkadian (*puḫur ilāni*) though not in Hebrew, is found frequently in
the Ugaritic myths, sacrificial lists, and god lists. It occurs
in different variations, all meaning the same thing: *pḫr ilm* (17:
7[= *CTA* 29. rev. 7]); *p[ḫ]r bn ilm* (51:III:14[= *CTA* 4.III.14]);
mpḫrt bn il (2:17, 34[= *CTA* 32.17,34] and 107:3[= *CTA* 30.3]);
and, finally, *pḫr m⁽d* (137:14, 15, 20, 31[= *CTA* 2.I.14, 15, 20,
31]). In at least one case (1:7[= *CTA* 34.7]) there is a reference to *p[ḫ]r b⁽l* (see below). Examination of these passages in
their context reveals an important fact. The term *pḫr/mpḫrt* appears to be a kind of semiofficial or formal designation for the
assembly, that is, the *name* of the council of the gods.[16] Its use
in mythological texts is confined to the two places in the Ba⁽al
and ⁽Anat cycle where there seems to be a kind of plenary session
of the gods. Elsewhere it occurs in lists of deities or lists of
sacrifices to them. This designation is by no means the only one
for the assembly or even the most frequent. By far the most common terms are *ilm*, "gods," and *bn il(m)*, "sons of El" or "sons of
the gods."[17] These are used everywhere to refer to the members of the assembly, but they do not seem to have the official
or formal quality belonging to *pḫr*, enabling it to be a part of
lists of the gods.[18] The tenth-century Byblian inscription of
Yeḥimilk indicates the same usage of the word.[19] In lines 3 and
4 the official gods of the city are invoked: Ba⁽alat Gebal; her
consort, Ba⁽al samem; and *mpḫrt ʾl gbl qdšm*, "the assembly/to-
tality of the holy gods of Byblos." The use of the phrase *pḫr
m⁽d* in Ugaritic is a significant one because it has the Akkadian

technical term *puḫur* and the Hebrew or Northwest Semitic technical term *mô͑ēd,*which is originally a political term[20] and in
at least one noted instance clearly refers to the assembly of the
gods. Isaiah 14:13 designates the place where the gods meet as
har-mô͑ēd. [21] The phrase *pḫr m͑d* in the Ugaritic texts would seem
to refer specifically to a plenary session of the divine council
and is best translated with Ginsberg as "the Assembled Body."[22]

Another term for the assembly of the gods similar in meaning
and usage to *pḫr* is *͑dt ilm*, "the council/congregation of the
gods." Already known in the Old Testament from Psalm 82:1, it is
found also in the Keret epic from Ugarit (128:ii:7, 11[= *CTA* 15.
II.7, 11]). Ba͑al beseeches El's blessing upon Keret before the
͑dt ilm (see below). The Keret epic and the sacrificial lists
reveal still another term for the divine council, *dr*, "family,"
"circle," which appears in two forms: *dr il*, "family or circle
of El," and *dr bn il*, "family or circle of the sons of El (that
is, the gods)." The former phrase, *dr il*, appears in parallelism
with *ilm* (128:iii:19[= *CTA* 15.III.19]) and along with *p[ḫ]r b͑l*
(1:7[= *CTA* 34.7]). The latter, *dr bn il*, appears in line with
mpḫrt bn il and *ab bn il* (2:17, 25, 34 [= *CTA* 32.17, 25, 34]; 107:
2[= *CTA* 30.3]). It is clear, therefore, that *dr (bn) il* is another designation for the pantheon at Ugarit, and one that indicates a close relationship with El. Finally, the term *bn qdš*
should be noted as a title for the gods meaning "sons of holiness"
or "sons of the Holy One," that is, "holy ones." Atirat's lackey
or messenger has this as a part of his name, Qdš-w-Amrr. Furthermore, *qdš* is a well-known alternate name for Atirat, which raises

the possibility of a special relationship of the *bn qdš* to this
deity.[23]

More recent texts from Ugarit have revealed that in Canaanite mythology, as in Mesopotamian, a group in the assembly, presumably the leadership or "upper house" of the council, was
designated "the great gods." In *PRU* II, 90, lines 1-2, the first
item on a list of jars of wine for distribution is "a *kd* for the
house of the *great gods* (*ilm rbm*)." This was the first reference
in the Ugaritic texts to a group called "the great gods." The
one occurrence in an administrative text might suggest that this
category played no role in the mythology of Ugarit; but the new
mythological texts in *Ugaritica* V contain at least two and possibly three references to *ilm rbm*, albeit in contexts that give us
little information about them. In one case we hear of *adn ilm
rbm*, "father/lord of the great gods."[24] In the other cases they
are referred to in one of the Ugaritic serpent charms in broken
contexts but after the description of the participation of the
various gods in assisting Šapš in "venom collection."[25] It is
likely that "the great gods" refers to the aforementioned deities
who also appear in the other Ugaritic serpent charm.[26]

Not surprisingly, "the great gods" appear again in the much
later Arslan Tash incantation text as a part of the council of
the gods.[27] Line 12 reads *wrb. dr kl. qdšn*, "And the great
(ones) of the council of all the Holy Ones."

There are other references to specific groups which apparently belong to the divine assembly and which are usually defined
or described only by their relationship to one of the major

deities. That is to say, a number of principal gods and goddesses are thought to have their own following or coterie of divine
beings, although these may be simply alternate designations for
the council as a whole or parts of it. These groups may overlap.

One such group about which the texts are often quite specific is the *messengers* of the gods called generally *mlakm, ǵlmm,*
or in Text 137 (= *CTA* 2.I), *t⁽ᶜ⁾dt.* These messengers, as far as
can be determined, travel generally in pairs and are usually associated with a particular deity. Yamm has two unnamed messengers who are sent to demand the surrender of Baᶜal by the assembly of the gods. Baᶜal has two messengers, Gpn and Ugr, who go
up and down the divine world on errands for their master, bringing messages to and from him. Qdš-w-Amrr is Aṯirat's attendant
but also carries a message from Baᶜal even as Gpn and Ugr carry a
message from Mot. Not all the gods had their own messengers;
ᶜAnat, for example, in Text 49:IV (= *CTA* 6.IV) delivers her message to Šapš personally and in correct form.

Some of the chief gods and goddesses had still larger contin-
gents. The divine assembly as a whole appears to have been regarded as belonging to El, its leader. The term *bn il(m)* may not
actually indicate that fact, but the designation *dr il,* "family
of El," seems to do so, especially when allied with the phrases
p[ḫ]r bᶜl and *ab bn il.*[28] El is the father (*ab*) of the gods. He
is also called *bny bnwt,* "creator of creatures" (49:III:5,11 [=
CTA 6.III.5,11]; 51:II:11[= *CTA* 4.II.11]; 51:III:32[= *CTA* 4.III.
32]; 2 Aq I: 25[= *CTA* 17.I.25]). The conception of the council
as peculiarly El's host on the basis of names for the council is

complicated by the question of Aṯirat's position as mistress
or mother of the gods. As indicated above, she was also known at
Ugarit and elsewhere as Quдšu, and it may be that *bn qdš* indicates a specific kinship with this goddess.[29] The principal epithet applied to Aṯirat is *qnyt ilm* (for example, 51:III:26, 30,
etc. [= *CTA* 4.III.26, 30]). In such instances it may refer to all
the gods or only to a group of them. The combination of these
names and epithets points to the fact that the council of the
gods was not only a separate entity and totality on its own
terms, but was also regarded as the host of El and his consort,
Aṯirat.[30]

   Aṯirat apparently had a separate aggregation of deities associated with her whether the whole divine assembly was regarded as
her family or not. One of the standard cliches of the Baᶜal-
ᶜAnat cycle is *aṯrt . wbnh . ilt . wṣbrt aryh*, "Aṯirat and her
sons/children, Elat and the band of her kindred" (49:I:12–13 [=
CTA 6.I.40–41]). The phrase *ṣbrt aryh* is a difficult one, but
the context and parallelism with *bn* and *aḫ* make the meaning clear
and in accordance with proposed etymologies.[31] The terms used
here do not in themselves point to the existence of a smaller
group of gods associated with Aṯirat, nor do their contexts; but
there is indication elsewhere of such a group, and it is quite
likely that the terms in this cliché refer to the same thing.
Mention has already been made of the *bn aṯrt* referred to frequently in the texts. In Text 51:VI:46 (= *CTA* 4.VI.46) they are designated as the *šbᶜm . bn . aṯrt*, "the seventy sons of Aṯirat."
The number must be taken seriously if not literally. It is possi-

ble that it is a poetic device referring to the totality of the
gods, but there is no numerical parallelism here of which this
would be a balancing part. In short, the term would appear to
refer to particular deities gathered around the figure of Aṯirat,
although reference to all the gods cannot be excluded. Whether
or not all uses of the phrases *bn aṯrt* or *ṣbrt ary* refer to this
possible sub-group cannot be determined.[32]

The rapid rise of Baᶜal to leadership in the council of the
gods -- a movement clearly evident in the Ugaritic texts -- makes
it natural enough that he also would have a coterie. We have already drawn attention to the expression *p[ḫ]r bᶜl* in Text 1:7 (=
CTA 34.7).[33] Pope is probably right in suggesting that the
phrase refers to an aggregation of deities around Baᶜal.[34] One
is tempted to see this as a later development representing a separate assembly under Baᶜal's rule and centering on Ṣaphon,
Baᶜal's abode, although such a supposition is quite conjectural
and made with great reservations.[35]

But there are further indications of a special coterie attached to Baᶜal.[36] Two references are made to the *šbᶜt ǵlmh/k*,
"his/your seven lads," or "his/your seven attendants" (49:VI:8[=
CTA 6.VI.8] and 67:V:8-9 [= *CTA* 5.V.8-9]). The first passage is
very broken and impossible to translate, but it has to do with
the battle against Mot and may have told about their aid in that
fight. The second passage is complete. *šbᶜt ǵlmk* is parallel to
ṯmn ḫnzrk. The word *ḫnzr*, though admittedly enigmatic, is usually translated "pig" or "boar." That translation is a peculiar
parallel to *ǵlm*,[37] but in the light of the frequent use of animal

names for nobles and leaders in Ugaritic and Hebrew, it may well
be correct.[38] New data possibly relevant to the problem have
been put forth by F. Løkkegaard.[39] He points to the presence of
ha-ni-za-rum in the Shemshara Tablets where, according to the
editor of the texts, it appears to be a military title,[40] or at
least the name of a high office of some sort, administrative or
military. It may be that this word is the same as $ḫnzr$ in the
Ugaritic texts even if the latter is an animal term.[41] The word
$ǵlmm$ may have a similar meaning at times, particularly in $ʿnt$:
II:4 (= CTA 3.II.4) where Driver translates "servitors"[42] and
Ginsberg translates "picked fighters."[43]

The new texts from Ugarit have revealed still another clear
and important reference to Baʿal's military retinue. In $Ugariti$-
ca V, Text 9, line 8 (RS 24.643) one finds in a list of sacrifices to the gods of the pantheon il . $tʿḏr$. $bʿl$, "the helper-gods
of Baʿal." That the designation is plural rather than singular
is confirmed by its presence in the Akkadian Ugaritic Pantheon
text as $ilanu^m$ til-la-$at^d adad$.[44] Although these gods do not play
any role under this designation in the mythological texts discovered so far, they do appear several other times in Ugaritic
pantheon lists.[45] They may have assisted Baʿal in various ways,
but comparison with the "helpers" of Marduk and of Tiamat who
marched at their side and the "helpers" of Rahab in Job 9:13 suggests that these gods were those divine beings who went forth with
Baʿal into battle.[46]

There may be yet another reference to the warrior retinue of
Baʿal in the difficult phrase [ ]dt ilm $tlt̲h$ in the Keret Epic

(128:II:7[= *CTA* 15.II.7]). Although usually translated -- albeit somewhat uncertainly -- "threefold," Svi and Shifra Rin have
suggested: "It would be plausible to assume, however, that *tlth*
is, like its cognate, ו ʾ וּ ʾ ? וּ , his lieutenants, his retinue,
that is, the *ᶜdt ilm*, the assembly of gods, Baᶜal's companions
or guards, such as each major deity has.... Thus *ᶜdt ilm*, *ǵlmm*
or *tlth* are the warriors accompanying a chief deity."[47]

All the above evidence makes it clear that Baᶜal was understood to be the leader of an indeterminate host apparently conceived in part as a military force.[48]

Evidence for the presence of a special following around other gods is not so strong, nor should one expect there to be such
evidence in every case. There are, however, a few references
(usually broken, unfortunately) which suggest the possibility.
ᶜAnat as Baᶜal's cohort and warrior goddess probably had such a
coterie, although her conflicts usually involved single combat.
Text 6:7 (= *CTA* 13.7), called by Cazelles a hymn to ᶜAnat,[49] refers to *mhrk*, "thy warrior(s)," which could be such a divine coterie, although the text is broken, and there is no way of being
certain whether the word is singular or plural. The Rephaim
texts make definite reference to *mhr* ᶜ*nt* (124:9[= *CTA* 22.B.9])
though again the number is uncertain.[50]

As for Mot and Yamm, the texts allow us to say very little.
In his battle with Baᶜal, Mot seems to make a reference to his
brothers (49:VI:10-11 [= *CTA* 6.VI.10-11]), although once again
the reader is stopped by a broken text, and the reference is completely enigmatic. Kapelrud conjectures about the likelihood of

Yamm's having an army behind him in his battle with Ba'al,[51] and comparison with the Marduk-Tiamat battle, which is closely akin, enhances that conjecture, as does the warlike character of his messengers (see below).

One should take note also of Text 2004:15 (= *PRU* V 4:15) where reference is made to *ršp ṣbi*, possibly to be translated "Rešeph of the army." Although we know all too little about Rešeph's active role in Ugaritic mythology, it is not surprising to find this god described as leader of a battle force.

There are other groups of divine beings in the council with specific names. The *rpum* mentioned above and the parallel term *ilnym* indicate one such group. Although more extended discussion is given in the next section, it may be pointed out that we have here one or two sets of deities connected with the netherworld and the dead spirits who may be comparable to the Anunnaki and the Igigi in Mesopotamian mythology.[52] Their association with chariots and horses and with the terms *mhr b'l, mhr 'nt* and possibly *ģzrm* (124:7-9[= *CTA* 22.B.7-9]) gives strong indication that the *rpum* functioned in some manner as a divine military host, although no texts as yet depict them in battle.

Notice should be given in passing to another particular group, the *ktrt*, or "skillful ones," whose main function may have been as birth goddesses, inasmuch as all their appearances are connected with birth or conception (Texts 77[= *CTA* 24]; 132 [= *CTA* 11]; and 2Aq[= *CTA* 17]).[53]

Finally, one may mention the *kbkbm/kkbm*, or "stars," as a constituent element in the divine assembly at Ugarit. The clear-

ndication of that fact is in Text 52:54 (= *CTA* 23.54)

šu . ᶜdb . lšpš . wlkbkbm

Lift up, prepare for lady Šapš and for the stars.

Furthermore, *kkbm* is parallel to *bn il* in Text 76:I:3-4 (= *CTA*
10.I.3-4), but the first parts of both lines are broken. Driver
reconstructs and translates reasonably:

[*wrgm*] *. d l [.] ydᶜ bn il*

[*d l ybn.*] *pẖr kkbm*

[and tell], that the son(s) of El may know

(and) [that] the host of the stars [may understand],[54]

Over against previous readings of the following line, Mlle. Herdner in her critical edition of the texts has rightly suggested
that line 5 probably reads [   ] *dr dt . šmm, [..]* "the family/
circle of the heavens," a very good parallel to the preceding
lines.[55] In this passage, therefore, the stars are thus related
to or identified with the gods and described with the same language as the divine assembly *(pẖr* and *dr).* In Text 6:13 (= *CTA*
13.13) Cazelles reads *kbkbm . tm . tpl . k . lbnt .* and sees here
possible signs of a myth whereby ᶜAnat gained dominion over the
stars by a victory. Such an interpretation is quite tentative,
however, particularly in light of the broken state of the text.
Philo Byblius also notes that the stars were a part of the Canaanite pantheon:

phusikous de hēlion kai selēnēn kai tous loipous planētas

asteras kai ta stoicheia kai ta toutois sunaphē theous

monous eginōskon [56]

But they knew as gods alone, natural things, the sun and

moon and the rest of the wandering stars (planets) and
the elements and the things united in these.

The Canaanite mythological fragment contained in Isaiah 14 also
appears to reflect the stars' position in the divine assembly
when it refers to the $k\hat{o}k^eb\hat{e}$ $^{)}\bar{e}l$, "the stars of El."[57]

As an assembly, the gods in the Ugaritic texts do not have
the widespread functions evidenced in the mythology concerning
the Mesopotamian divine council. There are two main passages in
which the gods are pictured as meeting as a body (Text 137 and
51:III[= *CTA* 2.I and 4.III]). Text 137 (= *CTA* 2.I) describes the
$p\dot{h}r$ m^cd gathered on Mount Ll[58] with El presiding, although he is
clearly not entirely in charge of things. In both contexts the
gods are dining and banqueting. The banquet, one of the few specific activities of the gods, is a dominant theme in their affairs and certainly influenced the development of later notions
of an eschatological banquet. Here as in other matters the world
of the gods and the world of man were a sort of mutual reflection,
each being the pattern for the other.

The gods as an assembly as well as individuals were responsible for blessing and protecting their worshipers,[59] who made
sacrifices to the assembly invoking their aid. When El blesses
Keret and insures progeny for him (128:II-III[= *CTA* 15.II-III]),
the gods are called together and as an assembly also give him
their blessing.[60]

The role of the individual gods and the assembly as divine
or cosmic warriors is discussed in the following sections.

Ba^cal and ^cAnat as Divine Warriors

The activities of the god Ba^cal and the goddess ^cAnat, the warrior deities par excellence in the Ugaritic texts, are intimately related and must be examined together. At the center of their affairs is a series of battles. These together with the divine epithets are the basis for study of this phenomenon in the Ugaritic corpus. The principal sources for investigation of that fact are the series of texts known as the Ba^cal and ^cAnat cycle.[61]

Ba^cal's initial conflict is with Prince Yamm, the Sea, narrated in Texts 137 (= *CTA* 2.I) and 68 (= *CTA* 2.IV), and it has been suggested that ^cAnat's reference to her conquests of *ltn, tnn,* and *šlyṭ* all have to do with this great battle.[62] This interpretation could be correct, especially in light of the fact that Tannin (*tnn*) appears as a sea-monster in the Old Testament (Ps. 74:13; Job 7:12), but this conclusion is not necessary, and there is strong evidence against it. Yamm is not equated with these three figures unless one assumes that because he appears first in the list all the other creatures named are to be identified with him. ^cAnat announced conquests over quite a few named enemies, not all of whom can be identified with one deity. There is nothing intrinsically wrong with the idea that Ba^cal and ^cAnat fought several battles, some of which may have been related to one another. Ba^cal's battles with Yamm and Mot are clearly two different conflicts, though they are aspects of a single mythological motif -- the conflict between cosmos or order and chaos.

The conflict between Ba^cal and Yamm is in many ways quite

similar to that between Marduk and Tiamat. One of these myths
is probably a reflex of the other, though it is difficult to
tell which was original.[63] It is necessary, therefore, in this
context to refer briefly to the relevant parts of Enūma eliš:
the election of Marduk, the combat with Tiamat and her forces,
and the events immediately following, particularly the building
of the palatial abode for Marduk -- Babylon and Esagila.

As Thorkild Jacobsen has shown, the democratic nature of
the assembly of the gods is a fundamental element in Enūma
eliš.[64] It places immediately to the fore the role of the assembly in the cosmic conflict. On both sides the attitudes and actions of the respective divine forces rank with and affect the
purposes of the principals involved. That is seen from the start
when the plan of Apsu and Mummu to destroy the gods was immediately communicated to the gods and apparently could not be kept
from them:

(Now) whatever they had plotted between them,
Was repeated unto the gods their first-born.[65]

The gods did not attempt on their own as an assembly or as
an army to oppose the forces that threatened them. What they
needed in the first place was a representative, a role taken by
Ea because of his wisdom and insight. Even more, they needed and
sought a leader in their battle against Tiamat, Kingu, and their
army.[66] But the role of the assembly itself was not a minor one,
as was recognized by Marduk when he sought kingship from the puḫrum, the assembly (Tab. II: lines 125ff.). Likewise Tiamat's
decision to march against the gods was at the instigation of the

deities around her, enraged at the other gods and set for combat.

When that decision was made, Tiamat's assembly lost no time in

planning the attack and equipping itself for battle. The lines

of the epic which recount these preparations make it clear that

her coterie was an army ready to march forth at her side with its

own commander-in-chief (Kingu), appointed by Tiamat and accepted

by the assembly.

> She has set up the Assembly and is furious with rage.
>
> All the gods have rallied to her;
>
> Even those whom you brought forth march at her side.
>
> They throng and march at the side of Tiamat,[67]
>
> Enraged, they plot without cease night and day.
>
> They are set for combat, growling, raging,
>
> They have formed a council to prepare for the fight.[68]

The democratic procedures of the assembly are clear. The gods

together, or at least a sizable segment of them, decided the

course of action and in this case, though not always, planned to

carry it out jointly. The dual nature of the *puḫrum* as delibera-

tive council or assembly and as an army is nowhere more obvious

than here where the two meanings have merged. Having met to draw

up its battle plans, the assembly has become an army prepared to

go out and do battle with the other gods. The familiar cliché

describing the going forth of the gods to aid in battle, which

appears in letters, historical inscriptions, and hymns is present

here also: *i-da-a-ša al-ku*, "they march at her side" (1.14).[69]

The appointment of Kingu is described as follows:

From among the gods, her first-born, who formed her

>Assembly,

She has elevated Kingu, has made him chief among them.

The leading of the ranks, command of the Assembly,

The raising of weapons for the encounter, advancing to

>combat

In battle the commander-in-chief. . .[70]

It was a diverse host that followed Kingu and Tiamat into

battle. Besides regular members of the divine assembly, there

were eleven new beings created by Tiamat, fearful to behold, mon-

ster serpents (II, 1.20), dragons (II, 1.23), and the like.

She has set up the Viper, the Dragon, and the Sphinx,

The Great-Lion, the Mad-Dog, and the Scorpion-Man,

Mighty lion-demons, the Dragon-Fly, the Centaur --

Bearing weapons that spare not, fearless in battle.[71]

On the other side of the conflict, Marduk was chosen as

leader by the members of the assembly, the Anunnaki (II, 88),the

Igigi (III, 126), and the great gods (III, 130) being specifi-

cally mentioned as among that body. Kingship was granted to him,

and in return he went forth with the gods who had crowned him to

battle Tiamat and her army (IV, 63-64). The vivid scene depict-

ing Marduk's preparation for battle makes clear that he assembled

various forces other than the gods of the assembly to his aid.

Functioning primarily as a storm god, Marduk summoned the winds,

the lightning, and the flood,[72] mounted his storm chariot drawn

by four steeds of destruction,[73] and backed by the gods and armed

with these cosmic forces, marched forth to meet Tiamat and her

army. He challenged her to single combat and in the ensuing
battle Tiamat was destroyed and her supporters captured. Victorious in the cosmic conflict, Marduk then created the universe,
and the gods erected a temple for him where he might dwell as
king.[74]

When one moves from *Enūma eliš* to the Ugaritic myth, it is
obvious that Ba'al parallels Marduk, the rising young god seeking kingship. That Yamm and Tiamat represent the same kind of
figure was already clear and is now confirmed by the equation *ym=*
^{d}*tamtu* in the "Ugaritic Pantheon" text.[75] Both myths represent
a type of rebellion among the gods and the struggle for kingship
or rule. Having said this, one must note also that the myths are
in a number of respects quite different. Each developed in its
own way.

Text 137 (= *CTA* 2.I) has as its setting a gathering of the
assembly in official fashion apparently for a banquet. The beginning of the text is broken, but enough remains to indicate
that the conflict between Ba'al and Yamm has already begun or is
foreshadowed here. With standard cliche Ba'al invokes the aid
of Ḥoron and 'Aṯtart against Yamm. Then the text switches abruptly to Yamm, who, in a clear-cut grab for power, sends his
messengers forth to the assembly to demand their surrender of
Ba'al to him. The terrifying effect of this message makes clear
that Yamm's action is not merely audacious; he is powerful enough
to frighten the whole assembly except Ba'al. Even El is scared.

At the sight of the messengers the gods cringe in fear:

(23) *tgly . ilm . rišthm . lẓr . brkthm . wlkht*

(24) *zblhm*

> The gods lower their heads upon their knees
>
> And on the thrones of their princeship.

But Ba^{c}al, not at all intimidated, rebukes (*yg^{c}r*, 1.24) the gods
and says:

(27) *šu . ilm . raštkm . lẓr . brkthm . ln . kht̠*

(28) *zblkm*

> Lift up, O gods, your heads from your knees,
>
> From the thrones of your princeship.

As Frank Cross has noted,[76] these lines form a very important
background for the warrior procession of Yahweh and his hosts in
Psalm 24:7 and 9. The cry of victory goes up:

> Lift up, O gates, your heads.

Cross assumes that this imagery cannot be explained on the basis
of raising the gates because to the best of our knowledge the
city had no gates that went up. This expression must have its
origin in the return of the victorious warrior god to the assembly after his defeat of the enemy. At Ugarit the shout is given
in the text prior to the battle, while in Psalm 24 it is uttered
on the return from battle. This is not as great a difference as
it might seem at first glance. On the one hand Ba^{c}al's cry is an
announcement of impending victory, an assurance that the messengers of Yamm need not be feared.   Even more important, in good
poetic and epic style it is to be expected that the cry, "Lift up
your heads, O gods," was repeated at Ba^{c}al's return. No record
of this repetition is left. One may suggest cautiously that the
shout of victory could have been repeated at the beginning of

Text 51 (= *CTA* 4) where about twenty lines are missing. This
break is just before the call for a castle for Ba⁽al, the natural result of his victory over Yamm. It is, of course, impossible to say for certain whether the repetition ever existed, but
there is no question that the cries in Text 137:27-28 (= *CTA* 2.I.
27-28) and Psalm 24:7, 9 are victory cries of the warrior god
and his host. The Old Testament version has been demythologized
only insofar as "the gods" are replaced by "the gates." The
imagery still remains that of the assembly, heads bowed in fear.
The conquest in holy war and cosmic war is followed by the triumphal return of the victor and his earthly or divine army.

There is no notice in these particular texts of an army with
the warrior god. That such was present in the context of Psalm
24 is obvious. In the Canaanite episode there certainly must
have existed a military retinue accompanying Ba⁽al. Other contexts reveal the presence of such a following with Ba⁽al. Lines
18 and 34-35 may suggest the same thing if one could be certain
to what ⁽*nn* and *hmlt* allude. The word ⁽*nn* in this case probably
refers to Ba⁽al's attendants, but whether there are two or a
larger group is unclear.⁷⁷ The comparable Marduk episode also
leads one to conclude that Ba⁽al was aided by a host of divine
beings. Whether these were the *ilm*, the *ǵlmm*, the *ḫnzrm*, the
rpum, the *il t⁽ḏr b⁽l*, etc., or all of these, one cannot tell.

The fright of the gods -- also to be compared with *Enūma
eliš* -- is due not only to the fact that Yamm has sent the messengers, but also to the appearance of the two messengers who
boldly interrupt the assembly.

(32) $i\check{s}t$. $i\check{s}tm$ $yitmr$

     $\d{h}rb$. $lt\check{s}t$ (33) $[l\check{s}/bym]nhm$

     A flame, two flames, they appear

     Sword(s) of sharpness, their tongue/in their right

     hands.[78]

The fear of the gods is understandable. The messengers of Yamm
appear as warriors, flaming and with swords. In another context
I have discussed this passage and the relationship of these fig-
ures to $i\check{s}t$ and $\underline{d}bb$ in ʿnt:III: 42-43 (= CTA 3.III.42-43) as well
as $Ph\bar{o}s$, Pur, and $Phlox$ in Philo Byblius.[79] For our purposes
here, however, it is important to stress again the significance
of these warrior messengers of fire, who strike fear into the
hearts of the gods, for the background of Israelite conceptions
of the heavenly host. There are numerous places in the Old Testament where the divine messengers or attendants are mentioned.
In quite a few of these cases they are pictured as warriors bearing sword in hand, for example, Genesis 3:24 where Yahweh places
the cherubim (the plural probably meaning two) at the east of the
Garden of Eden and a flaming, turning sword ($lah\d{a}t$ $ha\d{h}ereb$)
guarding the way of the tree of life. The cherubim and flaming
sword reflect the Canaanite fiery messengers or servants of Yah-
weh as $\bar{?e}\check{s}$ $l\bar{o}\d{h}e\d{t}$ (or better $\bar{?e}\check{s}$ $walaha\d{t}$) "fire (and) flame." The
several references to an angel or divine being with drawn sword
may also go back to this Canaanite conception. The $mal\bar{?}ak$ who
stopped Balaam (Num. 22:31), the commander of the army of Yahweh
(Josh. 5:13), and the $mal\bar{?}ak$ who brought pestilence as a result
of David's census (II Sam. 24:16ff. and especially I Chron. 21:

27, 30) all belong to this same imagery, although their swords
are not described as flaming.[80]

The other references to members of Yahweh's assembly reflect
the incendiary character of these mythological creatures themselves rather than of their weaponry. The account of Moses'
first encounter with Yahweh at Horeb says that the malᵃk Yahweh
appeared to him "in a flame of fire" ($b^elabbat$ᵉes).[81] The parallel with the $istm$ of Yamm is clear. The call of Isaiah takes
place in the context of the heavenly assembly of Yahweh. In the
vision Isaiah sees above Yahweh creatures (two?) called $s^erapîm$,
"burning ones (?)." These beings also may have originated in the
Canaanite imagery of the divine assembly and its fiery messengers.[82]

The above discussion has shown the significance of Text 137
(= *CTA* 2.I) for the portrayal of warrior motifs in the divine assembly at Ugarit as well as in the Old Testament. Text 68 (= *CTA*
2.IV) actually recounts the battle between Baᶜal and Yamm, although the end of Text 137 (= *CTA* 2.I) narrates a thwarted attempt by Baᶜal to strike the messengers of Yamm. Whether or not
Baᶜal and Yamm marched at the head of armies, the conflict itself
is one of single combat similar to the battle between Marduk and
Tiamat. Like Marduk, Baᶜal is provided with divine weapons whose
names reflect their purpose.[83] The object of the battles with
Tiamat and Yamm is the preservation and maintenance of kingship
over the gods.[84] *Ktr-w-Hss* says to Baᶜal before the battle (68:
10[= *CTA* 2.IV.10]):

tqḥ . mlk . ᶜlmk

drkt . dt drdrk

You will take your eternal kingdom

Your everlasting dominion.

And at the end of the battle (68:32[= *CTA* 2.IV.32])

ym . lmt . bᶜlm . yml[k   ]

Yamm indeed is dead; Baᶜal shall rule.[85]

This fact is confirmed by the cliché of the gods; "Our king is
Aliyan Baᶜal, our judge, and there is no one above him (51:IV:43–
44[= *CTA* 4.IV.43–44]).[86]

A necessary consequence of the establishment of kingship by
victory over the enemy, Sea, is the establishment of a palace or
sanctuary for the god as a sign of his victory and rule. Unlike
Enūma eliš where the gods immediately gave Marduk all he wanted,
Baᶜal has to beg, cajole, and threaten for his palace although
the other gods are regarded as already having palaces. In his
request, the account of which is narrated in Text 51 (= *CTA* 4)
and part of *ᶜnt* (= *CTA* 3), Baᶜal is aided considerably by ᶜAnat
and Aṯirat, and after the latter appeals to El, Baᶜal's wish is
granted.[87] *Kṯr-w-Ḥss* builds a magnificent palace, which is
burned until it turns into silver and gold, and a celebration is
prepared.

Then in column VII of Text 51 (= *CTA* 4) appears a crucial
passage which recounts the triumphal procession of the victorious
god to his palace. The first seven lines are broken, but they
appear to be further narration of the battle with Yamm (1, 4) in
which apparently Baᶜal once and for all does away with him. That

supposition is strengthened by the fact that henceforth Yamm is out of the picture, and Mot appears already by the end of this column as Ba^{c}al's principal antagonist. Furthermore, it is after the action described in these seven broken lines that Ba^{c}al makes his triumphal march to his palace establishing his rule. It is natural to suspect that this event took place *immediately after* his final annihilation of his enemy.

Lines 5 and 6 contain reference to Ba^{c}al's abode "on the mountain" (*bǵr*), "on Ṣaphon" (*bṣpn*) where his palace was established. Then beginning probably in line 7 is the actual narration of Ba^{c}al's march:

(7) $^c dr$. $1[--]$, $^c rm$

(8) $\underline{t}b$. $1pd[r?]$ $pdrm$[88]

(9) $\underline{t}t$. $1\underline{tt}m$. $a\underline{h}d$. $^c r$

(10) $\check{s}b^c m$. $\check{s}b^c$. pdr

(11) $\underline{t}mnym$. $b^c 1$. $[---?]$

(12) $t\check{s}^c m$. $b^c 1$. $mr[-?]$

(13) $bt[--]$ $b^c 1$. $bqrb$

(14) bt

(9)   Sixty-six cities he seized

Seventy-seven towns

Eighty (took) Ba^{c}al [   ]

Ninety Ba^{c}al of the sum[mit?]

[   ] Ba^{c}al in the midst of

the house

Having defeated Yamm, Ba^{c}al now marches victoriously to his palace conquering cities and towns on his way. It is quite probable

that Ba al was accompanied by his various military hosts, *il*
t‹dr b‹l, *ǵlmm*, *ḫnzrm*, *rpum*, etc.[89] He enters his house as the
mighty warrior,[90] hesitant no longer to put windows in the palace. The magnificent scene reaches its climax in lines 29-37:

(29) *qlh . qdš [.] b[‹l . y] tn*

(30) *ytny . b‹l s̩[at š]pth*

(31) *qlh . q[dš (?)]r . ars*[91]

(32) *[-----?] ǵrm . (.t/a) ḫšn*

(33) *rḫq [---------]*

(34) *qdmym . bmt . a [rs--]*

(35) tṯtn . ib . b‹l t(!)iḫd

(36) *y‹rm . šnu hd . gpt*

(37) *ǵr*

Ba‹al gives forth his holy voice;

Ba‹al repeats the utterance of his lips.

His holy voice . . . the earth,

. . . . . the mountains . . . .

Afar . . . .

East (and) west the high places of the earth?

wobble;[92] the enemies of Ba‹al take to

the woods; the haters of Hadd to the interior[93]

of the mountain.

Ba‹al stands in the midst of his palace as the storm god and warrior. The earth trembles at his holy voice. With Yamm destroyed
and all other enemies in flight, his rule is firmly established,
his palace is built, and he does not hesitate to challenge all
comers. The imagery of this scene is strongly reflected in the

warrior and storm concepts associated with Yahweh. Psalm 29,
generally regarded as a Canaanite hymn taken over into the Israelite cultus by the replacement of Ba^{c}al by Yahweh in the text,
pictures Yahweh in his palace (*hêkāl*, cf. Text 51 [= *CTA* 4] *passim*) surrounded by the gods, the divine ones. Enthroned upon the
flood, he gives forth his mighty voice, which causes the earth to
shake and tremble. If this psalm was originally a hymn to Ba^{c}al,
it must have been understood in the context of his victorious entry and enthronement in his palace (51:VII:42-44[= *CTA* 4.VII.42-
44]):

    (42) *bkm . ytb . b^{c}l . lbhth*

    (43) *umlk . ublmlk*

    (44) *arṣ . drkt yštkn*

        Thus Ba^{c}al is enthroned in his house

        Neither king nor no-king

        Shall establish the earth as a dominion.[94]

With these lines may be compared the climax of Psalm 29:10:

    yhwh lammabbûl yāšab

    wayyēšeb yhwh melek l^e^{c}ôlām

    Yahweh is enthroned on the flood

    Indeed Yahweh is king forever.

    The theophany passage of II Samuel 22 = Psalm 18 also has
striking affinities with the picture of Ba^{c}al in his palace. The
psalmist utters a cry, which is heard by Yahweh "from his palace"
(*mēhêkālô*, II Sam. 22:7). Then (Ps. 18:7):

    The earth did quake and shake,

    The foundations of the hills shuddered.[95]

Verse 14 is similar to 51:VII:29 (= *CTA* 4.VII.29). Even as "Ba^cal
gives forth his holy voice," "the Most High gives forth his
voice." Even as Ba^cal puts to flight his enemies and the ones
hating him, so it is said of Yahweh the warrior (II Sam. 22:18).

> He delivered me from my strong enemy,
>
> From the ones who hated me.[96]

The ancient war cry which was sung at the procession of the ark
to and from battle in the early holy wars of Israel is similar
to the description of the victorious Ba^cal in Text 51 (= *CTA* 4):

> Arise, Yahweh,
>
> Let thy enemies be scattered;
>
> Let the ones hating thee flee from before thee

Other passages could be pointed out, but enough has been said to
show that the picture of Yahweh as storm god, warrior, and king
bears striking resemblance to that of Ba^cal in the same roles in
Canaanite mythology.

The Ba^cal-^cAnat cycle gives further evidence of the role of
Ba^cal as warrior god, particularly in his conflict with Mot. This
conflict is essentially a fertility myth[97] involving the death
and renewal of life of both Ba^cal and Mot, but, as in the battle
with Yamm, the question of kingship is involved. Ba^cal's death
is cause for an attempt to produce a new king, but his return to
life is occasion for renewed battle to reestablish his kingship.
This conflict is recounted in columns V and VI of Text 49 (= *CTA*
6).

V   (1) *yihd . b^cl . bn . aṯrt*

    (2) *rbm . ymḫṣ . bktp*

(3)   *dkym . ymẖṣ . bṣmd*

(4)   *šḥr mt . ymṣẖ larṣ*

(5)   *[ytb.]b[ᶜ]l . lksi . mlkh*

(6)   *[bn dgn] lkẖt . drkth*

Baᶜal seizes the sons of Atirat.

Rabbim[98] he smites with a weapon (sword).[99]

Dokyam he smites with a mace.

Burning (?)[100] Mot he kicks to the earth.

The Son of Dagan sits on his throne of kingship,
          his seat of dominion.[101]

To gain his throne Baᶜal is forced to do battle with the sons of Atirat, among these apparently *rbm*, *dkym*, *mt*, who oppose him on other occasions. Having conquered these enemies, he then assumes his rule again, but another battle ensues, this time the final one between Baᶜal and Mot. This fight, recounted in column VI of Text 49 (= *CTA* 6), may have been a full-scale battle between Baᶜal and his coterie and Mot and his followers. There are references to the seven lads of Baᶜal (l. 8), the peoples (*limm*), and to beings whom Mot calls "my brothers." It is impossible to tell whether the plural verbs describing the battle refer only to Baᶜal and Mot or whether they may indicate the conflict between the two gods and their forces, but the fight results in the submission of Mot and the kingship of Baᶜal (ll, 34-35?).

There are other texts which refer to battles of Baᶜal, such as the fight with the "devourers" and "renderers" (Text 75[= *CTA* 12]) -- if it may really be called a fight -- and the references to Baᶜal's defeat of Tannin and Lotan (67:I:1ff.[= *CTA* 5.I.1ff.];

1001:1[= *PRU* II 1:1]). But the major battles are those with
Yamm and Mot when Ba'al fights for and with the gods with the
issues of kingship, sanctuary, and fertility at stake. The battle of the gods is the means whereby these three qualities of
world order -- divine and human -- are established.[102]

Ba'al's titles and epithets are further indications of cosmic warfare. The most important of these is *aliyn*, a hypocoris-
ticon from the verb *l'y*, "to prevail, be powerful." The title
also appears without the hypocoristic -- *ānu* ending as *aliy*. The
basic nuance of this epithet is clear; but the precision of meaning is hindered by two problems: what is the grammatical form of
the word without the hypocoristic ending; and to what extent does
the word *aliy(n)* originate in a longer cliché, which gives the
precise and original meaning?

As to the grammatical form and meaning of the word *aliy(n)*
two lines of thought are possible. One would be to view the word
as an elative adjective, "the most powerful,"[103] but several objections to that may be raised. Elatives, if they even existed
in Northwest Semitic, are at best quite rare in Canaanite.[104]
Furthermore, one would expect the form to be *'aqtal* rather than
'aqtil. Also the *-anu* ending would be unnecessary and peculiar
on the elative. A much more likely interpretation of the word is
that it is the first person imperfect of the *Qal* or G stem of *l'y*.
The pattern is precisely that of the third weak verbs, *'al'iyu*.
Its meaning would be "I prevail."

The *-anu* ending indicates that *aliy(n)* is a shortened form
of a longer phrase, a phenomenon quite common in Canaanite myth-

ology. The phrase is to be sought in the words which follow
aliy. Albright has proposed that the full formula may be seen
in the message of Ba°al to °Anat in°nt: III:11-12 (= *CTA* 3.III.
11-12) and IV:51-52 (= *CTA* 3.IV.51-52).[105] He maintains that the
full title was *ʾalʾiyu qurâdîma qâriyeya baʾarsi malḥamati*, "I
prevail over the heroes who meet me in the land of battle," but
Goetze has criticized this view by pointing out that *qryy barṣ
mlḥmt* is a part of the message itself, as evidenced by the fact
that °Anat replies in a series of first-person phrases beginning
with *aqry*.[106] In addition, it may be noticed that this message
is not given by Ba°al alone; El also repeats it (°*nt* pl. ix:II:
17-21[= *CTA* 1.II.17-21]).

    Goetze is probably basically right. The phrase *qryy barṣ
mlḥmt* must be separated from *aliy qrdm* unless one is to believe
that the meaning of the formula has been forgotten and part of it
cut off and associated with the message; but apparently out of
dissatisfaction with Goetze's interpretation of *qryy barṣ mlḥmt*,
Albright has maintained his original view. He has insisted correctly that the basic meaning of *qry* in Ugaritic is "to meet, oppose, encounter," as in Hebrew, rather than "to remove" as Goetze
maintains.[107] Goetze's analysis of *qryy* as an infinitive absolute also does not fully solve the problem of that word, which is
the *crux interpretatum* of the passage and does not appear to be
the same as the succeeding imperatives, *št* and *šk*.

    In any event, the parallelism: *thm aliyn b°l / hwt aliy qrdm*
indicates that the formula does not extend any further than *aliy
qrdm*. The presence of this parallelism in context where the mess-

age is different (67:II:10-11, 17-18[= *CTA* 5.II.10-11, 17-18];
51:VIII:32-35[= *CTA* 4.VIII.32-35]) makes it clear that the original epithet was *aliy qrdm*, "I prevail over the warriors."[108]
The title is a warrior epithet referring to Ba^{c}al's cosmic battles with the gods and, probably, to his aid in human conflicts.
Its connection with the gods is suggested not only by the narratives of Ba^{c}al's battles, but by the title or description he
gives his abode, Ṣaphon (^{c}nt: III:27-28[= *CTA* 3.III.27-28]):

(27) *bqdš . bǵr . nḥlty*

(28) *bn^{c}m . bgb^c tliyt*

    In the holy place, in the mount of my portion/

        inheritance

    In the pleasant place, in the hill of victory.[109]

The *gb^c tliyt* is not necessarily the place where the battles are
fought, but it is the locale of his rule and kingship won by battle.

Three other epithets appear to be connected with the warrior
characteristics of Ba^{c}al. One of these, *rkb ^{c}rpt*, "driver of the
clouds,"[110] arises out of the storm imagery associated with him
but reflects also his role as warrior and is often used when referring to him in this role.[111] The clouds are the war chariot
of the storm god as he goes to do battle.

Although attested in the mythological literature only once
and in a broken text then, the phrase *gmr hd* would appear to be
an epithet of Ba^{c}al meaning something like "Annihilator Hadad"
or "Avenger Hadad."[112] This phrase is also attested as a personal name in both Ugaritic and Akkadian texts from Ugarit. In *PRU*

II   4:16 and 107:12 *mgmr* appears as the name of a deity.

In Text 12, 1.4 of *Ugaritica* V there may appear a new Ba‘al
name -- *b‘l ‘rkm*. Virolleaud does not seek to translate the last
element but refers to the use of the plural participle of ‘rk in
Hebrew to refer to men equipped for battle (for example, I Chron.
12:34 and 36; cf. Jer. 6:23 and 50:42). One might also note the
divine appellation *yhwh ṣᵉbā’ôt ’ᵉlōhê ma‘arkōt yiśrā’ēl* (I Sam.
17:45) "Yahweh of hosts, God of the ranks of Israel." If ‘rkm
in the Ugaritic text is to be associated with these Hebrew uses
of ‘rk, then the name would be Ba‘al, the Man of War, or, better,
Ba‘al of the Ranks, referring to Ba‘al as a leader of armies like
ršp ṣbi.[113]

The name of Ba‘al in Philo's account is Demaros. This name
has been discovered in the Ugaritic texts in parallelism with
Aliyan Ba‘al and Hadad as *dmrn*. Pope connects this word with
Arab. *d̠mr*, "brave, mighty."[114] If he is correct, this title also
reflects the warrior nature of Ba‘al.[115] Two personal names
d̠mrb‘l (322:II:5[= *CTA* 102.II.5]) and *d̠mrhd* (322:VI:7[= *CTA* 102.
VI.7]) may be cited in this connection, meaning "Ba‘al/Hadad is
my warrior" or something similar.

Before looking at the role of ‘Anat as Ba‘al's warrior cohort, an examination of the Rephaim texts is in order here, as
possible further evidence of Ba‘al's military forces. These
texts are difficult to interpret and may not necessarily belong
to the Ba‘al-‘Anat cycle. They are usually associated with the
Aqhat legend, but there are important connections with Ba‘al and
‘Anat.

Because of the obscurity and very corrupt nature of the Rephaim texts (121-124[= *CTA* 20-22]) there will probably never be
complete agreement as to their   interpretation.[116]   There are
references to *il, b*l, *nt,* and *dnil,* but these do not greatly
illumine our understanding. The fact that *dnil* is mentioned has
led a number of scholars to connect these texts with the Aqhat
legend and the problem of Danel's progeny.[117] The etymological
basis of the word *rpum* has not been fully settled, but it has
been related to the roots *rpy,* "to sink, relax," and *rp*,*" "to
heal," with the latter root generally regarded as the proper etymology of the word. The *rpum,* commonly held to be shades or
ghosts, denizens of the world of the dead, are thought to heal in
that they restore to life. Thus Caquot concludes that the *rpum*
are the dead ancestors of Danel's family line; and these texts
are concerned with the restoration to life of Aqhat, who is
called "the healed one of Ba*al" (*rpu b*l*).[118]

This interpretation, which is masterfully argued, has many
plausible points, though not all are convincing. The following
comments are not meant to be an overall interpretation of these
texts from a different point of view but to emphasize particular
aspects of the *rpum* relevant to the conceptions of cosmic warfare among the Canaanites.[119] Regardless of the precise etymology of *rpum,* there are strong indications that these are divine
or semi-divine beings,[120] who function to some degree as a military coterie of one or more of the high gods, presumably Ba*al
and *Anat. The term *rpum* is regularly parallel to *ilnym,* a nominal plural form derived from a substantive *ln,* which survives

in Phoenician and means "god" (*ilnym* is parallel to *ilm* in *ᶜnt*:
IV:78-79[= *CTA* 3.IV.78-79]).[121] It may be, as has been suggested by Gaster, that the *ilnym* and *rpum* are the "upper" and "lower" gods of Canaanite mythology comparable to the Igigi and Anunnaki of Mesopotamian mythology.[122]

In Text 121:I:4 (= *CTA* 20.B.4) the *rpum* ride forth on their
chariots:

> *tᶜln . lmrkbthm . ti[ty   ]*

They mount on their chariots; they go

The picture of divine beings riding forth on chariots can hardly
be other than that of warriors riding out, even though in this
case they do not go to battle.[123] In addition, reference is made
more than once to *rpu bᶜl mhr bᶜl . wmhr ᶜnt*. Considerable disagreement exists among scholars as to whether *rpu* and *mhr* here
are singular[124] or plural.[125] While the problem cannot be solved
absolutely either grammatically or exegetically, since either
singular or plural is possible in the context, an interpretation
of the terms as plural is preferable because such interpretation
is consistent with the clear plural character of the term *rpum*
elsewhere and introduces no new problems such as the identity and
function of this new individual who is called *rpu bᶜl*.[126] If the
terms are plural, then these *rpum* are in some respects a military
host associated with Baᶜal and ᶜAnat, regardless of what other
function they may serve.[127] The noun *mhr*, as is clear from other
contexts, is to be translated as "warriors," "soldiers," or
heroes."

The fact that *rpu bᶜl* is paralleled by *mhr ᶜnt* as well as

mhr bᶜl is only one indication of the fact that ᶜAnat is a part-
ner in Baᶜal's fighting exploits. The Egyptian evidence for this
goddess shows her warlike character;[128] but even prior to her appearance in Egypt, the Ugaritic texts make clear the fact that in
the Canaanite religion and mythology of the second millennium B.
C. ᶜAnat was the warrior goddess *par excellence*. That was not
the only important aspect of her character; nor were the other
goddesses always peace-loving. A fluidity of personality and
character among the Canaanite goddesses makes it impossible to
separate out particular roles as belonging only to one or the
other. But in the Ugaritic texts as well as in Egypto-Canaanite
syncretism ᶜAnat's function as goddess of battle was primary.[129]

One of the basic aspects of this role was her association
with Baᶜal in his battles,[130] a fact most clearly brought out in
Baᶜal's address to her in Text 76:II:24-25 (= *CTA* 10.II.24-25):

(24) *nt̠ᶜn . bars̩ . iby*

(25) *wbᶜpr . qm . aḫk*

          We will plant my foes in the earth

          And in the dust those who rise against thy brother.
Baᶜal who is equipped for war with his bow and *qsᶜt* (arrows?)
calls ᶜAnat to join with him in battling his enemies.[131] That
she does so or has done so is seen in the fact that she partici-
pates in or claims participation in all of Baᶜal's major conflicts (*ᶜnt*: III:34-43[= *CTA* 3.III.34-43]):[132]

(34) *mn . ib . ypᶜ . lbᶜl .*

        s̩rt (35) *lrkb . ᶜrpt .*

        lmḫs̆t . mdd (36) *il ym*

        lklt . nhr . il . rbm

(37)   lištbm . tnn . išbm[n]h (?)

(38)   mḫšt . bṯn . ᶜqltn

(39)   šlyṯ . d . šbᶜt . rašm

(40)   mḫšt . mdd ilm . ar[š]

(41)   ṣmt . ᶜgl . il . ᶜtk

(42)   mḫšt . klbt . ilm . išt

(43)   klt . bt . il . ḏbb

        What enemy has risen against Baᶜal,

        Adversary against the Rider of the Clouds?

        Verily I smote the beloved of El, Yamm;

        Yea, I destroyed the River of El, Rabbim.

        Verily I muzzled Tannin, really muzzled him

        (And) smote the crooked serpent,

        Šalyaṭ of the seven heads.

        I smote the beloved of El, Ar[š]

        I exterminated the calf of El, ᶜAtak (ᶜtk).

        I smote the bitch of El, Fire;

        I destroyed the daughter of El, Flame.

Some of these creatures do not appear in conflict with Baᶜal. But

the only one of Baᶜal's opponents missing is Mot. Text 49 (= *CTA*

6) preserves in detail how ᶜAnat, enraged against Mot because of

his conquest of Baᶜal, made short work of him and scattered him

to fertilize the earth(?). It is therefore evident that much of

ᶜAnat's warring activity is in association with and in support of

Baᶜal and his forces.

    Yet ᶜAnat also fights on her own. One of the most unusual

and puzzling scenes in the Ugaritic texts is *ᶜnt*: IV (= *CTA* 3.IV),
her bloody massacre of many warriors. The context of this passage does not give a reason for the action. It may reflect some
sort of ritual associated with the cult of ᶜAnat, but the activity of the goddess appears to have little meaning along that
line. The most that can be said is that there is a type of blood
satiation here not entirely unknown elsewhere. A similar motif
is present in the attitude toward Kemoš reflected in the Mešaᶜ
Inscription as well as in some of the imagery associated with
Yahweh, such as appears in Isaiah 34. The important thing to
note is that the figures slaughtered by ᶜAnat, *lim* and *adm* (ll.
7-8) are human, not divine beings. This is the only occurrence
of the term *adm* except for the epithet of El, *ab adm*, which appears twice in Keret. The word *lim* occurs primarily in ᶜAnat's
epithet, *ybmt limm*. Whether there is any connection between this
puzzling epithet and the reference to *lim* in this context is a
tantalizing but unproductive question. In any event this passage
records the only occasion in the myths in which a god or gods are
engaged in battle with human beings. Furthermore, the human
beings are characterized as warriors: *dmr//mhrm* (ll.14-15) and
mhr//sbim//ǵzrm (ll.21-22).[133] It is thus important to note that
the pattern of the cosmic battle is sometimes projected onto the
realm of human life, producing conflict and battle between human
and divine elements.

The epithets of ᶜAnat, unlike those of Baᶜal, do not reflect
the warrior activity of this goddess. There may be, however, one
occurrence of an epithet pointing to ᶜAnat's bellicose character:

In Text 1004:12 (= *PRU* II.4.12) Virolleaud reads: *[l. e]lt . qb [l]*.[134] There can be no question about the first word, and the second is quite plausible. As Virolleaud points out, the Meso-potamian goddess Ištar bears the epithet *i-lat qab-li*, "Goddess of Battle."[135] If the reading is correct, the reference is sure-ly to ᶜAnat, the principal warrior goddess of the Ugaritic texts. ᶜAṯtart appears more than once in this text, and there is also a reference to *[   ] qdšt*, which would appear to be Aṯirat. ᶜAnat does not appear unless in line 12.

El as Divine Warrior[136]

Two excellent monographs have been written by Pope and Eiss-feldt on El,[137] so there is no necessity in this context for a lengthy general discussion of this deity. The thrust of most of the literature pertaining to him has been the assumption that while El is father of the gods and the "executive" deity of the pantheon at Ugarit, he is essentially a quiescent figure whose power seems rather limited when compared to that of other deities, whose fear of other gods is obvious, and whose gradual decline in the face of Baᶜal's rise to prominence seems clear. Pope espe-cially has pointed out that as far as the Ugaritic texts are con-cerned, El's actions and most of his epithets describe him as anything but a fierce warrior. Even a casual perusal of the texts reveals that fact and shows that El is on the way down, while Baᶜal, the young warrior, is on the way up.[138]

In the light of the published texts the above interpretation of the Ugaritic evidence is basically accurate. Some modifica-

tions in this general picture may be necessary, however, when
other sources are consulted and notice is taken of certain epithets and personal names. There is some evidence for a line of
tradition in Canaanite mythology which portrayed El in part as a
warrior deity or a deity whose might and power were recognized
and acclaimed.

That El still had a certain degree of power even in the
Ugaritic texts known at present is demonstrated in Text 49:VI:26-
31 (= *CTA* 6.VI):

(26)   *ik . al . yšm[ᶜ]k . ṯr* (27) *il . abk*

       l ysᶜ . alt (28) *ṯbtk*

       lyhpk . ksa . mlkk

(29)   *lyṯbr . ḫṭ . mṯptk*

(30)   *yru . bn . il < m > mt*

       ttᶜ . y (31) *dd . il . ǵzr*

How will Bull El, your father, not hear you?

Verily he will pull out the supports of your dwelling,

Yea overturn the throne of your kingship,

Verily he will break the scepter of your dominion.

Divine Mot was afraid,

Was fearful the beloved of El, the hero.[139]

In these lines the threat of El's hostility strikes fear into the
heart of Mot, but El's power is confined largely to the matter of
dispensing kingdoms, and Mot's fear is thus not of battle with
him but of loss of his rule. One could not conclude from these
lines alone that El was honored in any major way as a god of battle.

Yet the assumption that El was in no way a warlike deity leaves some questions unanswered. One could ask, for example, how El could ever have been king and ruler of the gods without some manifestation of his warrior might. In the human realm it was leadership in war that led to kingship or helped establish it;[140] so in the divine world one would expect such leadership, particularly in Mesopotamian and Canaanite mythology.[141] The status of El and Ba‛al, as well as of other gods, is in flux in the Ugaritic texts. The mythological world was no more a static phenomenon than the human world, though repetition and maintenance of the status quo were basic aspects of that world. It may have been, therefore, that the character of El was in process of change and that a warlike spirit was more manifest at one moment or place than at another.[142]

The second question concerns the relationship between El of Canaanite religion and Yahweh of Israelite religion. Did all the warrior aspects of Yahweh's nature come from nowhere or only under the influence of the image of Canaanite Ba‛al? Certainly there are clear and unmistakable similarities to Ba‛al as the storm god and warrior, and these are frequently pointed out. But the early associations of Yahweh, if one may speak of such, were with El more than with Ba‛al.[143] How does what is known of the warrior character of El or the lack of such fit in with that fact?

Philo Byblius' account of the "Phoenician History" of Sanchuniathon, the other basic source for Canaanite mythology, may give an answer or at least a clue. Accepting the need for caution, as stated earlier, one cannot ignore Philo's account when it gives a radically different picture of El (that is, Kronos) from that in most of the Ugaritic texts. In Philo-Sanchuniathon, Kronos is a much more arrogant, domineering god, who ruthlessly runs things his way, even dispatching his own progeny for the sake of expediency. The center of attention is focused upon this deity rather than upon Ba\`al/Demaros, as is the case in the Ugaritic texts, despite the fact that in the first millennium Ba\`al is the dominant deity in Syria-Palestine. Like Ba\`al, Kronos, as he is described by Sanchuniathon, does not hesitate to fight any of his enemies.

The particular passage most relevant to this discussion is *Praeparatio evangelica* I:10:17-21, concerning Kronos' first rebellion against his father, Uranos. Pope has convincingly stressed the similarity of this competition of the successive generations of gods to that recounted in the Kumarbi mythology[144] of Hurrian mythology.[145] He has also pointed out that the displacement of El/Kronos by Ba\`al/Demaros may be present in the Ugaritic texts.[146] The account, therefore, of Kronos' displacement of Uranos, which corresponds to Kumarbi's dethronement and banishment of Anu, would appear to be reliably archaic and authentic.

And Kronos having become a man, using the advice and assistance of Hermes Trismegistos -- for this one was his secretary -- he repels his father Uranos, avenging his mother. And to Kronos are born children, Persephone and Athena. Now the first died a virgin, but by the judgment of Athena and Hermes, Kronos made from iron a sickle and a spear. Then

Hermes, conversing in magic words with the allies of Kronos,
made (in them) a desire for battle against Uranos on behalf
of Ge. And thus Kronos engaged in war, drove Uranos away
from his sovereignty, and succeeded to the kingdom.[147]

El/Kronos is thus described in Philo as a god who does battle
against his enemies.[148]   In the total picture which Philo gives
of Kronos he is hardly less a warrior god than any of the other
deities. One of the most important pieces of information provided by this passage is that Kronos is regarded as having *allies*
around him -- *tois tou Kronou summachois*. This fact agrees with
the evidence of the Ugaritic texts. For the "allies" can hardly
be separated from the *pḫr il* or the *dr (bn) il* of these texts and
elsewhere and are to be compared with the *il t ͑dr b ͑l*, "the gods
who help Ba ͑al." The *il t ͑dr b ͑l* and the *tois tou Kronou summachois* are semantically equivalent, that is, the gods who help
Ba ͑al and the gods who kelp Kronos = El. The *summachoi* are the
divine assembly or at least a part of it. This relationship is
confirmed in Philo's account in paragraph 20:

   hoi de summachoi Ēlou tou Kronou Elōeim epeklēthēsan

And the allies of Elos, that is, Kronos, were surnamed Eloim.
The allies of El are specifically the gods. Here as elsewhere
Philo testifies to conceptions similar to or the same as those of
the Ugaritic myths. Another reference apparently to these divine
beings gives further information (*Praepar. evang.* I:10:37):

   *tois de loipois theois duo hekastō pterōmata epi tōn ōmōn
   hōs hoti dē suniptanto tō Kronō*

But to the rest of the gods two wings to each on the

shoulders in order that they might fly with Kronos.
In Canaanite and general Near Eastern religions,[149] wings were
a well-known characteristic of gods and goddesses, as well as of
subordinate beings, such as cherubim and seraphim. Here also the
gods are associated with El/Kronos as a sort of coterie accompanying him in his exploits.

The "allies of Kronos" are first mentioned when Hermes creates in them a desire to battle Uranos. The word *summachoi* (and
its related forms) has a definite military connotation. It means
"fighting along with, leagued, or allied with." In paragraph 17
reference is made to the alliance (*summachian*) of Ge, which enabled her to ward off the attacks of Uranos. The alliance in
that case refers definitely to a warrior host which fought along
with or for Ge. So also the result of Hermes' intervention with
the allies of Kronos is that Kronos makes war against Uranos and
drives him out. Thus there can be little question that it is
Kronos *and* his host who subdue Uranos, even though the allies are
not mentioned in the sentence which tells of the conflict. One
may see explicitly here what is perhaps implicit elsewhere, that
when a conflict ensues between two gods, it may be more than
single combat; the battle may involve the various divine or cosmic forces of the antagonists. Uranos also has allies (*summachōn*)
which he sends against Kronos on another occasion (para. 23).
These lines picture Kronos-El as a deity with a host that assists
him in battle. He functions in much the same way as Baʿal. His
belligerent nature is further reflected in his final *coup de
grâce* to Uranos and his murder of his son and daughter and his

brother. The picture of El in Sanchuniathon's history is thus
quite different from that in the texts from Ugarit.[150]

In the light of Sanchuniathon's description one is led to
ask whether there is further evidence of the might and warring
ability of El. Fragmentary and abbreviated though it may be,
such evidence is present in the names and epithets. One possible example is the name itself of the god -- ʾēl. Numerous suggestions for the etymology of the name have been proposed, some
incredible, others at least possible.[151] The most likely still
remains that of W. F. Albright, who says that the word ʾēl "was
almost certainly an adjectival formation (intransitive participle) from the stem ʾwl, meaning 'the strong, powerful one.'"[152]
Perhaps certitude is not possible at this point, but there is no
question that some etymology exists for the name of El as it
does for the other gods and goddesses of Ugarit and elsewhere.
Albright's proposal is plausible and not unlike other name formations of deities

Even more significant is one of El's most common appella-
tives at Ugarit -- *tr*, "Bull." This epithet has generally been
interpreted as referring to his procreative powers,[153] but such
an interpretation may be on the wrong track. To be sure, El has
other epithets, such as *bny bnwt*, "Creator of Created Things,"
and *ab adm*, "Father of Man." But neither of these is necessarily
to be taken as referring to procreation. The latter especially
is probably indicative of a social relationship rather than a
physical one.[154] El was of course the creator or begetter of the
gods, but in the one instance where we have any description of

his involvement in the procreation he does a very poor job and
hardly deserves the title "Bull."[155] And the fact remains that
in the Ugaritic texts Ba^cal, not El, is a fertility god and
proves his procreative powers, whereas El fails to prove his.

The bull, however, has a dual symbolism in the ancient Near
East. At times it is a symbol of fertility, but it is primarily
a symbol of strength, of might, and of fighting prowess, both in
the realm of the gods and in the realm of men.

The evidence of the Ugaritic texts agrees with this interpretation. Ba^cal is associated with the bull, albeit more in
artistic representation than in literary description. In Text
75 (= *CTA* 12) the "devourers" and "renderers" born to the "maid
of Athirat" are described as bulls with Ba^cal's face. The same
text later describes the fallen Ba^cal with the same language used
to characterize his attackers. ^cAnat too is spoken of as one
who has "horns of strength."

There is no question that the bull imagery in the Old Testament is indicative of might and strength. When applied to Yahweh it can hardly have anything to do with fertility. In other
contexts also the imagery of the bull and of the horns appears
as a symbol of strength and warring power. Elsewhere in the ancient Near East the bull is used to characterize gods, kings, and
pharaohs as strong warriors.[156]

Two other possible epithets of El suggest his role at some
time and place as a mighty or warrior god. If Frank Cross is
correct in his analysis of the name and figure of Yahweh,[157] then
El may have had as an early epithet *^ʾēl, ḏū yahwī sabaʾōt, "El

who creates the (heavenly) armies,"[158] which became *(dū) yahwī
sabaʾōt when Yahweh split off from El and is now preserved as
Yahwe ṣᵉbāʾot.[159] Similarly the phrase ʾēl gibbôr (Isa. 9:5),
which appears in a context that probably goes back to the early
days of the Israelite monarchy,[160] may also have been originally
an ancient epithet of the Canaanite El, that reflected his power
as warrior.

     Personal names having an ʾēl element have frequently been
dismissed as of little value because they tell us nothing significant about the deity.[161] This dismissal, however, may be a
little premature.[162] They at least can serve to corroborate information gained elsewhere and enlighten us as to various conceptions of the deity held by those who used such names. Certainly
it can hardly be doubted now that the ʾēl element frequently refers to the particular deity El rather than being always a generic term.[163] Of central importance in this regard is the appearance of the name ilmhr (UT 2029:18) in recently published
Ugaritic texts, a name which means "El is a warrior,"[164] but
there are a number of other names which suggest the might and
power of El, for example, Ugaritic mril, translated by Gordon,[165]
"God [El] is strong," and Old Testament Pagʿi-ʾel (Num. 1:13;
etc.), "El attacks" or "El strikes down."[166] A.R. Murtonen in
his list of West Semitic El names includes the following:[167] ʾlᶜz
(Old South Arabic, Hebrew), "El is strength"; ʾlpr (Nabatean),
"El is a bull (= strong)"; mr il (Arabic, Nabatean), "El has commanded"; *gbr(y)ʾl (Hebrew name appearing in Greek form), "El is
my strength"; grmʾl (Arabic, Nabatean), "El is strong"; dmrʾl

(Old South Arabic), [168] "El is strong"; ḥqm'l (Old South Arabic),
"El has strengthened"; yḥzq'l (Hebrew), "El is strong" or "El
strengthens"; sb'l (Arabic), "El is a lion (= strong)"; ᶜz(y)'l
(Arabic, Hebrew), "El is (my) strength"; Murtonen also mentions
the Amorite name *ṣb'')l, that is, Ṣi-ba-HAL (< AN), which he
translates "A Warrior of El." If his analysis of the element
ṣi-ba- is correct, a better translation would be "Army of El."
Huffmon, however, in his study of the Amorite names from Mari,
analyzes the element as a verbal form from *ṣbw -- "to desire."[169] Another uncertain name is ᶜzr'l or 'lᶜzr which may
contain either the root ᶜzr I -- "to help" or the root ᶜzr II --
"to be strong, mighty."

This list of names, to which others could perhaps be added,
covers a wide temporal and geographical span. Rather than vitiate the accumulated force of the listing, this fact simply makes
it even more clear that the deity El, worshiped in various forms
and in various places, was regarded as a deity of strength and
might.

New evidence for the strength and might of El may be found
in *Ugaritica* V, Text 2 (RS 24.252) where he appears as one of the
central figures, apparently bearing the title rpu mlk ᶜlm.[170] If
this appellation does refer to El, then we have in this text several references to the might of El. He is called in one place
gṯr wyqr, "Strong and Precious." In lines 6 and 7 of the *verso*,
which is broken, ᶜz and ḏmr, "strength and might," appear in
parallel and related to rpu mlk ᶜlm. Also in line 9 we have ᶜzk
ḏmrk l[a]⌈n⌉k, "your strength, your might, your [vic]tory,"

phraseology which in part may be compared with Exodus 15:2, a
most interesting parallel if the Ugaritic phrase refers to El.[171]
The Israelite poet in the song of victory with reference to Yahweh uses a word series familiar from Canaanite circles where it
was apparently applied to El.

Finally, it may be suggested that in light of the evidence
above, more significance is to be attached to El's role in *Krt* A
(= *CTA* 14). After the death of Keret's father, El comes to him
in a dream, giving him elaborate instructions about planning a
military expedition to seek another wife and describing at length
the preparations to be made for the army, the people and number
that are to march forth, and the way of the march. The fact that
elsewhere in the Keret epic El exercises special care of Keret,
who is also described as *bn il* (*UT* 125:20[= *CTA* 16.I.20]), does
not diminish in significance the fact that it is El here who commands Keret to go to war; and it is under his aegis that Keret --
after first sacrificing to both El and Baʿal, as well as engaging
in ritual purification -- marches out, even though battle is not
necessary in order to accomplish his desire for offspring. Regardless of the motive for the expedition, El is here found commanding a military encounter and receiving along with the warrior
god Baʿal the sacrifices necessary for its good outcome. This
account can hardly be separated from that body of evidence which
pictures the Canaanite deity El as strong and mighty, even a warrior at times.

Conclusion

In the mythology and religion of Canaan, as in Mesopotamia and elsewhere, notions of cosmic conflict were prominent: the warrior gods and goddesses who battled one another for the main- tenance of order, kingship, and fertility; the involvement of the gods in human conflict; the imagery of the divine assembly, or segments of it, as a warrior host marching with and helping the great gods. The Old Testament recognizes that from earliest times Israel's religion was strongly influenced by Canaanite mythology, and the Ugaritic texts further confirm this fact. Al- though constantly in reaction against the religion of Canaan, Israel drew upon this store of religious language and imagery to express her own faith even when it was in mortal combat with that of the Canaanites. For this reason the preceding pages have gone into great detail to describe the Canaanite conception of the di- vine warrior and his conflicts with other gods as a setting against which the early religious conceptions of Israel may be examined. There are many similarities, emphasizing once again that Yahwism did not develop in a vacuum but, as is true of all religious phenomena, related itself to its context and environ- ment by processes of integration, assimilation, subordination, and rejection.

Building upon the pioneer work of Alt, more recent studies by Eissfeldt and others have shown that the figure of Yahweh must be seen in strong relationship to the figure of Canaanite El. This discussion has taken a major step forward with the recent work of Frank Cross, who has demonstrated more forcefully than

ever the influence of the figure of El upon that of Yahweh, albeit along different lines and with somewhat different conclusions from those of Eissfeldt.[172] In the light of this work some
important conclusions may be drawn with regard to the Canaanite
deities El and Ba'al and the Israelite deity Yahweh.

There can be no doubt that in many respects the imagery associated with Yahweh is the same as that associated with Ba'al,
particularly with regard to Yahweh as warrior. He battles as the
storm god, riding or driving the clouds. He sends forth his
voice and the enemies flee. He battles the monsters of the deep
who represent death and chaos, as does Ba'al. Some of these
creatures have the same names in the Ugaritic texts and in the
Old Testament. Noting the similarities already mentioned (Text
137 [= CTA 2.I] and Ps. 24), one may assume that the direct contact with Ba'alism from an early period strongly influenced the
way Israel conceived its God.[173]

The question still remains, however, as to the role El
played in the understanding of Yahweh as warrior. That question
is emphasized by the strong rejection in normative Yahwism of the
worship of Ba'al, whereas from an early stage on, Yahweh seems
to have been strongly related to El, as Cross, Eissfeldt, and
others have shown. Part of the answer is to be seen in the fact
that Ba'al and El shared certain characteristics which must have
been assimilated in the character of Yahweh. Such could be the
case with regard to the role of war leader. At Ugarit, however,
it is Ba'al, the god rejected by Israel, who is war leader,
whereas El, who appears to have borne kinship with Yahweh, is not

primarily a warrior or the leader of a military host, although
in the preceding pages we have shown some indications of his warlike character even at Ugarit. The assimilation of Baʿal's
characteristics by Yahweh could easily have resulted from the
frequent tendency to syncretism and apostasy. One would expect,
nevertheless, that the El figure would have manifested more influence upon the warrior aspect of Yahweh's role, which was *central* to Israel's early conception of her god. The Ugaritic texts
in themselves do not suggest such influence. Philo, however,
paints a different picture of El and suggests that also in the
imagery of divine or cosmic warfare the association of Yahweh and
El may have been strong.

One can no longer explain the differences between the Ugaritic picture of El and that of Philo or Sanchuniathon by ignoring
the latter as erroneous; too much of Philo's account has been
shown to agree with the earlier material. It is especially in
the conflict with Uranos, the passage most relevant in this discussion, that Pope and others have shown strong ties with earlier
myths.

If the Canaanite mythology of Philo cannot be ignored or dismissed, the most plausible explanation of the conflicting pictures of El is that the description in Philo, which is literarily
the latest, actually represents an earlier stage in the tradition,
which was still discernible at Ugarit in epithets -- certainly
very ancient -- and an occasional personal name, as well as one or
two episodes in the Baʿal and Keret cycles, where the center of
interest in the theogony was passing on to Baʿal, but which may

have lasted on in the El religion of South Canaan and through
that carried over into the conception of Yahweh. Philo's account would thus represent a tradition from an earlier stage or
even a different area of Canaan and explain some of the differences in an otherwise rather homogeneous picture.

Pope has briefly hinted at this approach when he notes that
El "in his earlier years" may have been capable of the deeds ascribed to him in Philo.[174] More important still is his recognition that El's displacement by Ba^cal "need not have been general
over all the area in which El was worshiped. . . . The El of the
patriarchs was the god with whom YHWH was identified."[175] D. N.
Freedman has also pointed out that the identification of El and
Yahweh in the patriarchal traditions reflects an earlier stage
of Canaanite religion than that depicted in the Ugaritic
texts.[176] Sanchuniathon's picture of El as the warrior leading
his hosts into battle must belong to that earlier stage preserved
in South Canaan where, as Cross has noted, some sort of cultic
unity must have bound the patriarchal elements with those people
who in the Late Bronze Age formed a tribal confederation centering in the worship of Yahweh.[177] The centrality of El in the few
pieces of decipherable epigraphic material from southern Canaan
as well as the tendency to identify El with the strong creator
god, Ptah of Memphis, who was at his height at this time,[178] testifies further to the preservation of an El tradition similar to
that of Sanchuniathon in the area in which the relationship between El and Yahweh developed.

In this light, epithets such as *ʾēl gibbôr* and * *ʾel dū yahwī* *ṣabā'ōt* make more sense. Thus the imagery of Yahweh as warrior

god, leader of the cosmic armies (see next part) -- an imagery

central to Israel's religion from earliest times -- was a basic

aspect of the concept of deity in the ancient Near East but bore

special affinities to the warlike character of the Canaanite gods

El and Ba al with whom contact was intimate and from whom certain

other aspects were assimilated into the Israelite understanding

of Yahweh and his rule of the universe.[179]

PART TWO

COSMIC WAR AND HOLY WAR IN ISRAEL

The gods of Canaanite mythology and religion in particular
and of Near Eastern mythology in general fought their wars to
maintain or enhance their own positions in the divine world, to
save or punish peoples of the earth, and to ensure and preserve
order in the universe. In this interrelation of the cosmic and
the historical, such fundamental matters as kingship, salvation,
creation, and the building of temples were related to and depended upon the military activities of the gods and their armies.
So in Israel's understanding of deity, developed as it was in interaction with other cultures of the Near East, her early wars
were in fact "the wars of Yahweh." The primal acts of deliverance and the process of forming a people or nation centered in
these wars of Yahweh when as commander of the armies of heaven
and earth he fought for Israel. This imagery of the divine warrior thus became a major factor in the formation of Yahwism and
continued so throughout Israel's history.

The sources for this study are, first of all, Old Testament

texts from the early history of Israel into the tenth to ninth
centuries. Literary material that can be dated with a high degree of probability provides valuable historical control, so we
shall focus in this part on the early history.[1] When dealing with
language and imagery, and sometimes even with cultic matters,
however, one may eliminate valuable evidence by imposing precise
temporal restrictions, evidence which belongs to the subject matter under investigation and which often has an older history than
the present literary setting reflects. Thus passages which illu-
minate the subject but are somewhat later will also be used.
This material further serves the valuable function of confirming
the continuity in later traditions of the themes under study
here.

Both prose and poetry furnish significant data. Prose emphasizes more often the historical practice of holy war, while
poetry tends to emphasize the mythopoeic, the cosmic. It must be
noted, however, that these distinctions, to some degree inherent
in the nature of the material, are not rigid. Indeed, it is where
the situation is reversed and the prose narrative points to the
intervention of divine or cosmic elements while the hymnic literature reflects the mundane aspects of Israel's warfare along with
the activity of the divine warrior and his hosts (for example,
Judg. 5), that the fusion or conjunction of the human and the cosmic is most clearly seen.

Different types of poetic literature are relevant to the
subject at hand, indicating that while form-critical questions
are important, conclusions are not drawn merely by determining

the *Sitz im Leben* of a single particular genre.[2] Rather, the
various types, together with their language, provide the basis
for determining conclusions. The principal concern, therefore,
in the exegetical comments which follow is recognition within
the text of how Israel understood her god -- Yahweh as creator
and leader of the warrior hosts of the cosmos coming to Israel's
aid -- a conception determined both by the language, that is, the
imagery, and by genre and structure.[3]

The Divine Council in Israelite Thought
Nature and Function

In many respects the Israelite notion of a divine assembly
was quite similar to that of the surrounding cultures, particu-
larly Canaan and Mesopotamia, and assuredly adapted from them.[4]
As described in the Old Testament this assembly consists of a
largely nebulous array of divine beings called $\partial^e l\bar{o}h\hat{i}m/b^e n\hat{e}\ \partial^-\hat{e}l\hat{i}m$
$q^e d\bar{o}\check{s}\hat{i}m$, $b^e n\hat{e}\ \,^c ely\hat{o}n$ (Ps. 82:6), $\,^c b\bar{a}d\hat{i}m$ (Job 4:18; Isa. 44:26),
$m^e\check{s}\bar{a}r^e t\hat{i}m$ (Ps. 104:4), $m\bar{e}l\hat{i}\d{s}$ (Job 33:23),[5] $r\hat{u}ah$ (I Kings 22:21;
Ps. 104:3-4),[6] $\,^c\bar{e}d$ (Job 16:19),[7] or in totality $\,^c{}^a dat\ \,{}^> \bar{e}l$ (Ps.
82:1), $d\bar{o}r$ (Amos 8:14),[8] $s\hat{o}d\ q^e d\bar{o}\check{s}\hat{i}m$ (Ps. 89:8), $q^e hal\ q^e d\bar{o}\check{s}\hat{i}m$
(Ps. 89:6), $m\hat{o}\,^c\bar{e}d$ (Isa. 14:13), $s\hat{o}d\ yhwh$ (Jer. 23:18), $s\hat{o}d\ \,^>e l\bar{o}ah$
(Job 15:8), and $\,^c{}^a nan\hat{e}\ \check{s}^e mayy\bar{a}\,^>$ (Dan. 7:13).[9] The somewhat enig-
matic creatures called $k^e r\hat{u}b\hat{i}m$ appear to have been regarded as
mythical creatures belonging to the divine assembly (for example,
Gen. 3:24 where $k^e r\hat{u}b\hat{i}m$ guard the gate of Eden) as were the $\check{s}^e r\bar{a}$
$p\hat{i}m$ (Isa. 6:2-6).[10] The members of the assembly functioned al-
most entirely anonymously and as a whole, with the principal ex-

ceptions of the *śāṭān* of Job and elsewhere and the *mal'ak yhwh*, who plays a major role at many points and is often identifiable with Yahweh himself.

The host of heaven, *s^{e}bā' haśśāmayim*, also function as a part of the divine assembly.[11] Micaiah ben Imlah in his vision of the divine council sees standing about Yahweh "all the host of heaven" (II Kings 22:19). This host includes the sun, the moon, and the stars (Deut. 4:19 and 17:3) and is identified with the angelic host (Ps. 103:20-21; Ps. 148:2-3). In Job 38:7 *kôk-^{e}bê bōqer*, "morning stars," appears in parallelism with *b^{e}nê 'elōhîm*. G. Westphal in an old but very important article has pointed out the basic military connotation of the term *s^{e}bā' haśśāmayim*.[12] The shift here between "host," "army," and "council" appears in other Semitic languages, for example, Akkadian *puḫru*, which can mean either "assembly" (divine or human) or "army," that is, a military assembly.[13] The military function of the divine council, which is a primary one, is elaborated in detail in the following pages.

But the assembly served also as judicial court (Ps. 82; Job 1--2; Zech. 3).[14] Psalm 82 particularly presents the members of the council as responsible for giving justice to the weak, the poor, the fatherless, and pronounces a sentence of death against the gods because of their failure to administer that responsibility. This was one of the ways Israel dealt with the phenomenon of the presence of divine beings over against the fact of the total rule of Yahweh in the divine realm. Although in this context (probably a relatively early one) the gods were sentenced

to death, they nevertheless remained in Israelite thought as
ministers and servants of Yahweh. The centrality of the concern
for justice is nowhere more dramatically or forcefully presented
than in this psalm and testifies to the importance that the conception of the divine assembly held in Israelite culture.

The judicial role of the assembly relates also to another
important function, that of bearing the message of the deity Yahweh, a message which is often a judicial verdict. The assembly
itself may be addressed by Yahweh or one of his messengers and
called upon to perform a task. The opening sentences of Second
Isaiah (Isa. 40:1ff.) with their plural imperatives provide an
excellent illustration of Yahweh's addressing his messengers.[15]
In the following verses the herald voices transmit the directives
of Yahweh to the council. Often the *mal'ak yhwh* is named specifically as Yahweh's messenger who addresses either the council or
Israel.

In several instances the messenger of the council is a prophet. The most notable illustrations of this phenomenon are the
call of Isaiah in chapter 6, when he is cleansed and sent to proclaim to the people, and the vision of Micaiah (I Kings 22) which
is transmitted to the king. Other examples could be cited, but
it is sufficient to say that the conception of a divine assembly
around the throne of Yahweh formed a basic element in the Israelite understanding of prophecy. The prophet was one who stood in
the council of Yahweh. His task was the proclamation of the will
and message of Yahweh as declared in the heavenly assembly. It
is rather surprising, therefore, that the fundamental role of the

council of Yahweh in the nature and function of Israelite prophecy has been so little recognized by those who have dealt with
that subject.[16]   Not only are the passages cited above clear indication, but Jeremiah is very explicit about the fact that the
true prophet is distinguished from the false by the fact that the
true prophet has stood in the council of Yahweh.

> For who has stood in the council ($s\hat{o}d$) of Yahweh to see and
>   hear his word . . .
> But if they had stood in my council, they would have caused
>   my people to hear my words. (Jer. 23:18,22)

Finally, one may note the role of the council as a worshiping coterie in the divine theophany. The clearest example is the
early hymn Psalm 29 in which the $b^e n\hat{e}$ $\hat{e}l\hat{i}m$ are called to bow
down and worship Yahweh at his appearance. The theophany of Yah-
weh and his hosts in the wars of Israel is discussed below.

Comparison and Contrast with the Divine Assembly
of Other Near Eastern Religions

There are marked similarities and dissimilarities in the
conception of the divine assembly in the mythology and religion
of Mesopotamia, Canaan, and Israel. The basic notion of a council of divine beings grouped around a particular deity or deities
is common to all. So is the fact that these are largely anonymous
creatures, despite a tendency toward specific identification in
the more polytheistic religions. Also, the terminology is almost
exactly the same in Israel and Canaan, differences being rather
minor with one notable exception. The most common designation
for the assembly in both Mesopotamian and Canaanite mythology is

puḫur (Ugar. pḫr, mpḫrt) or, more fully, puḫur ilāni (Ugar. pḫr
ilm, pḫr bn ilm) -- terminology which appears nowhere in the Old
Testament. This absence is striking in view of the general du-
plication of terms and must have an explanation. It could be
that the absence of the term puḫru represents a conscious rejection of an aspect of Canaanite mythology, but such an hypothesis
is quite unlikely in view of the fact that there is little hesitation in using other terminology to express the same thing, some
of which must have appeared in Israel under direct Canaanite influence. A more likely explanation is that a lexical shift took
place in which puḫru fell out of use in Hebrew while the term
ṣābāʾ, a word foreign to Ugaritic and Akkadian as a designation
for the divine host, became the common one in Hebrew.[17]

One notes further the fact that the divine assemblies of
these cultures all included the heavenly host, the sun, moon, and
stars. A major difference, however, is the fact that Israel's
was basically a monotheistic faith in which these heavenly beings
were not independent, self-sufficient, major deities, but simply
a part of the large group of divine beings subject to the will of
Yahweh, whereas elsewhere they maintained independent status as
major deities. The fact, however, that the Israelite concept included the heavenly host (again an explanation within her own
framework of existence of divine phenomena in surrounding
cultures)[18] opened the door to a possible elevation of these elements to a status equal with Yahweh so that they might be worshiped in their own right. This is precisely what happened in
the seventh century (II Kings 21:5; 23:5).[19]

Another marked similarity, especially between Israel and
Canaan, is the imagery of the messenger to and from the god(s).[20]
The messenger is called a *mal⁾āk* in both Hebrew and Ugaritic,
although Ugaritic also uses the term *t⁽dt*. In the Ugaritic texts
messengers carry the proclamation of one god to another or even
to the whole council (for example, Text 137 [= *CTA* 2.I]). So
also as indicated above, Yahweh in the Old Testament sends
heralds with a message or command to the council. In both cases
we actually have the appearance of the messengers in the assembly
and see strong similarities in them, particularly in regard to
their rather warlike mien. In addition, one of the basic stylistic characteristics of the message formula in the Old Testament -- a series of imperatives -- is often a characteristic of
the message style in the Ugaritic texts.

There are also some differences between Israelite and Canaanite religion with regard to the messenger imagery. In Ugaritic these messengers often have definite names. That tendency
was a rather late development in Israel, reflecting a growing
preoccupation in later stages with the council and its constituency. Fierce competition with the Canaanite cult in Israel's
early history forbade this preoccupation with details in that
time. The messengers of Canaanite mythology also appear to have
moved in pairs, a fact which probably reflects actual practice on
the historical plane.[21] In the Old Testament where identification of the messenger is made, it is primarily only one figure,
although the plural *mal⁾ākîm* is often used as a general designation and sometimes more than one figure may appear (for example,

the three men who appear to Abraham and the two messengers who
appear to Lot -- Gen. 18 and 19).

The single messenger is the *mal'ak yhwh*. In various texts
this figure is often indistinguishable from Yahweh, and the proposal has been made that the *mal'ak yhwh* is merely an extension
of Yahweh, an aspect of Israel's notion of "corporate personality."[22] Without denying the close association of the *mal'āk* to
Yahweh in the Old Testament, one should note that the great
wealth of Canaanite mythology available now makes it clear that
the *mal'āk* originally was conceived of quite clearly as a distinct being within the council. Israel's tendency to identify
the *mal'ak yhwh* with Yahweh himself probably represents in some
contexts a tendency to avoid giving members of the council too
much individual status although it may not have been as conscious
an action as this would imply. The fact that the messenger was
called the "messenger of *Yahweh*" may have contributed to the tendency. This characteristic of identifying or associating the
messenger(s) with a particular deity Israel shared with Canaanite
mythology, although in the latter case more than one deity could
have a set of messengers, a phenomenon impossible in Israel. In
the Elohistic or northern tradition in Israel, however,the inter-
change of *yhwh* and *mal'ak yhwh* did represent a tendency to substitute the *mal'āk* or *šēm* in the accounts of the activities of
Yahweh himself. This tendency continued and was further elaborated in later Jewish tradition.

But more basic differences than these separated the imagery
of the divine assembly in Israelite lore from that of Canaan and

Mesopotamia.[23] At the heart of the matter lies the distinction
between a polytheistic development and a basically monotheistic
thrust, a distinction expressed in the fact that in Mesopotamia
and Canaan the council existed as a "primitive democracy,"[24]
whereas in Israel, Yahweh was the absolute ruler. In Mesopotamian theology each member of the council had a voice, and decisions were made by the whole body or by subgroups within the body.
Even "the great gods," "the seven gods who determine destinies,"
were subject to the will and decisions of the assembly.[25] At
Ugarit matters were decided largely at the whim and impulse of
various deities, the council as a whole acquiescing. But
Israel's religion knew no pantheon of ruling deities in competition with one another. The members of her divine assembly were
nebulous, anonymous beings who enjoyed no independent status,
ministers ($m^e\check{s}\bar{a}r^et\hat{\imath}m$) and servants ($^{c_a}b\bar{a}d\hat{\imath}m$) of Yahweh; all decisions and judgments were made by Yahweh and imposed upon the
rest of the council as well as upon Israel and other earthly powers.

The Israelite divine assembly knew no real distinctions between groups. Although different terms were used, most of them
could apply to the council as a whole. The divine assemblies of
Mesopotamia and Ugarit, however, consisted apparently of various
groups of gods, though again precise distinctions are not always
possible. In Mesopotamian mythology there were "the great gods"
and "the seven gods who determine destines." At Ugarit there is
no precise equivalent to the latter group, but *ilm rbm* appears
several times (see preceding part), and, as noted previously,

there were other associations often in identification with particular deities. Also the *rpum* and *ilnym* may have corresponded in
some manner to the Igigi and Anunnaki of Mesopotamian mythology.[26]

In short, the polytheistic impulse of surrounding cultures
tended to produce the conception of the divine assembly marked
by specificity, complexity, independence, and democratic rule,
whereas the monotheistic impulse of Israelite religion tended toward a notion of the council of Yahweh marked by anonymity, uniformity, powerlessness, and autocratic rule. It must not be
forgotten, however, that in terms of the dispensation of justice,
kingship, and the affairs of war the divine assembly of the Old
Testament must be looked at against the backdrop of the similar
imagery in the extra-biblical literature of the ancient Near East.
The last category, involving the warrior character of the god and
his host, is the particular focus of attention in these pages.

The Divine Warrior and His Army in the Early Poetry

Most of the material here belongs to the earliest literary
remains of Israelite history. While in the past some of these
poems have been regarded as quite late, the careful philological
and linguistic work of Ginsberg, Albright, Cross, Freedman, and
others has produced a growing consensus about the antiquity of
most of the poems of the Pentateuch and the historical books as
well as a number of the Psalms. Thus it is possible to say that
the phenomena and imagery of this literature reflect to a large
degree the early conceptions of Israelite faith. Precise dating,

however, is not the most important question. For that reason,
passages from the prophets and the other end of Israel's historical continuum as well as prose texts from various sources will
be examined in the following sections to demonstrate the rather
widespread character of the language and imagery of Yahweh and
his cosmic army. Although a number of texts are relevant, it has
already been recognized that many of them are related in terms of
theme and form, thus affording a certain amount of uniformity as
a basis for conclusions and some degree of variety as a basis for
checking the conclusions as well as the extent of influence of
the theme under discussion.

Deuteronomy 33:2-5, 26-29

For our purposes, investigation of these texts need not
start with the earliest (Ex. 15) because chronological sequence
within this corpus is not a significant consideration. The framework of the Blessing of Moses is representative of the themes
common to the picture of God the Warrior in the early material
and in its theophanic character is closely related to other passages. These verses (2-5, 26-29) present a hymn of praise to Yahweh, describing the conquest of Canaan in terms of a theophany of
Yahweh and his heavenly host leading the armies of Israel.[27] The
structure of the poem may be described simply:

1. Theophany of Yahweh and his heavenly army (vv. 2-3)

2. Establishment of kingship (vv. 4-5)

3. Israel's settlement in the land (vv. 26-29)

Verses 2-3[28]

    yhwh msyny b ᵓ

    wzrḥ mś ꜥyr l ⌜ꜥ⌝mw
                  lnw

    hwpy ꜥ mhr p ᵓrn

    w ᵓth-m rbbt qdš̌

    mymynw ᵓš̌d   ⌜ᵓ⌝lm

    ᵓp ḥbb ꜥmym

    kl qdš̌⌜ ⌝ bydk

    whmtkw lrglk

    yṣ ᵓ -m dbrtyk

    Yahweh from Sinai came

    (And) he beamed forth from Seir for his peo[ple][29]

    He shone forth from Mount Paran.

    (And) with him myriads of holy ones,

    At his right hand warriors of the gods,

    Yea, the purified ones of the peoples.

    All the holy ones are at thy hand,

    (Indeed) they bow down at thy feet;

    They lift up thy decisions.

The first tricolon is fairly straightforward. The only problem in the text is the form *lmw*, tentatively emended here to
l ⌜ꜥ⌝mw, on the assumption that a letter has fallen out.[30] Yahweh
is pictured as marching forth from Sinai and the south, as is
typical of the theophanic[31] passages in the early poetry.[32] The
most important form in the tricolon is *hôpîᵃꜥ*. This verb has as
its basic meaning "to shine, illumine" and is associated three

times in the Old Testament with the shining of light (Job 3:4;
10:22; 37:15). In at least one other instance (Job 10:3) the
context also clearly indicates the meaning "shine." All other
uses of this verb refer to Yahweh and his theophany and may best
be translated as "shine forth."[33] The verb yp^c has now been
found in the Amorite names of Mari and among the onomastica of
Ugarit.[34] These are theophorous names several times involving
the warrior god Ba^{c}al-Hadad as the divine element. Most instructive, however, is the use of yp^c in finite forms in the Ugaritic
texts. It appears in only two contexts. One of these is ^{c}nt:
III:34 // IV:49 (= *CTA* 3.III.34 // IV.49):

   mn . ib . yp^c . lb^{c}l .

   ṣrt . lrkb . ^{c}rpt .

What enemy has shone forth against Ba^{c}al,

(What) adversary against the Rider of Clouds?

In this context the term yp^c clearly refers to the conflicts or
battles between the gods. Text 137:3 (= *CTA* 2.I.3) which contains the other instance of a finite form of yp^c, is unfortunately broken. The context, however, is the conflict between Ba^{c}al
and Yamm. It is reasonable, therefore, to assume that its usage
is the same as in ^{c}nt. The proper name $yp^c b^c l$ points in the same
direction. Sparse though the data may be, one is forced to conclude on this basis that yp^c is a term of battle particularly
associated with deity. Aside from its presence in Job in a
rather late context there is nothing in the Old Testament to mod-
ify that conclusion. Psalm 80:2b-4 gives an illuminating example
of this meaning:

He who is enthroned on the cherubim, shine forth (hôpîʿāh)

Before Ephraim and Benjamin and Manasseh

Rouse up (ʿôrᵉrāh) thy might

And come to save us.

O God, restore us,

And make thy face to shine (hāʾēr)

That we may be delivered.

The context of these verses is clearly a call for victory in battle. Yahweh, who is enthroned on the Ark, is urged to "shine
forth" in battle to rouse up his might for a victorious deliverance. The precise meaning of hôpîʿāh is spelled out in 4b where
the victorious deliverance of the people is wrought by the shining of Yahweh's face.[35]

The first tricolon of Deuteronomy 33 is, therefore, a vivid
description of Yahweh's coming from Sinai, shining forth for battle from the south, the region that is not only the dwelling
place of the deity but also the line of march of the Israelites
in their conquest of the land.

Problems and difficulties abound in the second tricolon.
Not a single colon is without them. The translation of the first
is that of Cross and Freedman.[36] It is assuredly correct, producing good sense and good parallelism and supported at points by
the versions.[37] The term qdš as a basic designation for the divine beings in Ugaritic, Phoenician, and Hebrew has already been
discussed.

But the translation of the second colon is much less certain. Of the various possibilities two seem to be the most

plausible. One of these is the reconstruction of Cross and
Freedman, who assume an early damage to the text which produced
ʾšdt lmw for ʾšr ʾlm. The assumption is quite conjectural but
possible. It produces fairly good parallelism though not so
satisfactory as that of Milik, who reads ʾšrt as a noun, "company, retinue."[38]

Another reading of the text is possible, however, which
builds upon the work of Cross and Freedman together with a note
of A. F. L. Beeston suggesting a South Arabic cognate.[39] We
would propose to read as the original text with the early orthography:

  mymn ʾšd ⌈ʾ⌉lm

At his right hand the warriors of the gods
The only consonantal shift here is reading aleph for taw with
Cross and Freedman. The word ʾšd is, with Beeston, to be equated
with South Arabic (Sabaean) ʾsd, which frequently has the sense
"warriors." It is probably also related to Arabic ʾsd, which in
nominal form means "lion"; in verbal form, "to be bold like a
lion," "to be courageous," "to become strong, tall"; and in adjectival constructions "bold, daring (like a lion)." Furthermore
the same word appears at a much earlier time in Amorite.[40] If
this suggestion is correct, we would have then another possible
animal name for a (war) leader and a hitherto unrecognized hapax
legomenon in Hebrew with cognates in Amorite, Arabic, and Old
South Arabic.

Cross, Freedman, and Milik's recognition that the verse contains a reference to the divine beings is incontrovertible in the

light of the context, the parallelism, and the LXX *aggeloi*. That

holds true whether the solution proposed above is satisfactory

or not. If it is, then the first two cola of this tricolon

would be in excellent parallelism:

> With him myriads of holy ones
>
> At his right hand warriors of the gods[41]
>   (divine warriors)

The final colon poses problems also. We have suggested,

following Mendenhall and Cross, that *hbb* may best be interpreted

as a cognate of Akkadian *ebēbum/ubbubum*, "to be pure," "to puri-

fy."[42] The translation would read: "Yea, the purified (ones)

of the peoples" (or "his people," if reading with LXX). The

problem here is the intrusion of "the peoples," "the clans," in-

to a theophany of Yahweh and his hosts. Poetically the reading

is possible. The participle *ʾap* usually introduces a synonym or

climactic element.[43]   But *ʾap* can also connect elements that are

both contrasting and similar types, for example, "day" and

"night" (Ps. 74:16), "heaven" and "earth" (Ps. 89:12), "Yahweh

rules" and "the earth is established" (Ps. 96:10). The *ʿammîm*

thus are the opposite of the *ʾēlîm*, but in this context the two

groups represent parts of a single element -- the entourage of

Yahweh. The parallelism "warriors of the gods"//"purified of the

peoples" is exact in form. The parallelism of meaning is evident

too, for "the purified ones" must refer to those mustered and

sanctified for war. The rest of the hymn pictures the holy war-

riors of Yahweh's host and Israel's host as marching forth to

battle under the command of Yahweh with the conquest of Canaan their ultimate goal.

The third tricolon may be passed over quickly because it simply continues the imagery of Yahweh and his assembly, but two or three problems of text exist. The *qdšyw* of the first colon is probably to be read as the collective *qdš* (cf. LXX).[44] The verbal form of the second colon is quite problematic. Along with Cross and Freedman's proposal to read an infixed -*t* form of *mkk*, mention should be made here of Milik's interpretation of the first two words as being Ugaritic *hm*, "lo, behold,"[45] and the verb *tkk*, known from Syriac and Arabic and then preserved in Hebrew in the noun *tōk*, "oppression." He translated: "Ils se present à ta suite (litt.: à tes pieds)."[46] Whether or not the verb *tkk* may be translated in such a mild manner is open to question.[47] The final line of the verse -- if Cross and Freedman are correct in their interpretation -- notes the role of the members of the assembly as executioners of Yahweh's will whether in war, justice, or other areas. The similarity to the role of Enlil in the Mesopotamian assembly as well as to the messenger of the god(s) in Canaanite mythology and the Old Testament is immediately obvious. Here they are concerned with the affairs of war, although judicial connotations are not far away.

Verses 4-5

> *twrh ṣwh lnw mšh*
>
> *mwršh qhlt y'qb*
>
> *wyhw byšrwn mlk*
>
> *bht'sp r'šy 'm*
>
> *yḥd šbṭy yśr'l*

> Moses commanded for us torah,
>
> A possession of the assembly of Jacob.
>
> Then (Yahweh) became king in Yešurun
>
> When the leaders of the people gathered together
>
> The assembly[48] of the tribes of Israel.

Although these two verses are associated here with the archaic framework, verses 2-3 and 26-29, it is likely that verses
4-5 are the torso of an alternate ancient introduction to the
blessings which make up the main body of the poem, or a segment
of the framework misplaced from another context (conclusion?).
In that respect they were secondarily inserted into their present
location in the history of tradition of this poem and were considerably disturbed in the process. Thus one must recognize a
later stage when dealing with verses 4-5. This alternate introduction is, however, quite old in itself, as is the poem as a
whole. It is legitimate, therefore, to say that at an early
stage in Israel's literary history verses 4-5 were connected to
the archaic framework, and to look at the significance of that
fact, which is hardly by accident, despite the probable existence
of literary or composition devices, for example, catchword association ($y^e\check{s}ur\hat{u}n$, $s\hat{i}nay$).

The original character of the segment is unclear, and Cross
and Freedman do not even attempt a reconstruction of these verses. What they are about in their present form is well summarized by G. Ernest Wright: "As preserved, the verses refer to
the organization of the nation in the wilderness, when Yahweh became its king in the constituting assembly and when Moses gave the

law."[49] Especially significant is the fact that at the stage of
tradition in which the alternate introduction was attached to the
framework, or vice versa, Sinai was understood not only as the
mythological seat or abode of the god, as in surrounding cultures, but also as the place where the community was established
by covenant. Yahweh's marching from Sinai was seen not merely as
a mythological motif but in terms of the historical march of conquest from Sinai to Canaan. Equally important, in this action
Yahweh became king. Unlike the basic tenet of most Near Eastern
mythology, his kingship was established not primarily by the
mythological battle of the gods, but by the historical victories
of Yahweh and his earthly and heavenly armies over the enemies of
Israel. Overtones of the cosmic battle of the gods appear quite
strongly in other contexts, as is to be expected, but the basic
thrust is always that seen in this hymn.[50] Israel's creation and
deliverance were achieved by that fusion of the divine, or cosmic,
and the historical represented in the coming of Yahweh and his
heavenly army, not to fight other gods, but to fight the adversaries of Israel. This note is sounded further in the concluding
verses of the framework.

That these verses do not in themselves make an acceptable
transition into either the Blessings or the rest of the framework
has long been recognized. Cross and Freedman, along with others,
have suggested that verse 21b is probably to be connected with
verses 4 and 5, but they have not believed it possible to reconstruct with any accuracy. Seeligmann has sought to do so and
adds as a transition between verse 5 and verse 26 the following

cola:

> *wayy^etannû ṣidqôt yhwh ʿāśāh*
>
> *ûmišpāṭāyw ʿim yiśrāʾēl*
>
> to recount deeds of salvation performed by the Lord
>
> and His acts of deliverance on behalf of Israel:[51]

We cite this reconstruction, not from any certainty that it represents the original with exactness, but because of a conviction
in the light of the text and the direction of the whole framework
that the transition to verse 26 approximated this reconstruction.
The recognition of the *ṣidqôt yhwh*, as in Judges 5:11, is surely
correct and a conclusion to which I came independently before
reading Seeligmann. As he puts it, "The tribes assemble to extol
the glorious feats of deliverance performed for them by their
God. Then they raise their voices exclaiming: אֵין כָּאֵל יְשֻׁרוּן."
Yahweh is acclaimed as king in light of the victories which he
and his armies have wrought in the march of conquest.

Verses 26-29

After the interruption of the blessings these verses continue the hymn.[52] The point of focus in verses 26-29 is the conquest, the violent sacral wars of Israel under the command of
Yahweh.[53] The imagery is entirely that of Yahweh as the warrior,
but the warrior who brings historical conquest and deliverance
rather than primeval victory.

The first colon of verse 26, probably to be read: "There is
no god like the God of Ješurun," is to be compared with Psalm 89:
7ff. and Exodus 15:11 and stands as an answer to the question
cliché: "Who is like thee among the gods?"[54] Originally the

question and the answer must have been encomiums celebrating the
victory of a god over opposing gods.[55]   Psalm 89:7ff. still preserves that context.   But in Deuteronomy 33:26 as in Exodus 15:
11 Yahweh's cosmic or divine superiority is the result of his
victories over Israel's enemies.

The rest of verse 26 in archaic manner common to Near Eastern mythology[56]   describes Yahweh the warrior, rider of the
clouds and the heavens, driving his chariot to battle.   Verse 27
makes explicit the imagery, in terms of the conquest:

And he drove out before you the enemy

And said, Destroy. . . (or "And destroyed the Amorite").[57]
The vocabulary is common to the conquest accounts.   The verb
$g\bar{a}ra\check{s}$ is almost a technical term for Yahweh's activity in the
conquest (Ex. 23:28-31; 33:2; 34:11; Josh. 24:12, 18; Judg. 2:3;
6:9);[58] and the command to "destroy" must be understood in terms
of the $h\bar{e}rem$ against the Canaanites (Josh. 7:12; 9:24; 11:14; 11:
20; 24:8; Deut. 7:24; Amos 2:9).

In light of the above the expression ^{c}am $n\bar{o}\check{s}a^{c}$ $byhwh$ may be
translated in a military sense as "an army victorious in Yah-
weh."[59]   The following cola, referring to Yahweh as Israel's
shield and sword, carry on the imagery of Yahweh as the warrior
leading the army of Israel, and the rest of the passage is a description of Israel safely entrenched in Canaan, a picture which
connotes the Promised Land, the object of Israel's journeys, the
motive behind her holy war or conquest ideology.

The hymn of Deuteronomy 33 is a song of praise to Yahweh for
his aid in the march of conquest.   The center of the psalm is the

theophany of Yahweh and his hosts, but that theophany is a march
of war, as Yahweh and his hosts lead Israel into the Promised
Land. The origin of the theophany is Sinai and the south. The
references to Seir and Mount Paran, like the references to Edom
and Teman in parallel passages (Judg. 5:4-5 and Hab. 3:3), are
in part poetic devices, stylistic parallelism representing Yahweh's abode in the south. But, more than that, these geographic
designations refer to Israel's march through the wilderness.[60]
That fact is spelled out explicitly in the theophany of Psalm 68:
8 (see below) and is self-evident here when the hymnic framework
is looked at as a whole.

Parallels to this type of theophany often expressed in similar language are not uncommon in the literature of the ancient
Near East,[61] and Israel's poetic literature certainly came under
stylistic and thematic influence from these sources. In the
parallel texts of Mesopotamia, however, the theophany is generally in reference to the battle of the gods or the going forth of
Samaš, or the like. In the classic theophanic descriptions of
the Old Testament under discussion here, the divine assembly also
forms the background, echoes of the battle of the gods are heard
(for example, in Ps. 68 and Hab. 3), and indeed Yahweh is pictured as "shining forth" or beaming like the sun; but in these
descriptions the context and the warrior language reveal that the
theophany represents Yahweh and his heavenly host fighting with
the earthly armies to take the Promised Land or to conquer enemies after the original settlement. And the kingship of Yahweh
is established over Israel by his might and victory. This

picture in Deuteronomy 33 is further confirmed by other texts.

Judges 5

The Song of Deborah, which probably dates from the late twelfth or early eleventh century,[62] is a victory song similar to the hymn or psalm of praise, and in this respect is like the framework of Deuteronomy 33.[63] Like that passage also, the focus is on the victory of Yahweh and his armies over the enemies of Israel, although the movement of the song is not entirely consistent (as, for example, Ex. 15), and there are different forms within the poem. The song deals at times with the leaders, the tribes, individual feats, and the like; but the center of attention is -- the *ṣidqôt Yahweh*. Von Rad in his study of the holy war in ancient Israel has made this poem the point of departure and concludes, correctly no doubt, that the poem deals with one of the sacral wars of Israel within the context of the tribal league. The Song of Deborah belongs to a context of covenant, tribal league, and holy war set against the mytho-theological conception of the divine warrior's fighting with and for Israel. Without my going through all of the poem in detail, the following comments may make that context clear:[64]

Verse 2

> *bprᶜ prᶜwt byśrʾl*
>
> *bhtndb ᶜm*
>
> *brkw yhwh*
>
> When locks hung loose in Israel,
>
> When the people offered themselves freely
>
>> Bless Yahweh!

The first line of this verse has always been enigmatic, with the translation of the root *pr*ᶜ a subject of considerable disagreement. Hardly any two versions agree on the meaning of this line. The notion of "leading" and "leaders" is dependent upon Arabic roots and Septuagint translations. All uses of the noun in Hebrew relate to the hair of the head, and the verb is a normal Hebrew verb meaning "let go," "let loose," "unbind," sometimes having to do with the letting loose of the hair. Akkadian *pirtu* and Arabic *fr*ᶜ also refer to long or abundant hair.[65] There can be little question therefore, that the line is to be translated as it is above or in some similar manner.[66]

The problem then becomes one of meaning and interpretation. Here again the conclusion seems rather obvious though it is not often drawn.[67] The hanging loose of locks may refer to the wearing of the hair unshorn as a vow and a sign of holiness according to the custom of the Nazirite vow. The law of the Nazirite in Numbers 6:5 makes it clear that wearing the locks (*pera*ᶜ) of hair long is to sanctify oneself, to separate oneself as holy to Yahweh. This is the only context in which specific reference to the hair in Judges 5:2 makes sense. The reference must be to the long hair of a type or group of warriors who consecrated themselves to fight the holy wars of Yahweh. If so, Judges 5:2 contains the earliest reference to this custom and would seem to point to the fact that the Nazirite vow may have originated in the ritual of holy war or at least have been closely associated with that ritual at the beginning, although by the time of the presentation of the Nazirite law in Numbers 6 (P) that association had been lost.

The Samson story (Judg. 13--16) provides further possible evidence for this conclusion. Now greatly embroidered with legend and folktale,[68] this ancient story[69] probably centered about an authentically historical figure.[70] The key element here is Samson's long hair, the result of a Nazirite vow from birth and the only part of the vow which Samson seems to have observed throughout his life. The direct link between Samson's long hair and his great strength and ability as warrior would point again to the Nazarite as originally a type of holy warrior, especially inasmuch as he possessed a charisma also that contributed to his fighting ability (Judg. 14:19; 15:14).

But the same type of phenomenon may have been present among other peoples. Gunkel has pointed out parallels on the basis of comparative studies, but even more significant is the reference in Deuteronomy 32:42 to "the long-haired heads of the enemy (rôš parᶜôt ᶜôyēb). Two further pieces of data may be noted briefly although they are of necessity largely conjectural and may be put as questions. The LXX of I Samuel 1, now confirmed explicitly by 4Q Sam[a], preserves the tradition that Samuel was a Nazirite.[71] Even the MT of I Samuel 1:11 indicates that a vow was made that no razor should touch his head. There is no explicit sign of any warrior activity on Samuel's part, but could the clear dominance of Israel over the Philistines, which the Deuteronomist ascribes to his days of rule, have had anything to do with his Nazirite vow and its holy war connotations? Also one may ask whether the Rekabites, whose vow did not include the matter of unshorn locks,

could have had some similar relationship to the holy war tradition inasmuch as they were zealous warriors of Yahweh? At this
point, however, evidence ends and so must conclusions.

The second half of Judges 5:2 must then also relate to the
willingness of the warriors to consecrate themselves to Yahweh
in battle. If Cross is right that $n^e d\hat{\imath} b\hat{e}$ should be inserted before ʿam as in Numbers 21:18, then the reference would be only
to the leaders inasmuch as $n^e d\hat{\imath} b\hat{e}$ in Numbers 21:18 is parallel to
$\acute{s}\bar{a}r\hat{\imath}m$ (cf. Judg. 5:9).[72] This emendation, however, would not
alter the meaning. One should not assume that because the people
or their leaders were praised for their willingness to rally,
they were not expected -- or commanded -- to participate. The
fact that they were expected to join in does not preclude thanksgiving or self-congratulation at that fact, precisely because the
tribes did not always rally even though under strong obligation
to do so.

Verses 4-5[73]

yhwh bsʾtk mśʿyr

bsʿdk mśdh ʾdwm

ʾrs rʿšh

gm šmym ntpw[74]

gm ʿbym ntpw mym

hrym nzlw[75]

mpny yhwh zh syny[76]

mpny yhwh ʾlhy yśrʾl

Yahweh, when you went forth from Seir,

When you marched out from the field of Edom

> The earth shook;
>
> Even the heavens dripped,
>
> Yea, the clouds dripped water,
>
> The mountains streamed
>
> From before Yahweh, the One of Sinai,
>
> From before Yahweh, God of Israel.

These verses describe the theophany of Yahweh the warrior and as in Deuteronomy 33:2-3 form the appropriate beginning of the account of the victory of the divine warrior over Israel's enemies. Although no specific reference is made to the divine assembly, the picture is that of Yahweh, the warrior storm god, marching forth with his hosts to battle for Israel (see also Deut. 33: Ps. 68; Hab. 3). This passage is a key element in the hymn, linking the great theophany of Yahweh (and his army) to the holy wars of the people of Israel. Her wars were Yahweh's wars (I Sam. 18:17; 25:28; Num. 21:14), her victory dependent upon his mighty intervention. Although representing a particular genre or form found elsewhere, the theophany cannot be separated from its content; it describes Yahweh's coming to the aid of Israel against Sisera.[77]

Verse 8b[78]

> *mgn ʾm yrʾh wrmḥ*
>
> *bʾrbʿym ʾlp*[79] *byśrʾl*
>
> Was shield or spear seen
>
> Among the forty thousand in Israel?

Verse 8a is obscure and corrupt. The second half of the verse, however, is fairly straightforward and even the differences in the A and B texts of LXX are explicable in terms of the

reading in MT.[80]   The absence of weapons in Israel can make sense
only in the context of holy war where it was believed that weapons and numbers did not really matter because Yahweh came and
fought for Israel.[81]   This does not mean that in actuality there
was no fighting with weapons. Rather, it was in the ideology,
expressed so vividly in the poem, that weapons and human might
were regarded as being of minimal value. Thus, contrary to Albright's view, the Israelites might well "celebrate a great victory by boasting that they had no weapons at all."[82]

Verse 11c

>z yrdw lš‘rym ‘m yhwh

Then went down the people of Yahweh to the gates

In this brief description of the march of the army to battle
the phrase *‘am Yahweh* is worthy of comment. Here as elsewhere
(cf. v. 13), it refers to the troops of the tribal league, the
earthly army of Yahweh, levied for battle.[83] Similar uses of the
phrase are to be found in Judges 20:2 and II Samuel 1:12 (cf.
Num. 17:6; I Sam. 2:24; and II Sam. 14:13). Equally significant
is the fact that in the holy war instructions (1QM) at Qumran the
same designation in the form *‘m>l* continues as the name of the
forces of Yahweh which go out to battle (Col. I:5). The lead
banner, which goes before all the army, is inscribed "People of
God" (III:12). An early element of the holy war tradition is
carried over here into apocalyptic.

Verse 12

‘wry ‘wry dbwrh

‘wry ‘wry dbry šyr

qwm brq

wšbh šbyk

bn ᵓbynᶜm

Awake, awake, Deborah!

Awake, awake, utter a song!

Arise, Baraq,

And take captive thy captivity,

Son of Abinoam.

The MT of these verses offers no problem by itself. The B text of LXX also follows MT precisely. But the A text is quite another matter and introduces more complexity. Burney, who ably discusses and analyzes the variants, sees no reason for departing from the "lucid text" of MT.[85] Cross, however, pointing to the great variety in LXX without apparent basis in the MT and to the fact that a number of variants are pre-Hexaplaric, maintains that the A text of LXX must be taken into consideration. Because it is difficult to assume conflation, he suggests plausibly, though tentatively, a tricolon in the first line somewhat as follows:[86]

ᶜr ᶜr dbr

ᶜr dbr (w)šr

ᶜr rbt ᶜm
                   or
ᶜrr rbt ᶜm

Awake, awake, Deborah!

Awake, speak (and) sing (the battle song):

Awake, mistress of the people!
                                        or
Arouse the myriads of the people.

Then, following the A or Lucianic reading, Cross would add *ḥzq*
bᶜz or the like after *qûm* in the second line.[88]

This reconstruction does not solve all the problems, but it
probably is the best that can be suggested now. Moore has correctly recognized that the imperatives do not call for Deborah to
sing a victory song after the fight. Rather, the battle is at
hand, and Deborah is enjoined to sing a battle song to rouse the
people to fight for Yahweh, even as Baraq is urged to rise up and
capture the enemy.

The presence of the imperatives immediately raises the question as to who the speaker is. The common answer is that it is
the poet. In verse 23, however, the commands are uttered by the
malʾak Yahweh, so it is quite possible that in verse 12 also the
angel of Yahweh addresses Deborah and Baraq from the heavenly
assembly which marches with Yahweh.

The imperatives *ᶜûrî* and *qûm*, common terminology for initiat-
ing or stirring up battle, apply to Israel in her holy wars (Josh.
8:1; Judg. 7:9; 7:15; 18:9) when Yahweh commands her to arise and
fight because he has already given the enemy into her hand. But
the verbs refer also to the warrior activity of Yahweh. The ancient battle song of the Ark discussed below enjoins Yahweh to
rise up (*qûmāh*) and put his enemies to rout (cf. Ps. 7:7; 59:5;
80:3; Isa. 10:26; Zech. 13:7). Psalm 44, which is full of holy
war motifs, urges Yahweh to awake (*ᶜûrāh* -- v. 24), to rise up
(*qûmāh* -- v. 27) and come to the aid of his people. Isaiah 42:
13 pictures Yahweh the warrior as he goes forth:

    Yahweh goes forth as a warrior

As a man of war he rouses up ($y\bar{a}^c\hat{i}r$) his zeal.

The closest parallel to the language of Judges 5:12 is in Isaiah 51:9:

Awake, awake, put on strength, arm of Yahweh.

Awake, as in days of old, generations long ago.

In this instance, however, the military terminology describing Yahweh as a mighty warrior is in the context of his primordial cosmic battle with the dragon, in part historicized in terms of the Exodus.

Verses 13-18

It is not necessary to go into minutiae on this section. Verses 14-16 are very difficult and corrupt while verses 17-18 are fairly straightforward. The important thing to note is the formal listing of ten of the tribes in the tribal league. Only Judah and Simeon are definitely missing. Machir appears here for Manasseh. One is not inclined to expect Machir to represent all of Manasseh as it was classically represented east and west of the Jordan, but it is possible for it to do so. Or perhaps Machir represents Manasseh but only a part of it. In any event, the equation Machir = Manasseh is unavoidable for this poem,[89] and the same is true of Gilead = Gad. Here also the equation is not quite normal because one usually expects Gilead to indicate a larger area, but the territory of Gilead is definitely associated with Gad, which occupied a portion of it(Deut. 3:12; Josh. 13:24-28), as well as Manasseh (Num. 32:39ff.). Note also that the Syriac as well as some manuscripts of LXX have Gad for Gilead. The dropping of the *lambda* could easily explain that change in the

Greek but not in the Syriac.

Another alternative is to include Gad and Manasseh in the list, making an even twelve tribes. There are two places where this could be done. One possibility is the beginning of verse 16 where Albright would place Gad.[90] Also the fact that Zebulon is mentioned twice in two different places in the list might suggest that in one instance another tribe was once present.

The almost universal interpretation of this list of tribes has been that it is a compilation of words of praise for Ephraim, Benjamin, Machir, Zebulun, Issachar, and Naphtali for their participation in the battle, along with rebukes of Reuben, Gilead, Dan, and Asher for failure to respond to the call to fight. There are difficulties in this interpretation, and another one may be suggested that is equally plausible, if not more so.[91] It is possible to see in verses 13-18 simply an account of the mustering and marching of the tribes to holy war against Sisera, with no indication of anything but full and complete participation. The problems posed to this interpretation in verses 16-17 are not so difficult as might seem at first glance; the *lāmāh* of verses 16-17, upon which much of the weight of common opinion depends, may easily have been originally an emphatic particle *lo-mi*, "indeed, surely," or the like, as Cross has suggested. The orthography would have been the same.

Furthermore, the list is a compilation of blessings or tribal sayings similar to Genesis 49 and Deuteronomy 33. It is rather remarkable that the closest parallels between Judges 5 and these two poems are in Judges 5:16-17 and the blessings of

Zebulun and Issachar in Genesis 49:13-15. Different tribes are involved, but the blessings are remarkably similar. Reuben in Judges 5:16 and Issachar in Genesis 49:14 dwell "among the sheepfolds(?)" (*bên hammišpatayim*);[92] Asher in Judges 5:17 and Zebulun in Genesis 49:13 both dwell "at the shore of the sea" (*leḥôp yammîm*). Dan in Judges 5:17 and Zebulun in Genesis 49:13 are both situated at a place of "ships" (*ʾoniyyôt*). Only the comment on Gilead is unrelated to this section of Genesis 49. One is compelled, therefore, to see the poet of Judges 5 filling out his list from a blessings or sayings tradition reflected in Genesis 49, but not necessarily directly drawn from there -- a tradition which had nothing to do with war. Furthermore, the fact that these particular comments do not relate originally to the war may suggest an expansion at this point to include other tribes not originally here.

Strong credibility is given to this view by verse 23 where the town of Meroz (?) is clearly cursed for failure to respond. Here there can be no question of what is involved. The condemnation is strong and comes from the divine assembly itself (see below on vs. 23). Nothing in the tone of verses 16-17 compares with verse 23. One is thus led to see in 14-18 a list of blessings for the full cooperation of the tribal league as the traditions of sacral war demanded. The striking absence altogether of Judah and Simeon can best be explained on the assumption of their probable association at this time with a six-tribe league in the south which did not involve their participation with these tribes against Sisera.

Verse 20[93]

    mn šmym nlḥmw hkwkbym

    mm⌐z⌐ltm nlḥmw ʿm sysrʾ

    From heaven fought the stars

    From their stations they fought with Sisera

The reading of this verse poses no real problems. The emendation to *mimmazzᵉlōtām*, which was first proposed by Winckler and
may be seen in the LXX A text's *taxeōs*, "battle order," is now
generally accepted by scholars.[94] The interpretation of the
verse is fairly self-evident and need not be belabored, but it is
central to the understanding of the poem and its imagery. In
these lines the cosmic scope of the battle is hymnically elaborated. Not only the *ʿam Yahweh* (vv. 13ff.), but the starry hosts
of heaven, the servants of Yahweh in battle order, fight for Israel in her holy war. The elements of nature joined in as verse
21 also shows.[95] The Kishon reflects less the context of the divine assembly and more a naturalistic event connected with the
battle like the activity of the sea in Exodus 15, yet the verse
follows the same train of thought as verse 20 and points further
to the involvement of all the elements of the universe in the
battle.[96]

Verse 23

    ʾwrw <ʾrwr>[97] *mrwz*[98]

    ʾmr mlʾk yhwh

    ʾrw ʾrwr yšbyh

    ky lʾ bʾw lʿzrt yhwh

    lʿzrt yhwh bgbwrym

> Curse ⟨bitterly⟩ Meroz,
>
> Said the angel of Yahweh.
>
> Curse bitterly her inhabitants.
>
> For they did not come to the aid of Yahweh,
>
> To the aid of Yahweh among the warriors.

The setting here is clearly the divine heavenly assembly of
Yahweh. It reflects a particular type, the herald or messenger
Gattung, in which the council of Yahweh is addressed and commen-
ded.[99] The mention of the *mal'ak Yahweh* is immediate indication
of the form and context. The phrase *'āmar mal'ak yhwh* may be a
gloss although it fits in terms of accent and syllable count,
but if so, there is no reason to assume that it is not an early
one and properly belongs in its setting. Cross suggests that it
may have been a rubric, which correctly interprets the passage
and would have been quite primitive. The repetition of identical plural imperatives at the beginning points also to the fact
that the form is that of the messenger[100] who addresses the divine assembly and delivers Yahweh's command to curse the town or
clan of Meroz for violating the covenant demand to come to the
aid of the suzerain in battle.

The harsh quality of this command has been noted above. Verses 14-18 and 23 must be seen as a series of blessings and curses
which reflect the covenantal form of Israel's early faith and the
binding obligation of the tribes and clans to answer the call to
holy war. The assembly of Yahweh stands behind this passage and
the whole chapter both as participant in Israel's holy war and
witness against those who violate the covenant by not participat-

ing themselves. Here is an extremely early attestation of the
divine council background of the covenant lawsuit convincingly
spelled out in detail by G. Ernest Wright.[101]

There may be a further reference to the divine council in
this verse although here one speaks with much less certainty.
Meroz is cursed for failure to come to the aid of Yahweh *baggibbôrîm*. The common and logical interpretation here is that *baggibbôrîm* should be read as "with warriors," referring to the warriors of Meroz,[102] but another plausible interpretation is that
baggibbôrîm should be translated "among the warriors" (cf. LXX
en . . .) and that the reference is to Yahweh among his divine
warriors. The obligation of the tribes and clans to come to the
aid of Yahweh and his cosmic army is no more anomalous than their
obligation to come to the aid of Yahweh alone. Though not always
recognized, the word *gibbôrîm* is a perfectly good designation for
the members of the divine assembly. The clearest illustration is
Psalm 103:20 where the members of Yahweh's entourage are specifically labeled *gibbôrê kōaḥ*. This designation occurs also in Joel
4:11 and Isaiah 13:3, which are discussed below. There may be
other instances in the Old Testament,[103] but the above examples
are sufficient and are matched by the frequent use of this terminology for the angels in the Qumran literature. In 1QM xv:14 the
gbwry ʾlym are described as girding themselves for battle, and
Col. xii:7 also appears to contain a reference to the angels as
gbwrym. 1QH contains frequent reference to the *gbwrym* of the divine world: *gbwry šmym* (iii:35-36), *gbwry plʾ*(v. 21), *gbwry kwh*
(viii:11-12), (x:34). So also the Angelic Liturgy[104] and 4QBer

(unpublished).

> *Verse 31*[105]
>
> > *kn y'bdw kl*[106]
> >
> > *'wybyk yhwh*
> >
> > *'hby ⌜k⌝*[107] *ks't*
> >
> > *hšmš bgbrtw*
> >
> > Thus shall perish all
> >
> > Of thy foes, Yahweh.
> >
> > But thy friends be as the going forth
> >
> > Of the sun in its might.

This verse is often regarded as a later addition unconnected
with the original poem. There does seem to be a rather abrupt
break between verses 30 and 31, but that is no reason for elimi-
nating verse 31. It is a liturgical sentence climaxing and ending the poem and a paranetic extension and universalizing of the
specific victory celebrated in the song. It expresses the spirit
of the sacral war in which Yahweh vanquished his enemies and thus
stands firmly as an integral part of the poem regardless of what
particular moment it took its place. W. L. Moran, in his exposition of the covenantal background of the love of God in the Old
Testament,[108] points out the significance of the *'ōhᵃbeykā*, "thy
friends." The vassal was the "friend" and "servant" of the suzerain, Moran explains, and expressed his loyalty in terms of
"love" (*ra'āmu, ra'amūtu*). So also Israel, bound by treaty or
covenant to Yahweh, was his "friend" and depended upon that relationship of love for well-being. Moran has noted that *'hb* in
Judges 5:31 is one of the earliest uses of this verb, and that it

is to be interpreted in this light.[109] Along with the blessings
and curses of the chapter and its cosmic overtones reflecting the
council of Yahweh, the reference to the "lovers" of Yahweh places
the holy war traditions of the Song of Deborah squarely in the
context of the Israelite tribal league and its covenant relationship to Yahweh, the warrior and judge, the divine champion whose
victories were celebrated as the ṣidqot Yahweh.

Psalm 68

This ancient and confusing psalm has vexed scholars for centuries and has probably produced more comment and discussion than
any other single psalm. Its problems are too vast to be eluci-
dated to any large degree in this small scope, but recent discoveries and studies have produced new insights into the psalm.

Without going into all the suggestions that have been
made,[110] one may mention two views which represent the extremes
of contemporary interpretation of the psalm. In 1950 W. F. Albright produced a detailed discussion of Psalm 68, in which he
put forward the view, already tentatively suggested by predecessors, that the poem is a catalogue of *incipits* or first lines of
poems composed between the thirteenth and tenth centuries but put
in present form probably around the time of Solomon -- a conclusion based upon linguistic, orthographic, metrical, and comparative analysis. He sees the poem as a literary composition
apparently without a cultic setting in life.[111] In a full monograph written specifically as an answer to and criticism of Albright's interpretation, Sigmund Mowinckel, following the same
point of view with regard to the Psalms that he espoused for over

forty years, maintains that Psalm 68 is virtually a perfect
unity, belonging directly to the festival of the enthronement of
Yahweh.[112]   He disagrees emphatically with Albright at practically every point -- including metrical analysis -- except with
regard to the Ugaritic or Canaanite background of some of the
terminology and, strangely enough, with regard to date. Mowinckel also sees the psalm as an old one, having its origin in the
time of Saul.[113] His reason for dating, that is, the assumed
hegemony of Benjamin, is, however, quite different from that of
Albright.

Most discusssions since these works were published have
built upon them without following either all the way.[114] Mowinckel's attempt to find some sort of unity within a context of
worship is a valid endeavor, but with regard to this particular
psalm not necessarily a fruitful one. The possibility of an
older unified poem underlying this one cannot be completely
denied, but the present state of the text points much more clearly to a piecing together of isolated bits of poetry or *incipits*.
The fitting of every single verse into a clear scheme, such as
Mowinckel attempts, does not seem entirely feasible at this stage
of our knowledge. Here Albright is surely correct in seeing that
various parts of this psalm were not originally connected, even
if his atomizing into thirty or more incipits seems rather extreme despite precedent in Akkadian sources.

Central to the psalm is a series of war songs or pieces of
war poetry interspersed throughout the text.[115] They reflect battle or victory songs celebrating the victory of Yahweh and his

hosts either in the time of conquest or in the period of the
Judges. Their similarity to such poems as Deuteronomy 33, Judges
5, and Exodus 15 is marked. As in Judges 5 there are strong
signs that the psalm, or parts of it, had its setting in a cultic
context in which the wars of Yahweh and his armies were celebrated. The text as it now stands associates with these war songs
many other often baffling bits of poetry including adaptations to
the royal cultus at Jerusalem.[116] It is possible to see in the
pieces of war poetry a basic theme centering in the theophany of
Yahweh and dealing with the battle of Yahweh and his armies
against his foes and the foes of Israel. The cosmic background
of Israel's wars is everywhere present, and Yahweh's kingship and
the establishment of his sanctuary are themes which are also present in sections of the psalm.

Verse 2

yqwm 'lhym

ypw' 'wybyw

wynws mśn'yw mpnyw

Let "Yahweh" arise;

Let his enemies be scattered

And let the ones hating him flee from before him

This verse is part of the ancient Song of the Ark, a variant
of Numbers 10:35. Several points may be noted here. The verse
forms the appropriate beginning of this psalm.[117] It was sung as
Yahweh, enthroned on the Ark, went forth to holy war for his
people. The enemies are Yahweh's, not Israel's. Here theophany
and holy war are inextricably combined, casting Israel's under-

standing of warfare fully onto the divine plane and de-emphasiz-
ing the role of Israel, as the song of the return of the Ark in
Numbers 10:36 makes clear. The battle is between the divine warrior and his enemy. Tribal participation was expected and commanded, as this psalm, Judges 5, and other texts indicate, but
the invocation of the aid of the deity, a practice common in war
in the Near East and elsewhere, in Israel led to the theophany[118]
of Yahweh (and his hosts) -- a key element in her conception of
what went on in battle.[119]

Verse 5

The point of interest here is the epithet applied to Yahweh
in the second colon. The phrase $rōkēb\ ba^{\epsilon a}rābŏt$, perhaps to be
read $rōkēb^{\epsilon a}rāpŏt$, is a common appellation of Ba$^\epsilon$al in the Ugaritic texts (see preceding part), and refers properly to the driv-
ing of the clouds as a war chariot. Kapelrud,[120] Galling,[121]
Goetze,[122] and, most recently and extensively, Mowinckel,[123] have
shown that this phrase and other references to riding in the Old
Testament must be understood in terms of the driving of a chariot,
the principal vehicle of war in the second millennium. Again the
imagery is of Yahweh's driving the clouds, the cherubim, the
heavens, or other such vehicles into battle (see also v. 34; Deut.
33:26; Ps. 18:10; Isa. 19:1; Hab. 3:8; Ps. 104:3). The proper
interpretation of the term $rkb\ ^\epsilon rpt$ is further reinforced by the
fact that the members of Yahweh's council are pictured as riding
on chariots (for example, v. 18 of this psalm -- see below).

Verses 8-9[124]

$^{\textstyle ,}lhym\ bṣ^{\textstyle ,}tk$

lpny 'mk

bs'dk byšymwn[125]

'rs r'š

'p šmym ntpw

mpny 'lhym zh syny

mpny 'lhym

'lhy yśr'l

"Yahweh," when thou didst go forth

Before thy people,

When thou didst march from[126] the wilderness,

The earth shook,

Yea the heavens dripped

Before "Yahweh" of Sinai,

Before "Yahweh"

God of Israel.

The similarity between these verses and Judges 5:4-5 is immediately obvious. There are definite distinctions or differences
which led Albright to stress the separateness of the two occurrences; but these theophanies, virtually identical in form and vocabulary, must be kept together. In no way can one be said to have
priority over the other. Certainly it cannot be argued that Psalm
68:8-9 is secondary to Judges 5:4-5, because of historical references in the former, but these references are most illuminating.
In Psalm 68 Yahweh is pictured as leading his people, not from
Seir and Edom, but from the wilderness. This is the march of conquest. Yet Yahweh is pictured also as the one of Sinai. The
false dichotomy that results from separating the cosmic from the

historical, that is, Yahweh's coming from his cosmic mountain and his marching before the Ark through the wilderness, is clearly revealed when the theophanies of Judges 5, Deuteronomy 33, and Psalm 68 are looked at in their contexts. In the Song of Deborah the theophany of Yahweh's coming from a geographical location that might be construed as his abode is clearly in the context of a historical battle. The theophany can be only an echo of Yahweh's coming in conquest. Likewise the very mythopoeic theophany of Yahweh and his hosts from Sinai in Deuteronomy 33 is the center of a poem which recounts Israel's march from Sinai and the settlement in the land. Here in Psalm 68 where the imagery is clearly of Yahweh among his heavenly assembly (vv. 12, 18) and reference is made to Yahweh's battle against the cosmic enemies, Yamm and Bašan, the theophany is manifestly in terms of Yahweh's leading Israel. In all cases the picture of Yahweh and his council which is supposed to belong to the cosmic or mythopoeic realm, is set in a historical context and vice versa. Thus in these verses the fusion of the cosmic and the historical, the hosts of heaven and earth, in the conceptions associated with Israel's sacral wars and particularly the wars of the conquest is transparent. It is accentuated in what follows.

Verses 10-11[127]

These verses refer to the settlement of Israel in the Promised Land where Yahweh, associated here too with the storm god, provides for his people with rain and abundance. The marked resemblance in these verses to the content of Deuteronomy 33:26 further confirms the similarity of theme in these chapters.

Verses 12-13

> ʾdny ytn ʾmr
>
> hmbś́rwt ṣbʾ rb
>
> mlky ṣbʾwt
>
> yddwn yddwn
>
> The Lord gives a command;
>
> The bearers of the word are a great host.[128]
>
> The kings of the armies
>
> They flee, they flee
>
> . . . . [129]

Echoes of the messenger oracle appear here. The $m^e baśś^e r\hat{o}t$
are the members of Yahweh's assembly -- a great host -- [130] who
proclaim his commands for battle. Many assume that verse 13 is
the proclamation but we cannot be certain. As Albright recognized, the reference is probably to the kings of the Canaanite
city states and Israel's battles with them -- again in a fusion
of the divine and human, the cosmic and the historical. Yahweh's
action against the kings is picked up again in verse 15, though
its precise connection with verses 12-13 is a problem and may not
even have existed in the early stages of this composition.[131]

Verse 18

> rbb ʾlhym rbtym
>
> ʾlpⁿ śnⁿ n ʾdny
>
> bⁿbʾwⁿ msyny bqdš̌
>
> The chariots of "Yahweh" were two myriad,
>
> A thousand the warriors/archers of the Lord,
>
> When he came from Sinai with the holy ones.

Here the march of Yahweh and his hosts into battle is unmis-
takably present. "Chariots" can hardly refer to Israel's army at
any early stage in her history; it is obviously the divine army
here which marches forth to fight for Israel. Despite Mowinckel's difference of opinion, Albright has correctly solved the
problem of the *hapax legomenon* $šn^{\jmath}n$ by relating it to the word
which appears in the Ugaritic texts as <u>tnn</u> and in the Alalakh
texts as *šanannu* and refers to some class of warrior, possibly
"archers."[132] If my reading of Deuteronomy 33:2 is correct, the
šnn may be compared with the $^{\jmath}šd$ $^{\jmath}lm$ of that verse.

The imagery of the heavenly army is further clarified when
the difficult third colon is read correctly. The translation a-
bove builds upon that of Albright with only a change in the suffix, assuming instead of a third person plural a third person
singular referring to Yahweh. Recognizing $qdš$ as a collective
"holy ones" provides a clue to the proper reading. The resulting
tricolon is in good meter and parallelism and is reminiscent of
Deuteronomy 33:2-3.[133] Albright maintained that the question of
whether the warriors and chariots of the preceding cola are terrestrial or celestial is insoluble, although in light of II Kings
6:1[134] he favored celestial; and the new reading of the third
colon makes the celestial nature of this army the more likely. We
find, therefore, in Psalm 68 also the "ubiquitous motif" of Yahweh's march from the southern mountains (or Egypt) with his
heavenly armies.[135]

Verses 20-21 are praise to Yahweh for his victory and Israel's salvation. The last colon of verse 21 seems to contain a

reference to Yahweh's victory over Mot (Death), which may form a connecting link with verses 22-23 recounting his victory over his cosmic enemies.

Verses 22-24

> ˒k ˒lhym ymḥṣ
>
> r˒š̌ ˒ybyw
>
> qdqd "rš̌ˁ" (?)
>
> mthlk b˒š̌myw
>
> ˒mr ˒dny
>
> ˒š̌bm bš̌n⌐⌐
>
> ˒š̌bm mṣlwt ym
>
> lmˁn t⌐r⌐ḥṣ
>
> rglk bdm
>
> lš̌wn klbyk
>
> m˒ybym mnḥw

How "Yahweh" has smitten

The head of his enemies

The head of the "wicked(?)"

Roaming in his guilt.

The Lord said:

I muzzled the Serpent,

I muzzled the Deep Sea

That you may wash

Your feet in blood,

The tongues of your dogs

From the enemies their portion. (?)

The picture of Yahweh's battle against his enemies is present here also, but now the enemies are interpreted as cosmic.
Whether verse 22 refers to historical enemies, mythological monsters, or, more likely, both, cannot be determined. One of the
most crucial words -- $š^cr$ -- is highly uncertain.[136] But when
verse 23 is translated correctly, we see that Yahweh's enemies
are also the monsters of the cosmos. Albright in his earliest
treatment of this psalm was one of the first to call attention
to this theme in the verse and particularly to the mention of
the serpent Bašan. But the emendations proposed there are too
extreme and actually unnecessary. He refers to ^cnt: III: 35-44
(= CTA 3.III.35-44) as the basis for his readings, but does not
note the fact that this passage contains almost precisely the
equivalent of Psalm 68:23.[137] Dahood recognized the presence of
the verb $šbm$ in the second colon and correctly translated without
consonantal emendation: "I smote the deep sea."[138] A simple
transposition of the second and third elements of the first colon
produces the same results there, although Dahood does not so interpret it. Thus I would translate as above, a translation almost identical to ^cnt: III:37-38 (= CTA 3.III.37-38):

   ištbm tnn išbm⸢n⸣h

   mḫšt btn ^cqltn

   I muzzled Tannin, I muzzled him.

   I smote the twisting Serpent.[139]

The similarity between the gory character of verse 24 and
^cAnat's massacre of the peoples (^cnt: II = CTA 3.II) has been
pointed out more than once.[140] Albright's discovery of ^cAnat in

this line is, however, as he says, more ingenious than convincing.[141]   That there are mythological connotations can be inferred
from the preceding verse; but if the *ḥērem* can be understood as
in part a satiation of the deity, as appears to be the case in
the Mešaᶜ Stele and Isaiah 34, it is quite possible that verse 24
contains a reference to the *ḥērem* in the conquest.[142]

The remainder of Psalm 68 may be looked at as a whole, although it contains several parts not necessarily connected. Verses 25-28 describe the procession of Yahweh the king into his
sanctuary. Because of the separation and independence of most of
the elements in the poem, it is not possible to associate this
action definitely with the victory march of Yahweh and his hosts;
but comparison with a large part of the corpus of early poetry
would suggest that we have here the march of the victorious warrior into his sanctuary. As Albright has noted, verses 32 and 33
can hardly be dated before the time of David or Solomon (as is
true of the inserted reference to Jerusalem in v. 30). Verse 32
may have come into the poem because of the several references to
the bringing in of tribute.

These last verses from 29 on are a paean of praise to the
conquering warrior and a call for him to continue his triumphs,
to make known his strength and majesty. Verses 34 and 35 are especially significant because they again describe Yahweh as the
rider of the clouds and the heavens. The giving forth of Yahweh's mighty voice reminds one of the similar expression when
Baᶜal established himself in his abode after the victory over his
enemies (51:VII:28ff. = *CTA* 4.VII.28ff.) and testifies further to

the influence of Israel's milieu upon her conceptions of her warrior God.

Exodus 15

Yahweh the warrior, "terrible in glorious deeds," is nowhere
more vividly described than here in the Song of the Sea. Set in
the exodus and the conquest, the poem recounts Yahweh's deliverance of his people as he marches with his host from the south to
take the land for Israel. The type of theophany is not the same
as that in the passages previously analyzed; the divine assembly,
while apparent in the background, plays no major role; but the
motifs of battle, kingship, and establishment of sanctuary are
all here.

Once again Cross and Freedman have analyzed carefully the
details of the poem and clarified its relationship to mythological patterns and traditions of Canaanite literature.[143] More recently Cross has followed that up with two articles that treat
the poem along the lines that have been laid out here, making unnecessary a further exhaustive study of the poem in these
pages.[144]

The song begins as a hymn of praise to Yahweh for his victory over the Egyptians. Praise continues in the second verse,
but verses 2 and 3, which introduce the section recounting the
destruction of the Egyptians, identify by name and nature the God
who is praised.[145]

ᶜzy zmrt⸢y⸣ yh

wyhy ly lyšwᶜh

zh ᵓly wᵓnwhw

>*lhy* >*by* w>*rmmnhw*

yhwh >*yš mlḥmh*

yhwh *šmw* [146]

My might and my defense are Yah(weh)

He has saved me.

This is my God, whom I admire,

The God of my father, whom I exalt.

Yahweh is a man of war.

Yahweh is his name.

In these lines Yahweh, the object of Israel's praise, is characterized as the divine warrior. "This is my God," that is, the
one who is "my might" and "my defense," the one who is a warrior.
He has a name, Yahweh. He is also "the God of my father," the
ancient designation of the tribal or clan deity.[147] Summarizing
Alt, Cross aptly writes of this type of deity: "He may be described as an 'historical' god, i.e., one who guides the social
group in its peregrinations, its wars, in short through historical vicissitudes to its destiny."[148] Exodus 15 thus provides one
of the most ancient, if not actually the earliest, attestation of
the identification of Yahweh and the god of the fathers.

Furthermore, in the context of this song the identification
gains in importance. Although the imagery indicates Yahweh's destruction of the enemy by storm, and the heavenly hosts are referred to (v. 11), it is not primarily as the cosmic battler who
comes with his coterie in bright theophany riding the clouds,
giving forth his voice, sending his arrows, fighting the chaos
monster, who destroys the Egyptians. It is rather as the tute-

lary divine warrior whose right arm destroys the threat to his
people on the historical plane in holy war.

This does not mean the mythological dimension is absent. It
is there both in the themes and in the overall pattern, as Cross
has ably demonstrated.[149]   The focus on the sea reflects Israel's
use of available and influential mythic patterns as does the
storm god imagery. The heavenly army plays no role, but the assertion of Yahweh's incomparability is made vis-a-vis the "gods,"
the "holy ones." The content structure or themes of the poem
follow the familiar mythic pattern (see below). In the process
of recounting the redemptive activity of Yahweh and praising him
for it, the hymn fuses in partial fashion the themes of cosmic
warfare and holy war.

So it is Yahweh, the god of the fathers, the one feared
among the holy ones, who defeats the Egyptian army. The battle
is recounted in verses 4-10 followed by the coda of praise in
verses 11 and 12. The mode of destruction is the storm by which
Yahweh overturns the Egyptians and drowns them in the sea.[150]
From verse 13 onward the poem relates the march through the wilderness and the conquest. There is a definite progression which
reflects the "ritual Conquest" in the Gilgal narratives of
Joshua.[151]   That progression, together with the desert connotations of $n^e w\bar{e}h \; qod\check{s}ek\bar{a}$, "thy holy encampment," suggests that
verse 13 recounts the march to Sinai; but it is possible that the
verse refers to the battle camp at Shittim where Israel began the
conquest across the Jordan and where the Ark was taken across in
the Joshua traditions.[152]

Verses 15-16 stem from the traditions of holy war in which victory was believed to be accomplished, not by might of numbers and weapons but by terror (*ʾêmāh*; cf. Ex. 23:27f.; Josh. 2:9) and dread (*paḥad*; cf. Deut. 2:25; 11:25) which Yahweh wrought upon the enemy, that caused them to melt (*nāmōgû*; cf. Josh. 2:9, 24) before the Israelites.[153]

Then in verses 16b-18 the victorious march of Yahweh and his people is climaxed by the establishment of Yahweh's sanctuary and his kingship -- a motif familiar in Canaanite mythology.[154] Cross and Freedman cite ᶜ*nt*:III:26-27 (= *CTA* 3.III.26-27) for comparison here. Those lines read:

> *btk . ġry . il . ṣpn*
>
> *bqdš . bġr . nḥlty*

In the midst of my mount (who am) the god of Ṣaphon

In the holy place, the mount of my inheritance.

The final colon of this tricolon, which is not quoted by them, shows the close connection between the establishment of Baᶜal's sanctuary and his victories in battle:

> *bnᶜm bgbᶜ tliyt*[155]

In the pleasant place, in the hill of my victory.

A similar relationship with regard to Yahweh could be inferred from this parallel expression in Ugaritic, but Exodus 15 clearly shows the association of Yahweh's kingship and sanctuary with his victory over his enemies. The enemies of Yahweh, however, are not mythological; they are historical -- the very real enemies of Israel. Verse 16b is to be interpreted with Cross as the crossing of the Jordan. The sanctuary in verse 17 is Gilgal. It was

at this site presumably that the celebration of conquest and
holy war reflected in this song and in Joshua 3--5 took place.[156]

Thus, as Cross has pointed out, the Song of the Sea preserves a familiar mythic pattern: the combat of the divine warrior and his victory at the Sea, the building of a sanctuary on
the mount of inheritance, and the god's manifestation of eternal
kingship.[157]

We know this pattern well from the Ba^{c}al cycle at Ugarit and
the Creation Epic in Mesopotamia, but it is reflected with various modifications in the other poems discussed in the preceding
pages as well as in Psalm 24, which Cross has shown also contains
the same historic-mythic fusion of cosmic war and holy war.[158]
At the center of all these pieces there is usually both the march
into war and then the procession of victory as the divine warrior
and his hosts enter the sanctuary. This is the element which most
clearly unifies the poems studied both individually and collectively. The hosts of heaven and earth participate in the affairs.
The essential purpose of the divine warrior's activities -- and
the dividing line between these poems and their mythological background -- is the "creation" of a people (Ex. 15:16). Yet even
there the mythic pattern is not altogether absent, for creation
is an overt or implicit element in the Mesopotamian and Canaanite
myths.[159] The cosmogonic myths of kingship and salvation through
the work of the divine warrior have, therefore, profoundly moulded
the conceptual patterns of early Israel as reflected in her
poetry.

Habakkuk 3:3-15

The third chapter of the prophecy of Habakkuk belongs to a
much later period than Exodus 15. It is worth noting, however,
that verses 3-7 and 8-15 are two sections which probably come
from earlier sources.[160] The theophany of Yahweh the warrior here
is in many ways similar to that of Judges 5, Deuteronomy 33, and
Psalm 68. The picture is more detailed at points and is worthy
of note because the emphasis is much more heavily upon the mythological chaos battle, the conflict between Yahweh and the forces
of the sea and death.

Albright's translation of verses 3-8 is probably correct at
all points except possibly verse 4 where his emendations are
rather extensive.[161] This section of the hymn is entirely a theophany and begins, like Judges 5:4 and Deuteronomy 33:2, with
Yahweh's march from the south. The emphasis in verse 3 appears
to be upon the cosmic abode, but undeniably in the background of
these verses is the memory of Yahweh's march before the people
from Sinai. Paran is mentioned in this connection in Deuteronomy
33:2 and Teman is merely a synonym, both referring to Yahweh's
coming from the mountains of the south.[162]

The imagery is of Yahweh the warrior coming in his glory.
The elements of earth and heaven are violently disturbed. Peoples
and nations tremble. Whether verse 4 is meant to denote Yahweh's
fighting like a bull depends upon the validity of Albright's extreme emendation, which is open to question. The text is certainly corrupt in its present form. The first colon, the only
one that makes sense, may be correct inasmuch as Yahweh's

"brightness as the light" compares with the effulgence or radiance of the theophany in Deuteronomy 33:2.

Verse 5, as has been recognized many times, comes directly from Near Eastern mythology, both Canaanite and Mesopotamian. The closest parallel is the march of Marduk with servants at either side, these sometimes being the gods of plague and pestilence.[163] Rešeph especially is a well-known warrior deity of Canaanite origin.[164] Plague and pestilence here are personified members of Yahweh's host who accompany him into battle.[165]

The reference to Kušan[166] and Midian is perhaps significant. They may be simply other names for the southern region from which Yahweh comes in the theophany, but if these locations have any historical reference, another interpretation is plausible. Gerhard von Rad has demonstrated that the phrase "the day of Midian," which appears in the prophets (Isa. 9:3; 10:26), comes out of the traditions of holy war and the defeat of the Midianites in the period of the Judges.[167] It is, therefore, possible that the reference to Kušan and Midian may come from the same historical circumstances, although at a much earlier time than the Isaianic expression.

Verses 8-15 of this hymn are extremely corrupt, as any translation will show. Albright's effort involves many emendations -- some quite credible, others less so. Albright has recognized that for some verses translation perhaps should not even be attempted. Nevertheless, the picture of Yahweh the cosmic warrior battling the force(s) of chaos is certainly the thrust of the passage. The enemy is designated as River (*nāhār*, v. 8), Sea

($y\bar{a}m$, v. 8), the Deep ($t^e h\hat{o}m$, v. 10), Death ($m\bar{a}wet$, v. 13?), and possibly Earth ($^{\circ}ere\d{s}$, v. 12). As in similar descriptions, Yahweh bears a bow, arrows, and spear and rides or drives horses and a chariot.[168] Verse 9 appears to contain a reference to the satiation of Yahweh in battle, a note which is sounded in the apocalyptic vision of Isaiah 34. As in verses 3-9, Yahweh's advance in battle involves a great disturbance of the elements. The reference to the sun and moon is quite peculiar. They occupy a passive role, controlled apparently by Yahweh's spear and arrows. The details of the battle are described obscurely in verses 13b-15. It is important to note in this connection that in Yahweh's fight with the foes of Israel, described in the language of the mythological cosmic battle his opponent is understood to be accompanied by a warrior retinue ($przw$)[169] quite in keeping with mythological patterns of Canaan and Mesopotamia.

Most significant, however, is the fact that in the very center of this vivid description of the mythological chaos battle it is made clear that Yahweh's actions are for the deliverance of his people -- a note markedly absent in the battle myths of Ba^{c}al and El. His warfare is not only against mythological forces, but against nations, whom he crushes ($d\hat{u}\overset{y}{s}$) in order to save his people. Here again the cosmic and historical planes merge in Yahweh's warfare, but with different emphases. Whereas in the other texts examined, the focus has been upon the conflict of Yahweh's hosts against the enemies of Israel with the chaos battle brought in as a part of that conflict, in Habakkuk 3 the chaos battle dominates but its motive is for historical deliver-

ance of the ʿam Yahweh. The result is the same -- the theophany
of Yahweh and his various forces to fight the historical enemies
of Israel.

II Samuel 22:7-18 = Psalm 18:7-18

This royal psalm has been ably treated by Cross and Freedman,[170] but its striking similarity to previously discussed theophanic descriptions demands that it be noted here. Like most
of the texts we have examined, II Samuel 22 = Psalm 18 is relatively early. As a royal psalm it naturally belongs to the monarchy but probably about the tenth and no later than the ninth
or eighth century B.C.[171] As a whole, it treats of Yahweh's deliverance of the king in time of trouble and his training and
equipping of the king for war. The dominant image or quality
associated with Yahweh is again that of the warrior. The section
of the psalm under scrutiny is not necessarily a separate part
but is delimited here by its character as theophany and its comparative relationship to other such texts.

From his heavenly abode (mēhêkālô, v. 7) Yahweh hears the
cry of the king for help and comes to his aid. Unlike the theophanies of Deuteronomy 33 or Judges 5, Yahweh does not come from
a geographical point such as Sinai or Seir but from his "palace."
He does not *go forth* or *come* (yāṣāʾ, bāʾ, ṣāʿad), but descends
(yārad). The differences, however, are not as great as may seem,
since the gods' cosmic dwelling places were recognized to be lo-
calized at particular places, and the verb yārad is not uncommon
in theophanic descriptions, for example, Micah 1:3 where yārad
and yāṣāʾ appear in parallelism.

The appearance of Yahweh is again accompanied by the shaking
of the earth (*rā*ʿ*aš*, v. 8 -- cf. Judg. 5:4; Ps. 68:9) and the
shuddering of the mountains (*rāgaz*, v. 8 -- cf. Hab. 3:7). The
sources of the sea and the foundations of the world are laid
bare (v. 16). Yahweh himself is pictured as the warrior storm-
god breathing smoke and devouring fire (v. 9) and hurling his
arrows and lightning[172] to panic (*hāmam*) the enemy, a major element in the theory of holy war. If the first colon of verse 13
is correct as it stands, which is not certain, then there is reference here also to Yahweh's "consuming brightness" when he appears to do battle. Although the clouds are at his feet, the
chariot of Yahweh is not the clouds or heavens, as elsewhere, but
the cherubim on the Ark -- the palladium of holy war, on which
Yahweh rode to battle. Yet the cherubim were also members of
Yahweh's court. In verse 11 the deity is pictured as flying on
the wings of the wind. Verse 14 provokes the same comparison
with a central passage in the Baʿal myth that has been noted
elsewhere:

From the heavens Yahweh thundered,

And Elyon gave forth his voice.

From his heavenly abode (*hkl*) Baʿal, the storm god of Ugarit,
also gives forth his voice against his enemies according to Text
51:VII:27ff. (= *CTA* 4.VII.27ff.).

Here the result of Yahweh's violent epiphany is not a victory over mythological forces but the defeat of the king's enemies and the rescue of the king. The remainder of the poem
recounts this act and then details the role of Yahweh preparing

the king for battle.[173]

Joshua 10:12-13

   šmš bgbᶜwn   dwm

   wyrḥ bᶜmq ylwn

   wydm hšmš

   wyrḥ ᶜmd

   ᶜd yqm

   gwy ᵓybyw

   Sun, stand still in Gibeon

   (And) Moon in the valley of Aijalon!

   And the Sun stood still

   And the Moon stood

   Until he had executed vengeance

   Against the nation of his enemies.(?)[174]

Although this short poetic incipit is different from the
longer passages previously examined, it is probably an ancient
piece of epic poetry that tells again how the celestial bodies
participated in the battles which Yahweh fought for Israel. Brief
as they are, these lines have produced an extensive amount of
discussion, largely because they appear to be one of the most
singular miracle stories of the Old Testament. Most commentaries
and studies deal primarily with the nature of the miracle, often
seeking to rationalize or explain it. Such an approach would
seem on the face of it to be inherently wrong even though verses
13b and 14 attempt in part to do that themselves. The conjunction ᶜad in verse 13 suggests that the idea behind the poem was
that the sun stayed long enough in the sky for Israel to defeat

her enemies, but that is as far as one can go. And problems
still exist. What part does the moon play in these events? Is
a naturalistic interpretation necessary to explain its role also?

One of the more original and recent interpretations is that
of Jan Dus.[175] On the basis of several Old Testament texts he sees
Gibeon as a cult place of the sun god Šamaš. Then building upon
observations made by J. Heller, he interprets Joshua 19:12-13 as
originally entirely separate, referring to Šamaš and Yariḫ as two
deities venerated in Gibeon and Aijalon, who are commanded in a
curse not to give oracles but "to keep silence." The curse may
have originated in an Israelite sanctuary. Later, with the
spread of Yahwism and the decline in the worship of these deities
the true meaning of the poem was forgotten and it was connected
to Joshua's battle at Gibeon. The proposed interpretation builds
heavily upon the proposition b^e- in $b^e gib^c \hat{o}n$ and in $b^e {}^c emeq$ $\jmath ay$-
$y\bar{a}l\hat{o}n$, meaning "in Gibeon," and so on, rather than "over," for
which $^c al$ is always used. The prepositional usage is striking,
but had no special significance in view of the increased knowledge of the great flexibility of meaning and relationship of the
prepositions in early Northwest Semitic. Dus's views are interesting, but they depend too much on assumptions about sun worship
at Gibeon; also he ignores some of the problems in the passage,
being forced to maintain that the moon has no meaning here in its
present form and that $yidd\bar{o}m$ and $d\hat{o}m$ mean "be silent."

Easily the most credible interpretation of this passage is
that recently advanced by John S. Holladay, Jr.,[176] who sees
an astrological notion here. Comparing the poem with Assyrian

astronomical texts, he finds that the simultaneous appearance of
sun and moon in the sky can be a fortuitous omen and concludes:

> Within this context, the meaning of Josh. 10:12c-13b
> could hardly be more clear. The first stich is a prayer
> (or incantation) that the sun and moon will "stand" (*dmm* =
> *izuzzum*) in opposition (= *šitqulu*; hence the very necessary
> reference to Gibeon on the east and the valley of Aijalon
> to the west) on a day favorable to "the nation"(most proba-
> bly the fourteenth of the month) rather than to her enemies
> (the result if the moon were to "flee" from the approaching
> sun, thus delaying conjunction until the unfavorable fif-
> teenth of the month). The second and third stichoi, then,
> simply report a favorable outcome to the prayer, "the na-
> tion" in effect gaining its ascendancy over "its enemies"
> during those few fateful minutes of opposition when the
> great lunar and solar orbs "stood" in the "balance."[177]

Holladay would seem to be on the right track in getting at
the phenomena behind these lines. Some questions remain, however, and even by his interpretation the poem in its context must
be associated with the corpus of poetry already discussed. In
any accounting of the poem Joshua's praying to or commanding the
sun is strange, although of course not impossible. But even
though verse 12a begins: "Then Joshua said . . . ," one should
not jump too quickly to the assumption that the command was originally his. For one thing, Joshua speaks *to Yahweh*, as the
verse says; but even more important, as Holladay and others have
recognized, the poem must be looked at on its own terms as a sep-

arate unit which has been incorporated into the narrative. The

poem includes 12b and 13a but only the former could be Joshua's

prayer. The second line is clearly a poetic report of what hap-

pened as a result of the command in 12b. The two lines probably

were a part of a larger poem. As Noth has observed, the inser-

tion may have been due to the catchword "Gibeon" although, as he

also points out, the poem may have originally still referred to

this battle.[178]

The ʿad of verse 13a and, therefore, the understanding of

the whole line is not clearly explained by Holladay's interpreta-

tion. The examples he cites do not indicate that the good or bad

fortune will take place while the astronomical phenomena are hap-

pening but that they are indicators that such things *will* happen

in the immediate future. This may not be an impossible stumbling

block to Holladay's explanation, but it remains a problem.

The poem is a call to the celestial bodies to aid in battle

-- a motif reminiscent of Judges 5:20.[179] Representation of the

sun and moon as deities was common in the Near East.[180] In Is-

rael they were absorbed into Yahweh's assembly as a part of the

vast host gathered around him (for example, Ps. 148:3). Under

Canaanite influence they would have occupied a prominent place --

but as members of the council of Yahweh. The line was sometimes

so thin between acceptance of these as passive bodies under the

control of Yahweh and as separate beings worthy of worship that

in later times syncretistic tendencies in Judah produced worship

of sun, moon, and stars. Job 31:26 also testifies to the strong

temptation in Israel to worship the sun and moon.

Thus, although there is no sign of worship, it is not surprising to see the sun and moon personified in this context.
They are called upon to help Israel by standing still ($d\bar{a}mam$//
$^c\bar{a}mad$).[181]   A similar motif appears in Habakkuk 3:11:

> The exalted one, Sun, raised his arms, Moon stood ($^c\bar{a}mad$)
>
>> on his lordly dias;
>
> By the light of Thine arrows they move, By the lightning
>
>> sheen of thy spear![182]

Here again Yahweh goes forth to battle and, even as in Joshua
10,[183] the sun and moon participate. In light of the Habakkuk
passage where the standing still of the moon and sun is associated with Yahweh's warfare, there is the strong possibility that
the speaker and the actor of Joshua 10:12-13a are not Joshua and
Israel but Yahweh; and command to the sun and moon is more likely
to have come originally from the mouth of Yahweh or one of his
messengers than from Joshua. The collector or editor of the text
apparently recognized the peculiarity of the command's being ascribed to Joshua for he commented (v. 14): "There has been no
day like that one before it or after it when Yahweh listened to
the voice of a man." Then he added the recognition: "for Yahweh
fought for Israel."

This last statement further indicates that the subject of
$yiqq\bar{o}m$ in verse 13a is Yahweh rather than $g\hat{o}y$. The LXX reads
theos here, and Gruenthaner believes the reading may be original.[184]   The other versions, however, follow the MT, making one
hesitant to propose another reading, attractive as it may be.
Furthermore, Yahweh may be the subject in the text as it stands.

In the first place, the word *gôy* is a rather unusual, though not impossible,[185] designation for Israel, especially in this literature.[186] It generally refers to the nations who were Israel's enemy (*ʾōyēb*). The term *ʿam* would be much more likely if Israel is meant. In addition, with the single exception of this verse, the verb *nāqam* when it takes an object always takes a preposition with the object.[187] The most satisfactory explanation, therefore, seems to be that a *mem* (for *min*, which is common with *nāqam*) was lost by haplography from the original form of the text:

   ʿd yqm ⌜m⌝ gwy ʾybyw

which would translate:

> Until he had executed vengeance against the nation of his
>   enemies.[188]

The reading is not certain, but in my opinion it is more satisfactory. The incipit would thus refer to Yahweh's command that the sun and moon stand still to lengthen the day in the battle against the enemy (vv. 10, 14). However the text may have originally read, even in its present form it attests to Israel's understanding that these cosmic elements were involved in her holy wars as "Yahweh fought for Israel" (v. 14).

The Armies of Yahweh in Later Tradition

Early Prose Traditions

Joshua 5:13-15

This fragmentary episode, though listed here among later traditions, is probably fairly ancient,[189] reflecting early interpretation of how Israelite tradition viewed the conquest. It

has received relatively little attention outside the commenta-

ries,[190] although in some respects it is a focal point linking

the Gilgal events of Joshua 3--5 with the narratives of the con-

quest beginning at Jericho. There are quite a few problems in

the passage, not all of which are soluble. The question of lo-

cale is a difficult one. The text of verse 13 indicates that

Joshua was "in" or "by" Jericho ($b\hat{\imath}r\hat{\imath}h\hat{o}$). But inasmuch as verse

15 indicates that the locale is a holy place, especially in its

reference to a $m\bar{a}q\hat{o}m$, and in view of the relationship of the pas-

sage to the preceding episodes, it is possible to see also a con-

nection with the Gilgal sanctuary.

The text relates the appearance to Joshua of a man ($\hat{\imath}\check{s}$)

bearing a drawn sword, an immediate reminder of Numbers 22:23 and

I Chronicles 21:16 where an angel with drawn sword appears to

Balaam and to David.[191] In the Joshua passage, however, the fig-

ure has the appearance not of an angel but of a man arrayed as a

warrior. Joshua sees him only as a warrior and asks him a ques-

tion of a purely military nature: "Are you one of us or one of

our adversaries?"[192] -- the equivalent of the more modern: "Who

goes there, friend or foe?" The man answers that he is neither

but is the "commander of the army of Yahweh" ($\acute{s}ar\ s^e b\bar{a}^{\flat} yhwh$), and

Joshua immediately recognizes his heavenly visitor and worships.

Then comes the sentence paralleled in Exodus 3:5. As Noth and

others have recognized, the real message of the commander is now

missing. The words "Now I have come" indicate an official visit

and are meant to be followed by a message (cf. II Sam. 14:15ff.;

Dan. 9:22).[193]

At first glance the passage seems to be simply an isolated
incident brought in by the collector of these narratives, this
especially because of the truncated story that does not give the
actual purpose of the visit of Yahweh's commander. Noth's interpretation is largely along these lines.[194] He sees the event as
basically a type of cult legend associated with an unknown holy
place near Jericho, which went back to Canaanite times but was
used by the Israelites. The episode originally contained a longer message or conversation which has now been deleted by the
"collector" because of religious reasons. The remaining record
indicates that there were directions about the nurture and care
of the sanctuary.

Brief as it is, Noth's treatment of these verses is still
the principal one of recent times -- along with that of Abel --
and contributes several excellent observations. I find myself in
greater agreement with Abel, however, because, caught up as he is
with etiologies and *Ortsgebundenheit* (the association of traditions with places),[195] Noth fails to get at the core of the text
and its significance. He is correct in working on a history-of-
tradition basis, but he fails to see that in that history the associations of various traditions with other elements may have
been stronger. It is precisely the tradition history which forces one to associate this episode primarily with the events in
the conquest,[196] presumably even before the "collector" of the
traditions.[197]

The association with a cultic locale is correct, probably

even apart from verse 15, but Noth ignores too easily the nature
of the heavenly figure and the missing message. The earliest
possible record of the event identified the visitor specifically
as the "commander of the army of Yahweh," and apart from that
identification the episode is meaningless from the start. This
one is not designated as the *mal'ak Yahweh*,, though that figure
appears in a similar manner elsewhere. The title is very specific and unusual and must be taken seriously. His message must
originally have had to do with his nature and function. In the
parallel passages -- Exodus 3:5; Numbers 22:23; I Chronicles 21:
16 -- there is a message or purpose definitely related to the
context. There is no reason for assuming otherwise for the original Joshua episode or for assuming that the message has been
deleted, presumably because it was religiously offensive, though
Noth does not say so. The message was simply lost in transmission, and only the first two words of the text remain. The most
likely, indeed required, supposition is that the words of the
commander of Yahweh's army related to the conquest. The events
at Jericho were regarded as the first stage in the holy wars of
the conquest. This episode provides the transition point from
Gilgal to Jericho. Yet even apart from the missing message the
śar ṣᵉbā' Yahweh links the heavenly, cosmic army with Israel's
earliest holy wars, and the very presence of this figure declared
that the ensuing conquest was sacral and that Israel's army would
be led by Yahweh's divine army.

Genesis 32:2-3

As Gunkel and von Rad both have recognized, these two verses

are a fragment of an ancient tradition now etiologically connected with the name of the important city Mahanaim.[198] Abrupt and
succinct in their context, they tell of a meeting of Jacob with
the angels of God ($mal^{\prime a}k\hat{e}$ $^{\prime e}l\bar{o}h\hat{i}m$) and record that as he saw them
coming toward him, he exclaimed: "This is the army ($mah^{a}n\bar{e}h$) of
God," and therefore named the place Mahanaim. The fact that virtually nothing happens in the brief episode is strong indication
that this is only the remaining framework of what was once a
longer story.[199] The rest of the tradition would probably have
been very illuminating with regard to the character and function
of Yahweh's heavenly army in the patriarchal narratives, but this
fragment indicates that those ancient traditions understood the
host of Yahweh as a military force.[200]

II Samuel 5:22-25

Yahweh's peculiar reply when David inquires whether he
should go up against the Philistines is to be understood in terms
of this concept of the divine armies.[201] Yahweh tells David not
to go up until he hears the sound of marching ($s^{e\zeta}\bar{a}d\bar{a}h$) in the
balsam trees, but then to fight because Yahweh has gone forth be-
fore him ($y\bar{a}s\bar{a}^{\prime}$ $yhwh$ $lipneyk\bar{a}$) to smite the enemy. The language
(for example, $s^{e\zeta}\bar{a}d\bar{a}h$, $y\bar{a}s\bar{a}^{\prime}$) and imagery in the prose narratives
are virtually identical with that of the theophany of Yahweh and
his heavenly army in the early poetry and elsewhere and give
added weight to the notion in Israelite religious thought of a
heavenly or cosmic army coming to help in holy war.

Ninth-Century Prophets

Further examples may be seen in the narratives of Kings,

particularly in traditions relating to the ninth-century prophets.[202]   In his study of the oracles concerning foreign nations, R. Bach asks the important question as to how the summons
to battle and the summons to flight were carried over from the
early holy wars into the prophetic oracles and strongly agrees
with von Rad that the prophets of the ninth century in the Northern Kingdom must be understood out of the traditions of holy
war.[203]   He then wishes to look even further back to see if at
the earliest stages of prophecy there was a close relation between the prophet and the call to holy war. Whether that is so
or not, it is important here that the ninth-century prophets are
closely associated with the traditions of holy war and thus form
a link between the tribal league practices of holy war and the
later prophetic oracles.[204]   They also form a connection between
the early association of holy war theology with the heavenly army
imagery and the later association of prophetic eschatology and
the Day of Yahweh with that same imagery.

II Kings 6:15-19

In this episode Elisha's servant is terrified upon seeing
the great army of the Syrians who have surrounded them by night
and cries out, "Alas, my master, what shall we do?" Elisha re-
assures him with: "Fear not, for those who are with us are more
than those who are with them." The phrase "fear not" ($^{c}al\ t\hat{\imath}r\bar{a}^{\flat}$,
v. 16) is a familiar word of encouragement and battle cry of holy
war (Ex. 14:13; Josh. 8:1; 10:8, 25; 11:6),[205] the demand for
complete trust in Yahweh which lay at the very core of the theology and practice of holy war.[206]   The basis for the lack of

fear is not merely that Israel's army is greater than that of
the king of Syria -- a supposition that would probably be automatic if verse 17 were not in the text -- the army of Israel is not
even present in this context. Rather, the servant looks up and
sees on the mountain a mighty army of horses and chariots of
fire, none other than the heavenly army of Yahweh, which comes to
aid the prophet.[207] The imagery is especially similar to Psalm
68:18 where Yahweh is pictured as coming from Sinai with chariots
and warriors.

II Kings 7:6

After the siege of Samaria by Ben-hadad has lasted for some
time, four lepers decide their only hope is to go over to the
Syrian camp. When they enter the camp no one is there, "for,"
the record explains, "the Lord had made the army of the Syrians
hear the sound of chariots and of horses, the sound of a great
army, so that they said to one another, 'Behold, the king of Israel has hired against us the kings of the Hittites and the kings
of Egypt to come upon us.'" There can be little doubt that Israel understood in this account the sound of the heavenly army,
exactly as in the preceding story and in II Samuel 5:24.

In this light the chariot and horses of fire which separate
Elijah and Elisha at the former's ascent into heaven (II Kings 2:
11-12) are also seen to be representatives of the heavenly army
who fought for Israel.[208] Whether the expression was originally
so understood cannot be said definitely -- it is attributed also
to Joash the king as Elisha lay dying (II Kings 13:14) -- but in
the light of these passages it quite probably was. In any event

the designation is out of the holy war traditions, traditions in
which Elijah and Elisha firmly stood. Immediately after Joash
utters this cry over the dying Elisha, the prophet tells the king
to shoot an arrow out the window and as he does so, the prophet
cries out: "Yahweh's arrow of victory!" The cry is a sign of
Yahweh's intervention with symbolic or magical qualities similar
to Moses' raising his arms in the war against Amalek (Ex. 17:11)
and Joshua's pointing his spear toward Ai (Josh. 8:18). The
judgment of the anonymous prophet against Ahab for failure to
carry out the *hērem* against Ben-hadad (I Kings 20:35ff.) is also
strong indication that the ninth-century prophets played out
their roles in Israel's history against a backdrop of holy war
traditions.

Later Prophetic Writings

The warring armies of Yahweh appear in the prophetic writings
themselves, especially in the later eschatological and apocalyptic literature, a movement which reaches its full force in the
intertestamental period. If the Day of Yahweh has its origins in
the ancient holy war traditions of Israel[209] as they were carried
through the royal cultus,[210] then it is not surprising to see a
revival or carry-over of the fundamental element, that is, the
wars of Yahweh as a joint participation of human or earthly forces and divine or heavenly armies. In fact, this motif is precisely a central aspect of the end time. We shall not try to
deal with all the prophetic passages which portray the divine warrior, but shall focus rather on those which reflect our basic
theme, the march of Yahweh and his armies.

Isaiah 13:1ff.[211]

These verses, a doom oracle against Babylon, are part of a larger collection and may belong to a much later time than that of Isaiah.[212] They treat the Day of Yahweh as a great holy war involving the earthly and heavenly hosts. There are several problems in the text. The nature of the persons addressed in verse 2 is unclear. Is the verse a call to Yahweh's warriors to prepare for battle,[213] or is it an address to the enemy? It is even possible to interpret the commands as an address to the divine council, though that is not necessarily the best choice. In verse 3 Yahweh levies a mighty host for battle,[214] but here also it is impossible to tell whether these are heavenly or earthly hosts, or both. He calls them "my consecrated ones" ($m^e quddā\text{-}šay$), "my warriors" (*gibbôray* -- see below, note 218), and "my proudly exulting ones" ($ʿallîzê\ ga^ʾ{}^a wātî$). The use of the first person suffix might suggest that these warriors are indeed Yahweh's assembly. Most important is the use of the term $m^e quddāš$, "sanctified, consecrated," which belongs to the practice of holy war, in which the soldiers were purified and set under certain taboos before battle.[215] Then come the words:

Yahweh $ṣ^e bā^ʾ ôt$ is mustering ($m^e paqqēd$)[216] a host for battle.
They come from a far-off land, from the ends of the heavens,
Yahweh and the weapons of his indignation, to destroy the
whole earth.

(vv. 4b-5)

Using the ancient designation "Yahweh of hosts," the prophet announces that Yahweh has summoned a great army "from the ends of

the heavens"[217] to wipe out the whole earth. If indeed *kol-ha -*
ʾareṣ is to be interpreted as the whole earth, as seems to be the
case, the picture is one of final destruction -- wrought by Yahweh and his heavenly army (v. 5a) -- in the day of Yahweh. If
the reference is only to Babylon or some other individual nation,
then the army may be interpreted as a combination of earthly and
heavenly beings. Late though the text may be, the themes of the
passage are clearly in the tradition of Israel's understanding of
Yahweh's warfare as a divine-human, cosmic-earthly endeavor.

Joel 4:9ff.

This passage, similar to Isaiah 13 in form and content,
brings together a number of significant themes. Verse 9 begins
with a heraldic call to the divine assembly to proclaim holy war
(*qirʾû*). Then the proclamation of the assembly goes out to the
nations:

> qadd^e ṣû milḥāmāh / haᶜirû haggibbôrîm
> yigg^e ṣû yaᶜᵃlû / kōl ʾanṣê hammilḥāmāh
> Sanctify war! rouse up the warriors!
> Let them draw near and go up,
> All the men of war.

The language is again a call to arms, to purify the warriors
(cf. Josh. 3:5; II Sam. 11:11; I Sam. 21:6), to stir them up to
go to battle (cf. Judg. 5:12; Isa. 51:9; and so on). The apocalyptic element appears prominently in verse 10 where the prophetic
saying about the tools of war becoming the tools of peace is reversed, and plowshares and pruning hooks now become swords and
spears. The weak and timid become mighty warriors. The nations

are commanded to gather around. But then in the midst of this
command a significant change of address appears (v. 11b):

hanhat yhwh gibbôreykā

Bring down thy warriors, Yahweh.

As has been recognized, this can only be a call for Yahweh
to come forth with his heavenly army.[218] The divine beings who
make up the assembly of Yahweh are elsewhere called *gibbôrîm,*[219]
and the verb *nāḥat* confirms the fact that the heavenly warriors
are involved. They are brought down from above, whereas the nations are brought up (*wᵉyaᶜᵃlû,* v. 12) into the *ᶜēmeq yᵉhôšāpāt*.

The purpose of this warlike activity is made abundantly
clear in verse 12b:

kî šām ᵓēšēb lišpōṭ ᵓet-kol-haggôyim missābîb

For there I will sit to judge / all the nations round about.

Here is strong indication of the close connection between
the imagery of Yahweh as warrior and Yahweh as judge of the nations (cf. Judg. 11:27).

Two aspects of divine warfare are present in the succeeding
verses. The sun, moon, and stars are darkened (so also Isa. 13:
10), reminiscent of their participation in Judges 5:20; Habakkuk
3:11; Joshua 10:12-13). In verse 16 Yahweh comes roaring from
Zion "and the heavens and the earth shake" -- both aspects of
theophany seen in Judges 5; Psalm 68; Deuteronomy 33; II Samuel
22 = Psalm 18;and Habakkuk 3. The closing verses with their announcement of the return of paradise and a final proclamation of
doom against the enemies of Judah reflect much of the language
and imagery of the early poetic material.

It should be noted further that if Wolff is on the right track
in his interpretation of Joel 2:1-17, we may have there also a
vivid picture of the march of the divine army on the day of judgment. Wolff contends with strong arguments that 2:1-17 is not a
further description of the locust plague but a picture of the future, portraying an apocalyptic army modeled on the locust plague
but using other traditional motifs.[220]   In this graphic portryal
Yahweh commands a mighty army which marches forth wreaking destruction in the Day of Yahweh:

> The Lord utters his voice
>
>> before his army,
>
>> for his host is exceedingly great;
>
>> he that executes his word is
>
>>> powerful.
>
> For the day of the Lord is great
>
>> and very terrible;
>
> who can endure it?   (RSV)

If the locusts are excluded and the northern enemy, then it is
natural to assume that the prophet describes here the familiar
cosmic host, the military retinue of the divine warrior.[221]

   Isaiah 40:26 and 45:12

   Although these two verses do not involve the Day of Yahweh
or oracles calling for battle against the enemy, note should be
taken of Cross's observation that "here Yahweh is pictured as
marshaling and mustering his heavenly army."[222] This interpretation is given further support by Muilenburg who writes with regard to Isaiah 40:25-27:

> Mowinckel believes that Yahweh is portrayed here as
> the shepherd of the stars. More likely the figure is mili-
> tary . . . God, the captain of the host, calls out his myr-
> iads upon myriads of stars, and each star takes its appoin-
> ted place as its name is called. There they stand in their
> great battalions in response to the call of the captain.
> Not one is missing; each responds to the call of its own
> name.[223]

Christopher North has elaborated this observation most recently[224] by noting that we have here three military terms. One of
these is of course the $s\bar{a}b\bar{a}^{\,?}$, the host. The second is the Hiphil
of $y\bar{a}s\bar{a}^{\,?}$, which means in this case that "Yahweh leads them out
as a commander leads an army" (cf. 48:17; II Sam. 5:2; 10:16);
and the third, North says, is the term "by number" (cf. II Sam.
2:15 and Num. 1 [fourteen times]).

Zechariah 14

The motifs discussed throughout these pages reach their full
eschatological bloom in late prophecy in the final chapter of
Zechariah.[225] Incorporating the strong note of judgment that is
central to the Day of Yahweh traditions, Zechariah 14 describes
the final holy war when Yahweh's victory over all the nations
will be manifest.[226] The passage re-echoes the language and
themes of the ancient holy wars, for example, the $h\bar{e}rem$ (v. 11)
and the panic of Yahweh on the enemy (v. 13), and is, in fact, a
kind of recapitulation of the pattern we discerned in several
pieces of the early Israelite poetry, modified by other themes
and influences coming out of the royal theology and eschatology:

Yahweh goes forth ($y\bar{a}s\bar{a}^{\,\flat}$, v. 3) to fight (v. 3) against the enemies of Israel and returns victorious with his hosts ($q^e d\bar{o}s\overset{\text{Y}\!\wedge}{\imath}m$,
v. 5).[227] The result is Yahweh's kingship over all the earth
(v. 9), Israel's salvation and secure dwelling (vv. 5 and 11),
Yahweh's established sanctuary (the elevation of Jerusalem, v.
10). Finally, all the nations, not just Israel, shall go up to
the sanctuary to worship Yahweh the king.

Present also in this picture is clear creation imagery: the
waters of life flowing from Jerusalem, the elimination of the
seasonal alternations and day and night, the end of darkness.
This is a "paradise" scene. Although one finds no battle with
the chaos monster, chaos is again transformed into creation and
order.[228] Yahweh's battle is with historical enemies as always,
but the conflict is cosmic in scope and the cosmogonic battle
lies clearly in the background.[229]

Some Post-Old Testament Developments

A detailed examination of later developments outside the Old
Testament growing out of these lines of tradition and this conceptual framework does not belong to the scope of this work. It may
be of some value, however, simply to indicate areas where the
cosmic battle of Yahweh and his hosts comes to the fore and reflects earlier formulations and ideas.

The Book of Enoch is much concerned with angelology and the
day of judgment. It is no surprise, therefore, to find here
clear pictures of Yahweh and his hosts as the destroying army.
The best example is the opening passage with its theophany of the
divine warrior and his retinue, clearly dependent upon Old Testa-

ment imagery. God comes from his dwelling to tread upon the
earth, but here "from Sinai" has transformed into "on Sinai."
The notation is made that he appears "from his camp" (Ethiopic
has "and appear with his hosts"). In typical fashion the mountains shake and the hills melt like wax. Then in 1:9:

> And behold! He cometh with ten thousands
>
>   of His holy ones
>
> To execute judgment upon all,
>
> And to destroy [all] the ungodly[230]

The basis for these lines is obviously Deuteronomy 33:2. Similar
passages appear throughout the book.

The purpose of the coming of God and his hosts is no longer
historical victory in a particular battle with one of Israel's
foes, but the final judgment and destruction of the wicked and
vindication of the righteous. Here is the end stage of the ancient conception of the coming of the warrior host as mediated
through prophetic eschatology.

In a quite different way the heavenly army plays a minor
role in II Maccabees. For example, in 5:1ff. we are told of ap-
paritions of the divine army in the sky over Jerusalem: gallop-
ing horsemen, spearmen, cavalry, and so on. Then in 10:27 the
enemy forces see in the sky five warriors surrounding Judas Mac-
cabaeus. Their arrows and thunderbolts panic the enemy so that
they break up in disorder. The familiar panic of Yahweh which in
the early holy wars seized whole armies is explained specifically
here as the effect of the heavenly warriors. Then in 11:6ff.
Judas prays to God for a delivering angel who soon appears at

their head as a white horseman, and we read: "They advanced in
battle order, having their heavenly ally, for the Lord had mercy
on them."

All these episodes are typologically later but quite similar to the prose accounts in Joshua, Samuel, and Kings of the intervention of the army of God.

The fullest expression of these developments, however, is to
be found in the War Scroll from Qumran, which recounts the final
holy war between the Sons of Light and Sons of Darkness. All a-
long there have been signs that Yahweh and the heavenly host
fight alongside Israel in their battles, but here it is explicit
from the beginning:

> On the day when the Kittim fall there shall be a
> mighty encounter and carnage before the God of Israel, for
> that is a day appointed by Him from of old for a battle of
> annihilation for the Sons of Darkness, on which there shall
> engage in a great carnage the congregation of angels and the
> assembly of men, the Sons of Light and the lot of Darkness,
> fighting each in communion through the might of God with the
> sound of a great tumult and the war cry of angels and men
> for a day of doom. (1QM 1:9-11)[231]

Or in Col. xii:3-5:

> Mercy of blessing [for Thy thousands] and the covenant
> of peace Thou hast engraved for them with a stylus of life,
> so as to be king [over them] in all appointed times of eter-
> nity and to muster [the hosts of Thine el]ect by their thou-
> sands and their myriads together with Thy holy ones [and the

host] of Thine angels, for strength of hand in battle [to

subdue] them that have risen against Thee on earth by the

strife of Thy judgments, but with the elect ones of heaven

are [Thy] blessing[s].

Finally, in lines 6-8:

And Thou, O God, [art terrible] in the glory of Thy

majesty, and the congregation of Thy holy ones are amongst

us for eternal alliance, and we [(OR:they) shall render]

scoffings unto kings, scorn and derision unto mighty men,

for the Lord is holy, and the King of Glory is with us, a

people of saints; Migh[ty men and] a host of angels are a-

mong those mustered with us,the Mighty One of War is in our

congregation, and the host of His spirits is with our steps.

Then follows the call to the divine warrior to rise up and do

battle to establish his kingdom forever.[232]

These are only a few of the places that could be cited. The

elements of holy war are present throughout: the tribes summoned

to battle as the people of God, purification of the camp, the war

cry ($t^e r\hat{u}\Subset\bar{a}h$) and the panic ($m^e h\hat{u}m\bar{a}h$) of God. The language and

terminology of Deuteronomy 33 and Psalm 24 and the like are in-

voked. The ancient epithets of the divine warrior are recalled.

On the final day the mighty warrior God goes forth to battle,

leading the armies of heaven and earth against opposing earthly

and spiritual forces. The purpose of this apocalyptic encounter

is, as in days of old, the defeat of the wicked, the redemption

of Israel, and the establishment of God's kingship and kingdom

forever.

The Ark of the Covenant and Yahweh Sᵉbā'ôt

One of the most vexing problems in the history of Israel's religion has been the question of the nature and function of the Ark. It is not the purpose of this book to present an exhaustive study of the Ark in an attempt to solve all the difficulties associated with it[233] -- no one yet has succeeded in that task[234] -- but in this context it is important to point out that in the earliest texts having to do with the Ark it is clearly associated with the holy wars of Yahweh and perceived as a type of palladium in battle, embodying the presence of Yahweh as he marched to fight for Israel and acting as a security for victory over her adversaries. The starting point is the Song of the Ark in Numbers 10:35-36, the earliest testimony to the Ark now extant.[235]

There are two songs or incipits sung at the going out of the Ark to holy war and at the return. The first one is a variant of Psalm 68:2a. The meter, language, orthography, and context all lead to the conclusion[236] that these lines are archaic poetry:

qmh yhwh

[ ] ypṣw 'wybk

[ ] ynsw mśn'yk mpnyk

šwbh yhwh

<b> rbwt <qdš>

'lpy yśr'l

Arise, Yahweh,

Let thy enemies be scattered,

Let thy adversaries flee before thee.

Return, Yahweh,

∠With> the myriads of ∠holy ones>

With the thousands of Israel[237]

The warlike character of the Song of the Ark is self-evi-
dent. The imperative $q\hat{u}m\bar{a}h$ is standard terminology for the call
to initiate battle. In light of its usage here and in reference
to the Ark in Psalm 132:8 it is probable that the phrase $q\hat{u}m\bar{a}h$
$yhwh$ arose in connection with the going forth of the Ark to battle and then spread to other situations and contexts.[238] The going out of the Ark was in order to bring about the destruction
and flight of the enemies -- Yahweh's enemies, but unquestionably
historical foes of Israel.[239] Whether mythological motifs lie be
behind the language of verse 35 is difficult to determine. If
indeed the Ark was of desert origin, Canaanite influence would be
less expected. A striking parallel exists, however in UT 51:VII:
35-36 (= *CTA* 4.VII.35-36) in the context of Ba^{c}al's thunderous
theophany in his palace:

ib . b^{c}l . tihd . y^{c}rm .

šnu . hd . gpt . ǵr

The enemies of Ba^{c}al take to the woods,

The haters of Hadd to the edge(s) of the mountains.

The flight of the "enemies" and "haters" of the Canaanite storm
god is similar to the flight of the "enemies" and "haters" of
Yahweh. In the Ugaritic text as in the Numbers passage and in
other early poems elements of theophany and war are combined.

The return of the Ark to the Israelite camp is sung in verse
36. Attempts to separate verse 36 from verse 35 at an earlier

stage, which had nothing to do with the activity of war but referred only to the sitting still or resting of the Ark, are mis-
guided and depend less on the testimony of the Song itself than
on the context.[240] The leader god and war god were one and the
same.

These two verses are very archaic war songs forming a unity.
The present context associates them with the Ark -- an association which is certainly original -- and in the general context of
the march of Israel through the wilderness. In all likelihood
the brief songs were originally sung at the procession and return
of the Ark at the head of the people as an indication that Yahweh
the warrior and his hosts led them into battle. The present context in Numbers may not suggest accurately the origin of the
Song. It is not to be doubted, however, that at a very early
stage -- the wars in Canaan or before -- Israelite elements engaged in holy war with the Ark as the rallying point.

The conclusions drawn from Numbers 10:35-36 are borne out by
other passages. One of these, Numbers 14:39-45 (JE), must be
mentioned with some hesitation because its place in the history
of the tradition is not certain. Some see it as quite late,
though generally it is regarded as part of the epic tradition concerning the wilderness wandering and the beginnings of conquest.[241] In the account Moses warns the people not to go up a-
gainst the Amalekites and Canaanites for they will lose because
"Yahweh is not among you" (v. 42). The meaning of this sentence
is in verse 44: "Neither the Ark of the Covenant of Yahweh nor
Moses departed from the camp." The Ark was not in the battle, so

Yahweh was not there.

Judges 20 is generally recognized to be somewhat schematic and expanded with late elements introduced.[242] It certainly gives more detail on this battle than many of the others in the book. An explanation may be found, however, in the fact that the chapter is a very important one dealing with a holy war by the tribal league against one of its own members -- an inner Israelite conflict. Elements of holy war are present, for example, the levy of the tribes for war by sending out twelve pieces of flesh; inquiry of Yahweh; and the reply: "Go up, for tomorrow I will give them into your hand."[243] Parenthetically in verse 27 it is noted that the Ark was at Bethel. This reference may be a gloss, as is generally claimed, for it is the only reference in Judges to the Ark. Whatever its history, the reference conforms with the rest of our data and explains that the tribes had to go to Bethel to prepare for holy war because the Ark, the shrine center of Israel's sacral wars, was there.

The ark appears in the account of Israel's war against the Philistines in I Samuel 4, but there is indication that the Ark did not always go out to battle, as may be assumed anyway.[244] This tradition, however, may be the exception which proves the rule.[245] The Israelites, faced with impending defeat, sent for the Ark, but its arrival did not produce the expected victory. On the contrary, the rout was even greater. The narrator may well have been attempting to show the result when the presence of Yahweh in the battle was only a desperate afterthought on the part of the warriors.[246]

I Samuel 14:18 in the MT definitely associates the Ark with
Saul's holy war against the Philistines, which resulted in victory because of a (divine) $m^e h \hat{u} m \bar{a} h$ in the battle. The use of
this text may not be legitimate, however, inasmuch as most commentators follow the LXX and read "ephod" for "ark,"[247] because
the Ark was confined to Kiryath-jearim at that time. In any
event, if there is any possibility at all of reading "ark," its
setting in the ritual of holy war is clear.[248]

The procession of the Ark to Jerusalem in II Samuel 6 is not
ostensibly in a context of holy war, but it is my opinion that
the episode does indeed arise out of the traditions of holy war
-- the march with the Ark; the blowing of trumpets, the $t^e r \hat{u}^c \bar{a} h$,
David's dancing before the Ark.[249] But detailed analysis of that
passage belongs to a more extended treatment than we can give
here of the carry-over of the motifs and traditions of sacral
warfare into the royal cultus and theology.[250]

II Samuel 11:11 again reveals the Ark on the field of battle
with the tribal levies (not the king's soldiers) in the holy war
against the Ammonites which resulted in Uriah's death because of
his unwillingness to violate his state of purification and sanc-
tification -- an act which would have saved his life although he
did not know it.[251] On the other hand, in II Samuel 15:24ff.
David sends the Ark back into Jerusalem presumably because his
conflict with Absalom was not a matter of sacral war.

The two principal passages in the Psalms literature which
involve the Ark[252] -- both of which are probably early, though they
cannot be dated definitely -- indicate its warlike connotations

and associations. Psalm 24 makes no mention of the Ark, but

verses 7ff. are almost unanimously believed to have their origin

in the triumphal return of Yahweh and the Ark to Jerusalem.[253]

If this interpretation is correct, the verses speak for them-

selves with regard to the relationship of the Ark to Yahweh's

wars and to the name *Yahweh ṣᵉbā'ôt*. Likewise the explicit ref-

erence to the Ark in Psalm 132:8 which bears kinship to Numbers

10:35-36 designates the Ark as "the Ark of thy might" (*'ᵃrôn ᶜuz-

zekā*), an explicit reference to the warrior might and power of

Yahweh which produced victories for Israel. In both Psalm 24 and

Psalm 132 we have the Ark processional of Yahweh and his armies

either to or from battle.[254]

There are numerous references to the Ark in the conquest

narratives of Joshua 3-6, but these chapters are regarded as

quite expanded and heavily oriented to the cult, and so may be

dubious sources when dealing with such a matter as the Ark.[255]

But, as Cross has plausibly suggested, the celebration of ritual

conquest is at the base of these chapters;[256] and, noting the as-

sociations of the Ark with the holy wars of Israel in all other

relatively early texts, one is forced to see that same associa-

tion here. Regardless of the historical background of Joshua 6,

it can hardly be doubted, *contra* Noth,[257] that the Ark played a

central role in the earliest level of tradition about the march

around the city, although the very numerous references to it are

in part the result of expansion. The account of Joshua 6 relates

a schematized holy war with emphasis upon the miraculous activity

of Yahweh, and the Ark of the Covenant is inevitably set in that

context. The Gilgal traditions of Joshua 3--5 have a less warlike flavor to them, but they obviously involve preparations for
war.[258] In any event, nowhere in Joshua apart from the Deuter-
onomistic section 8:30-35 can the Ark be separated from the holy
wars of conquest.

The Ark plays no significant role in von Rad's analysis of
the theory of holy war, being confined to one citation and a
lengthy footnote.[259] He does associate it with the military activity of Yahweh in the early Song of the Ark, but goes no further than that, maintaining that the Ark appears in war only in
the later time (for example, I Sam. 4--6; II Sam. 11:11). But
more can be said than that. The Ark is at all points intimately
and directly associated with the wars of Yahweh. One can not assume that the Ark went out at every battle any more than one can
assume that the $h\bar{e}rem$ or any other aspect of holy war was always
present (a point von Rad has recognized). Nevertheless, the
unanimous witness of the texts relating to the Ark would suggest
that as a war shrine it played a central role in the sacral wars
of Israel's early history.[260]

The $s^{e}b\bar{a}{}^{\jmath}\hat{o}t$ epithet associated with Yahweh has drawn as much
disagreement and discussion as has the role of the Ark, and nu-
merous theories have been put forward to define it. The origin,
the meaning, and the grammatical explanation of the name in its
various forms have been matters of controversy; and the frequency of its occurrence (over 250 times) has compounded the question
rather than solving it. The problem of the term is so complex
that it has been the subject of an exhaustive, detailed disserta-

tion, which, however, has still not resolved the difficulties.[261]
The reader is referred to this work and to other more recent
studies for an analysis of the different opinions and theories
which have been proposed.

The term $s^e b\bar{a}^{\,\flat}\hat{o}t$ in this context has been said to refer
originally to the armies of Israel, the stars, angels, natural
powers, and all of creation. The basic point of agreement among
most scholars has been the fact that the epithet in its earliest
stages is to be associated with the Ark, the palladium of holy
war.[262] This conclusion is based on its early usage in the Samuel
narratives and is methodologically correct, but most analyses
have succumbed to methodological faults. The term has to be analyzed on the basis of its contexts, of course, but this methodological foundation stone eventually gives out because of the
great frequency of the epithet often in contexts which clearly
reveal nothing about the original meaning of the phrase. It is
necessary, therefore, to approach the term on a linguistic and
lexical basis and in light of comparative studies. Albright and
Cross separately have analyzed the term on this basis and thus,
as far as our present knowledge is concerned, have produced the
best interpretation of the divine name and epithet.

Two grammatical explanations of the name have vied for popu-
larity. One is that despite its infrequency beside the short
form, the longer form of the name -- $yhwh$ $^{\flat e}l\bar{o}h\hat{e}$ ($ha\d{s}$) $s^e b\bar{a}^{\,\flat}\hat{o}t$ --
is the original and that $s^e b\bar{a}^{\,\flat}\hat{o}t$ thus stands in genitival or con-
struct relation to either $^{\flat e}l\bar{o}he$ or $yhwh$. Certainly the longer
form must be explained in this manner. But if the short form is

original, as is most likely the case, then the explanation is
less satisfactory though not impossible. An alternate view es-
poused by Eissfeldt is that the words *yhwh* and $s^eb\bar{a}^{\flat}\hat{o}t$ are grammatically independent of one another. He views the latter term
as an abstract formation standing in apposition to *yhwh*, thus
producing *Jahweh der Zebaothhafte*, "Yahweh the Mighty One."[263]
This type of interpretation is not without precedent,[264] and is
grammatically possible. It remains, however, a rather forced
interpretation in light of the fact that $s^eb\bar{a}^{\flat}\hat{o}t$ is a perfectly
good word as is, meaning "hosts, armies."[265]

    The proper point of departure in the analysis of the name
is Albright's recognition that in common with numerous West Semi-
tic divine names, the name *yhwh* $s^eb\bar{a}^{\flat}\hat{o}t$ is a sentence name.[266]
The word is patently a verbal formation, duplicated often by al-
most identical name formations in the West Semitic onomasticon of
the second millennium.[267] It is a sentence name shortened to its
verbal element without hypocoristic ending. Gramatically, *yahweh*
is most likely a third person singular, causative imperfect of
"to be," that is, "to cause to be, create, procreate," or the
like.[268] The name originally would have meant "He causes to be"
or "He creates." Both Cross and Albright have argued that in
common with other divine names, *yahweh* originally was only one
part of a longer name. The Old Testament itself gives a clue to
its lengthier nature at an early stage in Exodus 3:14 where it
appears as $^{\flat}ehyeh$ $^{\flat a}\check{s}er$ $^{\flat}ehyeh$.[269] From this text and on the basis of comparative materials, Cross has demonstrated convincingly
that the original cultic name out of which the name and character

of Yahweh developed was $^{*}{}^{\jmath}el\ d\bar{u}\ yahw\bar{\imath}$, "El who creates.[270] Furthermore, because of sense and of parallel formations both in
Canaanite and Israelite literature, Cross and Albright have seen
that the verbal sentence must have had an object.[271] The most
likely candidate and the one most clearly preserved is $s^{e}b\bar{a}^{\jmath}\hat{o}t$.[272]

The meaning of the term $s^{e}b\bar{a}^{\jmath}\hat{o}t$ has been the question that
has drawn the attention of most scholars. That it encompassed
several meanings throughout the history of Israel's religion is
probably to be expected, but the primitive meaning of the term in
this cliché may not have been so all-inclusive. The word $s\bar{a}b\bar{a}^{\jmath}$
is basically a military term,[273] used most often to indicate an
army or warfare.[274] In the expression $yahweh\ s^{e}b\bar{a}^{\jmath}\hat{o}t$, then, must
be recognized a military force -- "He who creates the armies."
But in the original formation of the name were these armies divine or human? Because of the close association of the name with
the holy wars of Israel in I and II Samuel, and because "host of
heaven" is always singular $(s\bar{a}b\bar{a}^{\jmath})$ and never plural $(s^{e}b\bar{a}^{\jmath}\hat{o}t)$, it
has been assumed that the "hosts" referred to in the epithet $yah-$
$weh\ s^{e}b\bar{a}^{\jmath}\hat{o}t$ were originally the armies of Israel. The validity
of the first argument has been disqualified in this thesis, since
both divine and earthly hosts joined in Israel's armies. The
term $s^{e}b\bar{a}^{\jmath}\ ha\check{s}\check{s}\bar{a}mayim$ is actually strong indication that $s^{e}b\bar{a}^{\jmath}\hat{o}t$
originally referred to nonhuman participants. It is always sin-
gular because it is a technical term referring to a fixed and
specific group usually associated with astral elements.

The most valid interpretation has been given by Cross, who
sees in the term a clear reference to the beings who made up the

divine assembly (including the "host of heaven").[275] It is an

epithet of the god who was both warrior and creator and probably

arose out of the cult of El in the south when he was worshiped

both as the great creator god and the warrior god. The epithets

of El and Aṯirat which designate their creative or procreative

activities refer to their creation of divine beings, for example,

bny bnwt (El) and *qnyt ilm* (Aṯirat). One may assume, therefore,

that if Yahweh is recognized as originally a cultic name of El

and if we suppose that the god Yahweh "split off from El in the

radical differentiation of his cultus,"[276] then the name *Yahweh*

s^{e}bā$^{?}$ôt was probably a very archaic designation for Israel's God:

"He creates the divine armies." Despite its absence from the

books of the Old Testament prior to I Samuel,[277] the probable

history of the term, as well as its association with the Ark,

marks it as one of the earliest epithets for the God of the He-

brews.[278] Albright has demonstrated that the official name of

the Ark was probably "Ark of the Covenant of Yahweh of Hosts En-

throned on the Cherubim."[279] Thus the ancient shrine of holy war

and its name testify strongly to the fusion of the heavenly and

earthly armies in Israel's notion of holy war. Within this con-

text the ancient cultic title probably soon came to refer to both

the hosts of heaven and the hosts of Israel (cf. I Sam. 17:45).

The Pattern of Warfare in Early Israel

The use of the term "pattern" in this context is not meant

to imply that there was a set ritual which was carried out pre-

cisely in *all* battles. The texts do not indicate that such uni-

formity ever existed; even the schematized and elaborated narratives of Joshua 1--12 show differences among themselves. Nevertheless, there were certain elements central to Israel's war
activity and her conceptualization of it, and it may be of value
to sum up by setting these forth in the light of the discussion
presented in the preceding pages and that of other scholars.

Holy Warfare as a "Synergism"

At the center of Israel's warfare was the unyielding conviction that victory was the result of a fusion of divine and human
activity. As the centuries passed and the traditions grew, there
came a tendency to ascribe the victory solely to the miraculous
intervention of Yahweh apart from any participation of the people
but in the early period of Israel's history there was no such ab-
dication on the part of the people. While might of arms and numbers were not the determining factors (note the contrast in the
size of Gideon's army and that of the Midianites), it was yet
possible for the people to see themselves as going to the aid of
Yahweh in battle (Judg. 5:23). The emphasis, however, lay on the
activity of the divine, the involvement of Yahweh as warrior and
commander of the heavenly armies. The theophany of Yahweh and
his coterie was the foundation stone. Yahweh fought for Israel
even as Israel fought for Yahweh (Josh. 10:14; Judg. 7:20-22; and
so on);the battles were Yahweh's battles (I Sam. 18:17; 25:28).
Thus, as I have attempted to demonstrate in this book, Yahweh was
general of both the earthly and the heavenly hosts.

Holy War as a Sacral-Cultic Affair

Ritual or cultic aspects were present in Israel's early warfare, though some of the evidence for this fact is derived from later sources. Prior to battle, oracle inquiry of Yahweh was made to see if the army would be victorious. In this endeavor the priests may have taken charge, though it is often associated with the war leader. Because the war was sacral, a sphere of activity in which Israel's God was present, the camp and the warriors had to be ritually purified (I Sam. 21:6; II Sam. 11:11; Deut. 23:13-15; Josh. 3:5; 7:13). Undoubtedly the prophetic call to "sanctify war," which is present especially in passages announcing the Day of Yahweh (Joel 4:9; Jer. 51:27-28; Jer. 6:4), reflects the ancient command to prepare for holy war. Most important of all, however, was the practice of ḥērem, the devotion of the spoils -- both men and property -- to Yahweh.[280] The category of goods which fell under the ḥērem varies; so it is difficult to determine the presence of the ḥērem solely by what was destroyed. The biblical accounts do not indicate that the ḥērem was carried out in every instance of what was otherwise a sacral military affair, but it is quite likely that the practice was in effect at times even when not mentioned, just as in other instances reference to the ḥērem may have been inserted at a later date. The ḥērem had its origins in the offensive wars of conquest.[281] Israel fought at Yahweh's command, which included the ḥērem. The spoil and prisoners of war were holy and separated, even as the warriors who fought for Israel were holy.

March of the Ark and the Armies

The function of the Ark in Israel's wars also was a reflection of their sacral nature and of the fusion of divine and human

elements in these battles. The holy war palladium, the Ark of
the Covenant, was conceived of as the battle station from which
Yahweh, the divine warrior, the creator of the divine armies,
fought for Israel. Once again it must be stressed that the Ark
is not evidenced in all the accounts. In one instance (I Sam.
4) its presence was delayed until defeat was impending. Yet its
association with the holy wars is strongly indicated and the
march of the Ark and the divine warrior, Yahweh, is probably to
be seen even in texts where there is no specific reference to the
shrine itself. Deborah's shout to Baraq, "Does not Yahweh go
forth before you?" may refer to the procession of the Ark as Yahweh's throne. So also the poetic theophanies of Yahweh and his
heavenly armies are to be viewed at least in part in this context.
Psalm 68:8 is couched in almost identical terminology: "Yahweh,
when you went forth before your people." Thus the march of the
Ark with the armies occupied a place of importance both in the
ritual of holy war and in the conceptualization underlying it.

The Role of Yahweh and the Heavenly Army

The precise manner in which Yahweh and his hosts aided Israel is not always specified. Often merely the fact of the heavenly army's marching forth with Israel is all that needed to be
said, for example, Deuteronomy 33:2-3. Elsewhere the writers and
poets are more specific. The members of the assembly are described as warriors with drawn swords, riding in chariots.
Plague and Pestilence serve Yahweh. The astral beings fight for
Israel. Most important is the fact that Yahweh and his warriors
create an attitude within the enemy. They shake the earth and

disturb the elements. Tumult and confusion result. Yahweh thunders against the enemy and sends a panic upon them. In a quite definite sense Israel conceived of the victory as being primarily a divine one and indeed a cosmic one wrought by forces above and beyond any action on Israel's part, which, however, worked to Israel's benefit.

The Role of the People of Israel

The fact that victory was achieved by divine forces, and that Israel came to view this intervention as a type of miracle does not mean that the people themselves had no responsibilities. The narratives indicate that Israel was always engaged in very heavy fighting. Very few instances of battle show Israel as removed from true military engagement as does Joshua 6, and that narrative seems to reflect a later idealization of the battle. Yet even there where little emphasis is placed upon out-and-out fighting, the people still play a major and active role. The fact that the ʿam Yahweh saw itself often in this role as specifically a military grouping and that the clans were under obligation to "come to the aid of Yahweh" leaves no doubt that Israel understood herself as playing a vital role in war of Yahweh. The war leader, the earthly equivalent of the "commander of the army of Yahweh," filled with the divine spirit, led Israel forth to battle. The $t^e r\hat{u}^\zeta \bar{a}h$, the battle shout, was uttered by the people in the conflict. So also was the carrying out of the ḥērem. But primarily, as von Rad has recognized, Israel's role was to have faith in Yahweh and to fear not. Numbers and size of the army were regarded as less important factors. As long as Israel trusted in Yahweh, victory would be achieved. So Israel could

focus attention upon the might of Yahweh and his military coterie

and ascribe an almost passive role to her own involvement despite

the fact that in the narratives one sees that the wars of con-

quest and settlement in the land were bitterly fought.

The Primal March of Holy War

The journey of the Israelites into the land of Canaan ap-

pears to have been viewed throughout Israel's history from a very

early time as the holy war or Yahweh war *par excellence*. The

conquest in the Book of Joshua is schematically represented as

the ideal holy war. But that notion permeates much of the early

literature of Israel. It appears in the prose texts at all

levels where narratives of holy wars at various stages of the

journey from the wilderness on are related,[282] and it appears in

the very early poetic material where Yahweh is viewed as marching

from Sinai with his angels before him to aid Israel in battle.[283]

Although composed of many separate battles involving groups at

different times, the wars of the conquest were quite early viewed

as one great sacral war in which the *hērem* was carried out to se-

cure the land which Yahweh had given the people.

This original march of holy war had its origin in the theo-

phany of Yahweh at Sinai, from which he marched with his hosts to

aid Israel. Particularly in the poetic literature there are

mythological notions of the mountain as the dwelling place of

Yahweh, the cosmic abode of the storm god, but there is much more

here than simply the appearance of the storm god or the sun god

over the cosmos.[284] Yahweh does not go forth to fight mythologi-

cal monsters, nor merely to shine forth over the earth. He marches from Sinai to battle the historical enemies of Israel, and
all his army goes with him. Sinai, thus, is the abode of Yahweh
but it is also the region from which he goes forth to fight and
the place where he has covenanted with Israel and created the ˁam
Yahweh. Sinai, Seir, Edom, and Paran are vividly historicized
as the wilderness of Israel's journey.[285]

From Sinai, Israel and her God proceeded to Canaan, engaging enemies and adversaries along the way. The ancient poetry
sees the march through the wilderness as a military endeavor.
That picture is reinforced by the prose narratives (for example,
Num. 14:39ff.; Ex. 17:8ff.) but especially by the P account in
the early chapters of Numbers where the people of Israel are described as a force in military formation, each tribe being
rallied around its standard. The encampment is a battle camp.
The census of the men is for military purposes. That these chapters represent a later interpretation of the wilderness march in
many respects is certainly true, yet they cannot be dismissed entirely as a late fabrication. They fit too well into the general
pattern of earlier materials. Furthermore, recent scholarship
has been forced to take more seriously the details of the later
material in Numbers.[286] The same may be true of the larger
structures of the P material. Evidence for a military format to
the wilderness march has been seen elsewhere (for example, Ex.
18:24). The general alignment of the people who came from Sinai
through the wilderness in battle array is not incongruous with
the evidence both narrative and poetic.

The culmination of this primal march of holy war is the
crossing of the Jordan and the taking of the land. The result is
on the one hand the establishment of Israel in the land which had
been promised to her and on the other hand the establishment of
kingship and sanctuary for Yahweh.[287] In this respect the Israelite conception of divine warfare compares with basic motifs
in Near Eastern mythology, yet the assurance of Yahweh's kingship
and holy dwelling place is accomplished on a thoroughly historical plane. Yahweh and his armies go forth to fight not Tiamat,
Mot, Yamm, and other divine beings, but the Canaanites, the
Amorites, the Amalekites, and all the other people who stand in
the way of Israel's acquisition of her promised heritage. To be
sure, the battle of Yahweh against mythological forces appears at
points, but it is always a subordinate event fused with the more
political, historical aspect of the warrior god's activity -- the
defeat of Israel's enemies.

Israel's Warfare and Israel's God

In the origins of Yahwism and the worship of Yahweh in Israel two strains merged in the deity Yahweh, the tutelary clan
deity, the god of the fathers; and the high god El, the creator
of heaven and earth.[288] One may now note in light of the work of
Alt, Cross, and others on the development of this phenomenon and
in view of the detailed analysis in the preceding pages that the
combination of Israel's institutional conceptions of holy war with
the more mythological notions of cosmic warfare may have arisen
from the early fusion of the patriarchal tribal god who covenanted with the tribe(s) and led them in battle with the high creator

god who created and led the cosmic armies to war. Information
about the god of the fathers, especially his involvement in the
wars of the tribe, is quite limited, yet there are occasional
indications, some of them most important, as, for example, Exodus
15:2, where in a context celebrating Yahweh's deliverance of Israel in holy war he is called "the god of my father" and "a man
of war." Also connected with the Exodus events is the meaning
ascribed to the name of Moses' son, Eliezer: "The god of my father was my help and delivered me from the sword of Pharaoh" (Ex.
18:4). There can be little doubt that Israel's understanding of
her sacral warfare, a tribal and covenantal phenomenon, was intimately related to and derivative from the religion of the god
of the fathers.

        The other line of development which merges here, that of the
"high and eternal one, El the creator of heaven and earth,"[289]
who created the divine beings and led them forth into battle, the
high god (Baᶜal-Yahweh) who fought the monsters of the deep and
conquered them, has been discussed at length in these pages. It
is at this point that the phenomenon of the divine warrior and
divine warfare is placed on a cosmic level. It is in the fusion
of this element with the god of the fathers that one is to find
the origins of that particular Israelite conception of sacral
warfare viewed as a cosmic and earthly endeavor involving the
hosts of heaven and of Israel under the leadership of Yahweh. The
divine name Yahweh $\d{s}^e b\bar{a}{}^{\eng?}\hat{o}t$ is thus probably to be seen as a type
of cultic or liturgical "ancestor" of Yahweh, which reflects the
coming together of these two strains in the God of Israel, whose

suzerainty relationship with Israel encompassed this fusion of tutelary deity and cosmic warrior-creator.

As I have often stressed, these developments in Israelite religion were not by any means isolated events devoid of any outside influence. On the contrary, Israelite conceptions were very strongly allied with those of her neighbors. The notion of the divine warrior, the assembly of the gods as an army, and the chaos battle are all motifs which reflect outside influence upon Israelite thought, as is indeed to be expected. Yet it is necessary to recognize that like the surrounding cultures which, because of geographical, linguistic, and other factors, developed each in its own way, Israel also manifested its own peculiar character in its religious history. In Israel the creator god was the war god who marched forth to save his people. Basic to the other religions of the Near East in one form or another was the mythological battle to preserve order. Gods fought for man. In this respect there were many similarities to the figure of Yahweh which must not be overlooked. But by and large, there existed a separation between the historical battles of the kings aided by the god or gods and the mythological battles of the gods against the gods. The gods acted to save men, but at the center of the religious concern was the battle for order over chaos, life over death, fertility over sterility. At the center of Israel's faith, however, lay the battle for Israel's deliverance, a conflict involving the theophany of Yahweh and his mighty armies to fight with and for Israel. This encounter took place on a definitely historical level, but the forces of the cosmos were involved.[290]   Insofar as the mythological battle of the gods exis-

ted in normative Yahwism it was brought into this complex. The

mythological, etiological, and magical functions and purposes,

which were of primary concern in the divine warfare of Egyptian,

Mesopotamian, Hittite, Hurrian, and Canaanite religion, were sub-

ordinated in Israel to the historical purposes of election and

covenant so that the whole march through the wilderness to Canaan

was seen as a mighty holy war led by the divine warrior and his

armies.[291]   Finally and most important is the fact that the es-

tablishment of Yahweh's kingship and sanctuary and, in part, his

creation (Deut. 32:6) grew out of this cosmic, historical, sacral

war, whereas elsewhere these elements all resulted from and were

associated with the mythological battle of the gods. The Israel-

ite pattern subordinated all other beings to Yahweh and centered

its attention upon his activity on behalf of Israel. Central to

that activity was Yahweh's role as divine warrior, the "man of

war."

SOME CONCLUDING IMPLICATIONS

The Formation of the Epic Tradition

For some time the scholarly consensus on the growth or formation of the Pentateuchal or Hexateuchal traditions has been
based on the conclusions of von Rad in his form-critical study
of the Hexateuch, to the effect that Deuteronomy 6:20-24; 26:5b-
9; and Joshua 24:2b-13 represent a particular *Gattung* or genre,
"the small historical credo," which is "already a Hexateuch in
miniature" and which forms the basis or outline for the Hexateuch. Then in extended and brilliant fashion von Rad shows how
the Yahwist formulated his account of Israel's early history by
the processes of insertion, expansion, and addition of various
traditions.[1]

While von Rad's assertion that the Sinai tradition was not
an original part of the Exodus-Settlement traditions was early
and widely criticized, most scholars have accepted the hypothesis
of the archaic credo and then sought -- with varying degrees of
success -- to account for the absence of any reference to Sinai
in these credos.[2] More recently, rather severe and justifiable
criticisms have been raised against the prior hypothesis, that
is, that these three passages represent a single ancient form

which was the nucleus out of which the Hexateuchal traditions
were developed. The questioning voices have been numerous and
diverse: A. Weiser,[3] G. Fohrer,[4] L. Rost,[5] C. H. Brekelmans,[6]
Th. C. Vriezen,[7] B. S. Childs,[8] J. P. Hyatt,[9] C. Carmichael,[10]
and W. Richter.[11] There is no need to go into detail on the various criticisms. They have been well presented and with reference to other scholars in the work of Hyatt already cited.
Briefly stated, the passages under discussion, particularly the
basic one, Deuteronomy 26:5b-9, are heavily Deuteronomic in language and character; they are associated with three different
cultic occasions and cannot be dissociated from them; and they
probably represent different if related genres.

If von Rad's conclusions about the "credo" are now seen to
be questionable, it still may be that he was on the right course
in searching for a nucleus which was the principal basis for the
formation of the Hexateuchal traditions or, preferably, the epic
tradition.[12] Without assuming a monolothic schema of development
and allowing for the possibility of varying formulations, it is
quite likely that in some form or other the core of that early
experience and history was expressed in brief fashion, easy to
recount, then expanded and elaborated in various ways -- and probably at a quite early stage -- into the epic tradition. Such
brief recapitulation may have taken more than one form, but at
least one may be discerned whose credentials as a genuinely ancient recital of the saving events are far sounder than those of
the "credos." Von Rad himself has seen this evidence but for various reasons has regarded it as secondary to the Deuteronomic

credos.

I refer in this case to Exodus 15. In the preceding section
we pointed to the antiquity of this poem, a fact that can hardly
be contested any more. A hymn to Yahweh recounting his deliverance of Israel, the poem begins with and focuses on the defeat of
the Egyptians at the Sea, then recounts by stages the march
through the wilderness and into the promised land where Yahweh's
sanctuary is established and he rules as king. There is no certain reference to Sinai, though the "holy encampment" of verse
13 could refer to it,[13] but it is not necessary that specific
mention of Sinai be a part of every account. There are other
testimonies to it in other pieces of archaic poetry. Note further the reference in verse 2 to ᵓelōhê ᵓabî, "the God of my father." While no specific reference to the patriarchs is found in
the poem, I find here a link with those traditions in a reference
to what Alt and others have seen as the core of the patriarchal
traditions -- the worship of the God of the fathers.[14]

The poetic character of this passage is probably a pointer
toward its use as a foundation stone for the formulation of the
JE epic tradition. For, as many have remarked, it is quite likely that the earliest formulations of that tradition were poetic,
as indicated by the large amount of archaic poetic material in
the Pentateuch and the many signs of a poetic sub-stratum, particularly in the books of Genesis and Exodus.[15] Further, the cultic character of Exodus 15 would have contributed significantly
to its influence as an epic nucleus.[16]

Von Rad himself has cited Exodus 15 as one of the "free

adaptations of the creed in cult-lyrics."[17] But with the recognition of the relatively late character of the Deuteronomic "credo" and the early date of Exodus 15, it is preferable to start with the latter and see in it the basis for the later literary-theological activity of gathering and ordering the various traditions into a national epic. There may of course have been other early nuclei which played a part, such as the historical prologue of the covenant formulary.

We are led in this direction also by the recognition that in Exodus 15 we find a mythic-historic pattern which is found elsewhere in various forms in the early poetry: the march of the divine warrior to do battle with the enemies of Israel, the deliverance of the people and their establishment in the land, and the rule of Yahweh over Israel.[18] Its relationship to the cult is certain, but it also exercised a literary influence on other poems and hymns and presumably on the larger literary works. The hymnic framework of Deuteronomy 33:2-5, 26-29 may be cited as another example from the corpus of early Hebrew poetry. Again von Rad has referred to Deuteronomy 33:2-4 but as an example of the separation of the Sinai tradition. The problem in this case is that von Rad has assumed that verses 2-5 are to be understood by themselves, ignoring the fact that we have here the beginning of a framework which finds its ending in verses 26-29. There most explicitly one is dealing with the march of conquest and the settlement in the land. The basic elements of the mythic-historic pattern are there. They become also central elements in the epic unfolding of the story of Israel's origins.

It would be difficult to demonstrate in any conclusive and detailed manner how the epic tradition about Israel's beginnings came into being. Von Rad and Noth have both attempted to do this and indeed have provided valuable insights into the growth of the traditions, but one can hardly say that their important works have given us a consensus or even clear direction. Methodologically, it would be preferable to start with the earliest material and with the poetic, assuming all the while that in a complex history of tradition various influences would have come to bear from many directions and that the core or nucleus of the epic account could have been in several forms. Where it is not possible to work out the details, general hypotheses which rest upon a solid base of evidence will have to be formulated and used as tools or constructs for approaching the material afresh. The hypotheses of von Rad and Noth have served that function in a most valuable way, but it may now be necessary to suggest some new starting points and hypotheses. The most likely place to begin in such a case is with the early poetry of the wars of Yahweh.

At the Theological Center

An investigation of the theological meaning of God as warrior/fighter/commander is outside the scope of this book. Furthermore, I have dealt with some of the theological issues, albeit in relatively brief and preliminary form, in another context,[19] and more recently G. Ernest Wright has addressed himself to this theme in his Sprunt Lectures.[20] My aim in these concluding words is simply to call attention to the centrality of the divine warrior imagery and language in the Old Testament and the consequent need for a major focus upon it in any theological treatment of the Old Testament. Even as any attempt to work out the growth of the epic tradition needs to start out from the songs of Yahweh's and Israel's wars, so any theology of the Old Testament or any overall interpretation of the Old Testament should give significant attention to the conception of God as warrior and the role that it plays in the literature.

From beginning to end this theme in various forms and with various ramifications comes to the fore. It is not possible to dismiss it as "primitive" without in effect dismissing the Old Testament. Yahweh as warrior was indeed a very early part of Israel's understanding of deity and during that early period perhaps the primary imagery evolved. The principal concern of this study has been on the earlier materials, but the pre-monarchical and early monarchical periods were in many respects high points in Israel's history. Even more important, the language and understanding of God as warrior dominated Israel's faith throughout its course. In prophetic oracles, in psalms of the temple, and especially in the development of eschatological and apocalyptic literature, the centrality of Yahweh as the divine warrior and commander of the armies of heaven and earth is very much to the fore and grows out of the earlier theological formulations.[21] It would not be amiss to say that the most elaborated conceptions of the divine warrior come at the end of the Old Testament period. So wherever one turns one encounters this theme.

It is in this context also that myth and history come together and illustrate their interaction in a profound way in

Israel's religious expressions. The picture and patterns of divine warfare come out of the mythological world of the ancient Near East. The heavenly armies are a mythopoeic ingredient; the battle with the monsters of chaos a cosmogonic element. But the context in which these factors play their principal part is the theological conviction that Yahweh was working to save or to punish Israel in her various internal and external conflicts. The language by which the Israelites sought to speak of these conflicts and God's involvement was mythological, drawn from common ways of thinking in the cultures of the ancient Near East; but the sphere in which the divine armies were understood to be involved was not primarily an otherworldly, mythological sphere. The cosmic powers were present and effective in the vicissitudes of human history. It is fashionable in these times to play down the historical sphere as medium and place of revelation in the Old Testament. Certainly justifiable criticisms have been raised against efforts to squeeze the Old Testament completely into that definition. But it can hardly be gainsaid that much of Israel's experience and knowledge of her God came from the wars of her history and the theological reflection on their meaning, a reflection which appropriately and naturally used the available mythological tools.

The divine warrior imagery speaks theologically about some very significant dimensions in the understanding of God from the Old Testament perspective and presumably when one moves beyond that. Ernest Wright has ably elaborated this fact in his Sprunt Lectures, but it may be well to underscore three or four points

in order to demonstrate how central that imagery and its content
are in Old Testament theology.

Salvation. The notion of salvation can involve many kinds
of deliverance from a variety of oppressors. In early Israel,
salvation -- at least as a communal experience, which it was primarily -- was not spiritual but quite historical, the goal of the
warring activity of Yahweh. The victories are spoken of as the
ṣidqôt Yahweh (Judg. 5:11). As the "man of war" who fights for
Israel, he is the strength and defence of the people, indeed
their salvation (*yᵉšûᶜāh*, Ex. 15:2; cf. Ex. 14:30). As a result
of Yahweh's victory it is said that the people are "redeemed"
(*zû gāᵓāltî* Ex. 15:13) or "saved" (*nôšaᶜ*, Deut. 33:29; cf. I
Sam. 17:47). Yahweh fights for Israel quite simply to save them
from destruction and to give the people life and home. So at the
center of Israel's elaborated poetic and theological statements
about God the warrior was the salvation theme, the awareness of
having been saved this way, a conviction articulated not only
with the mythopoeic vocabulary of divine warfare but also with
the common theological vocabulary for salvation.

Or to put it in reverse form, at the center of the salvation
experience and theology of early Israel was the "man of war," the
divine warrior. If one wished to know concretely what salvation
meant in the early period -- and indeed in later times also --
it was simply: Yahweh fought for us and saved us.

Judgment. This does not need elaboration. It is the other
side of the coin, the negative dimension of the activity of the
divine warrior. As he fought for Israel to deliver her, so he

could and did fight against her to punish. The prophets especially drew this obvious conclusion from Israel's theology. And
it was this important assumption that kept the theology of Yahweh's wars from being purely ideological or a naive and simple
"God is on our side" faith. To speak about the judgment of God
in the Old Testament is to be confronted again with the imagery
of the divine warrior.

   Kingship. The same is true as far as the kingship and sovereignty of God is concerned. Whether over the gods or more particularly over Israel, it is the establishment of Yahweh's
eternal rule and sovereignty that is the ultimate goal of Yahweh's wars. It has long been thought that the kingship of Yahweh
originated out of the Jerusalem cultus, but that view is no longer tenable and in the light of extra-biblical material should
have been suspect from the beginning. It is precisely in the
early poetry of Israel that we see the kingship of Yahweh asserted (for example, Ex. 15:18; Deut. 33:5; Ps. 68:25; Num. 23:21;
Ps. 29:10; Ps. 24:9). Yahweh's sovereignty is established by his
victories over the enemies of Israel. He who defeats the foe
claims dominion. The conception of the kingship of God is therefore from the beginning fully wrapped up in the early representations of the divine warrior. It is not possible to talk of God
as king without talking of God as warrior.

   There are other elements of Israelite faith and Old Testament theology related to the subject under discussion here. It
is hoped that the matters mentioned above as well as the content
of the book as a whole are sufficient to indicate that Old Testa-

ment theology and the theological use of the Hebrew Scriptures by church and synagogue will have to wrestle with this fundamental theme.

Notes

Indexes

Part One. Divine Warfare in the Literature

of Syria-Palestine

1. For the question of homogeneity of religion in this area
see below. The religion of Israel is not the primary concern at
this point, though there are many relationships, some of which
will be discussed.

2. Note, for example, the Ugaritic Pantheon text equating
Canaanite and Mesopotamian deities (Jean Nougayrol, *Ugaritica* V,
42-64). Mitchell Dahood has argued that all three of the principal male deities at Ugarit, El, Ba‘al, and Dagan, *may* have been
of Akkadian or Hurrian origin rather than Northwest Semitic (M.
J. Dahood, "Ancient Semitic Deities in Syria and Palestine," *Le
Antiche Divinita Semitiche*, ed. Sabatino Moscati [Rome: Centro
di Studi Semitici, Universita di Roma, 1958], 65-94; cited hereafter as Dahood, *ASD*). Dahood himself opts for the Syrian origin
of Ba‘al but is uncertain about Dagan and regards El as belonging
to "the original Semitic pantheon" (p. 93). The designation of
Dagan as one of the three chief gods at Ugarit is not on the
basis of his very negligible role, if any, in the mythological
texts but on his apparently significant place in the cultus at
Ugarit evidenced by the temple and two steles dedicated to him as
well as his presence in two lists of sacrifices to the gods
(Texts 9:3 [= *CTA* 36.3] and 19:5 [= *CTA* 39.5]). Thus Dahood is
able to conclude: "In spite of the presence of numerous Akkadian
texts at Ras Shamra and the influence of Mesopotamian jurispru-
dence upon the legal system at Ugarit, the most ancient Northwest

Semitic religion was but slightly influenced by Mesopotamia"
(*ASD*, p. 93).

3. As an example of what was involved in this meeting of
Israel and Canaan, see the conclusions of Frank M. Cross in "Yahweh and the God of the Patriarchs," *Harvard Theological Review*,
55 (1962), 225-259.

4. William F. Albright, *Archaeology and the Religion of
Israel*, 4th rev. ed. (Baltimore: The Johns Hopkins Press, 1956),
p. 70; cited hereafter as *ARI*.

5. Marvin Pope, *El in the Ugaritic Texts* (Leiden: E. J.
Brill, 1955), pp. 4-5; cited hereafter as Pope, *EUT*. Cf. Albright, *ARI*, p. 70, who says: "Since not only the names of gods
and the mythological atmosphere, but also many details of Philo's
narrative are in complete agreement with Ugaritic and later Phoenician inscriptions, we are fully justified in accepting provisionally all data preserved by him, though we may often remain in
doubt as to the exact meaning of a passage or the original name
underlying Philo's Greek equivalent. We must, of course, also
allow for mistakes in interpretation made by Philo of his precur-
sors." Also Albright, *History, Archaeology, and Christian Human-
ism* (New York: McGraw-Hill, 1964), pp. 149-150.

6. This positive judgment does not offset Pope's wise
stricture that "the use of Philo of Byblos and other late sources
for the elucidation of the Ugaritic myths should be made with extreme caution" (*EUT*, p. 5). It should be noted that some Egyptian material is present and should be taken into account when
seeking to discern the originally Canaanite data.

7. "The stability of Canaanite religion throughout the Late Bronze Age and all phases of the Iron Age as well as of the Hellenistic period is not difficult to establish" (Dahood, *ASD*, p. 70). Cf. W. F. Albright, "Some Canaanite-Phoenician Sources of Hebrew Wisdom," *Wisdom in Israel and the Ancient Near East* (Leiden: E. J. Brill, 1955), pp. 1-2.

8. Emphasis upon the relative stability of Canaanite religion is not meant to deny the fact that over the centuries matters were in flux or transition even at Ugarit, a fact stressed by Pope and others and generally accepted by scholars in the field, or that certain areas emphasized the worship of particular deities (e.g., the Philistine worship of Dagon). But from an overall perspective the religion of Canaan was a unified, largely homogeneous entity.

9. Albright, Baumgartner, DeLanghe, de Vaux, Eissfeldt, and Pedersen, while not going to the extremes of other scholars, have all argued for a historical nucleus behind the Keret epic according to John Gray, *The KRT Text in the Literature of Ras Shamra* (Leiden: E. J. Brill, 1955), p. 1. H. L. Ginsberg has also stressed this fact in some detail in his *The Legend of King Keret*, *BASOR* (New Haven: The American Schools of Oriental Research, 1946), pp. 7-8. Cf. his excellent though brief discussion of the differences in style between Keret and the other two epics in the work just cited, p. 46.

10. There is still some uncertainty as to the relationship of some texts, e.g., *UT* 6 and 121-124 (= *CTA* 13 and 20-22) to the Baʿal-ʿAnat cycle or the other epics. Use of these texts, how-

ever, does not have to remain suspended until the question of proper locale is settled. Such settlement may be impossible in some cases.

11. Recent Old Testament studies which have given some attention to the divine assembly at Ugarit are Gerald Cooke, "The Sons of (the) God(s)," *ZAW*, 76 (1964), 22-47; J. L. Cunchillos Ylarri, "Los b[e]ne ha'elohîm en Gen. 6, 1-4," *Estudios Biblicos*, 28 (1969), 5-17; Ferdinand Dexinger, *Sturz der Göttersöhne oder Engel vor der Sintflut* (Wien: Verlag Herder, 1966), pp. 29-41; Hans-Winfried Jüngling, *Der Tod der Götter* (Stuttgart: Verlag Katholisches Bibelwerk, 1969), pp. 52-60.

12. This enumeration of the major deities in the pantheon is based solely on their appearances in the texts. As has been noted before, the actual evaluation in the cultus at Ugarit around 1200 B.C. as well as elsewhere may have been different. The fluidity of the three goddesses ʿAnat, Aṯirat, and ʿAṯtart compels one to name all three here even though ʿAṯtart does not appear nearly as often as the other two. The somewhat arbitrary division of deities into groups is according to their relative importance in the main texts. It does not correspond to any tripartite division of the pantheon, which may, however, have existed at Ugarit according to Gaster's interpretation of the phrase ʿdt ilm ṯlṯ in Text 128:II:7 (= *CTA* 15.II.7), cited in Dahood, *ASD*, p. 66, n. 3. For a different interpretation of this phrase see below.

13. The texts published in *PRU* II and V and in *Ugaritica* V show that Resheph played a greater role than previous texts had

indicated, though little can be said about this deity at Ugarit.
Cf. Dahood, *ASD*, pp. 83-85 and Albright, *Yahweh and the Gods of
Canaan*, p. 121.

14. See Michael Astour, "Some New Divine Names from Ugarit," *JAOS*, 86 (1965), 277-284, for a discussion of new gods appearing in the texts of *Ugaritica* V.

15. Syria-Palestine has not yet produced the number of deities (i.e., several thousand) that were worshiped in Mesopotamia,
according to the lists of Deimel and Tallqvist. See Dahood, *ASD*,
p. 65 and his remarks about the somewhat misleading impression
these lists give.

16. Pope, *EUT*, p. 48, is correct in saying that the use of
pḫr by itself "does not necessarily imply a plenary session or
perfect attendance," but it appears he goes too far in maintaining that *pḫr* "is used loosely of any considerable aggregation of
the gods." The contexts in which the word appears would indicate
that it has a more specific and definite usage.

17. Albright, *ARI*, p. 72, points out the fact that *bn il(m)*
means "'members of the *el*-group,' i.e., 'gods,' following a widely attested Semitic expression for members of a class or guild."
The occurrences of *bn il(m)* in Ugaritic are discussed in J. L.
Cunehillos Ylarri, *Estudios Biblicas*, 28 (1969), 5-17 and Jüngling, *Der Tod der Götter*, pp. 53-56.

18. The above comments do not mean that *pḫr* cannot mean
simply "totality" or "assembly" without reference to gods as is
often the case in Akkadian. It can and does.

19. A convenient publication and discussion of this in-

scription is that of W. F. Albright, "The Phoenician Inscription of the Tenth Century B.C. from Byblos," *JAOS*, 67 (1947), 156-157. Cf. Herbert Donner and Wolfgang Röllig, *Kanaanäische und aramäische Inschriften*, II (Wiesbaden: O. Harrassowitz, 1964), 6-7.

20. See its usage in the Tale of Wen-Amun and the discussion in F. M. Cross, "The Priestly Tabernacle," *The Biblical Archaeologist Reader*, I, ed. G. Ernest Wright and David Noel Freedman (Garden City, N.Y.: Doubleday and Company, Inc., 1961), 223-224.

21. Enticing as the suggestion may be, Ginsberg's attempt to read *b* <*p*> *ḥr mwᶜd* here is not convincing to me. See "Lexicographical Notes," *Hebräische Wortforschung* (Leiden: E. J. Brill, 1967), 79-80.

22. *ANET*, p. 130.

23. Note that Ugaritic apparently does not use *qdš* or *qdšm* by themselves as does the Old Testament, whereas the Old Testament does not use *bn qdš*, the Ugaritic term. This varying mode of terminology in the two sources is in contrast to references to *ilm* and *bn ilm*, which appear in both the Ugaritic texts and the Old Testament. The seventh-century incantation text from Arslan Tash uses the plural term *qdšn* in the phrase *kl dr qdsn*, "the council of all the Holy Ones," along with *bn ʾlm*, establishing this form as good Canaanite/Phoenician style even apart from its use in the Old Testament. For the latest transcription and translation of this text in the light of new photographs, see F. M. Cross and Richard J. Saley, "Phoenician Incantations on a Plaque of the Seventh Century B.C. from Arslan Tash in Upper Syria,"

BASOR, 197 (February, 1970), 42-49. The parallelism of *ilm* and

(*bn*)*qdš* is common to the style and language of the Ugaritic

texts and the Old Testament, e.g., Ex. 15:11; Deut. 33:2. On

the Old Testament examples see the following chapter.

24. Charles Virolleaud, *Ugaritica* V, 564, no. 6, lines 1-2

(RS 24.272). The reference appears to be to El.

25. *Ibid.*, pp. 574-580, no. 8, lines 26 and 31 (RS 24.251).

For extended discussion of these incantations, see Michael C.

Astour, "Two Ugaritic Serpent Charms," *JNES*, 27 (1968), 13-36.

26. These gods are as follows (according to Text 8): *[i]l*

w ḥrn, bʿl w dgn, ʿnt w ʿttrt, yrḫ w ršp ʿttr w ʿttpr, tt w kmt,

mlk b ʿttrt, ktr w ḫss, and *šhr w šlm.* In Text 8 not all of

these are paired this way and *ḥrn* appears at the end. But the

total list is the same except that *ʿttr w ʿttpr* is not in Text 7.

27. Cross and Saley have pointed out a number of lines of

continuity between the Ugaritic and Arslan Tash incantations.

28. Pope thinks that the phrase *dr il wpḫr bʿl* (1:7 [= *CTA*

34.7]) refers perhaps to "separate aggregations of minor deities,

one associated with El and the other with Baʿal (*EUT*, p. 90).

Such an assumption may well be correct. Certainly this particu-

lar expression points in that direction. He is wrong, however,

in stating flatly that the reference "can hardly be to the entire

pantheon, since the major gods are specified by name in text 1"

(*EUT*, p. 90). It is impossible to say definitely. But in Text 2

(= *CTA* 32) *dr bn il* appears several times along with *mpḫrt bn il*

apparently referring to the whole pantheon unless *dr bn il* is

only a part and *mpḫrt bn il* the whole, in which case why mention

the *dr bn il*? Furthermore, in Text 107 (= *CTA* 30) *pḫr ilm* appears in a list of gods in much the same way as *dr il* in Text 1
(= *CTA* 34), only without reference to sacrifices. Thus *dr* (*bn*)
il may refer to a subgroup within the council or to the council
as a whole.

29. Albright's explanation of the term *bn il* could, however, apply here also. See n. 17.

30. The growing relationship between Baʿal and Aṯirat evidenced in the Ugaritic texts is probably a necessary   part of
Baʿal's assumption of El's position. A list of sacrifices (Text
9 [= *CTA* 36]) mentions a sacrifice *lbʿl waṯrt* (1. 8). Baʿal's
taking over of El's consort, more fully evidenced in the Iron
Age, was part of his usurpation of El's role as leader of the
divine assembly.

31. For etymological discussion see W. F. Albright, "The
North-Canaanite Epic of ʾAlʾeyan Baʿal and Mot," *JPOS*, 12 (1932),
197, nn. 46 and 47; and Godfrey R. Driver, *Canaanite Myths and
Legends* (Edinburgh: T. and T. Clark, 1956), pp. 135, nn. 17, 30,
and 150; cited hereafter as Driver, *CML*. Dahood has raised the
possibility that *aryh* may be an animal name designation for nobles or warriors related to Hebrew ʾ*aryeh*, "lion" ("The Value of
Ugaritic for Textual Criticism," *Biblica*, 40 [1959], 161-162, n.
2). On this linguistic phenomenon in general see my "Animal
Names as Designations in Ugaritic and Hebrew," *Ugarit-Forschungen*, II (1970), 177-178.

32. In 51:VI:44-46 (= *CTA* 4.VI.44-46) *šbʿm bn aṯrt* is in
parallelism with *aḫh* and *a[r]yh*, the suffix referring to Baʿal.

33. *PRU* II 1: rev. 9-10 has two references to *pḫrk*. Unfortunately the broken text does not allow certainty about the
antecedent. It could be Ba⁽al or ⁽Anat inasmuch as both are
mentioned, and ⁽Anat is mentioned immediately after *pḫrk*. In
this context *pḫr* is parallel to *bt* and may not even refer to
the gods. Reference to the gods, the Rephaim (1. 2), and especially the phrase *w k mǵ ilm*, "and when the gods arrived," suggest, however, that a divine *pḫr* is involved.

34. See p. 16, n. 28.

35. If such a hypothesis has any validity, it would eliminate the problem of the combination of *har-mô⁽ēd* and *ṣāpôn* in
Isa. 14:13, which has caused Werner Schmidt (*Königtum Gottes in
Ugarit und Israel*, BZAW, 80 [Berlin: Alfred Töpelmann, 1961], p.
26) to contend that this passage contains originally different
traditions which have flowed together. The two terms *har-mô⁽ēd*
and *ṣāpôn* could be legitimately equated as referring to the locale of the *pḫr m⁽d* of Ba⁽al. Pope (*EUT*, pp. 102-103) has a solution somewhat similar to the one proposed here. He identifies
Mount Saphon with *ǵr ll* (137:20 [= *CTA* 2.I.20]), the place where
the assembly meets. This identification within the Ba⁽al- ⁽Anat
cycle itself is difficult, however, inasmuch as El is still head
of the *pḫr m⁽d* and is not generally connected with Saphon, whereas Ba⁽al resides at Saphon, and no activities of the pantheon
take place there in the Ba⁽al-⁽Anat cycle. If there was a *pḫr
m⁽d* at Saphon, it is preferable to see it as a separate or later
tradition representing the continued ascendance of Ba⁽al. The
matter is further complicated by the fact that *ṣpn* and *il ṣpn*

appear in god lists and in the Ba‘al-‘Anat cycle. The latter
term could refer to El, Ba‘al, Ṣaphon, or another deity altogether. There may have been confusion between El's abode and
Ba‘al's Mount Cassius. In the Ugaritic Pantheon text Ṣaphon is
equated with Ḫazzi, the mountain god of Hittite mythology (J.
Nougayrol, *Ugaritica* V, 44). The equation *spn* = Ḫazzi = Mt. Cassius was recognized as far back as 1940 by Goetze (Albrecht
Goetze, "The City Khalbi and the Khapiru People," *BASOR* 79 [Octo-
ber 1940], 32-34).

36. Text 137:18 and 34 (= *CTA* 2.I.18 and 34) appear to refer to Ba‘al's following, but the words *dtqh* and *dtqyn* are still
problematical. Gordon relates these to Arab. *wqy*, which means
"to keep, preserve," and in its eighth form "to fear, to honor
(God)." Driver suggests this root or the Hebrew *qāwāh*, *qiwwāh*,
"waited upon." There are problems in both cases. Most transla-
tors tend to translate, however, along these lines. Ginsberg may
be cited as an example:

> *tn . ilm . dtqh ./ dtqyn . hmlt*
>
> Surrender the god with a following,
>
> Him whom the multitudes worship:

All the words except "Surrender the god" are italicized by Ginsberg (*ANET*, p. 130).

37. Albright, *JPOS*, 12 (1932), 204 at first accepted Virolleaud's identification of *ḫnzr* with "wild boar," but later expressed himself otherwise: "Ḫnzr probably has nothing to do with
the word for 'swine'" ("Review of *Ugaritic Handbook* by Cyrus H.
Gordon," *JBL*, 69 [1950], 389).

38. See my article referred to in n. 31.

39. F. F. Hvidberg, *Weeping and Laughter in the Old Testa-ment*, ed. and trans., F. Løkkegaard (Leiden: E. J. Brill, 1962), p. 26, n. 1. Løkkegaard added notes to this edition based on the results of recent scholarship and his own study.

40. Jørgen Laessøe, *The Shemshara Tablets: A Preliminary Report* (Copenhagen: Munksgaard, 1959), pp. 77, 81, 83. Laessøe says that the word is not to his knowledge attested elsewhere and that it is "apparently an artificially Akkadianized form of a Hurrian(?) word" (p. 83). Hurrian terminology would not be un-usual at Ugarit where Hurrian influence was strong. Hurrian texts have been found, and Hurrian characteristics influenced the literary style of the Ugaritic texts according to W. F. Albright, "The Role of the Canaanites in the History of Civilization," *The Bible and the Ancient Near East*, ed. G. Ernest Wright (Garden City, N.Y.: Doubleday and Company, Inc., 1961), p. 357, nn. 62-63. On the basis of the Shemshara usage Løkkegaard suggests "yeoman?" as a possible translation for *ḫanizarum*.

41. Cf. Edouard Lipinski, *Le poème royal du Psaume LXXXIX 1-5, 20-38* (Paris: J. Gabalda and Co., 1967), p. 39, n. 6.

42. Driver, *CML*, p. 85.

43. *ANET*, p. 136.

44. J. Nougayrol, *Ugaritica* V, 45. Cf. M. Astour, "Some New Divine Names from Ugarit," p. 280, who is inclined to equate these gods with the "seven lads, eight boars."

45. C. Virolleaud, *Ugaritica* V, Text 9 (rev. 11) and Text 13, rev. 1 (only *il t*ᶜ*dr* written). Also to be restored

in *UT* 17:4 (= *CTA* 29, rev. 4) i[l t d̲]r b l.

46. W. F. Albright, *Yahweh and the Gods of Canaan*, p. 125, n. 89, proposes to render the designation "warriors of Baᶜal."

47. Svi Rin and Shifra Rin, "Ugaritic-Old Testament Affinities II," *Acts of the Gods* (Jerusalem: Israel Society for Biblical Research, 1968), p. xli.

48. Text 67:V (= *CTA* 5.V) also includes in Baᶜal's retinue *Pdry* and *Ṭtly* as well as various weather phenomena: ᶜ*rpt* (cloud), *rḫ* (wind), *mdl*(?), and *mṭrt* (rains). The ᶜ*rpt* here may have some relationship to the ᶜ*nn* (133:35 [= *CTA* 2.I.35]; 51:IV:59 [= *CTA* 4.IV.59]; 76:II:33 [= *CTA* 10.II.33]; ᶜ*nt*:IV:76 [= *CTA* 3.IV.76]) if the latter has anything to do with "cloud," as seems to be the case in terms of etymology. Further reference to Baᶜal's host and its military character may be seen in the enigmatic Rephaim texts discussed below.

49. Henri Cazelles, "L'hymne ugaritique à Anat," *Syria*, 33 (1956), 49-57. Cazelles thinks *mhr* means "young warrior" and refers to the king in this context as the warrior of ᶜAnat.

50. Cf. below on the Rephaim texts.

51. Arvid S. Kapelrud, *Baal in the Ras Shamra Texts* (Copenhagen: G. E. C. Gad, 1952), p. 109, n. 4.

52. Cf. Theodor H. Gaster, *Thespis*, 2d rev. ed. (Garden City, N.Y.: Doubleday and Co., Inc., 1961), p. 228. In an earlier context Gaster pointed out the parallelism between *rpi* and *pḫr* in Text 128:III:14-15 (= *CTA* 15.III.14-15), which he took to be evidence that the term denotes properly "members of the assembly" (Gaster, "The Canaanite Epic of Keret," *Jewish Quarterly Re-*

view, 37 [1946-47], 287-289). The only problem with that assumption is that the relationships appear to be *btk/bpḫr* or *rpi ar[ṣ]*
/*qbṣ dtn*. Even with that parallelism the word still appears to
have something to do with "gathering" or "assembly."

53. Cf. *UM*, Glossary, No. 989, and M. Pope and W. Röllig,
"Syrien. Der Mythologie der Ugariter und Phonizier," *Wörterbuch
der Mythologie*, ed. H. W. Haussig (Stuttgart: Ernst Klett Verlag,
1961-), I, 1, pp. 296-297; cited hereafter as Pope, *WM*.

54. Driver, *CML*, pp. 116-117. Cf. Job 38:7.

55. *CTA*, 10.I.5. The *d* of *dr* and the final *m* are the least
clear letters, but a careful examination of the photograph confirms Mlle. Herdner's reading.

56. K. Mras, ed., *Eusebius' Werke*, Vol. VIII, Pt. 1, *Die
Preparatio Evangelica*, "Die Griechischen Christlichen Schrift-
steller der ersten Jahrhunderte" (Berlin: Akademie-Verlag, 1954),
p. 42, para. 29; cited hereafter as Mras,*Eusebius' Werke*.

57. M. Dahood would compare with this *km hkkbm ᵓl* in l. 10
of the Phoenician inscription from Pyrgi, which he would translate "like the stars of El" ("Punic *hkkbm ᵓl* and Is. 14, 13,"
Orientalia, 34 [1965], 170-172). For the issues and problems involved, see Joseph Fitzmeyer, "The Phoenician Inscription from
Pyrgi," *JAOS*, 86 (1966), 295-296.

58. Cross, *HTR*, 55 (1962), 249, reads plausibly *ǵr <i> l*,
"Mount of El" for *ǵr ll*. Cf. Pope, *EUT*, p. 69.

59. This fact is evident also in the *Yeḥimilk* inscription
from Byblos and the Azitawadda inscription from Karatepe. The
most convenient translation of these texts is that of Franz Rosen-

thal, *ANET*, pp. 499-500.

60. Text 128:III:18-19 (= *CTA* 15.III.18-19) gives a valuable piece of information about the gods and their abodes. After
the gods bless Keret:

> *tity . ilm . lahlhm*
>
> *dr il . lmšknthm*
>
> The gods come/go to their tents,
>
> The family of El to their tabernacles/dwellings.

This passage along with 2 Aqhat V:31-33 (= *CTA* 17.V.31-33), which
says the same thing of *Ktr-w-Ḫss*, is further indication that the
Keret and Aqhat texts had their origin or context in a region
other than Ugarit. These terms (*ahl* and *mšknt*) are used only in
Keret and Aqhat and suggest strongly a semi-nomadic environment.
In the Baᶜal and ᶜAnat cycle the gods dwell in the following
structures: *bt* (51:V:75 [= *CTA* 4.V.75]), *hkl* (51:V:76 [= *CTA* 4.V.
76]), and *ḫẓr* (51:IV:51 [= *CTA* 4.IV.51) but never in *ahl* or *mškn*.
There are signs, however, that El dwelt in a tentlike structure
at least part of the time. In the Ugaritic texts El's abode is a
qrš, a term which indicates part of the tabernacle structure in
the Old Testament. In Hittite mythology Elkunirša is described
on one occasion as living in a "tent" (M. Pope, *EUT*, pp. 66-67).
Driver (*CML*, p. 37, n. 13) is correct in referring to II Sam. 7:6
in this connection, although he makes no comment about it. Yahweh tells David that he did not dwell in a *bayit* when he brought
the people of Israel up from Egypt, but rather moved about in an
ʾōhel miškān. The depiction of Yahweh's dwelling in the time of
the origins of Israel is not purely a nomadic and non-Canaanite

description but is reflected in Canaanite lore itself. This
fact along with the tenacity of Yahwistic tradition may help explain how the Israelite tent or tabernacle, originating in the
desert, was able to serve as the covenant sanctuary for so long
in Canaan itself before demands arose for a *bayit* or *hēkāl* as
Yahweh's "dwelling." Cf. F. M. Cross, *The Biblical Archaeologist
Reader*, pp. 214, 224-228; Samuel Loewenstamm, "Review of W.
Beyerlin, *Herkunft und Geschichte der altesten Sinaitraditionen*,"
IEJ, 12 (1962), 163; and W. Schmidt, "מְשָׁכְּךָ Als Ausdruck Jerusa-
lemer Kultsprache," *ZAW*, 75 (1963), 91-92.

61. There are still questions as to the number of texts
that belong to the Ba‘al epic and the precise order. General
agreement exists, however, as to which are the major texts, and
there is a basic amount of consensus about the order of the texts.
The main question on the order is whether Text 51 (= *CTA* 4) goes
before the ‘*nt* (= *CTA* 3) text or vice versa. Ginsberg places
Text 51 first because it still mentions Yamm as El's beloved,
whereas ‘*nt* mentions Mot in that position. Gordon, Driver, and
Pope put the ‘*nt* text first apparently because Ba‘al still does
not have a place in it. Ginsberg's argument does not appear to
be as strong inasmuch as Mot is also present and challenging
Ba‘al at the end of Text 51. One must agree, with Ginsberg, however, that final judgment is to be reserved.

62. Kapelrud, *Baal*, pp. 101-102; Schmidt, *Konigtum Gottes*,
pp. 37-38.

63. Thorkild Jacobsen, "The Battle between Marduk and Tiamat," *JAOS*, 88 (1968), 104-108, has argued cogently for the pri-

ority of the West Semitic Baᶜal and Yamm conflict.

64. T. Jacobsen, "Primitive Democracy in Ancient Mesopotamia," *JNES*, 2 (1943), 159-172; reprinted in T. Jacobsen, *Toward the Image of Tammuz and Other Essays on Mesopotamian History and Culture*, ed. William L. Moran (Cambridge: Harvard University Press, 1970), pp. 157-170.

65. Tablet I, ll, 55-56. *ANET*, p. 61.

66. Alexander Heidel, *The Babylonian Genesis* (Chicago: The University of Chicago Press, 1951), p. 21, n. 35.

67. A better translation of these two lines would be: "Along with those you yourselves created they are gone to her side./ Here they are massed(?), standing (lit. risen) here at the side of Tiamat."

68. Tablet II, ll, 12-18. *ANET*, p. 63.

69. For the Akkadian text the writer has referred to Rene Labat, *Le poème babylonien de la création* (Paris: Librarie d' Amerique et d'Orient, 1935).

70. Tablet II, ll, 33-37. *ANET*, p. 63.

71. Tablet II, ll, 27-30. *ANET*, p. 63.

72. See Heidel, *The Babylonian Genesis*, p. 38, n. 70, on the question as to whether this term refers to a dragon or not.

73. It is in the light of this depiction of Marduk, as well as other factors, that Jacobsen has argued that the battle between Marduk and Tiamat was probably a motif brought to Babylon from the West, presumably by the Amorites.

74. On the building of temples by victorious gods and kings, see now A. S. Kapelrud, "Temple Building, a Task for Gods and

Kings," *Orientalia*, 32 (1963), 56-62; and F. M. Cross, "The Divine Warrior in Israel's Early Cult," *Biblical Motifs*, ed. A. Altmann (Cambridge: Harvard University Press, 1966).

75. J. Nougayrol, *Ugaritica* V, 45.

76. F. M. Cross, "The Divine Warrior in Israel's Early Cult," pp. 23-24.

77. For a discussion of the problems in the interpretation of ʿnn in these lines, see Moshe Held, "Rhetorical Questions in Ugaritic and Biblical Hebrew," *Eretz-Israel*, 9 (Jerusalem: Israel Exploration Society, 1969), 72, n. 15. I would see here a class of deified beings, i.e., "clouds." The phrase rwḥy ʿnn appears in the angelology of Qumran (4 Q Ber) and the pseudepigraphical literature. See John Strugnell, "The Angelic Liturgy at Qumran - 4 Q Serek Šîrôt ʿÔlat Haššabbāt," *Congress Volume, Oxford, 1959* (Leiden: E.J. Brill, 1960), pp. 329, n. 1; 333. The ʿᵃnānê šᵉmayyāʾ of the council scene in Dan. 7:13 are to be viewed in this context also.

78. For discussion of the alternatives here, see Patrick D. Miller, Jr., "Fire in the Mythology of Canaan and Israel," *CBQ*. 27 (1965), 257, nn. 7 and 8.

79. *Ibid.*, pp. 256-261.

80. Note that in the LXX of Judg. 3:22 the handle of Ehud's sword is described as "flaming" although nothing of this is said in the Hebrew. One might expect that in other cases the sword may have been a flaming one even though no mention is made of such. The similarity to the Canaanite messenger pair is evident in any case. Cf. the expressions mlʾky ʾš and ʾly ʾwr in the

Qumran angelology and the *rwhy* *'š* of Jub. 2:2, all cited by
Strugnell, *Congress Volume*, *Oxford, 1959*, pp. 332-333. Note also the associations of fire with the throne of the Ancient One in
the council scene of Dan. 7.

81. Exodus 3:2. b^e*labbat- '$\bar{e}\check{s}$* = b^e*lahabat- '$\bar{e}\check{s}$*. Cf. the
versions, commentaries, and lexicons.

82. On the basis of Egyptian evidence, the $\acute{s}^e r\bar{a}p\hat{i}m$ appear
to have been *griffins*. R.D. Barnett (*The Nimrud Ivories* [London:
The Trustees of the British Museum, 1957], pp. 73-74) maintains a
Semitic origin for both the word and the creature. The relation-
ship of Ugaritic *bšrp il* (107:16 [= *CTA* 30.16]) to the $\acute{s}^e r\bar{a}p\hat{i}m$
of the Old Testament is impossible to determine at this stage due
to the difficulty of interpretation of this controversial but important text.

83. On these names see Cross, *HTR*, 55 (1962), 254.

84. On the kingship of Ba'al, see now Schmidt, *Konigtum
Gottes*, pp. 21-52.

85. Schmidt, *Konigtum Gottes*, p. 62, notes the close similarity between the last half of this line and the cry at the enthronement festival of Marduk: *marduk-ma šarru*, "Marduk is king!"

86. The use of the term *tpṭ*, "judge," is significant here
in that *tpṭ* is peculiarly Yamm's epithet. Recognition of Ba'al
as *tpṭ* and *mlk* is a recognition of his rule over the gods by his
defeat of Yamm.

87. The conflict between El and Ba'al is an undercurrent
here and at various places where El seems to favor Yamm while doing little to assist Ba'al. Cf. now Ulf Oldenburg, *The Conflict*

*between El and Ba*ᶜ*al in Canaanite Religion* (Leiden: E. J. Brill, 1969).

88. On lines 7-8 see the reconstruction of Driver, *CML*, pp. 100-101, which is certainly in part correct.

89. The probability that these lines depict Baᶜal marching at the head of an armed procession was pointed out in passing by F. F. Hvidberg, *Weeping and Laughter*, pp. 48, 55.

90. Ginsberg, *ANET*, p. 134, reads in italics: "Baᶜal] dwells in his house."

91. The reconstruction is fairly obvious except in the case of the verb in line 31. Driver reads *t/r* = Akk. *tararu*, "to quake, tremble." Another possibility, perhaps even better, is *ṯbr*, "to break, shatter," which occurs several times in Ugaritic and appears in a similar context in Ps. 29:5, with reference to the voice of Yahweh breaking the cedars.

92. The contexts in which this word is used give the meaning "to wobble, reel," or perhaps "to jump," which relates it to Arabic *naṭṭa*, "to jump," and Hebrew *nûṭ*, "to shake."

93. On *gpt*, see the lengthy note by W. F. Albright, "The North-Canaanite Poems of Alʾêyân Baᶜal and the 'Gracious Gods,'" *JPOS*, 14 (1934), 134, n. 175.

94. Lines 49-51 in this column may also be Baᶜal's announcement of his kingship, but there is difference of opinion as to whether it is Baᶜal or Mot who utters these words. It would seem to be Mot who calls out.

95. The translation is that of F. M. Cross and D. N. Freedman, "A Royal Song of Thanksgiving: II Samuel 22 = Psalm 18," *JBL*,

72 (1953), 23.

96. Cf. vs. 41.

97. There is no need in this context to deal with the difficult question of whether the fertility myth involves a yearly cycle, a seven-year cycle, or some other regular period. See the discussion in Pope, *WM*, pp. 262-264. A definite dissent against the interpretation of this myth as having to do with the cycles of fertility has been registered by Umberto Cassuto, "Baal and Mot in the Ugaritic Texts," *Israel Exploration Journal*, 12 (1962), 77-86. This article contains valuable insights into the nature of this myth particularly in his recognition that the questions of kingship and life and death are involved. Denial of fertility motifs, however, is not valid or at least argues from a very narrow definition of fertility. That is definitely a major part of what is involved in the struggle of life and death.

98. The words *rbm* and *dkym* are quite problematical. They may be adverbs, e.g., "greatly" and "crushingly." Pope, however, has questioned quite strongly the existence of adverbial accusatives ending in *-m* in Ugaritic ("Ugaritic Enclitic *-m*," *JCS*, 5 [1951], pp. 123-128). As Ginsberg's translation seems to indicate, it is difficult to separate these two words from *dokyam* and *mayim rabbîm* in Ps. 93:3-4. The context as well as the fact that elsewhere ʿAnat speaks of smiting *rbm* (ʿnt: III:36 [= *CTA* 3.III. 36]) would suggest that these lines refer to some type of monster such as *tnn*, *ltn*, etc. Frank Cross would interpret *dkym* as "Breakers of Sea" (oral communication).

99. In parallelism with *ṣmd* the word *ktp* here seems to re-

fer to some kind of weapon. See *UT*, Glossary, No. 983.

100. This word is uncertain but may be connected with ṣhrrt, which appears to have something to do with burning.

101. These lines can hardly refer to anything other than Ba⁽al's ascension to his throne.

102. A helpful treatment of the kingship battles of Ba⁽al is given in Norman Habel, *Yahweh Versus Baal* (New York: Bookman Associates, 1964), Chap. 3.

103. Pope, *WM*, p. 254, appears to interpret the word as an elative. He translates *aliy qrdm* as "Mächtigster der Helden" but does not comment grammatically.

104. H. Birkeland's early interpretation of the epithet as a broken plural noun form is subject to the same objections. Broken plurals are certainly scarce or nonexistent in Ugaritic. Birkeland's view is cited by Kapelrud, *Baal*, pp. 49-50.

105. Albright, *ARI*, p. 195, n. 11.

106. A. Goetze, "Peace on Earth," *BASOR*, 93 (February 1944), 17-20.

107. W. F. Albright, "The 'Natural Force' of Moses in the Light of Ugaritic," *BASOR*, 94 (April 1944), 34, n. 23.

108. The word *qrdm* can hardly be separated from the Akkadian words: *qardu*, *qarrādu*, and *qurādu*, all meaning "hero, warrior."

109. Cf. *ṣpn* = *ǵr tliyt* in Text 76:III:28-32 (= *CTA* 10.III. 28-32) and 1 Aq 84(?) (= *CTA* 19.I.84[?]).

110. Cf. Sigmund Mowinckel, "Drive and/or Ride in the Old Testament," *VT*, 12 (1962), 278-299.

111. Kapelrud, *Baal*, p. 62.

112. Driver, *CML*, pp. 81, 146. Cf. M. Dahood, "The Root GMR in the Psalms," *Theological Studies*, 14 (1953), 575-577.

113. Cf. Loren R. Fisher, "A New Ritual Calendar from Ugarit," *HTR*, 63 (1970), 488-490.

114. Pope, *WM*, pp. 255-256.

115. The equation Proto-Semitic $\underline{d}mr$ = Ugaritic $\underline{d}mr$ is quite legitimate as such. Ugaritic, however, has the word $\underline{d}mr$ referring to fighters or warriors and uses it fairly frequently always with $\underline{d}$ rather than d. One would expect, therefore, that *dmrn*, if it comes from *dmr*, would be written $\underline{d}mrn$. Because the consonant $\underline{d}$ is unstable at Ugarit and in the process of shifting, the words are probably the same. It is difficult to separate them in terms of meaning. On the problems of the spirant $\underline{d}$ in Ugaritic, see most recently Cross, *HTR*, 55 (1962), 249-250. The major difficulty, however, lies in the fact that Philo has d instead of z as regularly in Phoenician.

116. The many diverse points of view may be seen in the study of the Rephaim texts by Andre Caquot, "Les rephaim ougaritiques," *Syria*, 37 (1960), 75-93.

117. *Ibid*.

118. *Ibid*., pp. 91-93.

119. Kapelrud, *Baal*, pp. 107-108, takes brief note of the relationship of the *rpum* to Baʿal.

120. Contra John Gray, "The Rephaim," *Palestine Exploration Quarterly*, 81 (1948-49), 127-139, who views the Rephaim as the king and some of his officials.

121. Caquot, *Syria*, 37 (1960), 78.

122. T. H. Gaster, *Thespis*, p. 228, n.b.

123. Cf. Mowinckel, *VT*, 17 (1962), 295. In a similar manner Yahweh and his retinue are pictured in the Old Testament as riding on chariots (e.g., Ps. 68:17; Isa. 66:15; II Kings 2:11-12; 6:17).

124. E.g., Virolleaud, Dussaud, Caquot, Driver, and Gray.

125. E.g., Gordon and Kapelrud.

126. Hardly any two scholars who read *rpu* and *mhr* here as singular agree about the nature and identity of the person so designated. The problem has been complicated by the appearance of *rpu mlk ᶜlm* in RS 24.252 but the relation of that text to the *rpum* texts is unclear. I am inclined with others to identify *rpu mlk ᶜlm* with El.

127. Even if *rpu* and *mhr* are singular, they might simply be terms referring to the leader or chief of the *rpum*, who are also warriors in chariots. Cf. H. Cazelles, "L'hymne ugaritique à Anat," *Syria*, 33 (1956), 49-57.

128. Cf. the excursus on the goddess ᶜAnat in H. L. Ginsberg, "The North-Canaanite Myth of Anath and Aqhat," *BASOR*. 97 (February 1945), 8-10; and A. Kapelrud, *The Violent Goddess: Anat in the Ras Shamra Texts* (Oslo: Universitetsforlaget, 1969), pp. 48-63.

129. Ginsberg remarks that "sensuality and fecundity are primary, vigor and martial ardor secondary with Astarte; while the contrary is true in an even higher degree of Anath" (*ibid.*, p. 8).

130. Cf. Kapelrud, *Baal in the Ras Shamra Texts,* pp. 106-

107.

131.   It is possible that the verb here is to be interpreted as referring to past action.

132.   See Kapelrud, *The Violent Goddess*, pp. 54-63, for discussion of this passage and the various translations proposed.

133.   On *ǵzr* see my "Ugaritic *ǴZR* and Hebrew *ʿZR II*," *Ugarit-Forschungen*, 2 (1970), 159-175.

134.   The text is a list of deities to whom sacrifices are apparently offered.

135.   *PRU* II, 14.

136.   The following pages are drawn from my article "El as Warrior," *HTR*, 60 (1967), 411-431. For a somewhat more extended discussion and documentation the reader is referred to that source.

137.   Pope, *EUT*. Otto Eissfeldt, *El im ugaritischen Pantheon* (Berlin: Akademie-Verlag, 1951).

138.   Pope, *EUT*, pp. 27ff.

139.   Cf. Text 129:17-18 (= *CTA* 2.III.17-18) where the same threat is made to ʿAttar.

140.   Cf. T. Jacobsen, *ZA NF*, 17 (1957), 103ff. In these pages Jacobsen shows how in Mesopotamia the *lugal* was first the war leader in both the human and the divine realms.

141.   The classic example, of course, is Marduk, who was given kingship of the gods in order to do battle against Tiamat. So also Baʿal is king after his defeat of Yamm (*UT* 68:32).

142.   The best illustration of this phenomenon is the deity Dagon, who plays no role in the mythological texts from Ugarit

and yet must be reckoned as one of the principal male deities of that city in the light of his apparently significant place in the cultus of Ugarit evidenced by the temple and stelae dedicated to him as well as his presence in several lists of gods and lists of sacrifices to the gods as well as in the serpent charms published in *Ugaritica* V. That Dagon also was a significant deity in South Canaan is well attested from the Old Testament (I Sam. 5). Cf. M. Dahood, *ASD*, pp. 78-80; Hanna Kassis, "Gath and the Structure of the Philistine Society," *JBL*, 84 (1965), 265f.; and M. C. Astour, "Some New Divine Names from Ugarit," *JAOS*, 86 (1966), p. 279, n. 27. Thus inferences about the role of Dagon based only on the Ugaritic mythological texts would be somewhat misleading.

143. The strong association of Yahweh with El has been ably demonstrated most recently by Cross, *HTR*, 55 (1962), pp. 225-259.

144. Cf. the excellent summary of Hans G. Guterbock, "Hittite Mythology," *Mythologies of the Ancient World*, ed. S. N. Kramer (Garden City, N.Y.: Doubleday and Company, Inc., 1961), pp. 139-179. He notes the similarity to Sanchuniathon's account. The more extended treatment is his *Kumarbi*, "Istanbuler Schriften," XVI (Zurich-New York: Europaverlag, 1946), esp. pp. 110-115.

145. Pope, *EUT*, pp. 29-32 and 93f.

146. *Ibid.*

147. K. Mras, ed., *Eusebius' Werke*, p. 47, para. 17-19.

148. In his article on El in the *Theologisches Wörterbuch zum Alten Testament,* ed. by G. J. Botterweck and Helmer Ringgren, Frank Cross has noted the warrior character of El/Kronos and commented properly that his battles fit not so much in the context of

cosmogonic myth but in myths of theogony. Cf. in this connection
L. R. Fisher, *HTR*, 63 (1970), 489-490, n. 20.

149. Cf. Marie-Therese Barrelet, "Les déesses armées et
ailées," *Syria*, 32 (1955), 222-260, and specific reference in
Ugaritica V, Text 2 (RS 24. 252), p. 551, to ᶜAnat's flying.

150. Pope, *EUT*, p. 45, notes that there is at least one instance in the Ugaritic texts where El's nature appears kindred to
that of Kronos: "El is not always benevolent: in the lamentably
fragmentary and obscure poem BH he contrives the undoing of Baal
by a cunning and cruel stratagem, laughing inwardly as he sends
out his female agents, BH I 12ff." It is unfortunate that this
text (*UT* 75 [= *CTA* 12]) is as obscure and broken as it is. For
it might reveal even closer kinship to Philo's Kronos. El appears in it as a belligerent deity perhaps in command of "allies"
(gods?) who do battle for him against his protagonist. On the
bull imagery which appears here, see below.

151. Pope, *EUT*, pp. 16-19, gives a number of these suggested etymologies and maintains a rather strong skepticism about
all of them.

152. Albright, *ARI*, p. 72.

153. *Ibid.*, and Pope, *EUT*, pp. 35-42, who entitles this section of his book: "El as Bull: His Marital Relations." Eissfeldt,
El im ugaritischen Pantheon, p. 56; Gray, *The Legacy of Canaan*,
pp. 158f.; and W. Schmidt, *Königtum Gottes in Ugarit und Israel*
(Berlin: Alfred Töpelmann, 1961), p. 5, have seen that the term
_tr_ indicates strength more than procreation. In a more recent
article Gray argues for a somewhat stronger character and role

for El than he is sometimes given ("Social Aspects of Canaanite Religion," *Volume du Congres, Geneve, 1965*, Supplements to *VT*, 14 [Leiden: E. J. Brill, 1966], 170-192).

154. Gray, *The Legacy of Canaan*, p. 159.

155. On *UT* 52, see Pope, *EUT*, pp. 35-42.

156. For more detailed discussion and examples in all of these areas, see Miller, "El the Warrior," pp. 418-425.

157. Cross, *HTR*, 55 (1962), 250-259.

158. Cross's translation. He regards this as "a title of the divine warrior and creator," *ibid.*, p. 256.

159. *Ibid.*

160. Cross describes this as "a phrase from a 'liturgical' sentence name or protocol of a kind," *ibid.*

161. Pope, *EUT*, pp. 22-24; Gray, *The Legacy of Canaan*, p. 160.

162. As an example of the effective investigation of personal names in the study of Near Eastern religions, see Jimmy J. M. Roberts, *The Earliest Semitic Pantheon* (Baltimore: The Johns Hopkins University Press, 1972).

163. Cf. Gray, *The Legacy of Canaan*, pp. 160ff.; Eissfeldt, "Malkiel (König ist El) und Malkijah (König ist Jahwe): Gottesglaube und Namengebung in Israel," *Kleine Schriften* (Tübingen: J. C. B. Mohr, 1966), III, 384f.

164. The name also appears in Gordon's No. 321:I:9, although he reads it *ilmkr*. In Herdner's *Corpus des Tablettes en Cuneiformes Alphabetiques*, 211 (and fascimile), the name is read *ilmhr*. Cf. Eissfeldt, *El im ugaritischen Pantheon*, p. 46.

165. Gordon, *UT*, Glossary, No. 1545. Eissfeldt, *El im ugaritischen Pantheon,* 46, follows Virolleaud in questioning whether *il* at the end of this name represents the Semitic *il*.

166. T. Vriezen, "The Edomitic Deity Qaus," *OTS*, 14 (1965), 331.

167. A. Murtonen, *A Philological and Literary Treatise on the Old Testament Divine Names* אֵל , אֱלוֹהַ , אֱלֹהִים and יהוה (Helsinki, 1952), 95-103.

168. On *dmr* as applied to El at Ugarit, see below.

169. Herbert B. Huffmon, *Amorite Personal Names in the Mari Texts* (Baltimore: The Johns Hopkins Press, 1965), p. 256.

170. The identification of El with *rpu mlk ʿlm* is not absolutely clear. Virolleaud makes this equation, and it is most probable when the text is looked at as a whole. El is one of the two deities most prominent in the text. Immediately after the mention of *rpu mlk ʿlm* at the beginning, the text says that El sits with ʿAṯtart, rules, and judges with Hadd. Further, the title *mlk* is El's title. The term *rpu* is enigmatic here as elsewhere. It may be a sort of honorific, as appears to be the case in regard to Danel who is called *mt rpi*. Cf. *btk rpi ar[ṣ]* (*UT* 128:III:14 [= *CTA* 15.III.14]). It may be possible that we have here "Rapaʾu of the Eternal King," i.e., Rapaʾu of El, and thus one of the warrior Rephaim which appear elsewhere in association with Baʿal and ʿAnat. In an unpublished study of this text presented to the Colloquium for Old Testament Research, August, 1970, however, I have assembled the evidence which suggests rather strongly that the deity involved is El.

171. For a different interpretation of *dmr* in the Ugaritic
and Hebrew contexts discussed here, see S. E. Loewenstamm, "The
Lord is my strength and my glory," *VT*, 19 (1969), 464-470. On
the reading *l[a]* ⌐n⌐*k* see now Fisher, *HTR*, 63 (1970), 490, n. 20.

172. Cross, *HTR*, 55 (1962), 225-259.

173. Cf. W. F. Albright, *The Biblical Period from Abraham
to Ezra*, 4th rev. ed. (Harper & Row, 1963), pp. 38, 42. "It is
still unclear to what extent Baal was identified with Yahweh in
the period of the Judges, but the frequency of Baal names among
the families of both Saul and David (see below) makes it appear
likely that syncretism between Yahweh and Baal was already
favored in certain circles." And with reference to Gideon: "The
fact that his own personal name was formed with 'Baal' while that
of his father Joash was formed with 'Yahweh' vividly illustrates
the confused religious situation prevailing at that time in
north-central Israel."

174. Pope, *EUT*, pp. 44f.

175. *Ibid.*, p. 104.

176. "But the positive identification with El suggests a
period for the patriarchal traditions when El was the dominant
figure in the Canaanite religious pattern. This would take us
back to an earlier stage of Canaanite religion for the background
of the patriarchal narratives than that reflected in the Ugaritic
poems," David Noel Freedman and Edward F. Campbell, Jr., "The
Chronology of Israel and the Ancient Near East," *The Bible and
the Ancient Near East*, ed. G. Ernest Wright (Garden City, N.Y.:
Doubleday and Company, Inc., 1961), p. 206.

177. Cross, *HTR*, 55 (1962).

178. Albright, *The Biblical Period*, 13 and especially Cross, *HTR*, 55 (1962), 238.

179. Cross, *HTR*, 55 (1962), 258, lists the basic functions and traits of Yahweh in which kinship or comparison with El may be recognized. The one principal trait not listed is the warlike character of Yahweh. In light of this discussion that also may now be added.

Part Two.   Cosmic War and Holy War in Israel

1.   The various studies of Albright, Cross, and Freedman
are basic here.   In a Yale University dissertation entitled "Linguistic Evidence in Dating Early Hebrew Poetry" (1966), David
Robertson has analyzed the poetry of the Old Testament, coming
to cautious conclusions generally confirming those of Albright,
Cross, and Freedman, though not in every respect.   He would propose a working hypothesis that puts Ex. 15 in the twelfth century, Judg. 5 toward the end of that century, Deut. 32, II Sam.
22 = Ps. 18, Hab. 3, and Job 5 in the eleventh to tenth centuries
and Ps. 78 in the late tenth or early ninth.   Robertson acknowledges clearly the tenuousness of this reconstruction (see pp.
228-233) but maintains that the one clear conclusion is the early
dating of Ex. 15.

2.   This method has been put to good use recently by Robert
Bach, *Die Aufforderungen zur Flucht und zum Kampf im alttestamentlichen Propheten* (Neukirchen: Neukirchener Verlag, 1962).   He
examines a particular form in the oracles against the foreign nations and seeks to show its *Sitz im Leben* in the ancient tradition of holy war.

3.   The chapter does not attempt to examine every indication
of Yahweh as warrior.   That kind of general survey has already
been done by H. Fredriksson, *Jahwe als Krieger* (Lund: C. W. K.
Gleerup, 1945).

4.   For further discussion of the divine assembly and its
role in Israelite thought, see G. Ernest Wright, *The Old Testa-*

ment Against Its Environment (London: SCM Press, 1954), pp. 30-
41; G. Widengren, "Early Hebrew Myths and Their Interpretation,"
Myth, Ritual, and Kingship, ed. S. H. Hooke (Oxford University
Press, 1958), pp. 159-164; H. Wheeler Robinson, "The Council of
Yahweh," *Journal of Theological Studies*, 45 (1944), 151-157; F.
M. Cross, "The Council of Yahweh in Second Isaiah," *Journal of
Near Eastern Studies*, 12 (1953), 274-277; G. Cooke, "The Sons of
(the) God(s)," *ZAW*, 76 (1964), 22-47; H.-W. Jüngling, *Der Tod der
Götter* (Stuttgart: Verlag Katholisches Bibelwerk), 38-52.

5. This term for members of the divine assembly appears al-
so in the Karatepe Portal Inscription, col. I, line 8. Cf. Roger
T. O'Callaghan, "The Great Phoenician Portal Inscription from
Karatepe," *Orientalia*, 18 (1949), 173-205; N. H. Tur-Sinai, *The
Book of Job* (Jerusalem: Kiryath Sepher Ltd., 1957), pp. 269-270,
472; H. Neil Richardson, "Some Notes on ל י ץ and Its Derivatives,"
VT, 5 (1955), 169; and S. Mowinckel, "Die Vorstellungen des Spät-
judentums von heiligen Geist als Fürsprecher und der johanneische
Paraklet," *ZNW*, 32 (1933), 102, n. 14. The basic meaning of the
term is "interpreter, intermediary." *mēliṣ* in reference to the
angels also occurs at Qumran in IQH vi:13. Cf. the discussion of
Menahem Mansoor, *The Thanksgiving Hymns* (Grand Rapids: Wm. B.
Eerdmans, 1961), pp. 83-84, 143, n. 2.

6. Cf. Julian Morgenstern, "The Mythological Background of
Ps. 82," *Hebrew Union College Annual*, 14 (1939), 40, esp. n. 25.

7. Mowinckel, *ZNW*, 32 (1933), 103. Cf. Ugar. *t'dt*.

8. On the reading *dōr* here see F. Neuberg, "An Unrecognized
Meaning of Hebrew *Dōr*," *JNES*, 9 (1950), 215-217.

9. On the significant use of many of these terms in IQM see Y. Yadin, *The Scroll of the War of the Sons of Light Against the Sons of Darkness* (Oxford: Oxford University Press, 1962), pp. 230-232. Their frequency in the Apocrypha and Pseudepigrapha is well known. It is paralleled now in the Qumran literature. Cf. IQH.

10. The arguments advanced against inclusion of these beings in the assembly are not convincing. They are primarily arguments from silence and assume more differentiation in the membership of the assembly than the evidence warrants. Furthermore, winged divine beings were exceedingly common in ancient Near Eastern mythology. See Cooke, *ZAW*, 76 (1964), 37-38.

11. Cf. Cross, *JNES*, 12 (1953), 274, n. 1: "The heavenly bodies, given 'personality' in protological fashion, were conceived as part of the worshiping host of beings about the throne of Yahweh."

12. G. Westphal, " צבא השמים," *Orientalische Studien Theodor Nöldeke zum siebzigsten Geburtstag*, II, ed. C. Bezold (Giesen: Alfred Töpelmann, 1906) 719-728.

13. *Ibid.*; cf. T. Jacobsen, "Primitive Democracy in Ancient Mesopotamia," *JNES*, 2 (1943), 166, n. 44 = *Toward the Image of Tammuz*, p. 163; and W. Muss-Arnolt, *A Concise Dictionary of the Assyrian Language* (Berlin: Reuther and Reichard, 1905), pp. 796-797 where the use of *puḫru* in both senses is illustrated by examples from *Enūma eliš* in the preceding chapter.

14. See esp. Wright, *The Old Testament Against Its Environment*, pp. 30-41; H.-W. Jüngling, *Der Tod der Götter*, and J. S.

Ackerman, "An Exegetical Study of Psalm 82," Th.D. dissertation,
Harvard Divinity School, 1966. The divine council background of
the "lawsuit" oracle has been greatly illuminated by G. Ernest
Wright, "The Lawsuit of God: A Form-Critical Study of Deuteronomy
32," *Israel's Prophetic Heritage*, ed. Bernhard W. Anderson and
Walter Harrelson (New York: Harper and Brothers, 1962), pp. 26-
67. Cf. Herbert Huffmon, "The Covenant Lawsuit of the Prophets,"
JBL, 78 (1959), 285-295.

15.   Cross, *JNES*, 12 (1953), 274-277.

16.   Cf. J. F. Ross, "The Prophet as Yahweh's Messenger," *Israel's Prophetic Heritage*, pp. 98-107; and John S. Holladay, Jr.,
"Assyrian Statecraft and the Prophets of Israel," *HTR*, 63 (1970),
29-52. Cf. Cooke, *ZAW*, 76 (1964), 37-42.

17.   For illustrations of such lexical specialization see
Zellig Harris, *Development of the Canaanite Dialects* (New Haven:
American Oriental Society, 1939), pp. 85-86. The lexical selection may have been more complex, terms from a judicial ($^c dt$,
$mw^c d$), military ($ṣb^{\jmath}$, $alpm//rbtm$), and familial background having
replaced $pḫr/qhl$. The shift could indeed have been that complex,
but the question still remains as to why $puḫru/pḫr$, a word which
itself has judicial and military connotations and which existed
alongside most of these other terms in Ugaritic, should suddenly
disappear altogether. Aside from this particular phenomenon the
terminology is much the same in Ugarit and Israel. It may be
legitimate, however, to say that the specifically military terminology, $ṣb^{\jmath}$, $alpm//rbtm$, rises to the fore in Hebrew to a degree
not previously manifest.

18. Wright, *The Old Testament Against Its Environment*, p. 39.

19. I find it difficult to separate sharply, as does H.-W. Jüngling, *Der Tod der Götter*, two traditions -- the divine assembly and the heavenly host -- which are then joined together. That Assyrian influences were felt and affected Yahwistic conceptions of Yahweh's host does not alter the fact that, as at Ugarit, from an early time Israel regarded the heavenly beings as part of the court/coterie of Yahweh.

20. Cf. Cross, *JNES*, 12 (1953), 275, n. 8.

21. Cf. T. H. Gaster, *Thespis* (Garden City, N.Y.: Doubleday and Company, Inc., 1961), pp. 157-158.

22. Aubrey R. Johnson, *The One and the Many in the Israelite Conception of God*, 2nd ed. (Cardiff: University of Wales Press, 1961), pp. 28ff. Some valuable comments about the relationship and the problem of the one and many in Israelite thought are marred by an injudicious tendency to explain the Israelite understanding of the divine assembly, the *malʾak yhwh*, and even the prophet as messenger of the council almost entirely in terms of "an active 'Extension' of Yahweh's Personality" (p. 33). Extra-biblical evidence is used but not carefully, and often more important evidence is ignored. For example, the discussion of the use of the first person plural pronoun passages such as Gen. 3:22; 11:5ff.; and Isa. 6:8 (pp. 27-28)could have profited more by an examination of the use of the same grammatical form in Ugaritic texts dealing with the assembly of the gods, e.g., Text 49:I:20, 26 (= *CTA* 6.I.48, 54); 51:IV:43-46 (= *CTA* 4.IV.43-46); 68:29-30

(= *CTA* 2.IV.29-30); *'nt*: V:40-42 (= *CTA* 3.V.40-42). Cf. Cross, *JNES*, 12 (1953), 275, n. 4.

23. Cf. the general comment of Cross, *JNES*, 12 (1953), 274, n. 1: "While some of the imagery and poetic language featuring biblical allusions to the council of Yahweh find their ultimate origin in the assembly of the gods common to the mythological *Weltbild* of Mesopotamia and Canaan, the conception of the heavenly assembly was radically transformed on being incorporated into the faith of Israel. Even in the early literature Yahweh's council consisted of colorless, secondary supernatural creatures who served him."

24. The term was coined and elaborated by Jacobsen, *JNES*, 2 (1943), 159-172. It is not entirely applicable to the assembly of the gods at Ugarit, but the Canaanite conception in this respect is closer to the Sumero-Akkadian assembly of the gods than to the Israelite. Cf. Gaster, *Thespis*, p. 191, for a suggestive comparison of the assemblies of Canaanite and Mesopotamian mythology along these lines.

25. Jacobsen, *JNES*, 2 (1943).

26. Note also the "upper" and "lower" gods of Hittite mythology discussed by A. Goetze, *Kleinasien*, 2nd rev. ed. (München: C. H. Beck'sche Verlagsbuchhandlung, 1957), pp. 144-145.

27. It is not necessary to argue the separation of this hymnic framework from the blessings contained within. Form-critically the separation is clear and universally accepted. See, for example, the treatment of the theophany in these verses by Jörg Jeremias, *Theophanie* (Neukirchen: Neukirchener Verlag, 1965), 62-

64, 127-128, 140 and *passim*. The work of Cross and Freedman
("The Blessing of Moses," *JBL*, 67 [1948], 191-210) is fundamental to the following interpretation. A very helpful later study
is that of J. Milik, "Deux documents inédits du Désert de Juda,"
Biblica, 38 (1957), 245-268, esp. pp. 252-254. Cf. I. L. Seeligmann, "A Psalm from Pre-Regal Times (Dt. 33, 2-5, 26-29),"
VT, 14 (1964), 75-92. The eleventh to tenth century date proposed by Cross and Freedman is most likely.

28. The reconstruction of these verses is largely dependent
upon that of Cross and Freedman, *JBL*, 67 (1948), 193-196, and my
"Two Critical Notes on Psalm 68 and Deuteronomy 33," *HTR*, 57
(1964), 241-243, which is summarized in brief in the following
pages. There is no attempt here to reconstruct in terms of tenth
or pre-tenth century orthography. *Waws* and *matres lectiones* are
kept in place. Only the consonantal text is transliterated.

29. The *lāmo* of the Masoretic text is difficult as Cross
and Freedman, as well as most commentators, have noted. The
usual alternatives are *lānu*, "to/for us" (with the versions) or
lᵉᶜammô, "to/for his people." The arguments for reading "to/for
his people" are given by Seeligmann, *VT*, 14 (1964), 76. Whether
one reads *lāmô*, *lānû*, *lᵉᶜammô*, the meaning is clear.

M. Dahood, *Psalms I* (Garden City, N.Y.: Doubleday and
Company, Inc., 1966), p. 173, has pointed out several cases where
lāmô appears and the versions read "to/for us," but his assumption
that *lāmô* can therefore mean "to/for us" is questionable. Dahood
is too reticent to assume textual error. Paleographic confusion
between *mem* and *nun* or between *m* and *nw* is not unusual, as has

been pointed out in response to Dahood by E. Lipinski, "Le Dieu
Lim," *La Civilisation de Mari: XVe Rencontre Assyriologique In-
ternationale* (Liege: Universite de Liege, 1967), p. 156, n. 1.
The suggestion of the latter, however, that one should see the
god Lim in this word, though ingenious and well argued (e.g., the
chiastic parallelism of the first two cola), does not seem likely.

30. See the preceding note.

31. The more traditional term "theophany" is used throughout, although a case can be made for the term "epiphany" as a
more nearly accurate designation of what is described in these
passages. See the discussion in Claus Westermann, *The Praise of
God in the Psalms* (Richmond: John Knox Press, 1965), pp. 93-101,
esp. p. 99 and F. Schnutenhaus, "Das Kommen und Erscheinen Gottes
im Alten Testament," *ZAW*, 76 (1964), 1-22.

32. One should take note of the fact that the earliest
known occurrences of the name "Yahweh" are as a toponym in two
Egyptian inscriptions from the fourteenth century associated with
Seir in Edom. See R. Giveon, "Toponymes oeust-asiatique à So-
leb," *VT*, 14 (1964), 239-255.

33. Cf. Schnutenhaus, *ZAW*, 76 (1964), 1-22, and Jeremias,
Theophanie, pp. 62ff.

34. H. Huffmon, *Amorite Personal Names in the Mari Texts*,
pp. 212-213, and F. Gröndahl, *Die Personennamen der Texte aus
Ugarit* (Rome: Pontifical Biblical Institute, 1967), pp. 144-145.

35. Cf. Ps. 50:2 and 94:1 where the shining forth (*hôpî^{c}a*)
of Yahweh is for battle and judgment.

36. See Cross and Freedman, *JBL*, 67 (1948), 198, nn. 7-9, for details. Cross would now read *qdš* as it stands as a collective following the lead of H. S. Nyberg, "Deuteronomium 33:203," *ZDMG*, 92 (1938), 335-336. So also Milik, *Biblica*, 38 (1957), 253, n. 2. See F. M. Cross, "The Divine Warrior in Israel's Early Cult," p. 26, n. 49. The same form appears in Ex. 15:11 as indicated by the parallelism and the LXX. Cf. the preceding chapter, n. 23, and the reference there to the presence of this form in the Arslan Tash inscription.

37. "With him myriads" is reflected in LXX and "holy ones" in the Targum Onkelos.

38. Milik, *Biblica*, 38 (1957), 253. Milik's reading, however, does not give a basis for the corruption as do Cross and Freedman. He must assume a misreading of or damage to the *reš* and the omission of the *aleph*.

39. For a more detailed presentation see my article, *HTR*, 57 (1964), 241-243. Beeston's article is "Angels in Deuteronomy 33:2," *JTS* (1951), 30-31.

40. Huffmon, *Amorite Personal Names*, p. 169. (I failed to note the Amorite cognate in my original discussion. The article in the preceding note should be corrected to that extent.)

41. Cf. the similar idiom in the Qumran literature: *gbwry ʾlm*, "mighty ones of the gods" (1QM XV:14).

42. Miller, *HTR*, 57 (1964), 243, and Cross, "The Divine Warrior in Israel's Early Cult," p. 26, n. 50.

43. S. R. Driver, *A Critical and Exegetical Commentary on Deuteronomy*, *ICC* (Edinburgh: T. and T. Clark, 1902), p. 410.

44. See n. 36.

45. Johannes C. de Moor has recently contested this meaning for Ugaritic *hm*. See "Ugaritic hm-Never 'Behold'," *Ugarit-Forschungen*, 1 (1969), 201-202.

46. Milik, *Biblica*, 38 (1957), 252. His translation of the last colon is also worthy of note: "ils se mettent en marche derrière toi." He interprets *yiśśaʾ* as an ellipsis meaning "to lift up the feet and take off," citing Gen. 29:1 and *Krt* A: 98f. and 186f. (= *CTA* 14.98f. and 186f.). The form *dbrt* is understood as a preposition "behind" reflecting the primitive meaning of *dbr*, "to be last, behind," (p. 252, nn. 3-4). The parallelism which this translation produces is quite satisfactory. The imagery again would be that of the army of Yahweh marching behind him.

47. As background for the second colon note the idiomatic series of verbs *hbr*, *qll*, *šthwy*, and *kbd* (e.g., Text 49:I:9-10 [= *CTA* 6.I.37-38]), which are used in the Ugaritic texts to describe the attitude of any other divine being approaching El, the head of the pantheon, enthroned on his mountain.

48. Shemaryahu Talmon, " יתד a Biblical Noun," *VT*, 3 (1953), 135.

49. Wright, The Book of Deuteronomy: Introduction and Exegesis," *The Interpreter's Bible*, II (New York: Abingdon-Cokesbury, 1953), 529.

50. Gaster,("An Ancient Eulogy on Israel: Deuteronomy 33:3-5, 26-29," *JBL*, 66 [1947], 53-62), would see in verse 27 a reference to Yahweh's humbling the ancient gods. Seeligmann has fol-

lowed Gaster here arguing quite plausibly that such a motif may
well have "played a part in epic poems glorifying the Conquest."
I have reservations about Gaster and Seeligmann's reconstruction
but admit there are strong arguments in its favor (e.g., the resolution of some syntactical problems). We would not agree with
the judgment of Cross and Freedman, *JBL*, 67 (1948), 209, n. 84,
that Gaster's reconstruction "diverges too far from Israelite religious concepts to permit ready acceptance.

51. Seeligmann, *VT*, 14 (1964), 76-78 and 85-86. See his
discussion for indication of the valid parallels. The only way
in which he has altered the text in any substantial way is in his
reconstruction of the initial verb. That verb has been lost in
the transmission (although Seeligmann sees it in *wyt*'). There is
no orthographic problem in reading ṣidqôt for ṣidqat for this ancient poem.

52. The following paragraphs do not present any new reconstruction of the text. For translation and details see Cross and
Freedman, *JBL*, 67 (1948), 196, 209-210. It is possible to see in
the *ᶜezrekā* of vv. 26 and 29 a nominal form meaning "your
strength" from *ᶜzr II*. See Gaster, *JBL*, 66 (1947), and P. D.
Miller, Jr., "Ugaritic GZR and Hebrew ᶜZR II," *Ugarit-Forschungen*,
II (1970), 159-175.

53. Cf. Wright, *The Interpreter's Bible* II, 533-534.

54. Cf. Ps. 95:3; 96:4; 77:14 where I would tentatively
translate the first colon: "Thy dominion, O God, is among the
holy ones," etc. Cf. M. Dahood, *Psalms II* (Garden City, N.Y.:
Doubleday and Company, 1968), pp. 224, 230.

55. F. Stummer, *Sumerisch-Akkadische Parallelen zum Aufbau alttestamentlicher Psalmen* (Paderborn: Ferdinand Schöningh, 1922) p. 57, cites Sumerian Akkadian instances of the cliché: "Who is like you. . .?" An extended study of these formulas in their Near Eastern setting has recently been made by C. J. Labuschagne, *The Incomparability of Yahweh in the Old Testament* (Leiden: E. J. Brill, 1966).

56. Ugar. *rkb ʿrpt;* Akk. *rākib narkabati.* Cf. below the discussion of Ps. 68:5.

57. Cross and Freedman, *JBL*, 16 (1948), 210, n. 86. The alternate translation is that of Meek quoted by Cross and Freedman.

58. The common Deuteronomic term is *yāraš*.

59. T. H. Gaster, *JBL*, 66 (1947), 62.

60. Wright, *The Interpreter's Bible*, II, 332-333, 528.

61. Cross and Freedman, *JBL*, 67 (1948), 201-202, n. 19, cite one lengthy parallel. Others even more similar in language are given by Stummer, *Sumerisch-Akkadische Parallelen*, 38ff. Cf. Westermann, *The Praise of God in the Psalms*, pp. 93-96, who briefly notes the distinction elaborated here in more detail, and Joseph Blenkinsopp, "Ballad Style and Psalm Style in the Song of Deborah: A Discussion," *Biblica*, 42 (1961), 65ff.

62. See the most recent discussion of the date and historical context of Judges 5 by W. F. Albright, *The Biblical Period from Abraham to Ezra*, 4th rev. ed. (New York: Harper & Row, Publishers, 1963), pp. 39-40 and 102, nn. 82, 83. The presence of Dan by the sea as well as the linguistic and poetic elements of

the poem confirm this date.

63.   It is not possible or necessary to go into all the treatments of this poem.   Among the important studies in recent times are the form-critical and traditions history studies of Artur Weiser ("Das Deboralied.   Eine gattungs-und traditionsges-chichtliche Studie," *ZAW*, 71 [1959], 67-97) and Wolfgang Richter (*Traditionsgeschichtliche Untersuchungen zum Richterbuch* [Bonn: Peter Hanstein Verlag, 1963], pp. 65-112) and the partial lin-guistic study of Frank M. Cross (*Studies in Ancient Yahwistic Poetry* [Baltimore, 1950], pp. 27-42).   For treatments of the poem as a type of victory song, see *inter alia* C. Westermann, *The Praise of God in the Psalms*, trans. K. Crim (Richmond: John Knox Press, 1965), pp. 90-93; J. Jeremias, *Theophanie*, pp. 142ff.; and P. C. Craigie, "The Song of Deborah and the Epic of Tukulti-Ni-nurta," *JBL*, 88 (1969), 253-265.

64.   I am heavily indebted to the reconstructions of W. F. Albright, "The Earliest Forms of Hebrew Verse," *JPOS*, 2 (1922), 69-86, and F. M. Cross, *Studies in Ancient Yahwistic Poetry* (and oral communication).

65.   Cf. Egyptian *pr*ᶜ, "energetic, valorous, prowess," which may, however, be unrelated to the Semitic word.   Ugaritic eviden-ces the root *pr*ᶜ, but the contexts in which it appears are too broken or obscure to translate it with any certainty.

66.   Valuable linguistic notes following the line of trans-lation and interpretation given here are to be found in C. F. Burney, *The Book of Judges* (London: Rivingtons, 1918), pp. 105-109.   He even sees the connection with consecration for war.   Cf.

Albright, *JPOS*, 2 (1922), p. 81.

67.   Similar conclusions have been reached by Max Weber,
Ancient Judaism, trans. H. H. Gerth and Don Martindale (Glencoe,
Ill,: The Free Press, 1952), pp. 94-95, and to a lesser degree
Johannes Pedersen, *Israel III-IV* (London: Oxford University
Press, 1940), pp. 36-37, 264ff.   More recently and in briefer
scope may be cited R. de Vaux, *Ancient Israel*, trans. John McHugh
(New York: McGraw-Hill Book Company, Inc., 1961), p. 467, and J.
Blenkinsopp, "Structure and Style in Judges 13--16," *JBL*, 82
(1963), 63-66.   The comments of the latter are worth noting in
this context: "That the vow, i.e., Nazirite, moreover, was prim-
itively connected with the holy war of the amphictyony is also
inherently probable, and would be confirmed by the application of
nazir to the warlike Joseph tribe in the two ancient tribal poems
in Gen. 49:26 and Deut. 33:16, and by the fact that making the
vow is considered as essentially the act of a young man or warrior.   This is precisely the case with Samson.   (Note: In Judg.
14:10 he is *baḥûr*.   It might be worthwhile reopening the debate
on the semantic interpretation of *pr*^{c} as 'lock of hair' in the
title to the tribal poem of Deborah [Judg. 5:2] in the light of
the *nazir* vow.)"   Matthew Black has noticed a connection between
the Nazirite vow and the warriors of holy war in a discussion of
the Hasidim and Qumran in *The Scrolls and Christian Origins* (New
York: Charles Scribner's Sons, 1961), p. 16.   Cf. J. Gray, *Joshua,
Judges, and Ruth* (London: Thomas Nelson and Sons, 1967), p. 276.

68.   Cf. Hermann Gunkel, "Samson," *Reden und Aufsätze* (Göttingen: Vandenhoeck und Ruprecht, 1913), pp. 38-64.

69. See the judgment of George F. Moore, *A Critical and Exegetical Commentary on Judges, ICC* (Edinburgh: T. and T. Clark, 1908), p. 314: "Whether from J or not, the chapters undoubtedly belong to the oldest stratum of the book."

70. Cf. Jacob M. Myers, "The Book of Judges: Introduction and Exegesis," *The Interpreter's Bible*, II (New York: Abingdon-Cokesbury, 1953), 776: "While it cannot be doubted that some legendary accretions have attached themselves to the tales there can be little hesitancy in regarding Samson as a historical personality."

71. F. M. Cross, "A New Qumran Fragment Related to the Original Hebrew Underlying the Septuagint," *BASOR*, 132 (December 1953), 15-26. Cf. W. F. Albright, *Samuel and the Beginnings of the Prophetic Movement* (Cincinnati: Hebrew Union College Press, 1961), pp. 12-13.

72. Cross, *Studies in Ancient Yahwistic Poetry*, p. 27.

73. Verse 3 continues the declaration of praise already indicated in verse 1 and leads into the theophany of verses 4-5. On these verses and their relation to Ps. 68:8-11, see W. Richter, *Traditionsgeschichtliche Untersuchungen*; Lipinski, "Juges 5, 4-5 et Psaume 68, 8-11," *Biblica*, 48 (1967), 184-206; and J. Jeremias, *Theophanie*, pp. 7-11 and 142-150. On pp. 142-144 Jeremias has effectively answered the arguments of Richter and Blenkinsopp that verses 4-5 do not belong originally in the poem and has pointed to the thematic character of their content throughout the poem.

74. On the basis of some Greek manuscripts and the Hexaplar

where *etarachthē* appears Albright, *JPOS*, 2 (1922), 75, n. 1 read
namoṭṭû for *naṭ^epû*. He maintained that "drip" was an anticlimax
and the following phrase was added to explain the "absurd" pre=
ceding one. Cf. Moore, *Judges*, p. 141, and Burney, *The Book of
Judges*, p. 112, who proposes *namôgû*. The reading certainly im-
proves the metrical quality of the line producing a 2:2 line of
5 + 6 syllables. Since that time, however, Albright has changed
his mind. Recognizing that *nāṭ^epû* appears also in the parallel
passage in Ps. 68:8-9, he has given up any attempt to emend the
text but still prefers to see the word as meaning "quake, shake,"
or the like. He, therefore, derives the word from a stem *ṭpp*,
meaning something like "toss," on the basis of Arabic and Aramaic
cognates. See W. F. Albright, "A Catalogue of Early Lyric Poems
(Psalm LXVIII)," *Hebrew Union College Annual*, 231 (1950-51), 20.
Albright's feeling for the proper word is not to be ignored, but
the derivation is definitely forced.

75. Along similar lines as in the preceding note, Albright,
JPOS, 2 (1922), 75, n. 2, has also suggested on the basis of LXX
esaleuthēsan and the vocalization *hārîm nāzōllû* in Isa. 62:19;
64:2 that *nzlw* here should be vocalized the same way indicating
a verb *zll* belonging with Arab. *zlzl*, "quake, of earth," and *zll*,
"drip." His reading, which is in agreement with Burney, is much
more plausible here, and the imagery is more appropriate. Cf.
the reference of Myers, "The Book of Judges, p. 720 to Akkadian
ittarraru šadu.

76. The appellation *zeh sînay*, once considered a late gloss,
is now recognized as an ancient epithet, originally **zū-Sīnai*,

and similar to the Northwest Semitic formation of divine epithets
in the second millennium. Cf. Albright, "The Song of Deborah in
the Light of Archaeology," *BASOR*, 62 (April 1936), 30; and F. M.
Cross, "Yahweh and the God of the Patriarchs," *Harvard Theological Review*, 55 (1962), *passim*. Judges 5:5 still has metrical
problems unsolved. Albright, *BASOR*, 62 (April 1936), 30, proposes a reconstruction but one that is not entirely satisfactory.
Perhaps the first *yhwh* is to be deleted or else *ᵓelōhê* is to be
read *ᵓēl*. This would produce some order. But problems remain.
Cf. the reconstruction of the parallel verse in Ps. 68 in Albright, *HUCA*, 23 (1950-51), 13. Another possible reconstruction
of the middle cola suggested by Frank Cross is as follows:

$$ᵓrṣ \ r^c šh \ hrym \ nzlw$$

$$ancient \ variants \ \begin{cases} gm \ šmym \ ntpw \\ \\ ^cbym \ ntpw \ mym \end{cases}$$

   77. Cf. the summary statement of Jeremias, *Theophanie*, pp.
142-144. "Zunächst fällt am Deboralied auf, dass die Theophanieschilderung V. 4f. zwar eine Einheit für sich bildet. . ., dass
aber andererseits die Theophanieschilderung fest im Kontext des
Liedes verankert ist, ohne sich aus ihm lösen zulassen. Denn der
Tenor des ganzen Liedes weist ja darauf hin, dass es die Meinung
des oder der Sänger dieses Liedes ist, dass Jahwe focht und die
Schlacht entschied. Von Jahwes Heilstaten handelt das Lied (V.
11); die in die Schlacht ziehenden Israeliten waren nur seine
Hilfstruppen (v. 23, 13 txt. em.). Jahwe selbst schlug die
Schlacht durch die vom Himmel her kämpfenden Sterne (V. 20), und
durch ihn riss der Bach Kison die Feinde ins Verderben (V. 21)."

78. Verses 6-7 and 9-11 tell of the interruption of the caravan trade (see Albright, *Yahweh and the Gods of Canaan*, pp. 43-44) and describe the plight in Israel at the time. They are less germane to the song of battle except for *11b* where the singer(s) speak(s) of the recitation of the "triumphs of Yahweh" = "triumphs of his warriors (*prznw*) in Israel," one example of which is this song. On *pirzōnô* as "warriors" see Albright, *ibid.*, p. 43, n. 101.

79. On the military significance of *'elep* see G. Mendenhall, "The Census Lists of Numbers 1 and 26," *JBL*, 77 (1958), 52-66.

80. See Burney, *The Book of Judges*, p. 120 for textual analysis of the LXX here.

81. Cf. von Rad, *Der Heilige Krieg im alten Israel*, p. 9.

82. Albright, *JPOS*, 2 (1922), 76.

83. Von Rad, *Der Heilige Krieg*, p. 7. In addition to the bibliographical reference noted by him in n. 3 on that page, one might add C. Umhau Wolf, "Terminology of Israel Tribal Organizations," *JBL*, 65 (1946), 45, who notes that Akk. *ummānu* also means both "people" and "troops." The most recent discussion of the term *'am* is that of Ephraim Speiser, "'People' and 'Nation' of Israel," *JBL*, 79 (1960), 157-163. Cf. J. Wharton, "People of God," *IDB*, III, 727, who sees the probable origin of the phrase in the institution of holy war.

84. Cf. Y. Yadin, *The Scroll of the War*, p. 44.

85. Burney, *The Book of Judges*, pp. 120-122.

86. Oral communication.

87. The reconstruction is on the basis of a tenth-century orthography.

88. The structure of the second half of this verse is paralleled almost identically by 1QM xii:9:

qwmh gbwr   Arise, O mighty one

šbh šbykh   Take thy captives captive,

ʾyš kbwd   Men of glory.

As Yadin (*The Scroll of the War*, p. 317) has noted, the parallel of *šybkh* with *šllk* (1.10) is strong argument against reading *šbyk* "thy captors" in Judg. 5:12 as do some versions (i.e., Syriac, Arabic) and a number of commentators.

89. Cf. Burney, *The Book of Judges*, pp. 134-136, 142, 306-307; John Bright, *A History of Israel* (Philadelphia: The Westminster Press, 1959), p. 143.

90. Albright, *JPOS*, 2 (1922), 78.

91. The suggestion was made by Frank Cross. The elaboration given here has been worked out by myself.

92. The word *mišpatayim* occurs only in these two places. There is no certain meaning. The versions were nonplussed. Scholars vary between "sheepfolds" and "ashheaps." See the detailed discussion in Burney, *The Book of Judges*, p. 141. Note also the similar phrase in Ps. 68:14 where Albright plausibly equates the word with Ugar. *mtpdm* meaning "hearth" (*HUCA*, 23.1 [1950-51], 22).

93. Verse 19 poses no problems. It begins the account of the actual battle and gives the location.

94. For discussion of the Akkadian cognates, see Burney,

The Book of Judges, p. 146. To these should now be added the
Ugaritic forms *mzl* and *ymzl* in Krt A: 99, 188 (= *CTA* 14.99 and
188).

95. R. Smend comments: "The intervention of celestial
powers is directly decisive for the war of Yahweh in Judges 5:
20." (He compares also as ancient evidence Josh. 10:12-13, on
which see *infra*.). See R. Smend, *Yahweh War and Tribal Confederation*, trans. M. G. Rogers (Nashville: Abingdon Press, 1970),
p. 82.

96. On the textual reconstruction of v. 21 see Cross, *Studies in Ancient Yahwistic Poetry*, pp. 34-35. For similar ideas in
Egyptian and Akkadian, see Myers, "The Book of Judges," p. 726.

97. This reading has been proposed by Cross, *Studies in Ancient Yahwistic Poetry*, p. 36, who argues that the ʾ*rwr* has been
dropped out by haplography. The reading is definitely an improvement in terms of meter and parallelism.

98. The reading *mēroz* is quite problematical. No such
place is known. Probably Marom or Meron is to be read. Cf. for
discussion Albright, *JPOS*, 2 (1922), 79, n. 5; and "Some Additional Notes on the Song of Deborah," *JPOS*, 2 (1922), 284-285; A.
Alt, "Meros," *Kleine Schriften zur Geschichte des Volkes Israel*,
I (München: C. H. Beck'sche Verlagsbuchhandlung, 1953), 274-277.

99. On the characteristics of this genre see especially
Cross, *JNES*, 12 (1953), 274-277; also James F. Ross, "The Prophet
as Yahweh's Messenger," *Israel's Prophetic Heritage*, ed. B. W.
Anderson and Walter Harrelson (New York: Harper and Brothers,
1962), pp. 99-107.

100. Cross, *JNES*, 12 (1953), 275, n. 4.

101. Wright, *Israel's Prophetic Heritage*, pp. 41-49.

102. Cross, *Studies in Ancient Yahwistic Poetry*, pp. 30 and 37, reads *bgbrm* = *begibbōrêmô* "with their warriors" on the basis of the manner in which the text would be represented in early orthography. Cf. Albright, *JPOS*, 2 (1922), 79.

103. Including possibly the puzzling verse 13 of Judges 5, although it is too obscure to tell.

104. J. Strugnell, "The Angelic Liturgy at Qumran-4Q *Serek Šîrôt ꜤŌlat Haššabbāt*," *Congress Volume, Oxford, 1959* (Leiden: E. J. Brill, 1960), pp. 218-345, esp. 322 (4QS1 391 i:21) and 333. Strugnell also cites the use of *gbwrym* for divine beings in Enoch and Talmudic literature.

105. Verses 24-30 give the poetic account of Jael's killing of Sisera and may be omitted from the present discussion.

106. The arrangement of cola in this awkward verse is that of Albright, *JPOS*, 2 (1922), 83.

107. Reading with the Syriac and Vulgate. MT has *ʾhbyw*.

108. William L. Moran, "The Ancient Near Eastern Background of the Love of God in Deuteronomy," *CBQ*, 25 (1963), 77-87.

109. *Ibid.*, pp. 84-85. "Certainly the conclusion has an archaic ring, and the reference to the Israelites as Yahweh's 'friends' becomes perfectly intelligible in the light of our remarks on the covenant background of the term love. The Israelites are those bound to Yahweh in covenant, and therefore naturally opposed to his enemies; the war and victory described in the Song are those of the people of God. It is probable therefore

that the term love goes back to a very early period in the Israelite covenant tradition."

110. W. F. Albright refers to a monograph published in
1851, in which Edward Reuss brought together exegeses of the
psalm from over 400 commentaries. The studies and views put forward in the hundred or so years since then would make such a
monograph a multi-volume work. See W. F. Albright, *HUCA*, 23,
1 (1950-51), 7.

111. *Ibid.*, pp. 1-39. For a more recent defense of his position, see *Yahweh and the Gods of Canaan*, pp. 23-24.

112. Sigmund Mowinckel, *Der achtundsechzigste Psalm* (Oslo:
I Kommisjon Jacob Dybwad, 1953), pp. 1-78.

113. *Ibid.*, pp. 672-673.

114. See, e.g., the commentaries of Artur Weiser, *The
Psalms*, trans. H. Hartwell, The Old Testament Library (Philadelphia: The Westminster Press, 1962), pp. 277-290; Hans-Joachim
Kraus, *Psalmen* (Neukirchen: Neukirchener Verlag, 1960), I, 464-
477.

115. A purely form-critical analysis of the psalm, though
distinguishing the various elements, does not go very far in
solving its many problems. There are several types brought together here as in Judg. 5. For their elaboration, see Kraus.
Psalmen, I, 468-469. If any single form lies behind this compilation, it is probably a type of victory hymn. Its place in Israel's cult is another matter although the overall form may point
the way. Psalm 68 in its primitive form may have had its situation in life in a celebration of "ritual Conquest" such as Cross

posits in "The Divine Warrior in Israel's Early Cult," *Biblical Motifs*, pp. 11-30.

116. The reference to Jerusalem in v. 30 is surely a later addition. The whole verse is meaningless, as Albright shows. Some corruption has obviously taken place. As it now stands, there is no certain reference to the Jerusalem temple anywhere in the psalm (except v. 30), although vv. 25, 30, 33, and 18 (which contains no reference to the sanctuary even in its present state) were probably early so understood. Albright reaches a similar but more tentative conclusion in another context. In "The Psalm of Habakkuk," *Studies in Old Testament Prophecy* (Edinburgh: T. and T. Clark, 1957), p. 8, n. 28 he says that v. 30 "may not, however, have been included in the first Israelite form of the psalm." Albright seems to have changed his mind in his later study connecting the reference to Jerusalem with David's conquest of the city.

In their various studies of the early poetry Cross and Freedman have shown that in these contexts the various references to "shine," "sanctuary," "temple," not only do not have to apply to the Jerusalem temple but are properly understood as not having reference to the temple. They refer originally to the desert sanctuary, Yahweh's heavenly abode, or the amphictyonic tent shrine in Canaan. See Cross and Freedman, "The Song of Miriam," *JNES*, 14 (1955), 240; 248, n. 42; 249, n. 59; and "A Royal Song of Thanksgiving: II Samuel 22 = Psalm 18," *JBL*, 72 (1953), 23, n. 11.

117. That the part of the Song of the Ark referring to the

return is not used here may be by deliberate intention in the composition of the psalm, i.e., the psalm begins with God's going out to battle, not his return.

118. The second colon of v. 3 belongs intimately to the theophany imagery as comparison with Micah 1:4 reveals.

119. The problem, which Kraus, *Psalmen*, p. 475, raises, of how both the Ark and Sinai could be considered the seat or abode of Yahweh was probably less of a concern to the Israelite than it is to the scholar today and is in part resolved by the recognition of the war context of Yahweh's presence with the Ark. This is not to deny that the idea of Yahweh's abode on Sinai and his throne on the Ark did not originate in different contexts. One cannot say. But the evidence of these early poems is that Yahweh's coming from Sinai was represented probably at a very early time by the procession of the Ark. Cf. H. Eberhard von Waldow, "Theophanie," *Verkündigung und Forschung*, 14 (1969), 69-76, who argues for the original separation of Sinai and Ark. A fuller discussion of the whole question of the divine presence is given in R. E. Clements, *God and Temple* (Philadelphia: Fortress Press, 1965).

120. Arvid Kapelrud, *Baal in the Ras Shamra Texts* (Copenhagen: G. E. C. Gad, 1952), p. 61.

121. Kurt Galling, "Der Ehrenname Elisas und die Entrückung Elias," *Zeitschrift für Theologie und Kirche*, 53 (1956), 129-148.

122. In a communication to George M. A. Hanfmann, Albrecht Goetze remarks with regard to the phrase "rider of the clouds" that the clouds may be viewed as a chariot: "This is much more

likely because of the expression which finds its analogue in Akkadian." See G. M. A. Hanfmann, "A Near Eastern Horseman,"
Syria, 38 (1961), 252, n. 7.

123. Drawing upon Weiser's important work on chariotry in
the Near East and Europe as well as his own study of Old Testament materials, Mowinckel has convincingly shown in some detail
that *rkb* refers to "driving (a chariot)" rather than "riding (a
horse)." "Drive and/or Ride in the Old Testament," *VT*, 12 (1962),
278-299.

124. The arrangement of cola here is that of Albright,
HUCA, 23.1 (1950-51), 12-13.

125. *yšymwn* without the article is regularly a designation
for the wilderness wandering of Israel either in the Exodus or
the New Exodus (e.g., Deut. 32:10; Ps. 78:40; 106:14; Isa. 43:19,
20). For other notes on the details of the passage see the discussion of Judg. 5:4-5 above and Albright, *HUCA*, 23.1 (1950-51),
20.

126. Although it is impossible to be certain, comparison
with the theophany forms of Deut. 33:2-3, Judg. 5:4-5, and Hab.
3:3 suggests that the preposition *b* in *byšymwn* should be translated "from" as is often the case in Ugaritic and Hebrew.

127. The translation, especially of v. 10, is rather uncertain. See E. Vogt, "'Regen in Fülle' (Psalm 68, 10-11)," *Biblica*,
46 (1965), 359-361 for a discussion of the textual and structural
problems.

128. Another possible rendering is that of Albright in *HUCA*,
23.1 (1950-51), 37:

"Let * Y H W H give an oracle

Rejoicing a mighty host.

The verse would thus refer clearly to the holy war oracle prior to battle.

129. The precise translation of the second colon of v. 13 is difficult. It is certain that it has something to do with the division of booty.

130. Why $hamm^eba\acute{s}\acute{s}^er\hat{o}t$ should be regarded as referring to "maidens" (so Weiser and others) is difficult to perceive. The ending can be regarded as a collective in $-\hat{o}t$, as perhaps may be true of a $\d{s}^eb\bar{a}\,{}^{\prime}\hat{o}t$. See E. Kautzsch, *Gesenius' Hebrew Grammar*, ed. A. E. Cowley, 26th ed. (Oxford: The Clarendon Press, 1898), para. 122s.

131. Note the use of the archaic epithet $\v{s}adday$ for Yahweh. Its use in this context may indicate that at this time its primitive association with "mountain" was still known. If so, the verse provides valuable evidence for Cross's interpretation of El Sadday as "El, the Mountain One," especially in light of the fact that free use of the ancient names for Yahweh is not a characteristic of Ps. 68, this being the only one. See Cross, *HTR*, 55 (1962), 244-250.

132. Albright, *HUCA*, 23.1, 25 and "Notes on Psalms 68 and 134," *Interpretationes ad Vetus Testamentum Pertinentes Sigmundo Mowinckel* (Oslo: Land og Kirke, 1955), pp. 2-4. For $tnn(m)$ in the Ugaritic texts see Text 80:II:11 (= *CTA* 85.IV.1); 113:70 (= *CTA* 71.70); 303:1 (= *CTA* 116.1); Krt 91 (= *CTA* 14.91) and PRU II 26:4; 28:1; 30:1; 31:1. For $\v{s}anannu$ in the Alalakh texts see D. H.

Wiseman, *The Alalakh Tablets* (London: The British Institute of Archaeology at Ankara, 1953), nos. 145:43; 183:2; 226:6,11; 341: 1,9; 350:9; 352:6; 439:6,7, etc. and esp. p. 11, n. 4. Albright points out that the mistake in spelling could easily have arisen by dittography due to the series of letters *šn'n'*. Note also the Syriac *ḥyl'*, "troops," although this may be a guess. It at least recognizes what the word should mean. Mowinckel's unwillingness to accept this explanation of the word is rather puzzling. His own explanation is much more forced and difficult.

133. Cf. Cross, "The Divine Warrior in Israel's Early Cult," p. 26, and J. T. Milik, *Biblica*, 38 (1957), 253, n. 2, who reads "He comes from Sinai among the holy ones" (apparently *b' msyny bqdš*). The translation of Cross and the writer is preferable to that of Milik stylistically and by reason of comparison with the theophanies of Judg. 5:4 and Ps. 68:8 where *b* + infinitive to express a temporal clause is also used.

134. Albright, *Interpretationes* . . ., p. 5.

135. Cross, "The Divine Warrior in Israel's Early Cult," p. 25.

136. For the various possibilities see Albright, *HUCA*, 23.1 (1950-51), pp. 26-27. *ršc* seems the most likely option (cf. Hab. 3:13).

137. In his more recent work, *Yahweh and the Gods of Canaan*, p. 24, Albright accepts the translation of the two cola of v. 23 proposed by myself and by Dahood (see following notes).

138. M. Dahood, "*Mišmar* 'Muzzle' in Job 7:12," *JBL*, 80 (1961), 270-271.

139. See Patrick D. Miller, Jr., "Two Critical Notes on Psalm 68 and Deuteronomy 33," *HTR*, 57 (1964), 240.

140. Albright, *HUCA*, 23.1 (1950-51), 28-29; A. Haldar, *The Notion of the Desert in Sumero-Accadian and West-Semitic Religions* (Uppsala: A.-B. Lundequistaka Bokhandeln, 1950), p. 49.

141. Albright, *HUCA*, 23.1 (1950-51), 28.

142. So also Weiser, *The Psalms*, p. 289.

143. Cross and Freedman, *JNES*, 14 (1955), 237-240.

144. "The Divine Warrior in Israel's Early Cult", and "The Song of the Sea and Canaanite Myth," *God and Christ: Existence and Providence, Journal for Theology and the Church,* 5 (1968), 1-25. Cf. Norman Habel, *Yahweh Versus Baal*, pp. 58-62, and the bibliography cited in the second Cross article above, pp. 9-10, n. 27. Add to that the recent study of George Coats, "The Song of the Sea," *CBQ*, 31 (1969), 1-17.

145. See Cross and Freedman, *JNES*, 14 (1955), 243-244 and Cross, "The Song of the Sea. . .," p. 13 for details of text and translation. They advocate a transposition of $w^{e\,\flat}anweh\hat{u}$ and wa - $^{\flat a}rom^emenh\hat{u}$ for metrical reasons. I am not as certain as Cross and Freedman that v. 2 is a secondary interpolation. The argument is based on metrical considerations, which cannot be ignored, particularly in this poem. In terms of meaning or sense the verse fits where it is. Furthermore, it contains archaic terminology and formulae, as Cross and Freedman have pointed out. Most recently there has come to light the parallel Ugaritic expression, ^czk. *dmrk.* (*Ugaritica* V, Text 2 [RS 24.252], Verso, 1.9), "your strength and your defense," further testifying to the antiquity

of the language and clichés of the verse. On this line one
should note the discussion of S. E. Loewenstamm, "'The Lord Is
My Strength and My Glory,'" *VT*, 19 (1969), 464-470.

146. Cross and Freedman may be correct in regarding *gibbôr*
as a preferable reading to *ʾîš milḥamāh*. The meaning is the same
in any event.

147. See Albrecht Alt, "Der Gott der Väter," *Kleine Schriften zur Geschichte des Volkes Israel*, I, 1-78; F. M. Cross, *HTR*,
55 (1962), 225-259.

148. Cross, *HTR*, 55 (1962), 228.

149. "The Song of the Sea and Canaanite Myth," *passim*.

150. *Ibid.*

151. Cross, "The Divine Warrior in Israel's Early Cult,"
pp. 26f.

152. So Cross,"The Song of the Sea . . .," p. 23.

153. Cf. von Rad, *Der Heilige Krieg im alten Israel*, pp.
10-11.

154. Cf. Cross and Freedman, *JNES*, 14 (1955), 240, 249-250,
and Cross, "The Song of the Sea . . .," p. 24.

155. *tliyt* is clearly from the root *lʾy*, "to prevail" and
related to Baʿal's epithet Aliyan. The absence of a pronominal
suffix in clear parallelism to a word which contains one is not
uncommon in either Ugaritic or Hebrew. The word is to be read as
if it were *tliyty*, "my victory."

156. Cross, "The Divine Warrior in Israel's Early Cult."

157. Cross, "The Song of the Sea . . .," p. 24.

158. Cross, "The Divine Warrior . . .," pp. 19ff., and Part

One above, pp. 28-29. Cross regards Ps. 24:6-10 as a "tenth
century B.C. liturgical piece," although dating of this piece is
a little more precarious than in some other instances.

159. Cross, "The Song of the Sea . . .," pp. 8-9.

160. W. F. Albright, *Studies in Old Testament Prophecy*,
pp. 1-18. Albright says that vv. 3-7 were "probably taken with
little alteration from a very early Israelite poem on the theophany of Yahweh as exhibited in the south-east storm, the *zauba^cah*
of the Arabs" (p. 8). Verses 8-15 he regards as adapted from an
early poem or poems of Canaanite origin celebrating the triumph
of Prince Ba^cal over his enemies. Reference to "the anointed"
requires a time after David for vv. 8-15 (pp. 8-9). In addition
to Albright, David A. Robertson, "Linguistic Evidence in Dating
Early Hebrew Poetry," has shown that Habakkuk 3 has characteristic forms of early poetry along with those of later standard Hebrew.

161. For a more recent textual and philological study of
the poem -- albeit one that does not represent major improvements
over that of Albright -- see J. H. Eaton, "The Origin and Meaning
of Habakkuk 3," *ZAW*, 76 (1964), 144-171.

162. Albright, *Studies in Old Testament Prophecy*, p. 9,
comments with regard to vv. 3-7: "The historico-geographical
background reflects the period following the wilderness wanderings."

163. Johannes Hehn, *Hymnen und Gebete an Marduk* (Leipzig:
J. C. Hinriche'sche Buchhandlung, 1905), p. 314, ll. 4-5.

164. See R. Stadelmann, *Syrisch-palastinensische Gottheiten*

in Ägypten (Leiden: E. J. Brill, 1967), pp. 47-49.

165. Cf. the destroying angel who sends pestilence over the land in II Sam. 24.

166. Kušan probably represents a part of southern Trans-jordan south from the Arnon into Midian. W. F. Albright, "The Land of Damascus between 1850 and 1750 B.C.," *BASOR*, 83 (October 1941), 34. n. 8.

167. G. von Rad, "The Origin of the Concept of the Day of Yahweh," *JSS*, 4 (1959), 97-108.

168. The plural form "chariots" ($mark^eb\bar{o}teyk\bar{a}$) may refer to the chariots of Yahweh and his divine army. Cf. Ps. 68:18 and the pertinent discussion on that verse in the preceding pages.

169. On this word see Eaton, *ZAW*, 76 (1964), 155, and Albright's note on $p^er\bar{a}z\hat{o}n$ in Judg. 5:7 (*Yahweh and the Gods of Canaan*, p. 43, n. 101).

170. Cross and Freedman, *JBL*, 72 (1953), 15-34.

171. *Ibid.*

172. The casting of arrows of lightning is a common element in the iconography of the storm god in the ancient Near East. See e.g., *ANEP*, p. 168, no. 490; p. 179, nos. 531-532.

173. On this latter motif see Cross and Freedman, *JBL*, 72 (1953), 31, n. 80.

174. LXX reads "until *God* took vengeance on *their* enemies."

175. Jan Dus, "Gibeon -- Eine Kultstätte des Šmš und die Stadt des benjaminitischen Schicksals," *VT*, 10 (1960), 353-374. Among older studies see M. J. Gruenthaner, "Two Sun Miracles of the Old Testament," *CBQ*, 10 (1948), 271-290; Robert Eisler,

"Joshua and the Sun," *AJSL*, 42 (1926), 73-85.

176. John S. Holladay, Jr., "The Day(s) the Moon Stood Still," *JBL*, 87 (1968), 166-178.

177. *Ibid.*, p. 176.

178. Martin Noth, *Das Buch Josua*, 2nd ed. (Tübingen: J. C. B. Mohr, 1953), p. 65.

179. Cf. Rudolf Smend, *Yahweh War and Tribal Confederation*, trans. M. G. Rogers (Nashville: Abingdon Press, 1970), p. 82, n. 30.

180. On the sun and moon in Mesopotamian mythology, see Edzard, "Mesopotamien. Die Mythologie der Sumerer und Akkadian," *Wörterbuch der Mythologie*, ed. H. W. Haussig (Stuttgart: Ernest Klett Verlag, 1961-), Vol. I, pt. 1, pp. 101-103 and 126-127; Jean Bottero, "Les divinités sémitiques anciennes en Mésopotamie," *Le antiche divinità semitiche*, ed. Sabatino Moscati (Rome: Universita di Roma, Centro di Studi Semitici, 1958), pp. 44-48. On the sun and moon in Canaanite mythology, see Martin Pope and Wolfgang Röllig, "Syrien. Die Mythologie der Ugariter und Phönizier," *Wörterbuch der Mythologie*, Vol. I, pt. 1, pp. 302-393, 308-309; M. J. Dahood, "Ancient Semitic Deities of Syria and Palestine," *Le antiche divinità semitiche*, pp. 90-91.

181. The parallelism with $^c\bar{a}mad$ indicates $yidd\bar{o}m$ is to be read as "stand still" rather than "be silent."

182. This translation is that of Albright, *Studies in Old Testament Prophecy*, p. 12.

183. One of the weaknesses in Holladay's approach -- as is true of other treatments -- is that it does not take into account

this important parallel.

184. Gruenthaner, *CBQ*, 10 (1948), 279.

185. Holladay, p. 169, n. 15, cites the three examples in the Joshua *prose* traditions.

186. Cf. the lexicons and Speiser, *JBL*, 79 (1960), 156-163.

187. With one or two possible exceptions, this characteristic appears to be true of the noun also when used in the sense of "vengeance against."

188. A similar translation and interpretation is given by Noth, *Das Buch Josua*, p. 65, who notes that as far back as 1920 Delitzsch recognized a *mem* was missing.

189. So also basically Noth, *Das Buch Josua*, p. 23, who refers to "dieser alten Überlieferung."

190. Cf. F. M. Abel, "L'apparition du chef de l'armée de Yahveh á Josué (Jos V, 13-15)," *Miscellanea Biblica et Orientalia R. P. Athanasio Miller Oblata, Studia Anselmina*, 27-28 (1951), 109-113.

191. Note also the messengers of Yamm discussed in the preceding chapter and the cherubim and flaming sword in the Garden of Eden (Gen. 3).

192. Abel, *Miscellanea Biblica et Orientalis*, pp. 109-110, who notes that this translation is both grammatically and textually correct.

193. Noth, *Das Buch Josua*, p. 23.

194. *Ibid.*, pp. 23, 39-40.

195. Elsewhere Noth describes Josh. 1--12 as "ätiologischen Einzelüberlieferungen im Verein mit einigen wenigen Heldenerzah-

lungen." M. Noth, *Überlieferungsgeschichtliche Studien*, 2nd. ed. (Tübingen: Max Niemeyer Verlag, 1957), p. 41

196. The question of whether Joshua originally figured in this episode is not relevant.

197. Noth's *Sammler*, which he dates c. 900 B.C. Noth, *Das Buch Josua*, p. 13.

198. G. von Rad, *Genesis*, trans. J. Marks (London: SCM Press, 1961), pp. 308-309; Hermann Gunkel, *Genesis*, 2nd ed. (Göttingen: Vandenhoeck und Ruprecht, 1902), pp. 313-314.

199. LXX in v. 2 adds: "and looking up, he saw an army of God encamped (or arrayed for battle)."

200. I Chronicles 12:23 should be cited in this connection: "For from day to day men kept coming to David to help him until there was a great army like an army of God" ($mah^a n\bar{e}h$ $^e l\bar{o}him$). Wilhelm Rudolph, *Chronikbucher* (Tübingen: J. C. B. Mohr, 1955), p. 106, regards this as merely the expression of a superlative. In light of the prior use of $g\bar{a}d\hat{o}l$, the sentences make better sense when it is seen as a comparison between the greatness or size of David's army and the greatness or size of God's army, especially as the phrase $mah^a n\bar{e}h$ is already known as a designation for the heavenly army.

201. Cf. John S. Holladay, Jr., "Assyrian Statecraft and the Prophets of Israel," *HTR*, 63 (1970), 33, n. 21.

202. The material that follows in this section is taken from my article, "The Divine Council and the Prophetic Call to War," *VT*, 18 (1968), 100-107.

203. R. Bach, *Die Aufforderungen zur Flucht und zum Kampf*

im alttestamentlichen Prophetenspruch (Neukirchen: Neukirchener Verlag, 1962), pp. 102ff.

204. Cf. John Bright's description of Elijah in his *A History of Israel* (Philadelphia: The Westminster Press, 1959), pp. 227, 229-231.

205. G. von Rad, *Der Heilige Krieg im alten Israel*, p. 10.

206. G. von Rad, *Studies in Deuteronomy* (London: SCM Press, 1953), p. 48.

207. Holladay, "Assyrian Statecraft and the Prophets of Israel," p. 33, n. 21.

208. I. Benzinger, *Die Bücher der Könige* (Tübingen: J. C. B. Mohr, 1899), p. 131; Kurt Galling, "Der Ehrenname Elisas und die Entrückung Elias," *ZTK*, 53 (1956), 129-148; G. Westphal, *Orientalische Studien Theodor Noldeke*, p. 724. Rudolf Kittel (*Die Bücher der Könige* [Göttingen: Vandenhoeck und Ruprecht, 1900], pp. 188-189), who correctly sees the heavenly army as the basis for the chariots and horses of fire here and in chap. 6, does not put the warrior title of the prophet in that context, although he does admit there may be some relationship.

209. G. von Rad, "The Origin of the Concept of the Day of Yahweh," *JSS*, 4 (1959), 97-108.

210. F. M. Cross, "The Divine Warrior in Israel's Early Cult." Note his statement: "The ideology of holy war makes possible the transition from the cultus of the league to the cultus of the kingdom, and ultimately to the ideology of apocalyptic" (p. 27).

211. On this passage see now the monograph of Seth Erlands-

son, *The Burden of Babylon: A Study of Isaiah 13:2--14:23* (Lund: C. W. K. Gleerup, 1970).

212. Erlandsson, *ibid.*, in his extended study of the passage has challenged the general consensus at this point, arguing that Assyria was the enemy involved.

213. LXX apparently reads *pithû* "draw (a sword)," or the like for *pithê* in v. 2b, a reading that is probably to be followed. See Bach, *Die Aufforderungen zur Flucht*, p. 58.

214. *gam qārā'tî* at the beginning of 3b is possibly to be read: "loudly I have called." Cf. Mitchell Dahood, "Ugaritic Studies and the Bible," *Gregorianum*, 43 (1962), 70.

215. G. von Rad, *Der Heilige Krieg im alten Israel*, p. 7. Cf. von Rad, *JSS*, 4 (1959), 99.

216. The verb *pāqad* is used regularly for mustering the heavenly army in 1QM 12:4, 7. Cf. the discussion below of Isa. 40:26.

217. Erlandsson, *The Burden of Babylon*, p. 19, says: The expression מִקְצֵה הַשָּׁמַיִם instead of the more usual מִקְצֵה הָאָרֶץ seems due to אֶרֶץ being already used in the parallelism." He also cites the LXX use of *themeliou tou ouranou* where *themeliou* "was probably added to avoid giving the impression that the army came from heaven itself." But this is to miss the whole point that Yahweh's destroying armies did come from heaven as well as earth, as numerous examples in the preceding pages have indicated.

218. Cf. D. W. Nowack, *Die kleinen Propheten*, *KAT* (Göttingen: 1897), p. 110; Arvid Kapelrud, *Joel Studies* (Uppsala, 1948),

pp. 162-163. I would agree with the latter's textual discussion insofar as he prefers to read with MT rather than the versions. In his recent excellent commentary on Joel, Hans Walter Wolff emends the text on v. 11b but acknowledges that the conception of the heavenly armies is present in MT. He compares Isa. 13:3b; Zech. 14:5b; II Chron. 20:22; Enoch 56:5ff.; and 1QM 1:10f. *Dodekapropheton: Joel* (Neukirchen: Neukirchener Verlag des Erziehungsvereins, 1963), p. 88.

219. Ps. 103:20; possibly Judg. 5:23. The word frequently appears as a designation of the angels in the Qumran literature. In 1QM xv:14 the *gbwry 'lym* are described girding themselves for battle. Col. xii:7 also appears to contain a reference to the angels as *gbwry*! IQH contains frequent reference to the divine world: *gbwry šmym* (iii:35-36), *gbwry pl'* (v. 21), *gbwry kwh* (viii:11-12). So also the Angelic Liturgy and 4 Q Ber. See J. Strugnell, "The Angelic Liturgy at Qumran, 4 Q *Serek Šîrôt ʿÔlat Haššabbāt*, *Congress Volume, Oxford, 1959* (Leiden: E. J. Brill, 1960), pp. 318-345, esp. 322 and 333. Strugnell also cites the use of *gibbôrîm* for divine beings in Enoch and Talmudic literature.

220. Wolff, *Joel*, pp. 47-50. The similarities to Isa. 13 are pointed out by Wolff as well as by E. Kutsch, "Heuschreckenplage und Tag Jahwes in Joel 1 und 2," *Theologische Zeitschrift*, 18 (1962), 81-94.

221. One should compare in this connection Ezek. 30:9 where Yahweh's messengers go forth to terrify Cush "on the day of Egypt."

222. F. M. Cross, "The Council of Yahweh in Second Isaiah,"
JNES, 12 (1953), 277, n. 21.

223. James Muilenburg, "The Book of Isaiah, Chapters 40--
66, Introduction and Exegesis," *The Interpreter's Bible*, Vol. V
(New York: Abingdon Press, 1956), 442.

224. Christopher R. North, *The Second Isaiah* (Oxford: Oxford University Press, 1964), p. 88. Cf. George A. F. Knight,
Deutero-Isaiah (New York: Abingdon Press, 1965), pp. 41-42.

225. For a helpful analysis of the way in which older materials and themes are incorporated and interwoven and the cosmic
and historical combined, see Benedikt Otzen, *Studien über Deuterosacharja* (Copenhagen: Prostant Apud Munksgaard, 1964), pp. 199-
212. Cf. Sigmund Mowinckel, *Psalmenstudien*, *2*, 2nd ed. (Amster-
dam: P. Schippers, 1961), pp. 231-234. More recently Walter Harrelson, "The Celebration of the Feast of Booths According to Zech.
xiv, 16-21," *Religions in Antiquity*, ed. J. Neusner (Leiden: E.
J. Brill, 1968), pp. 88-96.

226. In a lengthy study of Zech. 14:1-5, H.-M. Lutz has investigated the history of tradition of this passage and demonstrated that its fundamental motifs or themes grow out of the ancient
holy wars or Yahweh wars (as Lutz prefers). His study does not
focus on the larger structure or context of the passage.(*Jahwe,
Jerusalem und die Völker* [Neukirchen: Neukirchener Verlag, 1968],
chap. 4). Most recently this chapter has been the subject of
Formanalyse by Magne Saebø who overemphasizes, however, the lack
of unity in the chapter and fails to take fully into account the
interrelationship of Yahweh's war, theophany, Day of Yahweh, Yah-

weh's kingship, etc. *Sacharja 9--14*(Neukirchen: Neukirchener Verlag, 1969), pp. 282-309.

227. I follow most critics in reading with LXX and the Syriac "with him" rather than "with you" in v. 5.

228. "The motif chaos-cosmos is clear throughout the chapter; the Lord is transforming the present world order by means of a convulsion of that order and the establishment of cosmos through and beyond the chaos" (Harrelson, *Religions in Antiquity*, pp. 90-91). Cf. Otzen, *Studien über Deuterosacharja*.

229. This passage is thus to be combined with those from II Isaiah which Cross has analyzed as combining notions of cosmic warfare with the theme of the Second Conquest or Exodus, and with the motif of the processional to Zion. See "The Divine Warrior in Israel's Early Cult," pp. 28-30. He comments (on p. 30): "In these and other passages it is necessary to recognize the wedding of two themes: one derived from the ritual Conquest, one from the procession of the Ark to Zion and the manifestation of Yahweh's kingship."

230. The translation is from R. H. Charles, *The Book of Enoch* (Oxford: The Clarendon Press, 1912), pp. 7-8.

231. The following translations are those of Yigael Yadin, *The Scroll of the War of the Sons of Light Against the Sons of Darkness*, trans. B. and C. Rabin (Oxford: Oxford University Press, 1962).

232. Cf. Cross, "The Divine Warrior in Israel's Early Cult," p. 30.

233. For examples of various approaches to the problem of

the Ark one may refer to W. Arnold, *Ephod and Ark* (Cambridge: Harvard University Press, 1917); Martin Dibelius, *Die Lade Jahves* (Göttingen: Vandenhoeck und Ruprecht, 1906); Julian Morgenstern, *The Ark, the Ephod, and the "Tent of Meeting"* (Cincinnati: Union of American Hebrew Congregations, 1945); Johannes Maier, *Das altisraelitische Ladeheiligtum* (Berlin: Verlag Alfred Töpelmann, 1965). For further bibliography on the Ark see Hans-Joachim Kraus, *Worship in Israel*, trans. Geoffrey Buswell (Richmond: John Knox Press, 1966), pp. 125-128; F. Langlamet, *Gilgal et les recits de la traversée du Jourdain (Jos., III-IV)* (Paris: J. Gabalda et Cie, Éditeurs, 1969), pp. 13-20; and G. Henton Davies, "Ark of the Covenant," *IDB*, I, 226.

234. Least of all is this true of J. Maier's study of the Ark where literary critical analysis is carried to extremes and produces very questionable results. Although my differences with Maier and objections to his approach may rest in part on prior assumptions or presuppositions, the problems of his work are more far-reaching than that. It has to be admitted that the problems with which Maier is dealing are among some of the most perplexing and disputed ones in Old Testament study. A detailed critique of his whole work is outside the scope of this section, but see below for some criticisms at a particular and important point. would agree with the judgments of Herbert Huffmon in his review of Maier's book in *Interpretation*, 20 (1966), 106-107. Although questioning some widely held assumptions about the Ark (including some held by myself), R. Smend is far more judicious and cautious in his chapter on this subject in *Yahweh War and Tribal Confeder-*

ation, pp. 76-97.

235. Maier, *Das altisraelitische Ladeheiligtum*, pp. 5-12
concludes that the "Ladesprüche" are two separate, independent
liturgical phrases in no way "uralte." They did not originally
belong to the Ark and are probably post-Exilic. Such judgments
run so counter to prevailing opinions worked out just as carefully by other scholars that it would seem unnecessary to respond.
But because Maier's is the latest major work on the Ark and he
has gone into such detail it is appropriate to voice some criticisms of his analysis of Num. 10:33ff.:

(a) Verse 34 may well be an interpolation belonging
elsewhere (i.e., after v. 36) as LXX indicates. But if LXX indicates a disturbance here, it does not do so in the rest of the
passage.

(b) Maier does not make a convincing case on v. 33b.
To begin with, it is not self-evident that vv. 35f. depend upon
v. 33b. One would assume *a priori* reference to the Ark, but that
does not make it necessary. Maier has shown *possible* signs of
lateness in 33b, but all of them are questionable. Further, 33b
may have originally said: "the Ark of Yahweh went before them"
with the rest of the verse later interpolation. The argument
that *ns'* is the verb for J and E in referring to the cloud and
the angel is no argument. It is used all through the strata and
is obviously the verb for journeying and for Yahweh's going before whether cloud, angel, or Ark.

(c) Maier's assumption that *ᵃrôn bᵉrît yhwh* is Deu-
teronomistic and therefore late cannot be demonstrated as clearly

as he assumes. His dating of all the Ark designations (pp. 82–
85) is more precise than the evidence allows. Note the judgment
of G. Ernest Wright in the light of the covenantal studies of the
last two decades that "a more reasonable case can be made for the
assumption that the title [i.e., "Ark of the Covenant"] is original and that the object was indeed the chest which held the
holy 'Words'" ("The Lawsuit of God: A Form-Critical Study of Deuteronomy 32," *Israel's Prophetic Heritage*, ed. by B. W. Anderson
and W. Harrelson [New York: Harper and Brothers, 1902], p. 50, n.
54). At least one cannot automatically say it is late.

(d) Psalm 68 is not late and post-Exilic as Maier assumes, but rather part of the corpus of early Hebrew poetry and
therefore an independent confirmation of the antiquity of Num.
10:35.

(e) Psalm 132 is ruled out too easily as depending on
the Temple situation and a special *Tendenz*. The fact is that
language clearly associated with the Ark in Ps. 132:8 is similar
to the imperative of Num. 10:35.

(f) Maier maintains that *ʾalpê yiśrāʾēl* is only in P
and literature dependent on that and is therefore late. This ignores the very careful and convincing study of George Mendenhall
on the census lists of Numbers 1 and 26 with particular emphasis
on the use of *ʾelep* in the P material which demonstrates the antiquity of the lists and the designation ("The Census Lists of
Numbers 1 and 26," *JBL* [1958], 52–66). There is, therefore, nothing requiring that this be judged late terminology. (Cf. next
paragraph.)

(g) Furthermore, Maier argues that $rib^e b \hat{o} t$ is to be
deleted or changed to $s^e \dot{b} \bar{a}^{\flat} \hat{o} t$. Much more likely is that a word
has dropped between $rib^e b \hat{o} t$ and $^{\flat} alp \hat{e}$. These two words are a
common word pair in Hebrew and Ugaritic. (See n. 237.) The
change to $s^e \dot{b} \bar{a}^{\flat} \hat{o} t$ is not necessary and violates the *lectior dif-
ficilior* rule in text criticism.

(h) With T. P. Sevensma, "Num. 10:35 and 36," *ZAW*, 29
(1909), 253-258 Maier regards the use of Piel participle of $\acute{s} \bar{a} n \bar{a}^{\flat}$
as late ("Alt ist die Verwendung des part. Pi‛el von $\acute{s} n^{\flat}$ aber
nicht."). Sevensma, on whom Maier relies more than once,, is,
however, a weak reed. He dates all the examples around the Mac-
cabean period, a position that no longer merits serious debate.
In actual fact the Piel participle of $\acute{s} \bar{a} n \bar{a}^{\flat}$ in this kind of context is *characteristic of poetry that is generally regarded as
quite early*, e.g., in addition to Ps. 68:2; Deut. 32:41; 33:11;
II Sam. 22:41//Ps. 18:41; and Ps. 89:24.

236. Among those more recent scholars who regard these ver-
ses as archaic and to be associated with the early wars of Yah-
weh, one may cite De Vaux, Cross, Smend, Eissfeldt, Beyerlin,
Bentzen, Lipinski, von Rad, Weiser, Ringgren, etc. In a recent
Kiel dissertation, W. Seeber comes to similar conclusions ("Der
Weg der Tradition von der Lade Jahwes im Alten Testament" [cf.
TLZ, 83 (1958), 722-723]). William McKane gives a helpful dis-
cussion of the early history of the Ark and its association with
Num. 10:35-36 and with the holy wars in his article "The Earlier
History of the Ark," *Transactions of the Glasgow University Ori-
ental Society*, 21 (1965-66), 68-76.

237. The reconstruction and translation are those of Cross, "The Divine Warrior in Israel's Early Cult," pp. 24-25, although the suggested reconstruction of the final line was independently proposed by myself several years ago also on the basis of Deut. 33:2-3 and Ps. 68:18. The parallelism (or combination) of $^{3a}l\bar{a}$-$p\hat{\imath}m$ and $r^e b\bar{a}b\hat{o}t$ is largely a characteristic of the Ugaritic texts (e.g., *UT* 51:I:27-29 [= *CTA* 4.I.27-29] and numerous other passages) and early Hebrew poetry (e.g., Gen. 24:60; Deut. 32:30; 33: 17; Ps. 68:18; I Sam. 18:7 = 21:12 = 29:5). The reversal of the two words in parallelism so that $r^e b\bar{a}b\hat{o}t$ is the A element and $^{3a}l\bar{a}p\hat{\imath}m$ is the B element is not unusual (e.g., Deut. 33:17 and Ps. 68:18). Metrically the line is improved by such a reading.

238. Cf. G. Henton Davies, "The Ark in the Psalms," *Promise and Fulfillment,* ed. F. F. Bruce (Edinburgh: T. and T. Clark, 1963), p. 60, who suggests that the commands of $q\hat{u}m\bar{a}h$ *yhwh* and $\check{s}\hat{u}b\bar{a}h$ *yhwh* elsewhere in the Psalms may refer to the Ark.

239. Cf. the designation "Yahweh's battles" for Israel's wars (I Sam. 18:17; 25:28).

240. This is the point of view of Hugo Gressmann, *Mose und seine Zeit* (Göttingen: Vandenhoeck und Ruprecht, 1913), p. 353.

241. Not only the passage as a whole, but the specific reference to "Ark of the Covenant of Yahweh" in v. 44b has been questioned (e.g., Maier, *Das altisraelitische Ladeheiligtum*, p. 4). De Vaux, however, sees no reason to deny the antiquity of Num. 14:44.

242. See, for example, the lengthy analysis of C. F. Burney, *The Book of Judges* (London: Rivingtons, 1918), pp. 442-458.

243. Von Rad, *Der Heilige Krieg* . . ., pp. 6-8. Cf.
Joseph Blenkinsopp, "Jonathan's Sacrilege, I Sm. 14, 1-46: A
Study in Literary History," *CBQ*, 26 (1964), 432.

244. So also R. Smend, *Yahweh War and Tribal Confederation*,
p. 78, n. 8.

245. W. McKane, "The Earlier History of the Ark," pp. 70-
71, has given cogent arguments against the view that the entry
of the Ark here is a last resort, indicating that it was not normal practice then for the Ark to accompany the warriors: "Even
if this were conceded, it would be proper to ask whether then
this had been customary at an earlier period and had been discon-
tinued except as an extraordinary measure. This would be an intelligible development and the question which has to be asked is
whether this is more credible than the proposition that I Sam. 4:
1f. is to be regarded as an absolute innovation. My own view is
that the reference in the book should be allowed more weight than
the silence in the period of the Judges which may be accidental
rather than significant. Hence von Rad's conclusion that the Ark
was not carried into war in the period of the Judges does not
seem to me to be soundly based."

246. The peculiar episode in I Sam. 5 concerning the Ark in
the temple of Dagon in Ashdod has attracted little attention. I
hope to treat this passage in a separate study, but a few comments are in order here. The story as it now stands is tied etiologically to a custom of stepping over the threshold. But mythological elements certainly lie hidden here though quite confused
and now obscured. The basic element is the battle of the gods --

in this case Yahweh and Dagon. The initial fall of Dagon may be
understood in one of three ways: (a) an act of worship; (b) an
act of fear similar to that of the gods of the assembly in Text
137 (= *CTA* 2.I); (c) a fall in battle. Cf., e.g., the battles
of Baᶜal and Yamm, Baᶜal and Mot. The cutting off of Dagon's
hands and head is strikingly similar to ᶜAnat's behavior in the
gory massacre recounted in ᶜ*nt*:II (= *CTA* 3.II) where ᶜAnat ties
the head and hands of her victims to her back and waist.

     Even here, however, where reflections of the cosmic
battle of the gods may be evident, the context is a definitely
historical one symbolizing and resulting in the destruction of
the Philistines. Yahweh's enemy is not a primordial monster, but
the national god of Israel's enemy -- a type of situation not
very frequent in the Old Testament. Cf. now the study of M. Del-
cor, "Jahweh et Dagon," *VT*, 14 (1964), 136-154.

     247. But cf. Moore, *Judges*, p. 111, who, although preferr-
ing the LXX reading, says: "Historically we could hardly object
that the presence of the Ark at Kirjath-Jearim would decide a-
gainst this text, because our author may not have known of its
detention at Kirjath-Jearim."

     248. On this passage see Blenkinsopp, *CBQ*, 26 (1964), 423-
449. Although he sees the incident clearly as a holy war, he
does not refer to the question of the Ark.

     249. Cf. Cyrus H. Gordon, "David the Dancer," *Yehezkel Kauf-
mann Jubilee Volume*, ed. M. Haran (Jerusalem: The Magnes Press,
1960), pp. 48-49.

     250. See Cross, "The Divine Warrior in Israel's Early Cult."

251. On this passage see the brief but excellent treatment by R. Smend, *Yahweh War and Tribal Confederation*, pp. 83-84. On p. 83, n. 37 he notes the possibility of reading $^{\jmath a}r\bar{o}n$ for $^{\zeta}\bar{a}r\hat{e}$.

252. G. Henton Davies, "The Ark in the Psalms," suggests other places in the Psalms where references to the Ark may be hidden. Some of his examples are quite convincing.

253. See the treatment of Cross, "The Divine Warrior . . .," pp. 19ff.

254. *Ibid.* Cf. the criticisms of Cross's interpretation of Ps. 132:8 by Delbert Hillers, "Ritual Procession of the Ark and Ps. 132," *CBQ*, 30 (1968), 48-55.

255. For example, Noth, *Das Buch Josua*, pp. 20ff.; von Rad, *Der Heilige Krieg* . . ., p. 28, n. 45.

256. Cross, "The Divine Warrior . . .," pp. 26-27.

257. Noth, *Das Buch Josua*, p. 41.

258. Kraus, *Worship in Israel*, p. 164, has recognized the possible holy war basis for the activity around the Ark in these chapters. The significance of the Ark here could be understood in three different ways according to Kraus: (1) the leading presence of Yahweh, which is connected with the Ark (Num. 10:35f.); (2) the significance of the shrine in the cultic events of the "holy war" (Num. 10:35f. also); (3) the character of the Ark as a procession shrine. In actuality, however, these three functions are intimately related in the early history of the Ark. Cf. on the Ark in these chapters the detailed analysis of F. Langlamet, *Gilgal*, pp. 104-123; 139-144.

259. Von Rad, *Der Heilige Krieg* . . ., pp. 9, 28, n. 45.

260. Cf. Smend, *Yahweh War and Tribal Confederation*, chap. 4.

261. B. N. Wambacq, *L'épithète divine Jahvé S^{e}bā,ôt* (Paris: Desclée de Brouwer, 1947).

262. For example, W. F. Albright, "Review of *L'épithète divine Jahvé S^{e}bā,ôt: Étude philologique, historique, et exégétique*," *JBL*, 67 (1948), 377-381; von Rad, *Old Testament Theology*, I, 18; Walther Eichrodt, *Theology of the Old Testament*, trans. A. W. Heathcote and P. J. Allcock (New York: Harper and Brothers, 1958), p. 55; Smend, *Yahweh War and Tribal Confederation*, p. 81. Wambacq, *Jahvé S^{e}bā,ôt*, and V. Maag, "Jahwäs Heerscharen," *Schweizerische Theologische Umschau*, 20.3/4 (1950), 32, disagree.

263. Otto Eissfeldt, "Jahwe Zebaoth," *Miscellanea Academica Berolinensia*, 2.2 (1950), 128-150. *Kleine Schriften*, III (Tübingen: J. C. B. Mohr, 1966), 103-123.

264. The word ,^{e}lōhîm has also been interpreted as an abstract noun, "deity, divinity," or the like, analogous to ḥayyîm, n^{e}ʿurîm, etc. Although this interpretation of s^{e}bā,ôt is not the most likely, B. W. Anderson's criticism that "it advocates an abstraction of thought which is not characteristic of the Hebrew mind" is not valid ("Hosts, Hosts of Heaven," *IDB*, II, 656).

265. For further criticisms of Eissfeldt's linguistic interpretation see the works referred to in Smend, *Yahweh War*, p. 83, n. 33. A new interpretation has been given by Matitiahu Tsevat ("Studies in the Book of Samuel, IV, Yahweh Seba,ot," *HUCA* 36 [1965], pp. 49-58), who regards the phrase as either noun plus

apposition or a nominal sentence, i.e., "Yahweh (the) armies" or
"Yahweh (is) Armies." This is an interesting interpretation but
does not seem a preferable solution. A nominal sentence name is
quite legitimate but not if the divine element is itself a verbal form. Tsevat wishes to keep separate the question of the
meaning of the name Yahweh and that of Yahweh $s^eb\bar{a}\,{}^{\jmath}\hat{o}t$, but we do
not believe that is the proper approach. The principal parallels
Tsevat cites (II Kings 13:14 and Num. 10:36) are subject to quite
different and more plausible interpretations as I have sought to
show. Finally, the question of the identification of the "armies" still remains and is a part of the total issue. Here it
would seem Tsevat has ignored the religio-historical perspective
presented in these pages, i.e., the involvement of the divine
armies in the wars of Yahweh. The same subject has been treated
by J. P. Ross, "Jahweh $s^eb\bar{a}\,{}^{\jmath}\hat{o}t$ in Samuel and Psalms," *VT*, 17
(1967), 76-92, but his approach has too many problems and does
not lay out any fruitful directions to follow.

266. Albright, *JBL*, 67 (1948), 377-381. Cross, *HTR*, 55
(1962), 250ff., has now marshalled a considerable amount of further evidence and examples.

267. Cross, *HTR*, 55 (1962), 250ff.

268. *Ibid.*, p. 253, n. 123.

269. *Ibid.*, p. 255.

270. *Ibid.*, pp. 255ff.

271. *Ibid.*; Albright, *JBL*, 67 (1948), 377-381.

272. David Noel Freedman, "The Name of the God of Moses,"
JBL, 79 (1960), 155ff., believes that prior to $s^eb\bar{a}\,{}^{\jmath}\hat{o}t$ the object

was probably *qin'ā* (Ex. 34:14) and/or *yir'ā* (Gen. 22:14).

273. See Westphal, *Orientalische Studien Theodor Nöldeke*, on lexical analysis.

274. In late literature it can be "toil, work" or "temple service."

275. Cross, *HTR*, 55 (1962), 256. Others have offered the same interpretation but on the basis of Old Testament materials alone while Cross has drawn in comparative materials from Canaanite mythology, which buttress this view considerably. Cf. the first chapter of this work.

276. *Ibid.*

277. The absence of the phrase in these books is not too unusual, as Albright and Eichrodt have recognized. The early sources are relatively fragmentary for one thing. It is also possible that the term could have been deleted for various reasons (so Eichrodt, *Theology of the Old Testament*, I, 194).

278. Cf. Albright, *JBL*, 67 (1948), 381, who says that one is safe in supposing that "the expression was originally at home in very ancient litanies from which it was taken as a most suitable formula with which to designate the holiest cult object of Israel, placed at the head of every army going forth to battle enemies of Yahweh on behalf of His people."

279. *Ibid.*, p. 378. There is, of course, considerable disagreement with Albright's conclusion.

280. See on this subject the detailed study of C. H. W. Brekelmans, *De Ḥerem in het Oude Testament* (Nijmegen: Centrale Drukkerij, 1959).

281. So also Brekelmans.

282. The P writer even speaks of the Red Sea events in the language of holy war (Ex. 14).

283. Judges 5, of course, deals with a later battle with the same imagery

284. Cf. the remarks concerning Judges 5 and Psalm 68 by J. Blenkinsopp, "Ballad Style and Psalm Style in the Song of Deborah: A Discussion," *Biblica*, 42 (1961), 65: "It is, in fact, the theophany which gives the specific religious note to the Song and unifies it on the theological level. We should notice here a profound cleavage, often overlooked or played down between the warlike procession of the 'Gewittergott' of antiquity and the Coming of YHWH from Sinai; the enemies of the former are the mythological monsters of the primitive ocean, those of the latter are players on the stage of real history. Here and in Psalm 68 the theophany is a triumphant procession to a real destination marked by triumphs which history records."

285. See esp. Ps. 68:8-9. Even Judg. 5:4-5 belongs to this context.

286. For a good summary of this new attention to the reliability of the P writer especially in Numbers, see F. M. Cross, "The Priestly Tabernacle," *The Biblical Archaeologist Reader*, ed. G. Ernest Wright and D. N. Freedman (Garden City, N.Y.: Doubleday and Company, Inc., 1961), pp. 209-212. Numerous studies have appeared since Cross's work pointing to the antiquity of elements in the P tradition, e.g., Mendenhall, *JBL*, 77 (1958), on the census lists of Numbers 1 and 26. In the most recent issue of *JAOS*

at the time of writing appear back-to-back articles by Moshe Weinfeld ("The Covenant of Grant in the Old Testament and in the Ancient Near East") and Jacob Milgrom ("The Shared Custody of the Tabernacle and a Hittite Analogy"), both arguing for the antiquity of material in this tradition (*JAOS*, 90 [April-June 1970]).

287.   See esp. Ex. 15; Josh. 2--5; Pss. 24,29 and 68; Deut. 33.

288.   Cross, *HTR*, 55 (1962), 259.

289.   *Ibid.*

290.   Cf. Ps. 82 for an involvement of the cosmic hosts on a life-or-death basis in the affairs of history and human activity. In this context it is a concern for social justice that is at issue.

291.   Cf. Cross and Freedman, *JNES*, 14 (1955), 239, where they point out that in Ex. 15 Yahweh uses the sea as a "passive" tool for fighting historical enemies -- Pharaoh and his army. He does not battle the sea as some "opposing divinity of darkness" (p. 239). In Ps. 68 and Hab. 3 the heavy overtones of the mythological battle of Yahweh and the cosmic chaos are still understood as a battle for deliverance of the people.

Some Concluding Implications

1. Gerhard von Rad, "The Form-Critical Problem of the Hexateuch," *The Problem of the Hexateuch*, trans. E. W. Trueman
Dicken (New York: McGraw-Hill Book Co., 1966), pp. 1-78.

2. For example, Herbert B. Huffmon, "The Exodus, Sinai,
and the Credo," *CBQ*, 27 (1965), 101-113.

3. Artur Weiser, *The Old Testament: Its Formation and Development* (New York: Association Press, 1961), pp. 83-90.

4 Georg Fohrer, "Tradition und Interpretation im Alten
Testament," *Studien zum alttestamentlichen Theologie und Geschichte (1949-66)* (Berlin: Walter de Gruyter and Co., 1969), p. 69.

5. Leonhard Rost, "Das kleine geschichtliche Credo," *Das
kleine Credo und andere Studien zum Alten Testament* (Heidelberg:
Quelle & Meyer, 1965), pp. 11-25.

6. C. H. Brekelmans, "Het 'historische Credo' van Israël,"
Tijdschrift voor Theologie, 3 (1963), 1-11.

7. Th. C. Vriezen, "The Credo in the Old Testament," *Studies on the Psalms: Ou Testamentiese Werkgemeenschap in Suid-
Afrika* (Potchefstroom: Pro Rege-Pers Beperk, 1963), pp. 1-11.

8. Brevard S. Childs, "Deuteronomic Formulae of the Exodus
Traditions," *Hebräische Wortforschung*, *SVT*, 16 (Leiden: E. J.
Brill, 1967), 30-39.

9. J. Philip Hyatt, "Were There an Ancient Historical Credo
in Israel and an Independent Sinai Tradition?" *Translating and
Understanding the Old Testament*, ed. Harry F. Frank and William
L. Reed (Nashville: Abingdon Press, 1970), pp. 152-170.

10. Calum Carmichael, "A New View of the Origin of the
Deuteronomic Credo," *VT*, 19 (1969), 273-289.

11. Wolfgang Richter, "Beobachtungen zur theologischen Sys-
tembildung in der alttestamentlichen Literatur anhand des 'klein-
en geschichtlichen Credo,'" *Wahrheit und Verkündigung*, ed. L.
Scheffczyk (München: Verlag Ferdinand Schöningh, 1967), pp. 175-
212.

12. That is, the primal, unified, probably poetic account
of Israel's early history, which lay behind the formulations by
the Yahwist and Elohist.

13. More likely, with Cross, "The Song of the Sea and Canaanite Myth," p. 23, it is the battle encampment of Shittim.

14. Cross, *ibid.*, p. 13, n. 42, is inclined to regard this
verse as a secondary interpolation on metrical grounds. While
acknowledging the metrical problems, I am less inclined to omit
it from discussion of the hymn. The combination $\varsigma\bar{o}z$ and *zimrāh*
is now familiar not only from later Israelite psalms but also
much earlier in the Ugaritic texts. The phrase $\,^{\vartheta e}l\bar{o}h\hat{e}\,\,^{\vartheta}\bar{a}b\hat{\imath}$,
while perhaps a secondary formulation in itself, is probably an
archaic reference to patriarchal religion.

15. For a recent discussion of this see W. F. Albright,
Yahweh and the Gods of Canaan, chap. 1, "Verse and Prose in Early
Israelite Tradition."

16. See Cross, "The Song of the Sea" and "The Divine Warrior . . . ." The former work is a seminal treatment of the use
of this poem in the formulation of later traditions. Albright,
Yahweh and the Gods of Canaan, p. 11, has called Ex. 15 a kind of

"Israelite national anthem."

  17. Von Rad, *The Problem of the Hexateuch*, pp. 8-11.

  18. Cf. Cross, "The Song of the Sea . . . ."

  19. P. D. Miller, Jr., "God the Warrior," *Interpretation*, 19 (1965), 39-46.

  20. G. E. Wright, *The Old Testament and Theology* (New York: Harper & Row, 1969), chap. 5.

  21. Cf. Cross, "The Divine Warrior . . . ." Also Paul Hanson, "Studies in the Origins of Jewish Apocalyptic" (Ph.D. dissertation, Harvard University, 1969).

Ugaritic Textual Index

Biblical References

Author Index

Subject Index